MW01120670

The Many Faces of Youth Crime

The Many Faces of Youth Crime

Contrasting Theoretical Perspectives on Juvenile Delinquency across Countries and Cultures

by
Josine Junger-Tas, University of Utrecht, Utrecht, The Netherlands
Ineke Haen Marshall, Northeastern University, Boston, MA, USA
Dirk Enzmann, University of Hamburg, Hamburg, Germany
Martin Killias, University of Zurich, Zurich, Switzerland
Majone Steketee, Verwey-Jonker Institute, Utrecht, Netherlands
Beata Gruszczyńska, University of Warsaw, Warsaw, Poland

with additional contributions from:
Sonia Lucia, University of Lausanne, Lausanne, Switzerland
Harrie Jonkman, Verwey-Jonker Institute, Utrecht, The Netherlands

Josine Junger-Tas
University of Utrecht
Utrecht, The Netherlands

Ineke Haen Marshall
Department of Sociology
Northeastern University
Boston, MA, USA
i.marshall@neu.edu

Dirk Enzmann
University of Hamburg
Hamburg, Germany
dirk.enzmann@uni-hamburg.de

Martin Killias
University of Zurich
Zurich, Switzerland
Martin.Killias@rwi.uzh.ch

Majone Steketee
Verwey-Jonker Institute
Utrecht, The Netherlands
msteketee@verwey-jonker.nl

Beata Gruszczyńska
University of Warsaw
Warsaw, Poland
b.gruszczynska@uw.edu.pl

ISBN 978-1-4419-9454-7 e-ISBN 978-1-4419-9455-4
DOI 10.1007/978-1-4419-9455-4
Springer New York Dordrecht Heidelberg London

Library of Congress Control Number: 2011936744

Printed on acid-free paper

Springer is part of Springer Science+Business Media (www.springer.com)

Preface

This book is dedicated to our inspiration and dear friend,

Josine Junger-Tas (1929 – 2011)

We have many people to thank now the second book on the results of the ISRD is complete. It is hard to know where to begin. We owe a debt of gratitude to Malcolm Klein who was our inspiration from the early beginnings of this project. Throughout the project, we have learned and benefitted from the many comments and suggestions we have received from our colleagues with whom we talked at conferences, or informally in the halls of our universities or research institutes. The International Self-Report Delinquency Study has been a truly international collaborative effort from its very inception. The results presented in this book were produced by tireless and generous cooperation and collaboration of more than 100 researchers from over 30 countries. The many workshops, personal meetings, and electronic communications together with tremendous energy of the entire ISRD-2 working group have generated an impressive amount of information about different dimensions of young people's life in Europe and several non-European countries. The ISRD-2 Steering Committee at times has tested the research partners' patience and understanding through adjustments and requests that sometimes took longer than desirable. Without the good cheer and positive attitude of the many national partners, this project would not have come to fruition. For all of us, the International Self-Report Study of Delinquency (ISRD2) has been a very rewarding learning process.

To the countless administrators, school principals, class room teachers, and research assistants in each ISRD country without whom this project could not have been completed, we say *Thank you*. And let us not forget the almost 70,000 students who were willing to participate in our study, without any promise or benefit. We are grateful to the European Union which through its Daphne project facilitated the participation of a number of new EU member countries in this study. We also thank the Swiss National Science Foundation which funded the study in Bosnia-Herzegovina and Russia. We appreciate the different national or local funding agencies that were willing to invest their scarce resources in this project because they recognized the importance of international and comparative research. We hope that – when these funding agencies read the results of our study – they feel that their money was well spent.

In this time of scarce public resources, it is particularly important that research has useful policy implications. As the last chapter of this book shows, we have tried to meet the needs of researchers as well as those involved with policy.

We also owe thanks to the Verwey-Jonker Institute for its generous practical and enthusiastic support of the ISRD-2 project. We thank Welmoed Spahr and Katie Chabalko from Springer who have shepherded us successfully and patiently through the process of completing the second book on the ISRD-2.

Finally, it took us a bit more time than we had originally planned to finalize the manuscript but we are happy with the results. Still, we had to leave many questions unexplored. We invite our colleagues – in Europe and beyond – to take up where we left off and continue the analysis of the rich ISRD-2 data set. Meanwhile, we have started preparations for the third International Self-Report Delinquency Study (ISRD-3).

Utrecht, The Netherlands Josine Junger-Tas

Contents

Part I Theory and Design

1 **Introduction to the International Self-Report Study of Delinquency (ISRD-2)** 3
Josine Junger-Tas and Ineke Haen Marshall

2 **Methodology and Design of the ISRD-2 Study** 21
Ineke Haen Marshall and Dirk Enzmann

Part II Extent and Nature of Problem Behaviour of Young People

3 **Delinquent Behaviour in 30 Countries** 69
Josine Junger-Tas

4 **Juvenile Victimization from an International Perspective** 95
Beata Gruszczyńska, Sonia Lucia, and Martin Killias

5 **Substance Use of Young People in 30 Countries** 117
Majone Steketee

6 **Social Responses to Offending** 143
Dirk Enzmann

Part III Testing Competing Explanations of Problem Behaviour

7 **The Importance of the Family** 185
Josine Junger-Tas

8 **The School and its Impact on Delinquency** 211
Sonia Lucia, Martin Killias, and Josine Junger-Tas

9 **The Lifestyles of Youth and Their Peers** 237
Majone Steketee

10 **The Neighbourhood Context** 257
Josine Junger-Tas, Majone Steketee, and Harrie Jonkman

11 **The Generalizability of Self-Control Theory** 285
Ineke Haen Marshall and Dirk Enzmann

Part IV Theoretical and Policy Implications

12 **Concluding Observations: The Big Picture** 329
Josine Junger-Tas, Dirk Enzmann, Majone Steketee, and Ineke Haen Marshall

Index 355

Part I
Theory and Design

Chapter 1
Introduction to the International Self-Report Study of Delinquency (ISRD-2)

Josine Junger-Tas and Ineke Haen Marshall

There is a growing interest in cross-cultural comparisons both among academics and among policy makers, which is related to general trends such as increasing globalization, the advantage of scientific collaboration in terms of building knowledge, and the need for policy makers to be informed about different kinds of solutions to comparable problems. The need for cross-national knowledge on crime is reflected in the United Nations Crime prevention and criminal justice programmes. Major efforts have been made by the United Nations to achieve comparisons between nations on the basis of police and criminal justice statistics (Vetere and Newman 1977; Pease and Hukkula 1990; Newman 1999; Aromaa and Heiskanen 2008). However, interpreting the results has always been difficult, because countries differ widely in the organization of their police and criminal justice system, the definition of legal categories, the counting rules, and the way they collect and present their statistics. Efforts have also been made by the Council of Europe to improve the accuracy and usefulness of international crime statistics and to confront the drawbacks of underreporting and non-standard indicators (*European Sourcebook of Crime and Criminal Justice Statistics* 1995, 2003, 2006, 2010). Many improvements have also been made with the International Crime Victimization Survey (ICVS) collecting victimization data from a large number of countries (van Dijk et al. 2008). A total of five "sweeps" of the ICVS (1989, 1992, 1996, 2000, 2005) have been conducted so far. Because of the multiplication of data sources both nationally and internationally, together with a growing understanding of the strengths and limitations of different measures of crime, we are now better capable of recognizing international diverging and converging trends (e.g. Junger-Tas 1996; Marshall 1996).

However, most of the international crime measures refer mainly to *adult* criminal behaviour, suggesting that juvenile criminal acts are not of particular interest. This is puzzling since youth crime is perceived as a major problem in many countries.

I.H. Marshall (✉)
Northeastern University, Boston, MA, USA
e-mail: i.marshall@neu.edu

J. Junger-Tas et al., *The Many Faces of Youth Crime: Contrasting Theoretical Perspectives on Juvenile Delinquency across Countries and Cultures*,
DOI 10.1007/978-1-4419-9455-4_1, © Springer Science+Business Media, LLC 2012

It is therefore no surprise that the need for more comparative knowledge on juvenile anti-social behaviour, as well as on juvenile crime, is increasingly felt.

Over the last several decades, a large number of self-report studies of offending and victimization have been conducted, mostly in the US, Canada, New Zealand, Australia, UK, and other European countries, but also in Japan, India, China, and South Africa. Indeed, the self-report method has long outgrown its infancy and by now appears a powerful and reliable research tool for criminologists. These self-report surveys of delinquency appear to have three different but often overlapping purposes: (1) *To measure the prevalence and incidence of offending*; (2) *To test theories about the correlates of offending*; and (3) *To describe the dimensions and trajectories of delinquent careers* (e.g. age of onset, seriousness, and versatility). Some of these are very sophisticated, extensive longitudinal surveys, while others are cross-sectional one-time small-scale studies. No matter their primary purpose or particular research design, self-report studies have proved to be a true treasure trove of insights into delinquency and victimization. They also have contributed to an extensive body of knowledge about the methodological challenges and requirements of survey research [i.e. sampling, validity and reliability issues, and psychometric properties of scales (see, e.g. Junger-Tas and Marshall 1999; Thornberry and Krohn 2000)]. It is one of the purposes of the International Self-Report Study of Delinquency (ISRD) to further contribute to the methodological development of self-report survey methodology, in particular the large-scale, cross-national variant which presents a number of additional challenges to the basic survey method. (See Chap. 2 on the methodological challenges of the ISRD-2).

Although self-report surveys of delinquency have been a mainstay of delinquency research for over half a century, these studies typically have been limited to one, or at the most, a handful of countries (e.g. Pauwels and Svensson 2008, 2010; Svensson et al. 2010; Vazsonyi et al. 2001; Wikstrom and Svensson 2008). The bulk of analyses that draw upon survey data from multiple countries is not explicitly comparative by design (Kohn 1987). For example, Thornberry and Krohn (2003) in *Taking Stock of Delinquency: An Overview of Findings from Contemporary Longitudinal Studies* discuss seven longitudinal studies of delinquency in the UK, USA, and Canada. These panel studies share a core set of design features, including repeated measurements and interviews with the focal group. There is no, however, explicit standardization of either the measurement instruments used or the sample selection. Another example is the International Dating Violence Study (Straus et al. 2004) which uses a standardized (translated) self-report instrument, but sampling is not standardized (convenience samples of college students in different countries). Thus, studies that use an explicitly comparative (cross-national) design are rather rare.[1] The ISRD-2

[1] At the European level, there are few comparative studies focusing on youth; one example is the European School Survey Project on Alcohol and Other Drugs (ESPAD) (see Hibell et al. 2004 http://www.espad.org/espad-reports). Another example is the Programme for International Student Assessment (PISA), an internationally standardized assessment of 15-year olds in schools, implemented in 62 countries worldwide in 2009. The WHO report on the Health Behaviour in School-Aged Children (HBSC) contains international self-report data on cannabis use, fighting, and bullying (Currie et al. 2008). Data on self-reported delinquency and victimization in six countries (Germany, Poland, Lithuania, Estonia, Finland, and Sweden) are reported in Dunkel et al. (2007).

study is one of the first large-scale cross-national studies of juvenile delinquency with an *explicitly* comparative design and methodology. A total of 31 countries participated in the ISRD-2.[2] ISRD-2's explicit comparative design intends to minimize the confounding impact of possible cross-national differences in study design and implementation on noted cross-national differences and similarities, through standardization: of survey instruments, sampling plan, and standardized data entry method. Such explicitly comparative design, we have argued from its inception some 20 years ago, is by far the strongest approach and has many advantages over other designs. The history and background of the ISRD-2 study has been discussed elsewhere (Enzmann et al. 2010; Junger-Tas et al. 2010), but below we want to highlight a few main points to provide the main methodological and theoretical contours of the ISRD-2.

1.1 The First International Self-Report Study (ISRD-1)

The International Self-report Delinquency study (ISRD) was launched in 1992 by the Dutch Research and Documentation Centre (WODC). The study was based on self-report delinquency data collected in 13 countries, most of which are Member States of the European Union. The objectives of the ISRD-1 project were as follows:

1. To examine cross-national variability in patterns of self-reported delinquent behaviour.
2. To measure the relative rank-ordering of prevalence of different types of juvenile delinquency in industrialized countries.
3. To study cross-national variability in the correlates of self-reported behaviour.
4. To contribute to the methodological development of the self-report method.

Participant researchers reached an agreement on a basic core instrument as well as on basic methodological requirements for achieving comparability. The validity and reliability of the ISRD-1 core questionnaire has been examined and found to be satisfactory (Killias 2001; Zhang et al. 2000; Marshall and Webb 1994).

Data collection took place in 1991 and 1992 in three Anglo-Saxon countries (Northern Ireland, England and Wales, and the USA, Nebraska), five countries from North-West Europe (The Netherlands, Germany, Belgium, Switzerland, Finland), and three countries from Southern Europe (Italy, Spain, Portugal). The first report, which consisted mainly of descriptive findings concerning the participating countries, was published in Junger-Tas. More advanced multivariate analyses and theoretical interpretations, based on the merged dataset of 11 countries, were presented in the second volume and published in November 2003 (Junger-Tas et al. 2003). The main comparative outcomes were presented at a conference held by the *European Society of Criminology* in Toledo (Spain), September 2002.

[2] Armenia, Aruba, Austria, Belgium, Bosnia, Canada, Czech Republic, Cyprus, Denmark, Estonia, Finland, France, Germany, Hungary, Iceland, Italy, Ireland, Lithuania, the Netherlands, Netherlands Antilles, N. Ireland, Norway, Poland, Russia, Scotland, Slovenia, Spain, Surinam, Sweden, Switzerland, United States, Venezuela.

1.2 The Second International Self-Report Delinquency Study (ISRD-2)

After ISRD-1 was completed, a number of reasons encouraged us to consider the possibility of repeating the study and even to start a series of such surveys.

- The interesting outcomes of the first comparative study, as well as the lessons learned with respect to the methodology of international comparative self-report measurement.
- Repeat studies would enable us to measure *trends* in youth delinquent behaviour over time.
- The relative lack of reliable data on youth crime in the new EU member states (from Central and Eastern Europe).
- Many countries now regularly collect self-report information on (types of) juvenile delinquent behaviour, so that the methodology of self-report surveys has been greatly improved.
- New insights in juvenile crime may be gained from comparisons with other countries.
- Cross-cultural comparison is an invaluable tool to develop our knowledge on stable correlates of crime and to test different criminological theories.
- Last but not least: the findings will allow policy makers to maintain, improve, or change their national youth policies.

One might consider ISRD-1 as a kind of pilot study, since it was the first time a standardized self-report delinquency survey was conducted with more than ten participants all over Europe and the US. Of all lessons learned from this first endeavour, the most important one was that we had to maximize standardization. Although, in the case of ISRD-1, we had achieved a valid and reliable questionnaire, and issued a number of clear instructions, some researchers introduced individual modifications, such as not asking all of the questions, changing some of them, or using different response categories. In addition, coding instructions were not strictly followed. Unfortunately, many researchers just did not realize the great importance of standardization for comparative purposes: the absence of exact similarity in the questionnaires made comparison extremely difficult, if not impossible.

So in order to avoid any future problems in future surveys, we took great pains to maximize collaboration among the participating countries. The ISRD-2 is not centrally funded, and was thus not able to provide financial support and/or incentives to its research partners. The ISRD project basically consists of a loosely coupled set of researchers from a number of countries who agreed to adhere to the ISRD protocol, and who were successful in securing local or national funding for doing the ISRD study. The ISRD protocol included the basic comparative design and methodology (i.e. survey instruments and sampling design, rules for data coding and data entry, and agreement to provide national data set for merging into international data set). The basic design and methodology were produced by the ISRD Steering Committee (SC), but a number of the specifics only were finalized after extensive discussions and consultations with participating researchers. An example is the decision to use seventh, eighth, and ninth graders as the target population (rather than the 14–21-year-old age group which was the focus of ISRD-1). The SC had settled on a school-based survey in principle, but it took a lengthy, often heated discussion during a workshop in Brigels, Switzerland with a large number of the ISRD partners to finally decide that these three grades offered the best opportunity to capture the 12–15-year-olds in most of the participating countries (because of compulsory education). In comparable fashion, it took several meetings and extensive internet discussions to finalize the ISRD-2 questionnaire (about 1 year and a half). Even an apparently simple issue, such as which response categories to provide for the question on family composition, turned out to be a rather complex question, that elicited several different suggested solutions. After the instrument was finalized, we required from participants – of which there now were 30 instead of the initial 13 – that from that point on absolutely nothing would be changed in the pre-coded questionnaire. There are many more examples of how we managed to make the project a truly collaborative and participatory experience, such as the decision to broaden the initial city-based sampling design to allow a handful of national samples for those research partners whose funding favoured such approach, on the condition that they oversample at least one large city in order to maintain comparability or the lengthy debates – and pilot data collection efforts in different countries – about which local and national structural indicators to collect. Needless to say, there was a continuous tension between the need for standardization (of questions, of sampling methods, of survey administration, of data coding and data entry) and the desire to make the project genuinely collaborative and participatory for all researchers involved, no matter in which country they lived. It should be remembered that adherence to the basic ISRD protocol was, basically, completely voluntary; it was therefore essential that all partners felt truly invested in the importance of maintaining the integrity of the ISRD comparative design. In the end, we feel confident that this is the case. And we are satisfied with the "flexible standardization" which most accurately describes the final outcome of our approach.

We depended on three tools to manage the project so as to maximize the adherence to research protocol in a standardized manner: (1) regular workshops; (2) electronic procedures to facilitate sampling and survey administration, and data coding and data entry (Lauritsen 2006); and (3) national technical reports.

1.2.1 Workshops

Starting in 2004, the SC has organized ISRD workshops twice a year.[3] These workshops had multiple functions. One function was to familiarize our partners with the basic ISRD methodology and design, and to explain the rationale behind some of its features. Not all partners had a comparable level of training or familiarity with survey

[3] Although usually well attended, not all partners were able to attend all meetings; some partners never physically were present. However, workshop papers and minutes were made available to all ISRD partners through the ISRD website and mailing list.

methodology, and these workshops provided the opportunity to field questions and suggest ways of dealing with problems. Throughout all meetings, the SC continued to emphasize the importance of maintaining a truly comparative design, even when local realities and time pressures threatened to overshadow this important ISRD objective. Perhaps of more importance was that these meetings also provided a forum for input and feedback from all partners: about problems faced in the field, or with sampling strategies, translation of questionnaire items, cooperation from schools, or data management. Partly because of these workshops, the study remained "a work in progress" throughout, since a number of unanticipated methodological and logistic problems were resolved as the project was already underway. The ISRD-2 project, from beginning to end, took about 6 years, and several national research teams changed composition during that time. The workshops helped to train and socialize researchers who joined the project when it was already underway. The workshops, in a sense, functioned as a form of "continuing education" for all involved. Last but not least, many new international collaborative relationships among groups of researchers were formed as a result of participation in these meetings.

1.2.2 Electronic Tools for Standardization

The ISRD has as its core a standard survey instrument (ISRD-2 questionnaire, see ISRD Workgroup 2005), as well as a standardized sampling plan, accompanied by instructions on administration and implementation in order to minimize national differences. In order to facilitate drawing comparable random samples (see Chap. 2), researcher partners had access to a pre-programmed software package ("Survey manager"). The "Survey manager" is an Excel program especially written for the ISRD-2 study to manage the list of schools and classes, to draw random samples of classes, and to manage survey administration. Standardized data entry was made possible by using the free EpiData software (Lauritsen 2006). This latter program ensured that all survey responses – regardless of the language of the questionnaire – were to be coded in exactly the same manner. Very detailed coding instructions were provided, with particular careful explanation about the differences between missing data, "no" responses, and "not applicable" categories. Keeping these categories distinct is particularly important when dealing with survey questions about offending ("did you ever …") and follow-up questions. Although there was some reluctance among some of the partners to utilize these tools, ultimately most of the data were indeed entered through the standardized data entry method.

1.2.3 National Technical Reports

It would have been naïve to expect complete standardization and full adherence to the general ISRD design by all countries. Realizing that no research project, no matter how small or large, succeeds in a perfect implementation of its research design, the ISRD project asked all participants to document all major methodological and other decisions made. The underlying philosophy was that some deviations from the design and methodology are inevitable, but they do not necessarily have to be fatal to the integrity of the larger project. That is, as long as there is detailed documentation about the kind of decisions that have been made (e.g. with regard to deviations from the sampling plan, or administration of the questionnaire), these deviations can be taken into account when interpreting the data. The partners were asked to write a national technical report, following a standardized outline, with details about sampling, survey administration, data entry, and so on.[4]

1.3 Theoretical Considerations

Comparative researchers have long argued that cross-national research provides a very useful method for generating, testing, and further developing sociological theories. In ISRD-1, where the major emphasis was placed on designing an instrument to measure delinquency, we limited the number of theoretical variables to some questions based on social bonding theory (Hirschi 1969), measuring school performance, school commitment, work commitment, bond with parents, supervision by parents, bond with friends, and organized leisure and sports participation. In the new rounds of ISRD surveys (ISRD-2), we have responded to the call for an expansion of the theoretical perspectives included (see Klein in Junger-Tas et al. 1994).

In considering the various options, we have chosen some of the strongest theoretical orientations regarding the genesis of delinquent behaviour: social control (social bonding) theory, self-control theory, routine activities/opportunity theory, and social disorganization/collective efficacy theory. These, mainly American theories, may now be tested in order to examine to what extent they may be valid in other countries than the Anglo-Saxon ones. Because of limitations to the length of the questionnaire, by necessity we were not able to include all possible measures pertaining to these theoretical perspectives, but we are satisfied that we have sufficiently relevant data to test the cross-national generalize-ability of these different perspectives.

1.3.1 Social Bonding/Social Control Theory

One of the most tested theories in criminology is social control – or social bonding – theory. It has been developed in the 1950s and has been systematized by Travis Hirschi (1969). In later years the theory has been considerably expanded (Laub and Sampson 2003; Sampson and Laub 1993; Sampson et al. 1997, 1999; Wikstrom 2004). Hirschi argues that delinquent acts are due to weakened or broken individual bonds to society. Social bonding is measured through four major elements:

[4] These technical reports are available on request.

attachment to significant others, such as parents, teachers, family, friends; commitment to act and achieve one's personal goals in a way that conforms to the social normative system; involvement in conforming social activities; and beliefs in the general social and moral norms and values of society. The general argument is that these four elements are significantly related to delinquency. The stronger they are, the lower the probability of delinquency. Hirschi claims that young people who have strong bonds with their parents would interiorize their parents' values and norms. As a consequence they would behave in a norm-conforming way, and since they would not want to disappoint their parents, they would try to do well in school and so there would be no incentive to play truant. Moreover, in meeting the demands from family, school, and the larger society, such juveniles would be rewarded by praise and privileges and a promising future. In this way they would develop a stake in conformity as well as strong inhibitions against delinquency involvement that might endanger such rewards. Hirschi also claims that such young people would select a few good friends with whom they would develop close bonds and resist to be involved with a large peer group, which runs a high risk to look out for mischief and troublesome behaviour "just for fun". However, this last point turned out to be one of the weaknesses in his theory, since later research showed that Hirschi had greatly underestimated both the group character of most juvenile leisure time interactions and the role of the peer group in facilitating deviant behaviour. For example, findings in some studies on the attachment to peers as well as their influence on behaviour are contradictory to the predictions made by social control theory (Junger-Tas 1992; Hindelang 1973; Johnson 1979). In addition, the theory does not consider the wider macro-structure of society, and consequently does not take into account the fact that children are raised in very different social and economic contexts, which may have an important impact on their parents socializing skills (Kornhauser 1978; Sampson and Laub 1993). However, since the main tenets of social control theory have generally been supported by research, we test the social control perspective in our study by measuring attachment to significant others, to school and to friends, as well as by the way the young person functions in several social sub-systems, such as the school and the family as well as with peers. Because of its central importance, all theoretically oriented chapters in this book (Chaps. 7–12) include a test of some aspects of social bonding theory, either alone or in combination with other perspectives. Chapters 7 (on the family) and 8 (on the school) in particular have social bonding theory as their central focus.

1.3.2 Self-Control Theory

A second theoretical perspective was developed by Gottfredson and Hirschi in their book "A General Theory of Crime", published in 1990. The principal thesis of the book is that a lack of self-control explains all possible types of deviant behaviour. According to the authors, low self-control in (young) people is not only predictive of crime but also of other types of comparable behaviours, such as excessive smoking and drinking, driving dangerously, and being involved in dangerous sports. As the authors note:

> … people who lack self-control will tend to be impulsive, insensitive, physical, risk-taking, short sighted and non verbal, and they will tend therefore to engage in criminal and analogous acts. Since these traits can be identified prior to the age of responsibility for crime, since there is considerable tendency for these traits to come together in the same people, and since these traits tend to persist through life, it seems reasonable to consider them as comprising a stable construct useful in the explanation of crime (Gottfredson and Hirschi 1990, 90–91).

The authors do not consider self-control as an innate characteristic, but claim that self-control becomes part of one's personality as a result of a training process by parents at a young age (acquired at age 8–10). If that training process fails, the lack of self-control will be a permanent characteristic of the child's personality, the consequences of which will be felt during his whole life. To test this, we included 12 items of the Grasmick et al. *self-control scale* (1993). Although empirical research so far has been rather supportive of the self-control theory, the question whether self-control theory is a true *general* theory of crime is still open (Pratt and Cullen 2000). Chapter 11 of this volume focuses explicitly on this particular theoretical perspective, although self-control is included in most theoretically oriented analyses throughout the book.

1.3.3 Routine Activities/Opportunity Theory

A quite interesting perspective, in particular with respect to juveniles, has been developed in Cohen and Felson's (1979) Routine Activities theory, which considers primarily the phenomenon of crime rather than that of offenders. The authors have studied the trends in crime over time, while considering the impact of technological and social change on everyday life and on the movements of people. They particularly consider criminal victimization in relation to situational context. The three main categories of variables, defining a situational context favouring a criminal act, are identified by Cohen and Felson as follows: (1) a motivated offender; (2) a suitable target; and (3) a lack of capable guardianship. They argue that these three categories of variables affect the likelihood of victimization (Cohen and Felson 1979; Felson 1998). Routine activities theory was later redefined into Opportunity theory, including additional theoretical elements predicting victimization, such as exposure, proximity, and the attractiveness of specific targets. Although findings tend to be supportive of most of its theoretical predictions, existing research has yet to test the full model of opportunity theory. Our study examines opportunities for young people to commit delinquent acts by looking at the (number of) peers, type of (collective) leisure activities, and belonging to a gang on the basis of a number of questions devised by the Eurogang group, an international group of gang researchers created by Malcolm Klein and his colleagues (Decker and Weerman 2005). Chapter 9 focuses explicitly on the role of opportunity and life style, but – again – most other chapters also include this important concept in their analyses.

1.3.4 *Social Disorganization/Collective Efficacy Theory*

Finally, more recently there has been a renewed interest in the possible impact of neighbourhood factors on delinquent behaviour (Bursik 1988; Bursik and Grasmick 1993; Kubrin and Weitzer 2003; Sampson and Laub 1993; Sampson 1987, 2006; Sampson and Groves 1989; Sampson et al. 1997; Wikström 1998). Families and children live under greatly varying social-economic conditions (Kornhauser 1978; Rutter and Giller 1983) and one's social class as well as the ethnic structure of society and its geographical distribution is of great importance. Kornhauser pointed out that disorganized neighbourhoods cannot transmit shared norms and values because they are unable to exercise social control on (adolescent) residents. Sampson and colleagues have further explored this idea by developing the concept of collective efficacy, linking social cohesion in a neighbourhood, as a function of mutual trust and solidarity, with the willingness of people to enforce social norms of behaviour (Sampson et al. 1997, 1999). The capability of neighbourhoods to realize a positive social climate is variable, and disorganized neighbourhoods in particular, with their concentration of poverty, minorities, and single parent families lead to isolation. Sampson and Laub further argue that the environment and living conditions of families have a great influence on parents' management skills in raising their children (Sampson and Laub 1993).

Research (Sampson et al. 1997) showed that neighbourhood social-economic deprivation, concentration of minorities, and high population turnover are negatively related to social control and positively to the level of violence. These factors are stronger predictors of violence than the (lack of) local services or friendship and kinship ties. Another finding is that social control on children is not exclusively exercised by their own parents, but that an important role is played by social organizational characteristics of the neighbourhood, such as mutual contacts between parents, exchange among parents, informal social control, and mutual support of residents (Sampson et al. 1999). The ISRD-2 study has added a number of questions on the characteristics of the neighbourhood the young person is living in, which are measured by a scale developed by Olweus (1996) and Sampson and colleagues (1999). Chapter 10 focuses explicitly on the central role of the neighbourhood, while the other theoretically oriented chapters also incorporate neighbourhood effects in their analysis.

1.4 ISRD-2 Methodology

Here, we just sketch some main features of the way we conducted this study. For more details and an elaborate review of all aspects of the ISRD-2 methodology, the reader should consult Chap. 2.

1.4.1 The Sample

Data were collected in 31 countries. The ISRD-2 has opted for city-based samples, rather than national random samples for a number of reasons. The primary purpose of the study was to examine the theoretical correlates of juvenile delinquency, which makes the representativeness of the sample of secondary importance (Maxfield and Babbie 2001). Furthermore, in order to test international similarities and differences of correlates of delinquency, city-based samples of secondary school students would be adequate. In addition, an important consideration for countries such as Germany, USA, Poland, and Russia was that data collection would be less costly and easier to handle in a handful of cities rather than in a random selection of schools all over the country.

So, the *core sample* was a school-based study with school classes as sampling units, including about 2,100 students per participating country. The sampling design required a minimum of five cities, the main selection criteria being size, degree of urbanization, demographic, and economic variables. Based on these criteria, there are three sub-samples including a metropolitan area, a medium-sized city, and some small rural towns. Samples would be stratified according to school type (academic or vocational) and grade level (seventh and ninth grade). The final sample would be a random sample of school classes. The number of students drawn from each school type was to be proportional to the proportion of children in each school type at city level. However, some countries had the possibility of funding a national random sample, based on a random sample of classes of all schools. This sampling design would make it possible to have national delinquency rates, but in order to obtain maximum comparability between participating countries, these countries did oversample one city according to the criteria mentioned. After the study was completed, we have a total of 67,883 student questionnaires, collected from 36 large and 32 medium size cities and 60 small towns (16 clusters of 2–9 small towns) in 31 countries.

1.4.2 The Instruments

The ISRD-2 uses paper-and-pencil self-administered questionnaires conducted in a school setting.[5] The ISRD-2 instrument was based on an expansion and modification of the ISRD-1 questionnaire. First, we wanted to make a rather comprehensive assessment of delinquent behaviour. To that end the following measures were used: *ever* (or lifetime) prevalence measures the percentage of youth who have ever committed a particular delinquent act; *current* prevalence measures the percentage of youth who have committed an offence in a given time limit, in our case the past year; *frequency* (or incidence) measures the number of times an offence has been

[5] Exceptions are Denmark, Finland and Switzerland where a computerized data collection method was used.

committed, while *variety* or *versatility* combines frequency and seriousness measuring the number of different types of acts committed. In addition, we asked probing questions to get more information on the circumstances of the event, co-offenders, victims, and place of occurrence, as well as social response to the act, including detection and reaction by parents, police, and others.

Second, a rather important measure according to the literature, *age of onset*, is also included in the instrument. Longitudinal studies suggest two general development trajectories for juvenile delinquency, early and late. Some self-report-based studies find that the frequency of offending is highest for those who have the earliest age of onset (Olweus 1979; Farrington and West 1990; Loeber 1991). Others argue that early and later onset offenders are qualitatively different (Moffit 1993).

Third, prior research has suggested that juvenile offending and *victimization* are closely related (Esbensen and Huizinga 1991; Lauritsen et al. 1991; Sampson and Lauritsen 1990, 1994; Schreck and Osgood 2008; van Dijk and Steinmetz 1983). In particular a delinquent lifestyle is viewed as a strong indicator of victimization. The ISRD-2 study did directly assess victimization experiences of respondents, which will allow us to conduct cross-national analysis of the relationship between juvenile delinquent acts and victimization.

Fourth, *ethnic minorities* are a group of growing importance in the study of crime (Junger 1989, 1990; Junger and Marshall 1997; van Hulst and Bos 1993; Junger-Tas 1997; Junger-Tas et al. 2003; Marshall 1997). "Minorities and crime" is a topic that is controversial, much debated, and often fraught with misconceptions. A key question in this respect – in both Europe and North America – refers to the extent of criminal involvement of foreigners, first- or second-generation immigrants, as compared to the youth population of origin. The ISRD-2 data allow us to address the theoretical relationship between minority status and self-reported delinquency.

Finally, the questionnaire includes variables related to the family, school, leisure time, peers, neighbourhood, and self-control (see previous discussion on theoretical considerations).

In addition to student surveys, we also collected a large number of national structural indicators for use in macro-level analyses. These structural indicators were collected from sources such as the International Crime Victim survey, World Values Survey, European Sourcebook, and a number of other international databases.

1.4.3 One Important Analytic Tool: Country Clusters

For both practical and theoretical reasons, we sought for an empirical method to cluster the 30 ISRD-2 countries into a smaller, more manageable number for our analyses. We have chosen for a classification of countries based on a theoretical perspective related to the different national welfare regimes (Esping-Andersen 1990; Saint-Arnaid and Bernard 2003). This view is based on the principle that all individuals provide for their needs by producing essentially goods and services in three different ways: (1) they work on the market place and get paid; (2) they pay taxes to the state and they may expect in return important public services and income transfers; (3) civil society (charities) and the family offer services and support (Esping-Andersen 1990; Saint-Arnaid and Bernard 2003). Depending on ideological orientation, different combinations of these three ways determine the social organization – or welfare regime – of any particular state. The first – qualitative – researcher to make a typology on this basis was Esping-Andersen (1990, 1999) who, adding cultural, economical, and institutional country differences, categorized societies into three types of social organization:

- The social democratic model (Scandinavian countries)
- The liberal model (Anglo-Saxon countries)
- The corporatist model (continental Europe)

The Scandinavian model is based on the idea of *equality* between citizens and is characterized by an extensive role of the state and an elaborate welfare system, reducing inequalities and fighting social exclusion. This results in high taxes and extensive income transfers providing among others free health care, free education, qualitatively good childcare, and generously paid parental leave. In this system, the state takes great responsibility for its citizens' well-being, reconciling – among others – the combination of employment and motherhood.

The ideological basis of the Anglo-Saxon liberal model is *freedom*, expressed in particular by the market economy. It is based on the view that income has to be generated either by participation in the labour market or by family support, and people would have to cover social risks by private insurance. Social security is seen as a last resort, social expenditures are limited, and benefits are low and restricted in time.

The – European – continental model considers first and foremost *the risks* of workers during their working life, such as unemployment or illness. This model provides for income on the basis of employment history and last earned income.[6] Specific organizations are responsible for taking care of social security benefits, but the state imposes social insurance through contributions from employers and employees. However, as Saint-Arnaud and Bernard (2003, 504) observe, in a system that is exclusively based on employment, those who do not work risk themselves to be excluded from the social welfare system.

Finally, other researchers added a fourth model to the three models proposed by Esping-Anderson, which they called Latin or Southern, since it was a type mainly found in South-European countries (Leibfried 1992; Ferrera 1996; Bonoli 1997; see also Smit et al. 2008). The South European model is more restricted than the continental model, since it is based on the principle of *subsidiarity*, in which the – extended – family is the principal source of providing for social security, with the church and charities forming a fall back position in case of extreme poverty. Of course these models are "ideal types", hardly existing in reality in its pure form, but nevertheless

[6] More recently pensions are based on the mean earned income over the years of employment.

they are very insightful and they led to fruitful analyses in ISRD-1 (Junger-Tas et al. 2003). Saint-Arnaud and Bernard (2003) have validated this typology in a quantitative model, using a large number of indicators, such as income taxes, social security contributions by individuals and employers, public expenditures on health and education, GDP annual growth rates, unemployment rates, and life expectancy at birth, to name but a few. Using these indicators, they were able to classify countries according to the original model designed by Esping-Andersen (1999).

Using the Esping-Anderson typology elaborated by Saint-Arnaud and Bernard (2003), we grouped the 30 ISRD-2 countries into six country clusters (two of which – post-socialist and Latin American – we added ourselves).

- The Anglo-Saxon cluster, including the United States, Canada, and Ireland.
- The West-European cluster, grouping Germany, France, Belgium, Netherlands, Austria, and Switzerland.
- The Scandinavian cluster, covering all Northern countries (Finland, Sweden, Norway, Denmark, and Iceland).
- The South-European cluster, including Spain, Italy, Portugal, and Cyprus.
- The Post-Socialist countries, which are considered as a category apart and comprise the Czech Republic, Poland, Hungary, Estonia, Lithuania, Slovenia, Bosnia, Armenia, and Russia.
- A rather heterogeneous Latin-American cluster, including Venezuela, Dutch Antilles, Aruba, and Surinam.

In making use of these clusters we do not mean to deny intra-cluster differences between countries, and throughout our analyses we do present and discuss country-specific data. However, we are confident that the significant practical as well as theoretical advantages of country clustering will become evident throughout the chapters that follow. Because of its central importance to our analysis, we will further expand on the use of the clustering approach in Chap. 2.

1.5 Structure of the Book

Part I (this chapter and Chap. 2) provides the general introduction of the study, including its organization, methodology, and design. Chapter 2 describes the many unexpected methodological issues that came up in this international comparative study bringing together 30 countries of highly different socio-economic and cultural background, and the solutions we found to these issues. This chapter will be particularly useful for researchers wishing to launch international comparative studies.

Part II (Chaps. 3–6) presents findings on the extent and nature of delinquency (Chap. 3), victimization (Chap. 4), substance use and abuse (Chap. 5), as well as the social response to offending and victimization (Chap. 6). Differences and similarities among individual countries as well as among country clusters are examined, mainly in a descriptive manner, but frequently supplemented by more in depth multi-variate analyses. Chapters 3–5 deal extensively with issues such as prevalence, frequency, versatility of the different behaviours (offending, substance use, and victimization) and their interrelationship. In addition, the association of these variables with gender, grade, age of onset, family structure, and ethnicity is examined, often finding considerable differences between country clusters. Chapter 6 focuses on the social response to victimization (i.e. reporting behaviour) and offending (i.e. detection and punishment) and draws conclusions about cross-national variability in social response and its implications for the validity of official crime data.

Part III (Chaps. 7–11) forms the heart of the ISRD-2 study because of its explicitly theory-testing approach: Chap. 7 focuses on the importance of the family; Chap. 8 analyses the impact of the school and the education system on delinquency and victimization; Chap. 9 centres around the role of the life-style and opportunity on young people's misbehaviour; Chap. 10 takes the neighbourhood as its central focus; and Chap. 11 tests different claims related to the concept of self-control. Although varying in their emphasis and focus, each of these chapters tests some claims derived from social control theory, self-control theory, social disorganization/ collective efficacy theory, and/or opportunity theory.

Part IV (Chap. 12) aims to pull together the complex and varied findings presented in the previous chapters. We place our findings in a broader macro-sociological perspective, and discuss theoretical implications as well as possible policy suggestions.

References

Arooma, K., & Heiskanen, M. (Eds.). (2008). *Crime and Criminal Justice Systems in Europe and North America 1995–2004.* Helsinki, Finland: HEUNI.

Bonoli, G. (1997) 'Classifying Welfare States: A Two Dimensional Approach', *Journal of Social Policy, 26*(3): 351–72.

Bursik, R., Jr, & Grasmick, H. (1993). Neighborhoods and crime. The dimension of effective community control. San Francisco: Lexington Books.

Bursik, R. J., Jr. (1988). Social disorganization and theories of crime and delinquency: Problems and prospects. *Criminology, 26*(4), 519–552.

Cohen, L. E., & Felson, M. (1979). Social change and crime rate trends: A routine activities approach. *American Sociological Review, 44*:588–608.

Currie, C. et al. (2008). *Inequalities in Young People's Health. HBSC International Report from the 2005/2006 Survey.* Copenhagen: World Health Organization.

Decker, S. H., & Weerman, F. (2005). *European Street Gangs and Troublesome Youth Groups.* Lanham, MD: Alta Mira.

Dunkel, F., Gebauer, D., Geng, B., & Kesterman, C. (2007). *Mare Balticum Youth Survey – Gewalterfahrungen von Jugendlichen im Ostseeraum.* Godesberg, Germany: Forum.

Enzmann, D., Marshall, I. H., Killias, M., Junger-Tas, J., Steketee, M., & Gruszczynska, B. (2010). Self-reported delinquency in Europe and beyond: First results of the Second International Self-Report Delinquency Study in the context of police and victimization data. *European Journal of Criminology, 7*(2), 159–181.

Esbensen, F., & Huizinga, D. (1991). Juvenile Victimization and Delinquency. *Youth and Society, 23*, 208–228.

Esping-Andersen, G. (1990). *The Three Worlds of Welfare Capitalism.* Princeton, NJ: Princeton University Press.

Esping-Andersen, G. (1999). Social Foundations of Postindustrial Economies. New York: Oxford University Press, pp 549–550.

Farrington, D.P & D.J. West (1990). The Cambridge study in Delinquent Development: a long-term follow-up of 411 males in: G. Kaiser, H.J. Kerner (eds) Criminality: Personality, Behaviour, Life History, Berlin, Springer.

Felson, M. (1998), Crime in Everyday Life – Insight and Implications for Society, 2nd edition. Thousand Oaks/London, Pine Forge Press.

Ferrera, M. (1996). 'The "Southern" Model of Welfare in Europe', *Journal of European Social Policy, 6*(1): 17–37.

Gottfredson, M. R., & Hirschi, T. (1990). *A General Theory of Crime*. Stanford, Stanford University Press.

Grasmick, H. G., Title, C. R., & Arneklev, B. J. (1993). Testing the core empirical implications of Gottfredson and Hirschi's general theory of crime. *Journal of Research in Crime and Delinquency, 30*, 5–29.

Hibell, B., Andersson, B., Bjarnason, T., Ahlstrom, S., Balakireva, O., Kokkevi, A., & Morgan, M. (2004). *The ESPAD Report 2003: Alcohol and Other Drug Use Among Students in 35 European Countries*. Stockholm: Swedish Council for Information on Alcohol and Other Drugs.

Hindelang, M. J.(1973). Causes of delinquency: a Partial Replication and Extension, *Social Problems, 20*(4), 471–487.

Hirschi, T. (1969). *Causes of Delinquency*. Berkeley:University of California Press.

ISRD2 Working Group (2005). *Questionnaire ISRD2: Standard Student Questionnaire*. Boston, Hamburg, Utrecht, Warsaw, and Zurich: European Society of Criminology.

Johnson, R. E. (1979). *Juvenile Delinquency and its Origins, an Integrated Theoretical Approach*. London, Cambridge University Press.

Junger-Tas, J., Marshall, I. H., Enzmann, D., Killias, M., Steketee, M., & Gruszczynska, B. (Eds.). (2010). *Juvenile Delinquency in Europe and Beyond: Results of the International Self-Report Delinquency Study*. New York: Springer.

Junger-Tas, J., Marshall, I. H., & Ribeaud, D. (2003). *Delinquency in an International Perspective: The International Self-Report Delinquency Study (ISRD)*. The Hague: Kugler.

Junger-Tas, J., & Haen Marshall, I. (1999). The self-report methodology in crime research. In M. Tonry (Ed.), *Crime and Justice: A Review of Research* (Vol. 25, pp. 291–368). Chicago: University of Chicago Press.

Junger-Tas, J. (1997). Ethnic Minorities and Criminal Justice in the Netherlands. In M. Tonry (Ed.), *Crime and Justice: A Review of Research* (Vol. 21, pp. 257–310). Chicago: University of Chicago Press.

Junger-Tas, J. (1996). Youth and Violence in Europe: a Quantitative Review, Studies on Crime and Crime Prevention, vol. 5, p.31–58.

Junger-Tas, J., Terlouw, G., & Klein, M. (Eds.). (1994). *Delinquent Behavior Among Young People in the Western World: First Results of the International Self-Report Delinquency Study.* Amsterdam: Kugler.

Junger-Tas, J (1992), Criminaliteit en Tijd, *Justitiële Verkenningen*, jrg.18, nr 3, 66–89.

Junger, M. (1990). *Delinquency and Ethnicity: an Investigation on Social Factors relating to Delinquency among Moroccan, Turkish, Surinamese and Dutch Boys*. Deventer/Boston: Kluwer Law and Taxation.

Junger, M. (1989). Discrepancies between Police and Self-report Data for Dutch Racial Minorities. *British. Journal of Criminology, 29*, 273–283.

Junger, M., & Marshall, I. H. (1997). The Inter-Ethnic Generalizability of Social Control Theory: An Empirical Test, *The Journal of Research in Crime and Delinquency, 3*(1), 79–112.

Killias, M. (2001). Précis de Criminologie, 2ème édition. Berne: Stämpfli.

Kohn, M. L. (1987). Cross-national research as an analytic strategy. *American Sociological Review, 52*(6), 713–731.

Kornhauser, R. R. (1978). *Social Sources of Delinquency: An Appraisal of Analytic models*. University of Chicago Press, Chicago.

Kubrin, C. E., & Weitzer, R. (2003). New directions in social disorganization theory. *Journal of Research in Crime and Delinquency, 40*(4), 374–402.

Laub, J. H., & Sampson, R. J. (2003). *Shared Beginnings, Divergent Lives: Delinquent Boys to Age 70.* Cambridge: Harvard University Press.

Lauritsen, J. L., Sampson, R. J., & Laub, J. H. (1991). The link between offending and victimization among adolescents. *Criminology, 29*, 265–292.

Lauritsen, J. M. (Ed.). (2006). *Epidata Data Entry, Data Management and Basic Statistical Analysis System.* Odense, Denmark: Epidata Association.

Leibfried, S. (1992) 'Towards a European Welfare State? On Integrating Poverty Regimes into the European Community', in Z. Ferge and J. E. Kolberg (eds) *Social Policy in a Changing Europe*, pp. 245–80. Frankfurt am Main: Campus.

Loeber, R. (1991). Antisocial Behavior: More Enduring than Changeable? American Academy of Child and Adolescent Psyciatry, vol.30, no. 3, p.393–397.

Marshall, I. H. (1996). How Exceptional is the United States? Crime Trends in Europe and the United States. *European Journal on Criminal Policy and Research 4*(2), 8–35.

Marshall, I. H. (1997). *Minorities, Migrants, and Crime: Diversity and Similarity across Europe and the United States.* Thousands Oaks, CA: Sage.

Marshall, I. H., & Webb, V. J. (1994). Self-reported Delinquency in a Mid-western American City. In J. Junger-Tas, G. Terlouw & M. Klein (Eds.), *Delinquent Behavior Among Young People in the Western World: First Results of the International Self-report Delinquency Study.* (pp. 319–342). Amsterdam, The Netherlands: Kugler.

Maxfield, K. G., & Babbie, E. (2001). *Research Methods in Criminology and Criminal Justice.* New York: Wadsworth.

Moffit, T. E. (1993). Adolescence Limited and Life Course Persistent Antisocial Behavior: A Development Taxonomy. *Psychological Review 100*, 674–701.

Newman, G. (1999). *Global Report on Crime and Justice: United Nations Office for Drug Control and Crime Prevention.* Centre for International Crime Prevention, Oxford University Press.

Olweus, D. (1979). Stability of Aggressive Reaction Patterns in Males: a Review Psychological Bulletin, vol. 86, no. 4, p. 852–875.

Olweus, D. (1996). Bully/victim problems at school: Facts and effective interventions. *Reclaiming Children and Youth: Journal of Emotional and Behavioral Problems*, 5(1), 15–22.

Pauwels, L., & Svensson, R. (2008). How serious is the problem of item non-response in delinquency scales and eatiological variables? A cross-national inquiry into two classroom PAPA self-report studies in Antwerp and Halmstedt. *European Journal of Criminology, 5*, 298–308.

Pauwels, L., & Svensson, R. (2010). Informal controls and the explanation of propensity to offend: A test in two urban samples. *European Journal on Criminal Policy and Research, 16*, 15–27.

Pease, K., & Hukkula, K. (eds.) (1990). Criminal Justice Systems en Europe and North-America. Helsinki: Helsinki Institute for Crime Prevention and Control.

Pratt, T., & Cullen, F. (2000). The empirical status of Gottfredson and Hirschi's general theory of crime: A meta-analysis. *Criminology, 38*(3), 931–964.

Rutter, M. and Giller, H. (1983). Juvenile Delinquency: Trends and Perspectives. New York: Penguin Books.

Saint-Arnaid, S., & Bernard, P. (2003). Convergence or resilience? A hierarchical cluster analysis of the welfare regimes in advanced countries. *Current Sociology, 51*, 499–527.

Sampson, R. J. (2006). Collective efficacy theory: Lessons learned and directions for future inquiry. In F. T. Cullen, J. P. Wright & K. Blevins (Eds.), *Taking Stock: The Status of Criminological Theory* (pp. 149–167). New Brunswick, NJ: Transaction.

Sampson, R. J., Morenoff, J. D., & Earls, F. (1999). Beyond social capital: Spatial dynamics of collective efficacy for children. *American Sociological Review, 64*, 633–660.

Sampson, R. J., Raudenbush, S. W., & Earls, F. (1997). Neighborhoods and violent crime: A multilevel study of collective efficacy. *Science, 277*(5328), 918.

Sampson, R. J., & Lauritsen, J. L. (1994). Violent Victimization and Offending: Individual-, Situational- and Community-level Risk Factors. In J. A.J. Reiss & J. A. Roth (Eds.), *Understanding and Preventing Violence: Social Influences* (Vol. 3, pp. 1–114). Washington, D.C.: National Academy Press.

Sampson, R. J., & Laub, J. H. (1993). *Crime in the Making: Pathways and Turning Points Through Life.* Cambridge: Havard University Press.

Sampson, R. J., & Lauritsen, J. L. (1990). Deviant lifestyles, proximity to crime and the offender-victim link in personal violence. *Journal of Research in Crime and Delinquency, 27*, 110–139.

Sampson, R. J., & Groves, W. B. (1989). Community structure and crime: Testing social-disorganization theory. *American Journal of Sociology, 94*(4), 774.

Sampson, R. J. (1987). Communities and crime. In T. Hirschi & M. Gottfredson (Eds.), *Positive Criminology* (pp. 91–114). Beverly Hills: Sage.

Schreck, C. J., Stewart, E. A., & Osgood, D. W. (2008). A reappraisal of the overlap of violent offenders and victims. *Criminology, 46*(4), 871–906.

Smit, P., Marshall, I. H., & van Gammeren, M. (2008). An empirical approach to country clustering. In K. Aromaa & M. Heiskanen (Eds.), *Crime and Criminal Justice Systems in Europe and North America 1995–2004* (pp. 169–195). Helsinki, Finland: HEUNI.

Straus, M. and International Dating Violence Research Consortium. (2004). Prevalence of violence against dating partners by male and female university students worldwide. *Violence against Women, 10*, 790–811.

Svensson, R., Pauwels, L., & Weerman, F. M. (2010). Does the effect of self-control on adolescent offending vary by level of morality? A test in three countries. *Criminal Justice and Behavior, 37*, 732–743.

Thornberry, T. P., & Krohn, M. D. (2000). The Self-Report Method for Measuring Delinquency and Crime. *Criminal Justice 2000* (Vol. 4, pp. 33–83). Washington D.C.: US National Institute of Justice.

Thornberry, T. P., & Krohn, M. D. (2003). Taking stock of delinquency. New York: Kluwer Academic/Plenum Publishers.

Van Dijk, J.J.M., and C.H.D.Steinmetz (1983). Victimisation Surveys: Beyond Measuring the Volume of Crime, Victimology: An International Journal, vol. 8, p. 291–301.

Van Dijk, J. J. M., van Kesteren, J., & Smit, P. (2008). *Criminal Victimisation in International Perspective: Key Findings from the 2004–2005 ICVS and EU ICS.* Hague, The Netherlands: Boom Legal Publishers.

Van Hulst, H., & Bos, J. (1993). *Criminaliteit van geïmmigreerde Curaçaose jongeren.* Utrecht: Onderzoek Collectief Utrecht.

Vazsonyi, A. T., Pickering, L. E., Junger, M. H., & Hessing, D. (2001). An Empirical Test of a General Theory of Crime: A Four-Nation Comparative Study of Self-Control and the Prediction of Deviance. *Journal of Research in Crime and Delinquency, 38*, 91–131.

Vetere, E., & Newman, G. (1977). International Crime Statistics: an Overview from a Comparative Perspective. Abstracts on Criminology and Penology, 17, 251–604.

Wikström, P-O. (1998), Communities and Crime, in: M. Tonry (ed.), The Handbook of Crime and Punishment, 269–302, New York, Oxford University Press.

Wikstrom, P. O. (2004). Crime as alternative: Towards a cross-level situational action theory of crime causation. In J. McCord (Ed.), *Beyond Empiricism:Institutions and Intentions in the Study of Crime. Advances in Criminological Theory* (Vol. 13). New Brunswick, N.J.: Transaction.

Wikstrom, P. O., & R., S. (2008). Why are English youth more violent than Swedish youth? A comparative study of the role of crime propensity, lifestyles and their interaction in two cities. *European Journal of Criminology, 5*(3), 309–330.

Zhang, S., Benson, T., & Deng, X. (2000). A Test-retest Reliability Assessment of the International Self-report Delinquency Instrument. *Journal of Criminal Justice 28*, 283–295.

Chapter 2
Methodology and Design of the ISRD-2 Study

Ineke Haen Marshall and Dirk Enzmann

The ISRD-2 as a comparative study of youth crime and victimization has two distinguishing features: (1) the rather large number of participating countries and (2) the explicitly standardized comparative design. There is no question that an explicit comparative design has many advantages over other designs. Yet, the cross-national standardized approach presents serious challenges and problems, methodologically as well as logistically. Some of these challenges we anticipated, some of them we did not. In a sense, because of its ambitious comparative design, our study has been "a work in progress" from the beginning – and continues to be so even at the stage of data analysis and – interpretation. The degree to which we have succeeded in achieving the goals of our study (i.e., to describe the cross-national variability in the prevalence and incidence of delinquency and victimization; to test for national differences in the theoretical correlates of delinquency and victimization; and to describe cross-national variability in selected dimensions of delinquency such as versatility, age of onset, co-offending) depends, to large extent, on the particular methodological choices we have made – at the onset of the project, and along the way. This chapter illuminates the problems, and our solutions to those problems considered solvable. Many challenges we encountered, however, are an integral (intrinsic) part of any type of cross-national research and simply cannot be solved. Awareness of these problems is the best weapon – and perhaps only – weapon against oversimplification or misinterpretation of the results.

It is the primary purpose of the chapter to discuss selected methodological issues in order to better understand the substantive chapters following this one. In that sense, it aims to provide a sort of technical guide. But, we hope to achieve more than that. Throughout, we take a "research as social activity" perspective: We provide context to illuminate the social processes which have shaped the ISDRD research process. As we have stressed before (Junger-Tas et al. 2010, p. 424), without such understanding of the research enterprise, the meaning of

I.H. Marshall (✉)
Northeastern University, Boston, MA, USA
e-mail: i.marshall@neu.edu

J. Junger-Tas et al., *The Many Faces of Youth Crime: Contrasting Theoretical Perspectives on Juvenile Delinquency across Countries and Cultures*,
DOI 10.1007/978-1-4419-9455-4_2, © Springer Science+Business Media, LLC 2012

particular data may be easily misconstrued. That is even more relevant in the cross-national context.[1]

The chapter is organized as follows. First, we briefly discuss the logic of comparative research methodology as it relates to the ISRD study (Sect. 2.1). Sections 2.2 and 2.3 focus on the most significant on the most significant sampling-related issues, and their implications for data analysis and interpretation. Discussion of instrumentation and measurement follows in Sect. 2.4, 2.5 and 2.6. The final section of the chapter evaluates questions related to the reliability and validity of the present study.

2.1 Comparative Research Methodology

As explained in the introductory chapter, the ISRD has multiple purposes, including the testing of criminological theories. There is no doubt that cross-national research provides a very useful method for generating, testing, and further developing sociological theories (see Kohn 1987). Comparative research is "an approach to knowing social reality through the examination for similarities and differences between data gathered from more than one nation" (Elder 1976, p. 210). It is well-known that the fathers of the social sciences, such as Durkheim, Marx, and Weber used comparative-historical approaches as the foundation for their insights. However, explicit discussions about the logic of the comparative method did not start to flourish until the 1960s and 1970s (Armer & Grimshaw 1973; Naroll 1970; Przeworski & Teune 1970; Rokkan 1968). Although there have been more recent elaborations of the debates that took place in the 1960s and 1970s, basically the same themes continue to dominate current discourse: the logic of the comparative method [Mill's methods of agreement or of difference (Lieberson 1991, 1994)], the equivalence of measures (i.e., the comparability of research variables across countries), the selection of nations (alike or dissimilar), and the meaning of "nation" (as an entity or as a set of variables) (see Loewenberg 1971). There is a vast literature on all these issues. All of these issues are relevant to our study, in one way or another, as will become evident throughout this – and all the subsequent chapters. Here, we briefly highlight how cross-national studies differ by the purpose of comparison (to show similarities or to show differences), and by the meaning of nation (as an entity or as a set of variables), because of the kinds of conclusions which may be drawn. The table below (adopted from Scheuch 1968, in Allardt 1990, p. 185) provides a powerful and concise overview of the different goals of comparative research (Table 2.1).

Comparative data provides an opportunity to test the universality of hypotheses in a situation of maximum differences (Przeworski & Teune 1970; Kohn 1987). Typically, comparative research is primarily interested in testing the assumption

[1] More detailed accounts of the particular methodological challenges encountered and decisions made by the individual country participants may be found in the country chapters in Juvenile Delinquency in Europe and Beyond: Results of the Second International Self-Report Delinquency Study, by Junger-Tas et al. 2010, Springer.

Table 2.1 Treatment of Nations

Purpose of comparison	Nation as an entity and historical unit	Nation as a set of variables
To show similarities	To identify universals	To prove general propositions
To show differences	To describe why societies are different	To specify time-space coordinates of propositions

that no national differences exist in variables of interest, for example, for present purposes, drug use or bullying. If differences are found, then national differences in observations are interpreted in terms of meaningful concomitant variations between the countries compared (Marsh 1967, p. 158). Since countries differ from one another on a great many variables, it is very difficult to determine which particular factor from among the many possible should be used to interpret the found differences. Obviously, more "similar" countries differ on fewer factors than more "dissimilar" countries. Therefore, the logic of the comparative design suggest that testing the universality of hypotheses (where there is no need to interpret differences)is best done in societies that are most dissimilar; specification of "time-space coordinates" (i.e., specifying under what conditions do particular hypotheses apply) is best accomplished in societies that are more similar (Marshall & Marshall 1983). The ISRD-2 data are mostly collected in Western societies (more similar), but also in a number of non-Western societies (more dissimilar). The ISRD design, then, maximizes the opportunity for hypothesis falsification as well as for theoretical specification. We will come back to this topic shortly.

2.1.1 Country Clusters

Some comparative studies focus on national *uniqueness* and cross-national contrasts, whereas other research studies are more interested in cross-national *similarities* and cross-national comparability. A third approach is primarily interested in "*cross-national subsets* and limited cross-national comparability" (Elder 1976, p. 210; italics ours). This third approach aims to avoid the danger of comparing phenomena outside their national contexts through the "identification of subsets of nations sufficiently similar (structurally or contextually) to permit meaningful within-subset comparisons. From these comparisons might emerge limited cross-national generalizations" (Elder 1976, p. 213). The ISRD study implemented this logic, by using six country clusters, incorporating Esping-Andersen's (1990) notion of levels of development of the welfare society. Our use of country clusters was already described in the Introduction (Chap. 1), but – because of its central importance to our analyses – it is important to highlight this issue once again. The criterion of decommodification, the degree to which individuals are protected from market forces when dealing with unemployment, disability and old age, is a very useful criterion to use in international comparative studies (Messner & Rosenfeld 1997; Savolainen 2000). Expanding on Esping-Andersen's ideas, Saint-Arnaud and

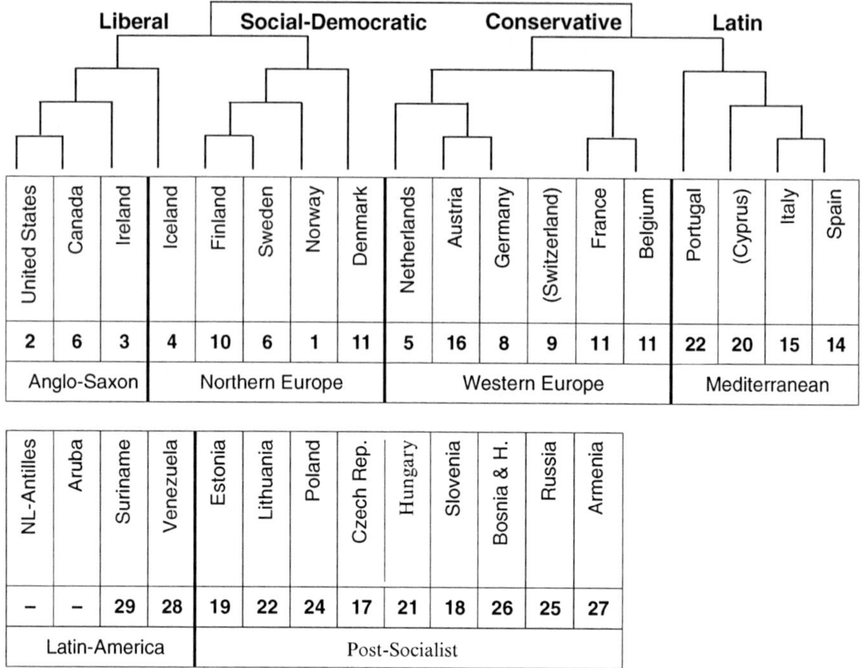

Fig. 2.1 Welfare regimes and rank of Human Development Index (HDI 2006, see UNDP, 2010) by Country clusters. *Notes*: Dendogram adapted from Saint-Arnaud & Bernard (2003, Fig. 4)

Bernard (2003) have developed an empirical grouping of countries, reflecting different welfare regimes (social democratic, liberal, conservative and "Latin," a family-oriented regime, where the family plays the determining role in ensuring material security). The clustering developed by Saint-Arnaud and Bernard is based on three distinct sets of social indicators: indicators of *social situations* (e.g., economic growth or life expectancy), of *public policy* (e.g., income tax or social security transfers), and of *civic participation* by citizens (e.g., voter turnout or level of trust). The ISRD has expanded the clusters by adding a Post-Socialist (see Lappi-Seppala 2007; Smit et al. 2008) and a Latin American cluster, thus grouping the countries into six clusters: Anglo-Saxon, Northern Europe, Western Europe, Mediterranean, Latin America, and Post-Socialist.

Figure 2.1 shows the clustering of countries into the four welfare regimes identified by Saint-Arnaud and Bernard (2003), the rank of the Human Development Index (HDI) of 2006 (UNDP 2010), and the actual clustering used in the following analyses. The HDI is a summary measure of health (life expectancy at birth), education (mean and expected years of schooling), and standard of living (GNI per capita). The figure illustrates that the HDI differs not only between ($F_{(5,23)} = 16.1$, $p < 0.001$) but also within countries. The human development (as measured by the HDI) is significantly lower in the Latin American and Post-Socialist countries as compared to the four clusters identified by Saint-Arnaud and Bernard, which validates our decision to set them apart.

One should note that apart from extending the classification scheme of Saint-Arnaud and Bernard by adding clusters of Latin American and Post-Socialist countries, we deviate from their classification of countries in three additional respects: Iceland that originally belongs to the cluster of liberal welfare regimes is placed into the Northern European cluster, Switzerland which was not part of Saint-Arnaud's and Bernard's analyses is placed within the Western European cluster, and Cyprus which was also lacking in their analyses takes the position of Greece.

The country clusters provide a very useful organizing framework to analyze a large number of countries simultaneously for several reasons. It makes analyses simply more manageable (i.e., rather than discussing differences and similarities between some 30 nations, it is now possible to focus on six country clusters instead). However, there are two additional advantages to the use of country subsets. First, as Elder (1976) argued, it provides a framework for *within-cluster* comparisons (i.e., comparing countries that may be assumed to be structurally more similar to one another, i.e., comparisons within the North European clusters, or within the Mediterranean countries). Comparisons between countries that are – in theory at least – more similar reduces the cultural variability and better allow the specification and refinement of theoretical propositions (see our discussion mentioned earlier). Having said this, we need to immediately add the precautionary note that the presumed similarity of countries within each cluster remains an important empirical question, and is well-illustrated throughout the different analyses in this book. A second strong point of the country cluster approach is that it allows to make *between-subsets* comparisons, testing the theoretical foundation (i.e., welfare regime combined with a regional criterion) of the clustering (and its implications for delinquency and victimization).

2.1.2 Multiple Levels and Units of Analysis

Much more could be said about the logic of the comparative design, including the use and meaning of countries – and subsets of countries – in comparative analysis. Instead, we hope to illustrate the different usages of "country" and country-level data throughout the substantive chapters of this book. In this context, it is important to stress that we designed our study with the aim to integrate micro-, meso-, and macro-levels of theorizing and analysis. The ISRD design allows us to address questions about the integration of micro-, meso- , and macro-levels of theorizing and analysis (Akers 2009; Johnson 2008; Wilcox et al. 2003), with the cross-national component adding an extra challenge, both theoretically and methodologically. Relevant units of analysis in our project are, respectively: individual pupils, classrooms, neighborhoods and schools (based on aggregated individual responses), cities and towns (aggregated individual responses as well as local indicators), countries (aggregated survey responses as well as national indicators we collected), and country clusters. This makes for a rather complex design at many different levels. Having said this, it should be noted that we have not used all of these possible units of analysis in this book. The challenges of sampling are discussed next.

2.2 Sampling

The ISRD design is complex, with analytic units at different levels. Sampling decisions were made at all respective levels of analysis: the selection of nations, cities and towns, schools, classrooms, and respondents (i.e., pupils).

2.2.1 *Nations: Meaningful Units or Simply Research Sites?*

Countries are more than simply research sites (i.e., places where data are collected); in a large cross-national study such as ours, they are meaningful units with a crucial role in the testing and specification of research hypotheses (Marshall & Marshall 1983). Typically, we do not think in terms of "sampling" when discussing the countries included in a comparative study. Still, as we discussed earlier in the chapter, which kind of countries are included (more similar or more dissimilar) has important implications for the kind of interpretations that may be drawn from the data. For our purposes, we were keen to expand the geographical coverage, in particular by including countries from Central and Eastern Europe. At the same time, we were also concerned with keeping the study manageable by maintaining the main focus on Europe. ISRD-2 was conducted in 15 western European countries, and ten Eastern and Central European countries. The USA (through cities and towns in four states) and Canada were also part of the study, as were some countries outside Europe and North America: Aruba together with the Netherlands Antilles, Suriname, and Venezuela. Obviously, the inclusion of these countries was not based on any kind of random sampling (from among the sampling frame of some 200 countries); rather, we simply tried to invite as many participants as possible through personal contacts and networks. In a sense, then, the ISRD-2 is a convenience sample (of nations), but a convenience sample with a strong concentration of "alike" (i.e., European) countries, and a handful of very dissimilar countries (which may be used for contrast).[2] Indeed, in analyses and interpretations of the ISRD-2 data, one should take maximum advantage of this particular combination of 31 countries. Comparisons between neighboring countries (like the Netherlands and Belgium) may be used for the specification of hypotheses (since the differences between these two countries may be more readily summarized), whereas comparisons between an European country

[2] We realize that this statement may be interpreted that we minimize the very real differences that exist even between very much "alike" countries. This is not the intention here. Rather, we see the "similar" and "dissimilar" countries approach simply as a very useful heuristic device which may be used to take full advantage of the types of countries that participate in a comparative study.

(say Germany) and a Latin American country (for example Venezuela) are more suitable to simply test the null hypothesis of "no national differences" (i.e., testing the universal applicability of theories). Attempting to specify the large number of national differences between Germany and Venezuela – national characteristics which may account for the observed differences in offending types, or victimization experiences for example – would be an impossible task. Similar logic may be used when examining *within*-country cluster differences, and *between*-country cluster differences.

2.2.2 City-Based and National Sampling Designs

In the introduction to this chapter, we made reference to the different purposes of self-report studies of delinquency: estimating the amount of offending and victimization, testing hypotheses related to correlates of offending and victimization, and describing the different dimensions of a delinquent "career." If the primary purpose of the study is to *describe the amount of crime* in a certain time period and region, there is no doubt that the "gold standard" is nationally representative samples. However, the description of the prevalence of delinquent behavior is but one of the objectives of the ISRD-2. A major goal of the ISRD-2 study is the *explanation* of offending behavior and victimization, and it may be argued that the (national) representativeness of the sample is less important (when focusing on testing correlates of offending and victimization) than the ability to obtain precise measurement of relevant covariates on the individual as well as on the meso- and macro-level (Junger-Tas et al. 2010, p. 6). To explain differences in prevalence rates and to test criminological theories, not only individual level data but also data on the local or macro-levels are needed. City-based samples offer the possibility to measure these variables that differ locally more precisely. For these, and several other reasons (e.g., more manageable and cost-effective; possibility for multilevel analyses), the ISRD-2 design preferred *city-based* random sampling to national random sampling. However, the individual objectives of the ISRD-2 participants were quite diverse, which resulted in a mixed sampling strategy. Those whose major objective was to use the ISRD-2 data to describe the amount of crime in their country or who live in a small country tended to prefer national random sampling, whereas those whose research interests were more focused on explaining local differences and testing criminological theories preferred city-based sampling (Junger-Tas et al. 2010, p. 7). With the exception of one country (Spain), the countries with a national sample oversampled at least one large city to make analyses on the level of cities possible for all countries.[3] Nine of the 31 participating countries had a national sample: Bosnia & Herzegovina, Czech Republic, Estonia, France, Hungary, Portugal, Spain, Suriname, and Switzerland (see Table 2.2 below).[4]

[3] For national reports the oversampled samples can be weighted down in order to make the overall sample nationally representative.

[4] It could be argued that the French samples are city-based samples and not nationally representative. Although Canada did participate, due to data protection policies of Statistics Canada it cannot be included in the following analyses, thus reducing the number of countries effectively to 30.

Table 2.2 Country samples by city size

		Small towns		Medium sized cities		Large cities		Not known	
Country	National sample	Cities	%	Cities	%	Cities	%	(%)	*n*
United States	No	2	40.8	1	39.4	1	20.5	–	2,400
Ireland	No	5	36.0	1	32.8	1	31.3	–	1,563
Iceland	No	–	–	1	100	–	–	–	591
Denmark	No	–	–	–	–	1	100	–	1,376
Norway	No	2	26.7	–	–	2	73.3	–	1,694
Sweden	No	2	22.2	–	–	1	77.8	–	2,282
Finland	No	–	–	–	–	1	100	–	1,364
Netherlands	No	9	35.3	5	23.9	1	40.8	–	2,330
Austria	No	5	34.5	1	28.8	1	36.7	–	2,994
Germany	No	3	31.6	2	29.0	2	39.4	–	3,478
Switzerland	Yes	–	–	1	6.2	1	26.9	67.0	3,643
France	Yes	(6)	18.3	(3)	8.5	3	73.1	–	2,398
Belgium	No	2	30.3	2	69.7	–	–	–	2,308
Portugal	Yes	–	–	1	8.9	1	23.9	67.1	2,616
Cyprus	No	3	39.0	2	61.0	–	–	–	2,310
Italy	No	5	22.7	6	41.7	4	35.6	–	5,300
Spain	Yes	?	71.9	1	12.6	3	15.5	–	1,789
NL Antilles	No	–	–	2	100	–	–	–	1,722
Aruba	No	1	100	–	–	–	–	–	705
Suriname	Yes	–	–	1	60.9	–	–	39.1	2,399
Venezuela	No	3	37.0	–	–	2	63.0	–	2,322
Estonia	Yes	–	–	1	10.5	1	29.5	59.9	2,611
Lithuania	No	3	36.1	1	32.0	1	32.0	–	2,175
Poland	No	5	39.4	1	27.4	1	33.1	–	1,458
Czech Republic	Yes	–	–	–	–	2	37.8	62.2	3,245
Hungary	Yes	–	–	–	–	1	17.4	82.6	2,203
Slovenia	No	4	66.8	1	33.2	–	–	–	2,233
Bosnia & H.	Yes	–	–	–	–	1	26.2	73.8	2,017
Russia	No	3	36.0	–	–	2	64.0	–	2,313
Armenia	no	3	32.9	1	31.3	1	35.9	–	2,044
Total	–	60	23.4	32	24.4	36	34.5	17.7	67,883

Note: In France two metro-areas are treated as large cities; in Spain no oversampling of large or medium sized cities occurred; number of cities or towns belonging to "not known" is not known

2.2.3 *Selection of Cities*

The city-based sampling design was based on a minimum of five cities or towns per country, the main selection criterion being size, degree of urbanization, and selected economic and demographic variables. The sampling guidelines recommended city-based sampling with about 2,100 respondents per country, where each sample would include at least 700 students from a large city or metropolitan area (about 500,000 inhabitants and more), a medium size city (between 96,000 and 144,000 inhabitants), and a cluster of three small towns (10,000–75,000 inhabitants).[5] The sampling design allowed for additional optional samples for those who wished to enlarge the scope of their sample (Italy, for example included a total of 15 cities and towns). Overall, data were collected in 36 large and 32 medium sized cities and 60 small towns (16 clusters of 2–9 small towns).[6]

Theoretically, each country should have attempted to select cities which could be considered typical for the country. Concern with selecting a "representative" city or town is based on the belief that there are significant differences (for purposes of the study of delinquency) between youth who live in different types of cities within a country. We used size (large and medium vs. small town) as one obvious and readily available criterion because we assume that, generally speaking, urban populations behave differently than rural, nonurban individuals. This, incidentally, is an empirical question which has been tested in our study (by comparing the small town sample against the more urban, city-based samples) and found some support. "Place" is significant, both in terms of its potential impact on its inhabitants, and in terms of the kind of people who live in a particular place (sometimes but not always through self selection; see Sampson 2006). If there are huge regional differences, or differences in culture, ethnic diversity, or economic prosperity between cities, then the students that are ultimately included in the (city-based) sample, may differ from the rest of their country's population. This possibility affects some of the ISRD samples more than others.

Most countries were able to meet the size criterion. Although valiant attempts were made to make the selected cities as comparable as possible to other cities/town of the same size, often the cities were chosen on the basis of convenience (i.e., not too far away from where the researcher lived, or where the researcher had professional contacts facilitating access to schools). City selection is a complex process, especially so in a cross-national study. In our view, and consistent with our earlier discussion, we argue that – as long as our aim is not to generalize estimates of prevalence rates across countries, but rather to explore the theoretical correlates of delinquency in different national settings, the ISRD-2 city selection processes are definitely not a problem. Indeed, some of the most influential self-report surveys of delinquency have taken place in one single city. Examples are the Glueck's study in Boston, USA (Glueck & Glueck 1950), Philadelphia Cohort Studies (Wolfgang et al. 1972; Tracy et al. 1990), the Cambridge Study in Delinquent Involvement (Farrington 1987), the Dunedin Multidisciplinary Health and Development Study (Moffitt 1993), the Denver Youth Survey (Huizinga et al. 1998), the Pittsburgh Youth Study (Loeber et al. 1998), the Rochester Youth Development Study (Thornberry et al. 1998), and the Project on Human Development in Chicago Neighborhoods

[5] For the present analyses the boundaries we set for city size are revised in order to adjust for the relative differences between countries with respect to what is considered a big or small city. Cities with 300,000 inhabitants or more are defined as large, cities with 100,000 to less than 300,000 as medium sized, and towns with 10,000 less than 100,000 as small towns.

[6] In seven national samples the size of the several cities or towns is not known; in further analyses we deal with this problem by treating these cities as a separate category.

(Sampson et al. 1999). These cities definitely were not randomly selected from all comparable cities, nor are they necessarily considered "typical" for a country. They mainly are viewed as research venues with clear geographic boundaries within which to randomly draw the sample. The insights based on these one-city studies typically are generalized towards the larger youth population, with usually only a perfunctory reference and caution that the results are only generalizeable to one particular place and time.

The ISRD-2 study has the advantage of including not just one, or a handful of cities, but a rather large number (68 cities with 100,000 plus inhabitants). Because of the standardization of sampling and instruments, there is relative comparability of data collected within these urban areas. Importantly, noted differences in (correlates of) delinquency prevalence between these cities may be explained by local structural differences (e.g., unemployment rate, divorce rate, youth policies). City-level structural indicators provide a tangible measure of the differences between ISRD-2 cities and towns, making the issue of representativeness of cities less relevance. In this context, it should be noted that our attempt to collect comparable local (i.e., city-level) structural indicators as part of the ISRD-2 study has only partially succeeded. In spite of lengthy discussions at our workshops, pilot studies to determine the availability of cross-nationally comparable indicators at the local level, and the valiant efforts of many countries' participants to complete the standardized structural indicator collection forms, at the time of the publication of this book, we still have not completed this task. A task which turned out to be more arduous than expected: We still have a lot of missing data beyond very basic information on population (number, gender and age composition), and some police and court information (mostly for the large cities). Local indicators are available for a limited number of cities and towns at this point; however, we have not made use of these data for any of the analyses in the current book.

City selection for cross-national comparative study is complicated by the reality that nations vary tremendously in the number and sizes of cities and towns. This fact is so obvious that it is surprisingly easily overlooked. Compare, for example, Iceland (with a population of 317,000 where data were collected in its one large city of Reykjavik), with Russia (141 million – or its captial Moscow ten million) and the USA (310 million), to take the other extreme examples. Imagine the process of selecting "typical" or "representative" cities from the literally hundreds of cities with more than 100,000 inhabitants in the vast regions of Russia or the US. And imagine further that the selection in principle needs to be limited to one large, one medium sized, and a cluster of three small towns. Smaller countries have the advantage of having a smaller number of cities and towns in the first place, and also, generally speaking, of being more homogeneous (thereby reducing sampling error). As a tentative hypothesis we may speculate, then, that the city-based samples of the smaller countries are likely more representative of their respective countries than those in large countries (where there is more variability). Thus, although the data are not representative for juveniles of the countries selected, they are fairly representative of juveniles living in the cities selected. When comparing countries, we actually are comparing cultural differences of cities shaped by the culture and social conditions of their countries.

Table 2.3 Percentage of survey participants per city size by country cluster

	Anglo-Saxon	Northern Europe	Western Europe	Mediterranian	Latin America	Post-Socialist	Total
Large cities	24.8	78.8	35.9	23.2	20.5	31.0	34.5
Medium cities	36.8	8.1	26.0	34.0	44.5	13.6	24.4
Small towns	38.5	13.1	23.9	28.2	21.9	21.5	23.4
Not known	0.0	0.0	14.2	14.6	13.1	34.0	17.7
Total	100.0	100.0	100.0	100.0	100.0	100.0	100.0
N	3,963	7,307	17,151	12,015	7,148	20,299	67,883

2.2.4 National Differences in the Size of City-Based Samples

Although the majority of participating countries planned to include equal samples in large, medium, and small cities, some participants drew predominantly large city samples (e.g., Norway, Sweden and Finland). Per definition, the countries that drew national samples do not have a small town sample, but rather, tend to have large or medium city samples (e.g., Switzerland, France, Portugal, Estonia, Czech Republic, Hungary, and Bosnia-Herzegovina).

In fact, all samples (except the isle of Aruba) include large and/or medium cities, but not all samples include small cities. The six country clusters differ significantly with regard to the size of cities sampled (see Table 2.3): Northern Europe has predominantly a large city sample with only about 13% of respondents living in small cities. In the Anglo-Saxon cluster, medium and small cities are slightly overrepresented (36.8 and 38.5%, respectively). In Western Europe and the Post-Socialist clusters, large cities are overrepresented (35.9 and 31.0% respectively). In the Mediterranean cluster and the Latin American cluster, medium size cities dominate (34.0 and 44.5%, respectively). Overall, the city-based samples are dominated by large cities (37.6%), with about equal representation of medium cities (30.9%) and small towns (30.9%). An additional complicating factor is that the size of the city-based samples differs significantly between countries. For example, Italy collected a total of 5,300 seventh to ninth grade students from a total of 15 cities and towns, whereas Iceland's sample was limited to 591 eighth graders from the largest yet medium sized city of Reykjavik. Needless to say, it is important to keep these differences in mind when drawing comparative conclusions. In the following paragraph, we explain how we have attempted to minimize the possibly biasing influences of national sampling idiosyncracies.

2.2.5 Methods to Resolve Problems Associated with the Mixed Sampling Strategy

The mixed sampling strategy (*city-based and national samples*) has implications for the proper use of the data. Add in the mix of different *sample sizes* of the country samples, as well as the use of country *clusters*, it quickly becomes apparent that there is a need to carefully decide on which subsample to use for which particular purpose. To recapitulate, the total sample (n=67,883)[7] is constituted, respectively of data collected in cities and towns (68 large and medium cities, 60 small towns) as well as in national samples (which includes oversampled cities). All the cases in the city-based samples (44,962) can be classified as from either a small town (n=13,454) or from a medium or large city (n=31,508).[8] For the national samples, however, it is a bit more complicated, because – aside from the 9,170 oversampled respondents in large or medium cities (excluding students of grade 10 and higher) – there is the "rest" category of the other 13,751 nationally collected cases, where the number of cases from a particular town or city was simply too small to be useful in city- or town-based analysis. Consequently, for most cases of this category the size of the city is not indicated and thus not known. In order to deal with these differences, we created three different data sets: (1) *total sample* (n=67,883); (2) students from *medium and large cities* only (n=40,678) including city-based as well as national samples; and (3) students from *small towns* (n=15,180), some of them are students from national samples (n=1,726). Apart from the data sets (2) and (3) there are still 12,025 cases from national samples where the city size is *not known*. In order to achieve a maximum sample size, in certain analyses these cases will be treated as belonging to the "not known" category of city size.

Each data set will be used for different purposes. In our analysis we have basically followed two strategies, which reflect the two primary purposes of the analysis. (1) For purely *descriptive* purposes (i.e., for describing the prevalence of delinquency or of victimization experiences) the comparability of samples across countries is important. Because on the level of cities sampling was random in nearly all participating countries, we base such analyses on students of large and medium sized cities only (be it city-based or national samples). One should note that the maximum comparability across countries is thus achieved at the expense of (a) restricting the generalizability to students from large and medium sized cities (which is not a huge price considering the fact that the majority of the population lives in urbanized regions), and (b) reducing the sample size from 67,883 to 40,678 cases. (2) However, for *theory testing* the comparability of samples across countries is not as crucial (assuming no interaction of the sampling location such as cities or the country side with relationships under investigation; see also Maxfield & Babbie 2001). Thus, for theory testing purposes (Chaps. 7–12) we will use the total and maximum sample.

Weighting. Country samples vary in number of cases (compare Italy to Iceland, for example), as do the six country clusters (see Table 2.3). Also, the number of countries in each of the clusters varies (Anglo-Saxon two; Northern Europe five; Western Europe six; Mediterranean four; Latin America four; Post-Socialist nine). When creating *descriptive* statistics (e.g., of prevalence or incidence rates of victimization or offending)

[7] Excluding Canada and cases of grade 10 or higher.

[8] Although all 705 cases of Aruba are actually sampled from a small town, they are effectively subsumed under large and medium sized cities because this small town represents the capital of the country.

for the total sample or for country clusters, weights have been used to give each country an equal weight. The weights were constructed by the formula

$$w_j = \frac{N}{k \cdot n_j}. \tag{2.1}$$

With

w_j = weight of sample j

N = total number of cases

k = number of (sub)samples

n_j = number of cases of (sub)sample j

The weights have the following two properties:

$$\sum_{j=1}^{k} w_j \cdot n_j = N \tag{2.2}$$

$$w_1 \cdot n_1 = w_2 \cdot n_2 = \ldots = w_k \cdot n_k \tag{2.3}$$

According to the first property, the sum of the weights over all cases equals the total number of cases; according to the second property, the weighted number of cases is equal for each (sub)sample j. Formula (2.1) was also applied to clusters of countries, with *k* equal to the number of countries per cluster and *N* equal to the total number of cases per cluster.[9] Since some analyses used only samples of large and medium sized cities, some analyses used only samples of small towns, and some analyses used the data of the total sample, weights were created accordingly.

2.3 Description of ISRD-2 Sample

Table 2.4 below shows how the samples obtained in the six country clusters differ with regard to gender, age, grade, and migration status. "Migration status" distinguishes three groups: First-generation migrants (born abroad), second generation migrants (born in the country but having at least one parent born abroad), and natives (including third generation migrants).

The distribution of gender is generally well balanced although there are somewhat fewer males than females. There are some age differences though (mean age: 14.0 years): while in most clusters the youngest age cohort represents under or about 10% of the sample, in the Mediterranean cluster this is about a quarter.

[9] This was only necessary when using software like SPSS which treated the weights as frequency weights; when employing software which was able to use population weights correctly (such as R, Stata or the complex samples module of SPSS), separate sets of weights for country clusters were not necessary.

Table 2.4 Background variables of sample by country cluster (%)

	Anglo-Saxon	Northern Europe	Western Europe	Mediterranean	Latin America	Post-Socialist	Total sample
Gender							
Male	52.5	48.5	50.5	49.4	47.4	48.7	49.2
Age							
<12	7.7	0.5	10.5	24.2	10.1	6.8	9.3
13	25.3	31.7	24.9	31.2	21.5	25.0	26.5
14	31.1	34.7	32.2	30.0	24.5	36.3	32.5
15	31.9	25.5	24.0	10.5	22.3	27.3	23.7
16+	4.1	7.7	8.4	4.1	21.6	4.5	8.0
Grade							
Grade 7	27.6	28.4	33.8	32.8	35.3	33.0	32.3
Grade 8	29.6	47.5	30.9	34.8	31.7	33.8	35.1
Grade 9	42.8	24.1	35.3	32.4	33.0	33.2	32.6
Migration							
First generation	5.5	6.2	10.7	6.8	12.2	2.4	6.8
Second generation	11.4	15.7	28.0	8.1	20.1	9.0	15.4
Natives	83.0	78.1	61.3	85.1	67.7	88.6	77.8

Notes: weighted data (see Sect. 2.5)

Also, Latin America has about 22% of juveniles in the age group 16 or older, compared to under or about 8% in the other clusters. Consequently, the Mediterranean cluster has a younger sample than the rest of the country clusters (mean age: 13.4), while the Latin American cluster is tending towards a slightly older sample (mean age: 14.3). In the four other country clusters the age distribution is more balanced. Looking at the distribution of samples by grades, the Anglo-Saxon cluster has relatively more kids in grade ninth (42.8%) than the other clusters, while 47.5% of the Northern European sample is concentrated in grade 8.[10] Some of the reasons for these differences will be speculated about in the next section. In order to compensate for some of these differences, we control in our multivariate analysis for age or grade.

Migration status is an important variable in the ISRD-2 study. According to the ISRD-2 sample, Western Europe has by far the highest percentage of migrants within its borders (38.7%), followed by Latin America (32.3%) and Northern Europe (21.9%); while in the other clusters, migrants (both first and second generation) form a much smaller proportion of the ISRD-2 sample. The West-European subset has also the highest percentage of second generation migrants (28%) – that is a young migrant population born in the host country – followed by the Latin American cluster (20%) and Northern Europe (16%).

[10] This is mainly due to Iceland, where only grade 8 students were surveyed. In Norway the nominal grade was decreased by one whereas in Poland it was increased by one because grade 7 to grade 9 students in these countries are about 1 year younger resp. older than in the other countries.

2.4 School-Based Survey[11]

It would be great if we could argue that the ISRD-2 cities and towns are truly representative of the population of students in the participating countries. That is likely not the case and we have tried to explain why this need not be considered a problem. To the contrary, we may actually view this as an opportunity to test meso (or city-) level hypotheses about the link between structural variables and delinquency and victimization. More commonly concerns are raised about the potential drawbacks – in terms of selection bias and threat to representativeness – of using a *school-based* design rather than drawing a sample randomly from the general target population in the desired age category (e.g., 12–15). Although there have been many critics of so-called "school criminology," there are several very sound reasons for using a school-based approach. Let's recapitulate the main arguments briefly. First, a school-based sample is more practical and less expensive than a population-based sample, particularly in larger countries. School samples are very common practice among a large number of well-respected and well-established youth surveys, in Europe and the US, Canada, Australia, and New Zealand. Although it has been argued that school-based samples do not include those youth who are most delinquent, who have learning problems, or who are truant, there are opposing arguments that school-based samples are as good if not better than population samples (Oberwittler & Naplava 2002). Unlike their older counterparts, our relatively young ISRD target group (12–15 year olds) is quite likely still enrolled in school, because of compulsory schooling up to the age in most countries. The school context is very important for youth, and in the ISRD design we do include information about the particular school context, which may be used for further analysis, as is illustrated in Chap. 8 of this book. Furthermore, it has been documented that the setting of the study is a crucial determinant of the quality and quantity of subject responses; overall, youth is likely to report higher (more realistic) incidence of delinquency and alcohol and drug use in school settings rather than at home (Brener et al. 2006). In sum, we feel strongly that our decision to use a school-based design was a sound one. However, as was to be expected, the *actual implementation* of the school-based sampling plan turned out to be not so easy for all partners.

All national research partners made a sampling plan, consistent with the ISRD sampling protocol. Although the ISRD-2 sampling protocol provided rather specific guidelines for sampling (of schools, classrooms and students), it quickly became apparent that we had to be quite flexible in the interpretation of these guidelines. We had decided to sample classes at compulsory school age to obtain a more representative sample with cross-national comparability. We soon found out that there were problems with the comparability of the different national school systems [see also Chap. 8]. There are differences in the age of compulsory education, major differences in number and types of secondary education (general, vs. technical, vocational or academic), national differences in grade repetition policy, national and local differences

[11] The discussion in this section draws from Marshall 2010; Junger-Tas et al. 2010; Enzmann et al. 2010.

in the organization of secondary education (e.g., not all students belong to a particular "class room"), and national differences in how special educational needs are met (Junger-Tas et al. 2010, p. 8–9). Apart from the lack of comparability of school systems, there were other realities which challenged the implementation of the classroom-based design in different countries, such as: (1) lack of availability of sampling frame (i.e., listing of seventh, eighth and ninth grade classrooms); (2) lack of cooperation of selected schools; (3) obstacles provided by the requirement to having active parental consent; and (4) ambiguity about how to define seventh, eighth, and ninth grade (resulting in disproportionate age groups in some countries). It is in the area of sampling, as in none of the other aspects of the ISRD-2 design, where our philosophy of "flexible standardization" became truly our guiding principle. Indeed:

> Sample designs may be chosen flexibly and there is no need for similarity of sample designs. Flexibility of choice is particularly advisable for multinational comparisons, because the sampling resources differ greatly between countries. All this flexibility assumes probability selection methods: *known probabilities of selection for all population elements*. (Kish 1994, p. 173).

Mindful of this admonition of survey expert Kish, throughout the entire project, we continued to stress to our national partners the importance of trying – in as much as possible – to keep true to the notion of probability sampling. Each country maintained a careful accounting of the exact procedures used in the sampling process, including deviations from the original sampling design.

2.5 Problems with Access to Schools and Pupil Cooperation: Cross-National Differences[12]

Ideally, the stratified, multistage sampling plan would go as follows: first, a listing of all secondary schools of the selected cities was created. This included public and private schools, vocational, technical, and academic schools. Then, a listing of all seventh, eighth, and ninth grade classrooms in these institutions was constructed. By selecting *classes* randomly from these listings, the number of students drawn was proportional to the number of students in each school type. All students in the randomly selected classrooms were to be asked to complete the ISRD questionnaire. It appears that the largest stumbling block on the way to probability sampling was the inability to get *access to the schools*. Indeed, it was lack of cooperation by the schools, rather than refusals of pupils, or their parents (with a few exceptions, such as the US and the Czech Republic) that proved to be the main source of nonresponse. A purely *random* exclusion of schools (or classrooms, or students) poses no particular threat; however, if there is a systematic, nonrandom self selection of schools (of classrooms, or students) at play, the possibility of nonrandom error looms large. This is particularly troublesome for cross-national research aiming to standardize procedures and methods

[12] This section is based on Ineke Haen Marshall, "Pour quoi pas?" versus "absolutely not!" Cross-national differences in access to schools and pupils for survey research, European Journal of Crime Policy and Research (Marshall 2010) 16:89–109.

(and thus sources of systematic error). If it is indeed true, as we have argued elsewhere (Junger-Tas et al. 2010), that self-reported survey research among youth in a school setting has a different meaning in different national contexts, it is possible that the national context itself may be a main source of nonrandom sampling error. The ISRD-2 experience suggests that this is a very real possibility.

2.5.1 School Cooperation

Table 2.5 (adapted from Marshall 2010, Tables 1 and 2) presents an overview of school, student, and parent cooperation in the ISRD countries. Consistent with the view that research should be viewed as a normal social activity (rather than as a

Table 2.5 School, parent, and student cooperation by country cluster

Country cluster	Country	Overall school participation rate-before substitution	Parental consent required	Parental/student refusal
Post-Socialist	Armenia	100%	None	NA
	Bosnia & Herzegovina	100%	None	NA
	Lithuania	100%	None	NA
	Slovenia	97%	Optional	4 parents
	Czech Republic	96%	Passive	10% overall Prague: 15% Pilsen:25%
	Poland	84%	Passive	22.5%
	Hungary	75%	Passive	no information
	Estonia	65%	None	NA
	Russia	43%[13]	None	NA
Northern European	Finland	100%	None	NA
	Sweden	97%	Passive (under 15 year)	13 students and/or parents
	Norway	70%[14]	No information	No information
	Denmark	55%[15]	Optional	None
Latin America	Surinam	100%	None	NA
	Netherlands Antilles	"Very good"	None	NA
	Aruba	76%		
	Venezuela	68%[16]	None	NA

(continued)

[13] Large city: 38.9%; medium city: 41.6%; small towns: 100.

[14] Information unavailable, estimation based on information provided in Kivivuori, 2007.

[15] Huge variations by district; highest refusal in large city.

[16] The refusal rate was higher in the large cities.

Table 2.5 (continued)

Country cluster	Country	Overall school participation rate-before substitution	Parental consent required	Parental/student refusal
Mediterranean	Cyprus	95%	Passive	No information
	Italy	84%[17]	Optional, passive	2% of parents and/or students
	Spain	81%	No information	"Low"
	Portugal	50%[18]	Not, except in large city	"Very few"
Western Europe	Switzerland	94%	Passive	None
	Austria	77.4%[19]	Passive	2 parents
	Germany	63%[20]	Passive	4% (144) parents and/or students
	Belgium Flanders	45–48%[21]	Passive	"Almost zero"
	Belgium Wallonia	50%[22]	Passive	2.3%
	Netherlands	15–18%[23]	Passive	None
	France	16%	Active	"About 20"
Anglo-Saxon	Canada	86%	Active	26.8% refusals, includes students absent
	Ireland	60%[24]	Passive, 2 schools active	No information
	USA	Very low	Passive, in medium and small towns	Overall noncon-sent: 32%
				Small towns: 8.3%
			Active, in large city	Medium city: 1.6%
				Large city: 67.9%

purely methodological exercise), Table 2.5 presents the data by the six country clusters. We find that these subsets of countries differ significantly, both culturally and structurally in ways that influence the response to school-based survey research. The ordering of the clusters (Post-Socialist on top, Anglo-Saxon cluster on the bottom) reflects the overall level of cooperation of schools, teachers, parents, and pupils. Space limitations do not allow us to discuss in great detail each and every

---

[17] Participation lower in larger cities.

[18] Variation by towns and cities.

[19] Large city: 58%; medium city: 75%; small towns: 100%.

[20] Variation by city and school type.

[21] Medium city: 45%; small town: 48%.

[22] Medium city: 53%; small town: 40%.

[23] Small towns: 18%; medium cities: 15%; large cities: 16%.

[24] Large city: 48%; medium city: 65%; small towns: 72%.

country, and its unique circumstances (for a more extensive discussion see Marshall 2010). We will simply highlight the most striking observations.

The first column "overall school participation rate – before substitution" reports the data (in as far as available) on the proportion of schools initially selected for participation that actually participated. Typically, the percentage of positive responses of contacted schools equals the participation rate, but not always. Sometimes, schools that initially agreed to cooperate, for a variety of reasons, dropped out at a later stage. There were also a number of instances where schools never responded to initial attempts of contact. These schools did not actively refuse to participate, but we view their lack of response as (passive) refusal. It must be noted here, that most of the national partners had a plan in place that allowed for the substitution of the initially selected schools that refused. Therefore, *the reported national participation rate should not be interpreted as the final national response rates*. In addition, the majority of the countries provide additional data and analysis to assess the degree of representativeness of their final sample (of schools, classrooms and pupils).

Table 2.5 shows that there is a considerable national variation in cooperation by the schools. A number of countries report perfect (e.g., Armenia, Finland, and Surinam) or near perfect (e.g., Cyprus, Sweden, and Slovenia) school cooperation. Unfortunately, there are also several countries who report low or very low school cooperation. The results of these national samples should be approached with due caution.

For instance, the USA was exceptionally unsuccessful with regard to gaining access to schools, and scores "very low" in Table 2.5. Why "very low" instead of reporting an actual rate for the US? In order to calculate a participation rate, one needs to know both the number of schools that participate (the nominator) and the total number of schools in the sampling frame (the denominator). The first part of the equation is easy; it is the second part that is problematic. What to do, for example, if – because of political local turmoil – one faces a blanket refusal of the school board responsible for all public schools in the selected city and one opts for a substitute US city – as happened in the US for the mid-size city? Do we include all public schools in the initially selected city as part of our refusal rate? The substitute mid-size city had a participation rate around 30%, but we base this on the number of eligible schools in that particular (substitute) city only. The US also had to find substitutes for the three small towns initially selected, because of lack of cooperation by the schools. It took several failed efforts and very hard work to locate two other – somewhat comparable – small towns where schools were willing to cooperate. The story with regard to the large US city is somewhat different. In this city with several million inhabitants, the US team followed standard external research proposal review protocols required by each school district. After lengthy reviews by each of the school district's Institutional Review Boards (consisting of representatives of school administration, teachers, community members and parents), the US team was denied access to conduct the survey in all but one school district. This school district serves a predominately minority population (Hispanic) and is one of the school districts within the city with the least resources; it represents a relatively small proportion of all eligible schools (about 20%). Thus, the US "large city" sample is definitely not representative of the population of the selected large US city. Still, comparisons of delinquency prevalence rates of the US ISRD-2 sample with two other nationally representative youth studies in the US shows that the rates are quite comparable (Marshall & He 2010). More about the US sample herein.

Another case in point is France. France's very low (15.5%) school participation rate reflects the unique social and political situation in France at the time of preparations for data collection: the urban riots that started in Clichy-sous-Bois, which made school principals very reluctant to participate (Blaya 2007). The Netherlands receives an equally low school participation rate (15–18%), mainly due to the timing of the study and oversaturation with requests for research.[25] Russia receives an overall participation rate of 43% based on cooperation of the schools that they actually contacted. As noted in their technical report, however, the Russian researchers could not include all schools in the large city (Moscow) in their initial sampling frame, for pragmatic as well as political reasons. Canada, with a rather high overall participation rate of 86% (of the contacted schools) however, excluded 25% of the target population because of lack of permission to include the Catholic students in Toronto. These examples provide the most striking illustrations of school noncooperation, but they illustrate the generally challenging nature of school-based surveys in many – but definitely not all countries.

School refusals may be problematic for a variety of reasons (in particular if we suspect that there is systematic nonresponse) but at least school refusal exclude both delinquents and nondelinquents alike (Kivivuori 2007, p. 36). But there is the additional problem of selective nonresponse of youth within – as well as outside the selected schools. A good argument has been made that those students who do not provide answers to the self-report questionnaire are more likely than average to engage in delinquency (Junger-Tas & Marshall 1999). Following Kivivuori (2007), there are at least three categories of missing pupils which may threaten the validity of self-report surveys.

First, some youth may be completely out of the school system, either because they are living in the streets, are in a youth detention center, or simply are not registered to attend school. In the bulk of the ISRD countries, that most likely is a minor problem, except in the Latin American cluster. For example, in Surinam (Bovenkerk and Wolf 2010), there is compulsory education but it is not enforced fully, if at all. An unknown number of children do not attend school because they are kept home to work in the informal economy, or they drop out for other reasons.[26]

Second, some kids are placed in special education schools because of disciplinary or learning problems. These may also be the youth who would score high on

[25] The Dutch technical report shows that the characteristics of the final sample are very comparable to those of the target population, suggesting that the high level of school nonparticipation most likely did not produce a biased sample.

[26] In Surinam, because of problems related to differences in languages (school vs. home), a large number of youth has to repeat grades, so that the average age of pupils in the seventh, eighth and ninth grade is also quite a bit higher than in the other clusters.

delinquency and other problem behavior (Kivivuori 2007). The ISRD project in general did not include the special education schools or classes – since this was done by all countries, this should not affect the comparative results – except possibly in terms of underestimating the total incidence (but probably not prevalence – see Kivivuori 2007) for the entire sample.

Third, on the day of the administration of the survey, invariably, some registered pupils are absent. It stands to reason to speculate that students who are absent with a valid excuse (i.e., sickness) may be different from those who simply decide not to show on a particular day (i.e., they are truant). Although the ISRD partners were to complete a standardized form about the different levels and reasons for nonresponse on the day of data gathering, it still is not always possible to make a distinction between students who were absent with – and those without – a valid reason. Using the data we do have available number on pupils' absenteeism during the time of ISRD data collection, we see a wide range of "pupils absent", from a low of less than 1% (Austria) and 2.8% (Portugal), to the higher end of 13% (Italy), 15% (Armenia), 16.7% Poland, 16.7% (Estonia), 17% Russia, and 18% Venezuela. In the remaining countries on which we have information, the rate of absenteeism on the day of data collection (for whatever reasons) is around 5–8% approximately.

2.5.2 *Pupil Cooperation*

The problems of missing pupil responses just discussed differ from the two types of pupil nonresponse that are explicitly linked to the *willingness* – either of the pupils or of their parents – to participate in the research, even after the school has given its consent. With regard to the students, the ISRD data suggest that very few students outright refused to participate. A large number of participants reported zero student refusals among the students, and the countries that reported some refusals indicated very low numbers (just a handful, see Table 2.5, third column). It does seem that pupil cooperation is pretty universal, albeit for different reasons in different national contexts (Marshall 2010). Although open refusal is quite uncommon, pupils may sabotage the study in other ways, for example by simply leaving the questionnaire blank, skipping major sections, or providing completely inconsistent and nonsensical answers. Screening for such "passive" refusal based on the proportion of unusable questionnaires per country, ranging from a high of 3.6% (Bosnia and Herzegovina) to 0.2% (Germany), shows that this did not happen in large numbers.

2.5.3 *Parent Cooperation*

The fact that, generally speaking, kids are willing to participate, regardless of where they are, may be because they are in a school setting, and/or because they are minors, unwilling or unlikely to object to the request by an adult. It is this very situation of dependency and relative powerlessness that has prompted a number of national and international professional organizations, research institutions, and government bodies to develop more explicit guidelines about research involving minors. Spurred by the horrific abuses of medical experimentation during the Second World War, concerns about ethical issues involved in research (i.e., preventing harm to subjects, informed consent) have expanded to include survey research involving minors. This in turn has produced a large body of scholarly work – particularly in the USA – on the effects of asking for parental consent on the response rates of pupils (see, for example, Esbensen et al. 1999, 2008; Henry et al. 2002; Ji et al. 2004; Pokorny et al. 2001; White et al. 2004).

Passive parental consent is generally viewed as the least intrusive: it simply means that a pupil is excluded from the research if the parent objects. *Active* parental consent lays the bar considerably higher: here the pupil only may participate if the parents explicitly provide evidence of their consent. In most cases, typically the pupil takes a form home from school (or the form is sent to the students' home) explaining the study: For passive parental consent, only if the parents do *not* want to child to participate should the form be returned to school (with parents' signature). On the other hand, for active consent, only those children who have returned the consent form with their parents' signature are allowed to participate in the study. Passive parental consent tends to produce much higher levels of student participation than active parental consent. The requirement to obtain (active or passive) parental consent strongly influences the response rates of pupils (Pokorny et al. 2001), and as such is of interest to comparative studies such as the ISRD. Table 2.5 presents an overview of the use of parental consent (second column), and the levels of parent refusal (third column), in the ISRD countries. For some countries, it is not possible to make a distinction between parental refusal and student refusal, or other grounds for student nonparticipation (e.g., Canada). Table 2.5 shows that in nine countries, parental consent was not used at all; in five countries, parental consent was used only occasionally; in 13 countries, some form of parental consent (mostly passive) was always used, and for two countries (Norway and Spain), there is no information available on the use of parental consent.

None of the countries in the Latin American cluster used parental consent procedures, as was also the case in slightly over half of the Post-Socialist countries. Furthermore, in one of the Post-Socialist countries (Slovenia), the use of parental consent was virtually nonexistent, with only two of the schools actually asking for parents' permission. The three other Post-Socialist countries did require passive parental consent. Here, Poland and Czech Republic stand out, because of their fairly high reported rates of parental refusal (22.5 and 10%, respectively). For Poland, that means that more than one in five pupils actually was not allowed by their parents to participate. In the Czech sample, 15% of the pupils' parents did not allow them to complete the ISRD survey, with an even higher proportion (25%) in Pilsen. This fairly high parental refusal rate in Poland and the Czech Republic stands in sharp contrast to the very low parental refusal rates found in the other country clusters (Northern Europe, Mediterranean, and Western Europe), with the exception of the Anglo-Saxon cluster. The Western European countries, without exception, reported always asking for parental consent. Passive parental consent was the norm, with the exception of France. France reports the use of active parental consent, with only a very small number of failures to consent of "about 20."[27] In view of the difficult circumstances under which the French ISRD study was implemented, this is an amazing rate of parental approval, definitely worthy of further exploration. Two other countries worked under conditions of requiring *active* parental consent: Canada and the USA (for the large city sample). Canada has very stringent requirements with regard to the protection of human subjects in research. As a matter of fact, concerns about the possibility that the identity of individual respondents might somehow be traceable if all collected data (including school and classroom information) were to be analyzed resulted in the final exclusion of the Canadian ISRD survey responses from the Toronto pupils in the merged international data set. Within the ISRD research study, Canada appears unique in its level of concern with the protection of confidentiality to this extreme degree.

The US sample is also impacted by the demand of parental consent. The US medium city and small towns were satisfied with passive consent, and the rate of parental refusal was quite reasonable, very low in the medium city (less than 2%), and a bit higher in the small towns (8.3%). There were major problems in the large city sample, where active parental consent was required. For a number of reasons (language problems, lack of interest and motivation), students only returned less than one third of the parental consent forms to their classroom teacher, resulting in a nonparticipation rate of about two thirds of the selected students. Add to this the only one of the large city school districts agreed to cooperate (the poorest district with the highest level of immigrant population), and it is very clear that the US sample should be approached with caution. However, once again we want to reiterate that comparison of the US ISRD-2 sample with other national US samples show rather similar prevalence rates on alcohol and drug use (Marshall & He 2010).

2.5.4 ISRD-2 Samples: Mostly Within Range of Normal Sampling Problems

There is no question that national context has an important influence on whether and how school-based self-report delinquency studies may be done. Of immediate relevance, though, are the implications for the representativeness of the school-based samples drawn in the ISRD-2 countries. As we discussed earlier, since student refusal overall is almost negligible, the two most important factors (threatening the representativeness of the samples) are: lack of school cooperation, and lack of gaining parental cooperation. Country samples with a relatively high score on one or both of these should be approached with more caution than those where school or parental cooperation was no problem. This observation also should be kept in mind when making comparisons between country clusters. Table 2.5 suggests that ease of

[27] Informal e-mail communication with the French research team leader (March 2010).

access to schools and use of parental consent are not randomly distributed across country clusters. The two clusters that appear to have the most problems with gaining access to schools (Western European and Anglo-Saxon) are also the only clusters where some form of parental consent is always required. Conversely, the clusters with the relative highest ease of school participation are more likely either not to require any form of parental consent, or – if they do – it is passive (and frequently optional) (Marshall 2010, p. 106–107).

It is not possible to calculate very precise estimates of the overall school cooperation rate for the *entire sample*, but we can make a rough estimate of the overall positive response rates of participating schools in the total sample, which is about 74% (before substitution, so the actual rate is higher). Combine this with the noted overall very low parent or student nonresponse or refusal rates being less than five percent for the total sample (with the exceptions of the Czech Republic, Poland, Canada and the US), and we can see that the total ISRD-2 sample has a response rate of somewhere between 65 and 70%, very much within the range of normal sampling experiences.

In sum, the shortcomings of the obtained samples do not need to be viewed as a critical flaw in our study. There are two reasons for this assessment. First, several of the national participants went to great length to compare the socio-demographic characteristics of the final achieved sample against the characteristics of the target population, and found a sufficient degree of overlap (e.g., Belgium, the Netherlands, Venezuela, USA). We find that the prevalence estimates of delinquency, alcohol use, and drug use based on the ISRD-2 samples are quite compatible with those found in other international surveys (see Chaps. 3 and 5).[28] Second, we want to reiterate our earlier view that a representative sample is of less importance when our primary interest is in hypothesis-testing and explanatory research, rather than in providing (generalizable) estimates of prevalence and incidence of delinquency and victimization. For these reasons, we are confident that the ISRD-2 survey results fall squarely within the normal range of sampling error typical for extant survey research on youthful offending and victimization.

2.5.5 Challenges of Cross-National Classroom-Based Sampling

The classroom-based sampling design produced a total of 67,883 questionnaires, collected in 30 countries (excluding Canada), in 1,536 schools, and 3,339 class rooms. The design also presented us with several challenges, directly related to the cross-national nature of the ISRD study. We select two of these challenges: (1) design effects and (2) age-effect in grades for brief discussion.

[28] The self-reported estimates of delinquency, alcohol and drug use in the US sample are generally speaking within the range reported by most comparable US surveys of delinquency (Marshall and He 2010).

2.5.5.1 Design Effects

The primary sampling units of the ISRD-2 study are school classes, not individual students. All students present in the school classes randomly selected (stratified by grade) were interviewed. Due to the clustering of students within school classes, characteristics of respondents within classes may be more similar or homogeneous than between classes. Dependent on the degree of homogeneity (as measured by intra-class correlations), tests of significance will tend to be too liberal (statisticians describe this phenomenon as design effect). Too liberal means that associations or differences will appear to be significant although they are not. But even when taking this design effect into account, small and *substantially* insignificant effects will still become *statistically* significant because of the huge sample size. Therefore, well endowed with a comfortable sample size, we decided to ignore the clustering of students within classes because for our analyses, the size of effects is anyway far more important than their significance. In our situation, not taking design effects into account in tests of statistical significance will practically not affect the interpretation of results. Only in Chap. 6, where more precision deemed necessary, design effects due to clustering (and also due to stratification by country and grade) were taken into account by employing special survey analyses software.

2.5.5.2 Age vs. Grade

Another consequence of using classes (not individual students) as primary sampling units is that the students are indeed representative samples of members of school classes of grades 7–9, but not necessarily representative samples of certain age groups. The sampling of school classes facilitated the practical management of respondent selection and also allowed us to get a greater level of cross-national comparability. That is, by focusing on classes at compulsory school age (for most countries ending in eighth or ninth grade), we expected to obtain a more representative sample with cross-national comparability. However, this comes with a price: In countries in which repeating a grade is related to the socioeconomic status or to problem behavior of students, consequently socioeconomic status or problem behavior is confounded with age (but not with grade). This can be demonstrated by investigating the percentage of repeaters per age group vs. grade (Tables 2.6 and 2.7). Whereas there is a substantial association of the percentage of repeaters with age (Cramér's V=0.40), the association is negligible as to the association of the percentage of repeaters with grade (Cramér's V=0.03). From one age group to the next the percentage of repeaters increases between 4.9% (≤12 to 13 years) and 40.1% (15 to 16+ years), although from one grade to the next – that on the average also corresponds to a difference of 1 year – the increase is only between 1.0 and 1.3%.

The relationship between age and repeating a grade is an artifact of the sampling design that takes classes as primary sampling units, not individual students: 12 year old students who did repeat a grade are overwhelmingly found in grade 6 instead of grade 7 (and are thus excluded from the survey), whereas 16 year old students who

Table 2.6 Rate of class repeaters per age group

	Age group					
Repeater	≤12	13	14	15	16+	Total
% No	98.0	93.1	87.8	79.9	39.8	84.5
% Yes	2.0	6.9	12.2	20.1	60.2	15.5
% Total	100.0	100.0	100.0	100.0	100.0	100.0
n	6,895	17,433	21,694	15,840	5,369	67,231

Notes: $\chi_{(4)}^2 = 10{,}546.7$, $p < 0.001$; Cramér's V = 0.396

Table 2.7 Rate of class repeaters per grade

	Grade			
Repeater	Grade 7	Grade 8	Grade 9	Total
% No	85.6	84.6	83.3	84.5
% Yes	14.4	15.4	16.7	15.5
% Total	100.0	100.0	100.0	100.0
n	22,202	22,297	22,732	67,231

Notes: $\chi_{(2)}^2 = 44.1$, $p < 0.001$; Cramér's V = 0.026

repeated a grade are overwhelmingly found in grade 9 instead of grade 10 (and are thus included in the survey).

This is the reason why we often will use grade instead of age in analyses where we want to know whether older students differ from younger students independently from socioeconomic status, school achievement, or likely problem behavior. In these instances grade will serve as a valid proxy for age.

2.6 ISRD-2 Measurement Instruments

Aside from sampling procedures, the quality of the *instruments* used to measure the variables of interest is of paramount importance for the ultimate quality of a study such as the ISRD-2. The ISRD-2 project uses several measurement instruments. The *student questionnaire* is undoubtedly the most significant data collection instrument used in the project. We also developed a *teacher questionnaire*, but unfortunately, this instrument was only used in a handful of countries. Most participants made use of the *administration form*, a questionnaire designed for interviewers to keep track of the response rates and other issues related to the process of data collection. Finally, a significant amount of effort was devoted to the development and completion of standardized forms to collect *local (city-level) and national structural indicators.*

2.6.1 Student Questionnaire

Developing and administering self-reported survey instruments to youth is a challenging process even in a relatively simple local study. Numerous publications on this topic exist (e.g., Fowler 2002; Presser 2004; Sudman et al. 1996). There are issues related to the reliability and the validity of the questions and/or the entire instrument, scale construction, question wording, question ordering, response categories, open-ended vs. closed questions, face-to-face interviews vs. self-administered, and computerized or paper-and-pencil, to mention but a few. Needless to say, these methodological and conceptual challenges are multiplied and magnified when these questionnaires are developed and administered simultaneously in a large number of different national contexts. In a cross-national study, the possibility of measurement error as a result of using invalid and/or nonreliable measurement instruments looms large because of the confounding effect of cultural context. One of the key challenges of comparative survey research is the *equivalence of measures*. Even if the ISRD-2 questionnaire, in its original English version, were a perfect instrument for the Irish or US sample, there still is no guarantee that it is equally valid and reliable when used in other ISRD-2 countries. However, we took great pains to ensure that the original questionnaire was used unaltered, in its original form by all countries, in order to increase the chance that the questionnaire captures the same phenomena in all countries. With a few exceptions, there were no changes in the order of the questions, or in response categories.[29] In this manner, we tried to minimize the possibility that cross-national differences in responses could be attributed to differences in the questionnaire (i.e., measurement instrument) rather than reflecting "true" national differences. Of course, careful evaluation of the psychometric properties of the main scales and indicators is one method to help us determine if there are systematic variations in the performance of these instruments by country or country cluster. Based on our preliminary assessments, we feel reasonably confident that the ISRD-2 student survey overall is a pretty robust instrument. This is shown, for example, by the analysis of the psychometric attributes of the self-control scale described in Chap. 11. A number of other analyses in this book report the reliability score (Cronbach's alpha) for most composite measures, and find these values to be in the acceptable range.

For the student questionnaire, we used several well-established measures that have been validated by others. We borrowed items and scales that already have been shown to "work," with occasionally some adaptations – after lengthy discussions at our workshops – to better fit our purposes.[30] Of course, it is an empirical question whether already well-established measures work equally well in a sample other than where the instrument was used originally. The very purpose of reliability analyses (e.g., calculating Cronbach's alpha), as well as validity assessments (face validity, construct validity, convergent validity) is to revalidate the original measures on other samples. Establishing validity (of an item, a scale, or a questionnaire) is difficult. There is evidence in the research literature of differential validity of the self-report method for some ethnic minorities, convicted offenders, and different age groups (Junger-Tas & Marshall 1999; Thornberry & Krohn 2000). Needless to say, the reliability and validity problems become more pronounced if instruments are used in a cross-national study such as the ISRD. To continue the analysis of how

[29] There are some exceptions (e.g., Canada and Ireland).

[30] There are some instances, however, where we do no longer know the original source of the question or scale.

our measurement instruments perform in different national setting is one of the key ambitions of our future research agenda. Herein, we discuss the main items and scales that have been used in the chapters that follow. If occasionally variables were operationalized differently than discussed here, it will be indicated in the relevant chapter. A copy of the questionnaire (ISRD2 Working Group 2005) is available through http://webapp5.rrz.uni-hamburg.de/ISRD/JDEB/.

2.6.1.1 Delinquency

The questions about self-reported illegal and risk behavior are modeled after the core measurement of self-reported delinquency utilized in the original National Youth Survey (Elliott et al. 1985); this instrument has been used quite extensively and successfully in several large-scale studies. The core questionnaire was developed in the first ISRD study, where the major emphasis was placed on designing an instrument to measure delinquency cross-nationally (see Chap. 1). The ISRD-1 measurement of delinquency has been validated several times (i.e., Zhang et al. 2000; Marshall & Webb 1994). Some of the screening questions ("Have you ever…") have been modified slightly (as result of discussions about cross-national adaptability), as have the follow-up questions. Self-reported delinquency was measured by the following 12 items[31]:

1. Did you ever *damage on purpose* something, such as a bus shelter, a window, a car or a seat in the bus or train, a car…? (*vandalism*)
2. Did you ever *steal something* from a shop or department store? *(shoplifting*)
3. Did you ever *threaten somebody* with a weapon or to beat them up, just to get money or other things from them? (*robbery/extortion*)
4. Did you ever *break into a building* with the purpose to steal something? *(burglary*)
5. Did you ever *steal a bicycle, moped or scooter*? (*bicycle theft*)
6. Did you ever *steal a motorbike or car*? (*car theft*)
7. Did you ever *steal something out or from a car*? (*theft from car*)
8. Did you ever *snatch a purse, bag or something else from a person*? *(snatching*)
9. Did you ever *carry a weapon*, such as a stick, knife, or chain (not a pocket knife)? *(carrying a weapon)*
10. Did you ever *participate in a group fight* on the school play ground, a football stadium, the streets, or any public place? (*group fight*)
11. Did you ever *intentionally beat up someone, or hurt him* with a stick or knife, so bad that he had to see a doctor? (*assault)*
12. Did you ever *sell any (soft or hard) drugs* or act as an intermediary? (*drug dealing)*

[31] Two questions dealing with computer hacking (item 60) and downloading music or film illegally (item 59) have not been used as part of the delinquency scale. In particular, the question about downloading music or films turned out to be confusing to youth. The question about "hacking" was less problematic and has occasionally been included.

All items were asked with two time frames: (a) *lifetime* prevalence ("Did you ever …"), and (b) *last year* prevalence ("Did you do this during the last twelve months") as well as incidence ("Yes, ___ times"). Each of these questions also included a number of follow-up questions (i.e., how old when doing it for the first time, did you do it during the last year, and if so, how many times, were you alone or with others, were you detected and by whom, and were you punished). Item 8 (snatching) appeared somewhat problematic in the translation: In some instances, it was translated to suggest "pick pocketing" or personal theft. With regard to item 3 (robbery/extortion), in some countries this offense is subsumed under robbery, in some under extortion.

There is ample discussion in the field of delinquency research about the proper use of any – or all – of these or comparable items to measure self-reported offending (Hindelang et al. 1981). There are several approaches to the use of these 12 delinquency items, and we use a number of them, either alone or in combination.

First, we analyze one (or more) of the items *separately* (i.e., shop lifting, or assault, or burglary). Although there may be national differences in the interpretation of the specific question, for example shoplifting or assault, it still is reasonable to assume that these questions are specific and focused enough to result in quite comparable responses cross-nationally.

Second, in many of our analyses we employ *composite* measures, making use of a number (but not all) of the items. The use of smaller and theoretically meaningful subscales is a very common practice, although there is no consensus about the best way to create such composite measures. We settled on two very common distinctions: minor and serious offenses, and property and violent offenses (Table 2.8). After lengthy discussion, we agreed to follow an empirical criterion to distinguish between *minor* and *serious* offenses. Although national criminal laws may classify some of these offenses differently, *minor offenses* are, generally speaking, the most *frequent* offenses: group fight, carrying a weapon, shoplifting, and vandalism. *Serious offenses* are the less frequent or *rare* offenses: assault, extortion, snatching, theft from car, car theft, bicycle theft, burglary, and drug dealing. We also distinguish between property and violent offenses. *Property* offenses are shoplifting, theft from car, car theft, bicycle theft, and burglary.[32] *Violent* offenses are: group fight, carrying a weapon, assault, extortion, and snatching.[33] It should be noted that the property offenses scale does not include vandalism, which could be considered either a violent or a property offense. It also does not include hacking. Similar to the single offense items, all composite measures come in three versions: Lifetime prevalence, last year prevalence, and last year incidence.

A third approach makes use of information on all 12 items. Often, it is used as a rather rough measure of delinquency involvement (*overall delinquency*); that is, if the respondent answers affirmative to *any* of the 12 items, he or she is considered as

---

[32] When occasionally distinguishing acquisitive crimes from other offenses, robbery/extortion and snatching can also be combined with the property offenses as mentioned.

[33] In the original English version, this is clearly a violent offense. Sometimes, it was interpreted as pick pocketing, sometimes as personal theft. Most researchers, however, interpreted it as a violent offense.

Table 2.8 Classification of self-reported offenses into composites

	Minor offenses	Serious offenses
Vandalism	Vandalism	–
Property offenses	Shoplifting	Burglary
		Bicycle theft
		Car theft
		Theft from car
Violent offenses	Carrying a weapon	Robbery/extortion
	Group fight	Snatching
		Assault
Drug dealing	–	Drug dealing

involved in delinquency. However, since the individual items differ significantly with regard to their level of seriousness (compare assault with shoplifting), this measure of overall delinquency is rather simplistic, and its usefulness is mostly limited to initial and rather broad comparisons. Much preferred is the use of the information of the total scale as a composite measure of *versatility*. Versatility is a combination of both seriousness and frequency. The research literature is very supportive of the robustness of the versatility (or variety) measure, and the results of our analyses further substantiate the usefulness of this versatile measure. We use three types of versatility scores: *raw versatility scores* (sum of prevalence of 12 offenses; for both lifetime and last year); *standardized versatility* scores (raw scores transformed to POMP (=percent of maximum possible) scores ranging from 0 to 100. This measure is invariant with respect to the number of offenses included; its correlation with the raw measure is about 1.0); and *categorized versatility* scores (0 = "no offense", 1 = "one offense", 2 = "two offenses", 3 = "three and more offenses"), both for ever and last year.

Measuring incidence or frequency Prevalence estimates pertain to the proportion of the sample who has been involved in a particular activity (e.g., assault). Another dimension is the frequency (incidence) of a particular act. It is by now well-established that incidence is an important measure of delinquent trajectories – as a matter of fact, the high frequency serious delinquent is a major policy concern. Also, when using self-report delinquency data as a supplemental measure of crime rates, the frequency of offending is more important than the prevalence estimates. Trying to get a valid and reliable answer to the question of "how often" is notoriously difficult (see, for example, Horney & Marshall 1991). We are not only dealing with unwillingness to respond, dishonesty, deliberate exaggeration, or deliberate underestimation, but also with honest inability to remember. As the example of the question on shop lifting (above) shows, we opted for an open-ended response category ("Yes, ___ times"). It took considerable work to clean the data and recode responses that appeared to be obviously exaggerated. Our general approach to the problem of possibly exaggerated or incorrect responses is explained in detail in Chap. 6, using the example of victimization and reporting to police. Because of a much skewed distribution (only few people report a high frequency), we frequently employed an incidence variable categorized into an ordinal measure, distinguishing the frequencies "never," "once," "twice to four times," "five times to nine times," "ten times and more."

2.6.1.2 Alcohol Use

Alcohol use and abuse is not included in our measure of delinquency. The reason for this is that we only wanted to include behavior that is illegal in all participating countries. Instead, we classify alcohol use – together with drug use and truancy – as *risk behavior* (see Sect. 2.6.1.4; also see Junger-Tas et al. 2010). Alcohol use was measured by the following two screening questions:

- Did you ever drink beer, breezers, or wine? (question 49)
- Did you ever drink strong spirits (gin, rum, vodka, whisky)? (question 50)

Follow-up questions asked about age of first use, whether or not the youth ever got drunk, and last month use (prevalence, and number of times). There was also an attempt to measure the amount of drinking (how many glasses, cans or bottles?), and whether the youth drank alone, whether drinking got noticed by adult (parents, police, teacher, or someone else), and whether or not they got punished. Some of these questions proved to be somewhat problematic because of the switch between the question of "Did you use it during the last 4 weeks?" and the next question which asked about "the last time" (did you use it alone or with others?). A more in-depth discussion of the alcohol (and drug) measures may be found in Chap. 5.

2.6.1.3 Drug Use

Drug use is not included in the delinquency measure, but drug dealing is (see Sect. 2.6.1.1). There were three separate questions about drug use and abuse: (1) weed, marijuana or hash; (2) drugs such as XTC or speed; and (3) drugs such as LSD, heroin, or coke. Follow-up questions asked about age of first use, last month use (including frequency), doing it alone or with others, whether or not use was detected (by parents, teachers, police or someone else), and whether or not youth got punished. Chapter 5 discusses some of the problems with these questions in more detail.

2.6.1.4 Risk Behavior

Youthful misbehavior includes a variety of phenomena, ranging from law violating behavior (such as those acts included in our measure of delinquency – see Sect. 2.6.1.1), to behavior such as drinking, drug use, and skipping school that is viewed as problematic because it may be a pathway to more serious illegal behavior. In the ISRD-2 study, youth who had at least two risk factors present (alcohol use and/or marijuana use and/or truancy (last month)) were considered to be at risk. It should be noted that all country participants created this variable for risk behavior and included it in the national chapter (Junger-Tas et al. 2010).

2.6.1.5 Victimization

The ISRD-1 study did not include questions about victimization, but in view of the importance of this concept (i.e., its overlap with offending, as well as its importance as an alternative to police data on crime), four items on victimization were included in the ISRD-2 questionnaire (question 15). Three of the questions concerned a criminal offense (robbery/extortion, assault, theft); the fourth item (bullying) is not a crime. In retrospect, the design of the question left something to be desired; we found that some youngsters had difficulty following the instructions. See Chap. 4 for more in-depth discussion of the questions on victimization, and Chap. 6 for a discussion of the questions related to the reporting of the victimization.

2.6.1.6 Social–Economic Status

Based on the discussions at the ISRD-2 workshops, we were reluctant to include questions on the type of job, income, or education of the youth's parents. Instead, we opted to include four questions which would provide a more indirect measure of the youth's relative affluence. These questions were initially developed for studying health-wealth relationships in cross-national health behavior research (Currie et al. 1997; see also Boyce et al. 2006). The number of positive answers to questions about having a room of one's own; having access to a computer at home; owning a mobile phone; and one's family owning a car were summed to obtain an indicator of *family affluence* (scores ranging from 0 to 4, transformed to POMP scores ranging from 0 to 100). Although these questions turned out to be among the most straightforward and simple to answer, we found that the value of this variable as a measure of affluence is debatable. Instead, it is conceivable that in affluent societies it measures the propensity to consume, instead. The internal consistency (standardized Alpha = 0.50) is low. There was relatively little variation between the kids: very few of them answered negatively on all items; most of the youth answered positively on three or four items (mean = 83.9, sd = 22.9). Exceptions were Armenia, Venezuela, and Suriname (mean = 54.0, 56.4, 60.6; sd = 32.5, 31.4, 30.5, respectively). We also used a more traditional measure of socioeconomic status by including two questions about whether the father or mother had a job (questions 8 and 9); i.e., *employment*. It took considerable debate to determine how to ask this question and which response categories to provide. The questions had a relatively large number of possible response options (eight in total), which were not necessarily mutually exclusive and exhaustive. Importantly, the different options (i.e., he has a steady job; he works at his own business, he sometimes has work, and so on) reflect the compromises made to accommodate the preferences of all national research partners. We found that the most useful way of recoding these variables was creating a dichotomous variable: is one of the adults in the household working or not (yes=93.2%; no=5.8%)?

2.6.1.7 Immigrant Status and Ethnic Minority Group

In ISRD-1, no questions were included about immigration status of the youth. However, some 15 years later when adjusting the questionnaire, there was unanimous agreement that we needed to obtain information about this variable. Whether the discourse is couched in terms of immigration status, ethnicity, citizens vs. noncitizens, minority status, migrant vs. native born, or even race is very much culture-dependent. For instance, in the USA, most of the debate about minorities has focused on race and ethnicity, rather than on immigration status. This is not necessarily so for most of Europe. It makes sense (as discussed in Chap. 3) to employ the general concept of *minority* status (i.e., a visible group with low power and subject to stereotyping and discriminatory treatment; see also, Marshall 1997). After lengthy debates, consensus was reached that a few simple questions about where the youth was born and where his or her father and mother were born (questions 3–5) would be the best way to capture this concept. Because of the open-ended question format, we obtained a wealth of data on the country of origin of the migrant youth. The data are available for the different (more than 100) countries listed, but for purposes of our analysis, we categorized the countries of origin into eight subgroups (Western and Northern Europe, Southern Europe, South-Eastern Europe, Turkey, Central and Eastern Europe, Asia, Africa, and North-/South-America). Chapter 3 provides a detailed analysis of this information.

Based on the responses to questions 3 (were you born in this country, etc.), question 4 (in what country was your mother born?), and question 5 (in what country was your father born?), we created the variable of *migrant*, which was sometimes used as a simple dichotomy (native born, vs. first or second generation migrant), and sometimes as a trichotomy (native born=77.8%, second generation migrant=15.7%, first-generation migrant=6.6% – see Chap. 3). Some additional questions were included which may be of interest, but they are not part of our core definition of ethnic minority group and/or migrant. For example, language spoken at home (question 7), experience of discriminatory treatment (question 8), and friends of foreign origin (question 35) may be used to shed more light on the issue of being a migrant or belonging to an ethnic minority group.

2.6.1.8 Family

Questions relate to the youth's family are a central part of most any youth survey. Some of the very same questions may be used as indicators for different theoretical perspectives (which also is true for questions related to friends, leisure time, school). Here, we provide a brief overview of those family-related questions which have been used in this book, recognizing that there are other ways in which these questions may be employed. There are also some other family-related questions on the survey which we do not discuss here. Some of these questions are taken from well-known sources (i.e., Hirschi's 1969 social bonding theory), others were formulated especially for our comparative study, in consultation with partner researchers. Also, there may be cases where we have adapted a question or scale, without being able to identify its original source. We apologize for this.

Attachment to parents was measured by the two questions [How well do you usually get along with your father (or stepfather), mother (or stepmother)] (questions 16 and 17). Values range from 1 (not at all) to 4 (very well). We included these two questions in a *family bonding scale*. The family bonding scale is a composite of four questions: (1) Frequency of family doing things together (1 = almost never, 6 more than once a week) (question 18); (2) frequency of eating dinner together (1 = never, 8 = daily) (question 19) ; (3) attachment to father (question 16); and (4) attachment to mother (question 17). The scores were converted to POMP scores, ranging from 1 (low) to 100 (high) (mean = 81.0, sd = 17.0, Cronbach's Alpha = 0.55).

Parental supervision is measured by the question of whether the parents usually know who the youth is with when they go out (question 20). In order to accommodate those youth who responded that they never go out, this variable was recoded as: (1) rarely or never, (2) sometimes; and (3) always or do not go out. A low value (1) reflects low levels of parental supervision, and a higher value (2 or 3) indicates more parental supervision. Occasionally, instead of parental supervision, we use the term *family control* (see Chap. 7).

Family disruption is measured by a scale comprised of answers to three questions on the life event scale. The Life Event scale (item 22) is an 8-item fixed response question (yes/no), asking if the youth "has ever experienced any of the following serious events …." Three questions related to the family are: Problems of one of your parents with alcohol or drugs, repeated serious conflicts or physical fights between parents, and separation/divorce of parents. The family disruption scale scores range from 1 (no disruption) to 100 (high disruption) (mean = 13.2, sd = 23.2, Cronbach's Alpha = 0.49).

Family structure or *family composition* is measured by one question (question 6). Not surprisingly, in view of the complex and changing living arrangements of young people today, we needed to provide a large number of response categories (eight, including an open-ended "other" category) in addition to the common category of living with both parents. We created three different recoded variables, ranging from five categories (living with both parents at home = 72.6%, living alternatively with father or mother = 4.9%, living with one single parent = 13.0%, living with a step-parent = 7.0%, and other = 2.5%) over four categories (collapsing "living alternatively with one parent" and "living with a step-parent") to two categories distinguishing between a complete family (with both parents at home) vs. "no complete family" (all other situations).

2.6.1.9 School

A number of questions tap the school-related experiences of the youth. There is the true-and-tried question asking "Do you usually like school?" (question 41), with four response categories ranging from "I like it a lot" (16.5%) over "fairly well" (45.0%) and "not very much" (27.5%) to "I do not like it at all" (11.0%) reflecting the level of *school attachment*. We also included an 8-item question asking the student: "How strongly do you agree or disagree with the following statements about your school?" (1 fully agree, 4 fully disagree). We used this question to construct two scales. First, we constructed a scale measuring *school climate or school bonding*, using the first four items (If I had to move I would miss my school; Teachers do notice when I am doing well and let me know; I like my school; and there are other activities in school besides lessons). This scale represents factors that normally belong to a positive school climate (mean = 69.0, sd = 22.5, Cronbach's Alpha = 0.61). The *school disorganization* scale is comprised of the last four items of this question (there is a lot of stealing in my school; there is a lot of fighting in my school; many things are broken or vandalized in my school). (mean = 37.9, sd = 25.1, Cronbach's Alpha = 0.75). These two scales do measure the students' *perception* of the level of school disorganization.

Two questions were asked related to students' *performance*: one objective (school failure, i.e., repeating a grade, question 42, see Table 2.7), and one subjective (self-assessment of achievement, question 44).

Since there is a lot of variation between countries with regard to the practice of repeating a class, the subjective measure of school performance proved to be a more useful variable. *Truancy* was measured by asking if student ever stayed away from school for at least a whole day without a legitimate excuse in the past year (question 43). A related question tried to capture the student's educational *aspirations* (question 46). The question asked about the student's plans after compulsory school. The age of compulsory education differs significantly between countries, as do the opportunities for continuing education. We tried to capture all possibilities by including a variety of responses (looking for a job; starting an apprenticeship; start training on the job; attending a school where a trade may be learned; continuing school to prepare for higher education, or other).

2.6.1.10 Neighborhood

We adapted a frequently used measure of the youth's perception of his/her neighborhood (Sampson et al. 1997; Sampson et al. 1999). This neighborhood scale (question 47) as initially used consists of 13 items. However, upon analysis, three of these items proved not useful (items 47.2, 47.4, 47.13). We created a *neighborhood quality* scale of ten items, transformed to POMP scores ranging from 0 to 100 (alpha = 0.77). Also, three subscales were constructed. *Neighborhood attachment* (or *neighborhood bonding*) is comprised of two items (If I had to move I would miss

Table 2.9 Descriptive statistics, internal consistency, and correlations of neighborhood scores

			Correlation matrix		
	Mean	sd	(1)	(2)	(3)
Neighborhood bonding (1)	74.7	29.5	(0.76)		
Neighborhood disorganization (2)	21.3	23.7	–0.067[a]	(0.82)	
Neighborhood integration (3)	61.6	28.4	0.459[a]	–0.180[a]	(0.82)

Notes: n (listwise) = 65,129; internal consistency (Cronbach's Alpha) in brackets
[a]$p < 0.001$

my neighborhood, 47.1; and I like my neighborhood, 47.3). A second scale measured *neighborhood disorganization*, using five items (47.5 through 47.9). The third subscale uses three items (47.10, 47.11, 47.12) to measure *neighborhood integration* (or *neighborhood cohesion*). The descriptive statistics, internal consistency, and the correlations of the subscale scores are shown in Table 2.9.

2.6.1.11 Lifestyle/Leisure Time

A significant portion of the questionnaire asked about leisure time activities of the students (questions 23 through 37). Routine activities and other opportunity perspectives stress the importance of unstructured and unsupervised activities. We tried to capture this in the *life style* scale, comprised of four questions: frequency of going out at night (item 23); time spent hanging out with friends (item 24.5); most free time spent with large group of friends (item 26); and having groups of friends who spend a lot of time in public places (item 29) (Cronbach's Alpha = 0.63). More details on this scale are presented in Chap. 9.

Deviant group behavior was measured by a subscale created from four items (37.3, 37.4, 37.5, 37.8) asking what kind of activities usually were happening when hanging out with one's friends (drinking a lot of alcohol, smashing or vandalizing for fun, shoplifting just for fun, frighten and annoying people for fun). The questionnaire also included six items to measure *gang membership* (items 27, 29, 30, 31, 32, and 33). These items were developed by the Eurogang (Decker & Weerman 2005), with the explicit objective of measuring gang membership in a comparative context. This is discussed in more detail in Chap. 9. A number of interesting analyses have meanwhile been conducted on this measure (see Gatti et al. 2010). Translation of the term "gang" proved to be problematic, for instance in France, one speaks of a "bande criminelle" rather than a "bande" (see also Chap. 9).

Closely related to lifestyle/leisure is whether or not the youth has friends involved in deviant or illegal behavior. Admitting to having *delinquent friends* is often used as an alternate way of asking about one's own involvement in delinquency: Respondents are often more willing to admit that they have friends who do undesirable things, rather than admitting to these things themselves. Research has shown that the self-reported delinquency of friends is strongly correlated with a youth's delinquent involvement (Warr 2002). In the ISRD-2 questionnaire, a 5-item question on the delinquency of friends preceded the section on self-reported delinquency and substance use, partly as a way of neutralizing the social desirability effect. This question asks about the number of friends one has who are involved in drug use, shoplifting, burglary, extortion, or assault (48.1–48.5).

2.6.1.12 Life Events

Serious events in a youngster's life may disrupt his or her normal development, which then may be expressed in misbehavior. In order to tap that dimensions, we asked if the youth had had an accident serious enough to get a doctor involved (question 40). Additionally, we included a *life events* scale (question 22). The eight items in this scale are not expected to correlate, therefore Cronbach's Alpha of 0.43 is no indication of unreliability. Rather, a high score on the life events scale indicates that the student has experienced a large number of negative life events. Two subscales were created: *family disruption* (see discussion under Sect. 2.6.1.8) and confrontation with *death and illness* (combining items 22.1 through 22.5: death of a brother or sister; of father or mother; of someone else significant; long illness of yourself; long illness of parents or someone close).

2.6.1.13 Attitudes Towards Violence

Subcultural theories of violence and delinquency assume that violent attitudes are a key explanatory component. Therefore, we included a well-established scale of attitudes toward violence (Wilmers et al. 2002) in the questionnaire. This 5-items question measures positive attitudes towards violence by asking respondents to agree (fully or somewhat) or disagree (fully or somewhat) that a bit of violence is part of the fun (38.1), one needs to make use of force to be respected (38.2), if one is attacked, one will hit back (38.3), without violence everything would be much more boring (38.4), and it is completely normal that boys want to prove themselves in physical fights with others (38.5). The responses were transformed to POMP scores (mean = 33.7, sd = 22.3, Cronbach's Alpha = 0.71).

2.6.1.14 Self Control

Low self-control has been one of the main theoretical perspectives on crime and delinquency since the general theory of crime was first introduced by Gottfredson and Hirschi (1990). We included an abbreviated version of the most frequently used self-control scale (Grasmick et al. 1993). The reliability coefficient for the total 12-item *self-control* scale = 0.83. There are four subscales: *impulsivity*, *risk-taking*, *self-centeredness*, and volatile *temperament*. The descriptive statistics, internal consistency, and the correlations of the subscale scores are shown in Table 2.9.

Table 2.10 Descriptive statistics, internal consistency, and correlations of low self-control scores

			Correlation matrix			
	Mean	sd	(1)	(2)	(3)	(4)
Impulsivity (1)	42.6	25.0	(0.57)			
Risk-taking (2)	38.7	29.3	0.490[a]	(0.78)		
Self-centeredness (3)	29.6	25.7	0.435[a]	0.395[a]	(0.68)	
Temperament (4)	45.2	28.4	0.384[a]	0.368[a]	0.378[a]	(0.69)

Notes: n (listwise) = 66,054; internal consistency (Cronbach's Alpha) in brackets
[a]$p < 0.001$

For further discussion of the psychometric properties of the self-control scale and the four subscales (Table 2.10), please consult Chap. 11.

2.6.1.15 Translation of the Questionnaire

English was used as the common language for the ISRD-2 project. The questionnaire was translated into 23 languages by the respective national participants. In some instances, the translated version was back translated in the English language, but this was not done routinely. Occasionally, incorrect translations of some of the words in a question became apparent during data merging or discussions at one of the workshops. Only one more serious translation problem became apparent, this is the translation of the delinquency item "snatching" (see Sect. 2.6.1.1).

2.6.1.16 Administration of the Questionnaire

In our earlier discussion of sampling, we discussed some issues related to the administration of the survey. A few additional comments should suffice (for details, see national chapters in Junger-Tas et al. 2010). Researchers were provided with guidelines concerning the proper administration of the survey. We also developed standardized forms (administration forms) which needed to be completed by the researchers detailing the conditions under which the surveys were completed (including presence or absence of teacher, students absents, and indication of any events or circumstances that might influence the survey results). Throughout the project, we stressed the need for standardized procedures during the administration of the survey, while realizing that we should expect *flexible* standardization. Indeed, researchers administrating a school-based survey in Surinam or in Moscow are likely to face different conditions than their colleagues in Switzerland or the Netherlands. By and large, though, we are satisfied that we have succeeded in a reasonable degree of uniformity in the administration of the survey. All of the surveys were concluded in a school setting, and all of them were self-administered (i.e., completed by the students themselves). Although countries vary with regard to the need for parental permission (see Table 2.5), the guidelines encouraged all participants to be respectful of the rights of both parents and children not participating in the survey. The survey instrument provided a standard introductory statement explaining the survey to the students, and stressing the anonymity of the responses. Although it was advised that the teacher should not be present during survey administration, this was not always possible or practical. Since teacher presence or absence was not country-specific, the amount of systematic bias resulting from teacher presence likely is minimal. In some countries, a professional survey company executed the survey, whereas in others the study was conducted by researchers associated with a university, or by a government agency, or a nonprofit research group. Based on our interactions with the national partners at the workshops and in later collaborative endeavors, we have no reason to expect that the affiliation or sponsorship of the study in any way had an impact on the quality of the administration of the survey.

The guidelines recommended that the surveys were to be completed by the students themselves, using pencil and paper. We had designed the questionnaire mindful of the need that it should be completed within one school hour period (around 50 min). The questionnaire was about 45 pages, and typically, most students were able to complete all questions within an hour, or sometimes even significantly faster. There were exceptions, where some of the students were not able to read the questions fast enough in order to be finished in time. Based on anecdotal evidence, this seemed to be true in virtually all countries, and we expect that no systematic biases result from this.

We opted for pencil-and-paper administration because we knew that many of the participants would not have access to sufficient computer capacity in order to use computerized data collection. There was one exception: Switzerland was able to collect the data through computerized self-administrated surveys. Details are provided in the Swiss national chapter (Junger-Tas et al. 2010; as to the comparability of computer administered surveys and paper-and-pencil questionnaires, see also Lucia et al. 2007).

2.6.2 National and Local Indicators Collection Forms

Student surveys provide data on the *individual* students, and these data may be aggregated to the level of classroom, school, city or town, or nation. However, we also wanted to collect national and local (city-level) structural indicators to supplement the self-reported survey information. These structural indicators provide a context for the findings, and are used in comparative analyses. Tests of macro-level comparative hypotheses routinely draw from secondary data sources and statistics provided by a large variety of government and nongovernment agencies (e.g., World Health Organization, World Bank). We invested tremendous time and energy in this part of the study, but we only partially succeeded in achieving our goal. We were quite successful in collecting and merging a large number of *national* structural indicators, but doing the same at the *local* level proved to be much more difficult.

The collection of *local* indicators was the responsibility of the national partners; they would have the local knowledge and network to collect – and interpret if needed – the information. We spent considerable time in workshops as well as in follow-up electronic communication discussing which structural indicators would be of interest to all participants, and if this information would indeed be readily available. We conducted a small pilot study, asking several of the participants to try to complete a draft form with local indicator data collected in the city or town where they had conducted the student surveys. Based on the feedback, we made revisions and then settled on a final *Local Indicators Data Collection Form*. The purpose of the form was to facilitate the collection of statistical data that are internationally comparable, readily available, and have a clear policy or theoretical relevance. The data collection form consisted of a series of tables designed to obtain primarily statistical data on the main local indicators for the period closest to the administration of the ISRD-2 survey. Indicators were to be collected for nine types of indicators – for each indicator, there was a "definition of terms" page, and three (blank) data tables (one for the large city, one for the mid-size city, and one for the small towns). Data were to be collected on basic demographics, population diversity, household composition, employment, income disparity and poverty, housing, education, officially reported delinquency and crime, and formal social control by police. Below each table was room for explanatory notes. If it was not possible to provide data as classified or defined in a table, an attempt should be made to collect data that are as close to the definitions as possible. In spite of valiant efforts of the national partners to provide the requested data on the local level, it turned out that large gaps in the obtained data remained. Because of space limitations, we do not want to further expand on the myriad of problems encountered throughout this particular stage of our research effort. We learned a lot about the idiosyncrasy of local statistics. We hope to still be able to produce a valid and workable data file with local data for at least a part of the approximately 120 cities and towns. Fortunately, there was one very positive by-product of our attempt to collect local indicators. That is, it helped us to better understand the geographical and political boundaries and definitions of the "local" areas used as to define the sampling parameters (small towns, city or metropolitan area).

We were much more successful in the compilation of national level structural indicators. A number of these indicators were collected by our national partners; they had the obvious advantage of having a more intimate knowledge and better understanding of the availability and meaning of the national level data sources. We complemented the nine basic indicators (similar to those collected at the local level) with macro-level indicators derived from sources such as the International Crime Victim Survey (ICVS), the European sourcebook, Transparency International, the World Values Survey, and the World Bank.

2.7 Summary and Conclusions

This chapter has highlighted some – but definitely not all – salient methodological and logistic issues and decisions which have shaped the ISRD-2 study. There is no doubt that we have overlooked some issues in our discussion; future analyses and debate may reveal new methodological and theoretical insights into the results of our study that we have not foreseen at this point. Actually, we hope and expect that this study – with both its strengths and its weaknesses – will contribute to the ongoing discussions among comparative methodologists about the challenges and benefits of cross-national social science research.

The ISRD-2 study was designed to take full advantage of the logic of the comparative design (see Sect. 2.1), which allows one to contribute to the development of theory through the testing and specification of hypotheses in a number of different national contexts. The flip side of conducting the study simultaneously in a large number of locales (i.e., national settings) is that the different results may be an artifact of the particular methodology employed (rather than reflect "true" national differences). If this were to be the case, the study would not be credible and lack validity. We opted therefore for an explicitly standardized design (sampling, measurement, data treatment) to be implemented uniformly by all national partners. From the very beginning of the study, however, in order to accommodate and take advantage of the particularities of different countries, we understood the design to be one of *flexible* standardization. Many of the final decisions with regard to sampling and instrumentation were the product of deliberation with a number of the research partners. In this chapter, we have explained a number of decisions made throughout the research process. We have good reason to believe that these decisions have produced reasonably valid data.

The ISRD-2 estimates of delinquency and alcohol and drug use have been validated by comparing them against the results of other comparable studies. Chapter 3 will make a case for the *convergent validity* of the ISRD-2 delinquency estimates. These estimates are compatible with those provided in the Petersborough Study (Wikström & Butterworth 2006), as well as with a Dutch self-report study (Van der Laan and Blom 2006). Cross-validation of the ISRD-2 measures of alcohol and drug use in a larger number of western countries (European School Survey Project on Alcohol and Other Drugs (ESPAD), see Hibell et al. 2004) provides additional support for the validity of the ISRD-2 data (see Chap. 5).[34]

Convergent validity is also at stake in discussions about to the international comparability of official police data, victimization data, and self-report data. We compared ISRD-2 offending and victimization rates with two other main sources of internationally available crime-related statistics: ICVS data and European Sourcebook (i.e., police-based) data. The analyses show a moderate level of support for a convergence of different measures (see Enzmann et al. 2010).

Reliability tests of the scales used in our analysis show alpha values quite within the acceptable range. Analysis of other psychometric properties of the scales (in particular the self-control scale, see Chap. 11) suggest that – generally speaking – these scales may be used in different national contexts. For example, Chap. 11 shows that the 12-item version of the Grasmick et al. self-control scale is one-dimensional

[34] Comparable results are reported for cross-validation of the ISRD-2 estimates for alcohol and drug use in the US ISRD sample (see Marshall & He, 2010).

and consists of four similar subscales in the total sample, in the six country clusters, as well as in most (but not all) individual countries.

The best way to judge if our methodological and conceptual decisions were on target is by looking at the *results* of the study. Do they add up and make sense? We certainly think so. Read through the substantive chapters following this one, and we will let the reader be the judge.

References

Akers, R. L. (2009). *Social learning and social structure: A general theory of crime and deviance*. New Brunswick: Transaction Publishers.

Allardt, E. (1990). Challenges for comparative social research. *Acta Sociologica 33,* 183–193.

Armer, M., & Grimshaw, A. D. (1973). *Comparative Social Research: Methodological Problems and Strategies*. New York: Wiley.

Blaya, C. (2007). *ISRD 2 Technical report: France*. Bordeaux: Université de Bordeaux 2, Observatoire Européen de la Violence Scolaire.

Bovenkerk, F., & Wolf, T. (2010). Surinam. In J. Junger-Tas, I. H. Marshall, D. Enzmann, M. Killias, M. Steketee & B. Gruszczynska (Eds.), *Juvenile delinquency in Europe and beyond: Results of the second international self-report delinquency study* (pp. 399–407). New York: Springer.

Boyce, W., Torsheim, T., Currie, C. & Zambon, A. (2006). The Family Affluence Scale as a measure of national wealth: Validation of an adolescent self-report measure. *Social Indicators Research, 78*, 473–487.

Brener, N. D., Eaton, D. K., Kann, L., Grunbaum, J. A., Gross, L. A., Kyle, T. M. & Ross, J. G. (2006). The association of survey setting and mode with self-reported health risk behaviors among high school students. *Public Opinion Quarterly*, *70*, 354–374.

Currie, C. E., Elton, R. A., Todd, J. & Platt, S. (1997). Indicators of socio-economic status for adolescents: the WHO health behaviour in school-aged survey. *Health Education Research, 12*, 385–397.

Decker, S. H., & Weerman., F. (2005). *European Street Gangs and Troublesome Youth Groups*. Lanham, MD: Alta Mira.

Elder, J. W. (1976). Comparative cross-national methodology. *Annual Review of Sociology, 21*, 209–230.

Elliott, D. S., Huizinga, D., & Ageton, S. S. (1985). *Explaining Delinquency and Drug Use*. Beverly Hills, CA: Sage.

Enzmann, D., Marshall, I. H., Killias, M., Junger-Tas, J., Steketee, M., & Gruszczynska, B. (2010). Self-reported delinquency in Europe and beyond: First results of the Second International Self-Report Delinquency Study in the context of police and victimization data. *European Journal of Criminology, 7*, 159–181.

Esbensen, F., Miller, M. H., Taylor, T. J., He, N., & Freng, A. (1999). Differential attrition rates and active parental consent. *Evaluation Review, 23*, 316–325.

Esbensen, F. A., Melde, C., Taylor, T. J., & Peterson, D. (2008). Active parental consent in school-based research: how much is enough and how do we get it? *Evaluation Review, 32*(4), 335–362.

Esping-Andersen, G. (1990). *The Three Worlds of Welfare Capitalism*. Princeton, NJ: Princeton University Press.

Farrington, D. P. (1987). *The origins of crime: The Cambridge Study of Delinquent Involvement*. London: Home Office Research and Planning Unit.

Fowler, F. (2002). *Survey Research Methods*. Thousand Oaks, CA: Sage.

Gatti, U., & Verde, F. (2010). *Gang membership and alcohol and drug use*. Paper presented at the American Society of Criminology, November 2010, San Francisco.

Glueck, S., & Glueck, E. (1950). *Unraveling juvenile delinquency*. New York: Harper & Row.

Gottfredson, M. R., & Hirschi, T. (1990). *A General Theory of Crime*. Stanford, CA: Stanford University Press.

Grasmick, H. G., Title, C. R., & Arneklev, B. J. (1993). Testing the core empirical implications of Gottfredson and Hirschi's general theory of crime. *Journal of Research in Crime and Delinquency, 30*, 5–29.

Henry, K. L., et al. (2002). The effect of active parental consent on the ability to generalize the results of an alcohol, tobacco, and other drug prevention trial to rural adolescents. *Evaluation Review, 26*, 645–666.

Hibell, B., Andersson, B., Bjarnason, T., Ahlstrom, S., Balakireva, O., Kokkevi, A., & Morgan, M. (2004). *The ESPAD Report 2003: Alcohol and Other Drug Use Among Students in 35 European Countries*. Stockholm: Swedish Council for Information on Alcohol and Other Drugs.

Hindelang, M. J., Hirschi, T., & Weis, J. G. (1981). *Measuring delinquency*. Thousand Oaks, CA: Sage.

Hirschi, T. (1969). *Causes of Delinquency*. Berkeley, CA: University of California Press.

Horney, J., & Marshall, I. H. (1991). Measuring lambda through self-reports. *Criminology, 29*, 471–495.

Huizinga, D., Weher, A. W., Menard, S., Espiritu, R., & Esbensen, F. (1998). *Some not so boring findings from the Denver Youth Survey*. Paper presented at the American Society of Criminology, Washington.

ISRD2 Working Group. (2005). *Questionnaire ISRD2: Standard Student Questionnaire*. Boston, Hamburg, Utrecht, Warsaw, and Zurich: European Society of Criminology.

Ji, P. Y., et al. (2004). Factors influencing middle and high schools' active parental consent return rates. *Evaluation Review, 28*, 578–599.

Johnson, D. P. (2008). *Contemporary Sociological Theory: An Integrated Multi-Level Approach*. New York: Springer.

Junger-Tas, J., & Haen Marshall, I. (1999). The self-report methodology in crime research. In M. Tonry (Ed.), *Crime and Justice: A Review of Research* (Vol. 25, pp. 291–368). Chicago: University of Chicago Press.

Junger-Tas, J., Marshall, I. H., Enzmann, D., Killias, M., Steketee, M., & Gruszczynska, B. (Eds.). (2010). *Juvenile Delinquency in Europe and Beyond: Results of the International Self-Report Delinquency Study*. New York: Springer.

Kish, L. (1994). Multipopulation survey designs. *International Statistical Review, 62*, 167–186.

Kivivuori, J. (2007). *Delinquent Behavior in Nordic Capital Cities*. Helsinki, Finland: Scandinavian Research Council for Criminology.

Kohn, M. L. (1987). Cross-national research as an analytic strategy. *American Sociological Review, 52*, 713–731.

Lappi-Seppala, T. (2007). Penal policy and prisoner rates in Scandinavia. In K. Nuotio (Ed.), *Festschrift in Honor of Raimo Lahti* (pp. 265–306). Helsinki, Finland: University of Helsinki.

Lieberson, S. (1991). Small N's and big conclusions: an examination of the reasoning in comparative studies based on a small number of cases. *Social Forces, 70*, 307–320.

Lieberson, S. (1994). More on the uneasy case for using Mill-type methods in small-N comparative studies. *Social Forces 72*, 1225–1237.

Loeber, R., Farrington, D. P., Stouthamer-Loeber, M., Moffitt, T. E., & Caspi, A. (1998). The development of male offending: Key findings from the first decade of the Pittsburgh Youth Study. *Studies in Crime and Crime Prevention, 7*, 141–172.

Loewenberg, G. (1971). New directions in comparative political research: A review essay. *Midwest Journal of Political Science 15*, 741–756.

Lucia, S., Herrmann, L. & Killias, M. (2007). How important are interview methods and questionnaire designs in research on self-reported juvenile delinquency? An experimental comparison of internet vs. paper-and-pencil questionnaires and different definitions of the reference period. *Journal of Experimental Criminology, 3*, 39–64.

Marsh, R. M. (1967). *Comparative Sociology: A Codification of Cross-Societal Analysis*. New York: Harcourt, Brace & World.

Marshall, I. H. (1997). *Minorities, Migrants, and Crime: Diversity and Similarity across Europe and the United States*. Thousands Oaks, CA: Sage.

Marshall, I. H. (2010). "Pourquoi pas?" versus "absolutely not!" Cross-national differences in access to schools and pupils for survey research. *European Journal of Crime Policy and Research, 16*, 89–109.

Marshall, I. H., & Marshall, C. E. (1983). Toward a Refinement of Purpose in Comparative Criminological Research: Research Site Selection in Focus. *International Journal of Comparative and Applied Criminal Justice, 7*, 84–97.

Marshall, I. H., & He, N. (2010). The United States. In J. Junger-Tas, I. H. Marshall, D. Enzmann, M. Killias, M. Steketee & B. Gruszcynska (Eds.), *Juvenile delinquency in Europe and beyond: Results of the second international self-report delinquency study* (pp. 138–158). New York: Springer.

Marshall, I. H., & Webb, V. J. (1994). Self-reported Delinquency in a Mid-western American City. In J. Junger-Tas, G. Terlouw & M. Klein (Eds.), *Delinquent Behavior Among Young People in the Western World: First Results of the International Self-report Delinquency Study* (pp. 319–342). Amsterdam, The Netherlands: Kugler Publications.

Maxfield, K. G., & Babbie, E. (2001). *Research Methods in Criminology and Criminal Justice*. New York: Wadsworth.

Messner, S., & Rosenfeld, R. (1997). Political restraint of the market and levels of criminal homicide: A cross-national application of institutional anomie theory. *Social Forces 75*, 1393–1416.

Moffitt, T. E. (1993). Adolescence Limited and Life Course Persistent Antisocial Behavior: A Development Taxonomy. *Psychological Review 100*, 674–701.

Naroll, R. (1970). What have we learned from cross-cultural surveys? *American Anthropologist 72*, 1227–1288.

Oberwittler, D., & Naplava, T. (2002). Auswirkungen des Erhebungsverfahrens bei Jugendbefragungen zu 'heiklen' Themen – schulbasierte schriftliche Befragung und haushaltsbasierte mündliche Befragung im Vergleich. *ZUMA-Nachrichten, 51* , 49–77.

Pokorny, S. B., Jason, L. A., Schoeny, M. E., Townsend, S. M. & Curie, C. J. (2001). Do participation rates change when active consent procedures replace passive consent? *Evaluation Review, 25*, 567–580.

Presser, S. et al. (Eds.) (2004). *Methods for testing and evaluating survey questionnaires*. Hoboken, NJ: Wiley.

Przeworski, A., & Teune, H. (1970). *The Logic of Comparative Social Inquiry*. New York: Wiley.

Rokkan, S. (1968). *Comparative Research Across Cultures and Nations*. Hague, The Netherlands: Mouton.

Saint-Arnaud, S., & Bernard, P. (2003). Convergence or resilience? A hierarchical cluster analysis of the welfare regimes in advanced countries. *Current Sociology, 51*, 499–527.

Sampson, R. J. (2006). How does community context matter? Social mechanisms and the explanation of crime rates. In P.O. Wikström & R. J. Sampson (Eds.), *The explanation of crime. Context, mechanisms and development* (pp. 31–60.). Cambridge: Cambridge University Press.

Sampson, R. J., Morenoff, J. D., & Earls, F. (1999). Beyond social capital: Spatial dynamics of collective efficacy for children. *American Sociological Review, 64*, 633–660.

Sampson, R. J., Raudenbush, S. W., & Earls, F. (1997). Neighborhoods and violent crime: A multilevel study of collective efficacy. *Science, 277*, 918–924.

Savolainen, J. (2000). Inequality, welfare state, and homicide: Further support for the institutional anomie theory. *Criminology, 38*, 1021–1042.

Scheuch, E. K. (1968). The cross-cultural use of sample surveys: Problems of comparability. In S. Rokkan (Ed.), *Comparative Research across Cultures and Nations* (pp. 176–209.). Hague, The Netherlands: Mouton.

Smit, P., Marshall, I. H., & van Gammeren, M. (2008). An empirical approach to country clustering. In K. Aromaa & M. Heiskanen (Eds.), *Crime and Criminal Justice Systems in Europe and North America 1995–2004* (pp. 169–195). Helsinki, Finland: HEUNI.

Sudman, S., Bradburn, N., & Schwarz, N. (1996). *Thinking about answers: The application of cognitive processes to survey methodology*. San Francisco, CA: Jossey-Bass.

Thornberry, T. P., & Krohn, M. D. (2000). The Self-Report Method for Measuring Delinquency and Crime. *Criminal Justice 2000* (Vol. 4, pp. 33–83). Washington D.C.: US National Institute of Justice.

Thornberry, T. P., Krohn, M. D., Lizotte, A. J., Smith, C. A., & Perter, P. K. (1998). *Taking stock: An overview of the findings from the Rochester Youth Development Study*. Paper presented at the American Society of Criminology.

Tracy, P., Wolfgang, M., & Figlio, R. (1990). *Delinquency careers in two birth cohorts*. New York: Plenum.

UNDP (2010). *United Nations Development Programme: International Human Development Indicators*. [http://hdrstats.undp.org/en/tables/default.html]

Van der Laan, A. M., & Blom, M. (2006). *Jeugddelinquentie. Risico's en bescherming: Bevindingen uit de WODC Monitor Zelfgerapporteerde Jeugdcriminaliteit 2005*. Den Haag: Boom.

Warr, M. (2002). *Companions in Crime: The Social Aspects of Criminal Conduct*. New York: Cambridge University Press.

White, V., Hill, D. J., & Effendi, Y. (2004). How does active parental consent influence the findings of drug use surveys in schools? *Evaluation Review, 28*, 246–260.

Wikström, P.-O. H. & Butterworth, D. A. (2006). *Adolescent crime: Individual differences and lifestyles*. Collumpton: Willan.

Wilcox, P., Land, K. C., & Hunt, S. A. (2003). *Criminal circumstance: A dynamic multi-contextual criminal opportunity theory*. New York: Aldine de Gruyter.

Wilmers, N., Enzmann, D., Schaefer, D., Herbers, D., Greve, W. & Wetzels, P. (2002). *Jugendliche in Deutschland zur Jahrtausendwende: Gefährlich oder gefährdet? Ergebnisse wiederholter, repräsentativer Dunkelfelduntersuchungen zu Gewalt und Kriminalität im Leben junger Menschen 1998–2000*. Baden-Baden: Nomos.

Wolfgang, M., Figlio, R., & Sellin, T. (1972). *Delinquency in a birth cohort*. Chicago, IL: University of Chicago Press.

Zhang, S., Benson, T., & Deng, X. (2000). A test-retest reliability assessment of the International Self-report Delinquency Instrument. *Journal of Criminal Justice, 28*, 283–295.

Part II
Extent and Nature of Problem Behaviour of Young People

Chapter 3
Delinquent Behaviour in 30 Countries

Josine Junger-Tas

Describing the nature and distribution of delinquency in 30 countries is an awesome task. In order to make this task more manageable, we make extensive use of six country clusters based on Esping-Andersen (1990) and Saint-Arnaud and Bernard (2003) (see Chaps. 1 and 2). We will start by presenting some of our results from the total combined sample as well as for the country clusters, for prevalence, incidence and versatility of self-reported delinquency.

3.1 Prevalence of Delinquency

Table 3.1 and Fig. 3.1 show the prevalence rates for delinquency[1] for the large and medium cities (n=43,141). Looking at "lifetime" and "last year" prevalence of delinquent behaviour, one can see that the highest prevalence rates are found in Anglo-Saxon and West-European countries, followed by the Scandinavian countries, Mediterranean Europe and the Post-Socialist countries. This is true as far as "lifetime" prevalence is concerned as well as "last year" prevalence. The new EU member states have lower delinquency rates than Western Europe. Low rates – both for lifetime and for last year prevalence – can be found in Cyprus, Portugal and Venezuela.

The means of the six clusters illustrate significant differences, particularly in the lifetime figures. There are large disparities between the Anglo-Saxon, W-European and N-European clusters and the remaining clusters. The rates for lifetime prevalence clearly demonstrate this. The largest differences in regards to last year rates are between the Anglo-Saxon and West-European clusters and the rest.

The total prevalence rate is somewhat misleading, because it is comprised of 12 different items (i.e. a youth may be considered delinquent if answering "yes" to the

[1] Measuring the % of youth who admitted to having committed any of the 12 offences (see Chap. 2).

J. Junger-Tas (✉)
University of Utrecht, Utrecht, The Netherlands

J. Junger-Tas et al., *The Many Faces of Youth Crime: Contrasting Theoretical Perspectives on Juvenile Delinquency across Countries and Cultures*,
DOI 10.1007/978-1-4419-9455-4_3,

Table 3.1 Lifetime and "last year" delinquency prevalence (%) in large and medium cities[a]

	N-lifetime	Lifetime prevalence	*N*-last year	Last year prevalence	Lifetime prev. per cluster	Last year prev. per cluster
Ireland	958	56.2	958	40.1		
United States	1,400	44.1	1,398	28.8		
Canada	3,290	36.5	3,290	20.1		
Anglo-Saxon					*45.6*	*29.6*
Germany	2,351	47.9	2,350	29.0		
The Netherlands	1,495	45.8	1,493	29.3		
France	1,921	47.3	1,918	28.9		
Belgium	1,569	41.0	1,566	25.1		
Switzerland	1,196	42.9	1,196	24.6		
Austria	1,948	40.6	1,947	22.1		
W-Europe					*44.3*	*26.5*
Denmark	1,302	43.0	1,300	26.5		
Finland	1,364	46.3	1,364	20.7		
Iceland	585	42.6	585	20.9		
Sweden	1,728	36.5	1,727	19.7		
Norway	1,196	33.3	1,196	16.6		
N-Europe					*40.3*	*20.9*
Italy	4,055	39	4,055	25.6		
Spain	495	37.2	495	21.4		
Cyprus	1,294	22.8	1,292	15.6		
Portugal	844	25.9	844	14.5		
Mediterranean					*31.2*	*19.3*
Czech Republic	1,212	39.7	1,211	24.5		
Armenia	1,357	29.8	1,357	22.0		
Estonia	1,023	37.5	1,022	20.8		
Hungary	382	45.3	382	27.0		
Lithuania	1,375	30.8	1,374	19.0		
Slovenia	728	28.7	727	17.2		
Poland	874	29.4	873	16.3		
Russia	1,460	29.5	1,460	17.7		
Bosnia-Herzeg.	522	24.5	522	16.1		
Post-Socialist					*32.8*	*20.1*
Aruba	664	47.4	663	25.5		
Dutch Antilles	1,696	40.3	1,695	20.1		
Surinam	1,440	36.0	1,438	16.2		
Venezuela	1,417	27.1	1,417	13.8		
Latin America					*37.7*	*18.9*
Total	*43,141*	*37.9*	*43,115*	*22.1*		

[a]Weighted data

question about vandalism, or answering "yes" to the question about assaulting somebody). Therefore, we want to examine the more specific rates of property offences and violence. These rates may be related to different lifestyle choices, such as variations in alcohol use or the way youth spend their leisure time. Herein we

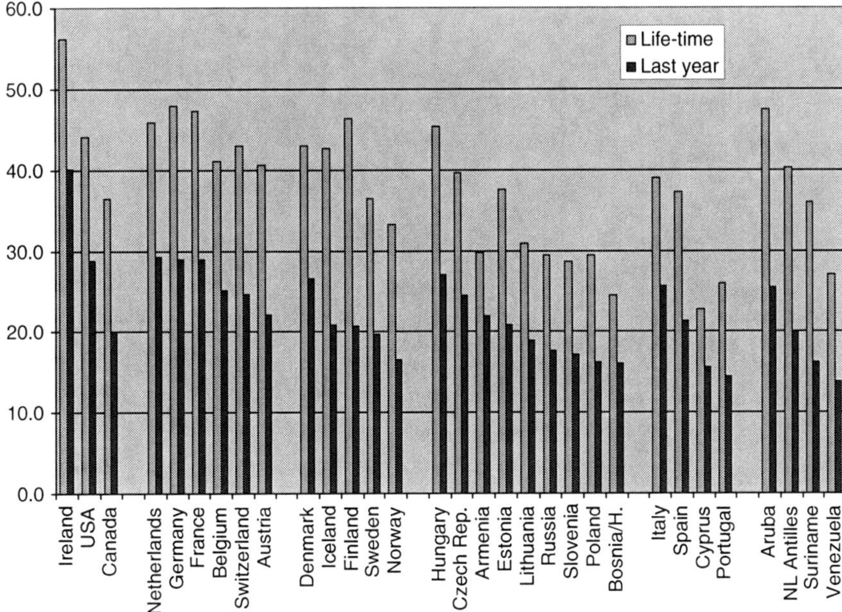

Fig. 3.1 Lifetime and last year delinquency prevalence in large and medium cities ($N=43{,}141$) (Cramer's V: lifetime = 0.15; last year = 0.13)

present comparisons of the rates (last year) of minor and serious property- and violent offenses (see Chap. 2 for definition; see also footnotes 3 and 4).

When we compare last year's property offenses and violent offenses prevalence rate, Figs. 3.2 and 3.3 show a significant difference between West-European countries and other countries, in that the former is much more prominent in property offending than in violence.[2] In terms of property offending, the prevalence rates decrease from the Western countries downwards to the Post-Socialist countries. However, in terms of violent acts there is much more variation. These findings suggest that while West-European children between the ages of 12 and 15 commit a considerable amount of property offenses and also take part in violent behaviour, juveniles in Mediterranean Europe, the new EU states and other less prosperous countries, tend to commit considerably more violent acts than property offenses.

To further illustrate the differences between country clusters, Fig. 3.4 illustrates that, with respect to minor and serious property offenses, Anglo-Saxon countries score highest, followed by West- and North Europe. There may be several explanations for the lower prevalence rates of property offences in the new EU member states and in non-member states. Perhaps big self-service shops and department stores – which create plenty opportunities for theft – are not as numerous in some of these countries; or maybe shops tend to be smaller, thereby increasing social control. Another reason might be that countries generally differ in levels of informal social

[2] Please note that Fig. 3.2 uses a different scale than Fig. 3.3.

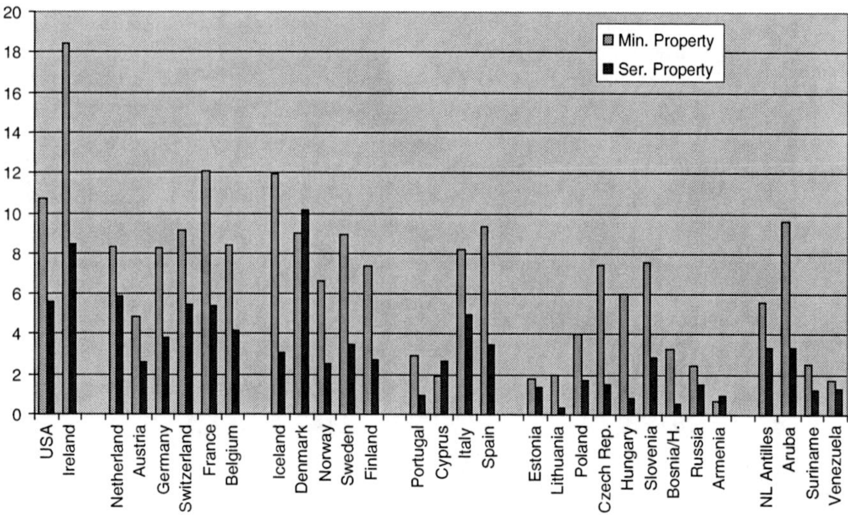

Fig. 3.2 Last year prevalence of minor and serious property offenses in large and medium cities (N=39,769) (Cramer's V: minor property 0.16, serious property 0.13)

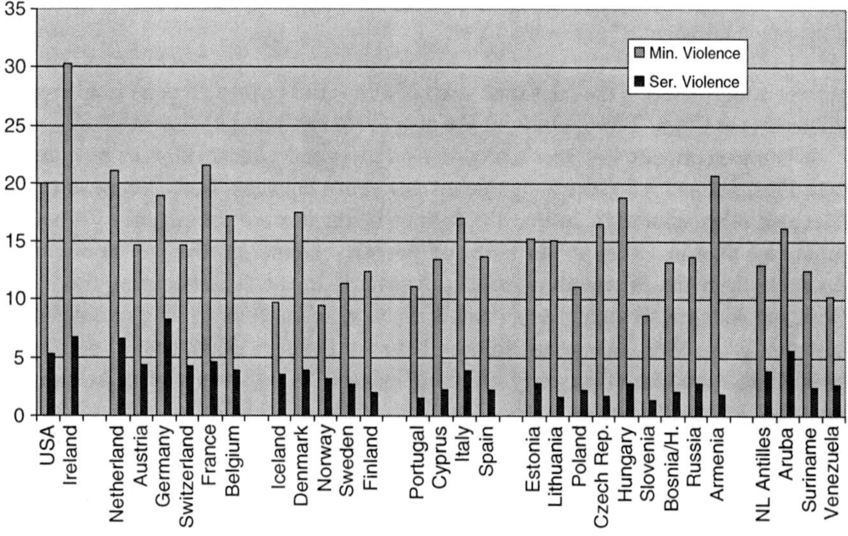

Fig. 3.3 Last year prevalence of minor and serious violent offenses (N=39,781) (Cramer's V: minor violence 0.12, serious violence 0.09)

control and surveillance exercised on young people. For example, greater geographical mobility (more mopeds, scooters, motorcycles, and so on), could decrease effective social control more so in Western- than in Post-Socialist countries. All these factors could explain their relatively high scores for property offenses in comparison to the remaining three clusters.

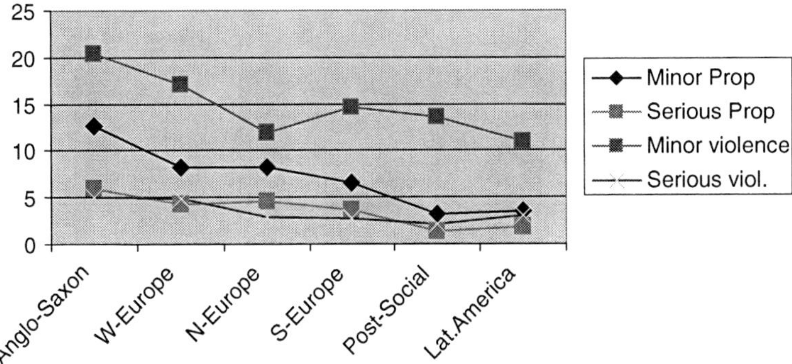

Fig. 3.4 Last year delinquency prevalence by country cluster (%) (N=40.638) (weighted data)

Nevertheless, in terms of minor violence, the picture is somewhat different. While it is true that the Anglo-Saxon and West-European clusters are first in rank, the differences between them and the other clusters are reduced (the line is much flatter) when compared to those related to property offenses, except for the Scandinavian countries which score exceptionally low on violent offending. Although the Mediterranean, Latin American and Post-Socialist clusters score low on property offending, their participation in violence is only somewhat lower than that of West Europe. This suggests that the main difference in delinquent behaviour between the first three clusters and the latter is essentially in property offending rather than violent behaviour. In regards to serious violence, the highest scores – about 5% – are again found in the Anglo-Saxon and West-European cluster, while the other clusters scored between 2 and 3.5%.

In order to get a better perspective on how serious offenses vary between countries, it would be useful to know how minor and serious offences are distributed among those who committed one or more offenses, while excluding those who did not report any offenses (see Fig. 3.5).

The analysis suggests that as far as minor offenses are concerned, almost all offenders (about 94%) in participating countries committed minor offenses.[3] Since there were hardly any differences between the countries we do not present the table. Thus, only 6% of the offenders reported only serious offenses. Interestingly, the rates for serious offenses[4] do show a variation. Consequently, the outcomes suggest that delinquency is not only more widespread in the three first clusters (as shown in Fig. 3.1), but offending patterns are also more serious (F=27,032, p<0.001). A Bonferroni test confirms that the differences are significant between the Anglo-Saxon, W-European and N-European clusters and the Mediterranean and Post-Socialist clusters.

[3] Minor offenses include shoplifting, vandalism, group fights, carrying weapon (knife), hacking.

[4] Serious offenses include theft, burglary theft of bike/motorcycle, auto theft, theft from car, robbery, assault, drugs dealing.

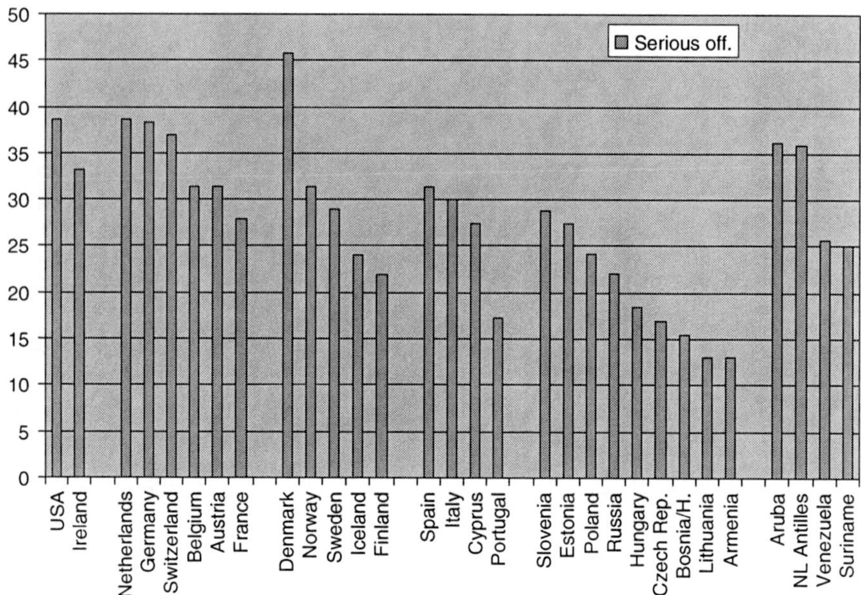

Fig. 3.5 Last year prevalence of serious offenses among youth with at least one offense ($N=9{,}007$) (Cramer's $V=0.18$)

Some countries within the clusters have much higher serious offense rates than others. This is the case for the United States, Germany, the Netherlands and Denmark, while the outcomes of the Latin America cluster are dominated by high rates in the Netherlands Antilles and Aruba.

3.2 Incidence (Frequency) of Offending

Considering the frequency of delinquent behaviour, it will come as no surprise that the non-serious offenses, such as vandalism, shoplifting, group fights and possession of a weapon – often a knife – are committed most frequently, while the more serious offenses occur rarely.[5] Among the serious offenses, assault and bicycle theft occur most frequently. Bike theft is mostly committed in countries where bicycles are commonly used as a means of transportation to school or the workplace – such as in the Netherlands and Denmark. Table 3.2 also shows that most offenses are mainly committed only once or 2–4 times. Higher frequencies (5 times or more) are rare and are mainly found among the non-serious offenses.

[5] As explained in Chap. 2, we used an empirical criterion to distinguish between serious (i.e. rare) and non-serious (i.e. frequent) offenses. This should be kept in mind throughout the interpretation of the results presented in this chapter.

Table 3.2 Total last year incidence of 12 offenses

	Once	2–4 Times	5–9 Times	>10 Times	Mean
Vandalism	2.1	2.9	0.7	0.7	0.42
Shoplifting	2.2	2.2	0.7	0.8	0.42
Group fights	3.9	4.3	1	0.8	0.57
Carry weapon	1.3	2.0	0.8	1.8	0.54
Snatching/theft	0.5	0.4	0.1	0.1	0.06
Bicycle theft	0.8	0.6	0.2	0.1	0.06
Burglary	0.3	0.3	0.1	0.1	0.04
Break in car	0.4	0.4	0.1	0.1	0.05
Car theft	0.2	0.1	0.1	0.1	0.03
Assault	0.8	0.5	0.1	0.1	0.11
Robbery/extortion	0.4	0.5	0.1	0.2	0.06
Drug dealing	0.5	0.6	0.2	0.4	0.23

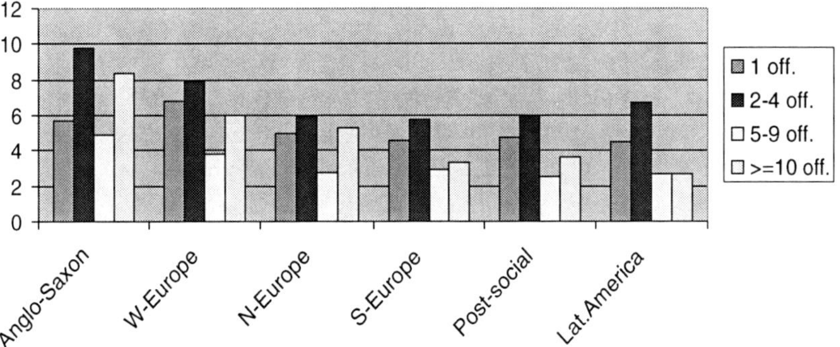

Fig. 3.6 Last year frequency of delinquent behaviour by country clusters ($N = 40{,}640$) (those with 0 offenses last year excluded) (weighted data)

In terms of the number of delinquent acts committed in the last 12 months, the highest frequencies, both for two to four and for ten or more offenses, occur in the Anglo-Saxon and West-European clusters (see Fig. 3.6). If we consider committing two to four delinquent acts as relatively non-serious, the difference between the first two clusters and the other four can be found in the higher number of occurrences. Not only do more young people in the Anglo-Saxon and West-European clusters commit five to nine offenses but they also score higher in the category of more than ten offenses. Thus, the difference between these two clusters not only relate to the nature of the crime (more property offenses), but also in terms of frequency.

It should be noted that a higher frequency of offending may simply imply that a juvenile has shoplifted more than 2–4 times or repeatedly vandalized objects, it does not necessarily mean that the juvenile is a serious delinquent.

3.3 Versatility

As shown in Table 3.2, frequency was measured simply by counting the number of times respondents committed specific offenses. However, this is not a very reliable measure since young people may only have a vague idea of the number of times they committed a non-serious offense, especially those offenses that occur on a frequent basis such as vandalism or shoplifting. Because of their saliency, serious offenses are likely to be remembered in greater detail and their accounts are thus more reliable. However, memory problems do continue to trouble self-report studies. A better measure that combines frequency and seriousness is diversity or versatility. We explained this measure in more detail in Chap. 2.

Figure 3.7 presents lifetime and last year versatility, and shows that in the period 2005–2007, 40% of young people aged 12–16 living in large and medium cities in 30 countries of the ISRD-2 study, had committed one or more different offenses during their lifetime. In the year that preceded the survey (i.e. last year versatility), this was about 24%. A second finding is that many of them do restrict their involvement in offending behaviour to one offense ("ever" 19% and "last year" 13.5%) or two different delinquent acts (8.5 and 5%, respectively). Three or more offenses have "ever" been committed by 10.5% of the respondents, and 5.5% of all respondents reported that they had committed three or more offenses "last year".

Although high versatility may be related to committing different non-serious offenses, such as vandalism, shoplifting or group fights, we expect (and we will explore later in the study) that this last group will include the most serious delinquents.

In general, more offenders committed three or more different types of offenses in the first three clusters than in the last three clusters (Fig. 3.8). This is illustrated with a gradually descending line within the categories of two and three or more types of offenses. This shows that not only do offenders in the Anglo-Saxon, N-European and W-European clusters commit more offenses than the other three clusters but

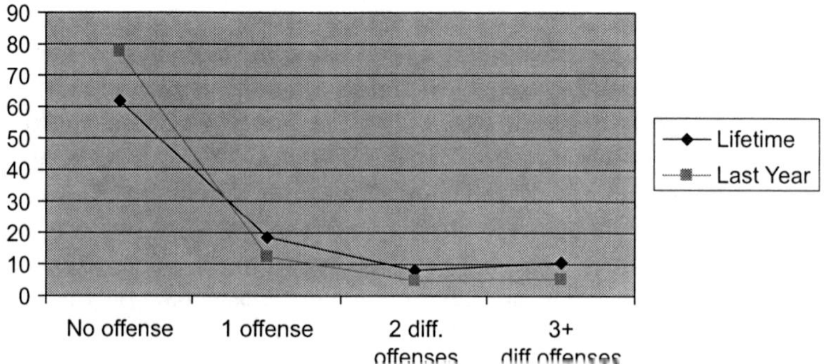

Fig. 3.7 Lifetime and last year versatility of delinquent behaviour in large and medium cities (N=40,700)

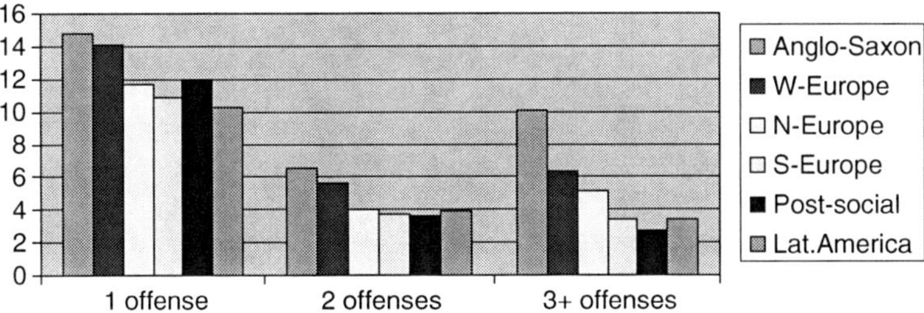

Fig. 3.8 Last year offending versatility of country clusters (%) (N=8,930) (weighted data; Cramer's V=0.06)

they also commit a larger variety of offenses, suggesting a more serious delinquency pattern. This supports our previous results which looked at the serious offense rates among offenders in all 30 countries (see Fig. 3.5).

3.4 Some Comparisons with Other Self-Report Surveys

It is interesting to compare a number of other large self-report surveys to the ISRD-2 study, to see whether our findings make sense in the light of other recent surveys that use the self-report method for their data collection.

In order for the comparison to be successful, we had to make sure that the sampling frames were comparable. This meant that these studies must also have used school samples based on a random selection of schools and classes. Furthermore, taking into account the strong correlation between delinquency and age, the studies also had to focus on school populations with similar grade levels that is grade 7–9. In addition, to make comparison possible there would have to be some similarity in regards to the nature of the offenses measured.

The first study that lends itself to such a comparison is the Wikström's Peterborough study (Wikström and Butterworth 2006). This cross-sectional study, was conducted among 2,000 schoolchildren aged 14–15 in Peterborough, a large city in the north of London. The authors used self-report methodology, and a paper and pencil questionnaire was administered in all 13 Peterborough state schools. The survey took place in 2000, which was 6 years before the ISRD-2 survey.

We can compare the Peterborough's delinquency outcomes most efficiently with those of the large and middle-sized cities of the two participating Anglo-Saxon countries: the United States and Ireland. Table 3.3 presents the "last year" prevalence of selected juvenile offenses which were used in both surveys. There may be some differences between the definitions of some offenses. For example, Wikström and Butterworth (2006) distinguish between residential burglary and non-residential burglary. Taking into account that residential burglary would be rather rare at age 14–15 (1.3%), we compared the ISRD-2 burglary item with non-residential burglary. Moreover, based on the explanation given in Appendix A, on the definition of

Table 3.3 Comparison "last year" prevalence of juvenile offenses between the Anglo-Saxon Cluster and the Peterborough study (Table 4.1)

	United States	Ireland	Peterborough
Shoplifting	10.7	18.4	13.9
Vandalism	10.3	19.1	17
Group fights/assault	12.7	26.9	24
Burglary (non-residential)	1.3	2.6	3.1
Break in car	3.5	4.1	3.2
Robbery/extortion	2.6	3.5	1.4

Table 3.4 Comparison "last year" prevalence of selected juvenile offenses between West Europe and the WODC study

	W-Europe ISRD	Belgium ISRD	The Netherlands ISRD	The Netherlands WODC
Shoplifting	8.5	8.4	8.3	8
Vandalism	9.1	6.7	8.9	10
Group fights[6]	14.1	13.5	16.4	25.3
Carry weapon[7]	9.2	9.4	11.2	5
Burglary	1.2	0.8	1.6	1.5
Soft drugs dealing	3.0	2.9	4.6	2.1

offending (Wikström and Butterworth 2006: 255–256), we assume that the Peterborough item of assault does correspond with the ISRD-2 item of group fighting.

It is clear from Table 3.3 that both studies show similar differences in prevalence rates between non-serious and serious offenses. In addition, the delinquency rates of the Peterborough study tend to be more similar to those of Ireland than those of the United States, in particular with respect to non-serious offenses. This is less clear in regards to serious offenses. On the whole however, the order of frequency in regards to the type of offenses committed is quite similar.

The second example compares ISRD-2 with a Dutch cross-sectional survey conducted by the Research and Documentation centre of the Dutch Ministry of Justice, which is routinely conducted every 2 or 3 years, beginning in 1987 (Van der Laan and Blom 2006). Usually, the survey is directed at young people between the ages of 12 and 17, but this time the group was between 10 and 17 years of age. The researchers used a random sample, which yielded 1,460 juveniles with a response rate of 68%. In 2005, the youth were questioned at home by a trained interviewer (Table 3.4).

We compared the ISRD survey with the Dutch ISRD survey, the Belgian ISRD study and total ISRD West Europe. The comparison has been standardized for ages 12–15. Again we see many similarities, taking into account some differences in the definition of the offenses, such as enlarging the definition of "group fights" and reducing it in the case of "carrying a weapon". The comparison shows that the relative rank-ordering across all studies is strikingly similar and the outcomes are quite

[6] WODC definition was to "beat or hit someone 'without' and 'with injuries' ".

[7] WODC definition was "carrying weapon only 'when going out' ".

consistent. The result suggests that the ISRD data are valid and support what is generally found in most self-report studies. Many youths commit offenses to a certain extent, but these are mostly minor in nature, and serious delinquency is rare.

These results can also be confirmed by another example given by Enzmann et al. (2010), who compared ISRD delinquency rates with data from the International Crime Victim Survey and from the *European Sourcebook*. This analysis found that police data and ISRD-2 data are correlated.

3.5 Delinquency by City Size

As shown in extensive international research (van Dijk et al. 2007), crime is generally more prevalent in cities than in rural areas. This is well known within the research community and may be related to the fact that there are many windows of opportunities in regards to committing offenses in large cities. Large cities surrounded by neighbourhoods have many shops, department stores, bars and cafes where criminal acts could take place. In addition, large cities imply an increase of anonymity, which makes it easier to commit offenses and to escape detection than in smaller ones.

Considering the prevalence of minor and serious delinquency, however, differences according to city size are small and only significant in the Anglo-Saxon and Mediterranean clusters (see Table 3.5). Both clusters have the highest rates of offenses in the large cities, which supports the literature, while the differences in the other clusters are rather limited. Interestingly, Latin America has the lowest minor offending rates, but in terms of serious offending they have rates that are comparable to North Europe and South Europe. The Post-Socialist cluster has the lowest last year prevalence rates of serious offending and the Anglo-Saxon cluster the highest, followed by Western Europe. The rates in the other clusters are in between.

Overall, the differences are small which might be related to the nature of the samples. For example, North Europe has large city samples, while Latin America predominantly has small city samples (see Chap. 2). Another factor might be the high degree of urbanization in the whole of Europe, which may eventually blur differences in delinquency involvement between urban and rural environments.

Table 3.5 Last year prevalence serious offenses by city size and country cluster (%) (N=40,638)

	Total minor offenses			Total serious offenses			
	Small	Medium	Large	Small	Medium	Large	Cramer's V
Anglo-Saxon	23.5	30.5	36.3	7.3	12.1	11.9	0.11–0.08
W-Europe	26.8	25.6	27.6	8.6	9.1	9.0	0.08–0.01
N-Europe	19.1	20.4	21.2	6.1	5.0	6.8	0.02–0.02
S-Europe	23.2	21.2	28.8	4.9	4.8	8.5	0.07–0.07
Post-Socialist	17.6	18.8	22.5	3.3	3.6	3.9	0.06–0.02
Latin America	16.8	17.8	17.3	5.2	5.8	3.5	0.01–0.04

3.6 Delinquency and Gender

Figure 3.9 illustrates the gender gap in property and violent offending by country cluster, showing a strong gender effect. This is not surprising in light of what we know from the literature (Felson 1998; Thornberry and Krohn 2003; Warr 2002). In most clusters, boys commit roughly twice as many offenses as girls.

This gender difference also includes Latin America although its prevalence offending rate is very low for boys as well as for girls. The Post-Socialist cluster is an exception, because in this group of countries, boys commit 3 times as many offenses as girls. Nevertheless, shoplifting remains a significant exception to the rule. Compared to the discrepancy between the sexes in minor and serious offending, differences in the prevalence of shoplifting (minor property) between the sexes are rather minimal.

As far as property offenses are concerned, the three first clusters have higher rates than the latter (see Fig. 3.9). Moreover, gender discrepancies are largest in the Anglo-Saxon and North European clusters, while they are much smaller in the other clusters. As for violent behaviour, it is worth remarking that when comparing the prevalence of property offenses to that of violent offenses, the overall gender gap is considerably more pronounced with respect to violence than to property offending behaviour.

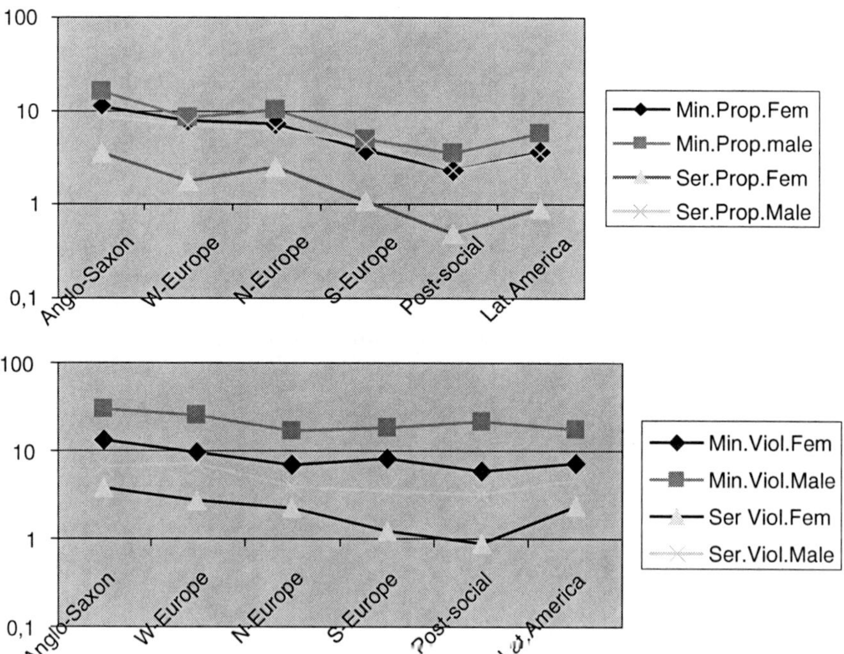

Fig. 3.9 Last year Prevalence of violent and property offenses by gender (log. scale) (weighted data)

In addition, differences in violent behaviour between clusters are also less pronounced than those in property offending.

3.7 Delinquent Behaviour by Age and Grade

Most students in our research population attend public and secular schools (60%). About 12.5% of the students attend private schools and 5% studies at religious, predominantly Roman Catholic, schools. We attempted to define the level of the education of our respondents, but because of the huge differences in school systems across participating countries, we did not succeed. This is unfortunate, since we know how important this variable is in explaining differential involvement in delinquent behaviour. The lower the level of education, the higher the involvement in delinquent offenses, and the more violence reported (Junger-Tas et al. 2003, 2008).

Normally one would expect a perfect correlation between age and grade. However, due to a number of factors, this is unrealistic. These factors include the increasing number of recent young immigrants in Europe, who are required to learn the language of the host country – often in special classes – and the fact that a sizable proportion of pupils have to repeat a grade. In fact, the correlation between age and grade is 0.70 ($p<0.01$) (see also Chap. 2).

By looking at offending prevalence rates by age (not shown), our results convey an expected trend: delinquency involvement increases with age. Delinquency usually starts around age 13, where delinquency involvement reaches its height at the ages of 14 and 15. This is common across all clusters. Figure 3.10 shows last year delinquency prevalence by grade. Indeed, comparing rates by grade with those by age roughly confirms the latter, with the lowest (last year) rates in grade 7, somewhat higher rates in grade 8 and the highest involvement in grade 9; this, with the exception of N-Europe where offending is more frequent in grade 8 than in grade 9.

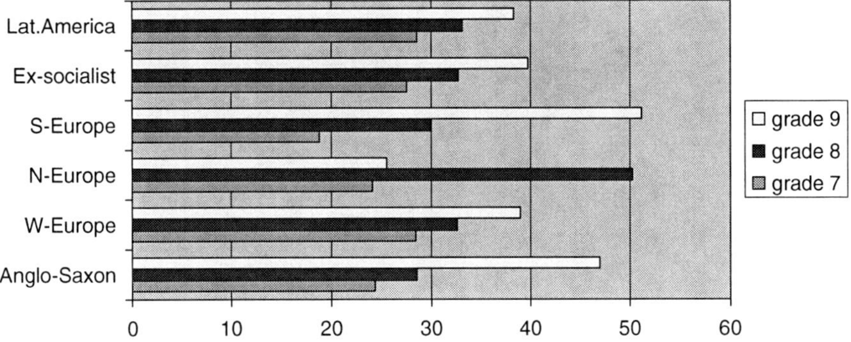

Fig. 3.10 Last year delinquency prevalence by grade (%) (weighted data)

3.8 Age of Onset

We also examined the age of onset by country cluster, to see whether there would be any differences indicating perhaps higher ages of onset in clusters of lower delinquency involvement in comparison to the more delinquent Anglo-Saxon and West-European clusters. Several observations can be made regarding Fig. 3.11. First, differences in the age of onset are either small or non-existent. This suggests that there is some degree of a universal trend in regards to the age at which young people start committing delinquent acts – as they tend to do this at about roughly the same age all over the world.

Second, a careful scrutinizing of Fig. 3.11 shows an overall slightly higher age of onset in the Latin American cluster in comparison to all the other clusters, but in particular to the Anglo-Saxon and W-European clusters. This illustrates that Latin American countries stand out within the total sample, as compared to the five other clusters. It also suggests that the Latin American cluster represents a different type of society as compared to the remaining ones, which are more similar to one another.

Third, one may note slightly increasing curves, starting with a lower age of onset for non-serious offenses such as vandalism and shoplifting and ending with a higher one for more serious offenses such as car theft and robbery, with the highest age of onset for drug dealing.

3.9 Age and Delinquency by Gender

Another interesting question is to what extent there are gender differences in the age distribution of offending. Since police, juvenile justice officials and researchers, including ourselves, consistently find lower rates of delinquency involvement of girls in comparison to boys, one might wonder whether girls, overall, start committing delinquent acts at an older age than boys. Furthermore it would be interesting to

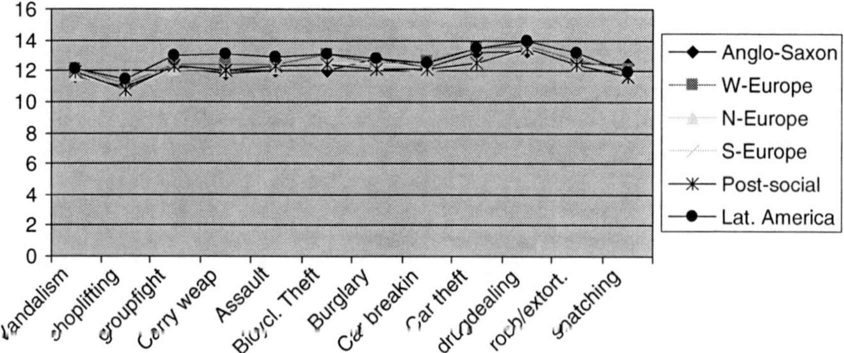

Fig. 3.11 Mean age of onset of offending by country cluster (%) (weighted data)

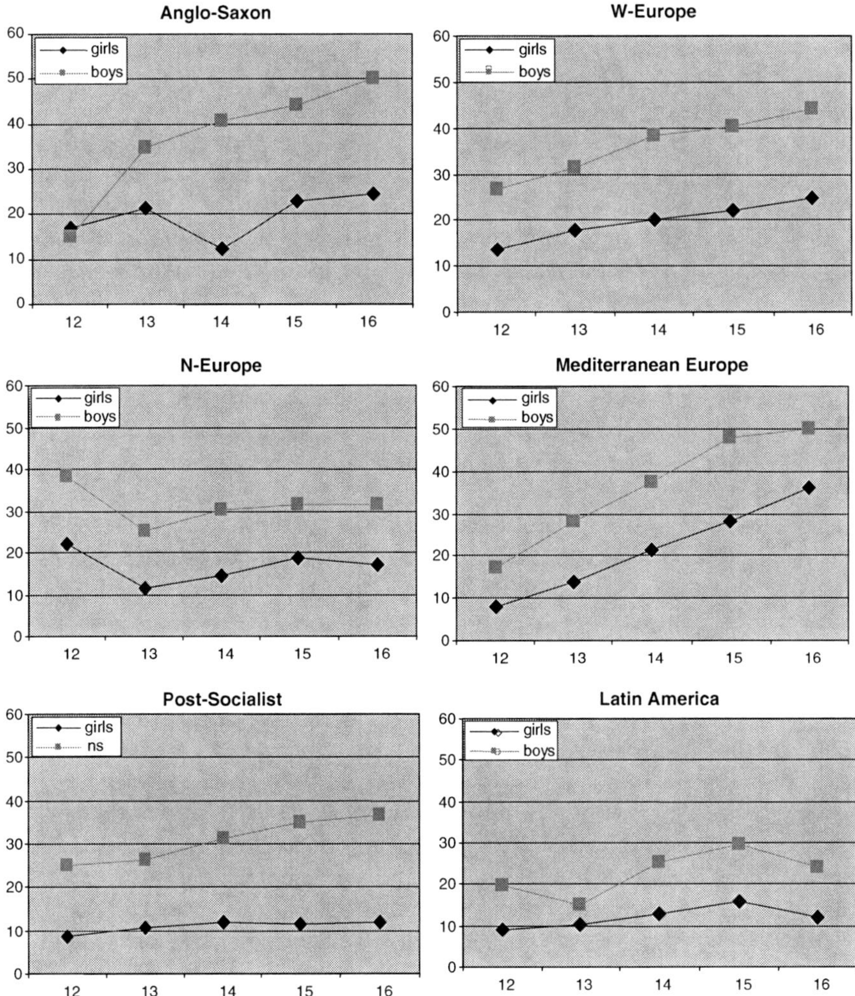

Fig. 3.12 Age distribution of delinquency by gender (%)

note whether any differences in this respect would also be related to a difference in the nature of the offenses committed. Again we compared the six country clusters, because there may also be cluster differences due to a diversity of social-economic and cultural factors.

One would expect that in general, girls start offending later than boys but the analysis reveals that this is not the case. Median age of onset of both boys and girls is 12; when using the mean age of onset, there is a very small difference between boys and girls (boys start 2 months earlier than girls). Figure 3.12 shows the age distribution of last year prevalence (of total offenses) by gender and country cluster.

In the Anglo-Saxon cluster, about the same percentage of boys and girls start offending at age 12.[8] However, after age 12, offending increases steeply among boys, which steadily increases the gap between the sexes. This differs greatly with West Europe, where there is also a gap between the sexes, but in this case, delinquent behaviour follows a quite parallel path for both genders. West-European girls are as delinquent as Anglo-Saxon girls, but West-European boys do not commit as many delinquent acts as Anglo-Saxon boys. The same tendency of parallel development is portrayed in North-Europe, but in that case there is something more remarkable going on.[9] The Mediterranean cluster has the same high level of delinquency, and girls follow the same pattern as boys, but at a lower level. The female level in the two last clusters (Post-Socialist and Latin America) is extremely low, while that of boys in the Post-Socialist cluster increases from 20 to about 40%. In Latin America, both sexes offend at quite a low level.

What conclusions might one make on the basis of these findings? Firstly, our data does not give us any indication that delinquency starts earlier in boys than in girls. Both genders involve themselves in delinquent behaviour at about the same age, but the main difference between the sexes lies in the extent and nature of the offending behaviour. Second, the data also suggests that the emancipation thesis should be rejected since the Nordic countries have embraced and based their society around the emancipation of women. Women in Nordic countries have gained importance in society and are increasingly represented in the labour market, government and parliament. However, juvenile crime in more traditional societies, such as in South Europe, increases much more rapidly by age than in North Europe. In the Post-Socialist cluster, where women have been active on the labour market for a long time, girls' delinquency, as opposed to that of boys, is very low. Yet, labour market participation does not necessarily go hand in hand with women's emancipation. Youth crime in Latin America is very low for girls and boys, a phenomenon which requires a multivariate analysis for clarification. One explanation could be the matrifocal structure of Latin American societies, where women often have the role of being the head of the family and are responsible for the family's income. This might also impact their daughters' behaviour. Interestingly, these family dynamics suggest a different type of women's emancipation than that of western countries. Our final and perhaps most important theoretical conclusion, derives from the sizable disparities in girls' delinquency between country clusters. The evidence suggests that the (differences in) male and female rates of delinquency are not simply a matter of biology because in that case the rates would be constant. Rather, cultural and socialization differences could play an even more significant role in explaining these differences, an important point that will be addressed later in this book.

[8] 11-year olds hardly committed any offenses.

[9] The relatively high proportion of youth starting at age 12 is caused by the extremely small number of 12-year olds (4 and 8) in the Scandinavian sample.

3.10 Juvenile Offending as Group Behaviour

From about age 12 until about age 18, when students leave the peer group and go their separate ways onto higher education, employment or while having steady relationships with the other sex, young people often come together and form groups. As the peer group gains importance, parental influence diminishes. Peer groups originate where many youths meet each other, at school or in their neighbourhood. Peer group activities do not necessarily imply delinquent behaviour: such groups also offer fun as well as social and psychological support in growing into adulthood (Muuss 1980; Warr 2002). In addition, the peer group teaches juveniles the norms and rules with respect to work, conflict resolution and appropriate behaviour with the other sex. Juveniles usually spend a lot of time with their peer group: they go out clubbing together, play music, drink and use drugs and sometimes they also commit offenses.

In the framework of this study we are interested in the question of which delinquent acts are committed in groups and which ones are committed individually? Table 3.6 shows that most juvenile offending is by far a group activity. There are, however, some differences according to the offense and country cluster.

First, considering the general offending pattern, some particular offenses, such as vandalism and breaking into buildings are typical group offenses; about 90% of all offenders commit these with their peers. However, the proportion of offenses committed in the company of peers is smaller for shoplifting (between 69.5 and 84%) and for snatching (a purse or bag – between 37 and 68.2%) and robbery/extortion (between 58 and 69.5%). These are offenses based on stealth, where more youths take precautions in order to refrain from being observed and may have a preference to commit the offense alone. Car theft on the contrary, often committed in public places, is an offense that gives status to offenders: such youngsters want to be seen and will thus, in majority, commit the offense with others (between 56.7 and 86.9%). The dealing of drugs is not an offense that would be openly committed, unless it concerns small scale dealing of soft drugs among peers. About 60% of soft drug dealers do this within their peer group, which implies that about 40% commit the offense on their own.

Table 3.6 Selected offenses committed last year in company of peers (%)

	Anglo-Saxon	North Europe	West Europe	South Europe	Latin America	Post-Socialist
Vandalism	92.3	89.8	91	88	76	89
Shoplifting	78.3	79.5	76.5	84	69.5	76
Car break	70	62.5	71.4	74.2	60.9	72.6
Snatching	68.2	65.8	51	55.6	37	53
Assault	74.4	54.5	50.7	65.3	47	61.4
Burglary	88.7	88.6	87.5	79	71.2	85.5
Robb./ext.	69.5	67.4	65.1	59.2	58	66
Car theft	84.3	86.9	84.8	77.3	75.6	56.6
Drug dealing	59.7	58.5	57	63.8	57	55.2

There are also some significant country cluster disparities. For example snatching (of a purse or bag) is committed more often with peers in the Anglo-Saxon and N-European clusters than in the others, while assault is predominantly only a group offense in the Anglo-Saxon cluster. This may be related to a generally higher level of violence in the Anglo-Saxon cluster, which could include a greater proportion of group violence. There were less multiple offender car thefts in the Post-Socialist countries, which could be explained by a lower presence of cars, making car theft, particularly in the form of joy-riding, more difficult.

Nevertheless, there is one clear exception to the general pattern. For almost all the selected offenses, the percentage of juveniles offending with peers is considerably lower in Latin America than in the other clusters, with the exception of drug dealing. An explanation for this particular oddity might be found in the geographical placement of this cluster relatively close to important drug producing states. This may possibly lead to a lesser degree of fear regarding repercussions and a more relaxed attitude with respect to drug dealing together with peers.

3.11 Delinquency and Migration Status

All European countries are inhabited by large groups of residents from different ethnic origins. The reasons behind the presence of ethnic minorities in these countries are similar and simple: the host countries have always felt the need for cheap labour. Some minority groups are descendants of slaves, imported in earlier times with the purpose of working on plantations. However, the largest category of immigrants consists of labour migrants. Since 1950, 18 million people have migrated to the United States, most of whom are of a non-European country, while 15 million people immigrated to Western Europe, the majority as so-called "guest workers" (Yinger 1994). Southern-Europeans were recruited by Switzerland, Belgium and the Netherlands. Germany and the Netherlands recruited large numbers of Turkish and Moroccan workers in the 1960s and 1970s. Another important category consists of immigrants from former colonies, who settled in their colonizers country of origin, usually in search of work. Examples are the West-Indians, Pakistanis and Bangladeshis in Great Britain, and the Surinamese and Antilleans in the Netherlands. Mexicans immigrants have a somewhat similar position in the United States and African immigrants particularly in France and Italy.

Finally, there is a growing category of people, which on the basis of political reasons, oppression and war have fled their country of origin, hoping to build a new future for themselves and their children in the host country. Since 1990, the numbers of newcomers, in particular asylum seekers and refugees, increased in all OECD countries. Others came in search for employment due to shortages in certain sectors, but immigration remained predominantly driven by hopes of family reunification. Although every country and every region has its own migrant population, the two main immigration countries are the United States – with 647,000 entries in 1999 – and Germany (674,000 entries). In France, the Netherlands and Switzerland,

Table 3.7 Region of origin of young migrants in ISRD-2 by country cluster[a] (%)

	Anglo-Saxon	West Europe	North Europe	Mediterranean Europe	Post-Socialist	Latin America	Total
	N=305	N=3,773	N=1,487	N=1,085	N=1,067	N=1,723	9,440
North West Europe	13.8	9.9	23.9	10.2	6.0	13.4	12.5
Southern Europe	1.0	13.1	3.5	8.1	1.0	4.2	7.6
South- East Europe	1.6	17.5	6.2	7.1	41.6	0.1	13.5
Turkey	0.7	18.5	5.1	0.1	0.1	0.1	8.3
Central East Europe	1.6	7.1	6.5	5.8	31.8	0.1	8.2
(Austral) Asia	15.7	11.0	34.2	12.0	17.3	4.8	14.5
Africa	5.6	13.4	12.2	28.8	1.2	0.2	10.9
North and South America	60.0	9.5	8.4	27.8	0.9	77.1	24.4

[a]Weighted data

immigration ranged from 65,000 to 78,000 persons, with Italy receiving a sudden influx of some 268,000 immigrants in 1999 (OECD Annual Report 2010:17–21).

Ethnic minority groups can be defined by the following characteristics:

- Their ethnic-cultural position differs from that of the original population
- They usually have a low social-economic status
- Their education level is low and many of them do not proceed further than the lower secondary level
- Their populations are too small in size in order to have much (political) influence on policy making
- Their unfavourable situation may last several generations

Returning to our study, the first question we want to ask is about the country of origin of the young migrants. In fact the countries of origin are as diverse as the countries participating in our study. Indeed, within the migrant population more than 100 different nationalities were represented, thus they were divided into geographic regional clusters. For the ease of comparative analysis, we reduced these clusters into eight regions: West- and North Europe, South Europe, South-eastern Europe, Turkey, Central and East Europe, (Austral)Asia, Africa, North and South America.

Table 3.7 illustrates that on the American continent (i.e. the Anglo-Saxon and Latin American clusters), the migration pattern is primarily regional, with a large majority of minorities migrating within the continent (60 and 77.1% respectively). For the European clusters, there is considerably more diversity with regard to the region of origin of migrant youth. The largest groups of migrants in Western Europe are originally from Turkey and South and East Europe, while in North Europe the greatest group of migrants are from Asian and African countries. This is also the

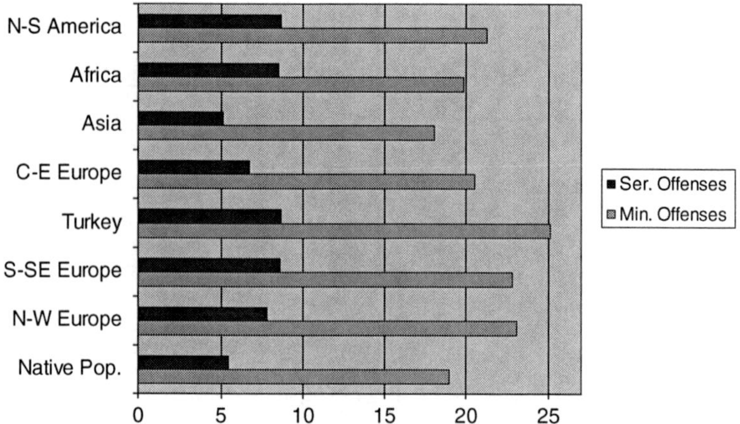

Fig. 3.13 Last year prevalence of minor and serious offenses among different groups of migrant and the native population ($N = 64,183$; weighted data; Cramér's V: minor offenses = 0.033, $p < .001$, serious offenses = 0.046, $p < .001$)

case in South Europe. For example, there are sizable numbers of North and Central African migrants in France, while Spain hosts many migrants from South America and Northern Africa. Finally, migrants in Post-Socialist countries are mainly from the region itself.

When looking at migration movements from a slightly different angle, we see that West Europeans – if they migrate – have a preference for North Europe (23.9%), which could be related to career options, notably in the agrarian sector. South and East Europeans, as well as Turkish migrants prefer to migrate to more prosperous Western Europe, while Asian migrants tend to resettle across (North) Europe and the United States. Figure 3.13 shows the distribution of prevalence (minor and serious offenses) by region of origin of migrant youth, by country cluster.

In many (European) countries, popular opinion claims that ethnic minorities are generally more involved in criminality than the native population. We examined this claim in all migrant groups that are represented in our sample. There is a possibility that ethnic minorities are differently involved in minor offending as well as in serious offending. A primary observation in this respect, which is portrayed in Fig. 3.13, is that there is no difference between minor and serious offending when comparing Asian immigrants to the native population. This is consistent with a common notion of rarely finding Asian immigrant youths in youth penal institutions or in child care.[10] The other immigrant groups (from different regions of origin) clearly do commit more minor\ as well serious offenses, while they do not differ a great deal among themselves. Turkey, however, stands out a bit among all the migrant groups, although this is essentially the case for minor offenses and not for the more serious ones.

---

[10] In this respect we should recall that the UK does not participate in ISRD-2. This country has problems with immigrants coming from Bangladesh and Pakistan.

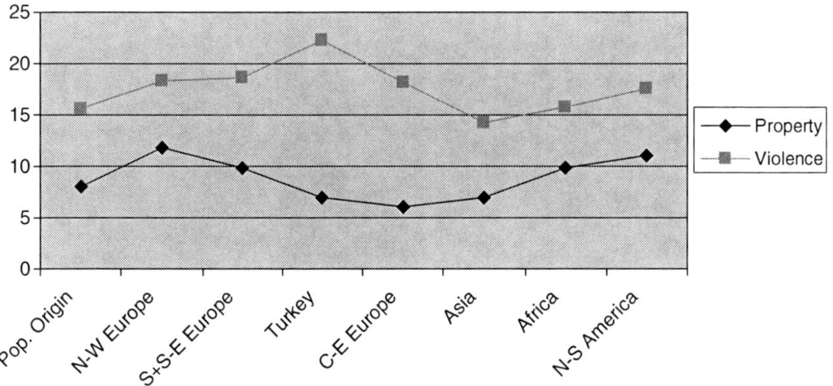

Fig. 3.14 Last year prevalence of total property and total violent offenses in native-born population and migrant groups (N=37,300) (weighted data; Cramer's V: property off.=0.04; violent off.=0.04)

Another question that we considered was whether some groups would concentrate on property offenses, while others might be more focused on those more violent in nature. Regarding this question, Fig. 3.14 reveals some surprising outcomes. First, migrant youth groups (with the exception of Asian youth) commit considerably more violent offenses than the native youth population. Second, young people from Asia, Turkey and Central and Eastern Europe commit fewer property offenses than the native population. However, most of the migrant groups, except Asia, commit considerably more violent offenses than the native population, and of these groups, the Turkish migrants are most overrepresented.

As mentioned earlier, an important part of violent offenses are "group fights", which are popular among all groups and includes all kinds of scuffles and horseplay on the school playground or in (semi) public places. Thus, it would be important to know whether the predilection for violence in some migrant groups is limited to minor violent offenses or would include more serious forms of violence.

Figure 3.15 shows that there are five migrant groups, which do commit more serious property offenses than the native population. Exceptions are youth from Asia and Central and Eastern Europe. As for serious violent offenses, all groups except youth originally from Asia, have higher rates than young natives.

We also see that youth from Central and East Europe and Turkey, in comparison to all other groups, commit considerably more serious violent offenses and relatively fewer serious property offenses, with again the Turkish youths having the highest scores. A tentative explanation might be that the youngsters coming from these regions may be influenced by their specific cultural background which tends to promote violence to deal with conflicts.

Clearly, information about country of origin produces interesting insights. A different dimension of immigration deals with differences between natives, first and second generation migrants, without consideration of the particular country of origin.

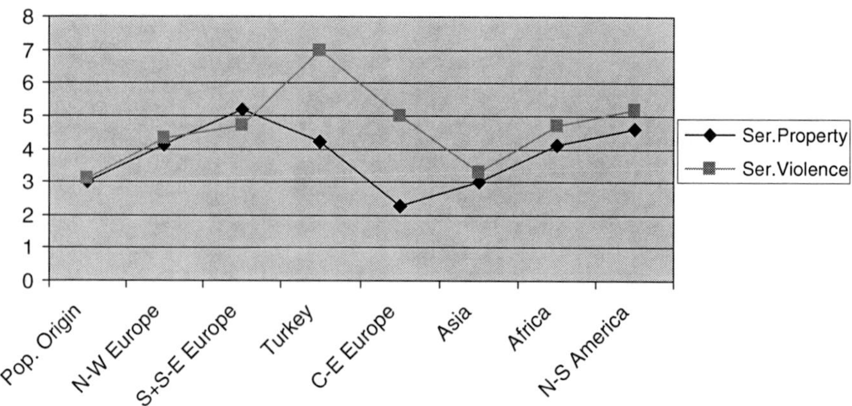

Fig. 3.15 Last year prevalence of serious property and serious violent offenses of migrant groups ($N=37{,}300$) (weighted data; Cramer's V: property = 0.04; violence = 0.05)

A distinction was made between first generation youths (who were born in a country other than the host country), and second generation youths (youth born in the host country but whose parent(s) were born abroad.). Table 3.8 illustrates the versatility statistics for first and second generation migrant youth. Our versatility measure as used here forms a scale of increasing seriousness of delinquency involvement. The dataset includes a total of 9,126 members of ethnic minority groups, of which about one third is first generation (32.5%) and two thirds were born in the host country (67.5%). This is the case for most migrant groups, regardless of region of origin.

However, some groups did migrate some considerable time ago and the study hardly includes any first generation kids, such as Turkish youths and to a lesser degree this is the case for a portion of the migrants out of Africa. A striking result shown in Table 3.8 is that there are hardly any differences in delinquency between first and second generation youth among almost all migrant groups, with the exception of Turkish youths ($\chi^2=12{,}75$, $p<.001$; Cramer's $V=0.13$). Second generation Turkish youths have committed considerably more offenses than the first generation, and as we have seen earlier, these tend to be violent offenses – rather than those related to property.

Overall however, differences in offending seriousness between first and second generation migrants are limited and do not greatly differ from versatility among native-born youths (13.8% committed 1 offense; 6.5% committed 2 different offenses; and 7.4% committed 3+ types of offenses; not shown in Table 3.8).

We also examined the country clusters to determine whether second generation migrants would cause more problems than first generation minority youths. The differences are limited both with respect to minor offenses and serious offenses (results not shown). There is a slight tendency for second generation migrants to commit more minor offenses than natives, except in the Anglo-Saxon and North-European cluster, and a similar tendency is apparent with respect to serious offenses in Latin America and the Post-Socialist clusters.

Table 3.8 Versatility of first and second generation ethnic minority groups[a] by region of origin (%)

	N-E Europe	S+S-E Europe	Turkey	C+E Europe	S+E Asia	Africa	N+S America
First generation							
	N=371	*N*=663	*N*=106	*N*=231	*N*=478	*N*=263	*N*=864
Offense	16.7	13.4	7.5	14.3	8.6	13.3	12.5
Diff. offenses	5.9	3.6	3.8	4.8	3.3	2.3	5.3
Diff. offenses	6.5	6.3	1.9	6.1	5.4	4.2	5.8
Second generation							
	N=775	*N*=1,297	*N*=646	*N*=511	*N*=828	*N*=736	*N*=1,357
Offense	13	12.8	15.3	12.5	12.7	13.5	14.2
Diff. Offenses	5.4	5.9	7.7	5.3	3.3	4.5	4.9
Diff. Offenses	7.2	7	6.7	3.7	4.8	5.7	6.5
χ^2 +	ns	ns	<0.001	ns	ns	ns	ns
Cramer's *V*	0.05	0.05	0.13	0.06	0.06	0.06	0.03

[a]Weighted data

3.12 Conclusions

We found that "lifetime" as well as "last year" delinquency rates are highest in Anglo-Saxon and West-European countries. Both North- and South-Europe have lower rates, and the lowest rates are found in the Post-Socialist countries as well as in the four Latin American countries. However, there are interesting differences in delinquent behaviour between countries in regards to property offenses, more so than in regards to violence. Property offense rates are especially high in Anglo-Saxon countries, W-Europe, and in North Europe (in that order), which are three very prosperous country clusters with a very mobile youth population that is difficult to control. As for violent behaviour, there is considerably more variation between countries and no clear patterns can be found. The same is true in regards to the relationship between delinquency and city size, but it should be noted that this may be due to the fact that most country samples are city samples with an overrepresentation of large and medium-sized cities. The only significant difference in the expected direction was found in the Anglo-Saxon countries.

Relating gender to delinquent behaviour showed lower rates for girls as compared to boys, which was to be expected. However, these refer in particular to serious property offenses and to violent offenses. There are small differences between the sexes with respect to nonserious property offenses in all clusters.

Clusters hardly differ when measuring the age of onset, which ranges between ages 12 and 14 for the different individual offenses. Age of onset appears to increase slightly from nonserious towards serious offenses. The only exception is Latin America, where the age of onset was a bit higher. Generally speaking, age of onset is also similar in both males and females.

Young people generally operate in groups, whether they join for sports, going out or committing offenses. That being said, the character and dynamics of group behaviour create higher prevalence rates for some offenses than others. For example, vandalism and breaking into buildings are more likely to be committed in groups, as well as car theft, perhaps for status reasons. Nevertheless, shoplifting is also done alone quite frequently (by 20–25%), and so is snatching a purse or robbery (by 30–40%). Small scale dealing in soft drugs is often a peer group activity among those who use soft drugs (60% of dealers). Yet 40% of those dealing (soft) drugs do this on their own and these might be more serious offenders. Peer group offending, in particular regarding violence, is more frequent in Anglo-Saxon countries than in Latin America, which might be related to generally higher violence rates in the former countries. Finally, we looked at delinquent behaviour of young migrants in comparison to the natives from the participating countries. The majority of young migrants in the sample came from regions that were not too far away from the host country. Migrants in the European clusters came from other European countries and those in Latin America came from the American continent. However, migrants from Asia (about 20%) were evenly spread over the different clusters, except in Latin America. In terms of delinquency, young migrants tend to commit more minor as well as serious offenses than native youths, but the differences are not that large. Migrant youths – whether first generation or second generation – commit essentially more violent offenses, whereas differences in property offenses remain slight. Disparities in violent offending between youth originating from Turkey and Central and East Europe and the other migrant groups are relatively large, the former having rather high rates. Finally, a comparison between first generation and second generation migrants did not reveal a substantial significant difference in regards to delinquency involvement. Second generation youths were only more delinquent than first generation youths in the Anglo-Saxon cluster.

References

Enzmann, D., Marshall, I. H., Killias, M., Steketee, M., & Gruszcynska (2010). Self-reported youth delinquency in Europe and beyond: First results of the Second ISRD in the context of police and victimization data. *European Journal of Criminology*, *7*, 159–183.

Esping-Andersen, G. (1990). *The Three Worlds of Welfare Capitalism.* Princeton NJ: Princeton University Press.

Felson, M. (1998), Crime in Everyday Life – Insight and Implications for Society, Thousand Oaks/London, Pine Forge Press – 2nd edition.

Junger-Tas, J., Marshall, I. H., & Ribeaud, D. (2003). *Delinquency in an International Perspective: The International Self-Report Delinquency Study (ISRD).* The Hague: Kugler.

Junger-Tas, J, Steketee, M. & Moll, M. (2008). Achtergronden van Jeugddelinquentie en Middelengebruik. Utrecht: Verwey-Jonker Instituut.

Muuss, R.E., (1980), Adolescent Behaviour and Society, New York, Random House.

OECD Annual Report 2010: The Secretary-General's Report to Ministers.

Saint-Arnaud, S., & Bernard, P. (2003). Convergence or resilience? A hierarchical cluster analysis of the welfare regimes in advanced countries. *Current Sociology*, *51*, 499–527.

Thornberry, T.P. & M.D. Krohn (2003), Taking Stock of Delinquency –an Overview of Findings from Contemporary Longitudinal Studies, Kluwer Academic/Plenum Publishers.

Van der Laan, A.M. & Blom, M. (2006). Jeugddelinquentie. Risico's en bescherming; bevindingen uit de WODC Monitor Zelfgerapporteerde Jeugdcriminaliteit 2005. Boom, Den Haag.

Van Dijk, J. J. M., Manchin, R., Van Kesteren, J. N., Nevala, S., & Hideg, G. (2007). The burden of crime in the EU: Research report: A comparative analysis of the EU International Crime Survey (EU ICS) 2005. Brussels: Gallup-Europe.

Warr, M. (2002), Companions in Crime – The Social Aspects of Criminal Conduct, Cambridge UK, Cambridge University Press.

Wikström, P.H. & Butterworth, D.A. (2006). Adolescent crime. Individual differences and lifestyles. Devon: Willan Publishing.

Yinger, J.M. (1994) Ethnicity. Albany: State University of New York, Press.

Chapter 4
Juvenile Victimization from an International Perspective

Beata Gruszczyńska, Sonia Lucia, and Martin Killias

4.1 Introduction

Delinquency and victimization are correlated. However, this does not imply that all victims are offenders, or that all offenders become victims of crimes. Elderly people and women especially commit substantially fewer offences, but nonetheless at times may experience victimization. However, among juveniles, the correlation between victimization and delinquency is generally assumed to be stronger, given that (young) offenders often expose themselves to increased risks of victimization. A delinquent lifestyle may indeed be among the strongest predictors of violent victimization. This in itself is one of many good reasons to look more closely at victimization among juveniles. A second motivation is that juveniles are being victimized disproportionately compared to other age groups, and crime is an essential aspect of the quality of life at this age. Many juveniles are obviously not regularly involved in delinquency, but are genuinely affected if violence occurs frequently in the age group they socialize with in everyday contexts. Since minors are notoriously poorly represented in national and international crime victimization surveys, this study offers a good occasion to look more closely at the factors which influence the probability of such experiences at this age, which may not necessarily be the same during later periods in life.

This chapter is divided into three parts. First, we shall present some descriptive statistics of the four types of victimization included in the ISRD-2 questionnaire: theft, bullying, robbery, and assault. Second, we shall look at the link between delinquency and victimization. In final part, multivariate analyses will be presented.

B. Gruszczyńska (✉)
University of Warsaw, Warsaw, Poland
e-mail: b.gruszczynska@uw.edu.pl

J. Junger-Tas et al., *The Many Faces of Youth Crime: Contrasting Theoretical Perspectives on Juvenile Delinquency across Countries and Cultures*,
DOI 10.1007/978-1-4419-9455-4_4, © Springer Science+Business Media, LLC 2012

4.2 Descriptive Statistics

The questionnaire included items on robbery, assault, theft, and bullying during the last 12 months.[1] Because in some countries, national samples were used, while in others the survey was restricted to cities (see Chap. 2), we shall focus on large and medium-sized cities. Small towns have been compared separately. It should also be noted that in some countries, the sample included older youths than in others – despite the fact that we only took into account students who were enrolled in grades 7–9.

4.2.1 Victimization and Urbanization

In the total sample of nearly 70,000 students, one in five (21.1%) became a victim of theft in the last 12 months. Bullying (including maltreatment, teasing, and mobbing) was somewhat less common (13.9%), followed by violent offences such as assault (4.2%) and robbery (4.2%). The overall victimization prevalence for the last 12 months was 31.4% including bullying and 23.9% without bullying. Thus, during the year preceding the survey, almost one in four students were victims of at least one criminal offence. As Table 4.1 shows, being victimized by any of the four

Table 4.1 Prevalence rate (in %)[a] by type of victimization and urbanization[b]

	Robbery	Assault	Theft	Bullying	Violent offences (robbery or assault)	Criminal victimization (all without bullying)	Overall victimization
Large and medium city (*N*=39,307)	5.4	4.3	21.6	14.2	8.7	25.9	33.6
Small towns (*N*=14,637)	2.6	4.0	17.4	14.1	6.0	20.7	29.1
Total national or all city sizes (*N*=65,614)	4.2	4.2	20.1	13.9	7.5	23.9	31.7

[a]All rates refer to averages of national rates; [b]Prevalence rate refers to valid answers

[1]Screening questions were as follows: "Thinking back over the last 12 months, did any of the following happen to you – … (a) Someone wanted you to give him/her money or something else (watch, shoes, mobile phone) and threatened you if you did not do it?; (b) Someone hit you violently or hurt you so much that you needed to see a doctor?; (c) Something was stolen from you (such as a book, money, mobile phone, sport equipment, bicycle …?); (d) You were bullied at school (other students humiliated you or made fun of you, hit or kicked you, or excluded you from their group?)".

offences considered here is slightly more common in large and medium cities than in small towns and in the entire sample (including rural areas).[2]

4.2.1.1 Inter-Cluster Comparisons

In order to look at the distribution of victimization internationally, we divided the countries into clusters, as suggested by Saint-Arnault (2003), discussed in Chap. 2. Rates of victimization are presented in Table 4.2 by clusters and by countries. The rates were weighed per cluster and only refer to valid answers.

Theft. In almost all countries, students were most likely to become victims of theft. Theft is most common in Slovenia, the USA, Aruba, Venezuela, Germany, and Switzerland. The lowest rates were found in Armenia and Russia, where only approximately one in ten students complained about being a victim of theft. Differences seem to be larger within the clusters than between them.

Bullying among peers varies substantially across countries. Differences within clusters outweigh those in between. The highest rate (almost 30%) was observed in Slovenia, in Estonia (about 25%), and in the USA (over 20%), while the lowest was found in Armenia (over 2%) and Portugal (4%). In Western European countries, bullying is most frequent in Germany and in France and the least frequent in Austria. In Southern Europe, about 14% of the students reported being victims of bullying, in Spain and in Italy, i.e. about 3 times the rate in Portugal. In Latin America, students from Aruba are bullied the most (about 20%), whereas the lowest rate is in Surinam (nearly 10%).

Robbery. The highest rates can be observed in some Post-Socialist countries, such as Hungary (13%) and Bosnia and Herzegovina (over 10%). Similarly, high rates have been found in Venezuela, Spain, and Portugal, as well as in Russia and Poland. At the opposite end of the scale are Armenia and Iceland (about 1%), the Czech Republic, Italy, Cyprus, and all countries in Western and Northern Europe (less than 5%). This, once more, underlines that differences between the clusters at time may be less important than those between countries within the same region.

Assault. The highest rates have been observed in a few Latin American countries (over 5%), such as The Netherlands Antilles and Surinam (over 7%), while Portugal and Spain (over 1%) have the lowest rates. These two Mediterranean European countries also had the lowest rates of violent victimization among 17 industrialized countries included in the International Crime Victimization Survey of 2000 (Gruszczyńska 2002). In other clusters, rates of assault oscillate between 3 and 6%, Sweden and Finland (about 2.5%) are somewhat below this threshold. Within the clusters, the rates of assault are more similar in comparison to the other types of victimization.

[2]In capital cities (of six new EU member countries) the overall victimization rate is over 35% (Gruszczyńska et al. 2008).

Table 4.2 Prevalence rates* (in %) by clusters and countries (medium and large cities)

	Robbery	Assault	Theft	Bullying	Total criminal victimization	*N*
Anglo-Saxon cluster	*5.9*	*4.3*	*26.4*	*18.4*	*29.9*	*2,314*
US (AS)	5.5	4.7	33.0	20.6	35.5	1,373
Ireland (AS)	6.3	4.0	19.6	16.2	24.1	941
Northern Europe	*3.0*	*3.2*	*20.9*	*12.0*	*23.5*	*6,177*
Iceland (NE)	1.2	4.1	20.4	9.3	22.5	570
Denmark (NE)	4.1	3.8	21.2	15.1	24.6	1,329
Nowary (NE)	2.7	3.6	23.3	13.4	25.3	1,200
Sweden (NE)	3.1	2.3	25.2	10.0	27.2	1,715
Finland (NE)	3.7	2.4	14.9	12.3	18.0	1,363
Western Europe	*3.7*	*4.3*	*23.2*	*14.9*	*26.8*	*10,341*
The Netherlands (WE)	4.1	4.9	22.9	14.4	27.3	1,487
Austria (WE)	3.3	4.2	25.1	9.7	28.3	1,887
Germany (WE)	4.8	6.1	29.1	18.5	34.2	2,268
Switzerland (WE)	4.0	3.4	27.0	12.4	29.8	1,203
France (WE)	3.4	4.3	15.7	17.7	19.7	1,838
Belgium (WE)	2.6	2.8	18.6	16.7	21.2	1,558
Mediterranean Europe	*5.5*	*2.1*	*15.4*	*10.6*	*19.0*	*6,613*
Portugal (ME)	8.6	1.2	14.2	4.0	18.3	825
Cyprus (ME)	1.7	3.2	14.6	9.8	16.7	1,336
Italy (ME)	2.6	3.0	16.8	14.6	19.1	3,951
Spain (ME)	8.9	1.2	15.9	14.0	22.0	501
Latin America	*6.3*	*5.7*	*27.2*	*15.1*	*31.8*	*5,780*
The Netherlands Antilles (LA)	4.8	7.7	27.5	17.1	32.4	1,675
Aruba (LA)	5.0	4.7	31.4	19.8	34.6	674
Suriname (LA)	6.3	6.2	21.1	9.7	26.3	1,374
Venezuela (LA)	9.3	4.0	28.6	13.4	33.9	1,364
Post-socialist countries	*7.5*	*5.2*	*20.3*	*15.2*	*26.3*	*8,775*
Estonia (FS)	8.0	6.8	25.0	24.8	31.0	981
Lithuania (FS)	7.7	2.8	14.4	18.5	20.0	1,384
Poland (FS)	8.2	6.1	19.3	13.9	25.9	792
Czech Republic (FS)	3.2	3.3	20.0	10.1	23.5	1,192
Hungary (FS)	12.9	5.9	25.7	17.9	33.2	382
Slovenia (FS)	7.2	5.6	34.1	28.0	38.2	725
Bosnia and Herzegovina (FS)	10.4	4.7	21.5	6.1	29.0	513
Russia (FS)	8.8	7.9	13.8	15.7	23.2	1,441
Armenia (FS)	1.1	4.2	9.1	2.4	12.9	1,365

*Prevalence rate refers to valid answers

Violent victimization. Due to the fact that robberies and assaults are both considered violent offences, a combined index has been created. Thus, the violent victimization index indicates the percentages of students who were either victims of robbery, assault or both. Figure 4.1 illustrates the differences across the clusters of countries.

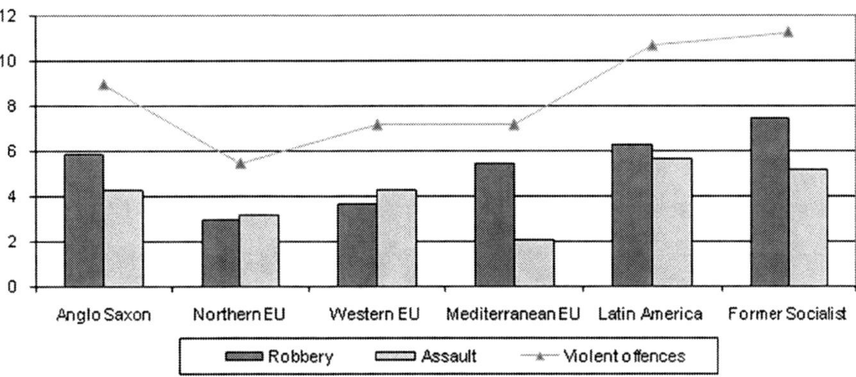

Fig. 4.1 Prevalence rate of violent victimization per cluster (weighted for clusters)

Violent victimization occurs most often in Latin American, post-socialist, and Anglo-Saxon countries. In Western and Southern Europe, over 7% of students reported such events. As for the differences within the clusters, they were largest among post-socialist countries, the front-runners being Hungary (about 16%) and Bosnia and Herzegovina, while Armenia and the Czech Republic (about 6%) are at the end of the scale.

4.2.2 Gender and Victimization

In the following analysis, we will look at differences between boys and girls regarding victimization. Indeed, gender turned out to be the most important socio-demographic variable in this context. In Fig. 4.2, we present victimization rates in the six clusters, by gender and crime type.

Robbery. On average, the ratio of victimization between boys and girls is about 3. In all countries, except for Armenia, boys were victims of robbery more often than girls. In some countries, boys faced even higher risks. For example, in Hungary, boys were victims of robbery 7 times more often than girls, in Cyprus over 9 times more, and in Denmark, Austria, Italy, Portugal, Czech Republic, and Poland 4 times.

Assault. Again, boys are more often assaulted than girls, but compared to robbery, the differences are less pronounced. Some post-socialist states have particularly high male–female ratios, namely Bosnia and Herzegovina (>6), Hungary (>5), and Poland (>4). On the other hand, there are also countries where the risk of being assaulted is greater for girls than for boys (USA, Denmark, The Netherlands, and Switzerland).

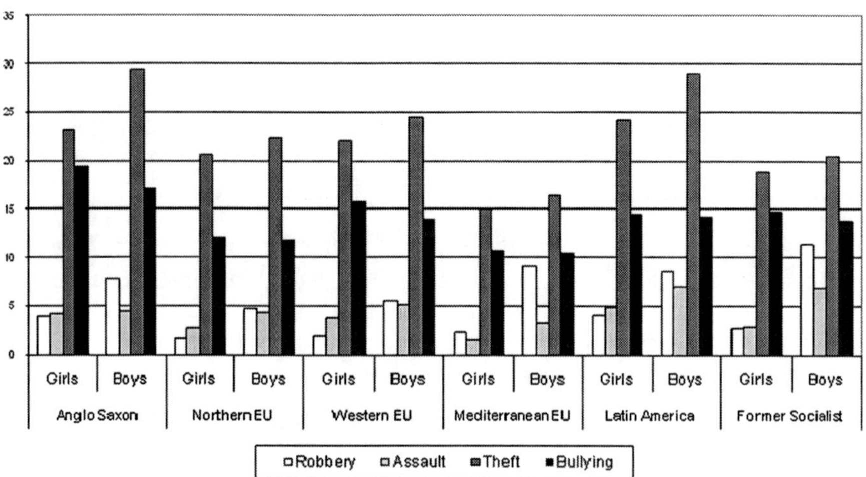

Fig. 4.2 Victimization rate by gender across clusters

Theft. Although in all countries, boys were more often victims of theft than girls, the differences were not large and were only significant in a few countries. This pattern is very consistent across countries and clusters.

Bullying. In many countries, bullying is gender indifferent. In some countries, girls are bullied more frequently than boys, whereas the rates are higher for boys in others. Overall, however, the differences are not large. This result comes as a surprise because other studies found that boys are generally more often victims of bullying than girls. This certainly has to do with the fact that, in our questionnaire bullying was measured by only one item, which included forms of harassment other than physical violence, such as being humiliated, ridiculed, or excluded from the group. It is plausible that wider forms of bullying are not necessarily related to gender-specific life-styles. In Portugal and Sweden, the study revealed that girls are more likely to become victims of mobbing behaviour, which includes being the dupe of false rumours, whereas boys are more often victims of physical violence (Smith et al. 1999).

4.2.3 Victimization and School Grade

School grade is obviously directly related to the age of the students and, indirectly, to behaviour and life-style. It is, therefore, an important variable in understanding victimization. Table 4.3, presents the changes in victimization in regard to grade level per cluster.

Table 4.3 Victimization rate* by school grade and cluster

	Grade	Anglo-Saxon	Northern EU	Western EU	Mediterranean EU	Latin America	Post-Socialist
Robbery	7	**2.4**	2.5	3.1	**3.9**	6.5	7.2
	8	**7.2**	2.7	4.0	**4.1**	6.6	7.6
	9	**7.1**	4.0	3.9	**7.5**	5.9	7.6
Assault	7	4.3	2.7	4.2	**3.2**	6.4	5,1
	8	4.4	3.6	4.5	**1.9**	5.6	5.7
	9	4.3	3.1	4.2	**1.5**	5.1	4.9
Theft	7	24.9	21.3	22.5	13.7	26.0	21.2
	8	23.4	20.6	22.6	16.1	28.6	19.9
	9	28.9	21.2	24.3	16.0	27.1	19.7
Bullying	7	19.9	**16.4**	**17.6**	**11.8**	**18.0**	**18.0**
	8	18.8	**10.5**	**15.2**	**12.0**	**15.5**	**15.1**
	9	17.4	**9.8**	**12.0**	**8.8**	**11.8**	**12.7**

*Weighted for clusters
Significant differences are in *bold* ($p<0.01$)

Robbery. In most countries, students in higher grades faced increased risks of robbery, probably because going out "normalizes" with age. Exceptions are the Czech Republic (where risk decreases with grade) and, Denmark, Norway, Holland, Germany, Switzerland, Antilles, Surinam, Estonia, and Russia (where risks are highest in the eighth (middle) grade).[3]

Assault victimization rates are not statistically dependent on students' age, except ME. In eight countries, students of the highest grade were assaulted more often than those of the lowest one. In eight countries, the youngest students were victimized most frequently. These different effects of grade (and age) may reflect country-specific changes in lifestyles across this age-period. If, generally speaking, older adolescents have more independence and spend more leisure time with peers and outdoors, this change may occur, in some countries, after age 16 rather than between 13 and 15.

Theft was not generally correlated with school grade, although in some countries rates did increase with grade. In Denmark, Belgium, and Italy the differences were significant. As suggested by the preceding analyses of gender effects, risks of theft may not be much related to lifestyle and are, therefore, more independent of gender and age.

Bullying differs from violent victimization in the sense that it mostly affects younger students, although the perpetrators may often be older students. In all clusters and countries, experiences of bullying decrease with grade – with no exception. The universality of this pattern calls, obviously, for a general explanation.

[3] No data from Iceland, Poland, Slovenia, and Bosnia and Herzegovina were taken into account in this analysis. For these countries, data were not available for all grades (from 7 to 9) due to differences in school systems.

The younger the students, the more potential bullies they may have at school. Moreover, it may also be that older students can defend themselves more efficiently against bullies, physical inferiority being a key variable in the explanation of such experiences (Olweus 1978; Smith et al. 1999). Since bullying is experienced at schools, its variations can hardly be explained by lifestyle and leisure-time preferences.

4.3 Individual and Social Correlates of Victimization

Beyond gender and age (or grade), risks of victimization may be correlated to family and school variables, neighbourhood characteristics, self-control and attitudes favouring violence, involvement in delinquency (overall, last year) and risky behaviours, such as truancy, drinking alcohol, taking drugs, or having delinquent friends. All significant associations between victimization and possible explanatory factors are presented in Table 4.4.[4] The variables introduced here will be explained later on in this section.

As Table 4.4 illustrates, gender, general delinquency, having delinquent friends, skipping school, social disorganization in the neighbourhood (i.e. frequent fights, thefts, dealing in drugs, as well as abandoned buildings and graffiti around one's home) and at least two risk factors (i.e. truancy, drinking alcohol and using cannabis) are highly ($p<0.01$) correlated with *robbery* in most of the countries.

The risk of *assault* is also significantly ($p<0.01$) correlated in many countries with the same variables (i.e. delinquency, having delinquent friends, skipping school, and neighbourhood disorganization), with the noteworthy exception of gender. Moreover, assault victimization is also correlated to self-control, i.e. the ability to restrain one's aggressive behaviour even in the face of provocation. This was significantly correlated with being a victim of assault in 20 out of 30 countries.

Thus, robbery and assault are largely related to the same independent variables and, primarily, to a problematic or even delinquent lifestyle. In regard to these two types of victimizations, the association of being robbed and the attachment to parents can only be observed in very few countries. Interestingly, parental supervision is only highly correlated with violent victimization in Austria.

Being a victim of *theft* is mostly correlated with delinquent friends, neighbourhood, and school disorganization. Although the relationship to parental supervision is only observed in 12 out of 30 countries, the pattern is rather consistent in Western Europe.

[4] Associations were considered significant if $p<0.01$. All variables were transformed into a dichotomous form.

Table 4.4 Significant correlates ($p < 0.01$) of robbery (R), assault (A), theft (T), and bullying (B) victimization

	Gender	School dis-organization	Neighborhood disorganization	Attachment to parents	Parental supervision	Self-control	Violent attitudes	2+ risk factors present	Delinquent friends	Last year delinquency	Skipped school
US	__T_	_ATB	RAT_	RATB	__T_	RAT_	R_T_	RAT_	RATB	RAT_	RAT_
Ireland	RAT_	_A_B	_A__	__T_	____	_A__	_A__	_A__	RAT_	RAT_	_A__
Iceland	____	__T_		R_TB	____	__T_	____	__T_	_AT_	__T_	__T_
Denmark	R___	____	RA_B	_ATB	____	RA_B	RA_	RAT_	RAT_	RATB	RATB
Norway	R___	RATB	RATB	_A_B	__T_	RATB	RAT_	RAT_	RAT_	RATB	RATB
Sweden	RA__	_ATB	_AT_	__TB	____	RAT_	RA__	RAT_	RAT_	RAT_	RAT_
Finland	RA__	__TB	RAT_	__TB	__T_	_ATB	_A_B	R_T_	RAT_	RATB	R_T_
Netherlands	R___	R_T_	RA__	_ATB	__T_	_A__	R___	__T_	RAT_	RAT_	R_T_
Austria	RATB	_ATB	RAT_	RATB	R_T_	_AT_	__T_	RAT_	RATB	RATB	RAT_
Germany	RA__	RATB	RA__	RATB	__T_	RAT_	RAT_	RAT_	RATB	RAT_	RAT_
Switzerland	R___	R_TB	RATB	__TB	__T_	R_T_	R_T_	RAT_	RAT_	RATB	RAT_
France	RAT_	R_TB	_A__	__TB	__T_	RA__	_A__	RA__	__T_	_ATB	RA__
Belgium	____	__TB	RA_B	__TB	__T_	R_T_	RA__	RA__	_ATB	RAT_	RA__
Portugal	R___	____	____	____	____	R___	____	____	____	R_TB	____
Cyprus	R_T_	R_TB	_ATB	__TB	____	_AT_	__T_	__T_	__T_	_AT_	_ATB
Italy	RA__	RAT_	RAT_	__TB	__T_	RAT_	RAT_	RAT_	RAT_	RAT_	RAT_
Spain	R___	____	____	____	____	____	____	____	_A__	R___	R___
NL Antilles	____	RATB	RAT_	RATB	____	_ATB	____	_A__	RAT_	RAT_	_ATB
Aruba	____	____	____	____	____	____	____	____	_A__	__T_	____
Suriname	R_T_	R_TB	_AT_	____	____	_A__	____	__T_	RAT_	RATB	RAT_
Venezuela	RAT_	__T_	_A__	___B	R___	_A__	_AT_	____	RAT_	RAT_	____

(continued)

Table 4.4 (continued)

	Gender	School dis-organiza-tion	Neighborhood disorganization	Attachment to parents	Parental supervision	Self-control	Violent attitudes	2+ risk factors present	Delinquent friends	Last year delin-quency	Skipped school
Estonia	RA__	RATB	RA__	R_TB	____	__T_	RA__	R_T_	RA__	RAT_	RAT_
Lithuania	R___	RA_B	____	__TB	____	_A_B	_A__	_AT_	_A__	RA__	_AT_
Poland	RAT_	_ATB	R_TB	__TB	__T_	____	____	_AT_	R_TB	_AT_	RA__
Czech Rep.	R___	__TB	RATB	__TB	____	_ATB	_A__	____	__T_	RATB	__T_
Hungary	RA_B	____	R_T_	R__B	__T_	____	____	R_T_	R_T_	R_T_	R_T_
Solvenia	R___	___B	____	__TB	____	____	____	_A__	__T_	RAT_	_AT_
Bosnia/H.	RA__	____	____	R_TB	____	____	____	____	RAT_	R___	____
Russia	R___	R_T_	RAT_	__TB	____	_AT_	_A__	RA__	_AT_	RAT_	RA__
Armenia	____	__T_	____	____	____	__T_	____	____	____	_AT_	__T_

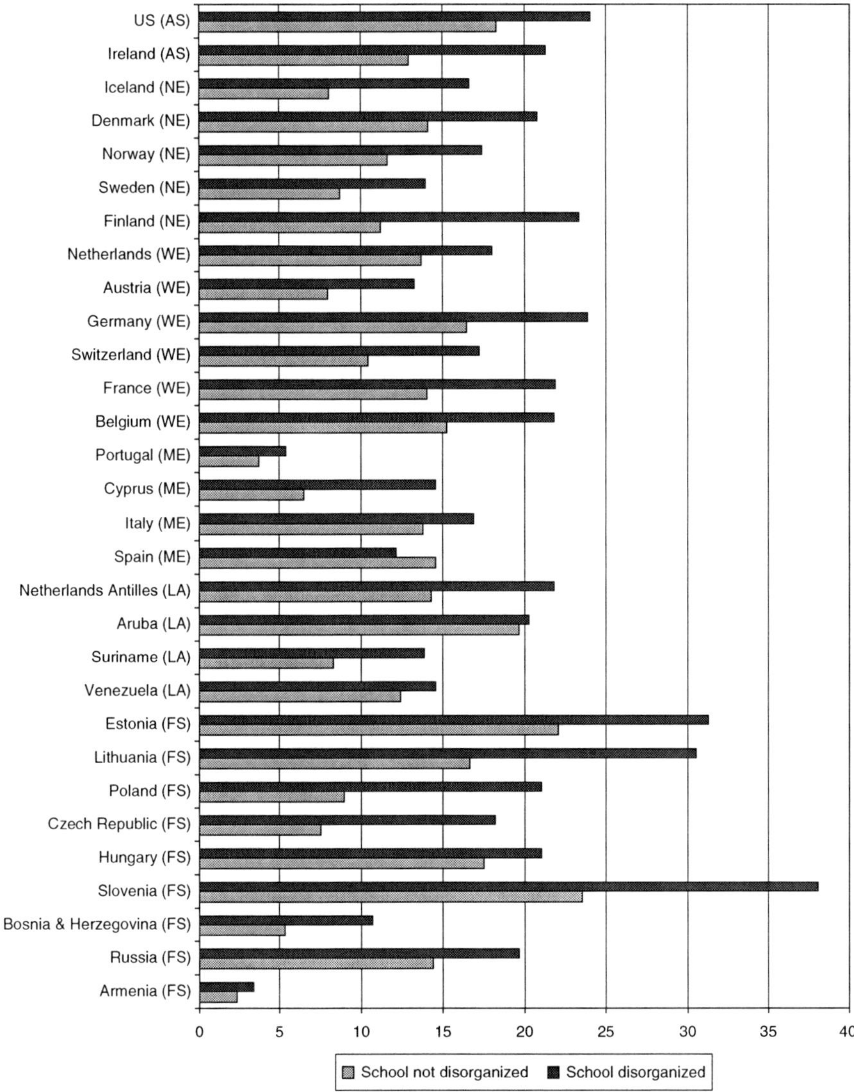

Fig. 4.3 Prevalence rates of bullying and school disorganization by countries

As illustrated in Table 4.4, *bullying* is consistently correlated only with school disorganization and attachment to parents. Other studies also show that school disorganization is correlated to bullying rates (Lucia 2009). For the other variables, the correlations are more random and difficult to interpret. Prevalence rates of bullying among students attending schools facing problems of disorganization or not are shown in Fig. 4.3.

Table 4.5 Delinquency and victimization, by type of offending (N=67,883)

	No offences committed	Committed at least one offence of any type	Committed shoplifting at least once	Committed at least one violent offence	Odds ratios
At least once victim of any offence	20.1	36.2			2.25
At least once victim of theft	18.9		35.0		2.31
At least once victim of a violent offence	6.7			23.2	4.19

Out of all the students who committed at least one offence (vandalism, shoplifting, burglary, bicycle theft, car theft, breaking into a car to steal something, snatching, carrying a weapon, extortion, assault, group fight, drug dealing) during the last 12 months, about 36% were also a victim of robbery, assault, or theft (within the last year), compared to 20% among those who have not admitted to any offences.

The relationship varies across the different types of offences. As the odds ratios in Table 4.5 show, the association between delinquency and victimization is substantially stronger between self-reported violent offences and violent victimizations (robbery and assault) than between overall offences and overall victimization, or between shoplifting and victimization of theft. Esbensen and Huizinga (1991) also found a stronger association between the ever rate of victimization and violent compared to property offences.

Once more, this confirms that not all victims of theft or other offences are simply delinquents, victimization is not merely the other side of the same coin. However, violent offenders may have a lifestyle that exposes them to violent encounters of all kinds. The next section will discuss this in more detail.

4.4 Multivariate Statistics

In this section, we will look at a variety of factors that may influence the three dependent variables (victimization of theft, robbery, and assault). As a preliminary step, we have identified variables that are significantly correlated with these types of victimization (Table 4.4).

4.4.1 The Variables

Seven groups of independent variables have been included in the multivariate analyses. They are defined as follows:

Demographic variables

- *Gender*: 0 = female, 1 = male
- *Age*: The youth included in the dataset are between 11 and 18 years old and they have been dichotomized into two groups (14 and younger = 0, vs. 15 and older = 1).
- *Migrants*: This variable has been constructed from the respondents' answers concerning their own and their parents' country of birth. A "non-migrant" has been defined as any respondent who was born in their country of residence and has parents who were also born in that same country. Respondents born abroad are also considered "non-migrants" if both their parents were born in his/her country of residence. All other respondents will be considered "migrants" (0 = non-migrant, 1 = migrant).

Variables related to the personality of the child

- The *self-control scale* is composed of 12 items (e.g. "I act spontaneously without thinking" and "I like to test my limits by taking risks"). The scale has been dichotomized at the quartile (0 = high self-control, 1 = low self-control).
- *Attitude towards violence*: In order to construct this variable, five items were used (e.g. "A bit of violence is part of the fun", "If somebody attacks me, I will hit him/her back"). The scale has been dichotomized at the quartile (0 = do not agree, 1 = agree).

Variables related to the family

- *Family structure*: "Are you living with your own mother and father?" (0 = traditional, 1 = broken home).
- *Attachment to parents*: "How do you usually get along with the man you live with?" and "How do you usually get along with the woman you live with?" (0 = strong, 1 = weak).
- *Parental supervision*: The question used asked whether the parents usually know with whom the child is with when he/she goes out (0 = always, or child does not go out, 1 = sometimes, rarely).
- *Life events*: In the questionnaire, respondents were asked whether they had experienced any traumatic events, such as "Have you ever experienced the death of a brother/sister?" and "Have you ever experienced a long and serious illness of one of your parents or of someone else close to you?" Out of the eight items, two have not been taken into account. The third item (death of somebody you love) had been discarded because 60% of the adolescents answered yes to having experienced the death of someone they loved. This can include the death of a grandparent or of their pet and is therefore, although an important event, not a traumatic one. Moreover, we also discarded the eighth item, which asks whether their parents had separated or divorced. This information was already included in the question concerning family structure (see above). This variable has also been dichotomized (0 = 0–1 life events, 1 = at least two life events).

School-related variables

- *School failure*: "Have you ever been held back, that is did you ever have to repeat a grade?" (0 = not having repeated a grade, 1 = having repeated at least once a grade).
- *School disorganization*: As for the preceding variable, the following four items have been combined into an index, namely "there is a lot of stealing in my school", "there is a lot of fighting in my school", "many things are broken or vandalized in my school", and "there is a lot of drug use in my school". Again, answers ranged from "I fully agree" to "I fully disagree". This index has been dichotomized in that we opposed the most "negative" quartile to the three remaining quartiles (0 = no, 1 = yes).
- *School climate*: To construct this variable, four items were combined into an index, namely "if I had to move, I would miss my school", "teachers do notice when I am doing well and let me know", "I like my school", and "there are other activities in school besides lessons (sports, music, theatre, discos)". Each question allows four answers, ranging from "I fully agree" to "I fully disagree". This index has been dichotomized in that we opposed the most "negative" quartile to the three remaining quartiles (0 = positive climate, 1 = negative climate).

Neighbourhood characteristics

The questionnaire included 13 items to measure the students' attachment to the neighbourhood, social control by neighbours, and signs of disorder and decay in the neighbourhood. Out of the 13 items, 3 were not taken into account and 3 subscales were constructed.

- *Neighbourhood disorganization*: Five items were used (e.g. "There is a lot of crime in my neighbourhood"). The internal consistency of the scale yields an alpha of 0.80. In order to represent neighbourhood disorganization, which is not common, the scale was dichotomized by opposing the most "negative" quartile to the three remaining quartiles (0 = disorganized, 1 = not disorganized).
- *Neighbourhood attachment*: Two items were used (e.g. "If I had to move, I would miss my neighbourhood"). This index was dichotomized, by opposing the most "negative" quartile to the three remaining quartiles (0 = strong attachment, 1 = weak attachment).
- *Neighbourhood integration*: Three items were used (e.g. "People in this neighbourhood can be trusted"). This index has also been dichotomized, by opposing the most "negative" quartile to the three remaining quartiles (0 = trustful, 1 = not trustful).

Variables related to lifestyle

- *Delinquent friends*: This variable is related to friends who display deviant behaviour and it is based on five items (e.g. "I have friends who used soft or hard drugs like weed, hash, XTC, speed, heroin or coke", "I have friends who entered a building with the purpose of stealing something"). The respondents were classified into "having delinquent friends" if they answered yes to at least two out of the five items (0 = no, 1 = yes).

- *Leisure time*: This item was measured by the question: "With whom do you spend most of your free time?" The variable has been dichotomized (0 = alone or with family, 1 = with friends).

Variables related to problem behaviour

- *Truancy*: "Did you ever stay away from school for at least a whole day without a legitimate excuse in the last 12 months?" (0 = never, 1 = at least once).
- *Being drunk*: Two questions were asked about the consumption of alcohol (beer/wine/breezers, and strong spirits). In each of them, a sub-question asked if the respondent had ever been drunk off of any one of these beverages and how many times it happened. Respondents were dichotomized in regard to whether or not they had been drunk at least twice while consuming any one of these types of alcohol (0 = no, 1 = yes).
- *Delinquency*: Two variables were constructed. The first one, "total minor offenses", is based on the following items: group fights, carrying a weapon, shoplifting, and vandalism. Respondents who admitted to having committed any one of these offences at least once were categorized as "minor offenders" (0 = no, 1 = yes). The second variable is "serious violent offenses" and is based on three items: assault, extortion, and snatching. Students who responded yes to one of these have been categorized as "having committed at least one serious violent offense" (0 = no, 1 = yes). The total of minor offences has been used when studying victimization by theft, whereas the variable "serious violent offenses" has been introduced in the robbery and assault models. The idea is that being a victim of theft (as a less serious offence) should be correlated, if ever, with other forms of "minor offenses", whereas becoming the victim of robbery and assault should be related to offences of a similar kind.

As the dependent variables are dichotomous, logistic regressions were applied. Each group of variables was controlled by the different socio-demographic variables. This resulted in seven models. This first step (model 1) allows us to keep the socio-demographic variables constant, in order to observe which group of variables is the strongest factor in regard to the dependent variable (i.e. the model with the larger χ^2 value). In order to perform this comparison, all missing values have previously been discarded (list wise deletion). This reduces the data from 67,883 to 51,015 subjects, thereby losing about 25% of the cases. The second step consisted of presenting the final model with all the variables (block 1 includes the socio-demographic variables and block 2 all the others variables). Because the data set is large, the variables are considered to be significant at the p-value of 0.01.

4.4.2 *Theft Victimization*

The results concerning the risk of becoming a victim of theft are presented in Table 4.6. Several models are compared. As the R^2 of Nagelkerke reveals (see Table 4.6, last row), all models except the final one explain only marginal fractions of the overall

Table 4.6 Odds ratios of the independent variables of theft victimization (Hierarchical logistic regression, $N = 51{,}015$)

Victimization of theft	Model 1: socio-demographic model	Model 2: individual variables	Model 3: family variables	Model 4: school variables	Model 5: neighbourhood variables	Model 6: lifestyle variables	Model 7: problem behaviour variables	Final model
Boys (*vs. girls*)	1.14*	1.10*	1.17*	1.11*	1.13*	1.12*	1.10*	1.11*
15–18-Years old (*vs. 11–14*)	1.14*	1.12*	1.05	1.10*	1.12*	1.00*	1.01	0.95
Migrant (*vs. non-migrant*)	1.44*	1.42*	1.38*	1.37*	1.41*	1.36*	1.42*	1.31*
Low self-control (*vs. high*)		1.43*						1.05
Positive attitude to violence (*vs. negative*)		1.11*						0.88*
Broken home (*vs. intact*)			1.25*					1.19*
Weak attachment to parents (*vs. strong*)			1.31*					1.21*
Parents do not know friends (*vs. know friends*)			1.41*					1.18*
Life events (*vs. 0–1 life events*)			1.66*					1.49*
School failure (*vs. never*)				1.06				0.98
School disorganization (*vs. no*)				1.75*				1.44*
Negative school climate (*vs. positive*)				1.12*				0.96
Weak neighbourhood bonding (*vs. strong*)					1.11*			1.05
Neighbourhood disorganization (*vs. no*)					1.42*			1.01
No neighbourhood integration (*vs. yes*)					1.12*			1.03
Delinquent friends (*vs. no*)						2.13*		1.54*
Going out in the evening (*vs. 0–3 times*)						1.11*		1.00
Hours spent with friends (*vs. 0–3 h/day*)						1.15*		1.05
Skipping school (*vs. never*)							1.31*	1.09*
At least drunk twice (*vs. less than twice*)							1.56*	1.18*
Total minor offences (*vs. never*)							1.80*	1.36*
Block test (X^2)	266.49	273.30	1,009.29	543.73	240.91	1,012.75	600.19	2,017.04
Model test (X^2)	266.49	539.78	1,275.21	810.22	507.40	1,279.23	866.68	2,283.00
Nagelkerke R^2 (in %)	0.8	1.7	4.0	2.5	1.6	4.0	2.7	7.0

$^*p \leq 0.01$

violence. Given the huge size of the sample, it is not surprising that the odds ratios as low as 1.10 can reach statistical significance.

When controlling for the socio-demographic variables, out of the six groups of variables, the family and the lifestyle variables are the most significant with substantively higher χ^2 values (respectively $\chi^2 = 1{,}009.29$ and 1,012.75). The two groups that follow are the problem behaviour variables and the school variables ($\chi^2 = 600.19$ and 543.73). Out of these groups, the variables with the strongest odds ratio are having delinquent friends, having committed at least one minor offence during the last 12 months, school disorganization, having experienced at least two traumatic life events, and having been drunk (odds between 2.13 and 1.56). Clearly, individual, socio-demographic, and neighbourhood variables are not strongly related to victimization of theft.

The final model explains 7.0% of the overall variance. Even when all variables included in the logistic regression are combined, we do not learn much about the distribution of risks of theft. The variables with the highest odds ratio are having delinquent friends and having experienced at least one traumatic life event. Those with friends who have committed at least two offences increase their risk to be victim of theft by 1.54. Having experienced more than 1 traumatic event in one's life increases the risk to be victim of theft by 1.49. Other variables are significantly and positively related to victimization of theft but with an even smaller odds ratio: school disorganization, having committed minor offences, being a migrant, a weak attachment to parents, low parental supervision, having been drunk at least twice, and being a boy all have odds ratios between 1.44 and 1.11. Interestingly, having a positive attitude to violence seems to be a protective factor since it decreases the risk of being a victim of theft (OR = 0.88). These weak and inconsistent odds ratios are obviously hard to interpret. The best explanation may be that theft, given its frequency, may hit juveniles more or less randomly.

4.4.3 *Robbery Victimization*

As for the victimization of theft, the χ^2 of the different models have been compared. The results are presented in Table 4.7. Here, the highest χ^2 score is observed for the socio-demographic and family variables (respectively $\chi^2 = 529.44$ and 405.25). The odds ratio of gender is impressive as boys are about 3 times more likely to be a victim of robbery than girls. Problem behaviour, lifestyle, and neighbourhood characteristics have similar χ^2 scores (χ^2 between 350 and 300). The variables related to school and individual characteristics are less strongly related to robbery. The next highest odds ratios after gender are neighbourhood disorganization, having committed serious violent offences, having delinquent friends, having lived two or more traumatic life events, truancy, a weak attachment to parents, and having been drunk at least twice (odds ratio between 2.20 and 1.53).

When looking at the final model, all the odds ratios decrease compared to those in the separate models, except for gender, which still has an odds ratio of about 3.

Table 4.7 Odds ratio of the independent variables of robbery victimization (Hierarchical logistic regression, $N=51{,}015$)

Victimization of robbery	Model 1: socio-demographic model	Model 2: individual variables	Model 3: family variables	Model 4: school variables	Model 5: neighbourhood variables	Model 6: lifestyle variables	Model 7: problem behaviour variables	Final model
Boys (*vs. girls*)	3.03*	2.81*	3.22*	2.89*	2.94*	2.96*	2.87*	3.05*
15–18-years old (*vs. 11–14*)	1.20*	1.16*	1.07	1.09	1.14	1.02	1.00	0.91
Migrant (*vs. non-migrant*)	1.16*	1.14	1.10	1.08	1.11	1.09	1.12	1.02
Low self-control (*vs. high*)		1.62*						1.09
Positive attitude to violence (*vs. negative*)		1.27*						0.96
Broken home (*vs. intact*)			1.34*					1.24
Weak attachment to parents (*vs. strong*)			1.55*					1.38*
Parents do not know friends (*vs. know friends*)			1.43*					1.10
Life events (*vs. 0–1 life events*)			1.88*					1.60*
School failure (*vs. never*)				1.28*				1.07
School disorganization (*vs. no*)				1.81*				1.29*
Negative school climate (*vs. positive*)				1.26*				1.01
Weak neighbourhood bonding (*vs. strong*)					1.14			1.08
Neighbourhood disorganization (*vs. no*)					2.20*			1.53*
No neighbourhood integration (*vs. yes*)					1.26*			1.14
Delinquent friends (*vs. no*)						2.06*		1.32*
Going out in the evening (*vs. 0–3 times*)						1.33*		1.14
Hours spent with friends (*vs. 0–3 h/day*)						1.26*		1.10
Skipping school (*vs. never*)							1.80*	1.42*
At least drunk twice (*vs. less than twice*)							1.53*	1.18*
Serious violent offences (*vs. never*)							2.12*	1.41*
Block test (X^2)	529.44	157.61	405.25	190.79	301.72	312.17	350.86	821.628
Model test (X^2)	529.44	687.05	936.43	720.23	831.17	841.61	880.31	1,352.804
Nagelkerke R^2 (in %)	3.8	4.9	6.6	5.1	5.9	6.0	6.3	9.6

$^*p \leq 0.01$

Other variables with odds ratios higher than 1.3 are life events, neighbourhood disorganization, truancy, having committed serious violent offences, a weak attachment to parents, and having delinquent friends. The final model explains 9.6% of the total variance, i.e. substantially more than our final model for theft victimization, but still a rather modest overall contribution to the understanding of becoming a victim of robbery.

4.4.4 Assault Victimization

The groups of variables with the highest χ^2 are problem behaviour and family variables (respectively $\chi^2=533.79$ and 502.13), followed by lifestyle variables, individual and neighbourhood disorganization (χ^2 between 400 and 300). The variables related to the school are more strongly related to assault than to robbery victimization.

In the final model, the variables with the highest odds ratio are having committed serious violent offences (OR=2.14), life events (OR=2.01), gender (OR=1.51), and neighbourhood disorganization (OR=1.42). It is interesting to note that gender is not as important here as in the robbery model, where the odds ratio was about 3. As for robbery, the total variance explained in the final model (9.0%) is rather modest (Table 4.8).

4.5 Discussion

Victimization is a serious problem in young people's lives. It may have crippling effects on the normal functioning of girls and boys. The four examined victimization types – robbery, assault, theft, and bullying – affect on average almost one third of the surveyed population of the 30 countries included. Students were most often victims of theft (20%) and bullying (14%) and less often of robbery (about 4%) and assault (4%).

In the analysis, social and demographic factors were taken into account, such as sex, grade, variables connected to family, school environment, neighbourhood, individual characteristics such as self-control, attitude towards violence, and variables of the so-called risk behaviours, such as drinking alcohol, taking drugs, as well as criminal histories in a broad meaning (crimes, petty offences, delinquency), and having friends involved in crime.

In the comparative analysis, individual countries and their clusters were taken into account. The grouping of countries into clusters was not without problems – intra-cluster differences were often as large, or even larger, than inter-cluster variations.

In most countries, boys were more often victims of violence and theft than girls. The exception was bullying: in some countries bullying affected girls more frequently.

Table 4.8 Odds ratios of the independent variables of assault victimization (Hierarchical logistic regression, $N=51,015$)

Victimization of assault	Model 1: socio-demographic model	Model 2: individual variables	Model 3: family variables	Model 4: school variables	Model 5: neighbourhood variables	Model 6: lifestyle variables	Model 7: problem behaviour variables	Final model
Boys (*vs. girls*)	1.59*	1.44*	1.67*	1.50*	1.53*	1.54*	1.45*	1.51*
15–18-Years old (*vs. 11–14*)	1.27*	1.21*	1.13	1.10	1.21*	1.07	1.04	0.93
Migrant (*vs. non-migrant*)	1.43*	1.39*	1.34*	1.30*	1.37*	1.33*	1.36*	1.21*
Low self-control (*vs. high*)		2.05*						1.36*
Positive attitude to violence (*vs. negative*)		1.31*						0.96
Broken home (*vs. intact*)			1.30*					1.18*
Weak attachment to parents (*vs. strong*)			1.30*					1.14*
Parents do not know friends (*vs. know friends*)			1.49*					1.10
Life events (*vs. 0–1 life events*)			2.39*					2.01*
School failure (*vs. never*)				1.57*				1.31*
School disorganization (*vs. no*)				1.92*				1.30*
Negative school climate (*vs. positive*)				1.20*				0.96
Weak neighbourhood bonding (*vs. strong*)					1.19*			1.14
Neighbourhood disorganization (*vs. no*)					2.26*			1.42*
No neighbourhood integration (*vs. yes*)					1.14			1.03
Delinquent friends (*vs. no*)						2.15*		1.26*
Going out in the evening (*vs. 0–3 times*)						1.33*		1.10
Hours spent with friends (*vs. 0–3 h/day*)						1.42*		1.19*
Skipping school (*vs. never*)							1.77*	1.36*
At least drunk twice (*vs. less than twice*)							1.59*	1.21*
Serious violent offences (*vs. never*)							3.35*	2.14*
Block test (X^2)	171.56	313.85	502.13	262.69	305.16	397.78	533.79	1,100.865
Model test (X^2)	171.56	485.41	674.04	434.25	476.73	569.34	705.36	1,272.782
Nagelkerke R^2 (in %)	1.2	3.5	4.8	3.1	3.4	4.0	5.0	9.0

*$p<0.01$

Table 4.9 Most important independent variables, by type of victimization

	Theft	Robbery	Assault
Demographic variables	Migrant	Boys	Boys
Individual variables			Low self-control
Family variables	Life events	Life events Weak attachment to parents	Life events
School variables	School disorganization		School disorganization School failure
Neighbourhood context		Neighbourhood disorganization	Neighbourhood disorganization
Lifestyle variables	Delinquent friends	Delinquent friends	
Problem behaviour	Total minor offences	Serious violent offences Skipping school	Serious violent offences Skipping school

Factors associated with lower victimization risks included, family bonding, sound neighbourhoods, and order at schools. Being in a school or neighbourhood where deviant acts occur on a daily basis can "normalize" crime (Wikström 1998) and give the impression that it is somewhat permitted, as suggested by the broken windows theory (Wilson and Kelling 1982). Furthermore, schools where crimes occur imply minimal intervention by guardians. As suggested by the routine activity theory (Cohen and Felson 1979; Felson 2002), a crime is more likely to occur when a motivated offender is in the same place, at the same time, as an attractive target, while in the absence of a capable guardian.

Table 4.9 gives an overview of the results of the multivariate analyses by presenting the most important variables (odds ratios higher than 1.3) related to each type of victimization in the final model.

Variables such as life events are related to all types of victimization. Moreover, victimization and delinquency are interrelated even when other variables are taken into account. Having committed theft is related to being a victim of theft, and having committed at least one violent offence during the last 12 months is related to robbery and assault. Finally, migrants are more at risk of being victims of theft, whereas boys are more vulnerable to violent offences such as robbery and assault.

4.6 Conclusions

As the bivariate analyses in the first part of this chapter have shown, risks of victimization are correlated with social background, individual or environmental variables, and a young person's lifestyle including deviance and delinquency. However, as the size of several correlations suggests and the multivariate analyses confirm, these variables influence risks of being victimized moderately at best. This should be viewed in relation to a relatively high homogeneity of lifestyle and living arrangements at the age of 13–15 when most of the time children are at school. Perhaps the social distribution of risks will change as young people become young adults, given that lifestyles and, particularly, the daily work and living arrangements become more diverse and, therefore, more open to varying influences and variable vulnerability. Whereas offenders act on their own will, at least to some extent, most victims are primarily vulnerable to decisions made by others and thus to influences they cannot fully control. Therefore, it seems plausible that victimization is to some degree a random event – or the result of the bad luck by simply having been at the wrong place at the wrong time. As the data suggests, this is more so in connection to property offences, whereas having committed serious violent offences increase the risks of becoming a victim of assault. This is quite probable since the risk of being physically attacked is obviously determined by the victim's – more or less violent – reaction to the conflict situation. Overall, however, the analyses show that despite some overlap between delinquency and victimization, victims are by far not always offenders. Most of them are simply the victims of bad luck.

References

Cohen, L.E., & Felson, M. (1979). Social change and crime rates trend: a routine actvity approach, *American Sociological review, 44* (4), 636–655.

Esbensen, F.-A., Huizinga, D. (1991). Juvenile victimization and delinquency. *Youth and Society, 23*(2), 202–228.

Felson M. (2002). *Crime and everyday life*. 3rd edition. London: Sage.

Gruszczyńska, B. (2002). Cross-national Perspective of Violent Victimization Risk, *Crime victimization in comparative perspective. Results from the International Crime Victims Survey, 1989–2000*, Boom Juridische uitgevers, Den Haag, 213–226.

Gruszczyńska, B., Burianek, J., Dekleva, B., Kalpokas, V., and Markina, A. (2008). Juvenile Victimisation, in: *Juvenile delinquency in six new EU member state. Crime, risky behaviour and victimization in the capital cities of Cyprus, Czech Republic, Estonia, Lithuania, Poland and Slovenia*, M. Steketee, M. Moll and A. Kapardis (eds.), Vervey-Jonker Instituut, Utrecht 2008.

Lucia, S. (2009). Multi-dimensional approach to bullying (2009). PhD Thesis, University of Lausanne.

Olweus, D. (1978). *Aggression in the school. Bullies and whipping boys*. Washington, DC: Hemisphere Press (Wiley).

Saint-Arnaud, S., & Bernard, P. (2003). Convergence or resilience? A hierarchical cluster analysis of the welfare regimes in advanced countries. *Current Sociology, 51*, 499–527.

Smith, P. K., Morita, Y., Junger-Tas, J., Olweus, D., Catalano, R. & Slee, P. (1999). *The nature of school bullying: a cross-national perspective*. London/New York: Routledge.

Wikström, P.-O. (1998). Communities and crime. In M. Tonry (Ed.), The Handbook of Crime and Punishment. Oxford University Press, 269–295, 269–301.

Wilson, J.K. & Kelling, G.L. (1982). Broken windows: The police and neighborhood safety, Atlantic Monthly, March, 29–38.

Chapter 5
Substance Use of Young People in 30 Countries

Majone Steketee

5.1 Introduction

Alcohol and drug use in relation to criminal activities has a long and colourful history. Several studies convey that problem behaviour such as heavy substance use and criminal behaviour are highly related (Gottfredson and Hirschi 1990; Junger-Tas et al. 1992; Franken 2003; Monshouwer et al. 2004). In accordance with these findings, this chapter will present and discuss the results of the relationship between substance use and delinquent behaviour.

In the ISRD-questionnaire we asked questions concerning alcohol and drug use and in this chapter we will present the prevalence of substance use of students in grades 7, 8 and 9 per country and for the clustered countries. Research on adolescent drug use and abuse and on effective prevention strategies have been dominated by studies of U.S. samples (e.g. Alsaker and Flammer 1999; Hunt and Barker 2001). This has prompted calls for studies on adolescent development and drug use behaviour that compare samples from two or more countries to distinguish between universal and context-specific influences on behaviour across countries and cultures (Brook et al. 2002; Jessor et al. 2003; Unger and Pardee 2002). Cross-national studies on the prevalence and aetiology of substance use and related behaviours can make significant contributions to the science of prevention (Beyers et al. 2004; Hosman and Clayton 2000). Therefore, this chapter will compare and analyze the differences and similarities between the countries and the country clusters in regards to juvenile alcohol use. First, we will look at the prevalence's for the use of alcohol, soft and hard drugs per country. This will be followed by an analysis of the relationship between substance use and criminal behaviour, and victimization.

Whether one wants to consider alcohol and drug use as delinquent behaviour or as problem behaviour, depends on each country's national law as well as on its

M. Steketee (✉)
Verwey-Jonker Institute, Utrecht, The Netherlands
e-mail: msteketee@verwey-jonker.nl

J. Junger-Tas et al., *The Many Faces of Youth Crime: Contrasting Theoretical Perspectives on Juvenile Delinquency across Countries and Cultures*,
DOI 10.1007/978-1-4419-9455-4_5,

prosecution policy, which in turn reflects the country's cultural climate. Due to the fact that all countries differ in their prosecuting zeal, especially regarding the use of alcohol and soft drugs, this study will consider drug use as problem behaviour.

5.2 Substance Use Among Youth

In Europe, there is a growing concern about the number of young people who drink alcohol or use drugs. Alcohol consumption among young people in Europe has risen during the past years. Several studies indicate that one quarter to one third of all adolescents drink alcohol (Hibell et al. 2009). Not only is the number of young people drinking alcohol growing, problematic drinking (e.g. drunkenness and binge drinking) is also an issue that raises concern. The use of alcohol has especially increased among 12–14 year olds. By this age, about half of the students (in some countries less) have already consumed alcohol 40 times or more in their lifetime, boys more so than girls. The prevalence rates of this behaviour do not differ much between the countries involved in the research (Hibell et al. 2004). According to the results of the European School Survey Project on Alcohol and Other Drugs (ESPAD) 2007, the highest proportion was reported in Greece (55%) and the lowest in France (39%). The number of students who drank 20 times or more in their lifetime differ substantially between the countries. Sweden ranks highest; in this country half of the students (49%) had this experience. In the three Mediterranean countries that took part in the survey, only one fifth of the students reported this. In the remaining three countries, Latvia, Poland and the Slovak Republic, about one fourth had been drunk that often. In all countries, this type of behaviour is more common in boys than in girls. Very frequent drinking (3 times or more during the past 30 days) is again reported most by the Swedes. These differences highlight the importance of different drinking styles: countries not only differ in how many juveniles actually use alcohol, but even more so regarding the type of alcohol, and ultimately, the quantities of ethanol that is being absorbed per drinking occasion.

The ESPAD also gives insight in regards to the use of illicit drugs. Overall, cannabis use dominates. There is however, a rather wide gap between the high and low prevalence countries. The highest prevalence rates for the use of hashish or marijuana are found in France (59%) and in Italy (43%). In Poland and the Slovak Republic, just over one third (around 38%), and in Latvia one fourth (26%) of the students reported to having used cannabis. However, in Greece and Sweden, only around 15% had ever used cannabis.

Empirical evidence from a large number of American studies has shown that early initiation predicts misuse later in life (DeWit et al. 2000; Grant and Dawson 1997; Kosterman et al. 2000; National Institute on Alcohol Abuse and Alcoholism 1997). Similar evidence has been found in European studies for both alcohol and marijuana use and later-related drug use problems (Anderson 2003; Kraus et al. 2000; Pitkanen et al. 2005). Studies have also shown that adolescent substance use is associated with other problem behaviours, such as delinquency and violence (Junger-Tas et al. 2003; Verdurmen et al. 2005), which in turn, are also predictors of future alcohol and drug dependence. Wikström and Butterworth (2006) found that cannabis use is a much better predictor of youth frequency in aggressive offending than drinking, while high-frequency alcohol use (being drunk) is a predictor of aggressive offending in parity to that of frequent use of cannabis. The findings indicate a correlation between the use of alcohol and drugs among prepubertal and teenage students, and the involvement of both groups in theft and vandalism.

Given this evidence, there is some recognition of the importance in delaying early onset of substance use in Europe. On the other hand, the primary assumption is that experimentation with alcohol and other substances is a normal and inevitable part of adolescent development and does not necessarily lead to problem use later in life. For instance, in the Netherlands the experience is that for most people, the use of alcohol and soft drugs (i.e. marijuana, cannabis, hashish, and mushrooms) is a passing phase in life, and most consumers abstain after trying soft drugs a few times (De Kort and Cramer 1999).

Several (inter)national studies have also shown that adolescent substance use is associated with other problem behaviours, such as delinquency and risky behaviour, which – in turn – are predictors of later alcohol and drug dependence. Alcohol and drug use, as well as anti-social behaviour, may be influenced by a weak or broken bond to society (Hirschi 1969; Sampson and Laub 1993). Low self-control can also explain risky behaviour such as smoking, alcohol use and other risky lifestyle choices (Gottfredson and Hirschi 1990). In addition, neighbourhood characteristics such as social disorganization and a lack of trust and solidarity, may affect anti-social behaviour as well (Hawkins et al. 1998; Loeber and Farrington 1998). Although we are starting to gain more insight about the relationship between covariates and risk factors and the development of alcohol use, drug use and anti-social behaviour, health and problem behaviour of young people as well as health policy go beyond curative youth care and individual behaviour. These are also population phenomena, not only individual affairs.

5.3 Substance Use Prevalence Among ISRD Youth

There are two questions in the ISRD-2 questionnaire about the use of alcohol and three questions about the use of drugs in terms of prevalence, incidence and other characteristics. The students were asked if they had consumed alcohol (beer, wine or Breezer's) or strong liquor such as vodka or whiskey. They were also asked if they had used soft drugs such as cannabis (marijuana or hashish) or hard drugs such as ecstasy or speed; and finally extreme drugs including LSD, heroin or cocaine. The recall period in the survey was lifetime use or the previous month (i.e. the last 4 weeks).

We found that the overall prevalence rate for alcohol use is quite high; 60.6% of all students in grades 7–9 had drunk alcohol in their lifetime and 27.7% in the last month. The youths in this study often consume low-alcoholic drinks (59.6% – lifetime and 26.5% – last month). The majority does not consume strong alcohol frequently. However, the number of students who do consume strong liquor frequently is qite high considering that the age of the students in grade 7 till 9 is

Table 5.1 Prevalence of substance use in large and medium sized cities of the countries (%)

	Beer/wine	Strong spirits	Hashish	Hard drugs	Abstinence
Lifetime	59.6	34.09	9.7	2.0	39.2
Last month	26.5	13.0	3.8	0.8	–

12–16 years old. One out of every three students (34%) has drunk strong alcohol at least once, and 13% has done so in the last month (Table 5.1).

The prevalence of drug use is much lower than alcohol consumption. In regards to drug use, the data illustrates that it is generally limited to soft drug use, predominantly the smoking of marijuana. 9.7% reported that they have used cannabis during their lifetime and 4% used it during the last month. The prevalence of hard drugs is 2.0% during a lifetime, and 0.8% in the last month.

There is also a large group of students who have not drunk or used any kind of drugs at all. The abstinence rate of all students is four out of ten (39.2%) (Table 5.1).

Looking at the prevalence's for lifetime and last month alcohol consumption, conveys that there are large differences between countries. The countries with the highest rates for alcohol consumption are Estonia (86.1–46.2), Hungary (85.4–48.3), Czech Republic (84.3–40.1), Lithuania (82.5–35.2) and Denmark (72.3–42.0). Although most of these countries are Post-Socialist, the lowest rates are in Bosnia Herzegovina (31.5–8.2) which is also a Post-Socialist country, but has a Muslim population. According to Islam, alcohol use is forbidden. Other countries with low consumption rates are Iceland (22.0–10.1) and some Mediterranean countries such as France (31.9–13.6) and Portugal (41.4–13.9) have also low alcohol consumption. For Iceland although only group eight was included in the sample, still the number of juveniles that have been drinking ever or during the last month is low.

It is remarkable that some countries have a high score on lifetime use of alcohol but have a low rate (below the average) for drinking during the last month. These countries are Venezuela, Aruba, Surinam, Russia and Armenia. Perhaps the cost or the lack of availability of alcohol can explain why more young people have ever drunk alcohol in their life but not recently.

As mentioned earlier, soft drug use among juveniles is less popular than the consumption of alcohol. On average, one out of ten juveniles has used marijuana or hashish (9.7%) and only 4% of all students have used it in the past 4 weeks. The use of hard drugs is much lower, yet considering the age range (12–16 years old), 2% have tried hard drugs like cocaine or heroin. There are some significant differences between countries. For example, students from Estonia not only report the highest rates for alcohol use, but also for the use of soft drugs (22.4%) and hard drugs (4.6%). This is twice as high as the average. Students from the Anglo-Saxon countries also report high rates for using soft and hard drugs. In the United States, 20% of the students report that they have used soft drugs in their lifetime and 4.4% have used hard drugs. In Ireland the rates are also quite high: 20.1% for soft drugs and 4.2% for hard drugs.

There are some countries where the number of students that use "soft" drugs is high but low for the use of "hard" drugs. Examples are the Netherlands (17.5 and 1.5%), Switzerland (19.2 and 2.7%) and Spain (18.5 and 1.8%). These countries

Table 5.2 Prevalence's of lifetime and last month alcohol use per country

	Alcohol life time				Alcohol last month			
	%	95% CI		*n*	%	95% CI		*n*
USA	46.7	42.5	50.9	1,329	16.6	14.0	19.6	1,329
Ireland	66.3	61.7	70.6	1,334	33.9	29.8	38.2	1,334
Iceland	22.0	17.4	27.3	1,338	10.1	7.0	4.4	1,338
Denmark	72.3	68.9	75.5	1,319	42	38.2	45.9	1,316
Norway	48.3	43.4	53.3	1,321	23.8	20.1	28.1	1,320
Sweden	54.2	50.9	57.5	1,327	22.3	19.7	25.1	1,325
Finland	70.7	68.2	73.2	1,356	32.4	29.3	35.7	1,356
The Netherlands	64.8	59.9	69.3	1,351	37.6	33.0	42.5	1,351
Austria	61.9	57.8	65.8	1,349	36.3	32.8	40.0	1,348
Germany	66.1	63.3	68.9	1,339	38.4	35.5	41.5	1,339
Switzerland	63.1	59.0	66.9	1,350	34.7	31.1	38.5	1,348
France	31.9	27.4	36.6	1,339	13.6	11.3	16.3	1,337
Belgium	61.1	57.1	64.8	1,331	34.4	30.9	38.0	1,329
Portugal	41.4	36.7	46.3	1,337	13.9	11.5	16.7	1,337
Cyprus	46.7	43.2	50.3	1,296	22.2	19.5	25.1	1,288
Italy	60.2	57.8	62.7	1,348	30.4	28.1	32.9	1,346
Spain	50.1	41.5	58.6	1,351	19.2	14.3	25.2	1,351
NL Antilles	65.9	63.0	68.7	1,341	23.9	21.6	26.3	1,339
Aruba	63.8	59.5	67.9	1,287	19	15.7	22.9	1,283
Suriname	78.7	75.8	81.3	1,344	19.5	17.1	22.1	1,327
Venezuela	76.0	72.0	79.6	1,334	23.4	19.6	27.6	1,330
Estonia	86.1	83.8	88.2	1,347	46.2	41.8	50.8	1,346
Lithuania	82.5	79.5	85.1	1,349	35.2	31.6	39.1	1,343
Poland	70.6	66.0	74.7	1,347	32	28.0	36.2	1,345
Czech Republic	84.3	81.4	86.8	1,355	40.1	36.7	43.6	1,352
Hungary	85.4	79.6	89.8	1,356	48.3	42.5	54.2	1,345
Slovenia	60.8	53.0	68.2	1,334	25.9	21.0	31.6	1,332
Bosnia Herzegovina	31.5	27.1	36.2	1,346	8.2	6.0	1.1	1,346
Russia	70.3	65.5	74.7	1,351	26.1	22.5	30.0	1,350
Armenia	71.8	68.3	75.1	1,347	26.9	23.7	30.2	1,347
Total	63.2	62.7	63.6	44,083	*27.9*	*27.2*	*28.7*	*40,077*

have a tolerant policy towards soft drug use and cannabis is widely available in local markets. The policy in these countries is more focused on harm reduction and prevention than on abstinence and repression. In the Netherlands, the drug policy consists of the depenalisation of the use and possession of small amounts of cannabis. The official goal of this policy is to prevent users from becoming marginalized and from being exposed to more harmful drugs by decriminalizing soft drugs and separating their market from hard drugs (Garretsen 2001, 2003; Verdurmen et al. 2005). So far, the evidence is weak as to whether or not such goals have been achieved. There are also some countries where the number of students that use hard drugs is quite high compared to other countries, but quite low on the consumption of soft drugs. Beyond the United States and Ireland, Post-Socialist countries such as Estonia, Poland and Hungary have high rates for the use of "hard" drugs (4.1 and 4.5%) but low rates for

Table 5.3 Life time and last month soft and hard drug use (%)

	Soft drugs life time				Soft drugs last month				Hard drugs life time			
	%	95% CI		*n*	%	95% CI		*n*	%	95% CI		*n*
USA	20.2	16.7	24.3	1,314	9.6	7.7	2.0	1,311	4.3	3.3	5.6	1,315
Ireland	20.1	16.9	23.8	1,307	7.5	5.9	9.5	1,304	4.1	2.8	6.1	1,309
Iceland	1.9	0.9	4.0	1,331	1.2	0.6	2.6	1,331	1.4	0.7	2.7	1,335
Denmark	11.8	9.6	4.4	1,298	2.9	2.0	4.2	1,294	2.3	1.6	3.4	1,307
Norway	4.5	3.2	6.3	1,300	1.7	1.0	2.7	1,299	1.4	0.9	2.3	1,305
Sweden	4.7	3.6	6.0	1,314	1.7	1.1	2.5	1,312	1.6	1.1	2.3	1,314
Finland	4.4	3.3	5.8	1,355	0.7	0.3	1.3	1,355	0.4	0.2	1.0	1,356
The Netherlands	17.5	14.1	21.6	1,345	8.3	6.5	0.6	1,344	1.5	1.0	2.4	1,346
Austria	9.9	8.1	2.1	1,343	3.3	2.3	4.7	1,341	2.2	1.5	3.0	1,346
Germany	9.7	8.2	1.5	1,334	3.4	2.6	4.4	1,333	1.5	1.1	2.2	1,334
Switzerland	19.2	16.7	22.1	1,335	7.9	6.2	0.0	1,331	2.3	1.5	3.4	1,348
France	8.7	7.1	0.6	1,327	3.9	2.9	5.1	1,324	1.9	1.3	2.7	1,330
Belgium	12.5	9.9	5.6	1,316	6.2	4.8	8.1	1,314	2.9	1.9	4.3	1,320
Portugal	1.5	0.9	2.7	1,329	0.7	0.3	1.9	1,329	0.6	0.3	1.4	1,331
Cyprus	3.4	2.2	5.1	1,256	2.1	1.2	3.5	1,253	2.5	1.6	3.8	1,263
Italy	8.6	7.4	0.1	1,341	4.1	3.3	5.2	1,340	1.6	1.2	2.2	1,343
Spain	17.5	12.3	24.2	1,326	8.5	5.2	3.8	1,326	1.8	0.8	4.0	1,334
NL Antilles	7.4	5.9	9.3	1,322	2.2	1.5	3.3	1,317	1.9	1.3	2.7	1,334
Aruba	6.4	4.6	8.8	1,264	2.4	1.3	4.7	1,264	1.5	0.7	3.2	1,267
Suriname	5.9	4.6	7.4	1,330	1.4	0.8	2.3	1,326	1	0.6	1.7	1,332
Venezuela	1.7	1.1	2.7	1,307	0.7	0.3	1.4	1,307	1.1	0.7	1.8	1,324
Estonia	22.4	19.4	25.7	1,339	8.2	6.0	1.0	1,334	4.5	3.2	6.2	1,331
Lithuania	11.4	9.3	3.9	1,338	3.4	2.5	4.6	1,335	2	1.3	3.0	1,342
Poland	7.4	5.6	9.8	1,341	2.5	1.6	3.9	1,339	4.1	3.0	5.6	1,342
Czech Republic	15.8	13.1	18.9	1,345	5.5	4.0	7.6	1,339	1.3	0.7	2.3	1,345
Hungary	14.2	11.2	17.9	1,342	4.2	2.4	7.4	1,342	4.5	2.3	8.5	1,345
Slovenia	8.6	5.6	2.8	1,325	2.3	1.3	4.1	1,323	1.4	0.7	2.7	1,332
Bosnia Herzegovina	0.8	0.3	1.9	1,320	0.4	0.1	1.6	1,317	0.8	0.2	2.5	1,338
Russia	8.1	6.0	0.9	1,344	2.2	1.5	3.3	1,342	1.9	1.3	2.8	1,342
Armenia	1.6	1.0	2.6	1,347	0.7	0.3	1.5	1,347	0.2	0.1	0.7	1,345
Total	*9.6*	*9.2*	*0.1*	*39,735*	*3.7*	*3.4*	*4.0*	*39,673*	*2*	*1.8*	*2.2*	*39,855*

use of "soft" drugs (7.4 and 14.1%). Since drug use is predominantly a matter of substance availability, it is hard to relate the higher rates in Eastern and Central Europe to market conditions. The data of our project, unfortunately, does not allow us to distinguish between the several types of "hard" drugs. However, according to the ESPAD survey, juveniles usually use ecstasy in countries with high prevalence rates of "hard" drug use (Hibell et al. 2009:90) (Table 5.3).

We have to mention that for some countries that has not asked for the use of LSD, they have only asked for heroin and coke. These countries are the Wallonia part of Belgium, Russia, France and Venezuela. So possibly the results for these countries can be lower.

A different question is whether a liberal policy on "soft" drugs increases its use, particularly among juveniles. Since ISRD-1, several countries whose policies were

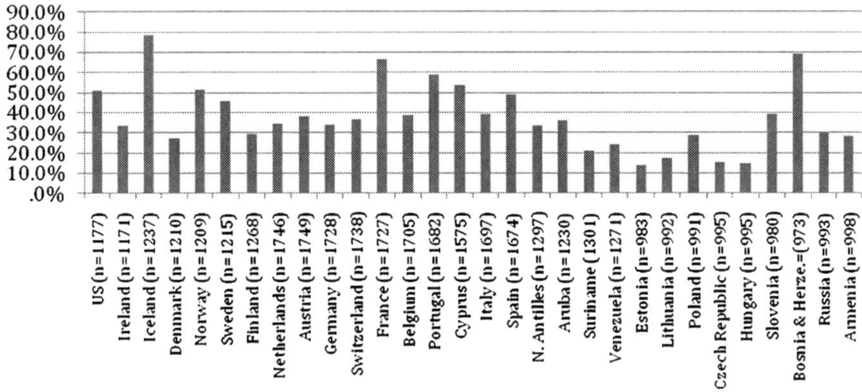

Fig. 5.1 Percentage of juveniles who have not used any alcohol or drugs (%)

relaxed during the following decade saw a sharp increase in the rates of "soft" drug use, such as the Netherlands, the Czech Republic and Switzerland.[1] This pleads for the assumption that liberal policies increase availability, which in turn, pushes demand. On the other hand, cannabis use is also frequent in the United States and Ireland where policy is certainly not tolerant, but where availability may still be high.

If we look at abstinence, the number of juveniles who do not drink or use any drugs at all, we see that Iceland has the highest rates of juveniles who have never used any alcohol or drugs (79.0%). In Bosnia Herzegovina (69.3%) and France, the number of students who have never used any substance is also high (67.1%). Furthermore, in the USA (52.6%), Norway (53.9%), Portugal (59.5%), Spain (56.5%) and Cyprus (57.2%) there are also a majority of juveniles who have not used any drugs. While in the Post-Socialist countries such as Hungary (15.4%), Estonia (15.7%), Czech Republic (16.2%) and Lithuania (18.1%) it is more common for juveniles to have consumed any type of substance (Fig. 5.1).

5.4 Additional Data Sources on Substance Use

We will first attempt to cross-validate the different measures of alcohol and drug use prevalence in Western countries. The ESPAD, especially, provides an interesting option for cross-validation. The purpose of ESPAD is to collect comparable data on substance use among 15–16-year-old European students by self-report in order to monitor trends within as well as between countries. The most recent ESPAD survey was conducted in 2007 (Hibell et al. 2004). The study targeted young people who became 16 years old in the year that the study was conducted (approximately 15.8

[1] See the retrospective data from the ESPAD surveys in Hibell et al. (2009):Table 6.1 (p. 374) and from the ISRD-1 of 1992 (Junger-Tas, Klein & Terlouw 1994:110, 196, 247).

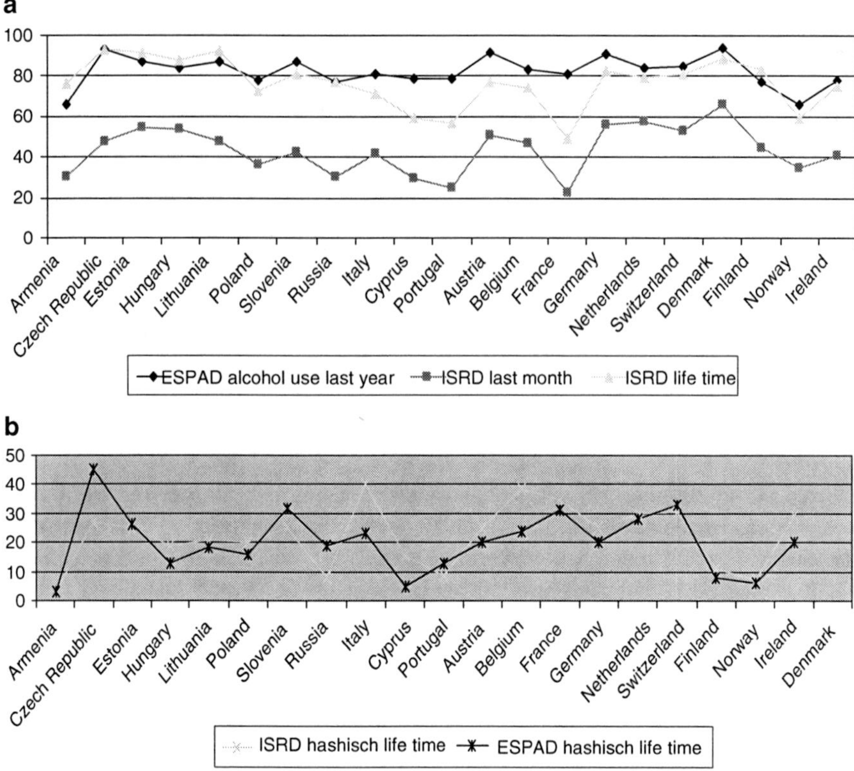

Fig. 5.2 (**a**) Comparison of the results on alcohol use from ESPAD and ISRD. (**b**) Comparison of the results on cannabis use from ESPAD and ISRD (The European Monitoring Centre for Drugs and drug addiction ESPAD 2009. The ESPAD report substance use among students in 35 countries)

years of age). In what follows, the ESPAD 2007 results are compared with the ISRD 2006 results. The difference between these two self-report studies is that the ESPAD data is based on national samples, while the ISRD-2 data is based on city samples as well. In regards to the comparison between the two studies we have limited the data to ninth graders. The ESPAD questionnaire asks about substance use during the last 12 months, whereas the ISRD-questionnaire differentiates between substance use during a lifetime and the last 4 weeks.

In all ESPAD countries, at least two thirds of the students have drunk alcohol at least once during their lifetime, with an ESPAD average close to 90% in the 2007 survey. The corresponding average figures for the past 12 months and the past 30 days are 82 and 61%, respectively. These figures remained relatively unchanged from 1995 to 2007 for lifetime and past 12 months prevalence's, while the past 30 days figures increased until 2003 before they dropped a little in 2007, especially among boys. Between the last two surveys there was also a clear decrease in the average proportion of students that had been drinking beer and/or wine during the past 30 days. The average figures as mentioned earlier are of course based on very divergent country figures. For example, alcohol use during the past 30 days was reported by 80% of the students in Austria and Denmark (limited comparability) but only by 31% in Iceland and 35% in Armenia.

If we compare the data from the two datasets we can see that there is a great similarity between the figures for ever use in the ISRD and last year use in the ESPAD survey. The number of students is somewhat higher than in the ISRD-survey, but the pattern is quite similar. Furthermore, in the ISRD-survey, Iceland and Armenia have a low score for alcohol use. For France and the Mediterranean countries such as Italy, Cyprus and Portugal, the difference is larger in that the ESPAD has some higher scores than the ISRD (Fig. 5.2a, b).

Although the number of students that use alcohol is higher within the ESPAD study, for the use of soft drugs (marijuana and hashish) the results of the ISRD are somewhat higher than the ESPAD study. Only in Czech Republic, Slovenia and Russia, the ESPAD study has higher rates. In the ESPAD study they used students that were born in 1991 and the mean age was 15.8 year. This would correspond with our ISRD data with the 16 years old students. So, we choose to compare the ESPAD study with the 16 years old students in the ISRD study.

5.5 Prevalence of Substance Use in the Country Clusters

The data analysis of substance use prevalence in the six country clusters reveals significant differences between the clusters. The Post-Socialist and the Latin American countries have the highest rates of students who have consumed alcohol at least once, while the number of students who have used alcohol during *the last month* is much lower, especially for all Latin American countries. The use of drugs is more prevalent in the Anglo-Saxon countries for lifetime and last month use, while in the Western European countries the use of alcohol is much more common (Table 5.4).

Table 5.4 Lifetime and last month use for the six country clusters (%)

	Anglo-Saxon	Northern EU	Western EU	Mediterranean EU	Latin America	Post-Socialist
Lifetime						
Beer/wine	55.1	52.9	57.3	47.9	69.8	71.1
Spirits	38.7	33.8	31.9	26.3	38.6	38.5
Hashish	20.2	5.40	13.0	7.8	5.3	10.0
Hard drugs	4.2	1.4	2.1	1.6	1.4	2.3
Last month						
Beer/wine	23.1	25.1	31.6	2.2	20.1	30.9
Spirits	16.1	14.4	13.9	10.3	10.4	13.8
Hashish	8.5	1.6	5.5	3.9	1.7	3.3
Hard drugs	1.6	0.6	0.8	0.9	0.4	0.7

Weighted for the clusters

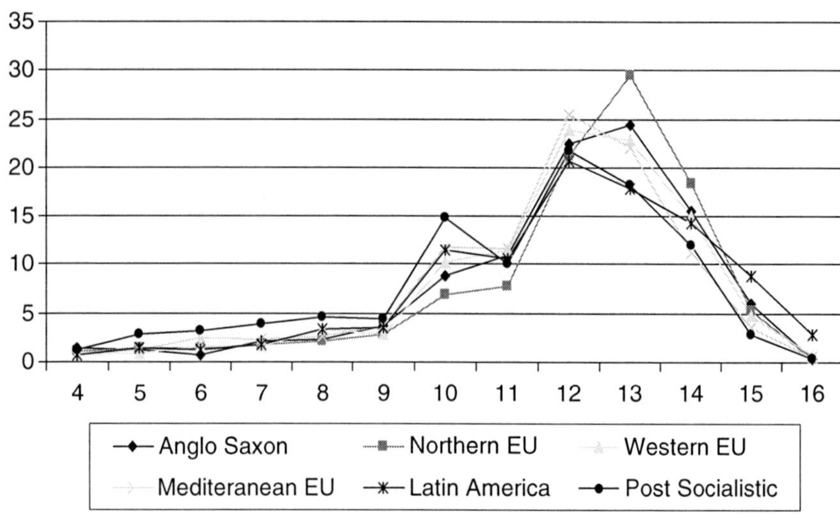

Fig. 5.3 Age of onset of drinking alcohol

5.6 Age of Onset

The age of onset of drinking alcohol and using drugs is a significant issue in the policy strategies of countries. A lot of research shows that starting at a young age is related to problematic drinking and using patterns in the future. As described earlier, empirical evidence from a large number of studies conveys that early initiation to alcohol (and drugs) predicts later misuse (DeWit et al. 2000; Grant and Dawson 1997; Kosterman et al. 2000). Therefore, it is important to be aware of when adolescents start drinking and what risks or protective factors are of influence on drinking and using behaviour. There is a question in the questionnaire about the first time they had used alcohol or drugs. We found no differences in the age of onset between the clusters. The average age for drinking beer or wine for the first time is 12 years. Only in the Northern European countries is the mean age 13 years old. The average age of onset for spirits is somewhat later, 13 years old (Fig. 5.3).

Most of the students start drinking between the ages of 10 and 15. The onset of using drugs starts at a later age, from 13 to 15 years old. The average age at which these adolescents first used drugs, is 13.25 years old for hashish or marijuana, and 13.22 years old for hard drugs. There are no large differences in the age of onset for soft and hard drugs between clusters (Fig. 5.4).

5.7 Problematic Alcohol Use by Juveniles

Not only is the increase of alcohol consumption by young people in Europe a problem, but problematic drinking (e.g. drunkenness and binge drinking) is also an issue of growing importance. A general trend among young people in Europe is "binge

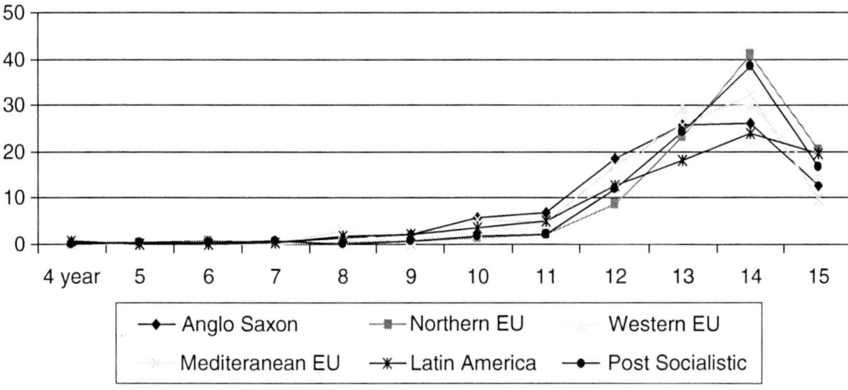

Fig. 5.4 Age of onset of marijuana or hashish (%)

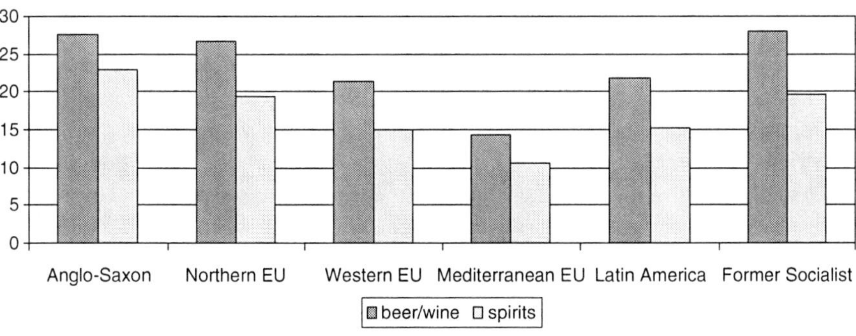

Fig. 5.5 Have you ever been drunk from alcohol (%)

drinking" or "coma drinking". Thus, we asked two questions about problematic drinking.

In the questionnaire there is a question about drinking. We asked if the students had ever been to school after consuming alcohol. One out of four students have ever been drunk from beer/wine (23.0%) and one out of six students from spirits (16.5%). There is a difference between the country clusters in regards to the number of students that report being drunk from alcohol. The highest percentages are found in the Post-Socialist countries (28.1 and 19.7%) and the lowest in the Mediterranean countries (14.3 and 10.5%). The countries where there is a zero tolerance policy towards alcohol such as Sweden and the US, also have high scores in regards to getting drunk (Anglo-Saxon 27.6 and 23%; Northern EU 26.7 and 19.5%) (Fig. 5.5).

The second question concerned the amount of alcohol that they had been drinking. We asked the students, if they had drunk alcohol in the last month and how many glasses they consumed the last time they drank. A common threshold for "binge drinking" is five glasses or more during a single session. The majority of the students who had been drinking, did so moderately and drank one or two glasses (53.4%). Some students had been drinking three or four glasses (23.7%), and more

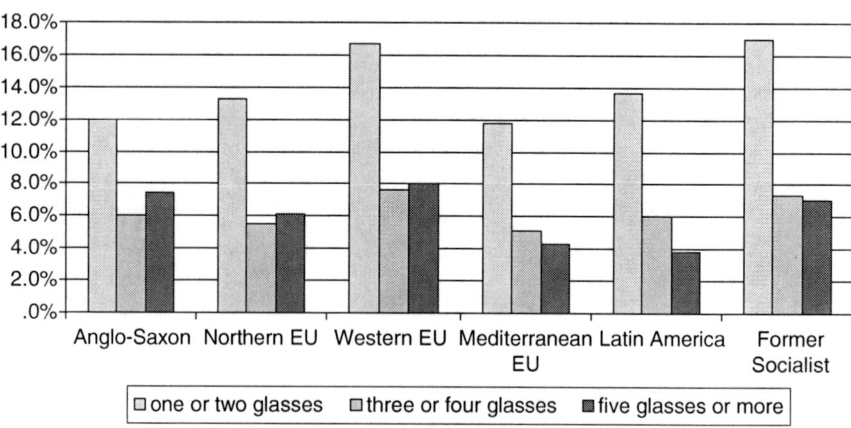

Fig. 5.6 The number of glasses of alcohol consumed the last time (%)

than one in five students (22.9%) had been binge drinking. We have to point out that we only asked about the *last time* they used alcohol. Most students drink heavily during the weekend when they go out (Trimbos 2007). So, if this question was asked on Monday or Tuesday, only 1 or 2 days after the weekend, the likelihood that they had been binge dinking is higher than if the question was asked on a Thursday of Friday, when they might have been drinking on a weekday when drinking behaviour is most likely to be more moderate.

When looking at the country clusters we can see substantial differences. In the Western European countries the number of juveniles that have been binge drinking (8.1%) is 2 times higher in comparison to the other clusters such as Latin America (3.9%). It is also higher than the Post-Socialist countries (7.0%) which have the highest rates of alcohol use. Estonia has the highest rates of students who have been binge drinking (19%). If we look at the number of students in Estonia who have consumed alcohol in the last month, more than a quarter (39%) has drunk six or more glasses. The other countries with high rates are Hungary (12.5%), Finland (11.7%) Switzerland (11.0%), Ireland (10.7%) and the Netherlands (10.1%) (Fig. 5.6).

There is a difference between the questions about being drunk and binge drinking. The second question is about alcohol use in the previous month and the first question asks whether the students have ever been drunk. Although the Post-Socialist countries have the highest scores on getting drunk, they have lower scores on binge drinking. This can be explained by the fact that there is also a difference between lifetime and last month use in those countries. The number of students who consumed alcohol in the last month is much lower in Post-Socialist countries and Latin American countries than it is for lifetime use, while this difference is smallest in Western European countries. One may conclude that when students begin drinking in Western European countries, this coincides with drinking more heavily and on a more regular basis. This is consistent with the question about how frequently they

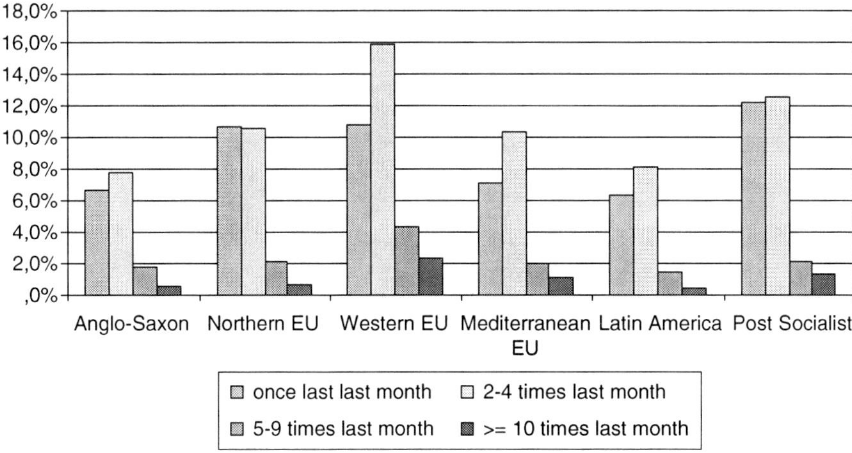

Fig. 5.7 Incidence juveniles have been drinking beer or wine during the last month (%)

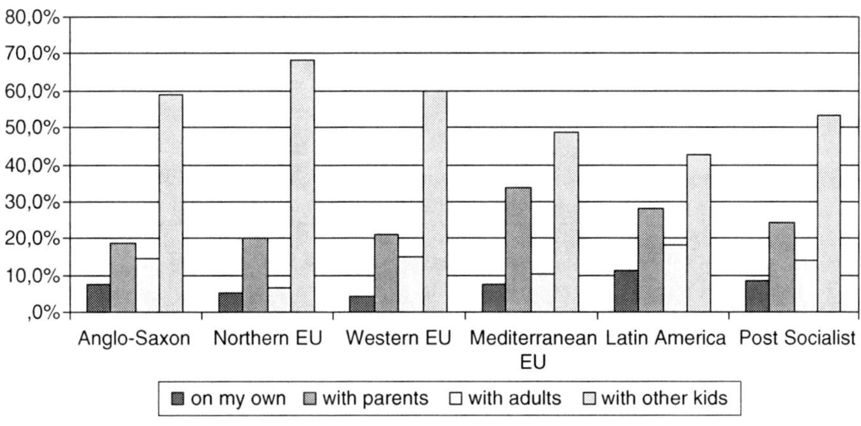

Fig. 5.8 Social context of drinking (%)

consumed alcohol in the last month (see Fig. 5.7). Most of the students have drunk alcohol once or twice in the last month. The students in Western Europe often drink more beer and wine than in Mediterranean and Latin American countries (Fig. 5.7).

5.8 Social Context of Substance Use

The majority of students drink alcohol with their friends (55.2%), predominantly beer or wine. In the Mediterranean countries students tend to consume alcohol more often with their parents (Fig. 5.8).

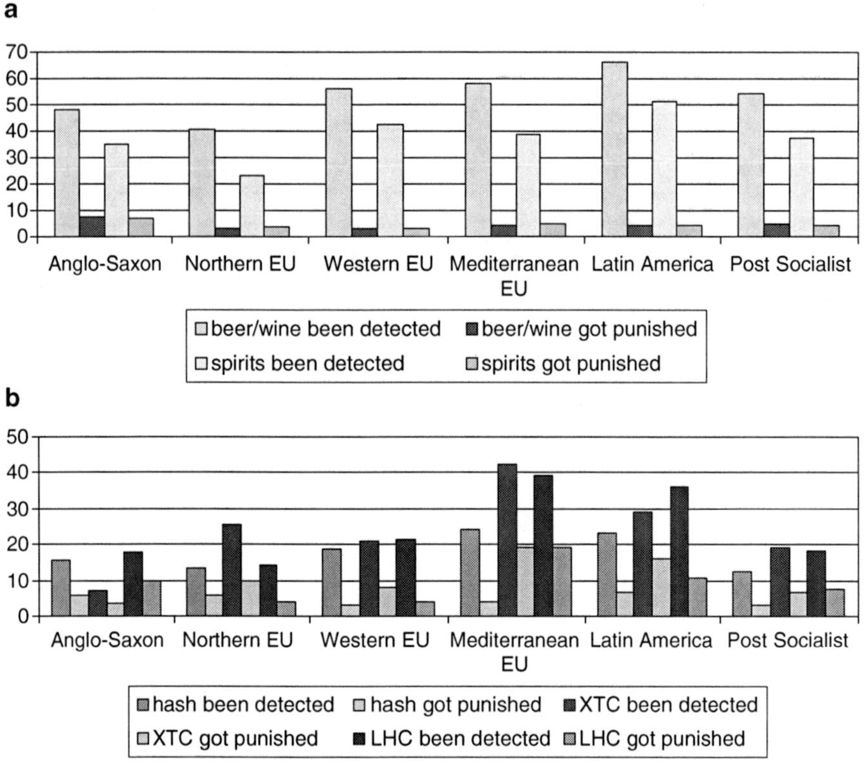

Fig. 5.9 (**a**) Percentage of students that were caught using alcohol the last time and were punished in the six country clusters. (**b**) Percentage of students that were caught using soft or hard drugs the last time and were punished in the six country clusters

There is a large difference between the country clusters in the number of students that get caught using drugs and get punished for their actions. Most parents are tolerant towards the use of alcohol (see Fig. 5.9a). Fifty percent of the students say that they were not punished for using alcohol (beer or wine) and one third was not punished for using strong liquor (33.6%). In regards to the use of soft and hard drugs, parents respond quite differently. In the Mediterranean and Latin American countries especially, parents punish their children for using soft or hard drugs. A large number of students say that they never got caught using hashish (84%). But for those who were detected almost three quarter were not punished (72%), only a small number of students reported they received any punishment. We see the same response for the use of hard drugs. Most of the students say that their parents do not know that they are using (80%). But if they their parents know that they are using hard drugs this does not mean that they were punished. Less than the half of them received some kind of punishment (42.1%).

5.9 Demographic Background

In the next section, we will look at gender-specific patterns in alcohol and drug use and whether they differ between one cluster to the other. In the past, it was common for boys to consume more alcohol than girls, but adolescent girls are catching up quickly. Some studies have found that girls in secondary school – especially those in the lower grades – now drink almost as much as boys in secondary school (MacKenzie 2000; Bonnie and Connel 2003). Our data also revealed that in general, boys show higher prevalence rates than girls for all types of use, yet the differences between boys and girls remain minimal (see Fig. 5.10).

Although the difference is not that considerable anymore, there is still a significant gender difference in regards to alcohol use in the last month. Boys drink somewhat more alcohol than girls, but if we look at problematic alcohol consumption; we see that boys are more likely to drink more glasses of alcohol. Boys (7.5%) tend to binge drink more than girls (5%), and they have been intoxicated more often from the consumption of beer (24.8 vs. 21.1) and spirits (17.2 vs. 14.9) than girls have. It is slightly more common for girls to abstain from alcohol and soft or hard drug use in their lifetime. If we look at the number of glasses the last time they drank alcohol, we see a similar pattern. Another difference is that boys drink alcohol significantly more frequently that girls. Furthermore, there is also a gender difference in regards to hashish or marijuana use. Boys use these soft drugs more often than girls do (odds ratio 1.72) (Table 5.5).

If we look at the country clusters there are some differences between boys and girls in our study within the clusters. In Anglo-Saxon and Northern European

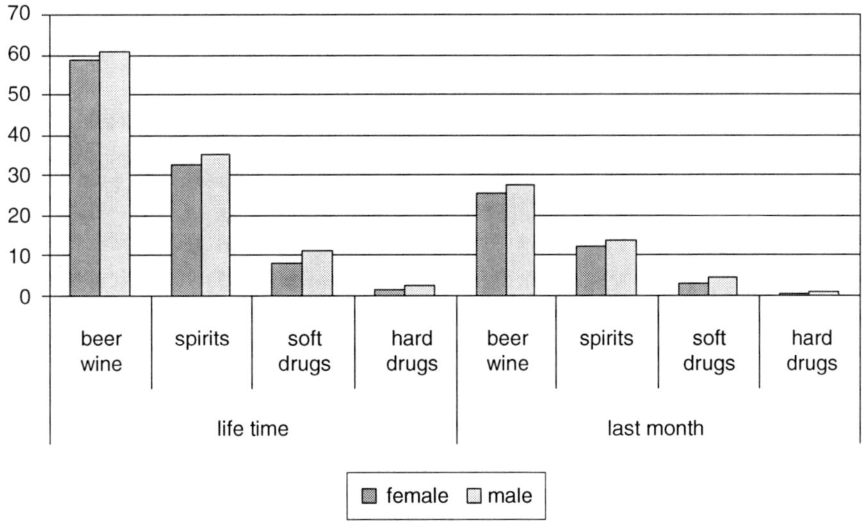

Fig. 5.10 Gender differences in consumption of alcohol or drugs (%)

Table 5.5 Logistic regression between gender and substance use

Male	Odds ratio	95% Conf. interval	
Alcohol last month	1.14***	1.11	1.18
Abstinence	1.12***	1.08	1.15
Binge drinking	1.41***	1.36	1.47
Drunk by beer	1.22***	1.17	1.26
Drunk by spirit	1.18***	1.14	1.23
Hashish last month	1.72***	1.58	1.88

*** $p<0.001$

Table 5.6 Lifetime and last month use for the six country clusters by gender (%)

	Anglo-Saxon (*N*=2,440)		Northern Europe (*N*=6,347)		Western Europe (*N*=10,619)		Mediterranean Europe (*N*=6,872)		Latin America (*N*=5,354)		Post-Socialist (*N*=9,051)	
	Girls	Boys	Girls	Boys	Girls	Boys	Girls	Boys	Girls	Boys	Girls	Boys
Life time												
Beer/wine	55.8	54.5	52.4	54.0	56.5	58.1	**44.1**	**52.0**	70.3	69.3	69.9	72.3
Spirits	40.0	37.7	33.9	34.2	30.8	33.1	26.2	24.5	**35.7**	**42.0**	**36.4**	**40.6**
Hashish	19.0	21.3	5.0	5.9	**11.0**	**14.9**	**6.3**	**9.4**	**3.9**	**7.0**	**8.4**	**11.8**
Hard drugs	4.3	4.2	1.4	1.5	1.7	2.4	**0.8**	**2.5**	***0.9***	***1.9***	***1.9***	***2.7***
Last month												
Beer/wine	22.4	23.8	26.0	24.3	31.3	32.0	**17.6**	**23.1**	19.8	20.5	**28.8**	**33.1**
Spirits	17.4	13.8	16.0	13.0	13.1	14.6	**9.1**	**11.6**	9.8	11.0	**12.2**	**15.5**
Hashish	7.5	9.5	1.7	1.6	**4.1**	**7.0**	**3.1**	**4.7**	**1.0**	**2.4**	**2.3**	**4.3**
Hard drugs	1.2	1.3	0.5	0.7	**0.4**	**1.1**	**0.1**	**1.6**	0.3	0.7	0.6	0.8

Bold $p<.001$
Bold and *italic* $p<.01$
Weighted for the clusters

countries there are no gender differences in the consumption of alcohol and drugs ever or in the last month. In the Western European countries there is only one gender difference: boys use more marijuana than girls and they used more hard drugs in the last 4 weeks. The girls in the Mediterranean countries drink significantly less than boys. Boys in the Mediterranean countries have tried alcohol and soft/hard drugs more often, although drinking spirits (probably cocktails) is more common among girls in these countries. In the Latin American and the Post-Socialist countries more boys use extreme substances such as liquor, soft and hard drugs. In the Anglo-Saxon and Northern European countries the drinking of hard liquor (probably cocktails) is also more popular among girls than among boys, especially in the last 4 weeks (Table 5.6).

The most important factor of alcohol consumption is age. The older a student is, the more likely he or she uses alcohol or drugs. Our sample consists of the first three grades of secondary school and it is clear that the higher the grade, the higher the likelihood of alcohol and drug use among the students.

Table 5.7 Logistic regression between grade and immigration status and alcohol and soft drug use last month

	Alcohol use last month		Soft drug use last month	
	Odds ratio	95% Conf. interval	Odds ratio	95% Conf. interval
Grade 8	1.81***	1.73–1.89	2.11***	1.84–2.41
Grade 9	3.29***	3.15–3.44	4.14***	3.66–4.69
First generation migrants	0.70***	0.65–0.75	1.17***	0.99–1.37
Second generation migrants	0.80***	0.76–0.84	1.37***	1.23–1.53

***$p<0.001$

Table 5.8 Lifetime and last use for the city size (%)

	Beer/wine	Strong spirits	Hashish	Hard drugs (XTC, LSD, heroin or coke)	Abstinence
Lifetime	59.5	32.8	8.8	2.0	40.8
Small town	58.4	31.7	7.4	1.9	52.2
Medium city	57.7	29.6	8.9	2.1	42.5
Large city	61.6	36.1	9.9	1.9	38.4
Last month	26.9	12.7	3.6	0.8	–
Small town	26.6	12.5	3.3	0.9	
Medium city	25.5	10.8	3.8	0.9	
Large city	28.2	14.3	3.6	0.7	

Weighted for the all sample

For all clusters there is a significant increase of students that use or drink between eighth and ninth grade (Table 5.7).

Another aspect relevant to this study is whether or not a student is a migrant within a country. The percentage of migrants of the whole dataset is 19.2%. Migrants are defined as students who were born in another country, or whose parents were born in another country. The places of origin of the migrants differ between each country. Within the West European countries they are mostly refugees or children of (im)migrant workers, but in the Post-Socialist countries like Estonia or Lithuania they or their parents came from Russia. Migrant youths drink significantly less alcohol. If we look at the ethnicity of migrant students we see that migrants from West, Central and Eastern Europe have the same consumption pattern for alcohol use as the native students. Among immigrants from Turkey, Africa and Asia, alcohol consumption is much lower which can be explained by the fact that the majority of them are Muslim. Nevertheless, the pattern for the use of soft drugs is not that different between migrant and native students. However, smoking hashish is more common among migrants, especially those of the second generation (see Table 5.7).

There is a difference in the consumption pattern according to the size of the city. It seems as though there are more juveniles who refrain from using alcohol or drugs in the small towns (52.2%) in comparison to medium (42.5%) and larger sized cities (38.4%). However, if we look at the last month use of alcohol, then the picture is somewhat different. The use of alcohol is the lowest in the medium sized cities, while the use of soft and hard drugs is the highest.

Yet, if we look at the different country clusters we see that the Western European cluster is the only group where substance use is higher in small cities than in large cities. In the Northern European countries, the only country in this cluster which has a medium sized cities in the sample is Iceland and they only have the 8 grade in the sample. So this probably explains why the substance use of the middle-sized cities is quite low.

5.10 The Correlation Between Substance Use and Juvenile Crime

We have looked at the association between substance use and offences committed by juveniles, by using a versatility scale which documents substance use in last year and in the previous month (see Table 5.9). The data reveals that using hashish has a stronger correlation with delinquent behaviour than problematic drinking or using hard drugs. This is consistent with the results of Wikström and Butterworth (2006) who found that using cannabis is a much better predictor than alcohol in regards to aggressive offending. The stronger correlation between serious offences and the use of hashish also supports Gottfredson and Hirschi's claim that criminal behaviour is risk behaviour, indicating a lack of self-control that is expressed in all kinds of other risk behaviours. This explains why delinquents not only commit offences but also

Table 5.9 Substance use last month for the clusters (%)

	Anglo-Saxon (*N*=2,440)	Northern EU (*N*=6,347)	Western EU (*N*=10,619)	Mediterranean EU (*N*=6,872)	Latin America (*N*=5,354)	Post-Socialist (*N*=9,051)
Beer/wine						
Small town	17.8	22.1	39.9	19.3	17.0	28.6
Medium city	20.3	9.6	25.7	21.8	20.9	28.5
Large city	27.8	29.8	26.9	23.4	21.2	31.3
Spirits						
Small town	13.2	11.3	16.9	11.1	9.6	11.0
Medium city	14.7	3.3	13.7	9.6	9.5	11.0
Large city	18.4	18.0	13.0	10.9	12.2	13.6
Hashish						
Small town	6.2	0.1	4.1	4.2	1.8	1.9
Medium city	8.8	1.2	5.5	3.0	1.9	2.6
Large city	8.2	1.7	5.0	4.4	0.7	3.3
Hard drugs						
Small town	1.8	1.0	1.1	1.3	1.0	0.5
Medium city	1.4	0.8	0.9	1.1	0.6	1.0
Large city	1.8	0.5	0.6	0.8	0.5	0.6

Weighted for the clusters

Table 5.10 Negative binomial regression between versatility last year and substance use

	IRR	95% Conf. interval
Alcohol use last month	1.82***	1.74–1.91
Hashish use last month	2.52***	2.34–2.71
Hard drug use last month	2.45***	2.23–2.71
Binge drinking	1.82***	1.72–1.92
Been drunk of beer	1.67***	1.58–1.77
Been drunk of spirit	1.25***	1.18–1.33

***$p<0.001$

drive dangerously, have more accidents, drink heavily and use drugs (Gottfredson and Hirschi 1990). Beyond the lifestyle explanation based on Gottfredson and Hirschi's work, this can also be explained by the fact that the increase of THC in generally available samples of cannabis has changed the pharmacological effects of the substance.[2] Interestingly, the correlation between the use of hashish and offences is stronger than for (problematic) alcohol use. Although it remains speculative at the time of this writing, one could argue that juveniles who regularly use cannabis face financial insecurity and, as a result, may turn to more to property offences. When we look at problematic alcohol use, there is a relationship with delinquent behaviour but there is no stronger relation than with alcohol use in the last month (Table 5.10).

Several (inter)national studies have also shown that adolescent substance use is associated with other problem behaviours, such as delinquency and risky behaviour, which – in turn – are predictors of future alcohol and drug dependence. Alcohol use, drug use as well as anti-social behaviour may be influenced by a weak or broken bond to society (Hirschi 1969; Sampson and Laub 1993). Also, low self-control can explain risky behaviour such as smoking, alcohol use and other risky lifestyle choices (Gottfredson and Hirschi 1990). In addition, neighbourhood characteristics such as social disorganization, and lack of trust and solidarity may also affect anti-social behaviour (Hawkins et al. 1998; Loeber and Farrington 1998).

There is no gender difference for the use alcohol, only for marihuana; more boys use soft drugs than girls. Being a migrant juvenile is a protective factor for alcohol but not for soft drugs. This is most likely due to the fact that many juvenile migrants are originally from Asia and Africa, where the use of hashish and marijuana is more common than the use of alcohol.

Several studies show that higher scores on self-control correlate with all kinds of personal behaviour and skills of juveniles. High self-control is also linked to a relative absence of problem drinking patterns (Tangney et al. 2004). In this study, we also found that higher levels of self-control is a protection factor, which minimizes

[2]The long-term increase of THC in cannabis products is well documented for several European countries. See J. Vuille, S. Hardegger and R. Steiger, Le taux de THC contenu dans le cannabis saisi par la police (1980–2008). Berne: Office fédéral de la santé publique 2009.

Table 5.11 Logistic regression predicting alcohol last month

	Alcohol use last month		Soft drug use last month	
	Odds ratio	95% Conf. interval	Odds ratio	95% Conf. interval
Male	1.04	1.00–1.08	1.39***	1.25–1.54
Grade 8	1.62***	1.54–1.70	1.82***	1.56–2.11
Grade 9	3.07***	2.91–3.22	3.42***	2.96–3.95
First generation migrants	0.62***	0.56–0.67	1.03	0.84–1.25
Second generation migrants	0.71***	0.67–0.74	1.06	0.93–1.20
Self-control	0.71***	0.69–0.73	0.69***	0.65–0.73
Attitude violence	1.10***	1.08–1.31	1.16***	1.10–1.23
Family bonding	0.87***	0.84–0.88	0.80***	0.76–0.73
Life events	1.13***	1.1–1.16	1.16***	1.11–1.21
School disorganization	1.03**	1.02–1.06	1.25***	1.18–1.31
Neighbourhood disorganization	1.01	0.99–1.03	1.30***	1.24–1.36
Life style	1.63***	0.99–1.04	2.09***	1.96–2.22

**$p<0.01$; ***$p<0.001$

the consumption of alcohol. The more self-control, the less likely students consumed alcohol in the previous month. We found identical results for the use of soft drugs. Attitudes towards violence are also related to the use of alcohol (odds ratio 1.10) and somewhat more with soft drugs (1.16).

The role of the family and especially family bonding is also a protective factor in adolescent problem behaviour (Hawkins et al. 1998; Kirby et al. 1999). Our data supports these findings and illustrates that family bonding is a protective factor which minimizes the use of alcohol and soft drugs. Significant life changing events also have an effect on substance use. The more drastic or frequent these life altering occurrences, the more likely students drink or use soft drugs.

Adolescent lifestyles, which can be defined by spending time in public places with a large group of friends, also influences substance use. In fact, this is the strongest predictor for the use of alcohol and soft drugs. School or neighbourhood disorganization is more related to soft drugs than alcohol use. There is no relationship between neighbourhood disorganization and the use of alcohol. This is because drinking alcohol is socially more accepted than smoking marijuana or hashish within families (Table 5.11).

Several studies which look at alcohol and soft drug consumption, show that the use of these substances is a significant predictor of youth involvement in violent crime (Harrison and Gfroerer 1992; Benda et al. 2001; Lennings et al. 2003).Thus, we looked at serious en minor violent offences and juvenile substance use in our study. The results illustrate that alcohol and soft drugs use is indeed a predictor. The relationship is strong and consistent for both minor and serious violent offences (see Table 5.12). Yet for serious offences, the likelihood that alcohol has been used is 4 times greater (4.00 odds ratio).

Table 5.12 Logistic regression for minor and serious violence offences last year and substance use

	Minor violence offences		Serious violence offences	
	Odds ratio	95% Conf. interval	Odds ratio	95% Conf. interval
Alcohol last month	3.11***	2.96–3.27	4.00***	3.61–4.45
Hashish last month	3.65***	3.30–4.04	4.19***	3.65–4.81
XTC last month	1.87***	1.38–2.53	2.83***	2.04–3.92
LHC last month	2.43***	1.73–3.40	2.95***	2.06–4.20

***$p<0.001$

Table 5.13 Logistic regression for minor and serious property offences last year and substance use

	Minor property offences		Serious property offences	
	Odds ratio	95% Conf. interval	Odds ratio	95% Conf. interval
Alcohol last month	3.32***	3.07–3.57	3.87***	3.47–4.33
Hashish last month	4.33***	3.86–4.86	6.09***	5.32–6.96
XTC last month	1.21	0.87–1.68	2.08***	1.49–2.92
LHC last month	2.44***	1.73–3.43	5.58***	3.94–7.93

***$p<0.001$

In regards to offences that are considered minor, such as property offences, alcohol also seems to be a predictor. Yet even in these cases, the use of soft drugs is a stronger guarantee. This is consistent with the results of Wikström and Butterworth (2006) who found that the use of hashish is a stronger predictor for property offences than alcohol (Tables 5.12 and 5.13).

If we look at the different clusters we can see that in the majority of them, the use of hashish during the last month has the highest correlation with delinquent behaviour. In the Mediterranean and Latin American countries, the use of alcohol is more strongly related to delinquent behaviour, while in the Post-Socialist countries and the Latin American countries the use of hard drugs has the highest correlation with offences. Problematic alcohol use, such as binge drinking or drunkenness only has a slightly higher correlation to delinquency in Anglo-Saxon, Northern and Western countries (Table 5.14).

There is no correlation between being a victim of theft, assault or robbery and substance use of youngsters.

5.11 Conclusion

There are a lot of students that have been using alcohol or soft drugs in Europe and the other countries. Nevertheless, 40% of all the students have not ever used any substance at all. Two thirds of the students have ever used alcohol and one third did so in past month. These figures are somewhat lower than the self-report from the

Table 5.14 Negative binomial regression for versatility last year and substance use

Versatility Last year	(1) Anglo-Saxon	(2) Northern EU	(3) Western EU	(4) Mediterranean	(5) Latin America	(6) Post-Socialist
Alcohol last month	1.71*** (6.66)	1.62*** (5.61)	1.61*** (11.36)	2.59*** (16.09)	2.31*** (8.23)	1.79*** (12.45)
Hashish last month	2.05*** (8.32)	3.03*** (8.24)	2.48*** (14.93)	2.14*** (7.32)	1.91*** (3.49)	2.04*** (10.12)
Hard drug, last month	1.83*** (5.40)	2.92*** (9.01)	2.45*** (10.37)	2.36*** (5.38)	2.86*** (5.46)	2.20*** (9.19)
Binge drinking	1.65*** (5.47)	1.67*** (4.66)	1.59*** (9.82)	1.80*** (7.10)	1.52*** (4.21)	1.67*** (10.10)
Drunken of beer	1.98*** (6.98)	2.03*** (5.83)	1.52*** (8.60)	1.84*** (7.48)	1.88*** (6.45)	2.04*** (13.90)
Drunken of spirit	1.16 (1.57)	1.13 (1.11)	1.34*** (5.66)	1.37*** (3.37)	1.62*** (4.52)	1.30*** (4.80)
N	3,615	6,712	16,268	11,186	6,411	19,205

Exponentiated coefficients; t statistics in *parentheses*

$^{***}p<0.001$

ESPAD where they asked whether the students had consumed alcohol during the last year. The figures of ever use of the ISRD and last year use of the ESPAD are quiet similar. However, these figures only represent, students aged 15–16 years old, and most of the students had been drinking alcohol since the 9 grade.

There are also large differences between the countries. For example, the students from the Post-Socialist countries have higher rates of ever having used alcohol. Countries with a low economic status, which includes, Venezuela, Russia, Aruba and Armenia have a high number of students who report that they consume alcohol but not on a regular basis. Perhaps the availability in those countries is low or the price of alcohol is relatively high.

The alcohol patterns for boys and girls are becoming more and more similar, yet boys seem to report more extreme alcohol use (number of glasses and times that they consume alcohol) than girls.

Juveniles seem to use alcohol mostly with their friends, but they are also more accustomed to drink a glass of wine or beer at home with their parents. In the Mediterranean countries drinking at home is more common.

The use of alcohol and drugs is unlikely delinquent behaviour not a stage but a something more kids do when they are older. Most of the students in grade 8 drink now and then and a quarter of the 9 graders have also used soft drugs. The use of hard drugs is rare in all grades.

Our study reveals that there is a relationship between alcohol and aggressive offences. Although there is a common understanding that alcohol plays an important role in violent behaviour, the use of hashish is of more influence in regards to delinquent behaviour. This is especially the case in serious offences and property offences.

References

Alsaker, F.D. & Flammer, A. (eds). (1999). *The adolescent experience: European and American adolescents in the 1990's*. Mahwah, NJ: Lawrence Erlbaum Associates.

Anderson, K.D. (2003). *The risk of alcohol: what general practice can do*. Nijmegen: Katholieke Universiteit Nijmegen.

Benda, B. B., Corwyn, R.F. & Toombs, N.J.(2001). Recidivism among Adolescent Serious Offenders - Prediction of Entry into the Correctional System for Adults. In: *Criminal Justice and Behavior* vol. 28, pp. 588–613.

Beyers, J.M. Toumbourou, J.W. Catalano, R.F., Arthur, M.W. and Hawkins, J.D., (2004) A cross-national comparison of risk and protective factors for adolescent substance use: The United States and Australia. *Journal of Adolescent Health, 35*, 3–16.

Brook, D.W., Brook, J.S., Zhang, C., Cohen, P. and Whiteman, M., (2002). Drug use and the risk of major depressive disorder, alcohol dependence, and substance use disorders. *Archives of General Psychiatry, 59*, 1039–1044.

Bonnie, R. and O'Connell, M.E. (eds), (2003). Reducing Underage Drinking: A Collective Responsibility. National Academies Press.

De Kort, M., & Cramer, T. (1999). Pragmatism versus ideology: Dutch drug policy continued. *Journal of Drug Issues, 29*, 473–492.

DeWit, D. J., Adlaf, E. M., Offord, D. R., & Ogborne, A. C. (2000). Age at first alcohol use: a risk factor for the development of alcohol disorders. *American Journal of Psychiatry, 157*, 745–750.

EMCDDA. *Summary of the 2007 ESPAD report EMCDDA*, ESPAD, Lisbon, March 2009.

Franken, I. H. A. (2003). Drug craving and addiction: integrating psychological and neuropsychopharmacological approaches. *Progress in Neuro-Psychopharmacology and Biological Psychiatry, 27*, 563–579.

Garretsen, H.F.L. (2001). Dutch alcohol policy developements: the last decades and present state of affairs. *Medicine and Law, 20(2)*, 301–312.

Garretsen, H.F.L. (2003). The decline of Dutch drug policy? *Journal of Substance Use, 8(1)*, 2–4.

Gottfredson, M. R. & Hirschi, T. (1990). A General Theory of Crime. Stanford University Press.

Grant, B.F. and Dawson, D.A, (1997). Age at onset of alcohol use and its association with DSM-IV alcohol abuse and dependence. Results from the National Longitudinal Alcohol Epidemiologic Survey. *Journal of Substance Abuse, 9*, 103–110.

Harrison, L. & Gfroerer, J. (1992). The Intersection of Drug Use and Criminal Behavior: Results From the National Household Survey on Drug Abuse. In: *Drug use and criminal behavior.* Volume 38, No. 4, p. 422–443.

Hawkins, J.D., Herrenkohl, T. Farrington, D.P., Brewer, D.D., Catalano, R.F., & Harachi, T.W. (1998) A review of predictors of youth violence. In: R. Loeber and D.P. Farrington (eds), *Serious and violent juvenile offenders: Risk factors and successful interventions.* (pp. 106–146) Thousand Oaks, CA: Sage Publications.

Hibell B., Andersson B., Bjarnason T., Ahlström S., Balakireva O., Kokkevi, A. & Morgan, M. (2004). *The ESPAD Report* 2003: *Alcohol and Other Drug use Among Students in 35 European Countries.* Stockholm: CAN; Council of Europe; Pompidou Group.

Hibell B., Guttormsson U., Ahlström S., Balakireva O., Bjarnason T., Kokkevi A., & Kraus, L. (2009). *The 2007 ESPAD Repost: Substance Use Among Students in 35 European Countries.* Stockholm: CAN; EMCDDA; Council of Europe.

Hirschi, T. (1969). Causes of Delinquency. Berkeley, Los Angeles: University of California Press.

Hosman, C.M. & Clayton, R. (2000). Prevention and health promotion on the international scene: the need for a more effective and comprehensive approach. In: Addiction Behavior, 25 (6) p. 943–954.

Hunt, G. and Barker, J.C., (2001). Socio-cultural anthropology and alcohol and drug research: Towards a indentified theory. *Social Science and Medicine, 53*, 165–188.

Jessor, R., Turbin, M.S., Costa, F.M., Dong, Q, Zhang, H. and Wang, C., (2003). Adolescent problem behaviour in China and the United States: A cross-national study of psychological protective factors. *Journal of Research on Adolescence, 13*, 329–360.

Junger-Tas, J., Klein, M.W, & Zhang, X. (1992). Problems and Dilemmas in comparative Self-Report Delinquency Research. In Farrington, P.D. & Walklate, S. (eds.) Offenders and Victims: Theory and Policy, British Society of Criminology, London.

Junger-Tas, J., Terlouw, G.J., & Klein, M.W. (eds). (1994). *Delinquent Behavior among Young People in the Western World: First Results of the International Self-report Delinquency Study.* Amsterdam: Kugler.

Junger-Tas,J., Haen-Marshall, I. and Ribeaud, D. (eds), (2003) *Delinquency in an international perspective. The international self-reported delinquency study (ISRD).* NY/The Hague: Criminal Justice Press/Kugler Publications.

Kirby, K.C., Marlowe, D.B., Festinger, D.S., Garvey, K.A., & LaMonaca, V. (1999). Community reinforcement training for family and significant others of drug abusers: A unilateral intervention to increase treatment entry of drug users. *Drug and Alcohol Dependence, 56*, 85–96.

Kraus, L., Bloomfield, K., Augustin, R., and Reese, A. (2000). Prevalence of alcohol use and the association between onset of use and alcohol-related problems in a general population sample in Germany, *Addiction, 95*, 1389–1401.

Lennings, C.J., Copeland, J. & Howard, J. (2003). Substance use patterns of young offenders and violent crime. In: Aggressive behavior. Volume 29, issue 5, p. 414–422.

Loeber, R. and Farrington, D.P. (1998). *Serious and violence juvenile offenders: Risk Factors and successful interventions.* Thousand Oaks, CA: Sage.

MacKenzie, D.L. (2000). Under the Influence? The Impact of Alcohol Advertising on Youth. Ontario, Association to Reduce Alcohol Promotion in Ontario (ARAPO).

Monshouwer, K., Dorsselaer, S. van, Gorter, A. Verdurmen, J. & Vollebergh, W. (2004). Jeugd en riskant gedrag. Kerngegevens uit het Peilstationsonderzoek 2003. Utrecht, Trimbos-instituut.

National Institute on Alcohol Abuse and Alcoholism, (1997). *Youth drinking: Risk factors and consequences, Alcohol Alert No. 37.* Washington, DC: National Institute on Alcohol Abuse and Alcoholism.

Pitkanen, T., Lyyra, A.L. and Pulkkinen, L. (2005). Age of onset of drinking and the use of alcohol in adulthood: a follow-up study from age 8–42 for females and males. *Addiction, 100*, 652–661.

Sampson, R.J. en Laub, J. (1993). Crime in the Making – Pathways and Turning Points through Life., Cambridge, Massachusetts, Harvard University Press.

Tangney, J.P, Baumeister, R.F. & Boone, A.L. (2004) High Self-Control Predicts Good Adjustment, Less Pathology, Better Grades, and Interpersonal Success. In: Journal of Personality. Volume 72, Issue 2, p. 271–324.

Trimbos Instituut. (2007).*Nationale Drug Monitor Jaarbericht NDM 2007*. Utrecht.

Unger, K.V. and Pardee, R. (2002). Outcome measures across program sites for postsecondary supported education programs. *Psychiatric Rehabilitation Journal, 25*, 299–303.

Verdurmen, J.E.E., Ketelaars, A.P.M. and Laar, van M.W. (2005). The Netherlands National Drug Monitor, Fact Sheet Drug Policy. Utrecht, The Netherlands: Trimbos Institute.

Wikström, P.H. & Butterworth, D.A. (2006). Adolescent crime. Individual differences and life-styles. Devon: Willan Publishing.

Chapter 6
Social Responses to Offending

Dirk Enzmann

Social responses to criminal offending were measured in the ISRD-2 survey in three different ways: (a) by asking victims of robbery, assault, or theft whether (and how many of) the offenses experienced in the last year became known to the police, (b) by asking offenders who reported having committed a certain offense during life-time whether they were detected the last time, and if yes, by whom (parents, teachers, police, and/or someone else); (c) by asking offenders additionally, whether they were punished the last time they committed a certain offense.

Reporting to the police, detection, and punishment are different indicators and aspects of social control. An analysis of reporting to the police shows which proportion of crime that actually happened finds its way into official police statistics and how factors influencing the decision to report may distort our view on crime. An analysis of detection turns the focus from victims to offenders and may show how different agents of social control perceive deviant behavior of their children, students, or the youth differently, and how the perception of the stereotypical offender is biased. To investigate whether offenders are punished sheds some light on the quasi objective risk of offenders being sanctioned and at the same time indicates indirectly how far certain offenses are regarded as serious or deserving punishment.

The detection and the reporting of crime are part of the process of the "social production of crime" (Brownstein 2000). Estimates are that between 77 and 96% of officially registered crime first come to official notice through members of the public (victims, representatives of victimized organizations, witnesses) (Coleman and Moynihan 1996). Thus, even the bulk of police statistics results from activities of institutions of informal social control rather than of formal social control. This does not mean, however, that crime in itself is a fiction or purely socially constructed. The comparison of standardized victimization reports or of self-reported offending as assessed with the ISRD-2 questionnaire with the amount of victimizations

D. Enzmann (✉)
University of Hamburg, Hamburg, Germany
e-mail: dirk.enzmann@uni-hamburg.de

J. Junger-Tas et al., *The Many Faces of Youth Crime: Contrasting Theoretical Perspectives on Juvenile Delinquency across Countries and Cultures*,
DOI 10.1007/978-1-4419-9455-4_6,

reported to the police or with the proportion of offenses detected (also assessed in the ISRD-2 study) only makes sense under the assumption that the answers of the respondents reflect (more or less) a reality. This comparison can reveal not only *that* official statistics and our knowledge of crime are biased but also the direction of bias, estimates of its amount, and some of its causes.

The analyses are organized into three sections investigating (a) reporting victimization experiences to the police, (b) rates of detection of self-reported offending by different agents of social control, and (c) the punishment of self-reported offending. Some analysis will use aggregated data on the level of countries and will relate these data to data from external sources such as the European Sourcebook (Aebi et al. 2010), the International Crime Victims Survey (ICVS) (Van Dijk et al. 2007), or the World Values Surveys (WVS) (World Values Survey Association 2009).

6.1 Reporting of Victimizations to the Police

Two measures of reporting to the police are available: Reporting rates based on prevalences, i.e., the percentage of *victims* whose victimization experiences became known to the police, and reporting rates based on incidences, i.e., the percentage of *victimization experiences* that became known to the police.[1] Whereas the *prevalence* of reporting to the police can be related to characteristics of the respondents, which allows us to investigate how persons whose victimizations were reported (at least once) differ from those whose victimizations were never reported, the *incidence* of reporting to the police allows to estimate how much of the *volume* of crime that actually happened (as told to us in the questionnaire) became known to the police. The latter can help to (re)interpret official crime statistics, especially when comparing countries, because the volume of crimes reported determines the major part of officially registered crime.

The estimation of the incidence-based reporting rate as a measure of the volume of crime reported is difficult because it rests upon two estimates of incidences: The incidence of victimization and the incidence of reporting. Incidence variables, however, have two problems. Because open response questions are asked, respondents can give fantastic and extremely improbable answers, especially if they do not take the survey seriously. Additionally, respondents who find it difficult to remember the number of events may give estimates that are too high (e.g., "30," when asked how many of the experiences of robbery during the last year were reported to the police). In this case it is likely that an event occurred frequently, although its frequency is questionable. Therefore, before calculating incidence-based reporting rates, the incidence measures have been adjusted by eliminating

[1] The questionnaire item asked "How many times was the incident reported to the police?" It is understood that respondents indicated how many of the incidents were reported.

extremely improbable answers (incidences of victimizations of robbery, assault, and theft: more than twice per week; incidences of reporting: more than weekly; concerning victimizations and reporting of bullying the thresholds were daily and weekly, respectively) in a first step, and by adjusting outlying values in a second step. This was accomplished by employing the following procedure separately for each country: Outliers are identified by fitting the empirical distribution of incidences (counts) to a negative binomial distribution with mean and overdispersion parameter estimated from the data. Values with an expected frequency of less than 1 are classified as outliers. Subsequently, outliers are replaced by random draws from the same negative binomial distribution under the restriction that they are higher than a minimum value that is normatively considered as being "frequent" (victimization and reporting of robbery: 4 times/year; victimization and reporting of assault or theft: 6 times/year; victimization of bullying: 12 times/year; reporting of bullying: 6 times/year). To preserve the rank order of cases, outliers sorted by size are replaced by random values sorted by size. Thus, replacements are guaranteed to be higher than the normatively fixed threshold of "frequent" events and are drawn from a distribution similar to the empirical distribution. Although replacement values are unlikely to be outliers, this is not precluded. The adjustment procedure results in estimates of incidence-based reporting rates that are unaffected by highly improbable and unlikely values and thus much more stable and reliable than unadjusted values.

Incidence-based reporting rates of all countries (grouped by country clusters) are shown in Table 6.1. Although victimization due to bullying (and the respective reporting rates) was also investigated (see Chap. 4), it will not be presented in greater detail because it is not considered to be a criminal offense. To achieve a bigger sample size and thus more stable estimates, data of the total samples (not only large and medium-sized cities) have been used. Even then, in some countries the number of cases (victims) is small, ranging from a minimum of 7 (Iceland) and 22 (Armenia) for robbery to a maximum of 815 (Switzerland) and 925 (Germany) for personal theft. Consequently, some of the 95% confidence intervals (CI) are rather wide.[2]

Results show that incidence-based reporting rates are rather low and that there is considerable variability of reporting rates across countries. Concerning robbery (weighted total reporting rate = 12.1%, 95% CI = 10.9–13.5), the lowest rates are found in Aruba (1.3%), Armenia (3.3%), Cyprus (4.8%), and Denmark (5.9%); the highest in Suriname (35.0%), followed by Portugal (21.1%), Italy (20.8%), and The Netherlands (19.6%).

The reporting rates concerning assault are similar (weighted total rate = 12.2%, 95% CI = 10.9–13.5), the variability a bit smaller. The lowest rates are found in Iceland (2.1%), Portugal (2.2%), Hungary (2.6%), and Armenia (3.6%); the highest in Suriname (34.2%), followed by Austria (20.7%), Cyprus (17.2%), and Aruba (16.7%).

[2] Because the base of the reporting rates are incidences of victimization *events* (not victims), deriving the sampling distribution of the reporting rates is difficult. Therefore, the 95% CIs were estimated by employing a bootstrap procedure (10,000 replications; bias-corrected and accelerated method).

Table 6.1 Reporting rates of victimizations

	Robbery				Assault				Theft			
	%	95% CI		*n*	%	95% CI		*n*	%	95% CI		*n*
USA	7.4	3.8	13.3	97	11.4	6.4	18.8	92	8.4	6.6	10.6	678
Ireland	8.1	3.7	14.7	73	9.6	4.4	17.5	55	6.3	4.4	8.7	339
Iceland	8.3	0.0	27.8	7	2.1	0.0	13.9	22	4.7	2.3	8.4	110
Denmark	5.9	2.1	12.9	53	7.0	2.9	14.5	48	6.7	4.3	9.9	254
Norway	9.7	3.5	25.8	41	9.5	4.6	16.9	55	9.4	6.9	12.7	359
Sweden	16.8	9.5	26.7	56	9.4	3.8	19.5	49	16.4	13.4	19.8	497
Finland	6.5	2.4	13.5	48	15.2	5.7	32.5	32	21.8	17.0	27.0	199
The Netherlands	19.6	11.9	33.3	67	13.4	8.3	20.6	104	18.6	15.6	22.1	461
Austria	12.9	7.4	20.9	79	20.7	13.8	29.0	114	15.8	13.2	18.8	650
Germany	12.8	8.4	18.8	132	10.0	6.5	15.5	198	10.3	8.5	12.5	925
Switzerland	12.4	6.8	21.3	84	12.1	7.2	19.3	86	17.5	15.2	19.8	815
France	19.1	12.3	27.3	71	13.6	8.7	19.8	102	11.6	8.5	15.4	324
Belgium	12.0	5.7	25.7	59	16.3	7.4	37.7	63	8.8	6.6	11.6	408
Portugal	21.1	15.3	29.2	143	2.2	0.0	12.2	33	14.3	10.8	18.7	298
Cyprus	4.8	1.4	13.7	36	17.2	5.9	45.0	60	10.8	7.9	14.6	279
Italy	20.8	14.3	29.3	108	13.7	7.8	25.0	140	16.0	13.5	19.0	765
Spain	10.4	6.0	17.0	109	13.8	5.6	33.3	56	15.2	11.2	20.5	242

NL Antilles	15.6	8.8	25.5	73	14.0	9.1	21.4	112	7.5	5.3	10.8	424
Aruba	1.7	0.0	6.7	33	16.7	6.8	33.3	30	9.5	6.2	14.0	200
Suriname	35.0	26.3	45.3	108	34.2	25.1	45.6	119	28.0	23.3	33.3	370
Venezuela	7.5	4.4	11.9	142	15.1	8.5	28.5	71	7.6	5.7	10.2	494
Estonia	11.3	6.9	18.0	120	10.5	6.3	16.9	130	14.2	11.0	18.8	486
Lithuania	12.7	8.3	18.6	127	10.3	3.8	21.9	46	8.8	5.8	14.5	251
Poland	14.0	8.1	22.2	79	13.9	7.3	26.8	76	21.8	16.9	27.3	213
Czech Republic	8.5	4.3	16.2	93	13.3	7.0	24.4	80	7.2	5.5	9.9	568
Hungary	17.1	11.0	25.0	85	2.6	1.0	5.9	125	9.9	7.7	12.9	484
Slovenia	11.1	6.8	16.9	102	7.3	3.4	13.8	126	11.1	8.8	13.9	602
Bosnia-Herzegovina	11.5	7.4	16.7	126	11.0	6.1	18.1	81	9.6	6.9	13.1	312
Russia	15.6	10.8	21.7	148	14.1	9.3	20.8	145	17.5	13.3	22.6	265
Armenia	3.3	0.0	17.1	22	3.6	0.9	8.6	89	2.4	1.0	4.8	173

Notes: Based on incidences; outliers adjusted

The reporting rates of theft are somewhat smaller (weighted total rate = 11.8%, 95% CI = 11.2–12.4), the variability is somewhat smaller, too. The lowest rates are found in Armenia (2.4%), Iceland (4.7%), Ireland (6.3%), and Denmark (6.7%); the highest again in Suriname (28.0%), followed by Poland and Finland (21.8%), and The Netherlands (18.6%).

It is commonplace to criminologists that only a fraction of offenses committed or victimizations experienced will be reported to the police. The data show that with respect to juvenile victims this fraction is rather small. The dark figure, i.e., the percentage of seventh to ninth grade juveniles' victimizations of robbery, assault, and theft not known to the police, is 88% across countries. However, when comparing the extent of crime across countries, the size of the dark figure is less important than its variability: The less one can assume the dark figure to be constant across place (or time), the less official crime statistics are suitable for comparisons.

The variability of reporting rates across countries is best illustrated combining all three offenses (Fig. 6.1). With the exception of Armenia and Suriname (both countries are clearly outliers whose reporting rates are far beyond the rates found in other countries), in each country cluster there is some overlap of the 95% confidence intervals. However, there are significant differences[3] of reporting rates within the clusters, especially within the clusters of Northern and Western European countries, but also within the cluster of the Post-Socialist countries.

For example, within the Northern European countries the rates of Iceland and Denmark are significantly lower than the rates of Sweden and Finland. Within the Western European countries, the rates of The Netherlands, Austria, and Switzerland are significantly higher than the rates of Germany and Belgium. Comparing the rates of the Post-Socialist countries (excluding Armenia), the rates in Poland and Russia are significantly higher than the rates of the Czech Republic, Hungary, Slovenia, or Bosnia-Herzegovina.

More important than the significance is the size of the differences (if significant) and its consequences for the volume of crime that becomes known to the police in comparison to the volume that did actually happen (as reported to us in the questionnaire): The overall reporting rate of Finland is nearly 3 times higher than the rate of Denmark, the rate of The Netherlands is nearly twice as high than the rate of Belgium, and the rate of Poland is more than twice as high than the rate of the Czech Republic.

As a consequence, the rank order of countries with respect to the volume of crime reported to the police corresponds only roughly to the rank order with respect to the volume of crime experienced. On the level of countries, the correlation (Spearman's ρ) between the number of reported crimes per juvenile and the number of victimizations experienced per juvenile is only moderately high ($\rho = 0.44$, $p = 0.014$); the exclusion of the outliers Armenia and Suriname does not change this

[3] If two CI error bars overlap by not more than half of the average arm length, the difference of reporting rates can be considered to be statistically significant at $p < 0.05$ (see Cumming and Finch 2005).

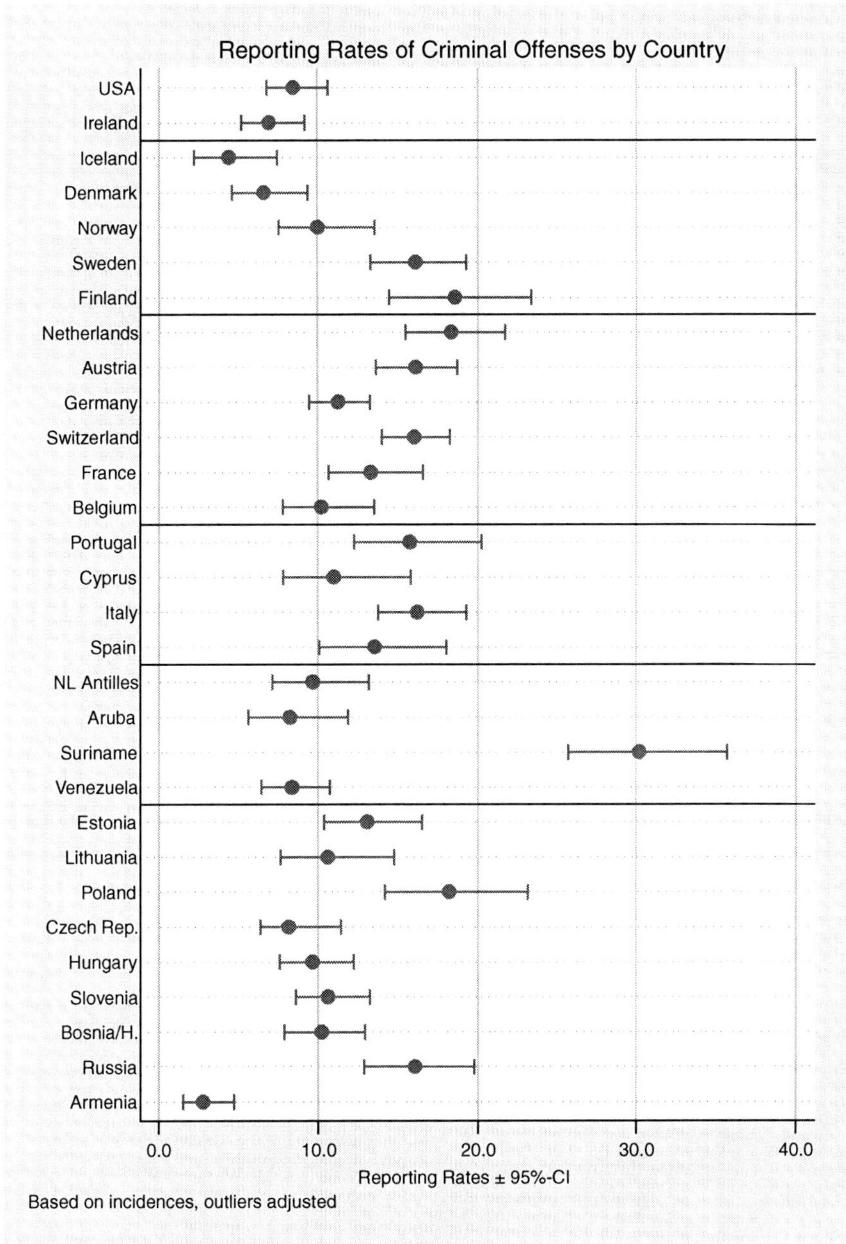

Fig. 6.1 Reporting rates of victimizations (criminal offenses total)

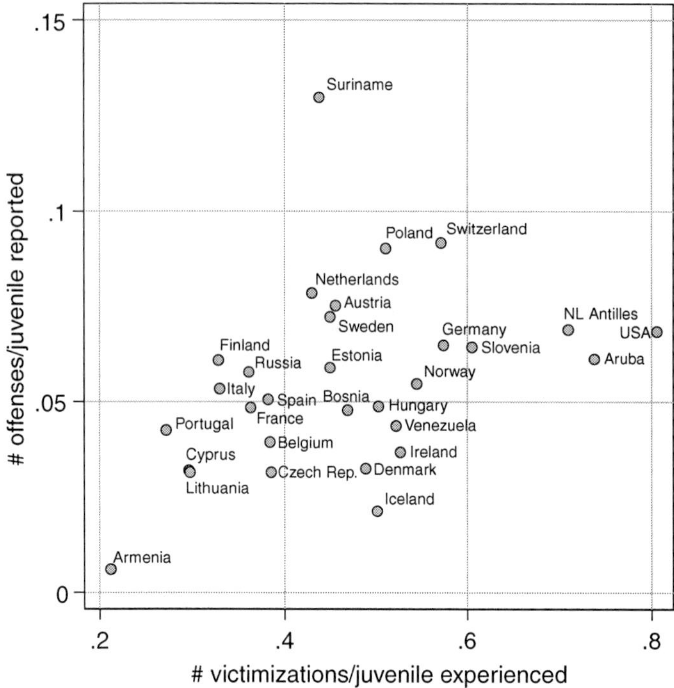

Fig. 6.2 Experienced vs. reported offenses per juvenile by country

(ρ=0.43, p=0.022). As Fig. 6.2 illustrates, if police statistics would record the *reported* victimization experiences of juveniles with respect to robbery, assault, and theft as investigated in the ISRD-2 studies, official statistics would reflect the rank order of the actual volume of crime only poorly: Whereas the actual volume of crime in the United States and Finland is vastly different (80.6/100 vs. 32.8/100), the volume of reported crimes is quite similar (6.8/100 vs. 6.1/100). On the other hand, the volume of crime experienced in Iceland and Poland is very similar (50.2/100 vs. 51.1/100), whereas the volume of reported crime is vastly different (2.1/100 vs. 9.0/100). This demonstrates that extreme caution is necessary when comparing the volume of crime based on official police statistics internationally, at least with respect to juveniles as victims.

Despite the considerable variability of reporting rates within country clusters, there are also significant differences between country clusters (Fig. 6.3). As to robbery, the reporting rates of the Anglo-Saxon, Northern European, and Latin American countries are significantly lower and about half the rates of the Northern European and Mediterranean European countries. The outlying countries Suriname and Armenia are excluded; including them changes the reporting rate of the Latin American cluster from 6.8 to 11.3% and the rate of the Post-Socialist countries from 12.9 to 12.7%. Similarly, as to personal theft the reporting rates of the Western European and Mediterranean European countries are significantly higher than

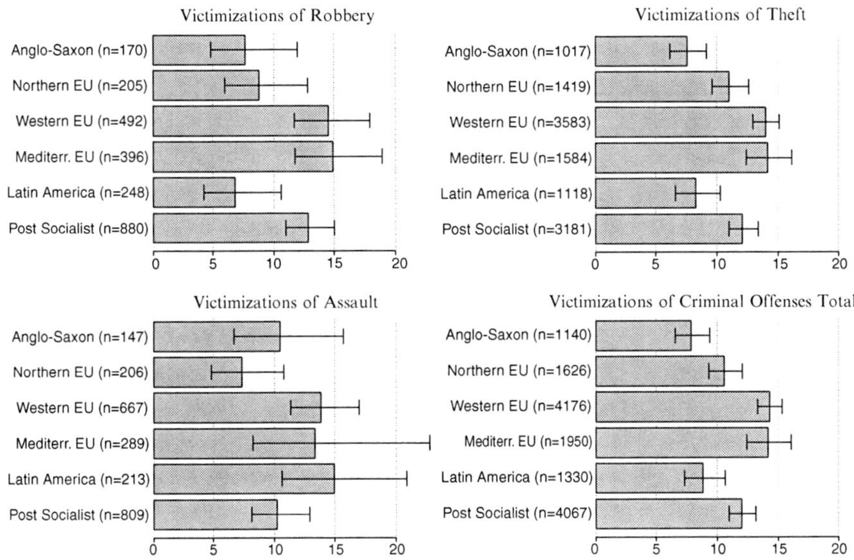

Fig. 6.3 Reporting rates based on incidences by country clusters. *Notes*: Weighted data, outliers adapted; total sample; excluding Armenia and Suriname; percentages and 95% confidence intervals

the rates of the Northern European countries. Again, the reporting rates of the Anglo-Saxon and Latin American countries are the lowest.[4] The overall pattern changes with respect to assault: As to this offense, the Latin American countries belong to those with the highest reporting rates, and the rates of the Northern European countries are the lowest.[5] This shows that the profile of reporting rates across country clusters is offense-specific. We know that an important factor determining whether a victimization will be reported or not is the (subjectively experienced) seriousness of the offense. One explanation might be that the average assault is actually more severe in the Latin American countries than in the Northern European countries. Although in Europe the sensitivity to violence is increasing while the seriousness of violent acts committed seems to decrease (Enzmann and Podana 2010), assaults in Latin American countries may be more severe.

In this context, it is interesting to note that more than 99% of victimizations of bullying (that is not considered to be a criminal offense) is *not* reported to the police (weighted incidence-based reporting rate across all countries=0.9%, 95% CI=0.8–1.2, n=7,382). The highest rate is found in Latin American countries (1.9%, 95%

---

[4]Including Suriname and Armenia, the reporting rates of the Latin American and post socialist countries change from 8.3 and 12.1 to 11.6 and 11.5%, respectively.

[5]Including Suriname and Armenia, the reporting rates of the Latin American and post socialist countries change from 15.0 and 10.3 to 19.7 and 9.7%, respectively.

Table 6.2 Reporting rates by country clusters (large and medium-sized cities)

	Based on prevalences				Based on incidences			
	%	95% CI		*n*	%	95% CI		*n*
Robbery								
Anglo-Saxon	13.0	7.4	21.8	132	8.4	5.0	13.4	127
Northern EU	15.9	11.1	22.4	194	9.3	6.4	14.0	192
Western EU	23.0	19.0	27.6	379	14.4	11.1	18.7	372
Mediterranean EU	24.8	17.3	34.2	237	19.8	14.4	27.5	233
Latin America[a]	10.9	7.6	15.5	232	6.6	4.1	10.1	226
Post-Socialist[b]	23.7	19.7	28.3	559	16.3	13.4	19.7	548
Total	*20.7*	*18.3*	*23.3*	*1,733*	*13.7*	*12.0*	*15.5*	*1,698*
Assault								
Anglo-Saxon	16.5	9.3	27.5	100	10.5	5.9	17.0	99
Northern EU	13.4	9.1	19.2	184	7.1	4.5	10.7	182
Western EU	20.3	16.6	24.6	455	12.3	9.7	15.5	448
Mediterranean EU	12.5	7.2	20.7	169	10.0	5.7	17.4	166
Latin America[a]	20.5	15.1	27.2	204	15.2	10.6	21.3	191
Post-Socialist[b]	12.8	9.5	17.1	380	9.7	6.8	14.0	373
Total	*15.8*	*13.8*	*18.1*	*1,492*	*10.7*	*9.1*	*12.5*	*1,459*
Theft								
Anglo-Saxon	13.2	10.5	16.3	631	8.9	6.9	11.2	617
Northern EU	17.3	15.3	19.6	1,278	10.8	9.4	12.4	1,250
Western EU	19.4	17.7	21.2	2,369	13.4	12.1	14.8	2,322
Mediterranean EU	19.4	15.8	23.5	1,016	14.8	12.2	17.8	1,007
Latin America[a]	11.2	9.4	13.2	1,028	7.9	6.2	9.8	990
Post-Socialist[b]	18.1	15.7	20.6	1,448	13.8	12.0	16.0	1,418
Total	*17.0*	*16.0*	*18.1*	*7,770*	*11.9*	*11.2*	*12.7*	*7,604*
Criminal offenses total								
Anglo-Saxon	14.4	11.7	17.6	712	9.0	7.2	11.1	697
Northern EU	17.5	15.5	19.6	1,464	10.5	9.2	12.1	1,436
Western EU	21.1	19.5	22.8	2,782	13.6	12.4	15.0	2,737
Mediterranean EU	19.9	16.4	23.9	1,223	15.6	12.9	18.9	1,213
Latin America[a]	13.3	11.5	15.3	1,219	8.5	7.1	10.3	1,173
Post-Socialist[b]	19.2	16.9	21.8	1,938	13.8	12.2	15.6	1,904
Total	*18.2*	*17.2*	*19.3*	*9,338*	*12.2*	*11.5*	*13.0*	*9,160*

Notes: Weighted data; incidences: outliers adjusted
[a]Excluding Suriname
[b]Excluding Armenia

CI = 1.1–2.9, $n=657$)[6] and the lowest in the Northern European countries (0.6%, 95% CI = 0.2–1.7, $n=673$).

Table 6.2 displays prevalence and incidence-based reporting rates of the three criminal offenses by country clusters for large and medium-sized cities only. The incidence-based reporting rates of large and medium-sized cities differ not much

[6]Excluding Suriname: 1.4%, 95% CI = 0.8–2.4, $n=522$.

from the rates of the total samples. In large and medium-sized cities, reporting rates of robbery are somewhat higher and the reporting rates of assault are somewhat lower than the total sample rates (robbery: 13.7% vs. 11.5%, assault: 10.7% vs. 11.5%).[7]

Prevalence-based reporting rates are on average about 50% higher than rates based on incidences (18.2% of victims vs. 12.2% of victimization events) because some victims experience more than one victimization and even victims who do report victimization experiences to the police do not report each event that happens to them.

Whether juveniles report a victimization experience to the police depends on several factors. The questionnaire did not ask for reasons of reporting or not reporting. However, from other studies we know that the frequency of reporting is related to the type of offense and that the most important factor for (not) reporting is its seriousness (Van Kesteren et al. 2000, p. 65 ff); other possible factors are the frequency of victimization, the level of familiarity between victim and offender, or the degree of confidence in the police. We investigate this issue further by using logistic regression analyses to predict the prevalence of reporting victimizations. To achieve maximum sample size analyses are based on the total sample, and robbery and theft are combined into the category "property offenses." Reporting of victimizations of assault, however, is investigated separately because especially among juveniles an overlap of offender and victim roles within one person – which should affect the willingness to report such events to the police – is more likely.

Apart from "membership of a country to one of the six country clusters" and the "gender of the victim" that both serve as controls, the model explores seven predictors:

- *City size*: Compared to smaller cities life in big cities is characterized by more anonymity and less integrated local networks and social bonds that would allow to solve conflicts informally. As a consequence, the size of a city is assumed to be related to higher rates of reporting to the police. A nominal variable distinguishes small towns (less than 100,000 inhabitants), medium-sized cities (100,000 to less than 300,000 inhabitants), and large cities (300,000 inhabitants and more). A fourth category distinguishes samples with mixed or unknown city sizes of those countries that opted for national instead of city-based samples.
- *Grade*: It is assumed that with growing age (and thus grade) the reporting rates should increase because older students tend to experience more severe offenses if they become a victim, tend to have more experience of reporting to the police, and are expected to have developed more autonomy that allows them to decide to report events to the police.
- *Native status*: First or second generation migrants are expected to be more reluctant to report victimization events to the police than natives.

[7]Including Suriname and Armenia: Robbery: 14.1% vs. 12.1%, assault: 11.4% vs. 12.2%.

- *Frequency of victimizations*: The more often (during the last year) a juvenile has become victim of an offense the more likely at least one of the victimizations should have been reported to the police. The frequency of victimization is categorized into "once," "2–4 times," and "5 times and more."
- *Delinquent peers*: Juveniles who are member of a delinquent peer group should be more reluctant to contact the police when victimized. Instead, juveniles with many delinquent friends are expected to consider notifying the police as inappropriate and to solve things by themselves.
- *Offender status*: Depending on the type of offense, there is a considerable victim–offender overlap: The odds of becoming a victim of property offenses are 2.3-fold higher for offenders of property offenses as compared to nonoffenders (95% CI=2.2–2.5) whereas the odds ratio for victimization of assault comparing offenders and nonoffenders is 3.2 (95% CI=2.9–3.4). It is conceivable that reporting rates of offenders and nonoffenders are different. Additionally, the probability that a victimization of an offender becomes known to the police might be increased for those whose last offense has been detected by the police compared to those whose last offense went undetected. A three category variable distinguishes nonoffenders from offenders whose last offense was not detected by the police and from offenders whose last offense was detected.
- *Going out at night*: A three category variable distinguishes juveniles who "never" go out at night from those who go out at night "1–4 times/week" or who go out "5–7 times/week." Going out at night belongs to a risky life style that increases the probability of victimization. Because the frequency of victimization is already a variable of the model, a positive net effect of reporting to the police related to going out at night could be due to intensified surveillance or presence of police at localities where youths tend to spend the night.

Table 6.3 shows the results of two multiple regression models to predict whether the juvenile or somebody else reported a victimization of a property offense or of an assault to the police that happened to the juvenile during the last year. Only three of the nine predictors contribute significantly to differences in the prevalence of reporting victimizations of assault, whereas nearly all predictors contribute significantly to differences in the reporting rate of property offenses. This discrepancy is predominantly due to the much smaller sample size with regard to victims of assault, only partly also due to smaller effect sizes (odds ratios). Most remarkable are differences concerning the effects of grade and the offender status of the victims. As to assault the increase of reporting rates with grade is stronger than with respect to property offenses (when controlling for all other predictor variables in the model so that any differences are most likely due to differences in grade alone): Whereas the predicted prevalence of reporting victimizations of property offenses increases from 15.5 and 17.5 to 19.7% (grade 7, grade 8, and grade 9), the increase is 11.7, 16.4, and 19.8% as to victimizations of assault. This may possibly be explained by larger changes in the (subjective) seriousness of the offense when comparing assaults to robbery or theft among younger and older victims. The explanation fits to the observation that reporting rates of adults are higher although the frequency of victimization

Table 6.3 Prediction (logistic regression) of the prevalence of reporting victimizations to the police

	Reporting property offenses		Reporting assault	
	Odds ratio	z	Odds ratio	z
Country cluster (base = Anglo-Saxon)	$\chi^2_{(5)} = 74.9$***		$\chi^2_{(5)} = 38.5$***	
Northern EU	1.60	3.73***	0.78	−0.74
Western EU	2.06	6.56***	1.20	0.70
Mediterranean EU	1.77	4.78***	0.80	−0.72
Latin America	1.62	3.93***	1.99	2.45*
Post-Socialist	1.32	2.40*	0.68	−1.39
City size (base = small towns)	$\chi^2_{(3)} = 22.2$***		$\chi^2_{(3)} = 3.3$	
Mixed/unknown	1.32	3.40***	1.40	1.69+
Medium cities	1.10	1.25	1.06	0.32
Large cities	1.32	4.11***	1.18	1.02
Gender (base = female)				
Male	1.23	4.23***	1.10	0.78
Grade (base = grade 7)	$\chi^2_{(2)} = 25.0$***		$\chi^2_{(2)} = 19.0$***	
Grade 8	1.16	2.49*	1.49	2.66**
Grade 9	1.34	4.99***	1.90	4.36***
Native status (base = migrant)				
Native	1.18	3.00**	0.91	−0.71
Frequency victimizations (base = once)	$\chi^2_{(2)} = 19.7$***		$\chi^2_{(2)} = 1.4$	
2–4 Times	1.18	3.26**	1.04	0.25
5+ Times	1.41	3.64***	1.30	1.17
Delinquent peers (base = no)				
Yes	0.85	−3.17**	0.84	−1.28
Offender last year (base = no)	$\chi^2_{(2)} = 0.9$		$\chi^2_{(2)} = 6.4$*	
Yes, not detected	1.00	0.01	0.88	−0.89
Yes, detected	1.11	0.92	1.44	1.87+
Going out at night (base = never)	$\chi^2_{(2)} = 13.2$**		$\chi^2_{(2)} = 1.3$	
1–4 Times/week	1.16	2.27*	1.12	0.70
5–7 Times/week	1.34	3.63***	1.24	1.15
χ^2 (df)	183.6 (19)***		74.9 (19)***	
n	12,788		2,332	

Notes: Unweighted data, total sample; +$p < 0.10$, *$p < 0.05$, **$p < 0.01$, ***$p < 0.001$

is less (cp. van Dijk et al. 2007). The second remarkable difference concerning the type of offense is the significantly higher prevalence of reporting victimizations of assault among offenders who were detected by the police the last time they themselves committed an assault (or group fight) as opposed to offenders whose last self-reported assault (or group fight) was not detected. The predicted prevalence rate of reporting is 21.1% among detected offenders compared to 14.3% among nondetected offenders ($\chi^2_{(1)} = 6.4$, $p = 0.012$). With respect to victims of property offenses, this difference is much smaller and not significant (detected offenders: 19.0%, not detected offenders: 17.5%; $\chi^2_{(1)} = 0.8$, $p = 0.362$). The victim–offender overlap *itself* is not a likely explanation because the reporting rates of victims only and those victims who also committed offenses but were *not* detected by the police are the same. The higher predicted reporting rate of offenders of assault detected by the police may possibly be explained by the fact that assaults more often than acts of robbery or theft occur among juveniles known to each other, and that police is more often mobilized to intervene when assaults happen in the public.

With respect to the prevalence of reporting property offenses to the police, results show that observed differences between country clusters cannot be explained by differences in city size, differences in the composition of the samples as to gender, grade, or native status, differences in the frequency of victimizations, contact with delinquent peers, offender status, or differences in life style behavior such as the frequency of going out at night. Prevalence rates of reporting are highest in Western European and Mediterranean countries (pred. = 21.4 and 19.0%) and lowest in Post-Socialist and Anglo-Saxon countries (pred. = 14.9 and 11.7%). The predicted prevalence rate of the Northern European countries is 17.5% (unweighted data). Excluding Armenia and Suriname, the results do not change substantially, although the predicted probability of the Post-Socialist countries is somewhat higher (15.8%) and decreases substantially in the Latin American cluster (from 17.7 to 11.0%).

As expected, the predicted reporting rates are higher in large cities as opposed to small towns (pred. = 19.1% vs. 15.1%; $\chi^2_{(1)} = 5.6$, $p = 0.018$). The higher reporting rates in large cities will exaggerate the observed higher victimization rate of large cities as opposed to small towns (see Chap. 4) in official police statistics. Victimizations of males are more likely to be reported to the police than victimizations of females (pred. = 18.9% vs. 16.0%), the difference cannot be explained by the higher frequency of victimizations of males (see Chap. 4) or differences in contacts to delinquent peers, own offender status, or the frequency of going out at night. Results show that migrants tend to report victimizations of robbery or theft less likely than natives (pred. = 15.9% vs. 18.2%). There are reasons to assume that migrants have less confidence in the police than natives, especially in view of tense relationships between migrants and the police in Western countries (e.g., France). In line with expectations, the frequency of victimization is an important factor that increases the probability that at least one of the events will be reported to the police (pred.: 16.5, 18.9, and 21.7% at one, two to four, and five or more victimizations last year, respectively). This increase shows that it is unlikely that the more frequent victimizations are less severe (as one could assume) because the most important factor for the decision to report to the police is the severity of the victimization. Juveniles who know delinquent peers or are member of a delinquent peer group tend to report victimization experiences less likely (pred. = 18.8% vs. 16.4% of juveniles without vs. with delinquent friends). Finally, with respect to robbery and theft, juveniles who go out more frequently at night are more likely to report victimizations to the police (pred.: 15.6, 17.6, and 19.7% of juveniles who go out never, 1–4 times, and 4–7 times/week). One should note that this increase is independent of the frequency of victimizations.

Overall, most of the factors that are associated with higher reporting rates of property offenses are also factors that increase the likelihood of victimization (see

Chap. 4). Four factors, namely male sex, higher age, larger city size, and high frequency of going out at night, are associated with an increased risk of victimization. At the same time, these four factors are also associated with higher reporting rates. A model calculation shows this: Reporting rates of older (grade 9) male juveniles living in large cities and going out at night more than 4 times/week are more than twice as high than the rates of younger (grade 7) females living in small towns and never going out at night (pred. = 25.4% vs. 11.7%). In effect, if official police statistics show higher victimization rates associated with the four factors mentioned, the picture of crime risks is not wrong but most certainly exaggerated. For completeness, one should note that some factors (Anglo-Saxon vs. Northern European country cluster, migration background vs. being native born, knowing delinquent peers) which are associated with higher victimization risks of property offenses are at the same time associated with lower reporting rates, thus playing down the risks of crime. However, factors producing an exaggeration are dominant.

The findings not only emphasize the well known fact that extreme caution is necessary when interpreting official police statistics but also show the direction of bias we may expect when comparing official victimization rates of certain groups. Nevertheless, the data do not explain how the considerable differences in reporting rates between countries come about: Even after controlling for factors displayed in Table 6.3 that might be interpreted as composition effects on the individual level there is still significant variability on the level of countries which is shown by an intraclass correlation of $\rho_{icc} = 0.049$ ($p = 0.001$). The issue remains of specifying context effects that may explain differences between countries. One route to an answer may be to examine whether local or national level indicators can explain the variability of reporting rates between countries. One might expect that police strength (sworn police officers per capita) is positively associated with reporting rates (compare Levitt 1998). However, using police per capita data of the European Sourcebook (Aebi et al. 2010), Spearman's rank correlation between police strength and incidence-based reporting rates of the ISRD-2 data on the level of countries is not significant ($\rho = -0.019$, $p = 0.929$, $n = 24$). The lack of correspondence between police strength and reporting behavior cannot be explained by the negative relationship found when relating police strength to general confidence of the public in the police: Using WVS data (World Values Survey Association 2009), the correlation is significant and comparatively high ($\rho = -0.553$, $p = 0.006$, $n = 23$). Examples of countries with a low rate of sworn police officers per capita and high confidence in the police are Denmark and Finland, a counter example of high rate of sworn police officers and low confidence in the police is Russia. The correlation of incidence-based reporting rates and confidence in the police, however, is not significant ($\rho = 0.077$, $p = 0.709$, $n = 26$). It seems as if ISRD-2 data are not correlated on the level of countries with data from other sources (European Sourcebook or WVS data). But this does not apply to all variables. For example, increased police strength (European Sourcebook) is associated with fewer victimizations per capita (ISRD-2 data) on the level of countries ($\rho = -0.455$, $p = 0.026$, $n = 24$). However, the correlation between the number of victimizations per capita that is actually reported to the police and police strength is weaker and not significant ($\rho = -0.341$, $p = 0.102$, $n = 24$), indicating that the apparent effectiveness of police strength in reducing the actual incidence of victimizations, is somehow obscured in official statistics. Overall, these preliminary analyses of ecological correlations show that clearly more research is needed to explain the variability of reporting rates across countries.

The analyses of incidence and prevalence-based reporting rates across countries show that alternatives to official police statistics in form of victimization surveys are necessary. But when comparing the reporting rates of the ISRD-2 data to results of the International Crime Victims Survey (ICVS) and the European Survey on Crime and Safety (EU-ICS), it becomes apparent that surveys of the general population cannot be generalized to juveniles and are no substitute for special juvenile delinquency studies that include victimization experiences of youth. Analyses show that Spearman's rank correlations of ISRD-2 reporting rates and the ICVS/EU-ICS offense-specific reporting rates (past 5 years, 18–19 countries; van Dijk et al. 2007, pp. 263–266) are indeed positive but rather low and not significant (robbery: $\rho=0.28$, $p=0.248$; assault: $\rho=0.37$, $p=0.122$; theft: $\rho=0.37$, $p=0.129$). The lack of correspondence is also apparent from the fact that Denmark belongs to the three countries with lowest overall reporting rates in the ISRD-2 study and Poland to the three countries with highest overall reporting rates,[8] whereas in the ICVS/EU-ICS samples it is the reverse. This also illustrates – vice versa – the truism that results of the ISRD-2 data are valid only for youth and must not be generalized to the total population.

6.2 Detection of Offending

Detection rates seem to be the counterpart to reporting rates when shifting the perspective from victims to offenders. Detection rates, however, are not simply the complement to reporting rates for at least two reasons: (1) Whether reporting victimization experiences to the police will result in offenders actually being caught by the police depends on several factors that are reflected ultimately in the clearance ratio of police statistics (which in itself is chiefly based on crimes reported). The cross-national comparability and reasons for the diversity of clearance rates are discussed in Smit et al. (2004). Clearance rates (ratio of crimes solved by crimes recorded) of minor offenses – as predominantly experienced or committed by juveniles – are well below 50%, mostly less than 20% (Smit et al. 2004). (2) Whether or not respondents of the ISRD-2 survey indicate that their offending behavior was detected depends much more on social desirability than the answer to the question whether their victimization experience became known to the police, because the question of detection is asked only when a respondent admits having committed an offense.

[8] Comparing only countries from which data of both, the ISRD-2 survey and the ICVS/EU-ICS are available.

From the perspective of the offender, detection by the police is not the sole and perhaps not the most important risk. For the prevention of offending behavior, detection by other institutions such as parents or teachers may be equally or even more important. After all, in most cases detection by some other person is a precondition for detection by the police. Whether institutions of formal social control will know of crimes committed essentially depends on detection by institutions of informal social control. Therefore, overall detection rates of offenses (by parents, teachers, or the police) are expected to be higher than rates of reporting victimizations to the police. Additionally to the rates of detection by the police, the ISRD-2 study allows to investigate rates of detection by parents and teachers.

It is important to note that the ISRD-2 questionnaire asked (per offense) only whether *the last* offense committed was detected (and by whom). The last offense, however, can be treated as a sample of all offenses that is (at least formally) independent from the number of offenses committed. This allows an estimation of the objective risk of detection per offense category and per agent or institution of detection (informal: parents; semiformal: teachers; formal: police). Because it is not sure how to interpret detection "by someone else" (among others, "someone else" could be the victims, neutral bystanders, or peers), we will not investigate this mode of detection. For the most part, we will focus on the comparison of rates of detection by parents and by the police: Parents because they are the most important agency of socialization and therefore also of informal social control, police because this agency shows how much of criminal activity of youths will become known to institutions of formal social control.

Because the detection of an offense is a comparatively rare event and consequently the number of juveniles concerned is small, analyses are based on the total sample, not on large and medium-sized cities only. For the same reason, offenses and their respective detection rates are collapsed into five groups of offenses: *Minor violent* offenses (carrying a weapon, group fights), *serious violent* offenses (snatching, extortion, assault), *vandalism*, *shoplifting* (minor property offense), and *serious property* offenses (bicycle theft, burglary, car break, car theft). Total offenses will additionally include dealing in soft or hard drugs. A "total offense" detection rate describes the percentage of offenders who were found out when committing an offense the last time for at least 1 of the 12 offenses.

6.2.1 *Rates of Detection by Different Agents of Social Control*

Figures 6.4 and 6.5 show rates of detection by parents and by the police for offenses total by country. The rates are grouped by country cluster and sorted within clusters by rates of detection by parents. Overall, the rate of detection by parents is nearly twice the rate of detection by the police (21.4%, 95% CI=21.7–22.0 vs. 11.4%, 95% CI=10.9–12.0). Especially noteworthy is the fact that the rate of detection by parents varies considerably on the level of countries, ranging from a low rate of 6.7% (Denmark) to high rates of 32.3 and 32.8% (Finland and Aruba). Its variability

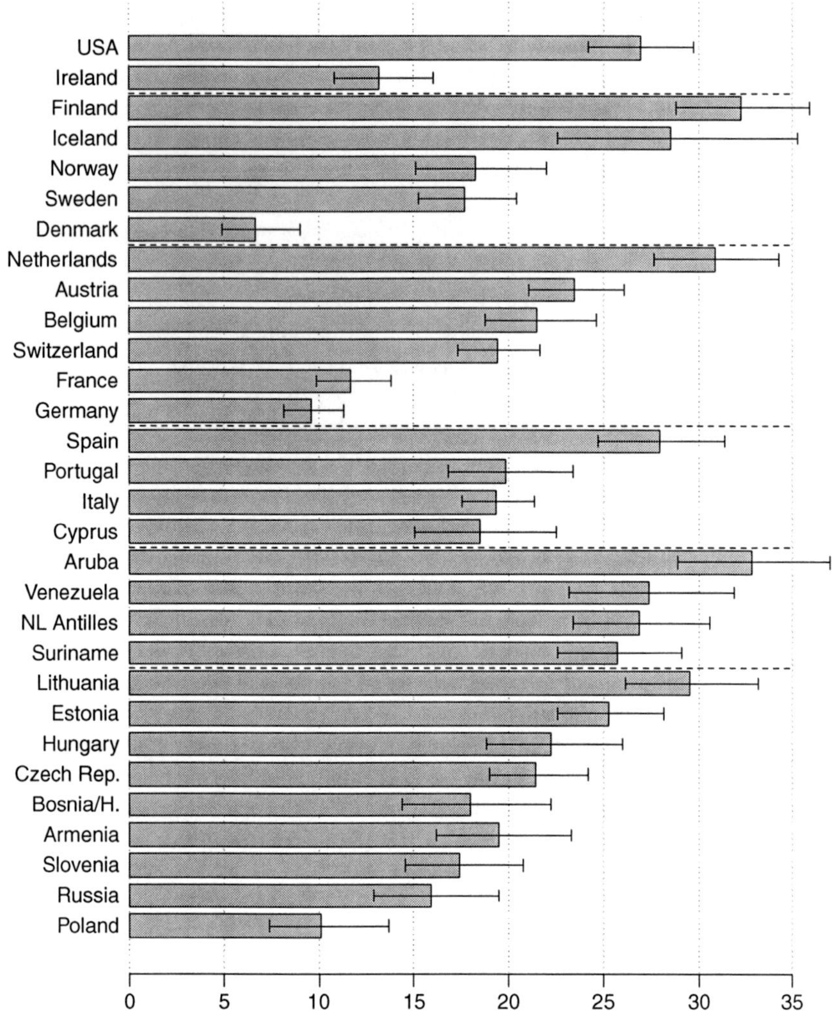

Fig. 6.4 Rates of detection by parents (offenses total). *Notes*: Percentages and 95% confidence intervals; n (total) = 23,468

is higher than the country level variability of rate of detection by the police, as shown by a significant intraclass correlation of the parental detection rate compared to a lower but still significant intraclass correlation of the police detection rate ($\rho_{icc}=0.055$, $p<0.001$ vs. $\rho_{icc}=0.034$, $p=0.001$). Additionally, on the country level there are significant differences of the rates of detection by parents within country clusters as shown by the 95% CIs in Fig. 6.4, whereas the within country cluster differences of the rates of detection by police are clearly less pronounced (Fig. 6.5).

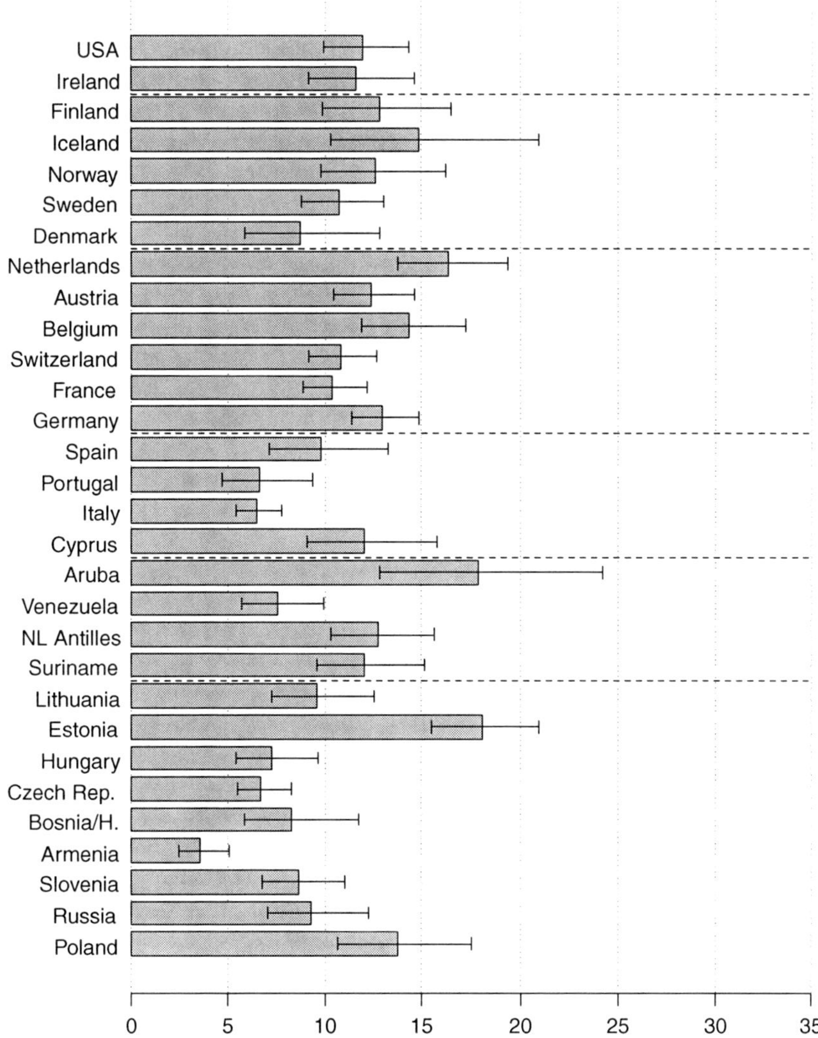

Fig. 6.5 Rates of detection by police (offenses total). *Notes*: Percentages and 95% confidence intervals; countries within clusters sorted by rates of detection by parents; *n* (total) = 23,470

As to detection by parents, the rates of Denmark, Germany, Poland, France, Ireland, Russia, and Slovenia belong to the lowest quartile of values, whereas the rates of Aruba, Finland, The Netherlands, Lithuania, Iceland, Spain, and Venezuela belong to the highest. The country cluster with the lowest average rate is the Anglo-Saxon cluster (18.8%, 95% CI = 17.0–20.9) followed by Western European (19.1%, 95% CI = 18.1–20.2), the Post-Socialist (20.3%, 95% CI = 19.2–21.4), the Mediterranean (21.5%, 95% CI = 20.1–23.1), and the Northern European cluster (21.7%, 95% CI = 19.9–23.7). The detection rate of the Latin American cluster is clearly the highest (28.7%, 95% CI=26.7–30.7). Although significant, the differences between country clusters are comparatively small (design-based $F_{(4.5,\ 14,559.4)}=18.2$, $p<0.001$).

Compared to the rates of detection by parents, the rank order of rates of detection by the police is somewhat different. Here, Armenia, Italy, Portugal, the Czech Republic, Hungary, Venezuela, and Bosnia-Herzegovina belong to the lowest quartile, whereas Estonia, Aruba, The Netherlands, Iceland, Belgium, Poland, and Germany belong to the highest. The cluster with the lowest police detection rate is the Mediterranean (8.4%, 95% CI=7.3–9.7), followed by the Post-Socialist (9.6%, 95% CI=8.8–10.4), the Anglo-Saxon (11.8%, 95% CI=10.0–13.7), the Northern European (12.1%, 95% CI=10.5–13.9), and the Western European cluster (12.9%, 95% CI=12.0–13.8). Again, the Latin American cluster shows the highest detection rate (13.5%, 95% CI=11.4–15.9). Compared to the rates of detection by parents, differences of police detection rates between country clusters are smaller (design-based $F_{(4.2,\ 13,476.3)}=7.2$, $p<0.001$).

The overall rate of detection by the police of 11.4% includes diverse types of offenses that differ in frequency, seriousness from the perspective of the victim, the public, or the law, visibility, and nature of victim–offender relationship – factors that contribute to the attention the offense attracts, the readiness to report to the police, and the likelihood of detection by police. As the first column of Table 6.4 shows, rates of detection by the police (and thus the objective risks of detection) differ considerably by offense type. At large, the rate of detection increases with the seriousness of the offense, the lowest detection rate is found for carrying a weapon (2.9%), the highest for car theft (17.9%). But detection also depends on the visibility or the victim–offender relationship as shown by the low detection rates of car break and drug dealing – the latter being a "victimless" offense. A comparison of the number of cases (i.e., the number of offenders) and detection rates shows that all in all the overall frequency of an offense is unrelated to the risk of detection. However, as it will be shown below, the latter is only true on the aggregate level of countries, not on the level of the offending juvenile.

The second and third pairs of columns of Table 6.4 confront the detection rates of only those countries that participated in both the ISRD-2 and the ISRD-1 study with results of the ISRD-1 study conducted about 15 years before (Junger-Tas et al. 2003).[9] Though the size of the detection rates and the rank orders of offenses with respect to their detection rates are similar when comparing the ten ISRD-2 countries selected here to the ISRD-2 countries total, the size of detection rates and especially the rank order of offenses of the ISRD-1 study differ considerably. Except for vandalism and burglary, the police detection rates of the ISRD-1 study are nearly twice the rates of the ISRD-2 study. Most likely the higher age of the respondents of the

[9] Despite differences of the design a comparison may be interesting. Countries participating in both studies and considered in Table 6.4 are Belgium, Finland, Germany, Ireland, Italy, The Netherlands, Portugal, Spain, Switzerland, and the United States. Data of the ISRD-1 study were collected in 1991 and 1992.

Table 6.4 Rate of detection by police (ISRD-2 and ISRD-1 studies)

	ISRD-2 total		ISRD-2 (ISRD-1 countries)		ISRD-1 total	
	%	*n*	%	*n*	%	*n*
Carrying a weapon	2.9	7,023	2.3	3,029	5.2	1,592
Snatching	3.8	1,670	3.3	860	8.5	129
Car break	4.6	1,551	4.3	802	8.8	354
Drug dealing	4.8	1,650	3.9	867	4.8	168
Bicycle theft	5.6	2,079	5.3	1,138	9.2	488
Shoplifting	6.5	10,678	6.5	5,110	12.1	2,417
Extortion	6.8	1,232	5.9	586	–	–
Vandalism	7.1	8,086	6.9	3,714	6.3	3,304
Group fight	10.0	12,066	10.0	5,432	16.4	1,883
Burglary	10.6	1,084	10.3	567	8.8	1,173
Assault	11.6	2,067	9.7	939	13.3	482
Car theft	17.9	604	20.8	282	35.8	179

Notes: Weighted data

ISRD-1 study (17.0 vs. 13.9 of the selected ISRD-2 countries) is responsible for this finding. All the more it is noteworthy that the detection rates of vandalism and burglary are higher in the ISRD-2 study – it is striking that these are the only offenses with a relatively small number of offenders as compared to the ISRD-1 study. Whether different crime prevention strategies are responsible for this is not clear.

The detection rates displayed in previous tables and figures are based on the total ISRD-2 samples without taking the city size into account. However, it is reasonable to assume that detection rates differ by the size of the cities. The factors that will determine the risk of detection in large cities vs. small towns are diverse and complex. On the one hand, the increased anonymity and cultural diversity of larger cities and their less integrated local networks and social bonds make detection of offenders by informal and formal agents of social control more difficult. At the same time, the readiness to solve conflicts informally or the ability to find informal ways of restitution will be reduced in larger cities, thus increasing the likelihood of notifying the police once an offense is detected. This is what we saw already with respect to rates of reporting victimizations to the police (Table 6.3). Whether the offender will be found out once an offense is detected (and reported) also depends on the offense: Whereas the likelihood of identifying the offender of snatching is rather low, the likelihood is very high in cases of shoplifting. Here, it is the policy of larger companies to immediately and unconditionally notify the police and to simultaneously transfer the offender to the police when reporting the offense.

Consequently, we find that differences in detection rates according to city size depend on the institution of social control as well as on the offense (Fig. 6.6): With respect to violent offenses the risk of detection by the police decreases with the size of the city, it clearly increases with respect to shoplifting. On the other hand, parents in larger cities detect a smaller proportion of the offense of their children than parents in smaller towns, showing that parental supervision and social control decrease with city size.

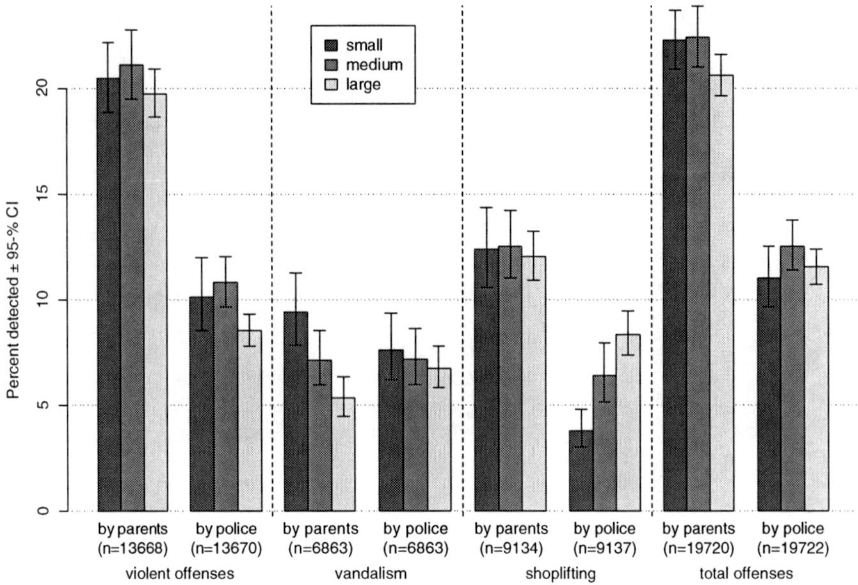

Fig. 6.6 Rates of detection by city size. *Notes*: Weighted data; total offenses including serious property offenses and drug dealing; *n* (small towns, total offenses) = 4,981; *n* (medium-sized cities, total offenses) = 5,810; *n* (large cities, total offenses) = 8,931

The risk of detection not only depends on the type of offense but also differs considerably by institution (parents, teachers, or the police). Figure 6.7 also shows that from the perspective of the agency of social control the delinquent behavior of their children, students, or the youth appears differently. Note that the bars do not show the total amount or the number of offenses per capita. Instead, the bars represent the estimated probability of detection (by the respective agent of social control).

Though parents recognize only about 20% of the delinquent behavior of their children, they still know twice as much as teachers or the police. The profile of offending behavior they recognize, however, is biased: They know comparatively much about violent offenses, be it minor or serious, but only little about vandalism committed by their offspring. The profile as it presents itself to teachers is still different: They detect a comparatively large proportion of minor violent and a smaller part of serious violent offenses, but are ignorant of other offenses such as vandalism, serious property offenses, and especially shoplifting. Although overall the police knows about the same amount of delinquent acts as teachers, their picture is the most balanced: They experience juveniles as committing serious property offenses, serious violent offenses, and minor violent offenses in nearly correct proportions although vandalism and shoplifting are still somewhat underrepresented. From the perspective of the offender, the risk of being found out at all is clearly highest as to violent offenses, least with respect to vandalism.

The different views on the problem behavior of juveniles are clearly determined by the different social roles of the agents of social control. The fact that teachers predominantly detect violent offenses and comparatively little of other problem

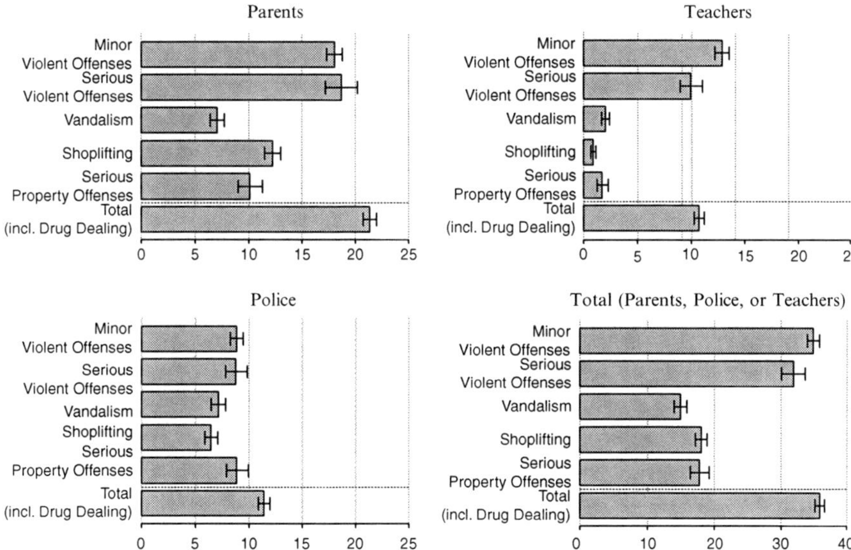

Fig. 6.7 Detection rates of different offense types by different institutions. *Notes*: Weighted data; percentages and 95% confidence intervals; $n = 15{,}094$ (min. violence), 3,967 (ser. violence), 8,088 (vandalism), 10,679 (shoplifting), 3,737 (serious property), 23,471 (total)

behavior is certainly due to the fact that the other behavior occurs outside the school context. In this sense, the perspective of teachers on problem behavior of their students is strongly biased toward violence. It shows that students with problem behavior may profit from social workers in schools. If they were aware of the delinquent behavior outside school, they could take measures in time to prevent students showing problem behavior from entering a criminal career. The data show that property offenses will be detected far more often by the police. Students thus carry a greater risk of reactions by institutions of criminal justice as might be recognized by teachers or other agents of informal social control.

The results also show that it is advisable not to consider the category "offenses total" but rather to consider offenses categorized into serious or minor violent or property offenses when analyzing the risks of detection by other factors such as gender, grade, aspiration level, migration status, offending as a group activity, or the frequency of offending. Investigating these factors, the following analysis will contrast the risks of detection by parents and by the police.

6.2.2 Factors Associated with Risks of Detection

If the risks of detection by the police differ for different groups of offenders, official statistics (police or court statistics) will be systematically biased, reporting too many or too few offenders per capita for certain groups. It is important to recognize such bias because it may show that the delinquent behavior of juveniles who enter

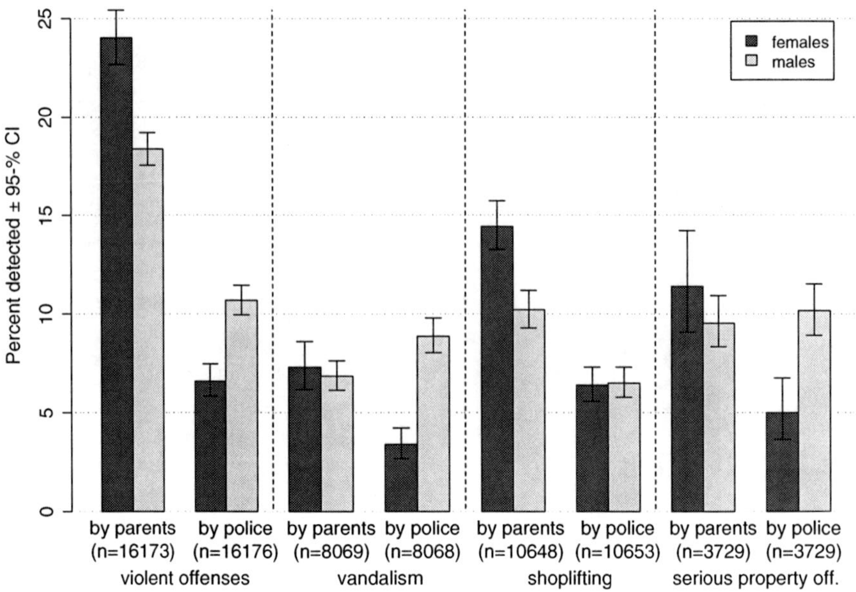

Fig. 6.8 Rates of detection by gender. *Notes*: Weighted data; *n* (females) violent offenses = 5,117, vandalism = 2,673, shoplifting = 4,941, serious property offenses = 933; *n* (males) violent offenses = 11,059, vandalism = 5,396, shoplifting = 5,712, serious property offenses = 2,796

the system of formal social control actually does not differ from the behavior of juveniles who only appear to be law abiding but are in fact equally delinquent. The analysis of detection by parents, on the other hand, may show the actual accomplishment of social control by the family. However, if there are group specific differences in parental detection rates, they may be not only due to differences in supervisory efforts of the parents but also due to the ability of some children to defy parental control. For example, we may expect that male or older juvenile offenders are found out by their parents less frequently than female or younger offenders.

In the following, we investigate factors that might be associated with the risk of detection by parents and by the police for different types of offenses. Factors investigated are gender, grade (as a proxy for age), school or aspiration level, migration status, group (vs. lone) offending, and the frequency of offending. The factor "school or aspiration level" tries to catch either the level of qualification the school degree offers (from "low" offering access to vocational education only, over "medium" to "high," offering access to universities or higher education) or (if not applicable or missing) the level of aspiration of the plans after school (from "low," looking for a job or start apprenticeship, over "medium," going to vocational school, to "high," preparing for academic studies). "Migrant status" differentiates three levels of first generation migrants, second generation migrants, and native born or third generation migrants.

Figure 6.8 presents differences between females' and males' rates of detection by parents and by the police for violent offenses, vandalism, shoplifting, and serious

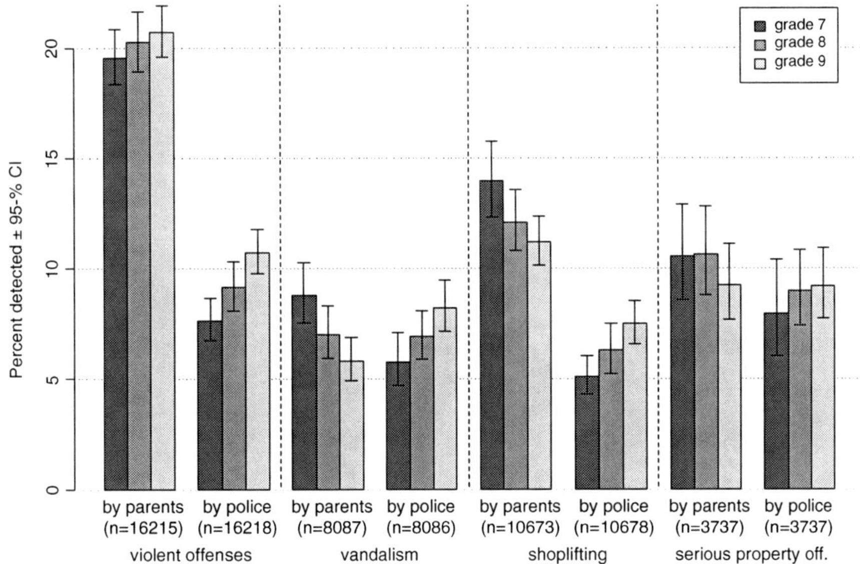

Fig. 6.9 Rates of detection by grade. *Notes*: Weighted data; *n* (grade 7, total offenses) = 6,384; *n* (grade 8, total offenses) = 7,880; *n* (grade 9, total offenses) = 9,207

property offenses. There are two remarkable results: (1) The risk of detection by parents is nearly always considerably and significantly higher for females than for males, indicating that parental supervision of females is more effective in the sense of recognizing delinquent behavior or that males succeed more in eluding parental control (see also Chap. 7). (2) Except for shoplifting, where detection rates of females and males do not differ, the males' risk of detection by the police is more than twice the females' risk. As a consequence, we expect that except for shoplifting the offending rates of males in official crime statistics are more than twice the actual proportion of males to females, thus grossly exaggerating the *de facto* more frequent delinquent behavior of males (see Chap. 3). The fact that police detection rates of shoplifting do not differ is perhaps due to automated surveillance systems and the restrictive policy of many shops to unconditionally report each theft detected to the police.

Inverse patterns of parental and police detection rates can also be observed concerning differences by grade (Fig. 6.9): As to vandalism and shoplifting rates of detection by parents decrease with grade, whereas rates of detection by the police increase significantly with respect to violent offenses, vandalism, and shoplifting. Two nonmutual exclusive reasons for the increase could be an increase in the seriousness of the offenses by age and the higher proportion of penal responsible juveniles in higher grades (in some countries).

Significant differences in police detection rates are also observable for all types of offense classes with respect to school or aspiration level (Fig. 6.10). The highest police detection rates are found among students of low or medium-level schools or

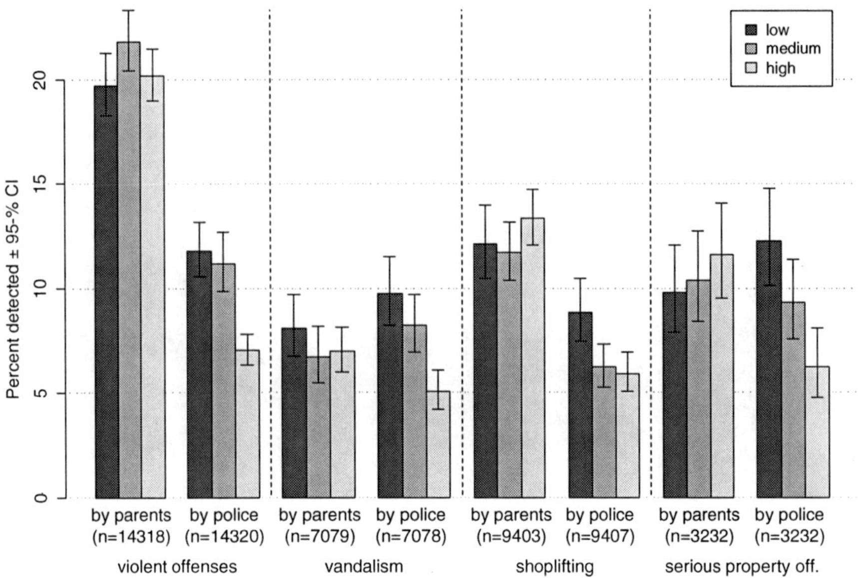

Fig. 6.10 Rates of detection by school or aspiration level. *Notes*: Weighted data; *n* (low, total offenses) = 4,238; *n* (medium, total offenses) = 7,378; *n* (high, total offenses) = 9,117

aspiration, detection rates of offenders with low aspiration levels are about twice the rates of students of high level schools or with highest aspiration. Rates of detection by parents, however, vary not systematically and do not differ significantly.

As to migration status, although there are smaller differences, the rates of detection of native offenders by the police are significantly lower with respect to violent offenses and vandalism (Fig. 6.11). Concerning parental detection, rates of first generation migrants tend to be the highest; significant differences are found with respect to vandalism and serious property offenses.

Analogous to the question whether they were found out having committed the last offense, students were asked whether they did commit the last offense alone or with others. For two offenses (carrying a weapon and group fight) this question was not asked. To investigate whether the rates of detection differ for lone or group offenders, the other offenses cannot be grouped into classes of offenses because then it would not be clear without ambiguity whether a respondent who was found out having committed an offense of a certain offense class committed the very offense that was found out alone or with others. Therefore, differences of detection rates by group offending are only analyzed for three single offenses with sufficient numbers of cases: assault, vandalism, and shoplifting. Results are presented in Fig. 6.12. As to the three offenses, parental detection rates of lone offenders are more than twice the rates of group offenders. Obviously, juveniles committing offenses in groups are less supervised by their parents or succeed better in eluding parental control than lone offenders. On the other hand the risk of group offenders being detected by the police is significantly higher than the risk of lone offenders.

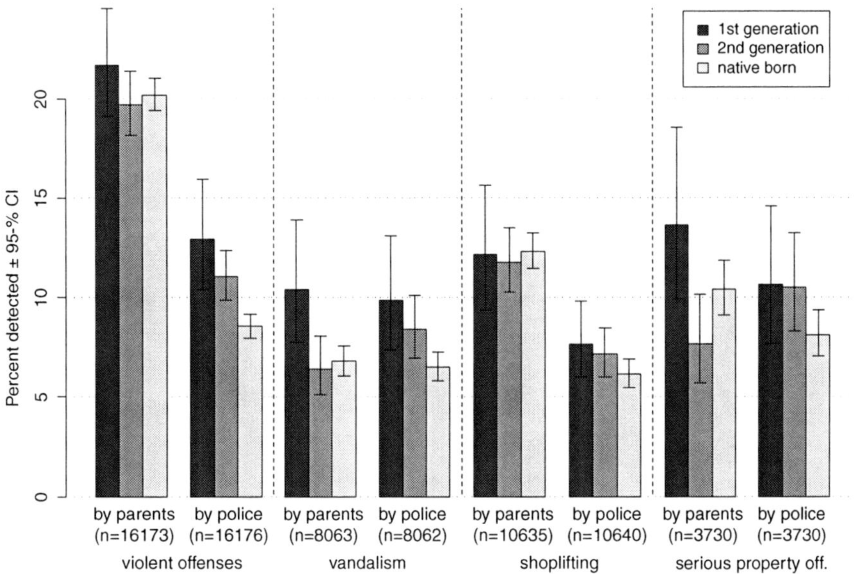

Fig. 6.11 Rates of detection by migration status. *Notes*: Weighted data; n (first generation, total offenses) = 1,707; n (second generation, total offenses) = 4,333; n (native born, total offenses) = 17,364

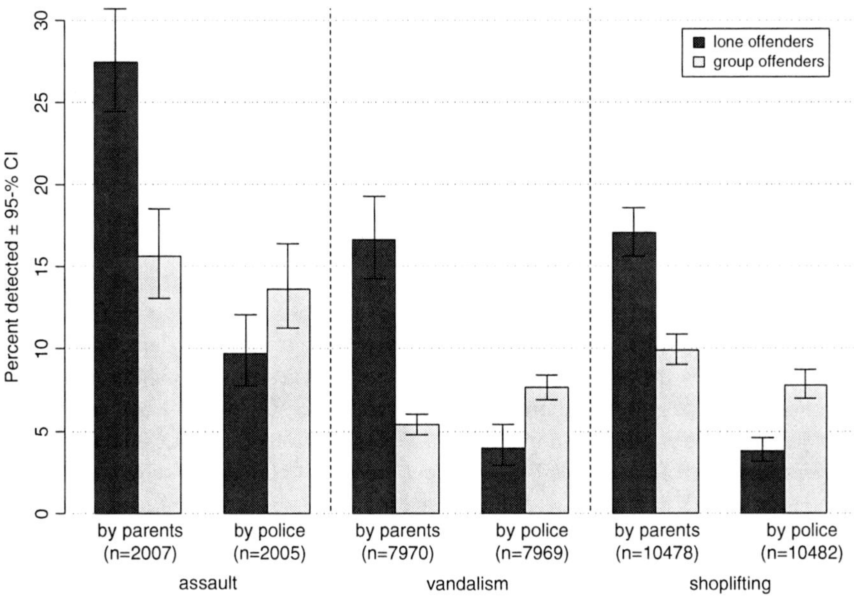

Fig. 6.12 Rates of detection by group offending. *Notes*: Weighted data; n (lone offenders) assault = 1,053, vandalism = 1,157, shoplifting = 3,452; n (group offenders) assault = 954, vandalism = 6,813, shoplifting = 7,026

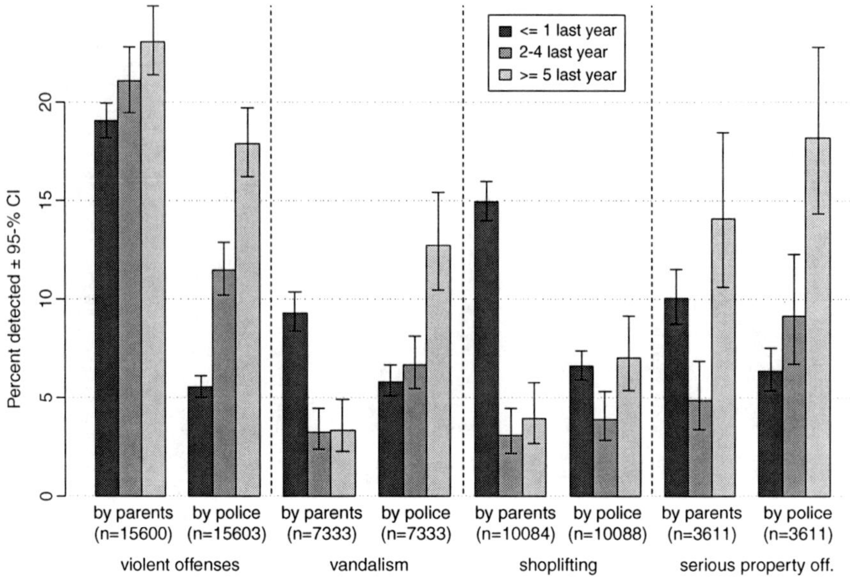

Fig. 6.13 Rates of detection (last time) by frequency of offending. *Notes*: Weighted data; *n* (≤1 last year, total offenses) = 14,338; *n* (2–4 last year, total offenses) = 4,191; *n* (2–4 last year, total offenses) = 4,636

Obviously, the risk of detection by the police increases with the number of persons involved in the offense.

When interpreting the results concerning the risks of detection and the frequency of offending, it is important to note that the question whether the student was detected refers only to the last offense committed. Estimating the risk of being found out this way makes the estimate formally independent from the number of offenses committed. If nevertheless the detection risks differ empirically among single (once or less[10] during the last year), multiple (2–4 times the last year), and chronic offenders (5 times and more the last year), it indicates that multiple or chronic offenders behave or are treated differently. The results are presented in Fig. 6.13. For all classes of offenses, there are significant differences in the rates of detection by parents as well as by the police. However, the often observed inverse pattern of a lower parental risk of detection and higher risk of detection by the police when comparing groups of offenders does not apply here. Concerning violent offenses and partly also serious property offenses, the higher detection risk of chronic offenders applies to parents as well as to the police. With respect to vandalism and shoplifting, however,

[10] It is possible that a respondent did not commit an offense during the last year but at least once during life-time. In that case the respondent can still answer the question whether he or she was found out the last time.

parents of chronic or multiple offenders detect offending of their children less likely. As to detection by the police, except for shoplifting the risk of detection increases significantly with the frequency of offending. The risk of chronic offenders is 2–3 times the risk of single offenders, and it is always considerably higher than the risk of multiple offenders. It seems likely that chronic offenders run a higher risk of becoming known to the police which again increases the risk of detection for an additional offense considerably. This implies that from the perspective of institutions of formal social control the discrepancy of the amount of crimes committed by chronic offenders as compared to multiple or single offenders appears much greater as it actually is. Additionally, because of the same bias, once detected as an offender the risk to enter a criminal career is increased not only due to the delinquent behavior itself but also due to its increased visibility.

6.2.3 Differences in Detection Rates and Bias in Formal Social Control

It is a remarkable result of the previous analyses that factors that are associated with higher rates of offending such as male gender, higher grade (i.e., age), first or second generation migrant (see Chap. 3) as well as lower aspiration level and group offending are also associated with a higher risk of detection by the police. As a consequence, actually existing differences in offending rates between certain groups become amplified when offenders enter the system of formal social control. The bias resulting from group-specific detection rates need not be an effect of intentional discriminatory behavior on the part of the police or other agents of social control but can just as well be explained by attempts to focus resources most efficiently on the most likely suspects. Thus the police is more likely to detect juveniles who conform to the image of the stereotypical delinquent, but this image in itself is not completely wrong. In a meanwhile classic article on the effects of socio-economic context on official reaction to juvenile delinquency, Sampson (1986) concludes that discrepancies between self-reports of deviance and official records are not simply due to errors in measurement but to structurally patterned sources of social control. He shows that bias in police control is less caused by discriminatory behavior directed against individuals but rather by structural level factors and allocation of resources to socio-economically deprived areas.

Although we cannot compare official records and self-reports of offending directly as Sampson (1986) did, the ISRD-2 data nevertheless allow to reproduce part of his analyses. An important hypothesis of Sampson's analysis was that residents of lower-class areas face a higher vulnerability to arrest – independently of their rate of (self-reported) delinquency and independently of their individual socio-economic status (SES). To test this he regressed (separately for males and females) the number of major police contacts recorded on the prevalence of self-reported delinquent behavior, the seriousness of delinquency, alcohol and drug use, neighborhood and individual SES, race, family composition (broken home), existence of

Table 6.5 Prediction (logistic regression) of detection by the police

	Males		Females	
	Odds ratio	z	Odds ratio	z
Frequency of offending (base: ≤1 last year)	$\chi^2_{(2)}=143.0$***		$\chi^2_{(2)}=50.8$***	
2–4 Last year	1.37	4.00***	1.36	2.66**
≥5 Last year	2.22	11.93***	2.18	7.12***
Risk behaviors (base: ≤1)				
≥2 Behaviors	1.87	10.43***	1.96	7.30***
Neighborhood disorganization (z-score)	1.20	7.18***	1.15	3.62***
Family affluence (z-score)	1.02	0.65	1.13	2.48*
Native status (base: migrant)	0.74	–4.93***	0.69	–4.12***
Complete family (base: no)	0.79	–4.02***	0.72	–3.70***
Parental supervision of going out at night (base: never)	$\chi^2_{(2)}=17.9$***		$\chi^2_{(2)}=0.0$	
Sometimes	0.75	–3.43***	0.99	–0.05
Always/don't go out	0.69	–4.20***	0.98	–0.15
Delinquent friends (base: no)	1.99	10.95***	1.57	4.65***
Gang membership (base: no)	1.27	3.84***	1.21	1.93⁺
χ^2 (df)	1,069.6 (10)***		314.5 (10)***	
n	13,084		8,368	

Notes: Unweighted data, total sample; ⁺$p<0.10$, *$p<0.05$, **$p<0.01$, ***$p<0.001$

delinquent peers, and gang membership. As a result, except for gang membership, family composition, and individual SES, all factors, most noteworthy neighborhood SES, contributed significantly to the number of police contacts supporting the hypothesis of ecological bias in police social control. Situational factors influenced male arrests more than female arrests. In a similar vein, using the ISRD-2 data we employed logistic regression analyses separately for males and females to predict detection by the police by the *frequency of offending* (three categories: ≤1 last year, 2–4 times last year, ≥5 times last year), *risk behavior* (two categories, ≤1 vs. ≥2 of the following behaviors: truancy last year, consumption of strong spirits, soft or hard drugs last month, and life-time drunkenness more than once), *neighborhood disorganization* (z-score), *family affluence* (z-score), *migration background* (first or second generation migrant vs. third generation migrant or native born), *completeness of family*, *parental supervision* when going out at night (three categories: never, sometimes, or always/respectively never going out), *contact to delinquent friends*, and *gang membership*. Any significant effect of these factors on the binary detection variable is an indication of bias in police control.

Results are presented in Table 6.5. The most important factor predicting detection by the police is the frequency of offending followed by contact to delinquent friends and two or more risk behaviors such as truancy or consumption of alcohol or drugs. The predicted proportion of male juveniles detected who did commit five offenses or more last year, reported at least two risk behaviors, and have delinquent friends is 35.0% (detection last time of at least one of the offenses committed) as opposed to

8.4% of male juveniles with two to four offenses last year, at most one risk behavior, and no delinquent friends (the corresponding rates for females are pred. = 22.1% vs. 5.5%). Obviously, police control focuses on groups with a higher risk of delinquent behavior. Migration status also contributes significantly to the detection by the police, although the effect is smaller (native born males: pred. = 11.6%, first or second generation male migrants: pred. = 14.7%; females: pred. = 6.5% vs. 9.1%). Parental supervision of going out at night and the completeness of the family have a strong effect on the detection risk for males, for females parental supervision is unrelated to the risk of detection by the police. Possibly, unsupervised males commit offenses later in the night which is associated with a higher risk of detection by the police, whereas even unsupervised females rather tend to stay home at night. This does not imply that parental supervision is not effective: Regression models using the same predictors to predict detection by *parents* show that – apart from a significant effect of gang membership – the effect of parental supervision is the only significant predictor for males and that it is even stronger for females (males: odds ratio = 1.12, $z=5.45$, $p<0.001$; females: odds ratio = 1.18, $z=6.23$, $p<0.001$). By the way, in the model for females the effect of family affluence on the detection by parents is significant and (as expected) negative (odds ratio = 0.93, $z=-2.37$, $p=0.018$).

The significant net effect of neighborhood disorganization on the risk of detection by the police is an important finding with respect to the hypothesis that police control is influenced by situational factors. The detection risk of delinquent juveniles living in disorganized neighborhoods is higher, even if controlling for the other individual factors. In this context, it is noteworthy that the family affluence of the individual student has either no effect (males) or even a small positive effect (females). All in all the results are remarkably similar to Sampson's findings, although the study design and the variables used are not identical.

6.3 Punishment of Offending

Already back in 1970, Black and Reiss tried to advance the sociology of social control by defining deviance in terms of the probability of a control response: "Thus, individual or group behavior is deviant if it falls within a class of behavior for which there is a probability of negative sanctions subsequent to its detection" (Black and Reiss 1970). Given the importance of detection and sanctioning, we know surprisingly little about the detection of offending behavior, and still less about the reality of punishment.

In the ISRD-2 study, students were asked for each type of offense by referring to the last offense committed whether they were punished (if found out). Although we do not know by whom and how offenders were punished, this still allows us to investigate not only the risk of punishment from the perspective of the offender but also the attitude toward the offense prevalent in society: Whereas the proportion of persons punished of the total number of offenders describes the overall risk of punishment, the proportion of persons punished of the total number of persons actually detected indicates how much a certain offense or offender deserves punishment and thus indicates indirectly also the severity of a certain offense from the perspective of the agency of social control. A comparison of the rate of punishment if found out across countries may thus show cultural differences that are important for comprehending differences in criminal behavior and social reactions to crime.

Figure 6.14 shows the overall risk of punishment and the rates of punishment if found out for different classes of offenses (note the differences in scale). From the objective perspective of the juvenile offender (i.e., the offender need not be aware of it), there are considerable differences between offenses: *Overall*, only 20.2% of all (last) offenses were punished, the highest risk of sanctioning is associated with serious violent offenses (19.4%) followed by shoplifting (15.3%) and minor violent offenses (12.8%). Punishment of serious property offenses (10.5%) and vandalism (9.9%) is least likely. The overall risk of punishment, however, is confounded with the risk of detection, which also varies considerably according to the type of offense (see above).

The risk of punishment *if found out* is more than twice as high (total risk: 43.5%). Once detected, the highest rate of punishment is associated with shoplifting (59.4%), the rates of serious violent offenses (48.2%), serious property offenses (45.0%), and vandalism (40.8%) are clearly lower. The rate of punishment for minor violent offenses (28.9%) is the lowest. Although significant for some offense classes, overall the differences of rates of punishment if found out between males and females are comparatively small (females: 42.0%, males = 44.4%, design-based $F_{(1,\ 2{,}885)} = 4.21$, $p = 0.040$); the differences are significant for minor violent offenses (females: 24.6%, males = 30.9%, design-based $F_{(1,\ 2{,}453)} = 21.31$, $p < 0.001$), vandalism (females: 33.7%, males = 43.4%, design-based $F_{(1,\ 1{,}219)} = 12.16$, $p < 0.001$), and serious property offenses (females: 36.4%, males = 47.7%, design-based $F_{(1,\ 616)} = 5.08$, $p = 0.025$), whereas the differences are not significant with respect to serious violent offenses and shoplifting.

Although we do not know by whom offenders were punished if found out, we nevertheless can investigate whether the fact that offenders were detected by the police has an impact on the risk of punishment. To unambiguously relate punishment to detection by the police, offenses cannot be collapsed into classes but must be analyzed separately. Table 6.6 presents the rates of punishment if found out of those who were detected by the police compared to those who were not detected – for offenses with a sufficient number of cases. As to violent offenses against persons (assault and group fight), the fact that offenders were detected by the police has no impact on the rate of punishment if found out. However, this is clearly different with respect to offenses affecting property such as vandalism and shoplifting: For these offenses the rate of punishment if found out increases significantly and substantially if offenders were detected by the police. Thus, whether involvement of the police increases the risk of punishment depends on the type of offense.

On the country level, the total rates of punishment if found out vary considerably as shown by a comparatively high intraclass correlation ($\rho_{icc} = 0.090$, $p = 0.002$). Because the number of cases is small, differences between country clusters dependent on the type of offense are investigated by collapsing the offenses into two categories (excluding carrying a weapon, vandalism, and drug dealing): Acquisitive

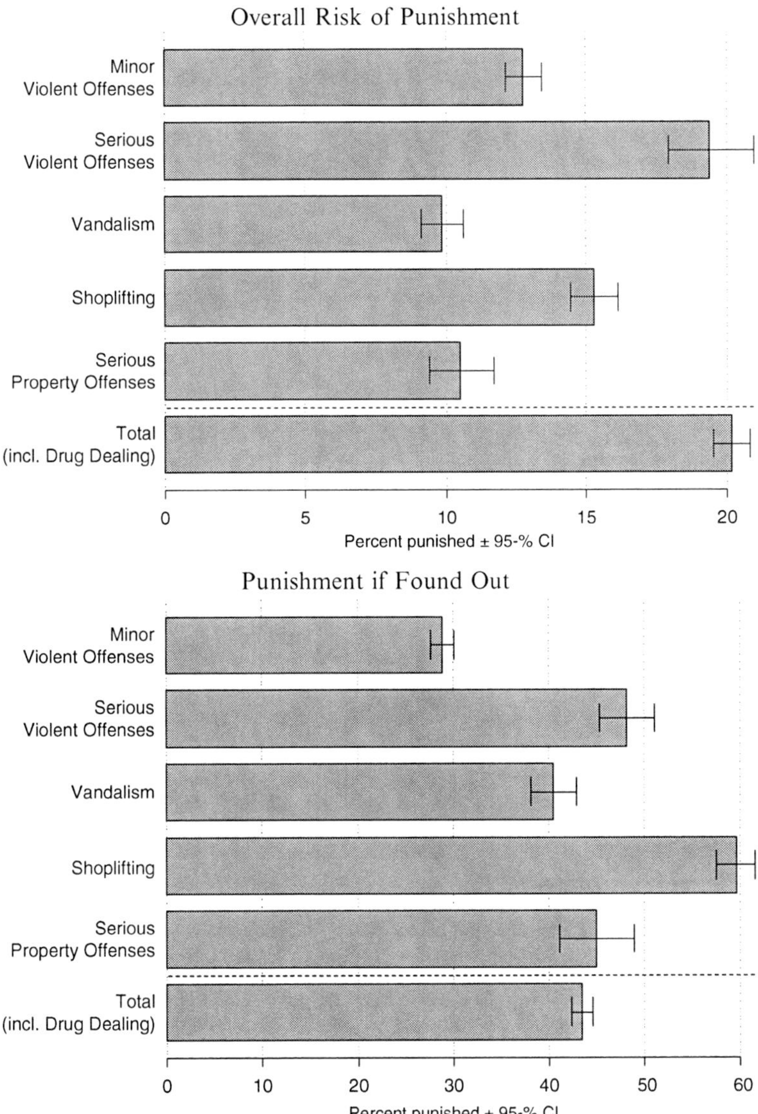

Fig. 6.14 Rates of punishment overall and if found out. *Notes*: Weighted data; percentages and 95% confidence intervals; *n* (overall risk): min. violence = 15,036, ser. violence = 3,939, vandalism = 8,051, shoplifting = 10,662, ser. property = 3,713, total = 23,421; *n* (if found out): min. violence = 6,572, ser. violence = 1,564, vandalism = 1,930, shoplifting = 2,698, serious property = 881, total = 10,736

property crimes (snatching, robbery, car theft, bicycle theft, car break, burglary, shoplifting) and violent crimes against persons (group fight, assault).

In Fig. 6.15 rates of punishment if found out are compared across country clusters for the classes of offenses against persons and of property offenses as well as for

Table 6.6 Rates of punishment if found out dependent on detection by the police

Offense committed	% Punished: Not detected by police	Detected by police	Cramér's V	Design-based F (df1, df2)	p	n
Assault	45.3	49.5	0.04	1.0 (1, 685)	0.329	962
Group fight	30.6	33.9	0.03	3.5 (1, 2,230)	0.062	5,248
Vandalism	36.0	54.4	0.17	43.5 (1, 1,210)	<0.001	1,895
Shoplifting	55.0	75.4	0.18	63.4 (1, 1,465)	<0.001	2,652

Notes: Weighted data

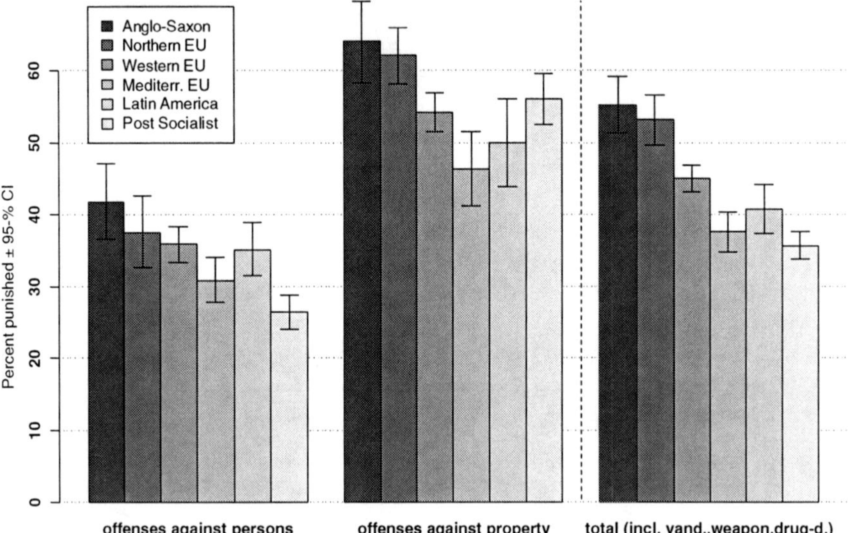

Fig. 6.15 Rates of punishment if found out by country cluster. *Notes*: Weighted data; n (offenses against persons) = 5,882; n (offenses against property) = 3,830; n (total, including vandalism, carrying a weapon, and drug dealing) = 10,769

offenses total including carrying a weapon, vandalism, and drug dealing. Three remarkable findings ask for an explanation: (1) Country clusters differ considerably as to the rates of punishment if found out (offenses against persons: Cramér's $V=0.10$, $p<0.001$; offenses against property: Cramér's $V=0.11$, $p<0.001$; total offenses: Cramér's $V=0.14$, $p=0.025$). Overall, punishment rates are highest in the Anglo-Saxon and Northern European cluster followed by Western Europe, they are the lowest in the Mediterranean, Latin-American, and Post-Socialist countries. The decline in punishment rates that is clearly visible with respect to offenses total seems to be related to differences in the welfare regime and perhaps to the overall affluence of the countries. (2) Rates of punishment are clearly and systematically higher for acquisitive offenses against property as opposed to violent offenses against persons.

Although we know that the police is comparatively less often involved in the detection of violent offenses (Fig. 6.7), results presented in Table 6.6 show that detection by the police alone cannot explain the overall higher punishment rates of property offenses. Differences in punishment rates are most likely related to differences in the appraisal of the seriousness of a property offense as compared to offenses against persons, reflecting a higher value our society attaches to the legal interest of property as opposed to the sanctity of a person. (3) The difference between the rates of punishment for acquisitive offenses against property and violent offenses against persons is about the same for all country clusters, except the Post-Socialist countries: Here, the difference is clearly the largest. A likely *post-hoc* explanation will be presented after having investigated differences in the overall punishment rates across countries in greater detail.

Country level differences in the rates of punishment if found out reflect differences in the perceived necessity of punishment that obviously is related to fundamental needs or values of the society. To explain differences in the rates of punishment between countries, the set of security vs. self-expression values (Inglehart and Baker 2000) seems to be especially relevant because it is linked to the process of modernization with increasing individualism and postmodernism. This process characterizes the change of values during the rise of the welfare state – note that the clustering of countries is primarily based on a classification of welfare regimes (Saint-Arnaud and Bernard 2003). In societies with continued economic development, socioeconomic stability, and security, a shift of value priorities has occurred moving from an emphasis on economic and physical security to values that emphasize trust, tolerance, subjective well-being, political activism, and self-expression. Research with the WVS studying this value change in 65 countries since the 1980s showed that the dimension of survival vs. self-expression values is strongly related to economic development and modernization (Inglehart and Baker 2000).

To explore the relationship between rates of punishment if found out and self-expression values on the country level, we use a respective measure of the most recent WVS (World Values Survey Association 2009). Figure 6.16 shows that there is a significant and strong positive relationship between punishment rates and self-expression values of 25 countries (Spearman's $\rho = 0.66$, $p < 0.001$).[11] Countries with lowest self-expression values are Russia, Estonia, Hungary, Armenia, and Lithuania, which belong to the cluster of Post-Socialist countries with the lowest rate of punishment if found out. Countries with highest self-expression values are Sweden, USA, The Netherlands, and Iceland, which belong to clusters with significantly higher punishment rates. When interpreting the relationship between punishment rates and self-expression values, one should note that ecological correlations must not be taken as relationships on the individual level. Furthermore, higher punishment rates do not imply more persons being punished or more severe punishment

[11] Denmark is excluded because it is clearly an outlier with a punishment rate if found out of 96.8 ($n = 107$). Including Denmark does not change the Spearman's rank correlation ($\rho = 0.67$, $p < 0.001$).

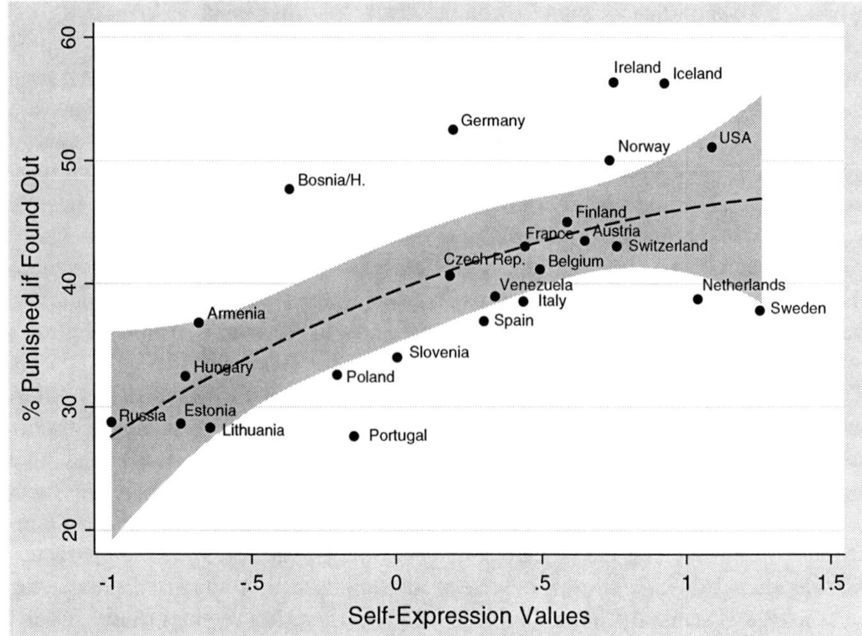

Fig. 6.16 Self-expression values and rate of punishment if found out. *Notes*: Denmark excluded; *shaded area*: 95% CI of fitted values; Spearman's $\rho = 0.66$, $p < 0.001$

but only more detected offenders being sanctioned. Note that the data do not reveal the agent of social control (parents, teacher, police, or others) that inflicts the punishment, nor the kind or severity of punishment.

At first glance a positive relationship between more emphasis on self-expression values and higher rates of punishment seems contradictory. From the perspective of sociological modernization theory, however, it is a remarkable finding which makes sense: Self-expression values develop only on the basis of a stable society. Delinquent behavior, however, threatens to destabilize a society that emphasizes individualism and self-determination. Sanctioning of antisocial behavior is thus functional and if applied rationally and carefully at an early age may promote an overall higher level of self-control. In fact, on the country level self-control is also positively correlated with self-expression values (see Chap. 12).

In this context two tendencies can be observed: In Western countries the increasing emphasis on individualism and self-expression goes hand in hand with globalization and a dominance of the market economy over other institutions of the society. This threatens to destabilize their welfare regimes. Here, we can observe that the emphasis on self-expression and individualism is linked to the idea of each citizen's responsibility for his or her own fate, creating a winner and loser society. With respect to juveniles, this means that youths are regarded as their own agents, responsible for their own acts: In this view, if they commit a crime they should bear the full consequences of the law. But on the other hand, in the same countries there is a *long-term* tendency to rely less on criminal justice and to become less punitive and repressive. In an increasing number of Western countries, in the context of juvenile justice reforms, alternative measures are adopted following the "minimum intervention" principle and using alternative sanctions, i.e., educational and restorative measures such as victim–offender mediation or reconciliation (Junger-Tas 2006). The same tendency can be observed with respect to parental punishment. In a growing number of countries, starting in Sweden in 1979 and spreading over Europe and beyond, physical punishment by parents is banned by law (Gershoff and Bitensky 2007; Commissioner for Human Rights 2009).

A more authoritarian educational style in countries with less emphasis on self-expression values may be a *post-hoc* explanation for the disproportionally higher rate of punishment for acquisitive property crimes in Post-Socialist countries. One should expect that the educational style in countries that emphasize self-expression values is less authoritarian and physical but place emphasis on respect for the needs of others and on efforts to reintegrate offenders. However, whether the sanctioning practices in postmodern countries are actually less harsh and more effective is an issue of further research.

6.4 Conclusions

Overall, the previous analyses of social responses to victimization and offending produced three major results: (a) Based on the ISRD-2 data estimates of reporting rates of victimizations, of rates of detection of self-reported offending, and of rates of punishment of self-reported offending were obtained, (b) the amount and direction of bias of police statistics and bias in the perception of delinquent behavior by different agents of social control as well as causes of bias became visible, and (c) it could be shown that rates of punishment differ according to the type of offense and according to basic values of countries and country clusters.

Incidence-based rates of reporting victimization events to the police that determine largely the amount of crime that becomes officially known are about 12% and are about the same for the three types of victimizations investigated (robbery, assault, personal theft). Thus, the dark figure is about 88% across countries. Countries, however, differ considerably as to the reporting rates, the overall rates range from 4.4 to 18.6% (excluding the outliers Armenia and Suriname). The Anglo-Saxon and Latin American country clusters show the lowest reporting rates of robbery and personal theft, the Mediterranean and Post-Socialist clusters the highest; with respect to assault the lowest rates are found in the Northern European and Post-Socialist clusters, the highest in the Latin American and Western European clusters. The huge differences of reporting rates change the rank order of countries as to the number of crimes known to the police (compared to the number of crimes actually experienced) considerably. Therefore, official crime statistics comparing rates of crimes per capita across countries must be interpreted with extreme caution.[12]

Compared to the rate of victimizations reported to the police, the overall rate of the self-reported last offenses committed that were detected by agents of social control such as parents, teachers, or the police is considerably higher (35.9%). The rate of detection by parents is clearly the highest (21.4%), detection rates of teachers (10.7%) and the police (11.4%) are lower. Clusters with the lowest overall police detection rates are the Mediterranean and the Post-Socialist countries, the Latin American cluster shows the highest police detection rate. The rank order of countries with respect to parental detection rates is somewhat different, here the cluster with the lowest rates are the Anglo-Saxon and the Western European cluster, but again the Latin-American cluster shows the highest detection rate.

Given the fact that nearly two thirds of the offenses are not detected by parents, teachers, or the police, the overall risk of punishment (referred to all offenders) is low as expected: Only 20.2% of all (last) offenses were punished, the risk of punishment is highest as to serious violent offenses and shoplifting (19.4 and 15.3%) and lowest as to serious property offenses and vandalism (10.5 and 9.9%). Of those detected, more than 50% are not punished. Here, the highest rates of punishment are found as to shoplifting and serious violent offenses (59.4 and 48.2%), clearly lowest is the rate of punishment for minor violent offenses such as carrying a weapon or group fights (28.9%).

Exploring factors that are associated with higher rates of reporting victimizations to the police or with higher rates of detection by the police shows that due to differential reporting or detection rates there is considerable bias in official statistics or social control according to city size, gender, age (grade), aspiration level, the native status of the victim or offender, the frequency of victimization or offending, the life-style of the victim or offender, or the neighborhood of the offender. With respect to the risk of detection by the police, the ISRD-2 data could reproduce findings of an earlier study (Sampson 1986) on the effects of socioeconomic context on official reactions to juvenile delinquency. Remarkably, whether victim or offender, the bias revealed does not completely distort the view on crime or offending but mostly amplifies the effects of factors that increase the risk of becoming a victim or offender. The findings thus show that processing stereotypes and routines resulting from real differences between victims and nonvictims or offenders and nonoffenders tend to be self-amplifying and to create self-fulfilling prophecies of agents of social control.

Finally, the analyses of rates of punishment showed that crimes against property are perceived as more severe, or rather as more deserving sanctioning, than crimes against persons, especially if the offense became known to the police. This seems to

[12]Often, reporting rates are calculated based on prevalences (i.e., the proportion of victims who did report at least one offense during the last year). The overall rate in our data is 18.2%, this is about 50% higher than the rate based on incidences. However, prevalence based reporting rates do not show how much of the volume of crime finds its way into official statistics.

reflect basic values of all societies investigated. Especially noteworthy from a sociological perspective is the finding of a strong positive ecological correlation between the rate of punishment and self-expression values. In countries that emphasize values typical for modernized and more individualized societies delinquent behavior of juveniles is more likely to be sanctioned. The social reaction to offending is based on and reflects basic cultural values that are changing with economic development. This development is characterized by a shift toward modernization and (in the long-run) hopefully toward values that are increasingly rational, tolerant, trusting, and participatory. The modern society requires social stability that rests on humane social control of deviance, as well as on the exercise of self-control by individualized and moral man.

References

Aebi, M. F. et al. (2010). *European Sourcebook of Crime and Criminal Justice Statistics – 2010.* Meppel, The Netherlands: Boom Juridische uitgevers. [http://www.europeansourcebook.org/ob285_full.pdf]

Black, D. J. & Reiss, A. J. (1970). Police control of juveniles. *American Sociological Review, 35*, 63–77.

Brownstein, H. H. (2000). The social production of crime statistics. *Justice Research and Policy, 2*, 73–89.

Coleman, C. & Moynihan, J. (1996). *Understanding Crime Data: Haunted by the Dark Figure.* Buckingham: Open University Press.

Commissioner for Human Rights (2009). *Children and corporal punishment: "The right not to be hit, also a children's right" (Issue Paper 2009).* Strasbourg: Council of Europe.[https://wcd.coe.int/com.instranet.InstraServlet?Index=no&command=com.instranet.CmdBlobGet&InstranetImage=1370686&SecMode=1&DocId=1206996&Usage=2]

Cumming, G., & Finch, S. (2005). Inference by eye: Confidence intervals and how to read pictures of data. *American Psychologist, 60*, 170–180.

Enzmann, D. & Podana, Z. (2010). Official crime statistics and survey data: Comparing trends of youth violence between 2000 and 2006 in cities of the Czech Republic, Germany, Poland, Russia, and Slovenia. *European Journal on Criminal Policy and Research, 16*, 191–205.

Gershoff, E. T. & Bitensky, S. H. (2007). The case against corporal punishment of children: Converging evidence from social science research and international human rights law and implications for U.S. public policy. *Psychology, Public Policy, and Law, 13*, 231–272.

Inglehart, R. & Baker, W. E. (2000). Modernization, cultural change, and the persistence of traditional values. *American Sociological Review, 65*, 19–51.

Junger-Tas, J. (2006). Trends in international juvenile justice: What conclusions can be drawn? In J. Junger-Tas and S. H. Decker (eds.), *International Handbook of Juvenile Justice* (pp. 503–532). Dordrecht: Springer.

Junger-Tas, J., Marshall, I. H. & Ribeaud, D. (2003). *Delinquency in an International Perspective: The International Self-Reported Delinquency Study (ISRD).* The Hague: Kugler Publications.

Levitt, S. D. (1998). The relationship between crime reporting and police: Implications for the use of Uniform Crime Reports. *Journal of Quantitative Criminology, 14*, 61–81.

Saint-Arnaud, S. & Bernard, P. (2003). Convergence or resilience? A hierarchical cluster analysis of the welfare regimes in advanced countries. *Current Sociology, 51*, 499–527.

Sampson, R. J. (1986). Effects of socioeconomic context on official reaction to juvenile delinquency. *American Sociological Review, 51*, 876–885.

Smit, P. R., Meijer, R. F. & Groen, P.-P. J. (2004). Detection rates, an international comparison. *European Journal on Criminal Policy and Research, 10*, 225–253.

Van Dijk, J., van Kesteren, J. & Smit, P. (2007). *Criminal Victimization in International Perspective: Key Findings from the 2004–2005 ICVS and EU ICS*. Den Haag: Boom Juridische uitgevers. [http://rechten.uvt.nl/icvs/pdffiles/ICVS2004_05.pdf]

Van Kesteren, J., Mayhew, P. & Nieuwbeerta, P. (2000). *Criminal Victimization in Seventeen Industrialised Countries: Key Findings from the 2000 International Crime Victims Survey*. The Hague: WODC/NSCR. [http://rechten.uvt.nl/icvs/pdffiles/Industr2000a.pdf]

World Values Survey Association (2009). *Word Values Survey 2005 Official Data File v.20090901*. World Values Survey Association. [http://www.worldvaluessurvey.org]

Part III
Testing Competing Explanations of Problem Behaviour

Chapter 7
The Importance of the Family

Josine Junger-Tas

7.1 Introduction

Regardless of the multiple theories concerning the aetiology or genesis of criminal behaviour in young people, the family, undoubtedly always plays a central role. This chapter will analyze the various ways in which families effect juvenile behaviour. In doing this we will examine the different hypotheses which attempt to explain the impact of family life on the behaviour of children and young people.

First, we will examine one of the most influential theories on the role of the family in this respect, Hirschi's social control (1969). Hirschi stated that young people who have strong bonds with their parents would interiorize the values and norms of their parents. As a result they would behave in a norm conforming way, and since they would not want to disappoint their parents, they would try to do well in school and there would be no incentive to play truant. Moreover, in meeting the demands from their family, school, and the larger society, such juveniles would be rewarded by praise and privileges and a promising future. In this way they develop a stake in conformity as well as strong inhibitions against delinquency involvement that might endanger such rewards. Hirschi also claimed that such young people would select a few good friends with whom they would develop close bonds and refrain from being involved with large peer groups involved in high-risk behaviour by attracting mischief "just for fun". However, this last premise turned out to be a weakness in his theory, because later research showed that Hirschi greatly underestimated both the group character of most juvenile leisure time interactions and the role of the peer group in facilitating deviant behaviour (see Chap. 9).

Parental management has been studied by many other researchers. For example, coercion theory (Patterson 1995) places a stronger emphasis on parental control than on attachment to parents while social control theory primarily views attachment

J. Junger-Tas (✉)
University of Utrecht, Utrecht, The Netherlands

J. Junger-Tas et al., *The Many Faces of Youth Crime: Contrasting Theoretical Perspectives on Juvenile Delinquency across Countries and Cultures*,
DOI 10.1007/978-1-4419-9455-4_7,

to parents as a condition for internalizing societal values as well as self-control. In this respect it should be observed that Loeber and Dishion (1983) found that the best predictor of delinquent behaviour was a shorter version of Glueck's measure of parental management, including the mother's discipline and supervision as well as family cohesiveness (Glueck and Glueck 1950). Loeber and Stouthamer-Loeber (1986; Loeber et al. 1998) also concluded that the strongest predictors of delinquency were parental involvement, monitoring, and rejection.

To test these hypotheses we used a bonding scale, based on questions concerning how well the juvenile gets along with his father and mother, how often he takes meals with his parents, and whether the family spends time together on outings, walks or on sports. These variables are combined in a scale labelled "family bonding". We also added questions about some serious life events, such as a serious illness of either parent, family disruption through alcohol or drug problems, serious parental (physical) conflicts and separation or divorce. In addition, we asked some control questions such as whether his parents know which friends he usually goes out with and, whether his parents gave him a curfew, which he obeys.

Second, we will test an important theory regarding the role of the family and self-control developed by Gottfredson and Hirschi from their book "A general theory of Crime" (1990). The principal thesis in this book is that a lack of self-control explains all possible types of deviant and extreme behaviour in addition to criminal behaviour, such as driving dangerously, being involved in dangerous sports or drinking heavily. The authors do not consider self-control as an innate characteristic, but claim that it becomes part of one's personality as a result of a training process activated by parents at a young age (somewhere between age 8 and 10). If that training process fails, the lack of self-control will become a permanent characteristic of the child's personality, the consequences of which will be felt during his whole life. To test this we used 12 items of the *Grasmick self-control scale* (Grasmick et al. 1993), (including items on impulsivity, risk seeking, self-centeredness, and temper). Parallel to this scale, we also measured young people's attitude towards violence (Wilmers et al. 2002) as well as to what extent parents have an impact on young people's self-control and aggressive attitude. More extensive test of self-control theory is presented in Chap. 11.

Third, we will examine the relationship between social structural factors and the family as well as with the behaviour of the juveniles in the study. One criticism of the classical social control theory is its micro-and meso-character. The theory does not take into account the wider perspective of society's social structure. Families and children live under greatly varying social-economic conditions (Box 1981; Kornhauser 1978; Rutter and Giller 1983). For example, the social class and ethnic structure of society and its geographical distribution were hardly considered. Kornhauser pointed out that disorganized neighbourhoods cannot transmit shared norms and values because they are unable to exercise social control on young people. Sampson and his colleagues explored this idea further by developing the concept of collective efficacy, which creates a connection between the social cohesion in a neighbourhood as a function of mutual trust and solidarity, with the willingness of people to enforce social norms (Sampson et al. 1997, 1999). The capability of neighbourhoods to realize a positive social climate varies and disorganized neighbourhoods, in particular, characterized by concentrations of poverty, minorities and single-parent families, often lead to isolation. Sampson and Laub further argue that the environment and living conditions of families are significant factors which influence parents' management skills (Sampson and Laub 1993).

Several other researchers have made efforts to remedy the shortcomings of classical Social control theory by adding exogenous variables such as social class and intelligence (Wiatrowsky et al. 1981). Others added structural social factors, such as unemployment and housing (Sampson and Laub 1993), or measures of economic hardship and single-parent families, or family process variables such as attachment, involvement, and control (Smith and Krohn 1995). According to the latter study, the impact of family socialization varies across different ethnic groups, a finding that will also be tested in our study. The authors also found indications that economic hardships and family structure are related to family process variables. *The Rochester Youth Development Study* showed that poverty, stress, and isolation have a negative impact on parental mood and this disrupts parent support and discipline, which is linked to adolescent internalizing and externalizing problems (Thornberry and Krohn 2003, p. 22). As Thornberry writes: "Overall, it is important to note that the social and family context plays a key role in producing delinquent and disrupted behaviour through its effect on parenting" (op. cit. p. 22).

One should be aware of the fact that a number of socio-demographic and socioeconomic factors that are related to criminal behaviour are also associated with physical illness, mental disturbances, and all sorts of accidents. For example, boys commit more offenses than girls, and have more accidents as well because they tend to take more risks. Low income and a low level of education are also related to fatal accidents by fire and in the home, including drowning. The same problem persists when the parents – the mother in particular – have alcohol-related problems (Rivera 1995). In addition, delinquents take great risks while driving and are therefore more often victims of road accidents (Gottfredson and Hirschi 1990; Junger et al. 1995; Yoshikawa 1994). Mortality among delinquents is also higher than non-delinquents. This is partly due to the fact that they are more prone to alcohol and drug abuse than non-delinquents (Stattin and Romelsjö 1995). The ISRD instrument includes some questions about the number of serious accidents and of serious illness(es) of the respondent and/or his family.

7.2 Social Background of Families in the Study

The *social structural background* of families was measured by four questions related to this concept. First, we measured family affluence by asking respondents whether they had a room of their own or whether they had to share a room with a sibling. We also asked whether the family owned a car, a computer, and whether the respondent had a mobile phone. These four variables were then combined in the scale *family affluence*. We also asked about *employment* of the father and/or mother.[1]

[1] We tried to construct a common SES measure combining employment with the parents' education level, but it was not possible to obtain a reliable consensus among participating countries concerning this measure.

Table 7.1 Pearson correlations of social background, family variables, and delinquency involvement

	Employment	Family affluence	Neighbourhood cohesion	Neighbourhood disorganization
Family bonding	0.09[a]	0.12[a]	0.21[a]	–0.18[a]
Family control	0.02[b]	–0.02[b]	0.09[a]	–0.19[a]
Minor offenses	–0.02[b]	0.04[a]	–0.06[a]	0.25[a]
Serious offenses	–0.01[b]	0.01[b]	–0.01[b]	0.08[a]
Versatility	–0.03[a]	0.03[a]	–0.06[a]	0.29[a]

[a]Significance at 0.01 level
[b]Significance at 0.05 level

In addition we used two *neighbourhood scales* based on earlier studies (Smith et al. 1999; Olweus 1996; Sampson et al. 1999). The original scale consisted of 13 items tapping into positive neighbourhood collective efficacy (*this is a close knit neighbourhood; people here can be trusted; people are willing to help each other*), and neighbourhood disorganization (*people generally don't get along; there are a lot of empty buildings; there is a lot of fighting; graffiti; drug dealing; and crime*).

The first question we want to examine is to what extent these background variables are directly related to delinquent behaviour.

Both structural variables – employment and family affluence – are positively correlated with family bonding, but they are hardly related with family control and versatility. Confirming the expectations of Sampson and Laub's theory, neighbourhood *integration* (collective efficacy) is strongly related to family bonding but less so to family control, and only weakly and negatively to versatility. This, while neighbourhood *disorganization* is negatively related to family bonding and family control, but has a positive correlation with all forms of delinquency and versatility,[2] as shown in Table 7.1 ($r=0.29$). The greater the problems in the neighbourhood, the lower the correlations with family bonding and parental control and the higher the juveniles' involvement in delinquency.

Unemployment of the family breadwinner in the 2006 study, was the lowest in S-Europe (6.3%) and in the Anglo-Saxon cluster (8.7%). Levels were slightly higher in the Post-Socialist countries (11%), N-Europe (11.4) and W-Europe (12.4%), while the highest levels were found in Latin America (13.4%). However, part of these discrepancies may be due to cluster differences in social organization, since the levels of unemployment may be related to the extent of social benefits regarding unemployment, illness and invalidity, as well as measurement differences. Generally speaking, the higher the rates for benefits on the basis of disability and illness in the population, the lower the rates for unemployment. Nevertheless this relationship varies considerably across countries. Moreover, it should be noted that unemployment is particularly high among single mothers in all country clusters as illustrated in Table 7.2.

[2] Versatility is highly correlated both with minor delinquency (0.68) and with serious delinquency (0.70). Since versatility takes into account frequency as well as seriousness of delinquent behaviour we will use this measure in most analyses.

Table 7.2 Unemployment by family structure and country cluster (%)

	Both parents	Alternative father/mother	Single parent	Cramer's V
Anglo-Saxon	7.1	7.9	22.6	0.21
W-Europe	11.7	10.6	26.5	0.16
N-Europe	7.7	9.0	26.4	0.21
S-Europe	4.3	5.9	18.6	0.21
Post-socialist	7.5	6.8	16.1	0.13
Latin America	8.1	9.7	15.6	0.14

Overall both the status of the family breadwinners' employment and family affluence are correlated with neighbourhood disorganization, in particular in the Anglo-Saxon, North and West European clusters, but not as much in the other clusters (table not shown). All three social background variables are also correlated with family bonding and family control, but neighbourhood disorganization has the strongest correlations. Although employment and family affluence are hardly correlated with delinquency involvement, neighbourhood disorganization, while showing substantial negative correlations with family bonding and, in particular, with parental control, has a large but somewhat variable impact on versatility. Positive correlations are the highest in the Anglo-Saxon cluster (0.42), followed by West and Northern Europe (0.33), Southern-Europe (0.28), the Post-Socialist countries (0.27). The lowest correlation is again found in Latin America (0.16). These cluster differences may be produced by three essential and often interrelated characteristics of neighbourhoods: first, the country's differential spatial distribution of social class; second, country differences in the housing market, which is related to the differential quality of housing; and third, the neighbourhood's degree of population heterogeneity (Wikström 1998).

In conclusion, it appears that employment of the family's breadwinner and family affluence are related to family bonding rather than to family control, while neighbourhood cohesion is related to both and is weakly and negatively associated with versatility. Of all three social background variables, it seems that the disorganization of the neighbourhood has the greatest impact on the families' control over juveniles as well their involvement in delinquency.

7.3 The Impact of Family Structure

Another important social background factor is *family structure*. The variation of family structures also tells us something about the cultural differences between country clusters (see Table 7.3).

For example, the highest percentage of families who consist of two biological parents (83.5%) and the lowest number of single parent families (8%), are found in Southern Europe – a cluster including countries with a rather strong Catholic tradition. In contrast, the low percentages of intact families are found in the Latin American (58%) and Northern European (64%) clusters. However, the consequences of this

Table 7.3. Family structure by Country cluster (%)

	Anglo-Saxon	North-Europe	West-Europe	South-Europe	Latin America	Post-Socialist
Biological parents	71.0	64.4	71.9	83.5	57.6	75.3
Alternative father/mother	5.6	15.0	6.3	3.3	3.2	1.6
Single parent	13.2	12.3	12.3	7.7	22.2	13.7
Stepparent	7.0	7.6	8.2	2.9	8.9	7.4
With other family	2.3	0.3	0.6	1.6	6.4	1.5
Other	0.9	0.5	0.7	1.0	1.7	0.5

Cramer's $V = .12$

situation differ greatly between the latter clusters. For example, the fact that Latin America is characterized by a high percentage of single mothers (22%) can be explained through the matrifocal family structure. This structure can be perceived as a long-term consequence of slavery which leads to the separation of many families, where child care became the responsibility of the mother. In North Europe, on the other hand, there are a rather high percentage of divorced parents. However, many separated parents agree to share parenthood (15%), meaning that the child lives alternatively with his father and mother. The percentage of families with a stepparent fluctuates around 7–8%, and is only 3% in South-Europe.

In situations where children are raised by other people than their biological parents, such as grandparents, other family members, foster families, or the child is cared for in a children's home, the three clusters with the highest number of such alternative arrangements are Latin America, South Europe, and the Anglo-Saxon countries. Interestingly, all three clusters do not have a well functioning welfare system which supports single mothers. Single mothers tend to be disproportionally burdened by unemployment and have to provide singlehandedly for the family income. In that respect, South Europe and Latin America have a long tradition of relying on the extended family (as well as on the church) for childcare and support.

So far we have looked at three family variables, but there are two other variables which combine serious family events which may also be important in regards to juvenile behaviour. The first refers to serious illness or death of a sibling, parent, or other family member, and the second refers to family disruption, based on questions about parents' alcohol or drug problems, serious conflicts or violence between parents, and separation or divorce. Referring to the first variable – death and illness – a comparison of the mean numbers of such events by country cluster hardly reveals any differences between N-, W-, S-Europe and the Post-Socialist countries (most juveniles experienced somewhat more than two such events in the past year). However, the mean number of such events reaches 3.0 in the Anglo-Saxon cluster and 2.5 in Latin America. Serious illnesses or death within the family occur more frequently in the latter two clusters than in the others. This outcome could be related to the qualitative differences in regards to the healthcare systems in Europe and the latter.

As for the second variable – family disruption – the lowest mean numbers of such events are found in S-Europe, which also has the lowest divorce rate, similar

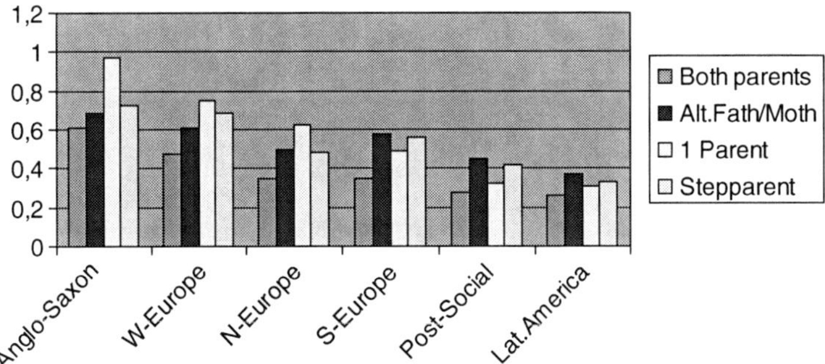

Fig. 7.1 Last year versatility means by family structure and country cluster (Anova)

to the Post-Socialist countries. N-Europe and the Anglo-Saxon cluster have the highest mean number of disruptive events, both clusters having high divorce rates.

Considering delinquency, juveniles who are raised in situations different from a nuclear family have the highest prevalence rates for both minor and serious delinquency in the Anglo-Saxon and N-European clusters. Since "other" may include "other family" but also foster family or foster home, this may partly explain the relatively higher rate of antisocial and delinquent behaviour in the western clusters as opposed to the other three clusters where there is a higher reliance on the family. Figure 7.1 shows the means of last year versatility by family structure, demonstrating clear country cluster differences as we already noted in Chap. 3. Cluster differences were analyzed by an Anova, all results being significant at the level of $p<0.001$, except in Latin America ($p<0.025$).[3] An interesting finding is that being raised by only one parent – in most cases the mother – is significantly and strongly related to delinquency in the Anglo-Saxon, W-European and N-European clusters, but much less so in the other three clusters, where being raised alternatively by a father and mother as well as having a stepparent seems to be more important in this respect. In these western clusters the presence of a stepparent (in many cases stepfather) tends to be less negative than being raised by a single mother, which is not the case in the other clusters. One reason might be that in Southern Europe and Latin America there is more family support available. In the latter countries, many children are still raised in the extended family while in Anglo-Saxon countries, North- and West Europe the nuclear family is the norm.

One of the consequences is that families are more isolated, so the mother has to provide for the family income and raise her children without support. This situation is particularly serious among the immigrant populations from Africa or South America where there is insufficient support for single mothers in the host country. It is worth noting that being raised alternatively by the biological father and mother

[3] Anglo-Saxon: $F=9.08, p<0.001$; W-Europe: $F=34.66, p<0.001$; N-Europe: $F=24.92, p<0.001$; S-Europe: $F=11.86$, $p<0.001$; Post-Socialist: $F=16.61$, $p<0.001$; Latin America: $F=2.78$, $p<0.025$.

Table 7.4 Family structure with social-economic background ($N=67{,}921$) (%)

	Both biological parents	Alternating father-mother	Single parent
Unemployment family head	8.5	8.0	21.0
Degree of neighbourhood disorganization			
Low	62.1	57.2	40.7
Somewhat low	17.8	22.0	26.2
Somewhat high	11.4	10.9	18.9
High	8.7	9.9	14.2

Cramer's V: unemployment 0.16; Disorganized neighbourhood 0.15

does not seem to be a particularly positive situation in regards to delinquency involvement of children. This is relatively high in all clusters but even more so in S-Europe and the Post-Socialist cluster. Post hoc analysis (Scheffe) showed significant differences between the presence of both biological parents and all other parental arrangements. This outcome is in line with earlier findings, which show that it is the number of parental attachments that counts (Rankin and Kern 1994). The authors found that a strong attachment to two parents had a greater preventive effect on delinquency than attachment to only one parent. Yet, this was particularly the case for non-serious offenses, which made the authors conclude that single-parent homes are only moderately associated with delinquency. This conclusion was confirmed in the ISRD study by a multiple regression, which conveyed that single parent families or children with a stepparent did not significantly contribute to the explained variance of versatility. This pattern is manifested in all clusters, except in Latin America where delinquency differences are limited. However, as may be expected, in terms of delinquent behaviour the best living situation for a child is when he/she lives with his/her family of origin consisting of two biological parents. One of the reasons may be that single parent families suffer more often than complete families, from unemployment and poverty and are they are often disproportionally concentrated in deprived neighbourhoods. This was confirmed by associating family structure with two variables unemployment and family disorganization. As mentioned earlier, unemployment is considerably higher among single parents than among families of origin or alternating parents. In addition, single parent families are more likely to live in disorganized neighbourhoods: 33% of single parent families are living in such neighbourhoods vs. 20% of families with both biological parents (Table 7.4).

What we have seen so far is that both family structure and neighbourhood disorganization are associated with delinquent behaviour, while this is hardly the case for the family heads employment and family affluence. Therefore, following Sampson and Laub's (1993) reasoning, the impact of neighbourhood disorganization on delinquency should be mediated by the association of social background variables with family bonding and family control. Of course it is not possible to draw any causal conclusions, as the study is cross-sectional. Nevertheless, the Pearson correlations between these variables show that, first of all, employment and family affluence are positively related to family bonding but hardly to parental control, and second, neighbourhood disorganization is negatively related with family bonding, as well as with parental control. We will examine this question more in detail in Chap. 10.

Summarizing our findings so far, in terms of delinquency involvement we have two sets of significant correlations. First, two social background variables *employment of the family head and family affluence* (*0.03*) are very weakly correlated with delinquency, while there is a strong correlation of neighbourhood disorganization with *versatility* (−0.30). Second, these background variables are also related to *family structure*. Indeed we found that single parents are more likely to be unemployed and living in disorganized neighbourhoods than two-parent families. Finally, in all country clusters *employment of the family head* and *family affluence* are related to *family bonding* but only very weakly to *parental control*.

7.4 Parental Socialization and Delinquency

Parents influence their children's behaviour in different ways: by affection, by supporting them, taking interest in their lives, monitoring their behaviour, and controlling them. Hirschi distinguished attachment to parents and monitoring and control (1969), but in more recent times the emphasis has been placed increasingly on control, as shown in Gottfredson and Hirschi's theory on self-control (1990). They argue that a lack of self-control, which they define as the propensity to commit crime, is the sole cause of all types of criminality. According to the authors, self-control is taught to children at a young age by careful monitoring, teaching them how to recognize rule breaking and by punishing adequately. This change into more controlling attitudes is also apparent in the increasingly repressive attitudes towards young people in general and juvenile delinquents in particular, both from the general public and from the juvenile court (Junger-Tas and Decker 2006). It is a remarkable thesis in view of the overwhelming evidence of the strong relationship between a juvenile's attachment to his parents and the effectiveness of the control exercised on him or her (Cernkovich and Giordano 1987; Hawkins et al. 1986; Loeber and Stouthamer-Loeber 1986). Another dimension, which is often forgotten, is parental social support, that is the extent to which they provide "emotional and instrumental resources to their children" (Wright and Cullen 2001, 678; Loeber and Stouthamer-Loeber 1986). Social support also refers to intimate communication and sharing activities (Rothbaum and Weisz 1994). Moreover, there are indications that attachment to parents, social support, and parental control are interrelated (McCord 1979; Wilson and Herrnstein 1985). This implies that parents who have a warm relationship with their children and support them are also better able to supervise them. Juveniles also tend to feel that the absence of parental supervision means that their parents do not care for them (Riley and Shaw 1985). The interrelation of these measures is an expression of what Wright and Cullen (2001) labelled "parental

Table 7.5 Pearson correlations of family measures

	Get along w. father	Get along w. mother	Family disruption	Freq. dinner w. parents	Freq. leisure w. parents
Get along w. father	1.00				
Get along with mother	.46	1.00			
Family disruption	–.24	–.15	1.00		
Freq. dinner w. parents	.16	.12	–.16	1.00	
Freq leisure w. parents	.24	.20	–.18	.24	1.00
Parental control	.15	.15	–.12	.19	.19

All correlations are significant at $p < .001$

efficacy", following Sampson et al's. (1999) label of "collective efficacy" for effective neighbourhood control on juveniles.

The ISRD-2 study includes two attachment variables (how does the respondent get along with his father and with his mother) two support variables (how often does the respondent engage in with his parents; how many days a week does he have dinner with his parents), and one combined measure of parental control (do his parents know his friends; do his parents give him a night-time curfew – if so – does he obey his parents). Table 7.5 first shows the Pearson correlations of these family measures to examine the extent to which they are associated. We added family disruption (serious conflicts between parents, physical abuse and separation divorce), since this might have a negative impact on all other parental measures.

As expected, the relationship with the father and mother are highly correlated (0.46), while the frequency of taking dinner and spending leisure time together is somewhat more strongly associated with getting along with the father than with the mother. Family disruption is negatively and moderately correlated with the relationship with the father and much less so with the mother. This suggests that in these cases, the father may be the source of the disruption. The frequency of having meals and spending leisure time with parents are also correlated and – interestingly – one notes a slightly higher correlation of parental control in regards to social support by parents than with attachment to parents. In fact Table 7.5 shows that family bonding – expressed according to the relation the respondent has with his parents – social support, parental control and in particular leisure spent together, are all interrelated.

Across the different clusters, the relationship with the father is also highly correlated to the relationship with the mother. The correlation is highest in South Europe ($r=0.59$) and lowest in Latin America ($r=0.42$). In all clusters, parental control has the highest correlation with family leisure, followed by attachment to parents. In terms of the association of versatility with family variables, parental control has the strongest negative correlation with versatility, suggesting the importance of this variable. Nevertheless, the strength of the association of parental control with parental social support moderates its impact. Spending leisure time with parents, however, does not seem that important in S-Europe, the Post-Socialist and Latin American countries, as compared to, for example, having dinner with the family or attachment to parents. One might speculate that in the framework of family norms and family

Table 7.6 Prediction of self-control and attitude toward violence and family variables

	DV: Self-control (betas)		DV : Pos. Attit. Violence (betas)	
Gender	–0.10***	–0.08***	0.24***	0.22***
Grade (base: 7)				
8 Grade	–0.05***	–0.03***	0.05***	0.03***
9 Grade	–0.07***	–0.03***	0.05***	0.02***
Migrant (base: native)				
first gen migr	–0.00	–0.01	–0.01	–0.01
Sec gen migr	0.02***	0.00	–0.06***	–0.04***
Fam. disruption		–0.06***		0.04***
Family bonding		0.14***		–0.10***
Parental control		0.24***		–0.20***
	$R^2 = .01$	$R^2 = .12$	$R^2 = .06$	$R^2 = .13$

*** $p < .001$

life, in the latter countries, spending leisure with parents is considered rather normal and accepted behaviour. This while in the Anglo-Saxon cluster, W- and N-Europe, having dinner and spending leisure time with parents may be more infrequent and may thus have a stronger impact on delinquency involvement. We recall that the latter have higher delinquency rates than the former (see also Chap. 3).

Finally, we examine the impact that parents might have on their children's attitude towards violence and self-control. Of course Gottfredson and Hirschi (1990) argue that self-control should be instilled in children during early childhood, while our sample is aged 12–16. However, the theory claims that if parents have had a significant influence on their children in this respect, it is likely that parental influence should also make itself felt in years to come. As a first step we regressed self-control – measured by part of the Grasmick scale (1993) – as well as attitude towards violence on the family variables (see Table 7.6).

Considering the lack of self-control, most variances are positively explained by parental control. The other variables' contribution is much weaker, which suggests that in addition to parental control, other variables may be more important. For example, self-control might be more situationally determined by peer group activities in the absence of adult supervision. This question will be further explored in Chaps. 9 and 11.

Where the attitude towards violence is concerned, the picture is different. As expected, parental control contributes most to the explained variance, but betas are also high for gender, indicating considerable differences in the attitudes towards violence between girls and boys. Explained variance is also considerably higher than in the case of self-control. The outcomes suggest that parental control has more influence on attitudes to violence than on a juvenile's self-control. The two variables are related (–0.43), but that does not explain everything. One may suppose that a positive attitude towards the use of violence would include a lack of self-control, but a lack of self-control does not necessarily include a positive attitude to violence.

Thus on the whole, these results do not appear to support the self-control theory. More on this topic about self-control will be discussed in Chap. 11.

7.5 The Family and Gender

As we have seen in Chap. 4, delinquent behaviour in girls does not differ very much from that of males in terms of minor delinquency, including the age at which they begin and the extent to which they engage in minor delinquency (except in South-Europe). However, with respect to serious offenses, girls commit considerably less delinquent acts than boys, and across clusters there is a tendency for girls to start at a later age than boys, with the exception of the Post-Socialist cluster.

In the 1970s, when studying delinquency in girls became prominent, the disparities between male and female delinquency remained constant, despite claims that female delinquency would slowly reach male levels (Adler 1975; Simon 1975; Austin 1993). However, the discussions in the media including those among politicians seem endless, especially because around 2,000 police figures all suggest that girls' delinquency is steadily increasing. Some claim that this is because girls are more likely to become victims of sexual abuse or family conflict than boys, which may result in problem behaviours such as running away or premature sexual activity. This may lead to juvenile justice intervention and institutional care and thus to higher delinquency rates for girls (Chesney-Lind & Pasko 2004; Cain 1990, Corrado et al. 2000). However, a far more likely clarification which could explain the decreasing gender gap are the net-widening policies of the police forces, public prosecutors, and juvenile judges, which are based on ever extending definitions of youth delinquency and greater police surveillance (Steffenmeier et al. 2005; Junger-Tas 2009).

There are a number of developments that may help clarify the formation of these policies. One is the repressive penal climate that has spread throughout the western world since the 1980s and 1990s, which is based on the postulate that minor delinquent acts, such as minor violence, petty theft, or disorders have to be "nipped in the bud". This is based on the idea that the earlier the intervention, the less likely a child's behaviour will evolve into serious delinquency. The consequence of this attitude is that the difference between delinquency and mere anti-social or disruptive behaviour diminishes (Steffenmeier et al. 2005) and non-serious acts such as fighting on the school playground will lead to police and prosecutor intervention. Another powerful trend can be described as the victim movement, in which considerable attention is paid to victim complaints and victim satisfaction at the expense of youth disorderly and delinquent behaviour. Finally, in a number of European countries, police focus is explicitly placed on youth and possible juvenile misbehaviour, leading to increased police action producing higher official delinquency rates, in particular of girls (Junger-Tas 2009).

In reality, self-report studies all over the world convey two things. First, there only is a small gender gap in regards to non-serious delinquency, where girls tend to commit shoplifting as often or only slightly less than boys (Chesney-Lind and

Sheldon 2004; Junger-Tas et al. 2003; Van der Laan and Blom 2006). Second, there is a large gender gap in regards to serious property and violent offending, where the differences in violence are particularly remarkable. The important question remains: how we can explain the gender gap in terms of delinquency?

The first possible explanation is based on biology. For example, some authors claim that because differences in aggression between males and females emerge very early in life and are applied across different cultures, they must have a biological origin (Maccoby and Jacklin 1980). Studies of siblings or twins are especially relevant in this respect. Those studies reveal that although delinquency predictors are similar for both genders, males show higher levels of delinquency because they are more vulnerable to disorders such as hyperactivity or conduct disorders, which are predictors of antisocial behaviour (Rowe et al. 1995; Rutter et al. 1998; Moffit et al. 2001). However, there are some problems with these types of explanations. For example, what we observe – mainly in cross-sectional studies – is essentially a phenotype of the behaviour that is behaviour as a result of continuous interactions between biological factors and environmental influences. We cannot observe the genotype in its original state at birth and even before birth, since even at that time, environmental influences have already had an impact on the foetus in the womb. In addition, there is considerable overlap in antisocial behaviour between males and females suggesting more similarities than differences. All in all, however, it does seem justifiable to state that given the universal character of gender differences in serious delinquency involvement, this may have at least some biological basis (Rutter et al. 1998).

On the other hand, causal explanations of misbehaviour in girls may differ according to the seriousness of that behaviour. Non-serious delinquency is widespread among juveniles, among males and females alike, and behaviour differences in this field are minor to non-existent. Nevertheless, there are signs which indicate that when girls become victims of physical and sexual abuse, they are more likely to become involved in serious delinquency or are more prone to becoming runaways (Chesney-Lind 2004; Acoca 1999). Other researchers claim that the gender gap can be explained according to differences in parental control, family bonding, and by prevailing social norms on acceptable behaviour as well as differences in opportunity to commit crime. In a study of 588 youths from the Boston area who had joined a peer group, Morash (1986) found that more girls refused to participate in the study (they were rather embarrassed about such contacts). Moreover, girls were older than boys when they joined the groups. Most of the groups did not have a regular meeting place and included more boys than girls. All in all, girls are less likely to join delinquent groups than boys. Giordano et al. (1986) found that girls are more likely than boys to develop intimate relationships implying that girl groups do not exercise the same influence on each other's behaviour as boys groups do, group norms promoting rather intimacy and self-disclosure. Girls also tend to take fewer risks than boys, where risk taking is directly related to increasing delinquency (Heimer 1995). Furthermore, high grades and positive self-esteem discourage risk taking, and thus delinquency in girls. In fact, what these authors suggest is that girls and boys have different pathways to delinquent behaviour. However, their studies are rather descriptive in nature and they do not attempt to explain in what way these different pathways emerge and effect delinquency.

Testing Gottfredson and Hirschi's *General theory of Crime* (1990), which takes a closer look at family and self-control, was attempted in a Canadian study of about 2,000 Canadian Secondary school students (LaGrange and Silverman 1999). Gottfredson and Hirschi (1990, 147) recognize differences in terms of self-control between the sexes, which, according to their theory, would also imply differences in criminal propensity. Since self-control, according to their theory is instilled by parents at a young age, this suggests differential socialization between the sexes. LaGrange and Silverman argue that actual offending is partially determined by opportunity and partially by the propensity to commit crime, which is defined by low self-control. They defined the opportunity to commit offenses by a lack of supervision and control by parents and considered differences in parental control between the sexes as one of the explanations of lower delinquency involvement of girls. In order to measure low self-control however, they did not use Grasmick's scale (Grasmick et al. 1993). Instead, low self-control was measured by impulsivity, risk taking, carelessness, temper, and whether the respondent was present oriented. Opportunity was measured by parental control and the amount of time the respondent spent with his peers in the absence of adult supervision. This study is interesting in light of the vast quantity of research on differential socialization of girls and boys, which indicated that low parental control predicts delinquency (LaGrange and White 1985; Rankin and Kern 1994; Hagan et al. 1985).

In general, parents all over the world tend to exercise more direct control over girls as portrayed by the first ISRD study and a large British self-report study (Junger-Tas et al. 2003; Graham and Bowling 1995). For example, even in the 1990s, twice as many males than females went on outings during the week-end (Junger-Tas and Terlouw 1991), while girls spent more time doing household chores and caring tasks. In addition, an interesting case in a small Dutch town showed that even before the age of six, little girls were only allowed to play in front of the house while little boys were allowed to explore the neighbourhood (Masson et al. 2002).

It would be interesting to examine this issue on the basis of the ISRD-2 material and we began, as illustrated in Table 7.7, by testing the effect of gender as to family bonding, parental control, family disruption as well as neighbourhood disorganization and self-control across the six Country clusters.

In all the clusters, boys appear to be more attached to their parents than girls, although the discrepancy is lowest in South Europe and in the Post-Socialist cluster. The outcome with respect to parental control is quite the opposite. One may conclude that even in 2006 – the year the survey was taken – parents tend to exercise considerably more control on their daughters than on their sons.

The results regarding family disruption and neighbourhood disorganization warrant closer inspection. While one may assume that there are no gender differences in regards to the frequency of family disruption, the fact that the girls' mean rates were higher suggests two things. First, girls are generally more disturbed by family conflicts and family disintegration than boys, yet girls may be more frequently victimized in such situations: either one or both may be the case (Table 7.7).

Table 7.7 *F*-tests on gender differences – Means of family variables, neighbourhood disorganization, violence, and self-control by gender and country cluster

	Family bonding		Parental control		Family disruption		Neighbourhood disorganization		Positive attitude toward violence		Self-control	
	Male	**Female**	**Male**	**Female**	**Male**	**Male**	**Female**	**Female**	**Male**	**Female**	**Male**	**Female**
Anglo-Saxon	80.0	77.7	72.9	77.5	13.5	16.7	23.7	20.4	48.5	36.6	55.6	59.4
W-Europe	83.5	81.8	71.8	77.1	15.1	18.8	18.3	15.2	39.2	28.6	63.9	69.4
N-Europe	83.1	81.7	72.7	79.6	12.9	16.0	21.5	16.7	36.4	26.4	59.2	64.0
S-Europe	83.8	83.0	83.5	86.8	7.4	8.6	24.9	18.9	35.4	25.5	61.0	66.3
Latin-Amer.	77.2	74.3	78.2	85.8	14.1	17.6	29.9	25.7	40.7	33.8	58.2	60.1
Post-Socialist	81.3	79.8	69.8	79.4	10.3	13.3	24.7	20.1	40.6	28.7	56.5	59.7
Total	81.7	80.1	73.8	80.8	11.9	14.9	23.6	19.2	39.4	29.0	59.0	63.1
ANOVA												
Gender	$F = 143.2$ ***		$F = 623.3$ ***		$F = 219.2$ ***		$F = 453.1$ ***		$F = 2999.5$ ***		$F = 553.2$ ***	
Cluster	$F = 153.2$ ***		$F = 244.8$ ***		$F = 194.0$ ***		$F = 249.3$ ***		$F = 267.6$ ***		$F = 335.3$ ***	
Gender*Cluster	$F = 4.2$ ***		$F = 19.0$ ***		$F = 3.4$ ***		$F = 4.6$ ***		$F = 17.9$ ***		$F = 12.3$ ***	

All gender differences are significant: $p < .001$

The different means in terms of neighbourhood disorganization, on the other hand, may be related to the fact that girls are more controlled by their parents and thus spend more time in the home and less time hanging out with a large group of friends. Thus, disorganization in their surroundings may have less impact on girls than on boys who spent more time on the streets.

The analysis of the responses to peer group involvement reveals differences between the first three clusters and the last three (table not shown). In the Anglo-Saxon, W-European and N-European clusters, the largest proportion of juveniles spent their time with a small group of one to three friends, while the second largest groups in W- and N-Europe spent their time with family. As an exception to the rule, the largest groups of juveniles in the Anglo-Saxon cluster, also primarily spent their time with small groups, however, the second place is occupied by a large group of friends instead of family. In the latter three clusters, youths spent most of their time with their family, suggesting that the families tend to have more significance in the lives of children from S-Europe, the Post-Socialist countries and Latin America. Furthermore, in all clusters – with the exception of the Anglo-Saxon one – more girls tend to spend leisure time with their families or with a small group of one to three friends than boys, and they are less likely to spend their free time with large peer groups. Comparing gender differences of attitudes towards violence and self-control by the *F*-test (Table 7.7) illustrates that gender disparities are considerable, both in regards to attitude towards violence and self-control. The most positive attitudes towards violence are found in the Anglo-Saxon cluster and the lowest is found in South Europe and Western Europe. Gender disparities in terms of violent attitudes are largest in the Anglo-Saxon cluster and in N-Europe, and they are lowest in Latin America. Note that levels differ between country clusters but gender disparities are very comparable (except for Latin-America). There are no gender differences in Latin-America. This suggests that in terms of violent attitudes, the latter girls and boys do not differ from each other a great deal. Finally, we regressed males and females separately on social background, family variables, self-control, and attitude towards violence in three steps. First, we considered how social background variables could be of influence, we then added family variables and in model three we added two important individual variables; self-control and attitude towards violence.

A primary finding was that the impact of neighbourhood disorganization on versatility somewhat reduces for males and females, once the family variables and the attitude towards violence and self-control are added in Model 2. This supports Sampson et al.'s theoretical approach (1997; 1999), which argues that neighbourhood disorganization has an indirect influence on delinquency, and is mediated by deficient parental control and the absence of community support (Table 7.8).

A second observation is that among girls, although parental control has the largest effect in decreasing versatility. Family bonding and also family disruption have a higher effect for girls than for boys. This suggests, what has been stated before: for girls, the bond with parents and family disruption are important predictors of versatility. Girls also seem to suffer more than boys from family disruption.

A third observation refers to the relatively high effect of positive attitude towards violence in model 3, both for girls and boys. In fact, this variable has the largest

Table 7.8 : Negative Binomial Regression of Versatility on Background-, Family- and Attitude Variables by Gender

Incidence Rate Ratios Females

	Model 1	Model 2	Model 3
Employment	0.78***	0.87*	0.87*
Family affluence	1.26***	1.27***	1.27***
Neighb. cohesion	0.88***	0.99	0.99
Neighbourhood disorganization	1.74***	1.56***	1.29***
Family bonding		0.79***	0.86***
Parental control		0.70***	0.82***
Family disruption		1.25***	1.21***
Self-control			0.61***
Pos. attitude to violence			1.41***
	$R^2 = .08$	$R^2 = .14$	$R^2 = .23$

Incidence Rate Ratios Males

	Model 1	Model 2	Model 3
Employment	0.85**	0.94	0.92
Family affluence	1.20***	1.20***	1.17***
Neighb. cohesion	0.92***	0.99	0.98*
Neighbourhood disorganization	1.70***	1.57***	1.30***
Family bonding		0.87***	0.91***
Parental control		0.71***	0.81***
Family disruption		1.12***	1.11***
Self-control			0.69***
Pos. attitude to violence			1.42***
	$R^2 = .10$	$R^2 = .15$	$R^2 = .25$

* $p < .05$; ** $p < .01$; *** $p < .001$

effect ion versatility. While self-control has a positive effect that it decreases the versatility, for boys a little more than for girls. Adding self-control and positive attitude toward violence into the model, it lowers the effect of the neighbourhood disorganization as well as the effect for family bonding and family control.

7.6 Ethnic Minority Groups and the Family

The question we want to discuss in this section is: To what extent are the results concerning the role of the family in most western countries with respect to juvenile norm conforming or rule breaking behaviour similar in families who migrated to these countries from other parts of the world? A second question is: Are the theories we executed in this chapter are also valid in the case of the different ethnic minority groups and to what extent can they be used to explain delinquency. We recall Chap. 3, which revealed that while there are no great discrepancies in minor delinquency

Table 7.9 Unemployment and Family structure by Immigrant group (%)

	N/W Europe	S-Europe	Turkey	C/E-Europe	Asia	Africa	N/S America	Natives
	N=993	N=2,677	N=1,019	N=876	N=1,587	N=1,015	N=1,769	N=53,270
Unemploym.	9.0	13.0	22.0	13.0	19.0	26.2	12.5	9.0
Cramer's V .10								
Family structure								
Both parents	62.8	78.6	86.3	65.4	78.5	63.3	52.5	73.7
1 parent	16.4	11.2	9.3	18.0	12.0	19.7	25.7	12.4
Stepparent	10.0	5.9	1.8	11.5	4.5	8.6	12.3	6.8
Cramer's V .06								
Family disruption								
Some	27.4	27.0	17.0	18.6	24.2	21.0	23.5	29.6
Considerable	11.0	11.0	6.7	6.0	14.4	8.0	10.7	12.5
Cramer's V=.16								

between natives and ethnic minorities, there are definite differences in serious offending, both in terms of property and violent offenses. Some groups in particular – Turkish immigrants and those from Central and East Europe – commit considerably more violent offenses. In addition, young people coming from South or East Asia have quite similar delinquency rates as native youths.

First, we will compare the youth native to the host country with immigrant groups in regards to unemployment, as an important background variable, and to family structure (see Table 7.9). As expected, unemployment is considerably higher among the families of ethnic minorities than the native population, in particular among Turkish and African family heads. Migrants from North and West Europe are an exception, since their unemployment rate is similar to that of natives.

The majority of immigrant youths from Turkey, S-Europe, and Asia live with complete families, which suggests a traditional and cohesive family life. This while groups whose origins are African, South American, as well as Central and East European, share troubled immigration histories, where family disintegration is more common. On the other hand, some immigrant populations, such as those coming from the Caribbean isles or from South America traditionally have many single-parent households.

Regarding family disruption, recall that this variable covers separation or divorce, repeated (physical) conflicts between parents and parent's alcohol, or drug problems. Table 7.9 shows on average, about 25% of the respondents experienced some family disruption, in most cases parent's separation or divorce, while 11–14% had been faced with considerable family problems. Among native youths, this percentage is about 30%, which may reflect the easy accessibility of divorce in western countries. Some immigrant groups, such as Turkish juveniles and children coming from Central and East Europe have experienced relatively little serious family disruption. Among the former, this may be a reflection of the cohesion often found in Turkish families, while the immigration history of migrant groups coming from, for example,

Table 7.10 Means of background-, family variables and versatility by immigration

	1st generation	2nd generation	Natives	
Employment	81.5	85.5	90.6	483.7***a
Family affluence	78.9	84.1	84.2	110.2***b
Neighb. disorgan	23.2	23.5	20.9	65.9***b
Family bonding	78.9	80.2	81.4	59.7***b
Parental control	74.2	75.6	78.2	64.7***b
Versatility	4.01	4.31	3.14	165.8***a

Notes: a) *Chi*²-Test; b) *F*-Test; *** $p < .001$

Asia, Africa or South America may have been characterized by relatively more severe family problems.

Most minority groups are plagued by unemployment and poverty. Therefore, it is no wonder that many of them are living in deprived neighbourhoods, where houses are cramped, vandalism is rampant, and crime is a daily occurrence. Table 7.10 shows the means of these variables over first and second generation immigrants in comparison to the native population. Table 7.10 shows that differences between the three groups in regards to employment and family affluence, while both first generation and second generation immigrants live in worse neighbourhoods than native youths. Second, differences between groups in terms of family bonding are smaller than to differences in parental control. The mean versatility of the native population (3.14) is lower than first (4.01) and second generation (4.31).

What can we conclude about the association of background, family, and neighbourhood with versatility among different ethnic groups? Among different migrant groups, the overall correlations of neighbourhood disorganization with versatility are rather high among all European and African migrants, while three immigrant groups – from Turkey, Asia, and N/S America – and the population of origin have correlations of similar strength as the native population. With respect to juveniles of Turkish origin, we recall our earlier findings, which showed that Turkish youths commit very few property offenses, and when they do offend it is likely to be a violent offense. In terms of family variables, an analysis of the variances show equal mean rates of family bonding between N–W European immigrants and natives and considerably higher rates among Turkish and S-European groups, both having very cohesive families (table not shown). All other groups have lower family bonding means. As for family control, considering the different immigrant groups, all of them except S-American groups, have lower mean rates than natives, suggesting that the main difference between native and immigrant families is in terms of parental control on children rather than in terms of family bonding. Moreover, family disruption in most immigrant groups, with the exception of Asian-, S-European, and especially Turkish families, is considerably higher than in native families. These outcomes perhaps underline the importance of family in the lives of young people in relation to conforming or antisocial behaviour, which supports the social control theory and suggests that the validity of the theory is not restricted to the United States or Europe but has a universal character.

Table 7.11 Negative binomial regression of versatility on social background, family variables, self-control, and positive attitudes to violence

	Model 1	Model 2	Model 3
First generation			
Employment	1.11	1.24	1.16
Family affluence	1.27***	1.27***	1.16***
Neighbourhood disorganization	1.74***	1.58***	1.22***
Family bonding		0.85***	0.86***
Family control		0.69***	0.80***
Family disruption		1.19***	1.17***
Gender			1.75***
Age			1.02
Self-control			0.67***
Positive attitude to violence			1.45***
R^2	0.08	0.14	0.26
Second generation			
Employment	0.77***	0.82**	0.75***
Family affluence	1.23***	1.23***	1.19***
Neighbourhood disorganization	1.86***	1.69***	1.36***
Family bonding		0.91***	0.95***
Family control		0.67***	0.80***
Family disruption		1.15***	1.17***
Gender			1.82***
Age			1.08***
Self-control			0.66***
Attitude violence			1.37***
R^2	0.11	0.16	0.28
Natives			
Employment	0.89**	0.99	1.00
Family affluence	1.25***	1.24***	1.21***
Neighbourhood disorganization	1.77***	1.69***	1.28***
Family bonding		0.86***	0.89***
Family control		0.68***	0.82***
Family disruption		1.13***	1.14***
Gender			1.92***
Age			1.09***
Self-control			0.66***
Attitude violence			1.42***
Pseudo R^2	0.08	0.14	0.26

**$p < .01$
***$p < .001$

7.7 A Final Test of Social Disorganization and Self-Control Theory

Finally, we tested social disorganization theory and self-control theory. Table 7.11 illustrates a regression model where we began introducing social background variables, successively adding family variables in model 2, and some individual variables in model 3, such as self-control and positive attitude towards violence, and as controls, age and gender. According to Sampson and colleagues (1997, 1999), these variables could act as mediators between the impact of the disorganized neighbourhood and versatility. For clarification, we restricted the analysis to first and second-generation immigrants as compared to native youths.

In our study we found similar results, in that the contribution of neighbourhood disorganization diminishes considerably when family variables are added in model 2 and when gender and age, self-control, and positive attitude towards violence are included in model 3. Out of all the family variables, family control contributes the most, while a positive attitude towards violence has an increasing effect, self-control has a decreasing effect in versatility. As we have established earlier in this chapter, gender also contributes to the explanation of versatility, while age hardly does.

In conclusion, it seems that overall our results support the disorganization theory, because the variables which reflect the parents' education process mediate much of the neighbourhood's direct impact on serious delinquency involvement. Self-control and positive attitude to violence makes a contribution in model 3, which does support Gottfredson and Hirschi's (1990) theory.

7.8 Conclusions

This chapter first discussed some descriptive findings concerning the social background of families and their relationship with family variables and juvenile delinquency involvement. We established that social background variables, such as employment and family affluence are hardly related to delinquent behaviour, but that neighbourhood disorganization is. As for family structure, we saw that in two clusters – N-Europe and Latin America – the number of families consisting of both biological parents is exceptionally low. In N-Europe this has resulted in mothers and fathers having to raise their children alternatively. In Latin America, 22% of the families are headed by a single mother, the other clusters having a percentage of 12–13% of single parent households. We also found that single parents have considerably higher unemployment rates and live disproportionally in disorganized neighbourhoods. With respect to juvenile delinquent behaviour, although the lowest rates are found among children living in complete families, all other arrangements showing higher rates, a regression analysis showed that single parents and stepfamilies only have a weak effect on delinquency involvement.

Moving on to our test regarding the theory on social control, it is of no surprise that our study also supported that theory (Hirschi 1969; Sampson and Laub 1993; Wikström 1998). However, that support is not without qualifications. As Wright et al. (2000); stated, emotional and instrumental parental support, intimate communication and sharing activities are just as important in affecting a child's behaviour as parental control. To test this with the ISRD data, we first found a strong correlation between family bonding and family control suggesting that the one cannot have an impact on behaviour without the other. Second, the data showed a strong correlation between the frequency of spending leisure with parents and the frequency of having dinner with them, the two variables indicating important family interactions. Third, we found that frequent leisure time with parents is not only highly correlated with attachment to the father and mother but also with parental control. All in all, the interrelationship of these variables suggests that we should consider family integration rather than parental attachment and parental control as two separate dimensions. When raising children, more emphasis should be placed on monitoring and supporting children rather than on pure control.

With respect to self-control theory (Gottfredson and Hirschi 1990), our data does support this theory. Self-control has a negative effect on delinquent involvement and it lowers the effect of family bonding and parental supervision. Self-control will be discussed further more in Chap. 11.

Sampson et al. (1997, 1999) and Sampson and Laub's theory (1993) cannot be satisfactorily tested in cross-sectional studies, or in survey research where the definition of neighbourhood cohesion and neighbourhood disorganization is created by respondents themselves. An attempt is made to specify the role of disintegrated neighbourhoods in furthering delinquent behaviour by a multi-level analysis in Chap. 11.

Nevertheless, what can be said on the basis of our findings in this chapter is that neighbourhood disintegration, as defined in this study by the presence of many abandoned buildings, graffiti, fighting, crime, and drug dealing in the respondent's neighbourhood, is strongly and positively correlated with serious delinquency involvement and negatively with family bonding and family control. In the regression analysis, where versatility is regressed on family variables also showed that neighbourhood disorganization makes the largest contribution, and this is true for all country clusters. This cannot come as a surprise, taking into account that unemployment and single parents are overrepresented in these neighbourhoods. All parents, and even more so single mothers, are struggling to provide a decent family income. Furthermore the negative association of neighbourhood disorganization with attachment to parents, but in particular to parental monitoring and support shows that many of these parents have difficulties in fulfilling all these tasks. The analysis of immigration groups confirmed these findings; it is not so much family bonding that is a problem but the lack of parental control, in terms of monitoring and support. This suggests that our data supports the Social disorganization theory, although we should be cautious not to overemphasize the results.

References

Acoca, L. 1999. Investing in girls: A 21st century strategy. *Juvenile Justice, 6*, 3–13.

Adler, F. (1975). *Sisters in Crime*. New York: McGraw-Hill.

Austin, R. L. (1993). Recent trends in official male and female crime rates: The convergence controversy. *Journal of Criminal Justice, 21*, 457–466.

Box, S. (1981) *Deviance Reality and Society*. London: Macmillan.

Cain, M. (1990). Towards transgression: New directions in feminist criminology. *International Journal of Sociology of Law, 18*, 1–18.

Chesney-Lind, M. & Pasko, L. (2004). *The Female Offender: Girls, Women and Crime*. Thousand Oaks, CA (2nd ed.): Sage.

Chesney-Lind, M., & Sheldon, R. G. (2004). *Girls, Delinquency, and Juvenile Hustice*. Belmont, CA (3rd ed.): Wadsworth/Thomson.
Corrado, R., Odgers, C. and Cohen, I. M. (2000). The Incarceration of female young offenders: Protection for whom? *Canadian Journal of Criminology, 42*, 189–207.
Cernkovich, S. A. & Giordano, P. C. (1987). Family relationships and delinquency. *Criminology, 25*, 295–321.
Giordano, P. C., Cernkovich, S. A, & Pugh, M. D. (1986). Friendships and delinquency. *The American Journal of Sociology,* 91, 1170–1202.
Glueck, S. & Glueck, E. (1950). *Unraveling Juvenile Delinquency*. Cambridge, MA: Harvard University Press.
Gottfredson M. R. & T. Hirschi (1990), *A General Theory of Crime*. Stanford, CA: Stanford University Press.
Graham, J. and Bowling, B. (1995). *Young people and crime*. Home Office Research Study No. 145. London: HMSO.
Grasmick, H. G., Tittle, C. R., Bursik, R. J. & Arneklev, B. J. (1993). Testing the core empirical implications of Gottfredson and Hirschi's general theory of crime. *Journal of Research in Crime and Delinquency, 30,* 5–29.
Hagan, J., Gillis, A. R. & Simpson, J. (1985). The class structure of gender and delinquency: Toward a power-control theory of common delinquent behavior. *American Journal of Sociology, 90*, 1151–1178.
Hawkins, J.D., Lishner, D.M., Catalano, R.F., & Howard, M.O. (1986). Childhood predictors of adolescent substance abuse: towards an empirically grounded theory. *Journal of Children and Contemporary Society, 8*, 11–47.
Heimer, K. (1995). Gender, race, and the pathways to delinquency: An interactionist analysis. In J. Hagan and R. D. Peterson (Eds), *Crime and Inequality* (pp. 140–173). Stanford, CA: Stanford University Press.
Hirschi, T. (1969). *Causes of Delinquency*. Berkeley, CA: University of California Press.
Junger, M., Terlouw, G. J., & van der Heijden, P. G. M. (1995). Crime, accidents and social control. *Criminal Behavior and Mental Health, 5*, 386–410.
Junger-Tas, J. (1995), Het raadsel van de Vrouwencriminaliteit. *Nemesis essays*, (September), 21–44.
Junger-Tas, J. (2009). Challenges to criminology in the 21st century. *Criminology in Europe: Newsletter of the European Society of Criminology, 8*(3), 3 and 13–16.
Junger-Tas, J., & Decker, S. H. (Eds.) (2006). *International Handbook of Juvenile Justice*. New York: Springer.
Junger-Tas, J. & Terlouw, G. J. (1991). Het Nederlandse publiek en het criminaliteitsprobleem. *Delikt en Delinkwent – Tijdschrift voor Strafrecht, 21*, 256–268 and 363–387.
Junger-Tas, J., Marshall, I. H., & Ribeaud, D. (2003). *Delinquency in an International Perspective: The International Self-Report Delinquency Study (ISRD)*. The Hague: Kugler.
Olweus, D. (1996). Bully/victim problems at school: Facts and effective interventions. *Reclaiming Children and Youth: Journal of Emotional and Behavioral Problems, 5*, 15–22.
Kornhauser, R. R. (1978). *Social Sources of Delinquency: An Appraisal of Analytic models*. Chicago, IL: University of Chicago Press.
LaGrange, T. C. & Silverman, R. A. (1999). Low self-control and opportunity: Testing the general theory of crime as an explanation for gender differences in delinquency. *Criminology, 37*, 41–72.
LaGrange, R., & White, H. (1985). Age differences in delinquency: A test of theory. *Criminology, 23*, 19–45.
Loeber, R., & Stouthamer-Loeber, M. (1986). Family factors as correlates and predictors of juvenile conduct problems and delinquency. In M. Tonry & N. Morris (Eds.), *Crime & Justice: An Annual Review of Research, Vol. 7* (pp. 29–149). Chicago, IL: University of Chicago Press.
Loeber, R., Farrington, D. P., Stouthamer-Loeber, M., & Van Kammen, W.B. (1998). *Antisocial Behaviour and Mental Health Problems*. New Jersey/London: LEA publications.

Loeber, R., & Dishion, T. (1983). Early predictors of male delinquency: A review. *Psychological Bulletin, 94*, 68–99.

Maccoby, E. E. & Jacklin, C. N. (1980). Sex differences in Aggression: a Rejoinder and Reprise. *Child Development, 51*, 964–980.

Masson, K., Karyotis, S. & de Jong, W. (2002). *De straat aan de jeugd: Een ontwikkelingsonderzoek naar drie jaar 'Thuis op Straat'*. Rotterdam: Aksant.

McCord, J. (1979). Some child-rearing antecedents of criminal behavior in adult men. *Journal of Personality and Social Psychology, 37*, 1477–1486.

Moffitt, T. E., Caspi, A., Rutter, M. & Silva, P. A. (2001). *Sex Differences in Antisocial Behaviour*. Cambridge: Cambridge University Press.

Morash, M. (1986). Gender, Peer Groups and Delinquency. *Journal of Research in Crime and Delinquency, 23*, 43–67.

Patterson, G. R. (1995). Coercion as a basis for early age of onset for arrest. In J. McCord (Ed.), *Coercion and punishment in long-term perspective* (pp. 81–105). Cambridge: Cambridge University Press.

Rankin, J. H. & Kern, R. (1994). Parental attachments and delinquency. *Criminology, 32*, 495–515.

Riley, D., & Shaw, M. (1985). *Parental Supervision and Juvenile Delinquency*. London: Home Office Research and Planning Unit.

Rivera, F. P. (1995). Crime, violence and injuries in children and adolescents: common risk factors? *Criminal Behavior and Mental Health, 5*, 367–386.

Rothbaum, F., & Weisz, J. R. (1994). Parental caregiving and child externalizing behavior in nonclinical samples: A meta-analysis. *Psychological Bulletin, 116*, 55–74.

Rowe, D. C., Vazsonyi, A. T., & Flannery, D. J. (1995). Sex differences in Crime: do means and within-sex variation have similar causes? *Journal of research in Crime and Delinquency, 32*, 84–100.

Rutter, M. & Giller, H. (1983). *Juvenile Delinquency: Trends and Perspectives*. Harmondsworth: Penguin Books.

Rutter, M., Giller, H., & Hagell, A. (1998), *Antisocial Behaviour by Young People*. Cambridge, MA: Cambridge University Press.

Sampson, R. J., & Laub, J. H. (1993). *Crime in the Making: Pathways and Turning Points Through Life*. Cambridge, MA: Havard University Press.

Sampson, R. J., Morenoff, J. D., & Earls, F. (1999). Beyond social capital: Spatial dynamics of collective efficacy for children. *American Sociological Review, 64*, 633–660.

Sampson, R. J., Raudenbush, S. W., & Earls, F. (1997). Neighborhoods and violent crime: A multilevel study of collective efficacy. *Science, 277*, 918–924.

Simon, R. J. (1975). *The Contemporary Woman and Crime*. Washington DC: National Institute of Mental Health.

Smith, P. K., Morita, Y., Junger-Tas, J., Olweus, D., Catalano, R. & Slee, P. (1999). *The Nature of School Bullying: A Cross-National Perspective*. London/New York: Routledge

Smith, C. & Krohn, M. D. (1995). Delinquency and family life among male adolescents: The role of ethnicity. *Journal of Youth and Adolescence, 24*, 69–93.

Steffensmeier, D., Bell, K. E. & Hayne, D. L. (2005) Gender and serious violence. Untangling the role of friendship sex composition and peer violence. *Youth Violence and Juvenile Justice, 5*, 235–253.

Stattin, H., & Romelsjö, A. (1995). Adult mortality in the light of criminality, substance abuse and behavioral and family risk factors in adolescence. *Criminal Behavior and Mental Health, 5*, 279–312.

Thornberry, T. P., Lizotte, A. J., Krohn, M. D., Smith, C. & Porter, P. K. (2003). Causes and consequences of delinquency: Findings from the Rochester Youth Development Study. In T. P. Thornberry, T. P. & M. D. Krohn (Eds.), *Taking Stock of Delinquency: An Overview of Findings from Contemporary Longitudinal Studies* (pp. 11–46). New York: Kluwer.

Van der Laan, A. M. & Blom, M. (2006). *Jeugddelinquentie. Risico's en bescherming; bevindingen uit de WODC Monitor Zelfgerapporteerde Jeugdcriminaliteit 2005*. Boom, Den Haag.

Wiatrowski, M. D., Griswold, D. B. & Roberts, M. K. (1981). Social control theory and delinquency. *American Sociological Review, 46*, 525–541.

Wikström, P.-O. (1998). Communities and crime. In M. Tonry (Ed.), *The Handbook of Crime and Punishment* (pp. 269–302). Oxford: Oxford University Press.

Wilmers, N., Enzmann, D., Schaefer, D., Herbers, D., Greve, W. & Wetzels, P. (2002). *Jugendliche in Deutschland zur Jahrtausendwende: Gefährlich oder gefährdet? Ergebnisse wiederholter, repräsentativer Dunkelfelduntersuchungen zu Gewalt und Kriminalität im Leben junger Menschen 1998–2000*. Baden-Baden: Nomos.

Wilson, J. Q. & Herrnstein, R. J. (1985). *Crime and Human Nature*. New York: Simon and Schuster.

Wright, J. P. & Cullen, F. T. (2001). Parental efficacy and delinquent behavior: Do control and support matter? *Criminology, 39*, 677–706.

Wright, J. P., Cullen, F. T., & Wooldredge, J. (2000). Parental social support and juvenile delinquency. In G. L. Fox & M. L. Benson (Eds.), Families, Crime, and Criminal Justice: Contemporary Perspectives on Family Research, Volume 2 (pp. 139–161). Greenwich, CT: JAI Press.

Yoshikawa, H. (1994) Prevention as cumulative protection effects of early family support and education on chronic delinquency and its risk. *Psychological Bulletin, 115*, 28–54.

Chapter 8
The School and its Impact on Delinquency

Sonia Lucia, Martin Killias, and Josine Junger-Tas

8.1 The School System as Social Environment

The school is an important social context for young people's socialization as they spend a considerable amount of time there. At school, they make friends and are supervised by their teachers. However, the role of the school in the lives of children is often underestimated. When compulsory education was introduced in most countries in the nineteenth century, the school taught – in addition to reading, writing and arithmetic- cultural norms and values, such as industriousness, hard work and how to behave according to the social norm. Teachers used to reward orderliness, diligence, self-control and respect for others, while they would punish children when they were careless or wouldn't pay attention. Virtues such as the love for God and one's country, a child's duties towards his parents, thrift and honesty found their roots in Christian morality and traditional conceptions of good citizenship. Even in contemporary times, the school represents a community of values, which are transferred and taught to children. Children are taught a certain degree of independence, when they are required to achieve an individual performance, for which they alone are responsible for, while abiding by objective criteria. Through processes such as these they learn how to cope with success and failure. Success bolsters self-confidence while repeated failure undermines it. Furthermore, the child is taught to distinguish universalism – being a member of a school class or of an ethnic group from specificity – being an individual member of one's family. In this way, children begin to see themselves and others as individuals who occupy a specific social position in society, an important distinction in social life. The significance of school learning has led some authors to believe that the school has replaced the family in terms of socializing youth in modern society (Gottfredson and Hirschi 1990).

M. Killias (✉)
University of Zurich, Zurich, Switzerland
e-mail: Martin.Killias@rwi.uzh.ch

J. Junger-Tas et al., *The Many Faces of Youth Crime: Contrasting Theoretical Perspectives on Juvenile Delinquency across Countries and Cultures*,
DOI 10.1007/978-1-4419-9455-4_8, © Springer Science+Business Media, LLC 2012

This chapter consists of two parts. In the first part we will test an important component of social control theory: the role of the school. We will examine how well the young people in this study perform at school and to what extent they are attached to the school. We will then examine which school variables are related to delinquent behaviour, including property and violent offenses. An important point to be considered is that violence within schools is not only associated with the characteristics of the young person, but also with the school itself and its system (Rutter et al. 1979). The second part of the chapter approaches the subject in a slightly different fashion, in that it will examine the impact of a tracking system on a child's school performance. The effects of tracking school performance levels and antisocial behaviour will be examined across the countries involved in a multilevel analysis.

8.2 School Functioning and School Bonding

The ISRD instrument includes a number of questions on school functioning. The most important questions included: "Did you ever have to repeat a grade"? "Did you stay away from school without an excuse for a whole day"? and "What are you planning to do after completing compulsory school"? In addition, two scales were made of four items, the first one expressed the bond with school: "If I had to move I would miss my school; I like my school; teachers do notice when I am doing well and let me know; there are all kinds of activities in school, such as sports, theatre or disco's" (Cranach's alpha=0.62). The other one measures school disorganization: "There is a lot of vandalism; there is a lot of fighting; there is a lot of stealing; and 'there is a lot of drug use in my school' (Cronbach's alpha=0.67)". It is worth observing that the strongest correlations in the first scale are between "considerate teachers" and "liking school" (0.30), while the strongest ones in the second scale are between "fighting in school" and "stealing" (0.51) and between "fighting in school" and "vandalism" (0.54). Table 8.1 presents the bivariate correlations between the school variables and three measures of delinquency. All correlations are significant at the 0.001 level, which may be explained by the large sample size.

One of the consequences for young people of repeating classes is that the more often they stay behind, the less often they think about their future after they have completed compulsory school. This suggests that students may feel a sense of failure, a lack of interest in school and, consequently, in what other educative options there eventually may be available. As such, however, repeating classes does not have a high correlation with any form of delinquency. The opposite is true for those who truant: truancy, which is related to repeating classes, has the strongest correlation with delinquency involvement in comparison to the other school variables. In addition, the data suggests that those who often truant, attend disorganized schools, are not greatly attached to school and even seem to hate their school. In accordance with this, planning for the future is associated with attending a well-organized school, having positive bonds with the school and liking school. Liking school, moreover, is rather strongly and negatively correlated with delinquency involvement. Finally, school disorganization is negatively correlated with all positive school variables and positively with truancy and delinquency versatility.

Table 8.1 Correlations of school variables and delinquency ($N = 39{,}452$)

	Repeat grades	Truancy	Future plans	Likes school	School bonding	School disorganiz	Total property	Total violence	Versatility
Repeat grades	1								
Truancy	0.11	1							
Future plans	–0.16	–0.10	1						
Likes school	0.02	–0.21	0.17	1					
School bonding	–0.07	–0.17	0.11	0.44	1				
School disorganiz	0.08	0.16	–0.13	–0.17	–0.12	1			
Total property	0.04	0.19	–0.07	–0.15	–0.11	0.15	1		
Total violence	0.08	0.23	–0.10	–0.18	–0.12	0.18	0.31	1	
Versatility	0.09	0.28	–0.11	–0.21	–0.15	0.21	0.66	0.71	1

All correlations $p < 0.001$

Table 8.2 Career planning after completing compulsory school by gender – in %

	Females	Males
Will look for a job	15.3	26.3
Vocational training	17.7	19.9
Continues his/her education	66.9	53.8
Cramer's V	0.16	

Considering the effect of gender, we found no great differences between boys and girls in regard to repeating grades and truancy. However, girls seem to like school more than boys (75% vs. 68%), and have stronger bonds with school (78% vs. 72%), though these differences are moderate. What really distinguishes the sexes from one another is the students' plans post-compulsory schooling. Girls clearly opt for pursuing a school career, which may lead to higher education, while considerably more boys withdraw from (higher) education in order to find a job (Table 8.2).

Immigration is another important variable that may lead to different choices in regard to school careers. In terms of liking school, first-generation immigrants have slightly lower scores than natives, but they commit truancy more often (35% vs. 28%) and repeat more classes (27.3% vs. 13 and 7%) than the natives. Consequently, fewer of them continue their education after compulsory school (51.7% vs. 62%), so in every respect they fare a lot worse than the natives. Although second-generation immigrants also repeat classes more often (22% vs. 13.7%) and would rather pursue vocational training schools instead of continuing their education (22% vs. 17.5%), overall they perform better than their first-generation counterparts in terms of repeating classes, truancy and pursuing employment instead of continuing their education. Thus, it is clear that gender and immigrant status are relevant to school-related variables and this may influence the noted bivariate associations between school variables and delinquency. Therefore we will now present the results of a multiple regression analysis, where we first introduced the control variables (age, gender, immigrant status), followed by the school-related variables.

Table 8.3 illustrates the results and allows for comparisons between the six country clusters with regard to the amount of explained variance (R square). Table 8.3 shows that in all clusters, when the control variables are presented alone, they have significant betas. However, when we added the school variables, only gender remained significantly related to versatility in all clusters, while ethnicity became weakly significant in the Anglo-Saxon cluster alone. In all other clusters, immigration did not contribute significantly to versatility. The strongest contribution in terms of explained variance came from the truancy in all clusters, although the betas differed per cluster. In the Anglo-Saxon (0.29), W-European (0.25) and N-European (0.28) clusters they were higher in comparison to the rest where the results varied between 0.21 and 0.17. The next highest betas referred to school disorganization, where the betas varied between 0.16 and 0.10, while liking school showed the last strongly and negatively significant betas. These ranged from −0.12 in the Anglo-Saxon, W-European and Latin American clusters to 0.09 in the N-European and the Post socialist clusters and 0.07 in S-Europe. Interestingly, repeating classes, is significant

Table 8.3 Regression on control- and school variables with versatility as dependent variable, by country cluster

	Model 1	Model 2
Anglo-Saxon		
Age	0.05[a]	0.02 (ns)
Gender	0.20[b]	0.16[b]
Immigrants	0.05[a]	0.05[a]
Repeating classes		–0.04[a]
Planning for future		–0.05[a]
Truancy		0.29[b]
Likes school		–0.12[b]
School bonding		–0.04[c]
School disorganization		0.16[b]
	R^2 0.04	R^2 0.24
West Europe		
Age	0.10[b]	0.01 (ns)
Gender	0.18[b]	0.14[b]
Immigrants	–0.01 (ns)	0.01 (ns)
Repeating classes		0.07[b]
Planning for future		0.02 (ns)
Truancy		0.25[b]
Likes school		–0.12[b]
School bonding		–0.02 (ns)
School disorganization		0.15[b]
	R^2 0.04	R^2 0.18
Northern Europe		
Age	0.05[b]	0.02 (ns)
Gender	0.15[b]	0.13[b]
Immigrants	–0.01 (ns)	0.02 (ns)
Repeating classes		0.03[c]
Planning for future		–0.03[a]
Truancy		0.28[b]
Likes school		–0.09[b]
School bonding		–0.03[a]
School disorganization		0.14[b]
	R^2 0.03	R^2 0.16
Southern Europe		
Age	0.13[b]	0.04[a]
Gender	0.16[b]	0.10[b]
Immigrants	–0.02[b]	–0.02 (ns)
Repeating classes		–0.01 (ns)
Planning for future		–0.05[c]
Truancy		0.21[b]
Likes school		–0.07[b]
School bonding		–0.07[b]
School disorganization		0.12[b]
	R^2 0.04	R^2 0.14

(continued)

Table 8.3 (continued)

	Model 1	Model 2
Post-Socialist		
Age	0.07[b]	0.02 (ns)
Gender	0.21[b]	0.16[b]
Immigrants	−0.03[a]	−0.02 (ns)
Repeating classes		0.04[b]
Planning for future		−0.06[b]
Truancy		0.19[b]
Likes school		−0.09 [b]
School bonding		−0.03[a]
School disorganization		0.11[b]
	R^2 0.05	R^2 0.13
Latin American		
Age	0.07[b]	−0.01 (ns)
Gender	0.14[b]	0.11[b]
Immigrants	−0.04[a]	−0.02 (ns)
Repeating classes		0.07[b]
Planning for future		−0.02 (ns)
Truancy		0.17[b]
Likes school		−0.12[b]
School bonding		0.02 (ns)
School disorganization		0.10[b]
	R^2 0.03	R^2 0.10

[a]$p<0.05$
[b]$p<0.001$
[c]$p<0.01$

only in W-Europe and in Latin America, both of which are clusters where repeating classes is a specific feature of the school system. In all other clusters its contribution is negligible. It should be noted that in all of the clusters, the pattern and order of betas that contributed the most to the explained variance of delinquency involvement were similar. This outcome confirms the universal validity of the importance of the school as suggested by social control theory, and is not only the case in the Anglo-Saxon cluster and Europe, but even in countries such as Venezuela, Surinam and the Antilles. The picture that arises from this analysis illustrates that overall, young people who attend disorganized schools are not attached to the school: they simply don't like being there. Although the responses we received regarding the question about disorganized schools, may partially be a reflection of the troublesome youngsters themselves, it can be said that such schools are unable to maintain a normative structure and an orderly teaching and learning environment with serious negative consequences for numerous students, including the most difficult ones. Youngsters, who must repeat a class, fail to make plans for their future, which suggests an unsatisfying school career. A consequence of which is that they become more vulnerable truancy, or leave school early in search of employment. According to Hirschi (1969), when a youngster is no longer attached to society – in this case a social institution such as school – he no longer feels the need to abide by its conventional norms and values and, because he has nothing to lose, he is free to break the law and commit offenses. Such young people tend to select or attract other marginalized youths as friends, resulting in a peer group that is more likely to fall into a trap of offending behaviour. They pursue such behaviour primarily out of boredom, for monetary reasons or out of the desire to take part in the youth culture.

8.3 Differences in School Systems Between Countries

The second part of this chapter considers an important characteristic related to the countries' different school systems, that is the existence of a system of "tracking" students according to ability. Youths who are striving for success but are structurally prevented from achieving it, may become frustrated and can turn to alternative pathways to success (Agnew 2005; Merton 1938). Tracking (streaming in British), or the division of students into instructional groups by ability, has become an educational practice in several countries. Within this system, the future perspectives of adolescents are determined by the track in which they are placed. The higher the academic track, the better the chances of finding a future profession. Other variables such as the school climate or the presence of delinquency at school can also increase the strain on students. Students assigned to lower tracks compared with those in higher tracks will exhibit less commitment to school and be more at risk of delinquency (Hirschi 1969). Jenkins (1995) found that students in low ability math groups were less committed to school and exhibited higher levels of involvement in school crime and misconduct. The theoretical work of Sutherland (1947) posits that behaviour is learned through intimate interaction with others. Once tracked, there is generally little opportunity for prolonged daily interaction among students from different tracks. Students spend much of their day in the company of other students who, according to the evaluation, share the same level of academic ability. Students in higher tracks are more likely to develop friendships with other students who share similar characteristics such as race and class background, as well as goals for educational and occupational success. In the lower tracks, it is common for students, who may themselves be unhappy, to encounter others who are disillusioned about school, disruptive to others in class, or those who have accepted their educational failure. Perhaps they may also encounter students who have developed other routes to success, which aren't academic in any way (i.e. involvement in delinquency). Thus, track location provides an environment in which likely friends are chosen (Febbo-Hunt 2003; Hallinan and Sørensen 1985).

In tracked systems, children are placed into different classes within a school, based on their academic abilities. Another type of tracked system is "setting" which involves assigning students to ability-grouped classes for one or two academic subjects while permitting them to be grouped heterogeneously for all other courses (Ansalone 2003). One aim of tracking is to facilitate instruction and to increase learning; however, it simultaneously creates unequal learning opportunities. Empirical research provides evidence to suggest that the quality and quantity of instruction increases with track level. Moreover, track levels have been connected to the social status of students as well as their self-esteem and motivation to learn (Hallinan 1994). In their meta-analysis of tracking, Kulik and Kulik (1992) reveal that high-ability students who have been placed in a tracked system, outperform compared with similar students in non-tracked classes. Supporters of the tracked system highlight its efficiency and ability to enhance self-development for students, since they can only directly compare themselves to similar-ability peers. This should not lead to lower self-esteem in lower-ability students, as would be the case if these students were placed in the same class as their high-ability peers. Since high self-esteem is correlated with high academic achievement, tracking should, theoretically, promote academic success for low-ability students. Critics, on the other hand, highlight that there is a class-bias; socially disadvantaged children and minorities are over-represented in low tracks (Ansalone 2003). However, when academic achievement is controlled, the effect of ethnicity and income on track assignments decreases, but does not disappear. Another and supplementary argument against tracking is that it can lead to a stigmatization of low-track students. In accordance with the labelling theory, it is believed that stigmatization has a negative impact on a students' academic performance. Moreover, track assignment depends on which school the students attend. Indeed, the assignment is not only based on academic factors, but also on teacher recommendations (Hallinan 1994). Through the selection process, teachers play a significant role in shaping the identity and self-esteem of the adolescents, which are continuously built upon on a daily basis. Career options, as well as friendship choices are largely determined by this selection process. Finally, once a student has been assigned to a specific track he or she can expect to remain in it (Kelly and Pink 1982).

The question about the link between the school system (tracking) and delinquency remains unanswered. Back in the early 1980s, Kelly and Pink suggested that the potential for offending at school is related to its organizational structure (Kelly and Pink 1982, p. 59). Allison (1992) reported that students from lower tracks admit to higher levels of cigarette, alcohol and cannabis use in comparison with students from an advanced level. This association is maintained even after controlling for gender, grade average, drug education lessons and pressure to use substances. Joseph (1995, 1996) found that lower track students experience greater failure, have an increased tendency to drop out of school, are more likely to misbehave and commit more delinquent acts, than higher track students. However, Wiatrowski et al. (1982) showed, that the correlation between tracking and delinquency is observed mostly in cross-sectional studies, while curriculum tracking did not change the probability of delinquency involvement in their longitudinal study among high school boys. This is supported by Febbo-Hunt (2003) who did not observe any direct effect of track placement on the frequency of delinquent behaviour (status, violent and property offenses). However, her analyses also show that tracking indirectly increases the propensity to commit more types of property offenses. It is interesting to see that the results differ depending on whether the instrument intended to measure the engagement or the abstention of delinquent behaviour (where logistic regression is applied) or the number of types of offenses committed (where Poisson or negative binomial regression techniques are applied). Results indicate that there is a direct and an indirect effect in regard to being in the lower track and the commitment of status offenses, whereas there are no direct or indirect effects of tracking on property offenses. In a Swiss national survey, being in the lowest track of the school system is not related to increased shoplifting or vandalism after controlling for socio-demographic and individual characteristics, as well as family and neighbourhood related variables (personal communication). However, tracking does increase exposure to non-delinquent peers and decreases the chance of dropping out for those placed in the academic track, but has little or no effect on the most disadvantaged segment of the population (Gottfredson 2001).

In the following section, we will explore the relationship between the school context and delinquency. Moreover, we will take advantage of the large international data set of multilevel analyses to determine the country-level effects on delinquency, after individual-level variables are controlled. In addition to the tracking dilemma, we will also draw some valid conclusions from the results of PISA, a large international study of national differences in educational achievement. Cross-national PISA means and standard deviations will also be used in order to assess the impact on delinquency of the school system's performance and its ability to integrate weaker students.

8.3.1 Methodology

Two dependent variables are used: serious violent offenses (assault, extortion, snatching), and serious property offenses (theft from a car, car theft, bicycle theft, burglary). We have two sets of independent variables: those at the level of the country (Sect. 8.3.1.1) and those at the individual level (Sect. 8.3.1.2).

8.3.1.1 Country-Level Variables

Each country has its own school system, which is not easy to characterize in simple terms. Therefore we have tried to assess, with the use of a small survey among all responsible researchers from the countries involved, how systems are organised per country in regard to tracking students based on their academic ability. According to the information collected, in nine countries, students between the ages of 10 and 13 have been subjected to such selection processes. In these nine countries, the best students will, from that age onwards, attend a "gymnasium"-type of school that qualifies them, at approximately age 18, to apply for university. A second track that usually lasts for about 3 or 4 years, prepares students for more demanding apprenticeships leading to qualified or technical jobs including banking. Finally, the lower tracks usually prepare students for manual and other less demanding jobs. However, 17 countries do not differentiate students according to intellectual abilities, at least not during the age groups included in our sample. Three countries have a *streaming system,* i.e. students follow some subjects, according to their ability, in different levels. The following table presents an overview of the situation based on the outcome of our survey. Most countries differentiate between two tracks, whereas a few have three, and others have a "streaming" system (Table 8.4).

Table 8.4 Ability-based tracking systems in schools

Countries	Number of tracks	% students in each track	Age of selection
Ireland	Streaming system	NA	NA
United States	Streaming system	NA	NA
Denmark	1	NA	NA
Finland	1	NA	NA
Iceland	1	NA	NA
Norway	1	NA	NA
Sweden	1	NA	NA
Austria	3	Low: 33% Medium: 28.3% High: 38.6%	10–11
Belgium	2	Low: 27.9% High: 72.1%	11
France	1	NA	NA
Germany	3	Low: 19.1% Medium: 40.6% High: 40.3%	10–11
Netherlands	3	Low: 46.1% Medium: 29.5% High: 24.4%	11
Switzerland	1, 2, 3 or 4, no tracks and setting	No tracks: 14.5% Low: 19.8% Medium: 37.6% High: 28.0%	12
Cyprus	1	NA	NA
Italy	3	No tracks: 62.8% (7 and 8 grade) Low: 11.3% Medium: 12.2% High: 13.7%	14
Portugal	1	NA	NA
Spain	1	NA	NA
Aruba	1	NA	NA
Netherlands Antilles	4	No indication	11
Suriname	No indication	No indication	No indication
Venezuela	1	NA	NA
Armenia	1	NA	NA
Bosnia and Herzegovina	1	NA	NA
Czech republic	2	Low: 83.6% High: 16.4%	11
Estonia	1	NA	NA
Hungary	3	Low: 67.5% Medium: 13.5% High: 19.0%	12–14
Lithuania	2	Low: 73.1% High: 26.9%	13–15
Poland	1	NA	NA
Russian Federation	1	NA	NA
Slovenia	1	NA	NA

NA not applicable

Table 8.5 PISA mean and standard deviation scores for 2006

List of countries	PISA mean	PISA standard deviation score
Slovenia	519	98
Russian federation	479	90
Poland	498	90
Lithuania	488	90
Hungary	504	88
Estonia	531	84
Czech republic	513	98
Spain	488	91
Portugal	474	89
Italy	475	96
Switzerland	512	99
Netherlands	525	96
Germany	516	100
France	495	102
Belgium	510	100
Austria	511	98
Sweden	503	94
Norway	487	96
Iceland	491	97
Finland	563	86
Denmark	496	93
United States	489	106
Ireland	508	94

For the following analyses, we used data from the 2006 PISA survey conducted in OECD countries. The domains of reading, mathematics and logical problem-solving were tested. The national PISA means and standard deviations are derived from the PISA site[1] and are presented in Table 8.5. The grand mean for the OECD countries is 500 and the standard deviation is 95. In our analyses, the PISA mean has been dichotomized: the countries with a mean above or equal to 500, vs. those below. The PISA standard deviation has been dichotomized into: countries with a standard deviation lower or equal to 95 vs. those higher than 95. PISA scores were not available for seven countries (Armenia, Bosnia-Herzegovina, Cyprus and the territories and countries in Latin America) because they did not participate in this test.

The PISA mean has no obvious (linear) relation to serious violent or serious property offenses (not shown). However, the standard deviation of PISA shows some correlation with serious violent and serious property offenses (Figs. 8.1 and 8.2). It expresses the variation among pupils at the PISA test. It is a good measure of how well-integrated pupils of various backgrounds are within the school system. In other words, a low standard deviation means that there are not very large differences in the intellectual performance of students, and that, therefore, social integration

[1] http://www.oecd.org/dataoecd/30/18/39703566.pdf (Table 2.1c).

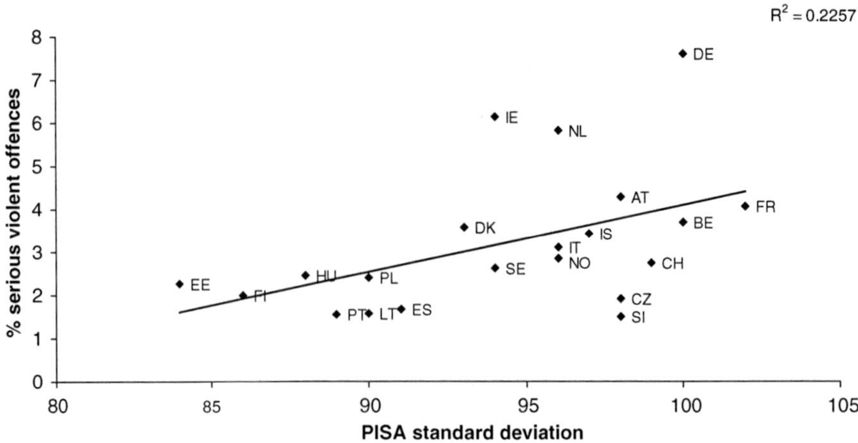

Fig. 8.1 Correlation between PISA standard deviation scores and serious violent offenses

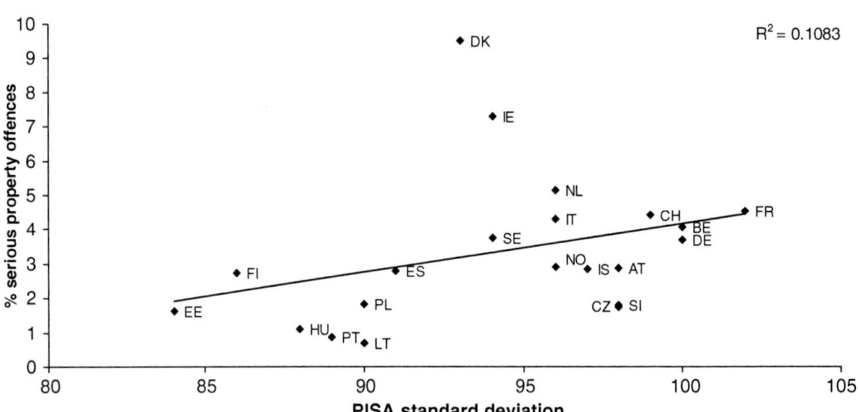

Fig. 8.2 Correlation between PISA standard deviation scores and serious property offences

is higher. Because some data of these variables were missing, we had to exclude 9 out of 31 countries and our analysis is therefore based on 21 nations. Bivariate correlation scatter gram plots suggest that this variable may have some potential in explaining cross-country variations in serious violent and serious property offenses (Figs. 8.1 and 8.2).

In addition to the PISA variables, we used the general unemployment rate. The latter has been dichotomized by separating the countries in almost two equal groups (46.8% have an unemployment rate higher or equal 7 and 53.2% have an unemployment lower than 7%). The data concerning these two variables was found on the

Eurostat site for the year 2006.[2] Finally, the variable "tracked system" has also been dichotomized: countries with a tracked system have been coded 1, and those without have been assigned 0.

8.3.1.2 Individual-Level Variables

As in the other chapters, we first looked at the important variables at the level of the country clusters. The results are given below in Table 8.6. The Latin American cluster as well as Armenia, Bosnia-Herzegovina and Cyprus are not included in the table as these countries did not participate in the PISA survey.

As Table 8.6 suggests, clusters differ with respect to serious offenses and PISA scores. However, PISA scores differ far more within than between the clusters. With the exception of the Mediterranean cluster, PISA scores hardly vary across clusters – but they do so across countries. Clusters vary more with respect to other school variables, such as the percentage of students having repeated at least one grade (this is very high in Western Europe and very low in Northern Europe), school disorganization, school-climate and PISA standard deviations. In general, students in Mediterranean countries have low PISA scores, view their performance as students more critically, but see the school climate as more positive and have higher long-term educational aspirations than students, e.g. in Western Europe. Serious property offenses are relatively rare in the former Socialist cluster and comparatively high in the Anglo-Saxon cluster. Serious violent offenses are twice as frequent in Anglo-Saxon and Western European countries compared with Northern and Mediterranean Europe or in Post-Socialist countries.

As for the country-level variables, all individual-level variables have been dichotomized as suggested by Farrington and Loeber (2000). One of the advantages of dichotomization is that the odds ratios are easier to understand and to interpret in comparison to regression coefficients.

Several socio-demographic characteristics, such as gender, age,[3] and migrant status, have been used in the following analyses. We also included selected school-related variables, such as the students' experiences with school and their school career. These variables have been defined in the following way:

- *School failure*: "Have you ever been held back, that is did you ever have to repeat a grade"? (0 = not having repeated a grade, 1 = having repeated a grade).
- *Attachment to school*: The question asked was "Do you usually like school"? The four possible answers have been dichotomized by combining the two most similar categories into one: 0 = strong attachment ("I like school a lot/fairly well"), 1 = weak attachment ("I do not like school very much/not at all").

---

[2] http://epp.eurostat.ec.europa.eu/portal/page/portal/eurostat/home/. The rate of unemployment for Switzerland and Iceland were obtained respectively from http://www.bfs.admin.ch/bfs/portal/fr/index.html and http://indexmundi.com/iceland/unemployment_rate.html.

[3] We used "age" rather than "grade", because it offered a larger variance. Coefficients were only marginally affected by this choice (see Chap. 3).

Table 8.5 Dependent and independent variables by country cluster

	Anglo-Saxon	Northern EU	Western EU	Mediterranean EU	Former socialist
% serious violent offences	5.1	2.9	5.0	2.7	2.1
% serious property offences	5.9	4.5	4.3	3.4	1.5
% truancy	28.5	30.7	22.2	27.6	28.0
% repeated grade	12.3	3.8	22.2	19.2	4.6
% self-assessment of achievement (below average)	8.3	6.9	10.4	12.6	10.6
% long-term educational aspirations	59.7	51.5	39.1	59.9	45.4
% weak attachment to school	38.2	35.0	36.4	39.2	51.7
% negative school climate	20.4	34.9	27.5	16.4	25.5
% school disorganization	37.2	17.3	28.6	20.0	21.7
Mean PISA	499	508	512	479	505
PISA standard deviation	13	31	10	8	18

- *School climate*: To construct this variable, four items were combined into an index, namely "if I had to move, I would miss my school;" "teachers do notice when I am doing well and let me know;" "I like my school", and; "there are other activities in school besides lessons (sports, music, theatre, discos)". Each question allows four answers, ranging from "I fully agree" to "I fully disagree". This index has been dichotomized by opposing the most "negative" quartile to the three remaining quartiles (0=positive climate, 1=negative climate).
- *School disorganization*: As for the preceding variable, the following four items have also been combined into an index, namely, "there is a lot of stealing in my school;" "there is a lot of fighting in my school;" "many things are broken or vandalised in my school", and; "there is a lot of drug use in my school". Again, answers ranged from "I fully agree" to "I fully disagree". This index has been dichotomized by opposing the most "negative" quartile to the three remaining quartiles (0=no, 1=yes).
- *Self-assessment of achievement*: Three possible categories of the question: "How well do you do in school compared to other students in your class"? have been dichotomized by combining the categories "I am doing better than most of my class mates" and, "I am an average student" and opposing these two to "I am not doing very well" (0=about or above average, 1="not doing very well").
- *Long-term educational aspirations*: For this variable we asked "What do you think of doing after you finish compulsory school"? Several response categories have been proposed. For the present purposes, the category "I shall continue my education preparing for higher education" has been opposed to the combined remaining categories (0=continue studying, 1=other).
- *Lowest level*: Pupils from the lowest track are coded 1 and all the others 0.

Listwise deletion has been chosen to deal with missing data. This method implies that only complete cases are taken into consideration for analysis and all incomplete cases are discarded. Out of the 49,654 pupils from the 21 countries, 44,710 remain, thereby losing about 10% of cases.

Analyses

As a first step, we looked at the bivariate correlations between PISA scores and several measures of integration of students at school that are usually considered relevant in the analysis of delinquency (Table 8.7).

As it turns out, countries with large PISA deviation scores (i.e. countries with more inequality among pupils) usually have tracking systems. This seems logical, since weak students may be achieving less in lower tracks, whereas students in the highest tracks may become even stronger as shown in the higher PISA scores. Countries with high PISA deviation scores also have a far higher proportion of students enrolled in the lowest track. Further, more students have repeated a grade in countries with large PISA deviation scores – again a "logical" finding since more students with below-average grades may be forced to repeat a year under elitist

Table 8.7 Correlations between PISA deviation scores and several school-related variables

	PISA deviation score		Significance	Association
	Small dispersion (95≤) (%)	Large dispersion (>95) (%)	Chi square	Gamma
System with tracks	22.8	76.2	0.000	0.830
Being in the lowest level	16.0	24.1	0.000	0.248
Have repeated a grade	10.9	14.8	0.000	0.175
Disorganization in the school	19.9	25.9	0.000	0.168
Self-assessment of achievement (below average)	9.6	10.4	0.003	0.047
Wish to study after school	51.7	43.9	0.000	−0.155
Have played truant	29.1	21.2	0.000	−0.206
Weak attachment to school	43.9	39.6	0.000	−0.088
Negative school climate	26.9	25.2	0.000	−0.042

systems. Interestingly, however, there are not a lot more students who assess themselves as being "weak" (or below average) in countries with more inequality at schools, and there are less students wishing to study after having finished school. Even school climate and attachment to school are at best weakly related to inequality, probably because students may not necessarily feel unhappy in countries with tracked systems and, thus, more homogeneous schools. School disorganization, however, is more frequent in systems with more inequality, probably because schools with larger gaps between strong and weak students may be less able to install discipline. On the other hand (and paradoxically), truancy is less common under homogeneous (i.e. non-tracking) systems.

Multilevel models will be used to account for the clustered nature of the sample, with pupils nested within countries (Bryk and Raudenbush 1992). The key research question is whether offense rates are invariant by country when controlling for individual sets of risk and protective factors. Because our dependent variables (having committed certain offenses or not) have been dichotomized, the models used are based on logistic regression (Snijders and Bosker 1999). Two types of hypotheses are investigated.

We expect that the offending rate differs between countries and that a certain number of variables explain the variability between countries in these prevalence rates, at least partially (random intercept model). Further, we shall investigate whether certain variables, such as sex, school failure, self-assessment of achievement and long-term educational aspirations, will have different effects per country (random slopes model).

In order to test the first hypothesis, we tested a Level 1 random-intercept model with fixed slope coefficients. This means that once the Level 1 variables are added,

Level 2 variables are tested one by one on the intercept (γ_{00}). For these models, Level 1 and 2 variables are uncentered. To test the second hypothesis, an evaluation of slope heterogeneity will be carried out. Here, Level 1 variables are group centred. Level 1 variables are added to the model, and the random effects of the slopes are tested one by one for significance. Then, the effects of Level 2 (country) variables on slopes are tested. As it turned out, none of these variables linked differently to the countries. Therefore, random slope models are not pursued any further in this chapter.

In the framework of this book, thc focus has been put on the comparison of clusters. However, such analyses cannot be carried out with only six clusters. Applying multilevel analyses with only 6 U (six clusters in all, out of which the Anglo-Saxon cluster includes only two countries) at Level 2, will not result in an accurate estimation between-group variances.

8.3.2 *Results*

8.3.2.1 Serious Violent Offenses

The question in the following analyses focuses on whether there is sufficient variability between countries that needs to be explained. In order to measure whether a given country has an effect on serious offenses, we examined the unconditional model (empty model) in which the lowest level of data (pupils) is modelled without any predictors. The empty model provides a partition of the variability in the data between the two levels. The empty model shows that 7.4% of the total variance is attributable to Level 2 (country), and that this country-level variance is significant ($p \leq 0.001$).

In the first Level 1 model, the intercept was specified as random and the slopes were fixed. Socio-demographic variables were added and all of them were significant, the variable with the highest odds ratio being gender (model 1). In model 2, school-related variables were introduced at Level 1, leading to a significant increase of the fit of the model (deviance decreases from 94,666 to 93,724). When adding the school-related variables, the odds ratio of the three socio-demographic variables decreased. Out of the seven school-related variables, only "being in the lowest track" was not significantly related to delinquency (OR = 1.08). Unexpectedly, having long-term educational aspirations was positively and significantly correlated with serious violent offenses (OR = 1.40). These two results may be related to the fact that students less motivated to engage themselves in long-term academic projects may not necessarily suffer from frustration, because they may perceive more realistic goals for their immediate future. Furthermore, being in a low track school may, despite limited perspectives regarding future job careers, not necessarily produce violent behaviour because daily frustration due to intellectual inferiority in comparison with peers may be less resented. The most impressive connection to serious violent offenses is "school disorganization". Pupils in a disorganized school are about 3 times more likely to commit serious violent offenses compared to those attending a school without such characteristics (Table 8.8).

Level 2 variables were added to the intercept and were tested one by one for significance (models not shown). Unemployment was not significantly related to serious violence, whereas the three variables related to educational inequality were significant at $p<0.05$, namely the existence in a country with a "tracked system", the PISA mean and the PISA standard deviation. When those three variables were simultaneously introduced into Model 3, all of them were significant (Table 8.9). Countries segregating weaker students into lower track schools seem to suffer from higher levels of serious violence (OR=1.46). Moreover, a low performance of the educational system, along with inequality between pupils (measured by standard deviation from the PISA mean), is also related to serious violent offenses. Indeed, the fact that the PISA mean is lower than the mean for all OECD countries (which is equal to 500) increases by 1.47 the risk of committing serious violent offenses and a large PISA standard deviation score (≥95) increase the risk by 1.46.

In sum, with the exception of gender, school-related variables such as frequent deviant acts at school ("disorganization"), the existence of a tracked system and high heterogeneity in intellectual performance among students (PISA standard deviation) are the strongest variables in the final model. The mean score of students of any country that was reached during the PISA tests is also significantly correlated with serious violent offenses (OR=1.47). In other words, countries with high-quality schools face lower rates of serious violence among their students.

8.3.2.2 Serious Property Offenses

Due to the fact that the variability between countries was significant, a multilevel analysis was applied. Indeed, 6.5% of the total variance is attributable to Level 2 (country).

In the first Level 1 model, the intercept was specified as random and the slopes were fixed. In model 1 for serious property offenses, the three socio-demographic variables behave similarly as in model 1 for serious violent offenses. They are all significant. Gender is closest related to serious property offenses (OR=3.93), i.e. being a boy multiplies the risk of committing such an act by 4 (Table 8.7), whereas the odds ratio for serious violent offenses is only 2.55 (Table 8.5).

In model 2, school-related variables were introduced at Level 1 leading to a significant increase of the fit of the model (deviance decreasing from 94′182 to 93′440). Out of the seven school-related variables, only "being in the lowest track" was not significant. As for serious violent offenses, the variables with the highest odds ratios included: gender, school disorganization and attachment to school. Surprisingly, youth with long-term educational aspirations appear to have a higher probability of being involved in serious property offenses than those without such aspirations (Table 8.10).

Level 2 variables were added to the intercept and were tested one by one for significance (models not shown). Two variables are significant at $p<0.05$: the "PISA

Table 8.8 Hierarchical generalised linear models for serious violent offenses: models at level 1

	Model 1				Model 2			
	B	S.E	Odds ratio	*p*-value	B	S.E	Odds ratio	*p*-value
Intercept	−4.625	0.306	0.01	0.000	−5.273	0.354	0.01	0.000
Boys (vs. girls)	0.938	0.066	2.55	0.000	0.758	0.054	2.13	0.000
14–18 years old (vs. 11–13)	0.909	0.147	2.48	0.000	0.569	0.104	1.77	0.000
Migrant (vs. non-migrant)	0.344	0.116	1.41	0.003	0.318	0.124	1.37	0.011
Repeated a grade (vs. did not repeat a grade)					0.450	0.035	1.57	0.000
Performs at school below average (vs. about/above average)					0.513	0.060	1.67	0.000
Has long-term educational aspirations (vs. no)					0.339	0.046	1.40	0.000
Weak attachment to school (vs. attached to school)					0.620	0.043	1.86	0.000
Negative school climate (vs. positive school climate)					0.414	0.053	1.51	0.000
School disorganization (vs. no school disorganization)					1.075	0.032	2.93	0.000
Not being in the lowest track (vs. yes)					0.078	0.071	1.08	0.272
		Variance component	Chi-square	*p*-value		Variance component	Chi-square	*p*-value
Random effect – country level								
Intercept		0.22291	578.73282	0.000		0.31267	810.3062	0.000
Deviance	94′667				93′724			

Table 8.9 Hierarchical generalised linear models for serious violent offenses: model 3

	Model 3			
	B	S.E.	Odds ratio	p-value
Fixed effects – individual level				
Intercept	−5.377	0.304	0.00	0.000
Boys (vs. girls)	0.758	0.054	2.13	0.000
14–18 years old (vs. 11–13)	0.574	0.104	1.78	0.000
Migrant (vs. non-migrant)	0.315	0.126	1.37	0.013
Repeated a grade (vs. did not repeat a grade)	0.451	0.038	1.57	0.000
Performs at school below average (vs. about/above average)	0.512	0.061	1.67	0.000
Has long-term educational aspirations (vs. no)	0.338	0.045	1.40	0.000
Weak attachment to school (vs. attached to school)	0.618	0.041	1.85	0.000
Negative school climate (vs. positive school climate)	0.416	0.053	1.52	0.000
School disorganization (vs. no school disorganization)	1.079	0.032	2.94	0.000
Not being in the lowest track (vs. yes)	0.113	0.069	1.12	0.102
Fixed effects – country level				
Predictor for intercept				
Tracked system (vs. no)	0.376	0.159	1.46	0.030
PISA mean lower than 500 (vs. ≥500)	0.387	0.182	1.47	0.048
PISA standard deviation <95 (vs. higher)	0.377	0.158	1.46	0.029
		Variance component	Chi-square	p-value
Random effect – country level				
Intercept		0.106	197.527	0.000
Deviance	93′722			

standard dispersion" and the "unemployment rate". But when added together on the intercept, the "PISA standard deviation" is no longer significant. Therefore the final model only includes the unemployment rate. This signifies that in countries with an unemployment rate under 7%, the risk of committing serious property offenses is increased by 2 (Table 8.11).

As for serious violent offenses, school disorganization and other school-related structural variables seem more influential than the personal characteristics of students, gender being the noteworthy exception.

8.4 Discussion

The data shows that at the individual level, the variables with the highest odds ratios are: gender, school disorganization and attachment to school. The data also shows that boys commit more offenses than girls. The risk is more significant for serious

Table 8.10 Hierarchical generalised linear models for serious property offenses: models 1 and 2

	Model 1				Model 2			
	B	S.E	Odds ratio	*p*-value	B	S.E	Odds ratio	*p*-value
Intercept	−5.085	0.185	0.01	0.000	−5.737	0.209	0.00	0.000
Boys (vs. girls)	1.368	0.074	3.93	0.000	1.205	0.081	3.34	0.000
14–18 years old (vs. 11–13)	0.999	0.116	2.72	0.000	0.697	0.125	2.01	0.000
Migrant (vs. non-migrant)	0.384	0.060	1.47	0.000	0.382	0.070	1.47	0.000
Repeated a grade (vs. did not repeat a grade)					0.329	0.100	1.39	0.001
Performs at school below average (vs. about/above average)					0.346	0.103	1.41	0.001
Has long-term educational aspirations (vs. no)					0.211	0.073	1.23	0.004
Weak attachment to school (vs. attached to school)					0.793	0.036	2.21	0.000
Negative school climate (vs. positive school climate)					0.284	0.073	1.33	0.000
School disorganization (vs. no school disorganization)					0.908	0.076	2.48	0.000
Not being in the lowest track (vs. yes)					0.069	0.069	1.07	0.314
		Variance component	Chi-square	*p*-value		Variance component	Chi-square	*p*-value
Random effect – country level								
Intercept		0.24543	333.26921	0.000		0.28817	408.047	0.000
Deviance	94′182				93′440			

Table 8.11 Hierarchical generalized linear models for serious property offenses: model 3

	Model 3			
	B	S.E.	Odds ratio	*p*-value
Fixed effects – individual level				
Intercept	–5.159	0.245	0.01	0.000
Boys (vs. girls)	1.205	0.081	3.34	0.000
14–18 years old (vs. 11–13)	0.695	0.123	2.00	0.000
Migrant (vs. non-migrant)	0.388	0.071	1.47	0.000
Repeated a grade (vs. did not repeat a grade)	0.339	0.102	1.40	0.001
Performs at school below average (vs. about/above average)	0.343	0.103	1.41	0.001
Has long-term educational aspirations (vs. no)	0.740	0.234	1.24	0.004
Weak attachment to school (vs. attached to school)	0.793	0.037	2.21	0.000
Negative school climate (vs. positive school climate)	0.285	0.073	1.33	0.000
School disorganization (vs. no school disorganization)	0.909	0.075	2.48	0.000
Not being in the lowest track (vs. yes)	0.054	0.070	1.06	0.435
Fixed effects – country level				
Predictor for intercept				
Unemployment rate <7% (vs. ≥7%)	0.740	0.234	2.10	0.006
		Variance component	Chi-square	*p*-value
Random effect – country level				
Intercept		0.18449	234.60191	0.000
Deviance	93′438			

property offenses than serious violent offenses. Being in a school where deviant acts are rather common may lead to the impression that crime is permitted in a certain way, as suggested by the broken windows theory (Wilson and Kelling 1982). Furthermore, a school where crimes occur either implies that there are no guardians, or they do not intervene, as suggested by the routine activity theory (Cohen and Felson 1979). A crime is more likely to occur when a motivated offender is in the same place, at the same moment, as an attractive target in the absence of a capable guardian. School disorganization is a very important variable in regards to other types of unruly behaviour, such as bullying (Lucia 2009). Attachment to school relates to Hirschi's social control theory (Hirschi 2002) which proposes that individuals who maintain close bonds to conventional institutions, such as school, are less likely to commit delinquent acts because they will care more about their teachers' expectations and will respect and adopt their norms and values. Moreover, the absence of long-term educational aspirations is negatively related to serious violent and property offenses. Furthermore, out of the seven school-related variables the only non-significant variable was "being in the lowest track". This finding is similar to those found by Wiatrowski et al. (1982) and Febbo-Hunt (2003). In other words, it is not simply "being" in a low track that is damaging (in terms of delinquency), at least not in a multivariate model where other variables are being taken into account.

At the country level, we observed that countries with a tracked system have higher rates of serious violent offenses (but not property offenses) as opposed to those schools where all students remained in one track (odds ratio 1.46). The presence of such an effect on the macro level and the absence of it at the micro level seems contradictory. However, an inequality of chances within the educational system may promote violence independently of individual strain. For example, a tracked system may lead to the segregation of weaker students into special school buildings – a fact that may affect behaviour even if individual strain may not increase through a more homogenous school environment. Perhaps even more interestingly, a high dispersion in the intellectual performance of students within a given country (PISA standard deviation) increases the prevalence of serious violent offenses by (equally) 1.46. Egalitarian school systems, thus, produce less offending than elitist styles of education. Finally, countries with a well performing school system (measured by a PISA score of more or less than 500) suffer less from serious violence than those where intellectual achievement is, on average, poor. Perhaps schools are, on average, performing better (and students are doing better during PISA tests) precisely because they are more successful at achieving good discipline and cooperation among their students.

Finally, the unemployment rate is negatively related to serious property offenses. At a first glance, this seems paradoxical since one might expect that theft and other property offenses increase during periods of economic recession. However, unemployment may also reduce certain leisure-time activities, such as going out, and thus decrease incentives as well as opportunities to steal. Similarly, in the Swiss national ISRD-2, we found that children from families with low levels of consumption had lower delinquency rates and consumed less alcohol, which made us presume that "wealthy" families offer many consumer goods to their children and may exert less control over their leisure-time (Killias et al. 2009; Lucia et al. 2009). In this context, it may be helpful to remember that pocket money is positively related to offending and theft. This was also observed in the Swiss ISRD-1 study, where a positive correlation between the availability of cash and delinquency was observed (Lorenz Cottagnoud 1996). Similar results were found in the Cambridge study where, compared to non-delinquents, young delinquents were found to have more cash available for their personal needs at age 20 (Farrington 1995). Other studies on self-reported delinquency in Switzerland (Eisner et al. 2000, p. 75) and in Germany reported similar results (Oberwittler et al. 2001).

There are several limitations in terms of the results presented here that should be kept in mind. First of all, our data is cross-sectional and we cannot, therefore, assess temporal order and, thus, causality. On the other hand, it does, intuitively at least, not make sense that characteristics of the school system should be the outcome rather than the cause of offending. There is neither a third variable present that might condition school variables and delinquency simultaneously. Therefore, there is good reason to assume that the school system may indeed play a causal role in the correlations observed in this chapter. A more serious limitation is related to the fact that we had to keep the number of variables introduced into our models to a manageable size. Beyond socio-demographic variables and those related to characteristics of school systems, individual variables (such as self-control) and family features (such as parental supervision, attachment to parents) or neighbourhood contexts were not taken into account in our models. The reader should, therefore, assess the results of this chapter in the light of the analyses presented in other parts of this book.

8.5 Conclusion

The analysis presented in this chapter underscores the importance of structural characteristics of school systems. As noted earlier by Rutter et al. (1979) and Gottfredson (2001), schools and their structural characteristics are probably more important than individual features of students, although school principals and policy makers tend to predominantly perceive delinquent and problem behaviour as the manifestation of individual problems. For policy makers, this information gives hope, as changing schools and making them more egalitarian (and responsive to the integration of weaker students) is feasible, whereas changing family and individual characteristics may be far more difficult and cost-intensive to achieve. We do not claim that integrating all students into one same system may be the ultimate solution. Students with more serious learning deficits and other inabilities would probably benefit more from a learning environment that is more specifically designed to meet their needs. Again, we would like to highlight that our results convey that students who are enrolled in the lowest of several tracks (under differentiated systems) do not commit more often serious violent or property offenses. It is not the individual fate of being in a low track, but the structural inequality that matters. Instead of focusing on promoting an elite of 10 or 20% of students, schools should also consider allowing intellectually less brilliant students to meet good average standards. This may not only be promising in terms of these students' motivation to achieve future educational and professional successes, but also for the prevention of delinquency and violence.

References

Agnew, R. (2005). *Juvenile Delinquency*. Los Angeles: Roxbury Publishing Company.

Allison, K. R. (1992). Academic stream and tobacco, alcohol, and cannabis use among Ontario high school students. *Substance Use & Misuse, 27*(5), 561–570.

Ansalone, G. (2003). Poverty, tracking, and the social construction of failure: International perspectives on tracking. *Journal of Children & Poverty, 9*(1), 3–20.

Bryk, A. S., & Raudenbush, S. (1992). Hierarchical Linear Models for Social and behavioral Research: Applications and Data Analysis Methods. Newbury Park: Sage.

Cohen, L. E., & Felson, M. (1979). Social change and crime rates trend: a routine activity approach. *American Sociological review, 44*(4), 636–655.
Eisner, M., Manzoni, P., & Ribeaud, D. (2000). Opfererfahrungen und selbst berichtete Gewalt bei Schülerinnen und Schülern im Kanton Zürich. Aarau: Sauerländer.
Farrington, D. P. (1995). The development of offending and anti-social behaviour from childhood: Key findings from the Cambridge study in delinquent development. *Journal of Child Psychology and Psychiatry, 36*(6), 929–964.
Farrington, D. P., & Loeber, R. (2000). Some Benefits of Dichotomization in Psychiatric and Criminological Research. *Criminal Behaviour and Mental Health, 10*, 100–122.
Febbo-Hunt, M. (2003). The Other Side of the Track: Curriculum Tracking and the Pathway to Delinquency. North Carolina: PhD, North Carolina State University.
Gottfredson, M. R., & Hirschi, T. (1990). *A General Theory of Crime*. Stanford, CA: Standford University Press.
Gottfredson, D. (2001). *Schools and delinquency*. Cambridge: Cambridge University Press.
Hallinan, M. T. (1994). Tracking: From Theory to Practice. *Sociology of Education, 67*(2), 79–84.
Hallinan, M. T., & Sørensen, A. B. (1985). Ability Grouping and Student Friendships. *American Educational Research Journal, 22*(4), 485–499.
Hirschi, T. (1969). *Causes of delinquency*. Berkeley: University of California Press.
Hirschi, T. (2002). *Causes of delinquency*. New Brunswick: Transaction Publishers.
Jenkins, P. H. (1995). School Delinquency and School Commitment. *Sociology of Education 68*, 221–239.
Joseph, J. (1995). *Black Youths, Delinquency, and Juvenile Justice*. Westport, CT: Praeger.
Joseph, J. (1996). School factors and delinquency. A study of African American Youths. *Journal of Black Studies, 26*, 340–355.
Kelly, D., & Pink, W. (1982). School crime and individual responsibility: The perpetuation of a myth? *The Urban Review, 14*(1), 47–63.
Killias, M., Aebi, M. F., Herrmann, L., Dilitz, C., & Lucia, S. (2009). Switzerland. In J. Junger-Tas, I. Haen-Marshall, D. Enzmann, M. Killias, M. Steketee & B. Gruszcynska (Eds.), *Juvenile Delinquency in Europe and Beyond: Results of the Second International Self-Report Delinquency Study*. Dordrecht: Springer.
Kulik, J. A., & Kulik, C. C. (1992). Meta-analytic findings on grouping programs. *Gifted Children Quaterly, 36*(2), 73–77.
Lorenz Cottagnoud, S. (1996). *L'argent de poche. Un des facteurs de la délinquance juvénile?* Unpublished Master's Thesis, Institut de Police Scientifique et de Criminologie, Lausanne.
Lucia, S. (2009). *Multi-dimensional approach to bullying*. Thèse de doctorat, Université de Lausanne.
Lucia, S., Egli, N., Aebi, M. F., & Killias, M. (2009). Les comportements déviants des jeunes en Suisse. Résultats d'un sondage national. *Crimiscope, 40.*
Merton, R. K. (1938). Social Structure and Anomie. *American Sociological Review, 3*, 672–682.
Oberwittler, D., Blank, T., Köllisch, T., & Naplava, T. (2001). Soziale Lebenslagen und Delinquenz von Jugendlichen. Ergebnisse der MPI-Schülerbefragungen 1999 in Freiburg und Köln. Freiburg i.Br: edition iuscrim.
Rutter, M., Maughan, B., Mortimore, P., & Ouston, J. (1979). *Fifteen Thousand Hours: Secondary Schools and Their Effects on Children*. London: Open Books; Cambridge, MA: Rarvard University Press.
Snijders, T. A. B., & Bosker, R. (1999). Multilevel Analysis: An Introduction to Basic and Advanced Multilevel Modeling. London: Sage Publications Ltd.
Sutherland, E. H. (1947). *Principles of Criminology*. Philadelphia: Lippincott.
Wiatrowski, M. D., Hansell, S., Massey, C. R., & Wilson, S. L. (1982). Curriculum tracking and delinquency. *American Sociological Review, 47*, 151–160.
Wilson, J. K., & Kelling, G. L. (1982). Broken windows: The police and neighborhood safety. *Atlantic Monthly, March*, 29–38.

Chapter 9
The Lifestyles of Youth and Their Peers

Majone Steketee

9.1 Introduction

Most children commit their first offence when they are 12, 13 or 14 years old (see Chap. 3). This is the adolescencet period where children seek autonomy and identity and are increasingly expected to make their own decisions and take more responsibility. Their need for independence means that parents become less important, while school and especially friends become more important. Therefore in this chapter we focus on the role of friends and their influence on the offending behaviour of adolescents.

Because juvenile delinquency and many other forms of deviant youth behaviour almost exclusively occur during leisure time, we also look at the role that lifestyle plays in offending. In criminology, there has been a strong focus on lifestyle in victimisation research (Wikström and Butterworth 2006; Van Dijk and Steinmetz 1983). The basic idea is that individuals' characteristics will influence their lifestyle, which in turn will influence the degree of exposure to risky situations (temptations or provocations), entailing a higher risk of victimisation as well as offending.

As described in Chap. 3, within this sample, most offences were committed in the company of others. Thus, we have examined the role of a deviant social network in delinquent behaviour in general and group delinquency (co-offending) in particular. We have also looked at extremely deviant social networks such as gangs. The ISRD-2 includes questions developed by Malcolm Klein and the Eurogang (Dekker and Weerman 2005) that ascertain exactly how many adolescents in the sample are active in a gang.

M. Steketee (✉)
Verwey-Jonker Institute, Utrecht, The Netherlands
e-mail: msteketee@verwey-jonker.nl

J. Junger-Tas et al., *The Many Faces of Youth Crime: Contrasting Theoretical Perspectives on Juvenile Delinquency across Countries and Cultures*,
DOI 10.1007/978-1-4419-9455-4_9, © Springer Science+Business Media, LLC 2012

9.2 Research on Lifestyles, Involvement in Deviant Peer Groups and Delinquency

On reaching adolescence, children are confronted with new developmental challenges. In their search for independence and autonomy, young adolescents seek distance from their parents and teachers, while peer relationships become more important. Thornberry (2005) states that in large part, peers replace parents, or at least are included with parents as major sources of reward for and approval of behaviour. However, because these peers also struggle with the same search for autonomy, adolescent peer groups become closed to adult authority and value behaviour that expresses rebellion from that authority: "One of the consequences is that the peer culture encourages and reinforces problem behaviour – deviant lifestyles, experimentation with alcohol and drug use, and involvement in minor forms of delinquency" (Thornberry 2005, p. 170). Thus, there is a group of adolescents whose "criminal career" is only temporary and related to experimental behaviour in the transition to adulthood. However, there is also a small group of adolescents for whom this leads to a serious and persisting career in crime.

The association between delinquent friends and delinquent behaviour is well established. Lacourse et al. (2003) found that youths who affiliate with delinquent groups during pre-adolescence or later during adolescence, as a group commit more violent acts than those who have never or only temporarily developed this kind of affiliation. The differential association theory developed by Sutherland (1947) proposes that through interaction with others, individuals learn the values, attitudes, techniques and motives behind criminal behaviour. Delinquency is a consequence of attitudes favourable to the violation of the law, attitudes that are acquired through intimate social interaction with peers. Thus, association with delinquent peers is an important predictor of delinquent behaviour (Sutherland et al. 1992). Others such as Hirschi (1969) argue that the onset of delinquent behaviour is preceded by the weakening of conventional attitudes or moral beliefs (see also Mergens and Weerman 2010). The outcomes of studies on the relationship between attitudes and behaviour are ambiguous. There is also evidence that associating with deviant peers is closely related to the deviant behaviour of adolescents (Garnier and Stein 2002; Weijters 2008). Warr and Stafford (1991) found that the effect of the attitudes of peers is small in comparison with the peers' behaviour, and the effect of peers' behaviour remains strong even when their attitudes and the adolescent's own attitude are controlled for.

Thus, although attitudes are a necessary condition for delinquency, without the opportunity, pro-delinquent attitudes will not be readily transformed into actual delinquent behaviour (Warr and Stafford 1991). Delinquent behaviour is also dependent on both motivation and opportunity (Cohen and Felson 1979). Another explanation of how peers can influence adolescents' behaviour is derived from the routine activity theory of Osgood et al. (1996). These authors have proposed that hanging around in non-supervised public places increases the likelihood of deviant behaviour. The study by Osgood and Anderson revealed that unstructured socialising with peers, measured as the average amount of time adolescents spent with their peers in an unstructured and unsupervised setting, has a significant effect on delinquency. Generally speaking, it may be assumed that if juveniles spend more time in public places it reflects a lifestyle in which they are more often presented with opportunities to offend or to be victimised (Wikström, 2006). Wikström and Butterworth (2006) found that individual routines and the related lifestyles of youth are strong predictors of offending. In particular, youth with high levels of peer-centred time use and activity, and also youth with low levels of family-centred time use and activity tend to be more involved in offending than others. The more that youth activities are peer-centred the more likely it is that there is a strong lifestyle risk, such as spending time with delinquent friends, spending time in public high-risk places and the frequency of substance use. They also found that lifestyle has a stronger impact on offending for some groups of youth than for others: "Youth with a high individual risk factor tend to offend regardless of their level of lifestyle, while youth with high individual protective factors only occasionally offend if they have a higher lifestyle risk. The group in between those with balanced risk-protective factors, seems to be the group of adolescents most influenced by their type of lifestyle. For this group of youths the level of offending increases with increased lifestyle risk" (Wikström and Butterworth 2006, p. 249).

In the ISRD-1, it was found that group membership seems to increase as the number of friends increases and with being enrolled in school (Junger-Tas et al. 2003). In other words, group membership is age-related and part of a social network created within a school setting. As such, it is unrelated to delinquency, since young people do a lot of things together without this necessarily leading to delinquent behaviour. For example, Junger-Tas et al. (2003) found that in southern Europe all leisure time is normally spent in groups outside the home, without this resulting in higher delinquency rates than in other countries. Whether a juvenile joins a delinquent group rather than a conventional one is to a large extent determined by their own functioning in the context of other conventional systems such as school. To the extent that the individual is marginalised he or she will seek the company of other marginalised youths, where alcohol and drug use are encouraged and delinquent behaviour is considered normal (Warr 2002; Thornberry and Krohn 2003). Children who are already aggressive will self-select peers that are similar to them at an early age. At the same time, there is evidence that aggressive children are likely to be rejected by their peers (Coie and Dodge: in Thornberry 2005), leading to isolation from mainstream peer networks and involvement in deviant peer networks, which can have an impact on the onset of delinquency during adolescence.

9.3 Characteristics of Leisure Time in the Six Country Clusters

According to the literature, the time youngsters spend outside their own home in public places has an influence on their delinquent behaviour. Therefore, we asked the sample about how many times a week they usually go out at night to events such as a party or a disco, or to places such as somebody's house or to hang out on the streets. The majority of the youths reported that they go out at least once a week

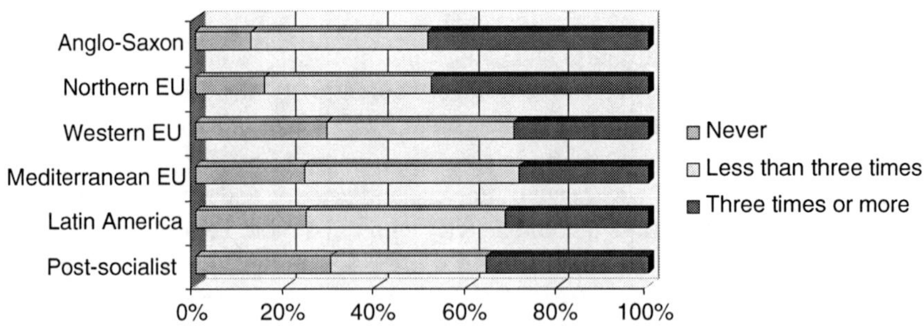

Fig. 9.1 Frequency of going out at night (%)

(74.6%). Most of them only go out once or twice a week, but almost one-quarter reported that they go out more often than they stay at home (22.6%) and close to 10% said they go out on a daily basis (9.6%). There is a small gender difference: more girls do not go out at night at all (27.6% vs. 23.2%) and more boys than girls go out more than 4 times a week (37.9% vs. 31.7%). Also, there is a tendency for more adolescents in grade 7 to stay at home compared with adolescents in higher grades. There is no difference between native born and migrant juveniles.

Having the opportunity to offend is indeed relevant. There is a relationship between going out frequently and committing a crime. Those juveniles who go out more frequently are more likely to commit an offence, perhaps this is because those who exhibit more delinquent behaviour are also more likely to go out at night. In particular, for those adolescents who go out on a regular basis (3 times or more per week), the chance that they will commit a serious offence is 6 times higher (odds ratio 6.55), than juveniles who do not go out as often. This relationship is almost equal for boys (odds ratio 6.13) and girls (odds ratio 6.28).

There is a difference between the country clusters. Within the Anglo-Saxon and Northern EU countries it is more common to go out frequently in the evening (48.9 and 47.8% respectively). In Mediterranean EU countries it is less common to spend time on a regular basis in public places (28.7%). In Western EU and Post-Socialist countries more children stay at home and do not go out at all in the evening. However, we should note that there is also a large difference between the countries within the clusters. For example, in Estonia more than half of the adolescents say that they go out at least 3 times a week (53.3%), which is comparable with Russian adolescents (50.0%), while in the Czech Republic and Armenia most do not go out at all in the evening (52.7% and 57.4%, respectively). Perhaps these differences between and within the clusters is due to differences in family and social cultures (Fig. 9.1).

As stated above, during adolescence friends become very important. During their transition to adulthood, adolescents become more distant from their parents, while the relationship with friends becomes more dominant (Thornberry 2005). To determine if an adolescent is more family-centred or peer-centred we asked them who they spend most of their free time with. There were four mutually exclusive answer categories: on their own, with their family, with a few friends (less than four), or

Table 9.1 Regression analysis of serious offences over the previous year and with whom the offenders spent their time

Serious offences last year	Odds ratio
Time on my own	1.08
With my family	0.48***
With 1–3 friends	1.63***
With larger group of friends	3.15***

***$p < .001$

with a large group of friends (four or more). Most of the respondents were peer-centred (56.5%), spending more time with a small (32.9%) or with a large group of friends (22.6%). Almost 10% of the adolescents spent most of their free time on their own, one third spent most of their free time with their family (35.2%). There was no difference between girls and boys, nor was there a difference based on migrant background. As expected, more of the respondents in higher grades report that they spend more time with friends and less with their family.

While adolescents belonging to a larger group are more likely to commit an offence, spending time with family is a protective factor in relation to delinquent behaviour (see Table 9.1). This is consistent with the study by Wikström and Butterworth (2006) which found that the more the youths are peer-centred and the less they are family-centred the more likely they are to be involved in criminal behaviour. Thus, spending time with your family is a protective factor and having a large group of friends means it is more likely that a youth will offend.

There is also a difference between the clusters. In Anglo-Saxon countries juveniles are more peer-centred and spend more time with their friends, while in the Mediterranean countries and Latin American countries it is more common to spend time with their family. This is consistent with the fact that adolescents from these countries do not go out so often in the evening.

It is of interest to determine what kind of activities the juveniles undertake in their leisure time. On an average school day, youths spend most of their free time hanging out with friends and watching television, or playing games or chatting on the computer. Playing a musical instrument or reading are not popular activities, and even reading a magazine or comics is rare. Most adolescents do their homework – only a small percentage (7.2%) say that they never do homework. Most spend half an hour to 2 h (83.1%) doing their homework.

There is a difference between girls and boys in the way they spend their leisure time. Boys spend much more time playing ($V=0.243$, $p<0.000$), while girls spend much more time on their homework ($V=0.180$, $p<0.000$) and reading books ($V=0.243$, $p<0.000$). There are no great differences in relation to the other activities. There are also no differences with respect to migrant background or school year.

In the literature it is assumed that juveniles who spend more time in public places are living a lifestyle in which they are more often confronted with opportunities to offend. In this study there is also a significant correlation between "hanging out with friends" and offending behaviour. If adolescents spend more than 3 h a day just

Table 9.2 Definition of lifestyle

Variables	−1	0	1
Going out at night:	Never	Once or twice	Three times or more
Hanging out with friends:	Less than a hour	One to two hours	Three or more hours
Time spent:	With family	On my own/with small group of friends	With a large group of friends
The group of friends spent a lot of time in public places:	No		Yes

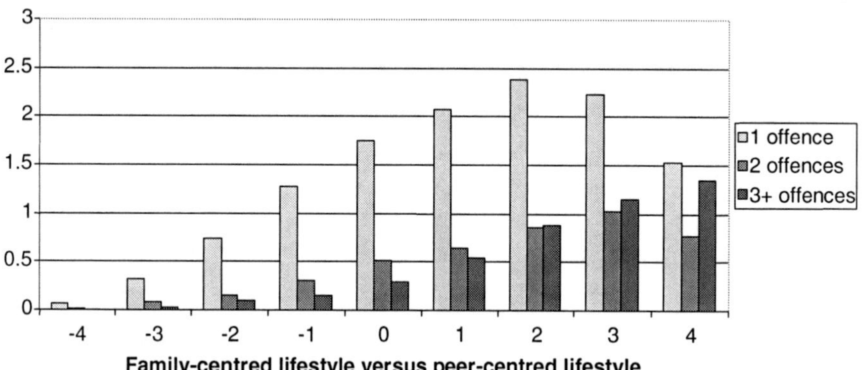

Fig. 9.2 Lifestyle of juveniles and versatility last year (%)

hanging out with friends in public places, the odds that they will also commit an offence are almost 6 times higher (odds ratio 6.55, $p>0.000$). With respect to those youths who spend time with a certain group of friends we also asked whether this group spends a lot of time in public places. There is a correlation between spending time in a group, doing so in public places and the prevalence of offending over the previous year (odds ratio 2.72, $p<0.000$). These are bivariate associations which may be spurious and disappear in controlled analysis later.

The results show that some elements of the leisure time of juveniles are related to their criminality. These are the frequency of going out at night, spending a lot of time hanging out with friends, being peer-centred, and spending a lot of time in public places with a group of friends. On the basis of these findings we created a lifestyle scale for youth, where each of the four variables was coded into a three-tiered scale of −1, 0 and +1. The final score varies between –4 and 4 (Cronbach's alpha=0.60) (Table 9.2).

If we look at the prevalence of offending over the previous year and lifestyles, Fig. 9.2 shows that having a more peer-centred lifestyle (frequently going out at night, frequently hanging out with a large group of friends in public places) is more related to offending behaviour. A more family-centred lifestyle – spending a lot of time at home with your family – is less related to delinquent behaviour.

9.4 Deviant Peer Behaviour and Its Impact on Offending

In the literature, there is evidence that one of the most powerful predictors of teenage drug use and delinquent behaviours is similar behaviour by peers (Garnier and Stein 2002; Warr 2002, 2003). One of the findings of this study is that most of the offenders have a companion in crime, with only a small proportion of juveniles offending alone (see Fig. 9.3). Even carrying a weapon is a violation reported to be undertaken with others (37.9%). However, in relation to more serious crimes such as assault, snatching or extortion, juveniles are more likely to commit them on their own. Usually co-offenders are also adolescents; however, in relation to drug dealing and car theft, an adult is more often involved.

The literature is inconclusive about whether boys differ from girls with respect to committing crimes with others (Warr 2002; Van der Laan 2006). Some studies show that both sexes appear to have an accomplice in crime, but there are also studies showing that girls commit crimes together more than boys. In this study, there is no difference between boys and girls in relation to committing the crime alone or with others for most offences. In relation to shoplifting, girls do commit an offence significantly more with others than do boys (70.4 vs. 64.4%, $p<0.001$). While girls steal bicycles or snatch purses more often with others and breaking into a car is more often done by boys in the company of others.

With respect to age or grade, there is only a significant difference in relation to vandalism ($p<0.000$). For almost all offences, having a companion in crime tends

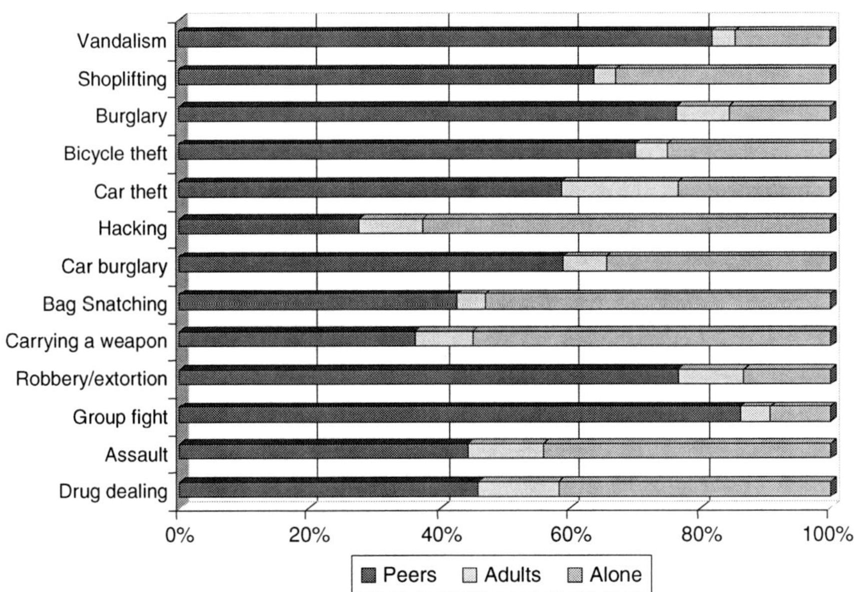

Fig. 9.3 The person with whom the offence has been committed (%)

to be highest at the age of 15, after which the number of juveniles who commit crimes on their own increases. There is no significant difference for juveniles from different ethnic backgrounds.

The need for acceptance by other adolescents is especially strong and this desire to belong to a group can lead adolescents to succumb to pressure to join undesirable groups or engage in undesirable activities (Connor 1994). In addition to lifestyle (opportunity) it is important to know whether adolescents actually belong to a group of friends who seek out and engage in risky or delinquent activities. Therefore, we looked at the variables of *risky group behaviour*, the *criminal involvement of peers*, and to what extent belonging to the group entails involvement in illegal activities.

First, we measured risky group behaviour using four items (Cronbach's alpha = 0.66). We asked whether, when hanging out with friends, the adolescent usually: (1) drinks a lot of beer/alcohol or takes drugs; (2) smashes or vandalises things just for fun; (3) shoplifts just for fun; (4) frightens and annoys people just for fun. Most of the youths were not involved in any risky behaviour (57.9%), and only a small number of youngsters engaged in more than two risky activities when hanging out with their friends (7%).

Because delinquent adolescents usually have delinquent friends (see Warr 2003; Wikström 2006), we also wanted to know if our sample had friends who were criminally involved. Five items in the questionnaire measured the extent to which a youth had friends who were more seriously engaged in criminality (Cronbach's alpha = 0.70). We asked whether they had friends who had engaged in illegal activities such as (1) using soft or hard drugs, (2) stealing from a shop or department store, (3) entering a building with the purpose of stealing something, (4) threatening somebody with a weapon or with violence to obtain money or something else from him or her, (5) beating someone up or hurting them badly with something like a stick or a knife. Most of the sample did not have friends who had done such things (59.25%). Almost 20% (19.46%) had friends who had engaged in one of these activities and close to 12% had friends that had engaged in two of these activities (11.71%). Only a small group had genuinely delinquent friends who had engaged in three or more illegal activities (9.59%).

There is a relationship between having friends who engage in illegal activities and the delinquent behaviour of the respondents themselves. The more items relating to offences committed by friends reported by the adolescent, the more likely it is that he or she will also have committed a crime. If we look at the substance use of friends, we see that having friends who use drugs makes it much more likely that the youth will also drink and use drugs. Smoking, in particular, is a group-related behaviour and it is more than 20 times likely that you smoke weed or marijuana if your friends do (Fig. 9.4).

There is not only a relationship between a friend's engagement in criminality and the involvement of the adolescent themselves, but also a relationship in terms of the type of offences committed. Having a friend who has shoplifted makes it more likely that an adolescent will steal something from a shop or department store (odds ratio 9.15, $p < 0.000$). The same can be said for burglary and assault. For extortion, the relationship is not as strong as for the other items. This is possibly due to problems with the translation of the term "extortion" in some countries, as was described in the methodology chapter (Table 9.3).

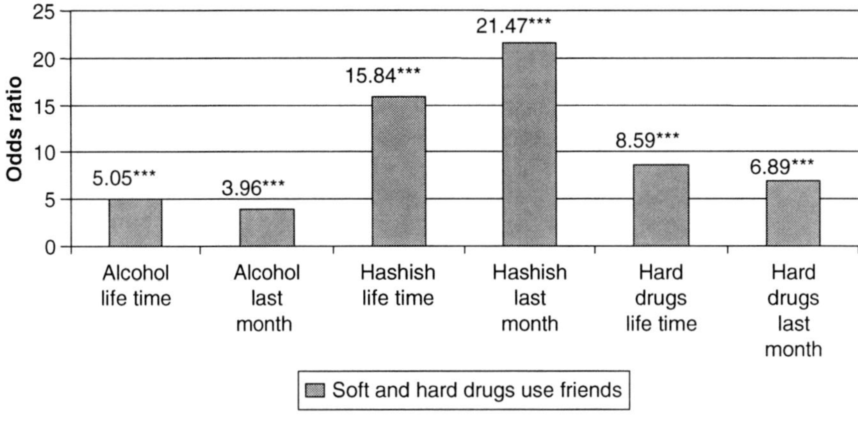

Fig. 9.4 Relationship between drug use of friends and the substance use of juveniles (logistic regression odds ratios). $***p<.001$

Table 9.3 Odds ratios for the relationship between friends' behaviour and the delinquent behaviour of the adolescents themselves

	Shoplifting	Burglary	Extortion	Assault
Friends' alcohol/drug use	1.77***	2.18***	2.01***	2.29***
Friends' shoplifting	9.15***	2.24***	1.98***	1.60***
Friends' burglary	1.87***	8.53***	2.01***	2.08***
Friends' extortion	1.07***	1.50***	3.46***	1.36***
Friends' assault	1.26***	2.04***	3.24***	5.63**

$***p<0.000$

Most adolescents have a certain group of friends with whom they spend time doing things or just hanging out (77.2%). In addition to risky group behaviour we also wanted to know if the group of friends consisted of "delinquent peers". When a group of delinquent adolescents band together it is usually defined as a gang. According to many researchers, being a gang member is an important factor influencing juvenile delinquency. The crime rates among the members of such groups are higher, especially for serious and violent crimes (Haymoz and Gatti 2010; Weerman and Esbensen 2005). In this study we used the Eurogang definition (Klein et al. 2002) to determine whether an adolescent belonged to a gang: "A street gang is any durable, street orientated youth group whose own identity includes involvement in illegal activity". The Eurogang definition consists of the following six questions:

- Do you have a group of friends?
- How long has this group existed (>3 months)?
- Does this group spend a lot of time together in public places?

Table 9.4 Percentage of youths who replied affirmatively to the questions relating to the Eurogang definition

	N=67.883
Do you have a group of friends?	76.3
How long has this group existed (>3 months)?	69.5
Does this group spend a lot of time together in public places?	75.4
Is doing illegal things accepted by your group?	19.8
Do people in your group actually do illegal things together?	16.8
Do you consider your group a gang?	14.4

Table 9.5 Percentage of youth who are members of a gang for the six country clusters, and differences between girls and boys

	Gang member	Boy gang member	Girl gang member
Anglo-Saxon	7.43	4.37	3.06
Northern EU	4.66	2.74	1.91
Western EU	5.05	3.37	1.68
Mediterranean EU	3.76	2.60	1.16
Latin American	2.19	1.67	0.54
Post-Socialist	3.07	1.99	1.09
Total	4.03	2.63	1.40

- Is doing illegal things accepted by your group?
- Do people in your group actually do illegal things together?
- Do you consider your group a gang?

An adolescent was considered to be a gang member only if he or she scored affirmatively on all six items. Cronbach's alpha for this scale is quite high at 0.77.

According to the research, only a small proportion of juveniles belong to a gang (4.03%, see Table 9.5 below). However, to better assess the meaning of this result we first recorded the frequency of affirmative answers for the six questions (see Table 9.4). It should be pointed out that all the percentages shown in the table refer to the whole sample and not only to those who said that they have a group of friends.

Here it is clear that a larger group of adolescents considered their group of friends to be a gang (14.4%) then are classified as a gang member according to the six-point definition by Eurogang (4%). These results reflect the usefulness of the different items for defining whether someone is a gang member, rather than using a single question regarding gang membership (see also Haymoz and Gatti 2010). Thus, for many youths, the term "gang" is probably more associated with an informal definition, referring to a group of people who associate regularly on a social basis – "The whole gang from the school went to the movie" – than with a gang considered as a delinquent group whose identity involves illegal activities. Haymoz and Gatti (2010) suggest that the term "delinquent youth group" is more appropriate than the term "gang".

There is a difference between the country clusters for the percentage of youths who are gang members (see Table 9.5). Especially Anglo-Saxon countries score high on the

Table 9.6 Gang membership and number of offences committed for the 13 items: over previous year (%)

	None	1 offence	2 offences	3+ offences
Whole sample	78.74	12.39	4.37	4.49
Gang members Anglo-Saxon	22.99	20.44	11.68	44.89
Gang members Northern EU	34.53	20.85	15.64	28.99
Gang members Western EU	23.66	19.83	15.53	40.98
Gang members Mediterranean EU	33.33	21.98	14.66	30.02
Gang members Latin America	33.80	14.79	13.38	38.03
Gang members Post-Socialist	39.70	20.77	16.42	23.12
All gang members	30.74	20.31	15.08	33.88

number of adolescents who belong to a gang (7.4%), but this is due to the extraordinarily high number of adolescents in Ireland who are gang members (16.8%). In the United States, the number of adolescents who are gang members is 3%. Other countries that score higher than average are France (8.5%), Belgium (6.3%), Sweden (6.6%), Hungary (6.5%) and Switzerland (6.2%). The lowest scoring countries are Armenia (0.4%), Iceland (0.7%) and Bosnia-Herzegovina (1%). In relation to the clusters, the Latin American countries have the lowest rates of adolescents belonging to a gang (2.19%).

Twice as many boys belong to a gang (2.6%) as girls (1.4%). This gender difference is smallest in the Anglo-Saxon countries and largest in the Latin American and Mediterranean countries, where almost 3 times more boys are gang members than girls. Although there are more boys involved in the gangs, these figures prove the involvement of girls in gangs and that the gang phenomenon is not the exclusive province of males. Of all the gang members, one third (34.7%) are girls and the groups are mostly mixed (68.1%). There are even a small proportion of gangs that consist exclusively of girls (4.5%).

If we look at the relationship between being a gang member and delinquent behaviour it is apparent that gang members are much more involved in delinquent acts than youths who do not belong to such groups. Indeed, being a gang member means that committing a crime is more likely and the number of offences committed is also much higher (see Table 9.6). More than two out of three gang members (69.2%) reported having committed an offence during the year prior to the survey, while the corresponding figure for the whole sample was about one out of five adolescents (21.3%). Not only have gang members committed an offence more often they also commit more kinds of offences. One third of the gang members had committed three or more different kinds of offences during the last year (34%), while only a small group of the whole sample showed the same delinquent behaviour (4.5%).

Being a gang member does not mean that individuals have actually committed an offence. Almost one third of the boys and almost half of the girls who are gang members had not committed a crime during the previous year. This is somewhat surprising because according to the definition of a gang it is not only acceptable to engage in illegal activities but the group actually commits illegal acts together. This pattern of

Table 9.7 Logistic regression model for being a gang member and specific variables

	Odds ratios	95% CI interval	
Male vs. female	1.10	0.998	1.229
Grade 8 vs. Grade 7	0.90	0.797	1.027
Grade 9 vs. Grade 7	0.94	0.832	1.065
First-generation migrants vs. non-migrants	1.30**	1.086	1.562
Second-generation migrants vs. non-migrants	1.39***	1.234	1.565
Lifestyle	2.75***	2.559	2.956
Deviant group behaviour	2.03***	1.945	2.133
Delinquent peers	1.3***	1.250	1.525
Self-control	0.83***	0.780	0.886
Attitude towards violence	1.38***	1.227	1.377
School disorganisation	1.13***	1.082	1.196
Neighbourhood disorganisation	1.22***	1.174	1.281
Truancy	0.95	0.890	1.013
Repeating grade	1.03	0.940	1.131
Family bonding	1.03	0.988	1.081
Life events	0.99	0.955	1.042

$^{**}p<.01$; $^{***}p<.001$

being a juvenile gang member but not having committed any offence in the previous year was apparent in all the clusters. However, there is a difference between the clusters in Anglo-Saxon and Western EU countries there were more gang members who had committed an offence than in Northern EU countries and Post-Socialist countries.

Most of the gang members are in the 14 (33%) or 15-year-old (30%) age groups. Most of them are native (70%), with only one third of the gang members being from other ethnic backgrounds. Only a small proportion of the ethnic gang members are first generation (8%), with most being second-generation migrants (22.2%). The migrants in the gangs come mostly from Western EU countries (45%) or American countries (17%). Migrants from Asia, Africa or Eastern EU countries are a minority within these gangs.

As mentioned, the groups are mostly of mixed gender (68.1%). Gangs that only consist of girls are rare (4.5%), but they do exist. Adolescents who are gang members have somewhat more friends with a different ethnic background (26.8%) than those who do not belong to a gang (20%).

A logistic regression analysis on gang members shows that a lifestyle that involves going out a lot and hanging out with a lot of friends correlates with being a gang member (see Table 9.7). Also, deviant group behaviour is highly associated with being a gang member. The delinquent behaviour of peers has less impact on being a gang member than lifestyle or deviant lifestyle. Interestingly, being a male, school year, truancy, repeating a year of school, family bonding or important life events were not significant. Having a high level of self-control was found to be the only protective factor in relation to becoming a gang member. A positive attitude towards violence is also more common among gang members. They also more often live in a disorganised neighbourhood and go to schools that are disorganised.

9.5 Impact of Lifestyle and Peer Group on Delinquent Behaviour

In the ISRD-1, it was found that in southern Europe all leisure time is normally spent in groups outside the home without this resulting in higher delinquency rates than in other countries. We could not replicate this result in the ISRD-2 study. There is definitely a difference between the clusters but it mainly concerns a difference between gang membership and delinquency. Having a lifestyle where you frequently hang out with a large group of friends in public places means that youths are more involved with delinquent behaviour in all clusters (see Table 9.7). This association is the strongest in the Mediterranean EU countries.

In all European countries, the effect of friends' behaviour on a respondent's delinquent behaviour is significantly strong, as is risky group behaviour. An exception is the Anglo-Saxon category, where being a gang member has a larger effect on delinquent behaviour. However, being a member of a gang is only highly significant in Anglo-Saxon and Western EU countries, while in Post-Socialist and Latin American countries it is significant but not very high. However, in the Northern EU and Mediterranean EU countries there is no significant relationship between being a member of a gang and delinquent behaviour.

In the Anglo-Saxon countries, having delinquent friends is less related to delinquent behaviour than other variables such as deviant lifestyle and being a gang member. In this model, lifestyle is mostly associated with delinquency in the Mediterranean EU countries and is least associated with delinquency in the Northern EU countries. Deviant lifestyle is most associated with delinquency in the Mediterranean EU countries and least associated in Western EU countries.

In all clusters, having delinquent friends is related to delinquent behaviour. However, as stated, having delinquent friends is of less influence in the Anglo-Saxon countries than being a gang member, having a deviant lifestyle, or lifestyle itself (Table 9.8).

9.5.1 Gender Differences for the Impact of Lifestyle and Peer Delinquency on Offending

Although in criminology the adolescent offending of boys is linked to their peers' delinquency, we know less about the role of delinquent peers in relation to girls' delinquent behaviour (Wikström and Butterworth 2006). When we look at the influence of their lifestyles and that of their peers, we can draw the conclusion that there is no significant difference between the boys and girls with respect to lifestyle. There is a difference insofar as risky group behaviour has a stronger impact on the offending of girls than boys, and this is also the case for peer delinquency, with its effect being more significant for girls than for boys (Table 9.9).

Delinquency among girls who are gang members is considerably higher than among other girls, also reaching a higher level than that of boys who do not belong

Table 9.8 Negative binomial regression model for versatility last year and lifestyles peer/group behaviour by the six clusters

	(1) Anglo-Saxon	(2) Northern EU	(3) Western EU	(4) Mediterranean EU	(5) Latin America	(6) Post-socialist
Gang member	1.56*** (5.16)	1.07 (0.75)	1.32*** (6.33)	1.29 (2.30)	1.26* (1.84)	1.25** (3.37)
Lifestyle	1.36*** (7.99)	1.23*** (5.18)	1.39*** (16.96)	1.46*** (13.72)	1.38*** (8.03)	1.34*** (14.61)
Risky group behaviour	1.57*** (16.41)	1.69*** (18.66)	1.48*** (27.25)	1.79*** (21.34)	1.57*** (13.11)	1.62*** (28.72)
Delinquent friends	1.47*** (15.68)	1.64*** (19.55)	1.64*** (36.96)	1.59*** (17.00)	1.53*** (16.22)	1.47*** (24.42)
N	3,631	6,075	16,449	11,312	6,432	19,444

Exponential coefficients; *t* statistics in parentheses

*$p<0.05$; **$p<0.01$; ***$p<0.001$

Table 9.9 Negative binomial regression model for versatility in previous year with respect to deviant lifestyle and peer delinquency for girls and boys

	Female	Male
Gang member	1.33***	1.31***
Lifestyle	1.39***	1.39***
Risky group behaviour	1.79***	1.52***
Delinquent friends	1.59***	1.40***

***$p < .001$

Table 9.10 Percentage of youth committing a crime when a gang member and gender

	Non-gang member		Gang member	
	Boys (%)	Girls (%)	Boys (%)	Girls (%)
Minor violent offences in last year	19.55	6.96	60.20	37.26
Serious violent offences in last year	3.63	1.49	24.93	13.86
Minor property offences in last year	5.49	4.52	28.37	27.69
Serious property offences in last year	3.61	1.13	27.49	9.93

to such groups. One can conclude that being a member of a delinquent group such as a gang has a more criminogenic effect on girls than on boys. Although boys commit more offences than girls if they are gang members, the difference between them and non-gang members is not as large as it is for girls (Table 9.10).

If we consider "being a gang member" a measure of peer pressure and a way of life, it is interesting to consider the impact of gang membership on delinquent behaviour in comparison to lifestyle, deviant lifestyle or the delinquency of peers. Table 9.11 examines risky group behaviour and the delinquent behaviour of peers. Model 1 includes some background variables that are related to delinquency. Being a boy has a predictive effect on delinquent behaviour among juveniles, as well as being in a higher grade and being a juvenile migrant. However, if we add being a gang member, lifestyle, deviant lifestyle or the delinquent behaviour of peers, the effect of these background variables is smaller (Model 2). For grade and being a first-generation migrant the effect is no longer significant. A deviant lifestyle is the best predictor of delinquent behaviour, followed by the delinquent behaviour of peers and a lifestyle dominated by a large group and hanging out in public places. Being a gang member is also of influence on the prevalence of offending over the previous year.

In Model 3 we have added some variables such as self-control, a positive attitude towards violence, and family bonding. Having greater self-control is a protective factor with respect to delinquent behaviour, so is having a positive bond with your family (as we saw in Chap. 7). A positive attitude towards violence is strongly related to delinquent behaviour, but this is also the case for disorganised neighbourhoods and schools and life events.

In Model 4 we see that being a gang member is less significant than in the other models, lifestyle is also less of a predictor in this model, as well as risky group behaviour and delinquent behaviour of peers. Nevertheless, these items have the highest degree of influence on the prevalence of offending over the previous year.

Table 9.11 Negative binomial regression models predicting delinquency (versatility last year) with conditioning effects

Variable	Model 1	Model 2	Model 3	Model 4
Male	2.53*** (0.057)	2.01*** (0.039)	1.87*** (0.040)	1.85*** (0.037)
Grade 8	1.35*** (0.038)	1.02 (0.024)	1.17*** (0.029)	1.03 (0.025)
Grade 9	1.56*** (0.041)	0.95 (0.022)	1.21*** (0.030)	0.96 (0.023)
First-generation migrant	1.28*** (0.056)	1.09 (0.042)	1.06 (0.042)	1.05 (0.039)
Second-generation migrant	1.41*** (0.039)	1.14 (0.028)	1.17*** (0.030)	1.09** (0.027)
Gang member		1.28*** (0.042)		1.10** (0.034)
Lifestyle		1.40*** (0.016)		1.28*** (0.015)
Risky group behaviour		1.61*** (0.014)		1.35*** (0.013)
Delinquent peers		1.46*** (0.011)		1.34*** (0.011)
Self-control			0.70*** (0.009)	0.80*** (0.010)
Positive attitude towards violence			1.37*** (0.016)	1.16*** (0.014)
Family bond			0.90*** (0.009)	0.95*** (0.009)
Know some friends			0.89*** (0.029)	0.99 (0.030)
Know all friends			0.59*** (0.020)	0.83*** (0.028)
School discipline			1.16*** (0.013)	1.07*** (0.011)
Truancy			1.43*** (0.019)	1.21*** (0.016)
Neighbourhood disorganisation			1.21*** (0.012)	1.08*** (0.010)
Neighbourhood integration			0.97 (0.010)	0.98 (0.009)

Weighted data; incidence rate ratios; standard errors of *b* in brackets; $^{**}p<.01$; $^{***}p<.001$

9.6 Discussion

The data shows that at the individual level, the variables with the highest effect on delinquency are gender, truancy, the lifestyle of the youngsters who have delinquent friends, and the deviant behaviour of the group. This risk is more significant in relation to serious crimes than for minor crimes. The ethnicity of the youth in this sample had some influence on the level of involvement in crime, which decreases when lifestyle and peer-group related items are added.

One of the findings of this study is that the lifestyle of adolescents influences their involvement in crime. Those adolescents who have a peer-centred lifestyle, measured in terms of time spent with a large group of friends in public places, are more likely to be involved in delinquent behaviour than those who are more family-centred. The more a youth is peer-centred the more likely it is that there is also a strong lifestyle risk, such as spending time with delinquent friends, spending time in high-risk public places and the frequency of substance use or other nuisance behaviour by the group. This is in accordance with the theory that spending a lot of time with friends in public places entails juveniles spending leisure time in a behavioural context unsupervised by adults, in which they may violate norms and conventions without much risk of interference from others (Wikström and Svensson 2008). During adolescence the bond with parents weakens, but it remains a protective factor with respect to offending (see Model 4, Table 9.11). In particular, supervision and monitoring by parents, and knowing who their children's friends are may influence the delinquent behaviour of these youngsters.

Another finding of this study is that juvenile delinquency mainly takes the form of group behaviour. When youths commit an offence they usually do so with co-offenders. In this study we distinguished between belonging to a gang (defined as a group that actually engages in delinquent acts) or to a deviant youth group (defined as risky group behaviour, heavy substance use, vandalism and harassment of people for fun). Both delinquent and risky group behaviour influence adolescents' levels of involvement in crime.

Joining a delinquent or deviant group is considered by some researchers to be a reaction to social marginalisation and exclusion (see Blaya and Gatti 2010). However, the reasons for joining a youth gang or a risky youth group are complex and multiple. A search for friendship and self-affirmation may be factors (Campbell 1987; Moore 1991), but social exclusion (Thornberry and Krohn 2003), early school leaving, living in segregated neighbourhoods and domestic violence may also play a role (Van Gemert 2001). In this study, the school, the neighbourhood and the bond with parents also have some explanatory value. Truancy and disorderly neighbourhoods and schools have a negative influence on adolescent offending, while family bonding and monitoring by parents have a more protective influence. Also, an individual's disposition, such as self-control and their attitude towards violence, have an influence on delinquent behaviour. The results of this study confirm one component of Wikström's Situational Action Theory of Crime (SAT). (We lack measures of the moral element of SAT theory). This theoretical framework incorporates the notion that criminal involvement is a consequence of an individual criminal propensity and the criminogenic features of the environment to which an individual is exposed (lifestyle, opportunity and routine activities). This is a newly developed general theory of moral action which aims to explain how specific personal and environmental characteristics interact to influence acts of crime.

In this study the variation between the country clusters with respect to the link between being a gang member and delinquency leads to the question of whether gangs in the United States or Ireland are more like the stereotyped image of a gang, namely an extremely violent and dangerous armed group that controls the neighbourhood (Haymoz and Gatti 2010). In our terms, these gangs are thus more likely to be "delinquent youth groups", while the image of the gangs in Europe is more one of "deviant youth groups". Haymoz and Gatti prefer the use of the expression "deviant youth group", arguing that it is less evocative than "gang" and more suited to the fact that European youth who belong to these groups not only commit more crimes, but might be involved in other types of deviant behaviour, such as alcohol and drug abuse and risky group behaviour. The findings of this research are in line with this argument, because there is a strong relationship between looking for risky situations (vandalism for fun) and being a gang member (odds ratio 2.03, see Table 9.7).

9.7 Conclusion

The adolescents involved in this survey vary enormously in their lifestyles and the way they spend their leisure time, factors which influence their level of involvement in delinquency. An adolescent with a peer-centred lifestyle – meaning they frequently hang out with a large group of friends in public places – has a greater likelihood of committing an offence than an adolescent who is more family-centred. In terms of the lifestyles of the adolescents, there were no differences with respect to gender or ethnicity.

In the first 3 years of secondary school, friends become more important for adolescents, who can become increasingly distant from their parents. Most young people have a group of friends whose behaviour has a strong influence on their own behaviour. One finding of this study is that juvenile delinquency is mainly a form of group behaviour. If an adolescent's friends are delinquent they are not only more likely to be delinquent themselves, but they are also likely to commit the same type of offence as their friends. Having a friend who has committed burglary increases the chances that you will also have been involved in burglary. Being part of a group of friends who engage in illegal or risky activities leads to a higher risk of committing serious offences. As a member of a delinquent group (gang), an adolescent will commit an offence more often than an adolescent who does not belong to a delinquent group. However, the effect of being a gang member with respect to engaging in risky activities when together is larger for girls than for boys.

The choice of a certain group of friends has not been investigated in this study but there are some indications that with increasing degrees of neighbourhood and school disorderliness more youngsters have delinquent friends. Whether a juvenile joins a delinquent group rather than a conventional one is to a large extent determined by their own predisposition. It is more likely that adolescence belonging to a deviant group have less self-control and a more positive attitude towards violence.

Although the family bond weakens over the period of early adolescence, supervision and monitoring by parents still remains important. It appears particularly important that parents know what their children are doing and who their friends are as this has a protective effect with respect to the delinquency of adolescents.

References

Blaya, C. & Gatti, U. (2010). Deviant youth groups in Italy and France: Prevalence and characteristics. *European Journal on Criminal Policy and Research, 16*, 127–144.

Campbell, A. (1987). Self-definition by rejection: The case of gang girls. *Social Problems*, vol. 5, p. 451–466.

Cohen, L.E. & Felson, J. (1979). Social Change and Crime Rate Trends: Routine Activity Approach. *American Sociological Review*, vol. 44, p. 588–608.

Connor, M.J. (1994). Peer relations and peer pressure. *Educational Psychology in Practice, 9*, 207–215.

Dekker, S.H. & Weerman, F.M. (eds.) (2005). *European Street Gangs and Troublesome Youth Groups*. New York: Altamira Press.

Dijk, J.J.M. van & Steinmetz, C.H.D. (1983). Victimisation survey: beyond Measuring the Volume of Crime. *Victimology: An International Journal*, vol. 8, p. 291–301.

Garnier, H.E. & Stein, J.A. (2002). An 18-year model of family and peer effects on adolescent drug use and delinquency. *Journal of Youth and Adolescence*, vol. 1, p. 46–56.

Gemert, F. Van (2001). Youth Groups and Gangs in Amsterdam: A pre-test of the Eurogang expert survey. In: Dekker, S.H. & Weerman, F. (eds.) *European Street Gangs and Troublesome Youth Groups*. New York: Altamira Press, p. 147–168.

Haymoz, S. & Gatti, U. (2010). Girl Members of Deviant Youth Groups, Offending Behavior and Victimization: Results of the ISRD2 in Italy and Switzerland. *European Journal on Criminal Policy and Research, 16*, 167-182.

Hirschi, T. (1969). *Causes of Delinquency*. Berkeley, Los Angeles: University of California Press.

Junger-Tas, J., Marshall, I.H. & Ribeaud, D. (2003). *Delinquency in an International Perspective: The International Self-Report Delinquency Study (ISRD)*. The Hague: Kugler.

Klein, M.W., Kerner, H.-J., Maxson, C.L. & Weitekamp, E.G.M. (2002). *The European Paradox: Street Gangs and Youth Groups in the U.S. and Europe*. Dordrecht: Kluwer Academic Publisher.

Laan, A.M. van der. (2006) Jeugddelinquentie: risico's em bescherming. Bevindingen uit de WODC Monitor Zelfgerapporteerde Jeugdcriminaliteit 2005. Meppel: Boom Juridische Uitgevers.

Lacourse, E., Nagin, D., Tremblay, R.E., Vitaro, F. & Claes, M. (2003). Developmental trajectories of boys' delinquent group membership and facilitation of violent behaviors during adolescence. *Development and Psychopathology*, vol. 15, p. 183–197.

Mergens, K.C.I.M. & Weerman, F.M. (2010). Attitudes, delinquency and peers: The role of social norms in attitude-behaviour inconsistency. *European Journal of Criminology*, vol. 7, p. 299–316.

Moore, J.W. (1991). *Going down to the Barrio*. Philadelphia: Temple University Press.

Osgood, W.D., Wilson, J.K., O'Malley, P.M. (1996). Routine Activities and Individual Deviant Behaviour. *American Sociological Review*, vol. 5, p. 635–655.

Sutherland, E.H. (1947). *Principles of Criminology*. 4th ed., Philadelphia: Lippincitt.

Sutherland, E.H., Cressey, D.R. & Luckenbill, D.F. (1992). *Principles of Criminology*. 11th ed., Dis Hills: General Hall.

Thornberry, T.P. (2005). Explaining multiple patterns of offending across the life course and across generations. *Annals*, AAPSS, 602, p. 156–195.

Thornberry, T.P. & Krohn, M.D. (eds.) (2003). *Taking stock of delinquency: An overview of findings from contemporary longitudinal studies*. New York: Kluwer Academic/Plenurn Publishers.

Warr, M. & Stafford, M. (1991). The influence of delinquent peers: what they think or what they do? *Criminology*, vol. 29, p. 851–866.

Warr, M. (2002). *Companions in Crime: The Social Aspects of Criminal Conduct*. Cambridge: Cambridge University Press.

Warr, M. (2003). The tangled web: Delinquency, deception and parental attachment. *Journal of Adolescence, 36,* 607–622.

Weerman, F.M. & Esbensen, F.A. (2005). A Cross-National Comparison of Youth Gangs. In: Decker, S.H. & Weerman, F.M. (eds.) *European Street Gangs and Troublesome Youth Groups*. Lanham: Altamira Press, p. 219–255.

Weijters, G. (2008). *Youth delinquency in Dutch cities and school. A multilevel approach*. Nijmegen: Print Partners Ipskamp Nijmegen.

Wikström, P.H. & Butterworth, D.A. (2006). *Adolescent crime. Individual differences and life-styles*. Devon: Willan Publishing.

Wikström, P-O. (2006). Individuals, settings and acts of crime: Situational mechanisms and the explanation of crime. In: Wikström, P-O. & Samson, R.J. (eds.) *The Explanation of Crime: Context, Mechanisms and Development*. Cambridge: Cambridge University Press, pp. 61–107.

Wikström, P.-O., & Svensson, R. (2008). Why are English Youths More Violent Than Swedish Youths?: A Comparative Study of the Role of Crime Propensity, Lifestyles and Their Interactions in Two Cities. *European Journal of Criminology*, 5, p. 309–330.

Chapter 10
The Neighbourhood Context

Josine Junger-Tas, Majone Steketee, and Harrie Jonkman

Since about the 1970s, a number of authors have called attention to the role of neighbourhoods in generating delinquency (Shaw and McKay 1942; Kornhauser 1978; Bursik and Grasmick 1993; Sampson and Laub 1993; Sampson and Raudenbush 1999; Sampson et al. 1997, 1999; Wikström 1998; Morenoff et al. 2001). If one wants to study whether growing up in specific neighbourhoods influences or effects young people, two immediate problems come to mind. The first concerns the definition of a "neighbourhood". Some researchers define neighbourhoods by using official statistical units, such as census tracts, or administrative units, such as postcode areas or wards (Boxford 2006). However, the problem with this kind of definition is that it may refer to large and mixed areas, parts of which may be inhabited by residents owning or renting their apartments or homes, and other parts consisting of low rent public housing estates. As Boxford states "...ward boundaries are artificial and do not exist in space" (Boxford 2006, 87). This is particularly the case in Europe where problem neighbourhoods are often confined to a small number of streets.

The second problem regards the "selection bias": does adolescent delinquency result from neighbourhood factors or from a differential selection of their families to specific neighbourhoods? Having been aware of this issue, Sampson refers to a housing experiment, which involved moving families from inner-city high poverty areas to low poverty areas (Goering and Feins 2003). Using a randomized assignment with two control groups, the authors compared the outcomes of families who moved with those who would have done so, had it been offered to them. Families who moved to low poverty areas witnessed an improvement of their sons' physical and mental health, well-being, safety and problem behaviour. Of course such an experiment does not yield sufficient evidence to abandon the selection bias theory. As Sampson observes, his study essentially conveys the importance of moving but does not delve into neighbourhood social processes that may produce delinquency. He suggests

M. Steketee (✉)
Verwey-Jonker Institute, Utrecht, The Netherlands
e-mail: msteketee@verwey-jonker.nl

J. Junger-Tas et al., *The Many Faces of Youth Crime: Contrasting Theoretical Perspectives on Juvenile Delinquency across Countries and Cultures*,
DOI 10.1007/978-1-4419-9455-4_10,

introducing measures at the neighbourhood level instead of dealing with individual families. This means that the question of whether it is the selection of problematic families into special neighbourhoods or the specific characteristics of problematic neighbourhoods, which play a decisive role in the genesis of delinquency is not yet resolved. On the other hand, neighbourhoods with low rent apartments obviously attract low-income residents, but this is not necessarily a criminal population. For example, Shaw and McKay's famous study on the ills that befall specific areas in big cities not only showed that these communities were characterized by high delinquency rates, but also by high rates of infant mortality, tuberculosis and child abuse (Shaw and McKay 1942). According to these authors, three structural factors lead to the disorganization of a local community and consequently to high rates of delinquency. These are low economic status, population heterogeneity and residential mobility. Since then health research has confirmed these findings (Junger et al. 2001). Studies have found that the lifestyle of persistent delinquents often result in more accidents, hospital visits, mental disturbances, and evidently they die earlier than non-delinquents (Rivera 1995; Stattin and Romelsjö 1995; Junger et al. 1995). They also found that these relations persisted over time, independent from population turnovers. For example, most migrant populations in Europe live in neighbourhoods that were already plagued by high rates of delinquent behaviour before World War II, a long-time before there were any migrant youths to be seen.

Kornhauser (1978) may be considered as "the founder of contemporary social disorganization theory" (Wikström 1998, 290). She rejects the concept of cultural deviance and proposes a social control model by relating communities with offending. She considers structural factors, such as poverty and ethnic heterogeneity as factors that produce high delinquency rates. Communities form a continuum, from wealthy, stable and cohesive communities, to poor, unstable and heterogeneous ones. The latter are unable to realize common values due to lack of or inadequate social institutions and collaboration among residents. This results in poor informal social control and inadequate socialization and supervision of children, both explaining a high rate of offenders in the community. Since then, community social control is perceived as a product of the social relationships between residents. For example, Bursik and Grasmick (1993) state that "the extensiveness and density of the formal and informal networks within the neighbourhood that bind the residents together as a social community" determines the effectiveness of social control (Bursik and Grasmick 1993, 4). This notion is also based on the concept of social capital, which was first presented by who expressed this particular concept as social ties among persons and positions, which Putnam (1993, 36) later defined as "...networks, norms and trust, that facilitate coordination and cooperation for mutual benefit". However, Morenoff et al. (2001, 519) observed that some neighbourhoods may have tight-knit social bonds and a high degree of social integration, but may be incapable of exercising social control, because of their isolation from mainstream society.

Some other contemporary researchers – those of whom Robert Sampson is the best known, more specifically examined the way in which socially disorganized neighbourhoods effect juveniles' social behaviour. They argue that these neighbourhoods are unable to realize the collective values of the residents and to exercise effective social control (see also Kornhauser 1978). Sampson and Groves (1989) built upon the three dimensions of community social organization that effect juvenile delinquency. First, community disadvantages increases parental stress and makes parental monitoring more difficult, the risk of which may be delinquent behaviour. Second, the ability of a community to supervise and control teenage peer groups decreases. This is important because delinquency is essentially a group phenomenon. In that respect, cohesive communities are better capable of controlling teenage groups than disorganized neighbourhoods (Shaw and McKay 1942; Sampson 1993). Finally, local friendships and acquaintanceship networks increase the capacity for community social control when residents know each other and form friendships. That capacity also improves when the rate of participation in formal and voluntary community organizations also increases (Sampson 1993). While Kornhauser (1978) writes about the instability and isolation of community institutions, in Europe we tend to refer to the social, health and youth services in communities as important mechanisms to maximize community organization and stability.

Therefore, in light of the increasing number of studies which focus on the impact of neighbourhood factors on adolescent behaviour, our perception is that the neighbourhood is really important in the genesis of rule breaking behaviour and we will try to test this by our analyses.

10.1 Neighbourhood Integration, Bonding and Disorganization

The ISRD-2 study allowed us to test Social disorganization theory, as we collected data concerning the community where the young people resided, as well other factors such as social control, school and the peer group. Since we had guaranteed the respondents that they would remain anonymous, we measured *neighbourhood integration* – or neighbourhood cohesion – by submitting them three statements (people around here are willing to help each other; this is a close knit neighbourhood; people in this neighbourhood can be trusted), *neighbourhood bonding* (I like my neighbourhood; if I had to move I would miss my neighbourhood; there is a lot of space for children to play) and *neighbourhood disorganization* (there is a lot of crime in my neighbourhood;… a lot of drug dealing;… a lot of fighting;… a lot of graffiti;… a lot of empty and abandoned buildings). All had scales from 0 to 100. Unfortunately, we were not able to conduct a parent survey, which makes it difficult to directly measure "collective efficacy" – a concept based on parents evaluating the relationship between residents and social control on juveniles in the neighbourhood. Our position is that young people are capable of recognizing neighbourhood disorganization, but they might be unable to provide us with a clear perspective of the social control component, an important aspect when measuring collective efficacy. Table 10.1 presents both the means of both neighbourhood integration and neighbourhood disorganization per country cluster, which are weighed for large and medium cities.

When we asked respondents about the cohesion of their neighbourhood, 95% of all 40,000 young people asked, rated this positively with a mean of 60. This suggests

Table 10.1 Means of neighbourhood integration, bonding and disorganization by country cluster large and medium cities (N=39.597)

	Neighbourhood integration	Neighbourhood bonding	Neighbourhood disorganization
Anglo-Saxon	62.5	74.3	27.0
Western Europe	60.3	70.0	21.4
Northern Europe	63.4	81.0	17.3
Mediterranean	62.4	72.6	23.0
Post-Socialist	56.7	75.3	25.6
Latin America	57.4	75.6	30.5
Total mean	60.1	74.2	23.3

that the majority of them generally coincide peacefully with their neighbours and other residents, which may guarantee a minimal level of neighbourhood social control. The scores on bonding are even higher, implying that whatever the problems that may have risen between some of them, all young people are greatly attached to their neighbourhoods, whether delinquent or not. After all, many grew up there which made them familiar with the composition of the neighbourhood, the residents, the shops, and made friends with whom they played with as kids and hung out with in the evenings. However, at the same time, they do not always resist in terms of contributing to neighbourhood problems. Two thirds – 68% – mentioned some or more problems with crime and disturbances they had been confronted with (mean score of 23.3). These findings tend to support what has been noted by Morenoff et al. (2001, p. 519), who stated that strong community ties may also impede the exercise of social control and that a high degree of social integration can go together with low levels of informal social control.

Interestingly, the highest mean for neighbourhood integration as well as bonding, and the lowest for social disorganization are those found in N-Europe. The lowest means for integration are found in the Post-Socialist countries and in Latin America. Conversely, neighbourhood disorganization appears to be the highest in Latin America, followed by the Anglo-Saxon cluster, but it is strikingly low in N-Europe, followed by W-Europe. One cannot help but wonder whether these results might be related to the breadth of the welfare state in N- and W-Europe, which take care of, among others, decent housing and safe neighbourhoods for most citizens. We will now explore what the possible implications are for the young people from our study living in disorganized as compared to living in cohesive neighbourhoods. Neighbourhood bonding will no longer be considered as it insufficiently differentiates between clusters and countries: all countries have bonding scores between 70 and 80, with only three outliers (Russia with a score of 50.1, Austria and Germany with scores of 61 and 63.7).

10.2 Impact of Degree of Neighbourhood Disorganization

In that respect we will begin by examining the kind of youth population residing in disorganized neighbourhoods.

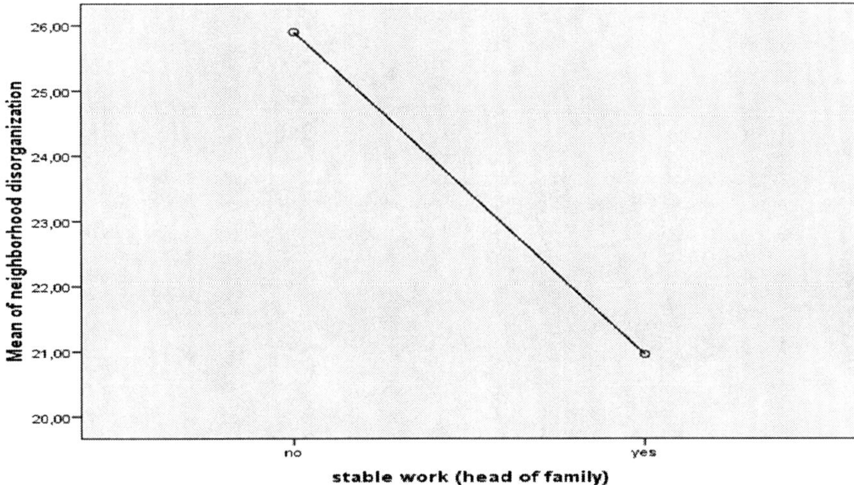

Fig. 10.1 Employment by Neighbourhood Disorganization Means. $F=272.22$, $p<0.001$, df = 1,66669

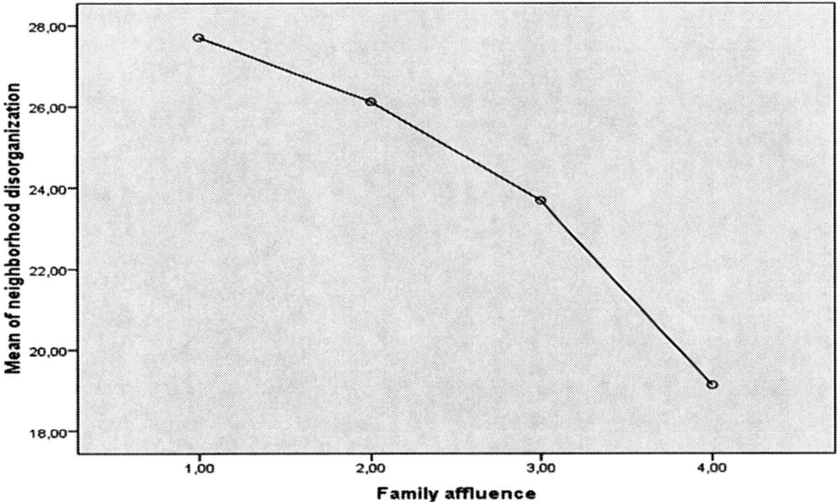

Fig. 10.2 Family affluence by Neighbourhood Disorganization Means. $F=264.74$, $p<0.001$, df = 3,39476

Figures 10.1 and 10.2 portray the relationship between employment and family affluence and the places where families live. Not surprisingly, our results show that unemployed and rather poor families tend to live in clearly worse neighbourhoods than those who are employed and more affluent.

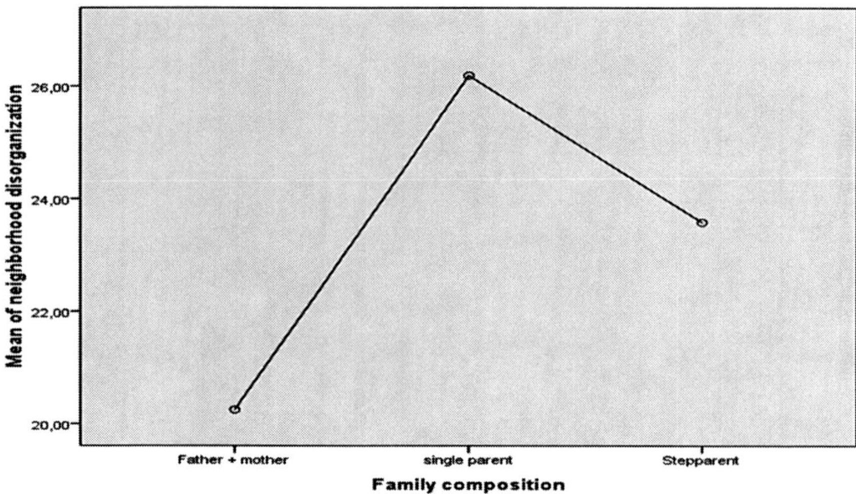

Fig. 10.3 Family structure by Neighbourhood Disorganization. $F = 254.96$, $p < 0.001$, df = 2,62032

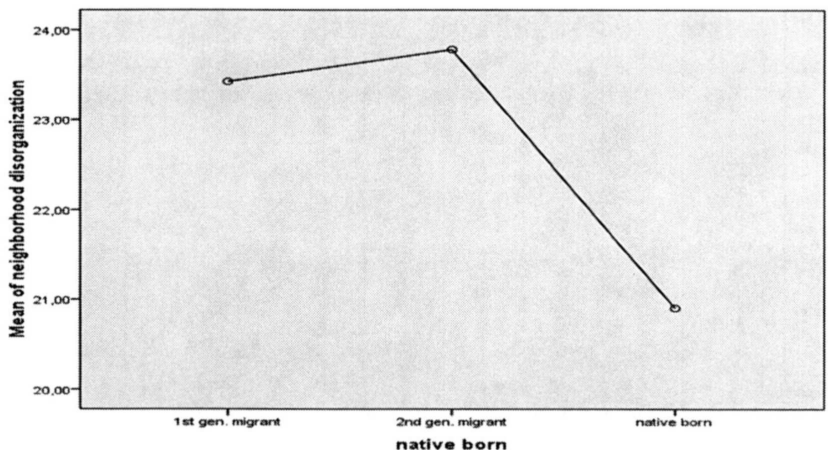

Fig. 10.4 Ethnicity by Neighbourhood disorganization. $F = 79.70$, $p < 0.001$; df = 2,67146

Turning now to family structure, Fig. 10.3 illustrates, as we noted before in Chap. 7, that single parent families are overrepresented in disorganized neighbourhoods, while – as shown in Fig. 10.4 – this is also the case for first generation and second generation immigrants.

It is worth recalling that the definition of a disorganized neighbourhood is based on the statements of the young people themselves, which makes it all the more remarkable that on this basis we may conclude that all conditions regarding a disorganized neighbourhood – as they appear in the cited literature – are fulfilled: population heterogeneity, unemployment, – relative – poverty, and family disruption.

10.3 Neighbourhood and the Family

The following section will focus on the question of how well families function in disorganized vs. cohesive neighbourhoods. This is significant because families play a key role in socializing children into conformity in terms of society's norms and values. Although in this respect informal family control is one of the most important predictors of delinquency (Cernkovich and Giordano 1987; Hawkins et al. 1986; Loeber and Stouthamer-Loeber 1986), social control is strongly related to the bond with parents (Wright et al. 2001: 678; Loeber and Stouthamer-Loeber 1986) and with social support, intimacy and trustful communication (Rothbaum and Weisz 1994).

In Table 10.2 we may first note that cohesive neighbourhoods correlate positively with family bonding – and leisure time with parents as part of bonding. Although parental control does not correlate highly with neighbourhood cohesion, delinquency versatility only has a weak and negative association. However, in disorganized neighbourhoods, all family variables are negatively associated with disorganization while versatility has a strong positive correlation. Furthermore, it should also be observed that cohesive neighbourhoods have a higher correlation with family bonding than with parental control, again suggesting that the bond with parents is a condition for effective parental control. This is not the case in disorganized neighbourhoods where the correlation between family bonding as well as parental control are both similarly negative, and leisure time with parents does not seem to be of great significance either.

Second, – as expected – family bonding is related to parental control. As noted, the high correlation between family bonding and spending leisure time with parents is because the leisure variable is a component of the family bonding scale.

Table 10.2 Pearson correlations of neighbourhood with family variables

	Neighb. cohesion	Neighb. disorg	Family disruption	Family bonding	Parent control	Leisure w. parents
Neighb. cohesion	1					
Neighb. disorg.	−0.14	1				
Fam. disruption	−0.12	0.12	1			
Family bonding	0.21	−0.17	−0.29	1		
Parental control	0.09	−0.17	−0.12	0.27	1	
Leisure w. parents	0.16	−0.12	−0.18	0.69	0.19	1
Versatility	−0.06	0.28	0.14	−0.17	−0.25	−0.13

Table 10.3 Multiple regression betas versatility regressed on social background and family variables by country cluster

	Anglo-Saxon	Western Europe	Northern Europe	Mediterranean	Post-Socialist	Latin America
Gender	0.19	0.14	0.13	0.12	0.15	0.13
Grade	0.002	0.02	−0.02	0.03	0.02	0.02
Ethnicity	−0.03	0.01	−0.01	0.02	0.01	0.02
Employment	−0.03	−0.01	0.01	0.01	0.002	0.01
Fam affluence	0.03	0.07	0.03	0.03	0.04	0.06
Neighb. integr.	0.04	0.02	0.01	−0.01	0.004	−0.01
Neighb. disorgan	0.37	0.27	0.25	0.22	0.22	0.13
Family bonding	−0.09	−0.11	−0.14	−0.07	−0.04	−0.07
Parental control	−0.18	−0.16	−0.13	−0.18	−0.15	−0.12
Fam. disruption	0.09	0.07	0.08	0.07	0.04	0.08
R^2	0.28	0.19	0.17	0.15	0.14	0.08

However, it apparently remains an important part, because how strong the bond is with parents, as well as the parents ability to control their offspring is made up of time spent with parents in intimate and enjoyable settings.

Family disruption combines three negative events in the children's lives. These include, separation of parents (23%), violent conflicts between parents (12%) and parent alcohol or drugs use (7%). This variable is obviously negatively associated with all family variables. Adding versatility to the correlation matrix conveys two relatively high correlations. First, a positive correlation with neighbourhood disorganization, and second, a negative correlation with parental control. This suggests that we have two key variables which explain delinquency involvement. A logistic regression later in this chapter will shed some more light on this affirmation.

Regressing versatility on all social background and family variables in the country clusters, reveals in Table 10.3 that the greatest contribution to the explained variance is from neighbourhood disorganization, betas varying between 0.37 and 0.22, with an exceptional 0.13 for Latin America. Betas range from −0.12 to −0.18 for parental control, while family bonding and family disruption contribute smaller Betas. Controlling for basic demographic variables illustrates that boys are considerably more involved in delinquency than girls.

According to Sampson and Laub's theory, social background cannot be directly related to delinquency, but is mediated by family bonding and control. In Table 10.3, we find that the family head's employment and family affluence are only weakly associated with delinquent behaviour, while they are positively related with family bonding (with employment 0.07; with family affluence 0.10), as the theory would predict. However, overall, the variance is rather low in most country clusters, suggesting that important variables are still missing in the analysis. Betas are highest in the Anglo-Saxon cluster and explained variance in that cluster is $R^2=0.28$, vs. 0.19 in W-Europe, 0.17 in N-Europe, 0.15 in S-Europe, 0.14 in the Post-Socialist and only 0.08 in the Latin American cluster. The Latin American cluster deviates from the rest, as we will see in all of our following analyses. It is not directly obvious what has lead to this outcome, but it should be noted that these countries have very different economic, cultural and social compositions in comparison to countries in the other clusters.

Testing Sampson and Laub's model in a more explicit way, we introduced some control variables in a first regression model, and then added neighbourhood disorganization in a second model and family variables in the third model. In the table, we also added the partial correlations in order to control the unique contribution of each variable. As presented in Table 10.4, gender is an important variable in all

Table 10.4 Versatility regressed on control variables, neighbourhood disorganization and family variables

	Model 1	Model 2	Model 3	
	Betas	Betas	Betas	Partial correlations
Anglo-Saxon				
Gender	0.20	0.18	0.18	0.21
Grade	0.01	0.04	0.01	0.01
Ethnicity	−0.03	−0.03	−0.03	−0.04
Neighb.disorgan.		0.42	0.36	0.37
Family bonding			−0.09	−0.09
Parental control			−0.18	−0.20
Fam. disruption			0.08	0.09
	R^2 0.04	R^2 0.22	R^2 0.28	
Western Europe				
Gender	0.18	0.15	0.15	0.16
Grade	0.06	0.05	0.03	0.03
Ethnicity	0.04	−0.01	−0.01	−0.01
Neighb. disorgan		0.32	0.26	0.27
Family bonding			−0.10	−0.10
Parental control			−0.16	−0.17
Fam. disruption			0.06	0.07
	R^2 0.04	R^2 0.14	R^2 0.19	
Northern Europe				
Gender	0.14	0.12	0.13	0.14
Grade	0.03	0.02	−0.02	−0.02
Ethnicity	0.01	−0.01	−0.02	−0.02
Neighb. disorgan		0.32	0.25	0.26
Family bonding			−0.13	−0.13
Parental control			−0.13	−0.13
Fam. disruption			0.08	0.08
	R^2 0.02	R^2 0.12	R^2 0.17	
Mediterranean				
Gender	0.16	0.12	0.12	0.13
Grade	0.09	0.07	0.03	0.04
Ethnicity	0.04	0.04	0.01	0.02
Neighb. disorgan		0.27	0.21	0.21
Family bonding			−0.07	−0.07
Parental control			−0.18	−0.18
Fam. disruption			0.07	0.08
	R^2 0.03	R^2 0.10	R^2 0.15	

(continued)

Table 10.4 (continued)

	Model 1	Model 2	Model 3	
	Betas	Betas	Betas	Partial correlations
Post-Socialist				
Gender	0.20	0.17	0.16	0.16
Grade	0.06	0.03	0.02	0.02
Ethnicity	0.02	0.01	0.01	0.01
Neighb. disorgan		0.26	0.22	0.22
Family bonding			–0.04	–0.04
Parental control			–0.15	–0.15
Fam. disruption			0.03	0.04
	R^2 0.04	R^2 0.11	R^2 0.14	
Latin America				
Gender	0.15	0.14	0.13	0.13
Grade	0.05	0.04	0.02	0.02
Ethnicity	0.03	0.04	0.03	0.03
Neighb. disorgan		0.15	0.12	0.12
Family bonding			–0.06	–0.06
Parental control			–0.12	–0.11
Fam. disruption			0.08	0.08
	R^2 0.03	R^2 0.05	R^2 0.08	

clusters and remains so in all models, but the explained variance of all control variables are low. Adding neighbourhood disorganization, however, substantially increases explained variance in the second model, although the size of the increase differs between clusters.

The partial correlation conveys the unique contribution of neighbourhood disorganization to the variance, which is hardly differing from its beta in model 3. In addition, although R^2 increases by adding family variables – with parental control making the largest contribution – the increase is not very substantial in most clusters. A cautious conclusion should therefore be that family variables have a moderate effect on delinquency, but that the direct effect of neighbourhood disorganization remains rather strong, giving only weak support to social disorganization theory.

10.4 Neighbourhood and the School

In Chap. 8 we saw how important the school is in children's lives. School achievement is related to the attachment to school as well as to planning what proceeds after finishing compulsory school, while failure is expressed in terms of repeating classes, having no future plans, and truancy. Chapter 8 also showed that it is not only a juvenile's talents, upbringing or motivation that might explain success or failure but also the education system and the school itself. Many schools are able to motivate students to learn and are capable of transferring society's norms and values into the minds of young people. These schools create an orderly and positive school climate, promoting study as well as good behaviour. However, not all schools are able to realize these values to the same extent. Some schools are sub-standard because of a lack of well-qualified teachers, which increases absenteeism among teachers, rapid teacher turnover, insufficient teaching material or poor school buildings. These are often (vocational training) schools at the bottom of the intellectual hierarchy, serving a deprived student population.

Like disorganized communities experiencing higher levels of crime (Bursik and Grasmick 1993), schools in such communities also hardly succeed in socializing young people effectively (Gottfredson 2001, 65). There are several factors that help explain their shortcomings. First, the educators' norms concerning appropriate behaviour, does not agree with those of the student body, which is unconventional, inconsistent and often poorly disciplined. Second, schools are not able to recruit parents to work productively with the school. Third, the social and emotional needs of students are so great that special efforts and support would be needed to make effective socialization possible. Finally, these schools have difficulties in terms of recruiting and keeping good teachers. The best teachers prefer to work with a well-trained, quiet middle class student population rather than an unstable, deprived and difficult student body in a poor and neglected environment. Results from correlational studies suggest that attending an effective school would raise young people's success rate 29–42% points above that of similar students in a sub-standard school (Gottfredson 2001, 81). In this respect, research also shows that community context and characteristics of the school's population correlate highly with school disorder (Gottfredson 2001).

The ISRD-2 study provides information about *school achievement, truancy, repeating grades* and the instrument includes two scales: *school bonding* (I like my school; if I had to move I would miss my school; teachers notice when I am doing well and let me know; there are other activities in school besides the lessons, sports, music, theatre…;) and *school disorganization* (there is a lot of stealing in my school; there is a lot of fighting…; vandalizing…; drug use in my school). Using these scales we accepted the respondents own definition, although we cannot rule out that part of that definition might be a reflection of their own behaviour.

Table 10.5 shows that the strongest correlation of neighbourhood cohesion is with school bonding, while the highest correlation in our whole matrix is between neighbourhood disorganization and school disorganization. This suggests that young people in deprived neighbourhoods are also attending sub-standard schools, where students are fighting, vandalizing and where stealing each other's possessions and drug use are rampant. Furthermore, it is of course no surprise that such students more often truant, repeat grades, have a low degree of school bonding and are more involved in serious delinquency. In addition and as expected, truancy and school disorganization also correlate positively with versatility.

Just as we did with the family variables, we will now test the impact of neighbourhood disorganization and school variables on delinquency involvement and we will do this in a two-model regression analysis.

First, we will compare the situation in cohesive neighbourhoods with that of disorganized neighbourhoods. Table 10.6 reveals that when controlling for gender,

Table 10.5 Correlations of neighbourhood with school variables

	Neighb. cohesion	Neighborh. disorganiz.	School achievement	Truancy	Repeat. grade	School bonding	School disorganiz.
Neighborh. cohesion	1						
Neighborh. disorganiz.	–0.18	1					
School achievement	–0.03	–0.06	1				
Truancy	–0.10	0.22	–0.05	1			
Repeated grade	–0.07	0.16	–0.11	0.11	1		
School bonding	0.25	–0.10	0.07	–0.17	–0.07	1	
School disorganiz.	–0.06	0.34	–0.10	0.16	0.08	–0.12	1

Table 10.6 Multiple regression of versatility on school variables

	Neighbourhood integration			Neighbourhood disorganization		
	Model 1	Model 2	Partials	Model 1	Model 2	Partials
Anglo-Saxon						
Gender	0.20	0.18	0.20	0.18	0.17	0.20
Grade	0.001	–0.04	–0.04	0.04	0.002	0.00
Ethnicity	–0.04	–0.05	–0.06	–0.04	–0.04	–0.05
Neighb. integr/disorg.	–0.09	–0.02	–0.02	0.43	0.32	0.32
School bonding		–0.10	–0.11		–0.08	–0.09
School disorgan.		0.18	0.19		0.07	0.08
Repeating grades		–0.03	–0.03		–0.05 (ns)	–0.06
Truancy		0.32	0.32		0.26	0.28
	R^2 0.05	R^2 0.22		R^2 0.22	R^2 0.30	
Western Europe						
Gender	0.18	0.15	0.16	0.15	0.13	0.15
Grade	0.06	0.00 (ns)	0.00	0.05	0.00	0.00
Ethnicity	0.04	–0.00	–0.00	–0.01	–0.03	–0.03
Neighb. integr/disorg.	–0.06	–0.01	–0.01	0.32	0.22	0.22
School bonding		–0.07	–0.07		–0.06	–0.06
School disorgan.		0.15	0.16		0.09	0.09
Repeating grades		0.07	0.08		0.05	0.06
Truancy		0.27	0.27		0.23	0.24
	R^2 0.04	R^2 0.17		R^2 0.14	R^2 0.21	
Northern Europe						
Gender	0.14	0.14	0.15	0.12	0.12	0.14
Grade	0.01	–0.02	–0.02	0.01	–0.02	–0.02
Ethnicity	0.01	–0.02	–0.02	–0.01	–0.03	–0.03

(continued)

Table 10.6 (continued)

	Neighbourhood integration			Neighbourhood disorganization		
	Model 1	Model 2	Partials	Model 1	Model 2	Partials
Neighb. integr/ disorg.	−0.04	−0.04	−0.04	0.31	0.22	0.22
School bonding		−0.07	−0.08		−0.07	−0.08
School disorgan.		0.14	0.15		0.07	0.08
Repeating grades		0.04	0.04		0.03 (ns)	0.04
Truancy		0.30	0.30		0.26	0.27
	R^2 0.03	R^2 0.16		R^2 0.12	R^2 0.20	
Mediterranean						
Gender	0.16	0.12	0.13	0.12	0.11	0.11
Grade	0.08	0.02	0.02	0.07	0.02	0.02
Ethnicity	0.04	0.03	0.03	0.04	0.03	0.04
Neighb. integr/ disorg.	−0.06	−0.02	−0.02	0.27	0.17	0.17
School bonding		−0.08	−0.08		−0.07	−0.08
School disorgan.		0.16	0.16		0.11	0.11
Repeating grades		0.02	0.02		0.00 (ns)	0.00
Truancy		0.25	0.25		0.22	0.22
	R^2 0.04	R^2 0.14		R^2 0.10	R^2 0.17	
Post-Socialist						
Gender	0.20	0.17	0.18	0.17	0.15	0.16
Grade	0.06	0.02	0.02	0.04	0.01	0.01
Ethnicity	0.02	0.01	0.01	0.01	0.00	0.01
Neighb. integr/ disorg.	−0.06	−0.03	−0.03	0.26	0.20	0.20
School bonding		−0.06	−0.06		−0.06	−0.06
School disorgan.		0.13	0.13		0.06	0.06
Repeating grades		0.04	0.04		0.03	0.03
Truancy		0.19	0.19		0.17	0.18
	R^2 0.05	R^2 0.12		R^2 0.11	R^2 0.15	
Latin America						
Gender	0.16	0.12	0.13	0.15	0.12	0.13
Grade	0.04	−0.01	−0.01	0.03	−0.01	−0.01
Ethnicity	0.03	0.02	0.02	0.05	0.03	0.03
Neighb. integr/ disorg.	−0.05	−0.02	−0.02	0.15	0.11	0.10
School bonding		−0.04	−0.04		−0.05	−0.05
School disorgan.		0.11	0.11		0.09	0.09
Repeating grades		0.08	0.08		0.07	0.07
Truancy		0.17	0.17		0.16	0.16
	R^2 0.03	R^2 0.08		R^2 0.05	R^2 0.09	

Neighbourhood integration: all betas significant, except (ns)

Neighbourhood disorganization: all coefficients $^{***}p<0.001$, except repeating grade in Anglo-Saxon ($p<0.01$), N-Europe ($p<0.05$) and S-Europe (ns) grade and ethnicity, children living in "no-problem" neighbourhoods run a relatively high risk of delinquency involvement if they attend disorganized schools and often truant with a moderate negative beta of school bonding. This while the two highest Betas, when kids live in problem neighbourhoods reflect the great impact of both the neighbourhood as well as truancy on delinquency versatility, resulting in higher explained variance. This is particularly the case in the Anglo-Saxon cluster but hardly in the Latin American one, which may be related to differences in the school system and school population.

If we compare Table 10.4 – neighbourhood disorganization and family variables – to Table 10.6 – neighbourhood disorganization and school variables – the decrease of the Betas of neighbourhood disorganization by adding family variables in model 2 – in Table 10.4 – is lower than that same decrease by adding school variables. While, at the same time the increase in explained variance by adding school variables is greater than by adding family variables. Consequently, drawing on our comparison it seems that apart from neighbourhood disorganization, the school has its own very important influence on the life of children. It is essentially the disaffection from school, as expressed in truancy that contributes most to versatility. All other school variables have considerably lower Betas, the highest among them being for school disorganization. The picture reveals that children, who live in integrated or disorganized neighbourhoods, attend schools which are sub-standard and are not capable of teaching and monitoring them, leading to an unsuccessful school career. As a result, children turn away from school, hang around with other marginalized juveniles and gradually become increasingly involved in delinquency. However, as we have seen in Table 10.5, this situation is more frequent in the case of young people living in problem neighbourhoods, while it is rather exceptional for young people living in integrated neighbourhoods.

An interesting survey in this respect was conducted by Kirk (2009), who studied 7,500 elementary Chicago school students as well as 2,000 elementary schoolteachers, examining the relative and interdependent impact of school, neighbourhood and family social control on young people's behaviour. As independent variables he chose: parental supervision, parent-teacher trust, student-teacher trust, school collective efficacy and neighbourhood collective efficacy, and as dependent variables: suspension and arrest. Kirk found a number of results that are also relevant to our study. For example, both suspension and arrests are significantly and negatively related to parental supervision, while more trusting bonds between teachers and students – a concept we measured by school bonding – are associated with a lower likelihood of arrest. Moreover, this association does not vary across schools and neighbourhood (Kirk 2009, 505). In addition, when combining the four measures of control together in one model, parental supervision and student-teacher trust were highly predictive of arrest, while this was hardly the case for school collective efficacy. Finally, the correlation between student-teacher trust and arrest is stronger in neighbourhoods with high collective efficacy than in disorganized neighbourhoods. In our study, the betas for school bonding did not differentiate much between neighbourhood quality, but they were negatively related to versatility. However, Kirk's study was performed in elementary schools, while our study deals with the three first grades of secondary schools. In this respect, Thornberry's (1987) argument that the direct influence of bonding with parents and parental control on their children's behaviour decreases when adolescents grow older and that other influences, such as the school and the peer group, take precedence, is of more relevance. This argument was tested by Jang (1999) by the means of a multilevel analysis of the data from the *National Youth Survey*. He found that the effects of school and the peer group on delinquency increase from early to middle adolescence, reaching a peak at age 13–15, and declines after that. Even though our ISRD-2 outcomes illustrated that the school, as opposed to the family had a greater impact on delinquency involvement, independent of the quality of the neighbourhood they live in, these outcomes do support this theory. Yet, whether this is also the case for the peer group will be examined in the following section.

10.5 Neighbourhood and the Peer Group

In their longitudinal *Rochester Youth Development Study,* Thornberry and colleagues studied the way in which young people associated with peers and committed delinquent acts. On the basis of that research, they concluded that adolescents who are involved in delinquency seek out friends who follow similar lifestyles. However, they also found that this association had an indirect effect on delinquency which was mediated by the reinforcement of the peer network. The authors concluded that there is in fact a reciprocal process of peer selection, leading to a delinquency stimulating and reinforcing environment (Thornberry et al. 2003, p.28). A process currently taking place which works similarly is the formation of gangs, which are based on a selection mechanism as well as on what they call facilitation, by which "norms, group processes and network characteristics of the gang facilitate involvement in delinquency and violence" (Thornberry et al. 2003, p.31). Pull factors, according to the youths, are being together with friends and participating in the fun and excitement of the gang. Push factors include structural disadvantages, living in deprived neighbourhoods, school failure and early involvement in delinquency.

10.6 The Influence of the Delinquent Peer Group

An initial question that comes to mind is whether youth living in disorganized neighbourhoods would be more likely than others to spend leisure time with a group of friends. The answer to that question is negative: the number of those who spend leisure time with a group of friends only increases from 75 to 84% (Cramer's $V=0.07$) according to the degree of neighbourhood disorganization, showing indeed that spending time with a peer group is normal youth behaviour (Warr 2002). However, this is not the whole story, since the type of group life differs a great deal with degree of neighbourhood disorganization.

Table 10.7 Percentage of delinquent friends by degree of neighbourhood disorganization in large and medium cities in %

	Degree of neighbourhood disorganization			
	1	2	3	
Friends committed	*N*=25.900	*N*=9.601	*N*=3.229	Cramer's V
Assault	6.1	15.2	31.8	0.25
Burglary	5.6	11.6	26.5	0.21
Threats w. violence	3.7	10.2	25.2	0.24
Shoplifting	28.1	40.5	54.1	0.17

Table 10.8 Serious offenses last year by having delinquent friends or not by degree of neighbourhood disorganization in large and medium cities – (%)

	Neighbourhood disorganization		
	1	2	3
Friends committed[a]	*N*=25.900	*N*=9.601	*N*=3.229
Assault	18.4 (2.6)	28.2 (5.7)	43.5 (11.7)
Burglary	18.0 (2.7)	28.7 (6.5)	46.7 (12.8)
Threats w. violence	20.0 (2.9)	30.2 (6.7)	47.0 (13.3)
Shoplifting	8.5 (1.6)	16.5 (4.1)	33.2 (8.4)

[a]Serious offenses of those without delinquent friends are placed between brackets

A second question is whether there is a connection between the number of delinquent friends a juvenile has and the neighbourhood he lives in. In this respect, one might hypothesize that in worse neighbourhoods young people have more delinquent friends than those living in better neighbourhoods. As Table 10.7 shows, we find that the more disorganized the neighbourhood, the more delinquent friends juveniles have.

Table 10.7 also shows that the offense of shoplifting is committed most frequently in a youth population aged 12–15. This is even the case in neighbourhoods with a low degree of disorganization, where more than a quarter of juveniles have friends who have shoplifted. Nevertheless, in the most disorganized neighbourhoods over half of their friends had shoplifted.

A final question regarding this subject is what the relationship is between living in a disorganized neighbourhood, having delinquent friends – or not – and committing serious offenses. As might be expected, those with delinquent friends commit considerably more offenses than those without such friends. Furthermore, Table 10.8 illustrates that according to the degree of neighbourhood disorganization, the number of juveniles committing serious offenses increases. It not only increases among young people with delinquent friends but also among those without such friends, doubling at each higher degree of disorganization. This again conveys the great impact the type of neighbourhood may have even on young people without delinquent friends. Finally, there is a disparity between having friends who commit assault, burglary or threaten with violence, and friends who only shoplift, resulting in fewer serious offenses among the latter than among the former. This is also the case among young people who do not have any shoplifting friends: they commit substantially fewer serious offenses and seem to limit most of their delinquent behaviour to minor offending.

As we have seen earlier, the concept of "gang" does not seem to have the same significance in Europe as it has in the United States where its origin lies. This is because a number of youths claimed that they were members of a gang but did not report any offenses. Out of all of the young people reporting no gang membership, 19.5% did commit at least one minor offense in the past year. Among gang members, this was 41%, and in the former group, 5.3% did commit at least one serious offense in the past year vs. 17% of the latter. So, although the concept does seem a bit questionable, the two groups clearly differed in terms of delinquency involvement, which does support those European researchers who claim that Europe, does not have any real gangs and they are better identified as "troublesome groups" (Dekker and Weerman 2005). In our case we suspect that a number of youths claimed gang membership because they associated it with being "cool", without having a clear idea about what it really implies.

Given the fact that, according to degree of neighbourhood disorganization, the nature of the peer group differs both in the number of illegal acts committed and in the number of youths who consider their group as a gang, the question then is how frequent and how serious delinquency involvement is in the different groups. This is shown in Fig. 10.5, which indicates that there are substantial differences in versatility of delinquent behaviour by neighbourhood disorganization. An Anova analysis showed significant differences ($p<0.001$),[1] with the highest versatility scores in the worst neighbourhoods. Considering those who have a large group of friends, versatility is 5 times as high in the most deprived neighbourhoods than in the least deprived. Among those whose peer group meets in public places, it is 4 times as high; among those who consider their group as a gang it is more than 3 times as high; and among those whose peer group admits to committing illegal acts it is more than twice as high. In other words, in the least disorganized neighbourhood, rates of versatility increases fourfold from having a group of friends (6.5%) to the group that commits illegal acts (23%); at the second stage of disorganization these vary from 16.3 to 35.5%, that is more than twice; and in the worst neighbourhoods these vary from 33.5 to 48.2%, which is one and half times higher. These outcomes suggest that with increasing deprivation, the impact of the delinquent peer group grows and the impact of the degree of disorganization of the neighbourhood diminishes.

Nevertheless, it is clear that there are interaction effects. To examine these we conducted different two-way Anova analyses, looking for interaction effects of neighbourhood disorganization with "peer group meets in public places", "considering

[1] Group meets in public places, $F=363.83$, $p<0.001$.
Group commits illegal acts, $F=0.936,80$, $p<0.001$.
Group is considered Gang, $F=610.0$, $p<0.001$.

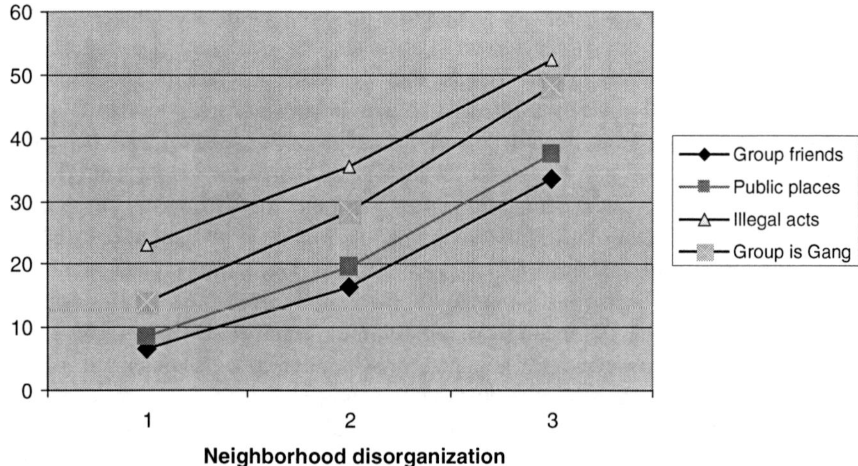

Fig. 10.5 Last year versatility by Peer group, time spent outdoors and degree of neighbourhood disorganization (%)

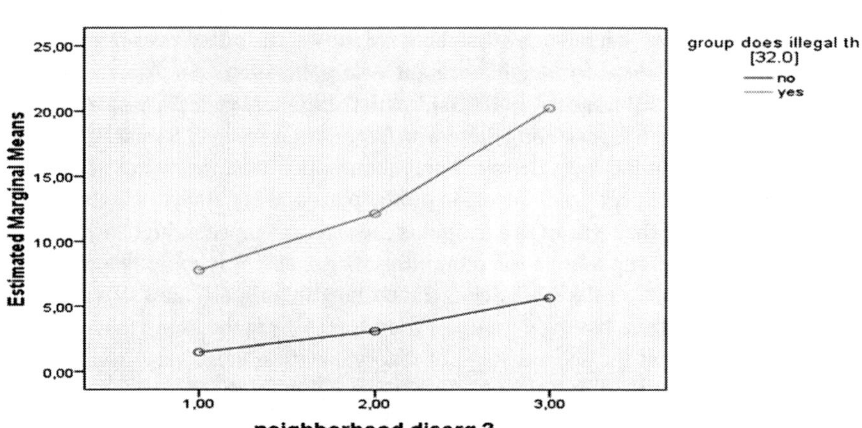

Fig. 10.6 Interaction of two independent variables – Peer group committing Illegal Acts and neighbourhood disorganization – on versatility

the peer group as a gang", and with "group commits illegal acts". Figure 10.6 illustrates these results, with a significant interaction effect of $F=263.40$, $p<0.001$.

Taking into account that most young people spend leisure time with a peer group, Fig. 10.6 shows that when that peer group does not commit illegal acts the degree of neighbourhood disorganization has a limited effect on delinquency involvement, where delinquency involvement only increases slightly. On the other hand, when the peer group does commit illegal acts, versatility increases strongly with degree of neighbourhood disorganization, in particular in the worst neighbourhoods. A similar interaction pattern was found while introducing the variables "considers group a gang" ($F = 190.17, p < 0.001$), and "group meets in public places" ($103, 20, p < 0.001$). The latter interaction being weaker in light of the fact that meeting in public places does not differentiate so much between delinquents and non-delinquents. However, since young people living in the worst neighbourhoods have a more extensive delinquent peer group (see Table 10.7), our tentative conclusion would be that the impact of the peer group does dominate the impact of the neighbourhood in causing serious delinquent behaviour.

10.7 The Whole Picture

To recapitulate our findings so far, Table 10.9 presents the correlation between neighbourhood disorganization and the main variables relating to the family, the school, the peer group, and two individual characteristics of the young people in all country clusters: attitude to violence and self-control.

The correlation with family disruption is positive but overall rather low, indicating that the role of family separation or divorce in causing delinquency is not as important as older criminologists have argued. Both correlations with family bonding and, in particular, parental control are higher and negative in all clusters as expected.

Table 10.9 Correlations of neighbourhood disorganization with some selected variables by country cluster

	Anglo-Saxon	Western Europe	Northern Europe	Mediterranean	Post-Socialist	Latin America
Family disruption	0.15	0.13	0.19	0.10	0.12	0.13
Family bonding	−0.15	−0.17	−0.20	−0.18	−0.18	−0.15
Parental control	−0.22	−0.20	−0.20	−0.23	−0.21	−0.10
School bonding	−0.15	−0.12	−0.11	−0.16	−0.13	0.03 (ns)
School disorganization	0.40	0.35	0.33	0.33	0.35	0.24
Repeating grades	0.16	0.17	0.10	0.19	0.09	0.13
Truancy	0.29	0.24	0.25	0.26	0.18	0.15
Group meets in public places	0.13	0.22	0.19	0.16	0.14	0.11
Group comm. illegal acts	0.29	0.27	0.30	0.29	0.27	0.17
Considers group a Gang	0.32	0.28	0.11	0.23	0.18	0.16
Posit. attitude violence	0.45	0.32	0.30	0.31	0.26	0.22
Self-control	−0.31	−0.21	−0.27	−0.24	−0.22	−0.20
Versatility	0.43	0.34	0.32	0.28	0.28	0.16

All correlations sign. at $p < 0.001$ except one

With respect to the role of the school, there are two important correlations. The first is with school disorganization, which again suggests that in the whole of Europe, children who grow up in deprived neighbourhoods are likely to attend disorganized schools. The schools' disorganization to some extent may be a by-product of the rather difficult school population. Nonetheless, these schools are clearly unable to maintain an orderly, learning environment. This is supported by the rather high correlations with truancy in four of the six clusters, with the exception of the Post-Socialist and the Latin American cluster. As for the peer group, having friends who commit illegal acts is rather strongly correlated with neighbourhood disorganization in five of the six clusters. This while being a gang member is also highly correlated with neighbourhood disorganization, but only in the Anglo-Saxon and the W-European cluster. Exceptionally low is the correlation between gang membership and neighbourhood disorganization in the Nordic countries, suggesting that the phenomenon of gangs is pretty rare in these countries. Finally, the correlation between living in a deprived neighbourhood and having a positive attitude towards violence is high, while the level of self-control is somewhat lower. However, as observed before, the two are rather strongly correlated (0.43).

In order to obtain a more precise idea of the contribution that each variable gives to versatility – combining frequency and seriousness of delinquency involvement – we conducted a logistic regression, where we recoded all variables, including the dependent one, into dichotomized variables.

Table 10.9 reveals that the likelihood of committing frequent and serious offenses is highest when the peer group commits illegal acts. This is rather obvious, but it was also high when respondents viewed violence positively, self-control inhibiting that likelihood – and when they reported to have friends who were committing assaults. The likelihood of delinquency involvement continues to increase when a juvenile's peer group usually meets in public places, when he is truanting from school and when he has friends committing burglary. All these variables, except the attitude towards violence, but probably including truancy, refer to the influence of the peer group and to its quality. That influence reaches a peak between the ages of 12 and 17, and decrease after that age, but it might go a long way in explaining the tremendous effect on behaviour shown in our sample of young people aged 12–16 (Warr 2002; Thornberry et al. 1991; Thornberry and Krohn 2003).

Furthermore, neighbourhood disorganization increases the likelihood of delinquency and so does school disorganization and repeating grades. Together with truancy, these Betas suggest that independently of the impact of the peer group, the school also plays a significant role in the genesis of delinquent behaviour.

Finally, young people who experience family disruption are somewhat more likely to be involved in delinquency, while family bonding and parental control decrease that likelihood. Nevertheless, overall the family variables do not have a very great impact, confirming findings in other studies showing that in adolescence, the influence of parents diminishes while that of the school and the peer group increases (Thornberry 1987, 1992; Warr 2002) (Table 10.10).

Table 10.10 Logistic regression of family, school, peer group and individual variables; dependent variable is versatility

	B	Wald	Exp(B)
Gender	0.967	317.472	2.63***
Ethnicity	–0.020	0.105	0.98 (ns)
Age group	0.073	2.959	1.08 (ns)
Family disruption	0.110	4.212	1.11*
Family bonding	–0.142	2.932	0.87*
Parental control	–0.375	48.772	0.67***
School bonding	–0.261	23.300	0.77***
School disorganization	0.343	32.006	1.41***
Truancy	0.463	79.577	1.60***
Repeating grades	0.179	7.430	1.20**
Friends commit assault	0.895	202.850	2.45***
Friends commit burglary	0.435	45.117	1.55***
Friends commit extortion	0.177	5.765	1.19*
Friends commit shoplifting	0.859	218.967	2.36***
Peer group meets public places	0.518	62.911	1.68***
Peer group comm. illegal acts	1.125	447.138	3.08***
Posit. attitude to violence	0.908	131.722	2.48***
Self-control	–0.237	19.541	0.79***
Neighbourhood integration	0.001	0.577	1.00 (ns)
Neighbourhood disorganization	0.279	60.278	1.32***
Constant	–5.412	961.037	0.004***

$*p<0.05$, $**p<0.01$, $***p<0.001$
Correctly classified: 90.6% of cases; Nagelkerke = 0.42

10.8 Neighbourhood and Delinquency in a Multilevel Analysis

From the findings presented in previous paragraphs, we can conclude that the neighbourhood where young people live has an influence on (delinquent) behaviour. In this final paragraph we will examine the question of whether the neighbourhood has the same influence in all thirty participating countries. The central question is: are there similarities and/or differences between the countries in terms of the influence a neighbourhood has on delinquency involvement and to what extent this may be related to the quality of the neighbourhood in which these children grow up? To begin with, we controlled whether there was sufficient variability in terms of delinquency between the countries in our study.

The first model in our multilevel logistic regression (Model 0: Intercept model) is an empty model, which illustrates the delinquency level of students and the variability between countries. This model indicates that the general level of overall serious offenses committed is 6.08%, while the total variance of serious offenses explained by the different countries is 7.2%.

Table 10.11 Linear multilevel regression models for serious delinquency and the impact of the neighbourhood

	Model 0: intercept only	Model 1: with background Predictors	Odds	Model 2: with neighbourhood Predictors	Odds
Intercept	−2.854 (0.095)	−5.993 (0.202)		−5.980 (0.217)	
Grade		0.306 (0.216)	1.36	0.267 (0.022)	1.31
Male		1.00 (0.037)	2.72	0.915 (0.038)	2.50
Migration		0.046 (0.008)	1.05	0.024 (0.008)	1.02
Neighb. disorgan.				0.755 (0.179)	2.13
Neighb. integration				−0.133 (0.017)	0.89
Nihdi					
Random					
Var (intercept)	0.258 (0.07)	0.235 (0.065)		0.293 (0.08)	
Var (n disorg)					
Covariance					
Rho	7.2%				
Log-likelihood	−14834.819	−13423.833		−12263.849	

	Model 3: with random slope Nhood. disorganiz.	Odds	Model 4: with structural predictor	Odds
Intercept	−5.999 (0.219)		−7.05 (0.256)	
Grade	0.269 (0.022)	1.31	0.274 (0.023)	1.31
Male	0.915 (0.384)	2.50	0.932 (0.04)	2.54
Migration	0.035 (0.008)	1.03	0.027 (0.009)	1.03
Neighb. disorgan.	0.761 (0.031)	2.14	0.78 (0.029)	2.18
Neighb. integration	−0.112 (0.017)	0.89	−0.117 (0.018)	0.89
Nihdi			0.364 (0.055)	1.44
Random				
Var (intercept)	0.548 (0.079)		0.33 (0.053)	
Var (n disorg)	0.125 (0.03)		0.10 (0.029)	
Covariance	−0.167 (0.252)		−0.142 (0.284)	
Log-likelihood	−12256.784		−11652.299	

The large variation between students who committed serious offenses in the past year and live in the participating countries, justifies a multilevel analysis with, in our case, special attention to the neighbourhood and its influence on delinquency. In other words, we want to examine whether delinquent behaviour can not only be explained by the country the kids live in, but also whether this is the case for the neighbourhood they grew up in.

In the first model, we added some important socio-demographic variables, such as gender, migrant status and grade (see Table 10.11). All of them are significant and were controlled per country level. For example, boys are 2.72 times more likely to commit delinquent acts than girls. As we have also seen in Chap. 3, age and grade are significant. The likelihood of eighth grade students to commit offenses is 1.35 times higher than that of seventh grade students, and the likelihood of ninth graders to offend is also 1.35 higher than that of eighth graders. Similarly, immigrant juveniles are overall more likely to have committed serious offenses than native youths. However, in this respect, differences between groups are more important. For example, immigrant youths from Central Europe (OR = 12) and from Australia (OR = 12.8) show the highest levels of serious delinquency as compared to native students, although the Australian immigrant group is small. Prevalence of serious delinquency among young immigrants from Eastern Europe is also higher than that of native youths.

In Model 2 (with neighbourhood predictors), we added the following variables – neighbourhood integration, neighbourhood bonding and neighbourhood disorganization – which we were particularly interested in. These three neighbourhood scales decreased the fit of the socio-demographic variables in Model 1, and since they were significant we left them in the Model. More specifically, neighbourhood disorganization increases the likelihood of serious offending with OR 2.13. Neighbourhood integration might be seen as a protective factor and decreases the likelihood of serious delinquency with 11%.

Neighbourhood bonding, on the other hand is not significant and thus has been excluded from further exploration.

We now know that delinquency varies between countries and that the quality of the neighbourhood has an effect on serious delinquent behaviour of the students in the thirty countries. Nonetheless, it is important to know whether this effect not only varies between the countries but also between the specific neighbourhoods in which the students live. Subsequently, we also want to explore in which direction the variance of the relationship between countries and neighbourhood is likely to move towards. Therefore, in Model 3 (with "neighbourhood disorganization") we used a random slope model to unravel this relationship. We introduced a slope for the variable, neighbourhood disorganization, and fixed the other significant variables with the intention of examining whether Model 3 is stronger than Model 2. On the basis of the log-likelihood test we were able to decide that the slope model was an improvement. The fixed part of the model did not change much, but the random part of the model showed that the variance could partly be explained by the country where student lives as well as by neighbourhood disorganization.

The negative covariance between the intercept (country) and the slope (neighbourhood disorganization) implies that in countries with high levels of delinquency, the influence of the neighbourhood is less important. This while in countries with low crime levels, the influence of a disorganized neighbourhood is stronger. It is important to understand why the impact of neighbourhood disorganization on serious delinquency varies with the level of delinquency involvement. Multilevel analysis allows us to add structural factors at the second level – that of the country – which might provide us with a better explanation.

Thus, we added several structural indicators that provided more information on the country level. We used the following indicators: the Human Development Index, Life expectancy at birth, the Education Index, Expenditures in social protection, the Gross Income Inequality Index-Gini coefficient, Percentage Urbanization, Percentage Unemployed under 25-years and GDP per capita. Out of these eight structural indicators, The Human Development Index has the strongest effect on serious delinquency of youngsters. The Human Development Index is measured annually by the United Nations Development Program (UNDP). The Index provides a 100-point standard scale of societal modernization, combining levels of knowledge (adult literacy and education), health (life expectancy at birth), and standard of living (real per capita gross domestic product).

While adding the Human Development Index in Model 4 (with Structural Predictor), we not only found that these structural variables had a strong influence on delinquency (OR = 1.44), the other variable remaining also significant, but we also discovered that the variance components decreased and the model indictor (log-likelihood) improved significantly.

A likely explanation for our findings is that the more affluent countries have higher levels of youth delinquency than the less affluent ones. In addition, in affluent countries (mainly West-European and Anglo-Saxon countries) differences in quality between neighbourhoods are not as great as they are in poorer countries. In the latter countries, although differences between disorganized and non-disorganized neighbourhoods are much larger, the level of delinquency is overall lower. How can we explain these unexpected outcomes?

One might expect that less affluent countries would have more young people willing to acquire desired goods by illegal means or by committing violent offenses. Complementary research reveals that income inequality – as measured by the Gini coefficient – is one of the most important correlates of violent crime, such as threats, assault and robbery (Van Wilsem 2009; Van Dijk et al. 2008). However, in terms of property crime, the outcome is quite different: countries experiencing an economic boom also experience an increase of property crime. *In fact* "trends in crime over time are strongly and positively related to levels of affluence" (Van Dijk et al. 2008, 102). This is the case, for example, in rapidly developing countries, such as Ireland, where sudden affluence coincided with an increase of (property) crime. Several reasons may help explain the increase in property crime in wealthy countries.

First, increasing wealth is often accompanied by a multiplication of desirable, easily available, and concealable goods, such as, electronic equipment or mobile phones (Mayhew 2003). Second, in the second half of the twentieth century, the level of supervision by controlling agents in a number of social and economic institutions, such as the public transport system, self-service shops, schools and sports clubs have drastically reduced, thereby also reducing social control on young people. In addition, in affluent countries young people are increasingly geographically mobile, which facilitates offending. Third, social control not only decreased in society at large but also in the home, where both parents are employed more than before. This makes it more difficult to monitor one's children on a permanent basis and makes it easier for young people to withdraw from adult supervision. Confirming opportunity theory (Cohen and Felson 1979; Felson 1998, 2006) all these circumstances create plenty of opportunities to commit offenses, in particular property offenses. Since we know that the bulk of youth offending (and this goes also for adults) is property offending, and since in affluent countries neighbourhood differences are not as extreme in comparison to poorer countries, the outcomes of the multilevel analysis should not really come as a surprise.

10.9 Summary and Conclusions

All children view their neighbourhood (very) favourably in a way that "neighbourhood bonding" hardly differs between the respondents. However, young people do differ in terms of how they define their neighbourhood as integrated or disorganized, with North-Europe scoring exceptionally low on neighbourhood disorganization, and the Latin American and Anglo-Saxon clusters scoring the highest. In addition, confirming what we know from the literature about this subject, this study also finds that an accumulation of unemployment, relative poverty, family disruption and population heterogeneity are common in disorganized neighbourhoods.

From examining the neighbourhood and the role of the family in a two-model regression, we were able to conclude that the influence of neighbourhood disorganization decreases when we add family variables – confirming social disorganization theory – but both neighbourhood and family, in particular parental control, also continue to independently contribute to the explained variance.

This is even more so when we consider the correlation between the neighbourhood and school. The data suggests that the influence of the school is more important than that of the family, which may be related to the age group in our study, 12–16 year olds. This supports the research literature which confirmed that when children reach adolescence, the school and the peer group become of more importance at the expense of family influence. Another important finding from our study is that children living in disorganized neighbourhoods are also more likely to attend disorganized schools, crippled by vandalism, theft, and violence.

Most young people tend to spend their leisure time with a group of friends. However, our study revealed that the higher the degree of neighbourhood disorganization, the more delinquent friends youngsters have and the higher the likelihood is that they will commit (serious) delinquent acts themselves. This is particularly the case when their friends have already committed assault, burglary or robbery. However, young people whose friends are shoplifting also tend to shoplift, but since shoplifting is widespread among young people, the majority of them mostly limit their offending behaviour to minor offenses as opposed to serious offenses. Interestingly, this is independent of the degree of neighbourhood disorganization.

On the other hand, higher levels of neighbourhood disorganization is accompanied by a higher likelihood of youngsters meeting in public places. This also leads to an increase of peer group illegal activity, where the majority of them tend to declare that they are gang members. They also score higher on versatility, a combination of frequency and seriousness of delinquency. Of course there are interactions between neighbourhood disorganization and "peer group meeting in public places; committing illegal acts and; seeing their group as a gang". Although caution is warranted, when one analyzes these interactions and compares them with the outcomes when such peer groups are absent, the results suggest that the impact of the peer group on generating delinquency is stronger than the influence of the neighbourhood. In fact, a logistic regression confirms the significance of the peer group in regards to stimulating delinquent behaviour, followed by impact of the school, followed by the family.

Finally, a multilevel analysis considered the similarities and differences between countries in terms of the neighbourhood impact on delinquency, and examined a number of macro-structural variables which might help explain eventual differences. Finding that delinquency varied between the countries and that the neighbourhood had an effect on serious delinquent behaviour, different models were examined. The outcome revealed that only one structural variable had a strong impact on delinquency in the many neighbourhoods, which was the Human Development Index, showing that affluent countries have the highest levels of juvenile delinquency and poorer countries the lowest levels. At the same time, neighbourhood quality differs less in affluent countries than in poorer countries.

Several theories were examined in this chapter in regards to the neighbourhood, the most important of which is social disorganization theory. We found that disorganized neighbourhoods are commonly characterized by poverty, unemployment, single mothers and ethnic minorities, and conveyed that much of the neighbourhood impact was indirect and operated through the family, which supports the theory. This is also partly the case for the school. Young people living in disorganized neighbourhoods are more likely to attend disorganized schools. Nevertheless, besides the influence of the neighbourhood, the independent impact of the school on school behaviour, such as academic achievement and truancy, appeared to be stronger than that of the family.

Where the peer group is concerned, social control theory predicts that "birds of a feather flock together", and indeed peer group delinquency is associated with the delinquent behaviour of juveniles themselves. However, as stated before, Hirschi greatly underestimated the role of the peer group. Our data illustrated that that role is extremely substantial, confirming Thornberry's interaction theory, which claims that although selection is important when joining a peer group, subsequently that group exercises a powerful influence on a group members' behaviour. We found significant interactions between the neighbourhood, peers' delinquency and gang membership in generating serious delinquency, suggesting that the peer group is a major influence on the behaviour of adolescents.

Finally, as word of caution, it must be noted that the ISRD-2 sample is a fairly representative sample of young people in Europe aged 12–15. Most delinquency consists of non-serious trivial acts such as shoplifting and serious, violent delinquency is rare. Property delinquency is widespread in affluent European countries, where ghetto-like neighbourhoods are exceptional. Although this does not invalidate our findings with respect to differences in behaviour as they are related to differential degrees in neighbourhood disorganization, this consideration should be kept in mind.

References

Boxford, S. (2006). *Schools and the problem of crime*. Cullompton, Devon

Bursik, R., Jr, & Grasmick, H. (1993). Neighborhoods and crime. The dimension of effective community control. San Francisco: Lexington Books.

Cernkovich, S. A., & Giordano, P. C. (1987). Family relationship and delinquency. *Criminology, 25*, 295–319.

Cohen, L. E., & Felson, M. (1979). Social change and crime rate trends: A routine activities approach. American Sociological Review, 44.

Dekker, S. H., & Weerman, F. M. (eds). (2005). *European Street Gangs and Troublesome Youth Groups*. New York: Altamira Press.

Felson, M. (1998), Crime in Everyday Life – Insight and Implications for Society, Thousand Oaks/ London, Pine Forge Press – 2de edition.

Felson, M. (2006).Crime and Nature, Sage publications, Thousand Oaks.

Gottfredson, D.C. (2001), Schools and Delinquency. Cambridge University Press, Cambridge.

Goering, J. & Feins, J.D. (2003). Choosing a Better Life? Evaluating the moving to opportunity social experiment. Washington. The Urban Institute Press.

Hawkins, J. D., Lishner, D. M., Catalano, R. F., & Howard, M. O. (1986). Childhood predictors of adolescent substance abuse: Toward an emprically grounded theory. *Journal of Children in Contemporary Society, 18*(1/2), 11–48.

Jang, S. (1999). Age-Variability Effect of Family, School and Peers on Delinquency: a multilevel Modelling Test of International Theory: *Criminology, 37*, 643–686.

Junger, M., R.West & R.Timman (2001) Crime and Risky behaviour in Traffic: an Example of Cross-situational Consistency, Journal of Research in Crime and Delinquency, 38, 4, 439–459.

Junger, M.,G-J. Terlouw & P.G.M. van de Heijden (1995).Crime, Accidents and Social Control, Criminal Behavior and Mental Health, vol.5, no.4, 386–410.

Kirk, D. S. 2009. "Unravelling the Contextual Effects on Student Suspension and Juvenile Arrest: The Independent and Interdependent Influences of School, Neighborhood, and Family Social Controls." Criminology 47(2), forthcoming.

Kornhauser, R. R. (1978). Social Sources of Delinquency: An Appraisal of Analytic models: University of Chicago Press: Chicago.

Loeber, R., & Stouthamer-Loeber, M. (1986). Family factors as correlates and predictors of juvenile conduct problems and delinquency. Crime & Justice., 7, 29.

Mayhew, P. 2003 'Counting the costs of crime in Australia', Trends and Issues in Crime and Criminal Justice, no. 247, Australian Institute of Criminology, Canberra.

Morenoff, J. D., Sampson, R. J., & Raudenbush, S. W (2001). Neighborhood inequality, collective efficacy, and the spatial dynamics of urban violence. *Criminology, 39*, 517–560.

Sampson, R. J. (1993). "The Community Context of Violent Crime". In W. J. Wilson, (ed.) *Sociology and the Public Agenda* (pp. 267–274). Newbury Park, CA: Sage.

Sampson, R.J. & Groves, W.B. (1989). Community structure and Crime. Testing social disorganization theory. The American Journal of Sociology. Vol 94 (4). P. 774–802.

Sampson, R. J., & Laub, J. H. (1993). Crime in the Making: Pathways and Turning Points Through Life. Cambridge: Harvard University Press.

Sampson, R.J. & Raudenbush, S.W. (1999). Systematic social observation of public spaces: a new kook at disorder in urban neighbourhoods. *American Journal of Sociology, 105*, 603651.

Sampson, R. J., Morenoff, J. D., & Earls, F. (1999). Beyond social capital: Spatial dynamics of collective efficacy for children. *American Sociological Review, 64*, 633–660.

Sampson, R. J., Raudenbush, S. W., & Earls, F. (1997). Neighborhoods and violent crime: A multilevel study of collective efficacy. *Science, 277*(5328), 918.

Shaw, C. R., & McKay, H. D. (1942). Juvenile delinquency and urban areas: A study of rates of delinquency in relation to differential characteristics of local communities in American cities: University of Chicago Press, Chicago.

Stattin, H. & Romelsjö, A. (1995). Adult Morality in the Light of Criminality. Substance use and Behavioral and family Risk Factors in Adolescence. *Criminal Behavior and Mental Health, 5*(4), 279–312.

Thornberry, T. P. (1987). Toward an interactional theory of delinquency. *Criminology, 25*(4). 863–887.

Thornberry, T. P. 1992. The development of delinquency and drug use. UNAFEI Resource Material Series, No. 40, December, United Nations Asia and Far East Institute, Tokyo.

Thornberry, T. P., & Krohn, M. D. (2003). T*aking stock of delinquency. An Overview of Findings from Contemporary Longitudinal Studies*. New York: Kluwer Academic/Plenum Publishers.

Thornberry, T. P., Lizotte, A. J., Krohn, M. D., Farnworth, M., & Jang, S. J. (1991). Testing international theory: An examination of reciprocal causal relationships among family, school, and delinquency. *Journal of Criminal Law and Criminology, 82,* 3–35.

Putnam, R. D. (1993) 'The prosperous community: social capital and public life' in the American Prospect, 4:13.

Rivera, F.P.(1995). Crime, Violence and Injuries in children and Adolescents: Common Risk Factors?, Criminal Behavior and Mental Health, vol.5, no.4, 367–386.

Rothbaum, F., & Weisz, J. (1994). Parental converging and child externalizing behaviour in non-clinical samples: A meta-analysis. *Psychological Bulletin, 116*, 55–74.

Van Wilsem, J. 2009, Urban Streets as Micro Contexts to Commit Violence : D. Weisburd et al. (eds.), Putting Crime in its Place, Springer Science Business Media, LLC 2009, 199–216.

Van Dijk, J. J. M., van Kesteren, J., & Smit, P. (2008). Criminal Victimisation in International Perspective: Key Findings from the 2004–2005 ICVS and EU ICS. The Hague, the Netherlands: Boom Legal Publishers.

Warr, M. (2002), Companions in Crime – The Social Aspects of Criminal Conduct, Cambridge, Cambridge University Press.

Wikström, P.-O. (1998). Communities and Crime. In M. Tonry (ed.), *The Handbook of Crime and Punishment* (pp. 269–302). Oxford: Oxford University Press.

Wright, J. P., Cullen, F. T., & Miller, J. T. (2001). Family social capital and delinquent involvement. *Journal of criminal justice, 29,* 1–9.

Chapter 11
The Generalizability of Self-Control Theory

Ineke Haen Marshall and Dirk Enzmann

In the preceding chapters, we made frequent use of Hirschi's social bond theory, first presented in the classic *Causes of Delinquency* (1969). This theory argues that delinquent acts are inhibited to the extent that an individual is connected to a conventional life through social bonds – to family, school, and peers; and delinquency results "when an individuals' bond to society is weak or broken" (Hirschi 1969: 16). Social bonds theory has been one of the most influential and enduring theoretical paradigms in the study of delinquency, both in its original formulation and through more recent revisions. A case in point is the expanded "age-graded theory of informal social control" developed by Sampson and Laub (1993) "the true inheritors of social bonding theory" (Paternoster and Bachman 2010: 127). There is no doubt that social bonds theory – in one form or another – is still alive and well forty years after its initial formulation. This in spite of the well-known fact that the ideas of the original author of social bonds theory, Travis Hirschi, did take a different direction after *Causes of Delinquency*, as evidenced by his 1990 book, *A General Theory of Crime,* written together with Michael Gottfredson. Their general theory – usually referred to as self-control theory – is much broader than social bonding theory: it is "a theoretical explanation of criminal offending at all ages, in all places, as well as an explanation of non-criminal acts that were thought to share important conceptual grounds with crime and delinquency (smoking, drinking, accidents, obesity, gambling)" (Paternoster and Bachman 2010: 126). In the general theory of crime, the earlier (1969) notion of social control through *social bonds* is replaced by that of *self-control.* The focus of this chapter is on the key concept of the 1990 general theory of crime: low self-control. The ISRD-2 is one of the first studies to measure self-control in a large sample of youth from 30 different countries. This provides a unique opportunity to evaluate several claims which have been made – explicitly or implicitly – about the concept of self-control in a comparative context.

I.H. Marshall (✉)
Northeastern University, Boston, MA, USA
e-mail: i.marshall@neu.edu

J. Junger-Tas et al., *The Many Faces of Youth Crime: Contrasting Theoretical Perspectives on Juvenile Delinquency across Countries and Cultures*,
DOI 10.1007/978-1-4419-9455-4_11,

11.1 Theoretical Background and Purpose of Chapter

One of the central assumptions of the general theory of crime is that "relative differences in the tendency to deviant behavior are *stable* over the life course" (Hirschi and Gottfredson 2000: 58, emphasis ours). The theory basically endorses a *population heterogeneity* perspective, which assumes that there are stable individual differences across people. The theory posits that all criminal and analogous behavior is the manifestation of a single underlying cause, a propensity for criminal behavior, termed "low self-control." This underlying propensity for crime is established early in life and remains stable over time. Later debates about the viability of the general theory of crime have often contrasted the population heterogeneity perspective with the assumption of *state-dependence* (Nagin and Paternoster 2000). Unlike the population heterogeneity perspective, state-dependence rejects the notion that there is stability in propensity for deviant behavior over the life-course, and instead, assumes that situational factors shape and influence changes throughout the life-course.

The stability assumption of the general theory of crime is intimately connected to the distinction between *crime* and *criminality*: "Crimes are short term, circumscribed events that presuppose a peculiar set of necessary conditions (e.g., activity, opportunity, adversaries, victims, goods). Criminality, in contrast, refers to stable differences across individuals in the propensity to commit criminal (or equivalent) acts." (Hirschi and Gottfredson 1986: 190).[1] Whether a crime actually will be committed depends not only on the criminal propensity (criminality) of the potential offender, but also on the available *opportunities*, as well as the *age* of the person. There is no question that the general theory of crime is a very parsimonious theory, consisting of two main concepts: self-control and opportunities, although age (maturation) also plays a key role.

11.1.1 Age

It is hard to imagine how the general theory of crime could have developed without the contentious and interesting debate about the posited invariance of the age–crime curve. The age–crime curve basically shows that offending increases during adolescence, then reaches a peak in the early twenties, and then consistently declines as people mature. In a 1983 article, Hirschi and Gottfredson published an article in which they made the interpretation that "the age effect is invariant across social and cultural conditions" (Hirschi and Gottfredson 1983: 560). They claim that there is a universal decline in crime resulting from the "inexorable aging of the organism" (Gottfredson and Hirschi 1990: 141), while the basic propensity to crime (i.e., low self-control) remains unchanged (i.e., the population heterogeneity view).

[1] They later replaced the 'criminality' concept by 'self-control', see section 11.1.2.

Crime declines with age, for everybody. This "maturational reform" happens equally to all offenders as they age and is not causally related to changes in the social bonds, or other situational conditions that may vary over one's life. This position is counter to the life-course (or state-dependence) perspective which argues that there is a considerable amount of change ("turning points" and "transitions") over one's life-course and offenders easily may become nonoffenders, while others may not start offending until later in life (Laub and Sampson 2003). Thus, in the latter view, the age–crime curve is not made up of basically the same population (i.e., those with high criminal propensity), but rather reflects an ever-changing population composed of different types of offenders (see for example, Moffitt 1993). In Gottfredson and Hirschi's view, a person's self-control is established around age 8–10, and after that age, there is no expectation of chance. The ISRD-2 sample has a fairly narrow age range (12–16), but within the limitations provided by our data (i.e., limited age range, and sampling based on grade rather than age – see comments in Chap. 2), we do include this important variable in the analyses presented in this chapter, using grade as a proxy of age.

11.1.2 Self-control

The general theory of crime views the problem of crime as a problem of low self-control. Self-control is the concept developed to account for stable individual differences in criminal and analogous behavior (i.e., population heterogeneity). Given the foundational nature of this concept, it is not surprising that much has been written about it (Mutchnick et al. 2009: 307). Actually, the very authors of the general theory themselves have – over time – revised their interpretation of self-control to some degree. Their initial conceptualization was presented in their 1990 book. Here, low self-control is constituted by six constitutive traits."[T]hese traits can be identified prior to the age of responsibility for crime, … [they tend] to come together in the same people, and … [they] tend to persist through life" (1990: 90–91). They include an inability to defer gratification and lack of interest in long-term achievement (*impulsivity*); a deficit in diligence, tenacity, or persistence (a *preference for simple tasks*); adventure-someness, recklessness (as opposed to cautiousness), and *risk-seeking*; a preference for *physical activities* as opposed to cognitive and verbal activities and skills; indifference and insensitivity to the needs and suffering of others (*self-centeredness*); and, finally, a minimal tolerance for frustration (*volatile temper*) (pp. 89–90). In later writings, "a smaller conceptual fence seemed to be built around the idea of self-control": self-control is now seen as a tendency to be tempted by behaviors that promise short-term pleasure at the expense of long-term costs. "People who engage in crime are people who tend to neglect long-term consequences" (Hirschi and Gottfredson 2001: 90). Hirschi (2004: 543) explicitly has shifted and simplified the original 1990 definition to "the tendency to consider the full range of potential costs of a particular act." In the 2008 response to a critical assessment of self-control theory by a variety of authors, Hirschi and Gottfredson write that their interpretation of self-control has evolved over time. In view of the central importance of the concept, we reproduce the following quote:

> We began with *criminality*. At one point we tried *propensity* – and still occasionally used it for ease of exposition (Gottfredson 2006). At one point we dug up and quickly reburied *criminality*. We even briefly considered *conscience* before settling finally on *self-control*. As we have come to use the term, self-control is the choice version of the *causal* concept of propensity (and/or criminality). It is our new and improved version of a discarded concept (p. 222, italics in the original).

In spite of the changing interpretations and definitions, the basic idea has not changed: self-control "is a relatively time-stable trait of persons that consist of the inability to resist immediate gratification and avoid the long-term costs of one's behavior" (Paternoster and Bachman 2010: 126). Self-control is viewed as a "latent trait," the "tendency to avoid acts whose long-term costs exceed their momentary advantages" (Hirschi and Gottfredson 1994: 3). Important to remember is that low self-control is not a personality trait that compels criminal or other acts, but rather it is an "orientation that shapes choice" across situations (Hirschi and Gottfredson 2008). In response to a criticism by Akers and Sellers (2004: 124) that they do not define self-control separately from propensity, they argue that self-control is not a "motivating force underlying criminal acts" but is instead a "barrier that stands between the actor and the obvious momentary benefits crime provides" (Hirschi and Gottfredson 1993: 53). A substantial part of our analysis revolves around the measurement of this key concept of the general theory of crime (see Sect. 11.2).

11.1.3 Opportunities

Once a theory is published, its original authors lose control over its interpretation. This appears to be the case for the role of opportunity in the general theory of crime. Gottfredson and Hirschi suggest in their 1990 book that, when the *opportunity* presents itself, individuals with low self-control are more likely to choose immediate gratification, without regard for the long-term consequences for themselves or others (Gibbs and Giever 1995: 248). While low self-control may be viewed as a distal cause of crime, opportunities have been interpreted as the proximate cause (e.g., Goode 2008: 14). Hirschi and Gottfredson have objected to making "opportunity and self-control equal or even competing explanations of crime (Grasmick et al. 1993)." (Hirschi and Gottfredson 2008: 219). They object that "[A] concept we all but ignored had risen to coequal status with a major concept of the theory" (2008: 219), something which was not their intention. Because the precise role of opportunities remains controversial and "a largely unexplored element of the theory" (Simpson and Geis 2008: 50), we make this element a central component of our analyses (see Sects. 11.3 and 11.4).

11.1.4 The Generality of Deviance

Self-control theory attempts to explain short-term self-interested behavior that entails the risk of long-term sanctions (Hirschi and Gottfredson 2001: 94). Consistent with the idea of self-control is the belief that "individuals will tend to engage in (or avoid) a wide variety of criminal and analogous behaviors – that they will not specialize in some to the exclusion of others, nor will they 'escalate' into more serious or skilful criminal behavior over time" (Hirschi and Gottfredson 1994: 3). This argument provides a strong rationale for the frequent use of *variety* measures of delinquent involvement, used in many empirical tests of the theory, including ours (see Sect. 11.4).

Self-control theory proposes to explain why "reckless, deviant, criminal and sinful acts tend to go together, to be committed by the same people" (Hirschi and Gottfredson 2001: 89). The theory does not only claim to apply to a variety of crimes and analogous behavior, but it also is a theory that is applicable across cultures and places, across racial groups, and across gender. Of particular relevance for current purposes is the claim of cultural invariability. Our data collected in a variety of national settings allow a straightforward test of the hypothesis of cultural invariability.

11.1.5 Purpose of Chapter

This very cursory introduction to self-control theory has highlighted the ideas and interpretations primarily as they are conceived by the original authors of the general theory of crime. But theirs are not the only voices that have shaped the development of self-control theory. Since the introduction of Gottfredson and Hirschi's (1990) general theory of crime, low self-control has become one of the most frequently examined theoretical correlates of delinquency, risky behavior, and victimization. Some have even labeled the general theory of crime as representing a "paradigm shift" (Mutchnick et al. 2009: 322), which has helped to shape the theoretical and research agenda of an entire discipline. The amount of theoretical debate and empirical research on self-control theory is huge and continues to accumulate. Ever since its first formulation two decades ago, attempts have been made to refine, expand, integrate or, conversely, reject self-control theory (e.g., Goode 2008). Generally speaking, the evidence seems to suggest that there is considerable empirical support for the main tenets of self-control theory (e.g., Pratt and Cullen 2000; Akers and Sellers 2004; Gottfredson 2006).

Most of the research and theoretical debate on self-control theory has been published in North America, but there is a growing number of studies that are based on data collected outside the US (e.g., Vazsonyi et al. 2001; Pauwels and Svensson 2008, 2009; Wikstöm and Svenssson 2008; Ribeaud and Eisner 2006; Rebellon et al. 2008; Oberwittler and Naplava 2002; Paternoster and Brame 1998; Romero et al. 2003). We are in a unique situation to contribute to the comparative research on self-control theory through our large international database. There is no way that we can address all or even most of the theoretical and empirical issues that are still open to debate. In this chapter, we will select three issues from among the large number of potentially interesting research questions which may be derived from self-control theory: one of them mainly of a methodological and descriptive nature (Sect. 11.2) and two of which are of a substantive and predictive (Sects. 11.3 and 11.4).

The first question to be tackled revolves around the measurement of the concept of self-control (reliability, validity, and dimensionality) and the degree to which an abbreviated version of a commonly used scale (i.e., Grasmick et al. 1993) is applicable in different countries and country clusters. This section will also present descriptive statistics on the distribution of low self-control over the different ISRD countries and will allow us to draw some tentative conclusions about national variations in self-control. Section (11.3) examines commonly used predictors of low self-control (e.g., gender, migration status, grade (as an indicator of age), family- and neighborhood factors) in a comparative context. Thereafter (Sect. 11.4), we evaluate the cross-national generalizability of a theoretical model of the impact of low self-control on delinquency, while taking into consideration commonly used variables related to the family, the neighborhood, as well as opportunity. We conclude the chapter (Sect. 11.5) with a brief summarizing comment.

11.2 Measurement of Low Self-control

A major debate revolves around the *meaning* of the concept of "self-control" and we saw (Sect. 11.1.2) that Gottfredson and Hirschi themselves have been active participants in this discussion about the conceptual definition of self-control. This discussion is intimately related to the *measuremen*t of self-control, and there are literally hundreds of empirical studies which pertain, either explicitly or implicitly, to the measurement of self-control controversy.

A main debate concerns *attitudinal* versus *behavioral* measures. Gottfredson and Hirschi (1993: 48) have expressed a preference for behavioral measures. Examples are "whining, pushing and shoving (as a child); smoking and drinking and excessive television watching and accident frequency (as a teenager); (and) difficulties in interpersonal relations, employment instability, automobile accidents, drinking and smoking (as an adult)" (Hirschi and Gottfredson 1994: 9). In other work, they have argued that "the best available operational measure of the propensity to offend is a count of the number of distinct problem behaviors engaged in by a youth" (Piquero 2008: 28). Indeed, they are quite critical of the use of attitudinal measures, not the least because survey responses may be biased by the possible impact of self-control on survey participation and responses. As is pointed out by Ribeaud and Eisner (2006: 35), however, one of the most thorough meta-analyses of self-control theory (Pratt and Cullen 2000) shows no difference in the power of either type of measure in predicting delinquency. Other studies which compared attitudinal versus behavioral measures (e.g., Tittle et al. 2003; Marcus 2003) also find roughly comparable results. (For more discussion on attitudinal versus behavioral measures, see Ribeaud and Eisner 2006; Geis 2000; Tittle et al. 2003; Piquero 2008). Of particular relevance to the present chapter is Ribeaud and Eisner's conclusion that both types of potential bias in attitudinal measures (i.e., negative self-selection and biased responses of low self-control respondents) are less likely to occur in school-based paper-and-pencil surveys (compared to home-based face-to-face interviews) (2006: 36). The ISRD2 data are exclusively conducted in a school setting, primarily through paper-and-pencil surveys.

The most widely used attitudinal measure of self-control is the scale developed by Grasmick et al. (1993). Hirschi and Gottfredson have repeatedly expressed their displeasure with the fact that, presently, the Grasmick et al.'s attitudinal measure is now viewed as *the* measure of self-control: "We believe it is illegitimate to see or treat this scale as the embodiment of the theory" (Hirschi and M. Gottfredson 2001: 230). Their objections notwithstanding, the current study does follow in the footsteps of the bulk of empirical studies which rely on the Grasmick et al. attitudinal self-control scale.

Grasmick and colleagues (1993) have developed a 24-item self-report scale to reflect the six dimensions of low self-control as first described in the 1990 publication of the general theory of crime: impulsivity, risk-taking, self-centeredness, volatile temper, preference for simple tasks, and preference for physical (over mental) tasks. Grasmick and colleagues (1993) used exploratory analyses to conclude that their scale – consisting of these six dimensions – appeared to measure one underlying factor ("low self-control"). Since then, a number of studies have been published focusing on the psychometric properties of the Grasmick et al. (1993) scale – or some modified version of this scale. The general theory of crime assumes that self-control is linked to crime in the same way across all demographic groups and cultures which implies "that the measure of self-control is similarly structured and has similar scale properties across all demographic groups" (Piquero 2008: 29). Thus, the main methodological research questions have been the factor structure of the scale, scale invariance, and reliability (e.g., Arneklev et al. 1999; Grasmick et al. 1993; Longshore and Turner 1998; Higgins 2004; Longshore et al. 1996; Piquero and Rosay 1998; Piquero et al. 2000). The findings are inconsistent. Some evidence shows scale reliability and the presence of one underlying factor or a one-dimensional structure (Nagin and Paternoster 1993; Piquero and Tibbetts 1996; Piquero and Rosay 1998), while other studies support the presence of multiple dimensions (Longshore et al. 1996; Vazsonyi et al. 2001; Romero et al. 2003; Ribeaud and Eisner 2006). Most of the analyses regarding the scale's dimensionality are based on classical factor analytic methods, but more recent studies have used a Rasch model (Piquero et al. 2000; Gibson 2005) which allows the joint consideration of item difficulty and person ability. It has been found, for example, that scale items function differently for low and high self-control groups (Gibson 2005: 9). The present study allows us to validate the Grasmick et al (1993) scale in the context of a large international data set.

In order to keep the length of the questionnaire manageable and appropriate for our young target group, the ISRD-2 used a short (12 item) version of the Grasmick et al. (1993) scale. We included three items for those four dimensions which had been shown to be the most robust in previous work (impulsivity, risk-taking, self-centeredness, and volatile temper), excluding preference for simple tasks and preference for physical – over mental – tasks. Because of the importance of these four subscales, we list the three questions asked for each of the four "elements" (Hirschi 2004). Response categories ranged from fully agree (1) to fully disagree (4). Scale scores were transformed to a range from 0 to 100 (where a high score indicates a high degree of impulsivity, risk-taking, self-centeredness, and volatile temper).

- Impulsivity (IM):
  - I act on the spur of the moment without stopping to think.
  - I do whatever brings me pleasure here and now, even at the cost of some distant goal.
  - I'm more concerned with what happens to me in the short run than in the long run
- Risk-taking (RT):
  - I like to test myself every now and then by doing something a little risky.
  - Sometimes I take a risk just for the fun of it.
  - Excitement and adventure are more important to me than security.
- Self-centeredness (CE):
  - I try to look out for myself first, even if it means making things difficult for other people.
  - If things I do upset people, it's their problem not mine.
  - I will try to get the things I want even when I know it's causing problems for other people.
- Volatile temper (TE):
  - I lose my temper pretty easy.
  - When I'm really angry, other people better stay away from me.
  - When I have a serious disagreement with someone, it's usually hard for me to talk about it without getting upset.

We created a self-control score, consisting of a simple summation of the 12 items. For ease of interpretation, we transformed the scores on the SC scale, ranging from 0 (low self-control) to 100 (high self-control).[2]

[2]It should be noted that – for the four subscales – higher scores indicate a higher degree of impulsivity, volatile temperament, and so on, thus implying a lower level of self-control; conversely, for the total self-control scale, higher scores mean higher self-control.

The analysis of the psychometric properties of the self-control scale (as well as its subscales) is presented in the three Sects. 11.2.1 (dimensionality), 11.2.2 (reliability), and 11.2.3 (validity) that follow. The first part of the chapter (on the concept of self-control and its measurement) is concluded by a presentation of the results of comparative analysis of self-reported levels of self-control across countries and country clusters (Sect. 11.2.4). These analyses provide the groundwork for the remainder of the chapter, focusing first on the predictors of self-control (Sect. 11.3), followed by the comparative testing of a multivariate theoretical model of delinquency (Sect. 11.4).

11.2.1 Dimensionality of the Self-Control Scale: Results of Exploratory Factor Analyses

In order to evaluate if the 12-item scale indeed consists of four distinct "elements" (impulsivity, risk-taking, self-centeredness, and volatile temper), we conducted exploratory factor analysis (principal axis factoring) for each of the 30 countries. We found that according to parallel analysis criteria (Preacher and MacCullum 2003), a four-factor solution was obtained for the majority (27) of countries. Exceptions were Italy (five factors), and Russia and Lithuania (3 or 5 factors). Oblique rotation of the factor loadings (Promax) showed that – consistent with theoretical expectations – the factors are, overall, highly correlated. The lowest factor correlations were in Surinam (0.28 between factor IM and TE) and Armenia (0.29 between factor IM and CE); in the majority of countries, the lowest correlations were found in the 0.4 and 0.5 range. In most of the countries (22), the highest correlations were in the 0.6 range, with Cyprus (0.7 for factor IM and RT) and Portugal (0.7 for factor IM and RT) as positive outliers.

In 26 out of the 30 countries, the loadings of the items corresponded to theoretical expectations: three items measuring impulsivity (IM), three items measuring risk-taking (RT), three items measuring self-centeredness (CE), and three items measuring volatile temperament (TE). These findings suggest that, generally speaking, the self-control scale (SC) appears to perform quite well. However, in four countries (Armenia, Lithuania, the Netherlands, and Surinam), the results were less straightforward. Analysis of the results for these four countries suggests that impulsivity is the most problematic scale: it failed to present itself as a distinct three-item factor in all four countries. Specifically, impulsivity shared variance with risk-taking (Armenia, Lithuania, and Surinam), volatile temperament (Lithuania and the Netherlands), and self-centeredness (Lithuania). Risk-taking failed to present itself as a distinct subscale in three countries (Armenia, Lithuania, and Surinam). Volatile temperament failed to manifest itself as a separate factor in only two countries (Lithuania and the Netherlands). On the other hand, factor analysis failed to identify self-centeredness as a distinct factor for only one country (Lithuania). These observations are consistent with additional scale analysis (shown below) which suggests that (1) some of the scales are more robust than others, and (2) some scales perform better in some countries than others.

Our analysis thus far seems to support the theoretical notion that impulsivity, risk-taking, self-centeredness, and volatile temperament may be viewed as distinct elements (or dimensions) measured by the Grasmick et al. (1993) scale. A closely related issue concerns the question whether these four elements reflect *one or more than one underlying (latent) dimensions* (e.g., Nagin and Paternoster 2000; Piquero and Tibbetts 1996; Piquero and Rosay 1998; Longshore et al. 1996; Vazsonyi et al. 2001; Romero et al. 2003; Ribeaud and Eisner 2006).

We answered this question for the ISRD2 data by factor analyses of the subscale scores and visual inspection of the plots produced by parallel analysis (not shown). The results of our visual inspection are unequivocal and straightforward. For the six country clusters (Anglo-Saxon, Northern Europe, Western Europe, Mediterranean Europe, Latin America, and Post-Socialist), as well as for the total sample, the SC scale appears to be one-dimensional. Of course, whether this one underlying factor indeed captures the essence of "low self control," and thus may be considered valid, is a question which is not answered simply. We will report on the results of our attempt to validate the Grasmick et al. scale in Sect. 11.2.3 below. Since no scale can be valid unless it is also reliable, we now first turn our attention to the question of the *reliability* of the self control scale, as well as its four subscales.

11.2.2 The Reliability of the Self-Control Scale

The reliability of a scale concerns the *consistency* of its performance. A number of researchers have examined the reliability of either the original Grasmick et al. (1993) scale (e.g., Arneklev et al. 1993, 1999; Longshore and Turner 1998; Longshore et al. 1996; Piquero and Rosay 1998) or a modified version of this scale (e.g., Burton et al. 1998; Evans et al. 1997). There is a limited amount of research literature assessing the reliability of self-control measures outside the USA (Rebellon et al. 2008: 335). These studies tend to conclude that the Grasmick et al. (1993) self-control scale – or some modified version thereof – is a reliable measure of self-control across a number of different national settings (e.g., Paternoster and Brame 1998; LaGrange and Silverman 1999; Vazsonyi et al. 2001; Vazsonyi and Crosswhite 2004; Ribeaud and Eisner 2006; Rebellon et al. 2008).

Our primary interest is the reliability of the 12-item SC scale (both in individual countries as well as in the six country clusters; but we are also interested in evaluating how the four subscales fare with regard to reliability, in the total sample, in individual countries as well as in the six country clusters. We are, of course, also curious to explore the cross-national comparability of the SC total and the IM, RT, CE, and TE subscale means and standard deviations (this issue will be discussed in Sect. 11.2.4).

Since it was the original intention of the ISRD2 design to use the 12-tem SC scale, rather than the four subscales, we included only three items for each of the four dimensions in our questionnaire. It should be noted that a scale with a small number of items (such as the IM, RT, CE, and TE scores with only three items each) will attain lower alpha values than scales with a large number of items such as the total SC score.

11.2.2.1 Reliability for Total Sample

For the entire sample, the reliability coefficient (alpha) is quite good (0.83). None of the individual items appears particularly problematic, so the alpha value would not be improved if we were to drop any of the 12 items – good reason to continue our analysis with the complete 12-item SC scale. Examination of the item-rest correlations for the SC scale shows that they are all in a good range: The lowest (0.37) is for the question "I am more concerned with what happens to me in the short run than in the long run" (part of the IM scale), and the highest (0.57) is for the question "Sometimes I will take a risk just for the fun of it" (part of the RT scale).

The alpha for the SC scale is better than for the four subscales (which is not surprising in view of the larger number of items which make up the SC scale). Risk-taking has the highest alpha (0.78), and impulsivity the lowest (0.57), with self-centeredness (0.68) and volatile temperament (0.70) in between. For each of the four three-item scales, the alpha value would not be improved if we dropped one of the items, suggesting that there are no problematic items: they belong together.

11.2.2.2 Reliability for Individual Countries

As we already noted earlier, factor analysis suggests that the SC and the four subscales do not perform uniformly in the 30 individual countries. Therefore, we examined the reliability coefficients as well as the item-rest correlations for those countries which were shown to deviate from the general pattern (Armenia, Italy, Lithuania, the Netherlands, Surinam, and Russia).

Armenia. The alpha for the SC scale for Armenia (0.78) is reasonable and would not be improved if we were to drop any of the items. The most problematic is item three (part of the IM scale) (I am more concerned with what happens to me in the short run than in the long run), which is true for all countries. The alpha for IM (0.36) is quite low, followed by RT (0.59), TE (0.63), and CE (0.73).

Italy. This country (which has a five-factor solution – see Sect. 11.2.1) has an SC scale alpha of 0.84, slightly higher than the total sample. In Italy, the alphas for the subscales (RT, TE, and CE) are not worse than the overall sample, with the exception of IM (0.30), again with item 3 performing poorest.

Lithuania. This is an interesting case. Remember, that Lithuania was the one country where none of the four dimensions appeared to manifest themselves as distinct (see Sect. 11.2.2). Still, the reliability of the SC scale (0.81) in Lithuania is comparable to the overall sample alpha; the alpha would not improve if any of the 12 items would be dropped. Not surprisingly, IM has the lowest alpha (0.47). Among the four subscales in Lithuania, RT has the highest alpha (0.78), followed by CE (0.68) and TE (0.61).

The Netherlands. This country also deserves some discussion, in view of the fact that in previous analyses only two (out of four) dimensions manifested themselves as theoretically predicted. The overall alpha (0.81) for the SC in the Netherlands cannot be improved by eliminating any of the items. The alpha for IM is the lowest among the subscales (0.51), but the IM alpha would increase slightly if the first item (I act on the spur of the moment without stopping to think) were to be dropped rather than the commonly more problematic item 3 (More concerned with short run than long run). It is possible that this represents a problem with the translation (from the original English into Dutch), since this first item also appeared to be problematic in Surinam (which also used the Dutch translation). For the Netherlands, RT (alpha 0.81) is the most reliable subscale; the alphas for CE and TE, respectively, are 0.64 and 0.66.

Surinam. In Surinam, IM alpha is 0.46, and the other subscales are also lower in reliability than in other countries (RT 0.63, CE 0.65, TE 0.61). The reliability of SC scale in Surinam (0.76) is also slightly lower than in the total sample.

Russia. Finally, although parallel analysis showed some ambiguity in the number of dimensions of the Russian responses to the CE scale (3 or 5), it appears that the reliability of the SC is quite comparable to the other countries (0.84). In Russia, like in virtually all other countries, eliminating an item would not improve the alpha value of the SC scale. The alpha (0.56) for IM is quite low in Russia (as in other countries), as is the reliability coefficients for TE (0.68). On the other hand, RT (0.75) and CE (0.75) appear to be quite reliable for the Russian sample.

The country-based results, not surprisingly, confirm the results based on total sample analysis: Among the subscales, RT has the highest overall reliability (median alpha=0.78) and IM performs the worst (median alpha=0.61), and the reliability of the total SC scale is quite reasonable (median alpha=0.84). Although some countries show some interesting variations on this general pattern, there appears to be quite an impressive degree of cross-national comparability in the reliability of the SC scale, as well as its four subscales.

11.2.2.3 Reliability for the Country Clusters

Analysis of the six clusters further supports the idea that the four subscales (IM,TE, RT, and CE) belong together. Factor analysis for the six clusters, using the four subscales as the constituting items for the SC scale, suggests that the structure of the SC scale is quite similar in the different clusters. As already mentioned, visual inspection of the plots produced by parallel analysis indicated that – in the six clusters – the SC scale has one underlying dimension. Furthermore, examination of the item-rest correlations indicates that – for all six clusters – the highest item-rest correlations are for IM, while the lowest are for TE. The reliability coefficients for the six clusters, for the SC scale (using IM, RT, SC, and TE subscale scores as input items), range between 0.69 (for Latin American cluster) and 0.78 (for Anglo-Saxon cluster). The lower value of alpha for the SC scale in the cluster analysis (as compared to the analysis of the total sample) can be explained by the smaller number of items (4 instead of 12).

In sum, it seems that the reliability of the SC scale used in our large international sample is quite high and is definitely comparable to the findings reported in other comparative studies, which tend to base their findings on a much smaller number of countries. An exception to the limited geographical coverage is the recently published study by Rebellon et al. (2008), which tested the reliability of their six-item self-control scale on a 32 nation nonrandom sample of college students. They derived six items from the instrument used in their International Dating Violence Study (IDVS) to create a self-report scale, capturing Selfishness, Trouble with Rules, Life Goals, Risk-Taking, Often Hurt, and Bad Temper (2008: 338–339). Based on confirmatory factor analysis, they conclude that their IDVS self-control scale is reliable across the 32 national settings. Of 192 factor loadings (six items by the 32 settings), 187 were statistically significant, with an average factor loading of 0.50. Their measure of overall reliability (alpha) was 0.53 (compared to the ISRD alpha of 0.83). The lower reliability coefficient for the IDVS scale may be partly due to the smaller number of items (6) as compared to the ISRD scale (12). However, even when we reduced the SC scale to four subscale scores (examining the reliability for the six clusters, using the four subscales as the constituting items for the SC scale), the alpha varied between a low of 0.69 (for the Latin American cluster) to a high of 0.78 (for Anglo-Saxon cluster). The ISRD SC scale consists of 12 items taken from the Grasmick et al. (1993) scale, whereas the IDVS self-control scale used items which were originally intended for other purposes. Still, in spite of differences in study design, sampling method, and characteristics of the self-control scale, our results further support Rebellon et al.'s (2008) conclusion that "the scale appears generally reliable in a range of national setting both inside and outside the West" (p. 355).

11.2.3 Validity of the Self-Control Scale: Correlation with a Behavioral Measure

Much more challenging than trying to establish the reliability of the SC scale for comparative analysis is the question of validity. How do we know whether the SC scale indeed measures the elusive concept of low self-control? We already discussed how Gottfredson and Hirschi, the originators of low self-control theory, have cast serious doubt on the validity of Grasmick and colleagues' attitudinal self-control scale (see also Hirschi 2004 for a critical analysis of the Grasmick et al. 1993 scale). They clearly prefer behavioral measures of low self-control, such as smoking, drinking, and accidents (see Sect. 11.2 for more discussion). Fortunately, the ISRD2 study includes the following question which may be used to (theoretically) validate the SC scale: "Did you ever have an accident that was so serious that you had to see a doctor (e.g., a sports or traffic accident, not a simple cut or wound?)." Answer categories were: never, once, more than once. We would expect that, if the abbreviated version of Grasmick et al.'s self-control scale is valid, youth with higher scores on the SC scale also should report more experiences with accidents. Analysis of variance showed a clear, significant, and consistent correlation between accident proneness of youth and their scores on the SC scale (see Table 11.1 below)

There are significant differences between the mean scores on the SC scale between those youth who never had a serious accident (63.26), those who report one such accident (59.61), and those who report having had a serious accident more than once (56.11). Thus, youth who have a lower score on the SC scale are more likely

Table 11.1 Relationship between accident proneness and mean responses to SC scale and subscales

Serious accident in past	Self-control	Impulsivity	Risk-taking	Self-centeredness	Volatile temperament
Never	63.26	40.55	34.48	28.18	43.74
Once	59.61	43.94	40.80	30.55	46.27
More than once	56.11	46.93	48.18	32.59	47.82
F-value	605.69	316.34	1030.34	143.41	107.72

to report having experienced one or more serious accidents. Looking at the subscales, values on the risk-taking scale appear to show the strongest correlation with accident proneness: Youths who report having had a serious accident more than once score significantly higher on the RT scale (mean RT value: 48.18) compared to those who report having had a serious accident only once (mean RT value: 40.80) and those who have never had a serious accident (mean RT value: 34.48). Impulsivity also is significantly – and in the expected direction – related to accident proneness, as are self-centeredness and volatile temperament. Although admittedly limited in scope, the results of this analysis suggest that the SC scale (as well as its subscales) may be considered to have a reasonable degree of construct validity, using a (self-reported) behavioral measure of self-control.

11.2.4 How Do Countries and Country Clusters Differ with Regard to Self-Control?

Thus far we have established that we may be satisfied that the ISRD2 measures of self-control meet the standards of reliability as well as validity. The psychometric attributes of the SC scale are interesting and important, and (comparative) psychometric analysis is required prior to further analysis of the survey data. Indeed, psychometric analysis may be viewed as a necessary evil which needs to be taken care of before we can move on to the much more interesting – and substantive – findings of our study. For instance, if low self-control is indeed a significant predictor of criminality and analogous behaviors, then the comparative criminologist is immediately presented with the question of whether this characteristic is evenly distributed across countries. This issue is the focus of this section. Later in this chapter, we will explore the related question of whether low self-control is correlated with the same predictors across countries (Sect. 11.3), and if the same theoretical model (using family, neighborhood, and opportunity variables) may be used to account for the variation in delinquency across countries (Sect. 11.4).

11.2.4.1 Differences of Self-Control by Countries

Fig. 11.1 presents the mean SC values for the 30 ISRD-2 countries (using large- and medium-sized cities only). Fig. 11.1 also includes the 95% confidence intervals for the SC means. As usual, the countries are arranged by country cluster

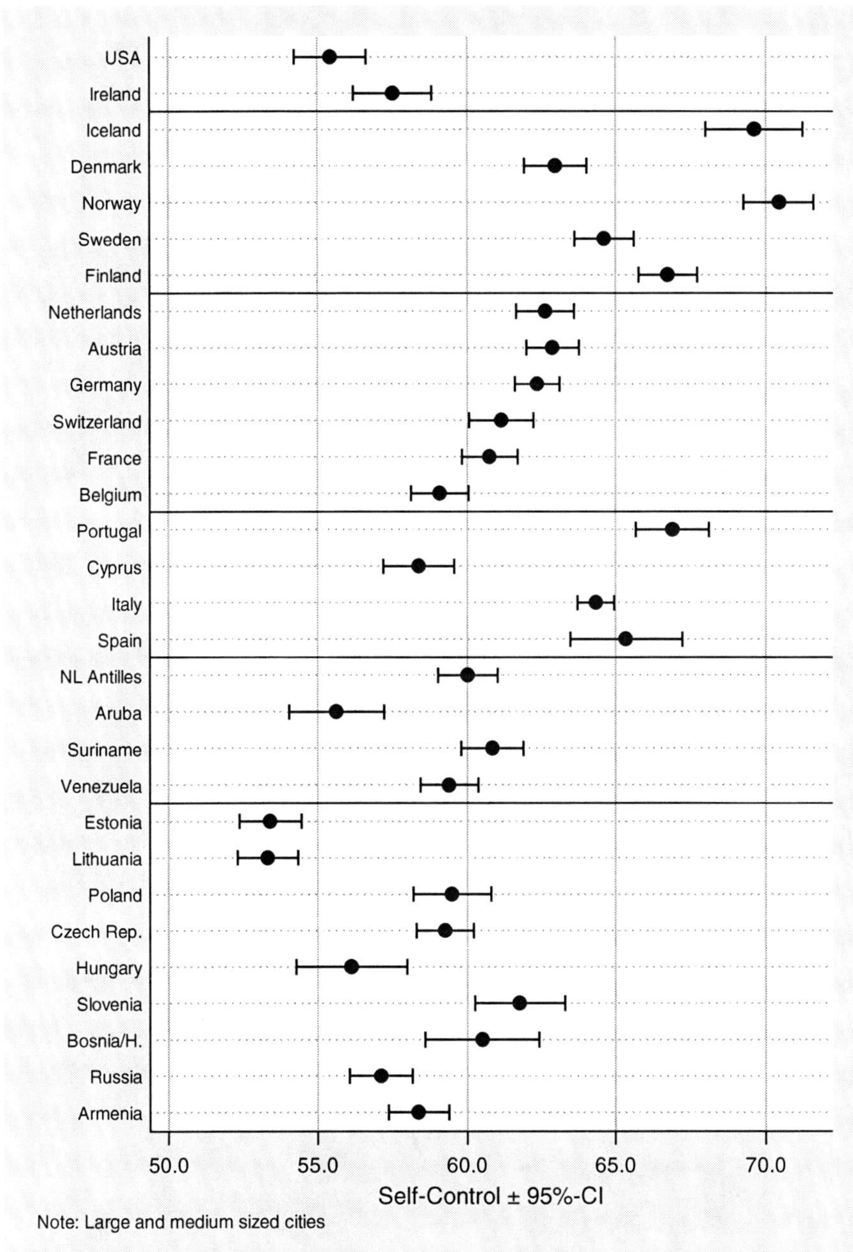

Fig. 11.1 Self-control by countries

Table 11.2 Self-control by country cluster

Country cluster	Mean	SD	Lower 95% CI	Upper 95% CI	*N*
Anglo-Saxon	56.5	21.9	55.6	57.3	2398
Northern EU	66.9	20.1	66.4	67.4	6216
Western EU	61.5	19.7	61.1	61.9	10474
Mediterranean EU	63.8	20.8	63.3	64.3	6767
Latin America	59.0	20.3	58.4	59.5	5202
Post-Socialist	57.7	19.6	57.3	58.1	8945

(Anglo-Saxon, Northern Europe, Western Europe, Mediterranean, Latin America, and Post-Socialist). Although theoretically, the SC values range between 0 and 100, visual inspection of Fig. 11.1 shows that although there is considerable variability between countries, the spread of SC values is fairly narrow (18 points, between 53.3 and 70.4). Clear outliers are Estonia (53.4) and Lithuania (53.4), with a relatively low level of self-control, and Iceland (69.6) and Norway (70.4), with a relatively high level of self-control. Fig. 11.1 also shows that there is considerable variation within country clusters, a point which we will discuss shortly.

Table 11.2 presents SC statistics (mean, SD and 95% confidence intervals, as well as sample size) for the six country clusters. A striking observation is that the mean SC values differ significantly between all six country clusters, thus providing additional validation of the usefulness of the clustering approach suggested by Arnaud et al. The Anglo-Saxon countries show the lowest level of self-control (56.5, SD 21.9). It should be noted, though, that this cluster consists of only two countries: USA (55.4) and Ireland (57.5). The mean level of self-control of the US sample is roughly comparable (using 95% confidence intervals) to that of Ireland, Aruba, Estonia, Lithuania, Hungary, and Russia. The Anglo-Saxon cluster is closely followed by the Post-Socialist cluster (57.7, SD 19.6). In the Post-Socialist cluster, there is considerable variability (scores ranging between 53.4 for Estonia and 61.8 for Hungary). The Latin American cluster (59.0, SD 20.3) also shows a relatively low level of self-control, with Aruba (55.6) scoring considerably lower than the three other Latin American countries. Within this cluster, Surinam has the highest level of self-control (60.8). The Western European cluster represents a middle position with regard to the reported levels of self-control (mean value 61.5, SD 19.7); there is a fairly narrow range of values within this cluster. Belgium (59.1) has the lowest mean level of self-control within the Western European cluster, and Austria (62.9) reports the highest level of self-control, with Germany, Switzerland, the Netherlands, and France having means between 60.8 (France) and 62.6 (Netherlands).

The Mediterranean cluster shows a relatively high level of self-control (63.8, SD 20.8). In this four country cluster, Cyprus (58.4) is a clear (low) outlier compared to Spain, Italy, and Portugal which each reports a considerably higher level of self-control (respectively 65.4, 64.3, and 66.9). Finally, Northern Europe appears to have the highest mean level of self-control (66.9, SD 20.1). Norway (70.4) and Iceland (69.6) show the highest level of self-control among all 30 ISRD countries. The only other cluster where there is no score below 64 is that composed of the Mediterranean countries. The Northern European cluster averages a full ten points above the Anglo-Saxon cluster.

What are the implications of these comparative differences in levels of self-control? Does it necessarily mean that countries with lower levels of self-control also will have lower levels of delinquency? That is a question that will be explored later in the chapter, but at this point we speculate that – although the *levels* of self-control may differ by country or country cluster – it is possible that the *effects* of low self-control may be similar across countries and country clusters.

11.2.4.2 Differences of Self-Control Subscales Between Country Clusters

Although we have shown that the total 12-item SC scale is a reliable and likely valid measure of low self-control in our 30 country sample, the exploration of how countries – and country clusters – *differ* with regard to their scores on the four distinct *subscales* (risk-taking, impulsivity, self-centeredness, and volatile temperament) is a worthwhile endeavor in and of itself. Fig. 11.2 below shows the self-control subscales by country cluster.

Risk-taking: Recalling our earlier discussion, the subscale with the highest reliability score was risk-taking. Fig. 11.2 shows that both the Anglo-Saxon cluster and the Post-Socialist cluster have the highest mean level of self-reported support of risk-taking. Western Europe occupies a more intermediate position, but is still considerably closer to the other clusters (Northern Europe, Mediterranean, and Latin America) than to either the Anglo-Saxon or Post-Socialist clusters. Northern Europe, Western Europe, Mediterranean, and Latin America together score significantly lower on the risk-taking dimension than either the Post-Socialist countries or the Anglo-Saxon cluster.

Impulsivity: With regard to impulsivity, Fig. 11.2 suggests that – again – both the Anglo-Saxon cluster and the Post-Socialist cluster are outliers in the direction of a higher level of impulsivity; there is no significant difference between these two country clusters. Northern Europe, on the other hand, clearly stands by itself with a relatively low level of impulsivity. Western Europe, the Mediterranean cluster, and the Latin American cluster occupy a middle position; these three clusters do not appear to differ significantly with regard to impulsivity.

Self-centeredness: Whereas impulsivity and risk-taking showed a fairly clear and consistent picture, the situation becomes a bit more muddled when examining self-centeredness. Fig. 11.2 suggests that, this time, it is not the Anglo-Saxon and the Post-Socialist cluster which score highest, but rather, the Latin American cluster stands by itself showing the highest levels of self-centeredness. Northern Europe reports the lowest level of self-centeredness, followed by the Mediterranean countries. The middle position is shared by the Anglo-Saxon, Western European, and Post- Socialist cluster; their mean scores are not statistically significantly different.

Volatile temperament: An interesting picture emerges when one examines Fig. 11.2 for the country clusters' responses to questions measuring volatile temperament. Consistent with cultural stereotypes, the Latin American clusters scores significantly higher on the volatile temperament dimension than all other clusters,

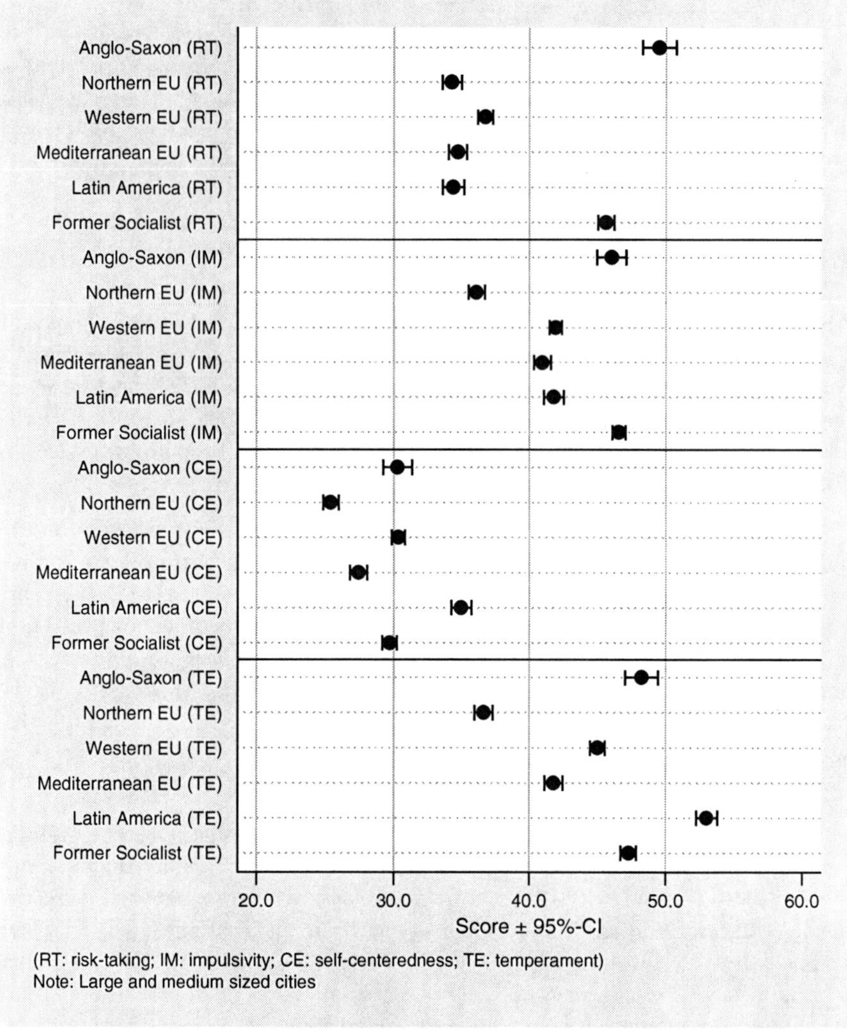

Fig. 11.2 Self-control subscale-scores by country cluster

whereas the Northern European cluster has the lowest mean value. At the same time, and once again showing the complexity of social reality, we see that the relatively low value for the Mediterranean cluster belies the cultural cliché that there is such thing as a southern explosive temperament. The Anglo-Saxon and the Post-Socialist cluster rank below the Latin American countries, but score significantly higher than the Western European and Mediterranean countries.

This analysis does show that it is useful to more closely examine the different dimensions of low self-control. Impulsivity, risk-taking, self-centeredness, and volatile temperament do not manifest themselves uniformly in all countries and country clusters.

11.3 What Are the Predictors of Self-control? Self-Control as Dependent Variable

The psychometric assessment of the self-control scale, together with our analysis of the cross-national distribution of low self-control (and its four elements of impulsivity, risk-taking, volatile temper, and self-centeredness), has provided a sound foundation for the next logical step in our exploration: that of the cross-national variability of the predictors (or "causes") of self-control.

11.3.1 Family and Self-control

A well-known assertion made by Gottfredson and Hirschi (1990) is that self-control is pretty well established by the age of 8 or 10, and "the differences observed at ages 8–10 tend to persist from then on" (Hirschi and Gottfredson 2001: 90). They do acknowledge that children learn from many sources to consider the long-range consequences of their acts, but "[T]he major sources of self-control, … , are the actions of parents or other responsible adults" (Hirschi and Gottfredson 2001: 90). In their view, the four needed elements of successful socialization are: care, monitor, recognize (deviant behavior), and correct (90). When any of these elements is missing, "continued low self-control may be the result" (90). They cite neglect, abuse, single parenting, large number of children, and parental criminality as "measures of the extent of parental concern for the child or … conditions that affect the ability of the parents to monitor and correct the child's behavior" (90). The child's level of self-control reflects the degree of effectiveness of the parenting that a child receives. To speak with the authors of a recent review of the role of parenting in self-control theory: "Self-control is instilled early in life as a result of parents who care enough about their children to make the effort to effectively discipline them. This [*parental management thesis*] is a strong proposition because it asserts that *self-control has no other major sources*." (Cullen et al. 2008: 62; italics ours). A corollary to the parental management thesis is the *parental mediation* thesis: the notion that any parental management mediates the impact of family factors and all other factors on self-control, which then leads to crime and analogous behaviors, and these factors have no other direct effects on self-control or crime, and their effects on self-control are not mediated by any other intervening variable (Cullen et al. 2008: 65).

A number of studies have examined parental disciplinary practices and other family characteristics as predictors of self-control and/or correlates of delinquency (e.g., Burt et al. 2006; Cullen et al. 2008; Gibbs et al. 1998; Hope and Chapple 2004; Hope et al. 2003; Latimore et al. 2006; Nofziger 2008; Perrone et al. 2004; Phythian et al. 2008; Pratt et al. 2004; Wright et al. 2008). Considerably smaller is the number of studies which have examined specifically the parental management and the parental mediation thesis (see Cullen et al. 2008: 70–71 for an overview and listing of studies). The pattern of results of these studies is generally consistent with the parental management thesis: various measures of effective parenting tend to be related to levels of self-control (Cullen et al. 2008: 68). A complete review and discussion of these studies is beyond the scope of this chapter. However, because of the immediate relevance for the present ISRD study and the analyses presented in this section, we highlight one study which provides a careful designed test of the parental mediating thesis, that is, the study by Hope and colleagues (2003). This study shows that "the structural family background variables exert their influence on self-control through the family process variables of attachment and supervision" (p. 307 quoted in Cullen et al. 2008: 69). Inconsistent with self-control theory in their view is the finding that "even with parental supervision in the model, gender, age, and parental education continue to exert significant influences on self-control" (Cullen et al. 2008: 69).

The ISRD2 study does not have a direct measure of parental discipline, but there are several indicators of the potential of effective parenting. Four measures of family life are used in our analysis. First, and most consistent with the general theory of crime, we use *parental supervision* (i.e., do parents know with whom the youth spends time when going out). A second measure related to effective supervision is whether or not there are two parents in the home (i.e., *intact family*). Gottfredson and Hirschi argue that it is more difficult to supervise children if there is only one adult available. Also consistent with self-control theory is the third variable of *family bonding* (whether or not the youth usually gets along with father or mother). This attachment variable is viewed as a necessary condition for effective parental disciplining. A similar logic may be applied to the fourth variable: that of *family disruption* (e.g., whether or not there have been repeated serious conflicts or physical fights between the parents, see Chap. 2). Parental supervision is more likely to be effective if the youth is raised in a family with a minimum of parental conflicts. We believe that it is reasonable to argue that these measures of family life – although taken when the youth is in 7th, 8th, or 9th grade – are not independent of the quality of family life at an earlier age.

11.3.2 Neighborhood and Self-control

There are different variants of control theories: *individual level theories* (such as self-control and social bonding theories) and *community or neighborhood-level control theories* (Paternoster and Bachman 2010). The most influential current versions of neighborhood control theory are Bursik and Grasmick's systemic theory of community (1993) and the theory of *collective efficacy* developed by Sampson and colleagues (e.g., Sampson 2006, see also the discussion in Chap. 10). The literature on this topic is voluminous and far beyond the scope of this chapter, but there are a few points of direct relevance here. First, there is evidence of contextual (i.e., neighborhood) effects on individual development (Sampson 2006: 52), which raises the possibility of such effects on the development of self-control. A complicating matter is the possibility of *selection bias*: how do we know that area differences in any outcome of interest, such as adolescent delinquency – or self-control, "are the result of neighborhood factors rather than the differential selection of adolescents or their families into certain neighborhoods" (Sampson 2006: 47). There are good reasons to speculate that there may be a neighborhood effect on self-control. For example, disorganized neighborhoods may undermine parents' ability to provide effective supervision; they may attract adults with low self-control who may be less effective in parenting their children. In a 2004 article, Pratt, Turner, and Piquero examined the effects of parental socialization and community context on self-control. The results of their study indicated that self-control was predicted by both parental socialization and adverse neighborhood conditions; that the total effect of adverse neighborhood conditions on children's level of self-control was just as strong as the total effect for indicators of parental socialization; and that important race differences did emerge, particularly with regard to the interrelationships between the neighborhood-level measures and parental socialization.

Self-control theory would predict that family variables are stronger predictors of self-control than neighborhood-level variables. In our analysis of the "causes" of self-control, we will therefore include three measures of the neighborhood: (1) neighborhood bonding; (2) neighborhood integration; and (3) neighborhood disorganization (see Chap. 2 for a more detailed explanation of these three indicators).

11.3.3 Socio-demographic Variables and Self-control

According to the general theory of crime, the universal, persistent *gender* differences in delinquency and crime may be explained by differences in levels of self-control. That is, females are posited to have a higher level of self-control, possibly as a product of closer supervision and thus more effective socialization than their male counterparts (Hirschi and Gottfredson 2008: 225). Females also may have less access to criminal opportunities. In recent writings, Hirschi and Gottfredson argue in favor of a "choice perspective" over opportunities: From this perspective, "gender is a situational factor of considerable significance in the actor's decision to commit a criminal act" (p. 225). There are numerous empirical studies on gender as a "cause" of self-control: i.e., do boys have – generally speaking – less self-control than girls, and if so, why? (see, e.g., Burton et al. 1998; Mason and Windle 2002; Greenberg 2008). Our analysis will use gender as one of the control variables.

The role of *age* in self-control theory is rather straightforward: Self-control is assumed to be established around the age of 8 or 10, and it is assumed to remain relatively unchanged after that. A number of recent studies have challenged the premise of the stability of self-control and argue that self-control actually may fluctuate or change throughout the person's life-course (Turner and Piquero 2002). This claim may be empirically assessed in our study, even though we have a rather limited age range in our sample (12–16 years). As explained in Chap. 2, we substitute *grade* level for the age variable. If the assertion of self-control theory is true, then there should be no significant differences in levels of self-control between pupils in either 7th, 8th, or 9th grade. The analysis will include grade as one of the control variables.

Gottfredson and Hirschi tentatively suggest that race differences in crime could be due to racial differences in self-control. Several studies have tested this hypothesis (Vazsonyi and Crosswhite 2004; Love 2006), with mixed results. When Gottfredson and Hirschi discuss race and crime, they limit their discussion to differences between Blacks and Whites (Greenberg 2008: 46). The ISRD2 data do not have information on race; rather, data are collected on the *immigration status* of youth. Although the empirical evidence on the criminal involvement of first- and second-generation immigrants – as compared to native youth – is mixed, the logic of self-control theory suggests that there may be differences in level of self-control between these groups of youth. This is an assertion that we are able to test with our data; we will use immigration status as one of our control variables.

The general theory of crime claims that the more affluent classes in society tend to exhibit higher levels of self-control; they argue that people with low self-control are unlikely to succeed in white-collar type occupations (i.e., inability to plan and to forego immediate pleasures for long-term gain). Following this logic, there should be a link between the socio-economic position of a youth's family and their level of self-control. Therefore, we use as the family's *level of affluence* as a fourth control variable.

It may be argued that a big city environment is less conducive to the effective parental supervision of youth, thereby lowering the development of self-control. This is consistent with the frequently found higher levels of delinquency of big city youth. In our analysis of the predictors of self-control, *city size* is introduced as a control variable.

Finally, and of great importance in the current study, we employ the six *country clusters* as control variables. In the previous Sect. (11.2.4), it was shown that country clusters differ with regard to their level of self-control (e.g., the Anglo-Saxon and Post-Socialist clusters have lower levels of self-control than the Northern European country cluster). Remember, a main research question in this chapter revolves around the issue of the cross-national generalizability of self-control theory. In the present analysis, by introducing the country clusters as control variables, we will be able to determine if the particular country cluster in which the youth resides has an effect on the level of self-control, independent of the family and neighborhood variables, gender, grade, immigration status, family affluence, or size of city.

11.3.4 Results of Regression Analysis: Family, Neighborhood, and Country Cluster Effects on Self-control

Table 11.3 below shows the results of the regression analysis, using levels of self-control as the dependent variable. There are four regression models: Model 0 with the group of socio-demographic control variables (city size, gender, grade, immigration status, family affluence, and country cluster); Model 1 with both the control variables and the family variables; Model 2 with both the control variables and the neighborhood variables; and Model 3 with the control variables, family variables, and neighborhood variables.

Table 11.3 Predicting self-control by controls, family-, and neighborhood factors

	Model 0	Model 1	Model 2	Model 3
City size				
Small	0.014** (2.59)	0.002 (0.40)	0.007 (1.39)	0.000 (0.06)
Medium	0.005 (0.95)	−0.003 (−0.48)	0.024*** (4.61)	0.014** (2.74)
Large	0.001 (0.21)	−0.001 (−0.23)	0.057*** (10.33)	0.043*** (8.10)
Gender				
Male	−0.099*** (−24.96)	−0.084*** (−22.16)	−0.069*** (−18.46)	−0.060*** (−16.37)
Grade				
8th grade	−0.053*** (−11.42)	−0.030*** (−6.80)	−0.038*** (−8.67)	−0.023*** (−5.59)
9th grade	−0.071*** (−15.26)	−0.024*** (−5.30)	−0.047*** (−10.68)	−0.016*** (−3.80)
Migrant status				
First-generation	0.002 (0.25)	−0.005 (−0.79)	0.006 (0.87)	0.001 (0.21)
Second-generation	0.040*** (5.78)	0.019** (2.91)	0.027*** (4.15)	0.015* (2.44)
Family affluence (*z*-score)	−0.000 (−0.05)	−0.008* (−2.00)	−0.028*** (−7.09)	−0.028*** (−7.34)
Country clusters				
North Europe	0.134*** (20.55)	0.130*** (20.95)	0.100*** (16.13)	0.103*** (17.23)
West Europe	0.094*** (11.73)	0.072*** (9.46)	0.072*** (9.47)	0.056*** (7.62)
Mediterranean Europe	0.109*** (14.95)	0.058*** (8.32)	0.121*** (17.59)	0.077*** (11.50)
Latin America	0.034*** (5.38)	0.020*** (3.40)	0.058*** (9.71)	0.041*** (7.16)
Post-Socialist	0.002 (0.28)	−0.001 (−0.18)	0.007 (0.88)	0.002 (0.23)
Intact family				
1 Parent		−0.016*** (−3.50)		−0.017*** (−3.84)

(continued)

Table 1[illegible].3 (continued)

	Model 0	Model 1	Model 2	Model 3
Family disruption z-score		−0.075*** (−16.42)		−0.056*** (−12.63)
Family bonding z-score		0.142*** (34.66)		0.116*** (29.05)
Parental supervision		0.229*** (58.14)		0.192*** (50.22)
Neighborhood bonding z-score			0.024*** (5.54)	0.009* (2.14)
Neighborhood integration z-score			0.014*** (3.37)	−0.019*** (−4.53)
Neighborhood disorganized z-score			−0.326*** (−83.28)	−0.275*** (−71.47)
Adjusted R^2	0.034***	0.131***	0.137***	0.198***
F	158.5	521.0	580.0	728.1

Standardized beta coefficients; t statistics in parentheses
$^{*}p<0.05$, $^{**}p<0.01$, $^{***}p<0.001$

The first model (Model 0) shows that, although there are several variables with a significant beta value, the total amount of explained variance by the socio-demographic background variables is quite low ($R^2=0.034$). We need to keep in mind that because of the large sample size, it is very easy to obtain statistically significant beta values. Consistent with expectations, males are slightly more likely to report a lower level of self-control than females (−0.099), as are youth in grades 8 and 9 (−0.053 and −0.071, respectively) compared to 7th graders. Native-born youths are slightly more likely to report a higher level of self-control compared to second-generation immigrant youth (0.040). Contrary to expectations, youth with higher levels of family affluence report lower levels of self-control. All country clusters report a significantly higher level of self-control compared to the Anglo-Saxon country cluster. The Post-Socialist country cluster is an exception, which is not surprising since our earlier analysis showed that the level of self-control in this cluster is quite comparable to the Anglo-Saxon cluster.

Model 1 adds the cluster of family variables to the regression equation. The amount of explained variance increases significantly ($R^2=0.131$). The control variables which were shown to be significant in Model 0 retain their significant betas. The impact of the family variables is mostly consistent with theoretical expectations. The effect of close parental supervision on self-control is the strongest (0.229). As expected, youths with a higher level of family attachment (0.142) report higher levels of self-control. Youths who have experienced more conflict in their family tend to report lower levels of self-control (−0.075). In as far as Model 1 may be seen as a test of Gottfredson and Hirschi's parental management and mediation thesis of the "cause" of self-control, these result seem consistent with this thesis.

Model 2 replaces the cluster of family variables with our measures of neighborhood (neighborhood bonding, neighborhood integration, and neighborhood disorganization). The total amount of explained variance ($R^2=0.137$) is about the same in Model 1 (family variables). In this model, two additional control variables (city size and family affluence) obtain weak but significant beta values. That is, higher levels of self-control are reported by youth from middle and large cities, and those from less affluent families. All three indicators of neighborhood are significant predictors of self-control. Neighborhood bonding and neighborhood integration are rather weak predictors (0.024 and 0.014, respectively). The independent effect of neighborhood disorganization is quite strong, however (−0.326). In so far as Model 2 may be viewed as a test of the community-level theory of the predictors of self-control, our findings seem to support this interpretation.

Model 3 allows us to determine the independent effects of both the family and neighborhood indicators as well as the socio-demographic background variables. It is not surprising that the total amount of variance explained is higher ($R^2=0.198$), because the total number of variables included in the model has increased. Although there is a high number of significant betas (18 out of 21), most of the beta values are rather low. The highest beta (−0.275) is for neighborhood disorganization: youths who experience their neighborhood as disorganized tend to report lower levels of self-control (the two other indicators of neighborhood have very low beta values). Parental supervision (0.192) and family bonding (0.116) are next in relative magnitude: youths with stricter parental supervision and a higher level of parental attachment report higher levels of self-control than their counterparts with less supervision and lower parental attachment (the measure of family conflict is very weakly related to self-control). Among the control variables, the country clusters appear to have the strongest independent effects: youths from the Northern European cluster are more likely to report a high level of self-control compared to those from the Anglo-Saxon cluster (0.103), and so are youth from the Western European cluster (0.056), the Mediterranean cluster (0.077), and the Latin American cluster (0.041). Gender also makes a difference: males report lower levels of self-control than females (–0.060). Very weak effects – in the expected direction – remain with regard to (second-generation) immigration status (0.015). There are a few results that are counterintuitive: Youths from medium and large cities report higher levels of self-control (0.14 and 0.43, respectively); 8th and 9th graders report lower levels of self-control than their younger 7th grade counterparts (–0.023 and –0.016, respectively); and youth from more affluent families report lower levels of self-control (–0.028). The very low values of the betas may render these observations substantively irrelevant, in view of the large sample size.

In sum, the results are supportive of the parental management and mediation thesis (Gottfredson and Hirschi), neighborhood effect theories (e.g., Sampson), and gender effects. Also, and of particular interest to the comparative researcher, country cluster retains an impendent effect on self-control, holding family and neighborhood variables constant.

11.4 Low Self-Control and Delinquency: Cross-national Evaluation of a Theoretical Model

One of the objectives of this chapter is to assess the cross-national applicability of self-control theory. We already saw that the *level* of self-control varies between and among countries and country clusters (Sect. 11.2.4). We speculated that – although the levels of self-control vary nationally – it may very well be possible that the *effects* of self-control are similar across countries and country clusters. In order to test this assertion empirically, in this last part of the chapter, we test a theoretical model of self-control theory which will include a test of the cross-national generalizability of the model. The number of studies empirically testing the effect of self-control on delinquency and analogous behavior is huge (see references listed in previous sections) and there is no way we can incorporate all suggested revisions and modifications and additions in our theoretical model. Most researchers now acknowledge that different measures of family, school, neighborhood, peers, as well as opportunities all play a role in the generation of delinquent behavior, together with low self-control. The common approach is to include low self-control as one of the explanatory variables, together with social bonding, social learning, opportunity, and strain variables, and then to assess the independent contribution of low self-control to variations in the outcome variable (delinquency, risk behavior).

The choice we have made for this chapter is to further expand on the theoretical model developed in the previous section (family and neighborhood variables as predictors of self control), by adding the opportunity factor. The role of opportunity "is unclear in self-control theory" and it remains "conspicuously untested," according to Simpson and Geis (2008:50) in their critical review of empirical research on opportunities and self-control theory. We see this as a call to take advantage of our large international database to contribute to the clarification of the role of opportunity.

From the very beginning, opportunity has been of particular interest for students of the theory of low self-control. Although, in their original work (1990), as well as in later work (2003), Gottfredson and Hirschi argued that opportunities play a negligible role in their theory, research has shown that opportunities amplify or moderate the effect of low self-control on crime. For example, in a recent article in *Criminology*, Hay and Forrest (2008) make a strong case for the notion that low self-control likely has effects that are conditioned on the supply of criminal opportunities. Drawing from routine activities theory, they develop a theoretical statement of how opportunity should be incorporated into self-control theory. They employ "standard" delinquency variables such as unsupervised time from home, time with peers, and adult absence as indicators of delinquent opportunities. Using data from the National Longitudinal Study of Youth, they find that effects of low self-control partially depend on availability of criminal opportunities, measured by *the time juveniles spend with their friends or away from the supervision of their parents.* The ISRD data set does include this measure, which we will use to tap one of the dimensions of opportunity.

In this context, we also want to mention Wikström's *Situational Action Theory of Crime* (SAT). This theoretical framework incorporates the notion that criminal involvement is a consequence of individual criminal propensity (self-control) and the criminogenic features of the environment to which individual is exposed (lifestyle, opportunity, routine activities). Wikstöm views self-control as a situational concept (Wikstöm and Svenssson 2008).[3] The cornerstone of SAT is the assertion that human actions are an outcome of how individuals perceive their "action alternatives" and make their choices as a result of the interaction between their individual characteristics (propensities) and features of the environment. The proposed key individual characteristics are an individual's morality and their ability to exercise self-control. The ISRD data set does not include any measures of individual's morality, but it does include indicators comparable to those proposed by Wikström to measure "criminogenic features of the environment." A crucial environmental characteristic is the particular behavior-setting in which youths find themselves (environmental inducements, measured by *lifestyle*). Wikström associates lifestyles with exposure to criminogenic behavior settings. He defines "lifestyles" as an individual's preference for and active seeking out of particular sets of activities and related

[3]It should be noted that Hirschi and Gottfredson adamantly reject the notion that self-control may be a situational concept. See Hirschi and Gottfredson (2008).

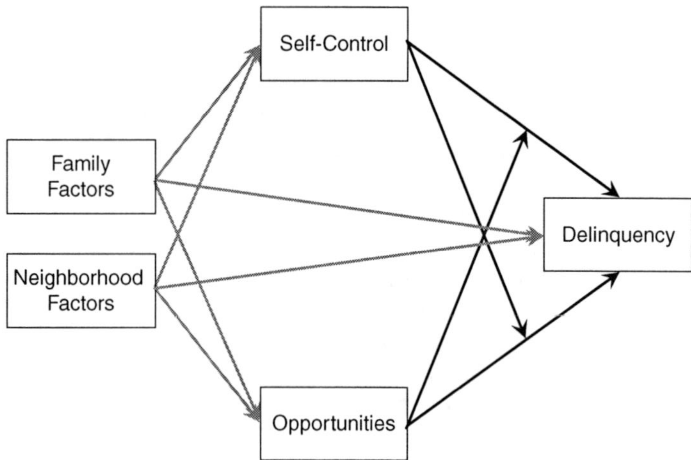

Fig. 11.3 Theoretical model predicting delinquency

attributes (Wikström and Svensson 2008: 312). Lifestyles in which youth spend significant time in public and semipublic behavior settings in which they informally socialize and are unsupervised by adults, in a behavioral context in which they may express violations of norms and conventions without much risk of interference from others, may be considered high-risk lifestyles (p. 313). In the 2008 study, high-risk lifestyle is measured by an index "on how frequently they spend time in city centre public settings, the extent of their peers' criminal involvement and their own self-reported frequency of alcohol consumption" (p. 313).

There are other studies, besides Hay and Forrest (2008) and Wikstöm and Svenssson (2008), which have explored the role of lifestyle/opportunities (cites), but we highlighted these authors because of their discussion of the operationalization of opportunity, closely paralleling the indicators available in the ISRD data set. We will come back to this shortly, but first we present our theoretical model, in the form of a path model, reflecting our assumptions about causal priority of different variables (Fig. 11.3).

The dependent variable is *versatility*, a simple count measure of the number of different delinquent acts committed. This measure is particularly appropriate for a test of self-control theory, because of its assertion of the generality of deviance (i.e., no specialization).The effect of *family* is measured by the two variables which were shown to be the strongest predictors of self-control in our earlier analysis: family bonding and parental supervision. Similarly, *neighborhood* characteristics are measured by neighborhood integration (e.g., the degree to which people look out for one another) and neighborhood disorganization (e.g., the level of visible signs of crime and graffiti in the neighborhood). The measure of s*elf-control* has been extensively discussed before (12-item SC scale).

Our measure of *opportunities* is an expansion of the lifestyle variables, discussed in Chap. 9. In Chap. 9, a lifestyle scale was developed, based on responses to four items: going out a night (never, once or twice, three or more), amount of time hanging out with friends (less than an hour, 1–2 h, or 3 or more hours), leisure time spent with family, by oneself or with a small group of friends, or with a large group of friends, and whether or not the group of friends spent a lot of time in public places (no or yes).[4] Each of the four variables were coded into three categories (−1, 0, and +1), with a final score varying between −4 and +4. We added a fifth indicator, consistent with Wikstöm's and others' operationalization of "opportunity": whether or not the youth has delinquent friends. Youths were assigned −1 if they had no delinquent friends, 0 if they had at least one delinquent friend who had ever assaulted somebody, and +1 of they had at least one friend who had ever committed an acquisitive crime (shoplifting, burglary, or robbery/extortion). Having friends involved in acquisitive crime should weigh heavier in terms of an opportunity perspective, than having friends who have hurt others. The opportunity measure ranges from −5 to +5.

The path model posits the following links:

Family – a direct link to self-control and to versatility (as would be expected based on existing theory and research). In addition to the posited main effects of family on self control and versatility, our model also proposes an indirect effect from family to versatility through self-control (in other words, self-control is a mediating factor). We also propose a direct effect of family on opportunities, as well as an indirect effect of family on versatility, with opportunity as a mediating factor.

Neighborhood: A direct link to self-control (see our previous discussion in Sect. 11.3) and to versatility (consistent with literature and research). The model also proposes an indirect effect of neighborhood on versatility through self-control and through opportunities. In our earlier discussion, we made an argument to support the association between neighborhood variables and self-control; it has also been argued before that opportunity is influenced by neighborhood characteristics.

Self-control is presumed to have a direct (main) effect on versatility, but an additional link is the interaction between self-control and opportunity (on versatility). This part of the model is consistent with recent interpretations that self-control should buffer the effects of opportunities on crime (or that opportunities should amplify the effects of low self-control). Thus, although opportunities should increase crime, this should be even more the case when self-control is low. Likewise, the positive effect of low self-control on crime should be stronger when opportunity is high (Hay and Forrest 2008: 1047). The Hay and Forrest analysis confirms this expectation: they found that the effects of low self-control on delinquency partially depend on the availability of criminal opportunities. Wikstöm found comparable results. Finally, *opportunity* is also presumed to have an independent, main effect on versatility, an expectation grounded in a large number of empirical studies as well as theoretical argument (routine activity theory among others).

[4]It should be noted that – although we distinguish between *opportunities* and *lifestyle* – these two terms are often used interchangeably in the delinquency literature. However, when directly related to tests of self-control theory, opportunity seems the preferred term.

Analyzed but not shown in the path model are the control variables (city size, gender, grade, migrant status, and family affluence). We do not include country clusters as control variables in this model; rather, we present the results of the comparative test of our theoretical model (using the country clusters) in a separate analysis (Sect. 11.4.3).

11.4.1 How Well Does the Theoretical Model Fit to the Data? Results of Multivariate Analyses

As our theoretical model suggests, we had to perform three separate regression analyses, the results of which are shown in Table 11.4 below.

First, employing OLS regression analysis, we regressed self-control on the control variables, family variables, and neighborhood variables (Model 1). Column 1 in Table 11.4 shows the results. This basically repeats the OLS regression shown in Table 11.3, but we are using a more parsimonious model here. We do not use country clusters as controls, and we use only two family indicators and two neighborhood indicators (those who have been shown to be the most robust on earlier analyses). Migration status is now dichotomized (natives are the reference group). By and large, the results are comparable to those discussed in Sect. 11.3.

The second column of Table 11.4 shows the effects of the control variables, family, and neighborhood factors on opportunity (Model 2). Interestingly, gender fails to reach statistical significance. This seems a rather anomalous finding, as is the positive relationship between family affluence and opportunities (0.138). Not unexpected is the comparatively strong effect of parental supervision (−0.273): youths with low parental supervision score higher on the opportunity scale. Neighborhood disorganization also appears to have a significant effect on opportunities: youths who live in disorganized neighborhoods appear to have more opportunities for delinquency (0.187). Not surprising is the finding that youths in higher grades tend to have more opportunities for delinquency than youths in 7th grade (0.060 for 8th grade and 0.099 for 9th grade; see F-test). The total amount of variance explained by all variables of Model 2 is about 18%.

The third column of Table 11.4 shows the result of a negative binomial regression with versatility as the dependent variable (Model 3). In addition to the controls, family, and neighborhood variables, Model 3 includes self-control and opportunity (main effects), as well as the interaction effect of self-control and opportunity. The estimate of explained variance is about 31% (pseudo $R^2=0.306$). Here, the effect sizes are expressed as incidence rate ratios (IRR): the factor by which the versatility score increases if the independent variables increase by one. If the z statistic is negative, then the effect size can be displayed as the reciprocal 1/coefficient, indicating the factor by which versatility *decreases*. Gender (i.e., being male) has the strongest effect on versatility (2.204), followed closely by opportunity (2.017) and self-control (0.599, or 1/1.669). We also see a significant and substantial effect (1.067) of the interaction term (opportunity × self-control), confirming our theoretical expectations. We will come back to this shortly.

Table 11.4 Coefficients of path model predicting versatility

	OLS regression		Negative binomial regression
DV	Self-control (z)	Opportunities (z)	Versatility
City size (base = national sample/unknown)	F(3, 62,510) = 96.3***	F(3, 62,510) = 39.4***	Chi²(3) = 76.1***
Small towns	0.041 (3.58)***	0.112 (9.79)***	1.164 (5.32)***
Medium-sized cities	0.084 (7.44)***	0.035 (3.10)**	1.234 (7.54)***
Large cities	0.164 (15.44)***	0.080 (7.55)***	1.241 (8.24)***
Gender (base = female)			
Male	–0.113 (–15.36)***	0.003 (0.40)	2.204 (43.66)***
Grade (base = grade 7)	F(2, 62,510) = 17.6***	F(2, 62,510) = 269.6***	Chi²(2) = 30.4***
Grade 8	–0.046 (–5.15)***	0.128 (14.32)***	1.120 (5.13)***
Grade 9	–0.047 (–5.17)***	0.208 (23.03)***	1.106 (4.62)***
Migrant status (base = native)			
Migrant	–0.020 (–2.32)*	0.049 (5.59)***	1.170 (7.93)***
Family affluence (z-score)	–0.015 (–4.00)***	0.138 (37.63)***	1.104 (10.29)***
Family	F(2, 62,510) = 2,429.9***	F(2, 62,510) = 3,450.8***	Chi²(2) = 458.7***
Family bonding (z-score)	0.127 (32.82)***	–0.098 (–25.23)***	0.888 (–14.42)***
Parental supervision (base: never)			
Sometimes/always	0.412 (53.03)***	–0.559 (–71.90)***	0.784 (–13.22)***
Neighborhood	F(2, 62,510) = 2,698.9***	F(2, 62,510) = 1,217.0***	Chi²(2) = 689.7***
Disintegration (z-score)	0.006 (1.63)	–0.040 (–10.51)***	1.059 (6.57)***
Disorganization (z-score)	–0.278 (–72.97)***	0.187 (49.19)***	1.217 (24.54)***
Self-control (z-score)	–	–	0.599 (–45.46)***
Opportunities (z-score)	–	–	2.017 (60.44)***
Self-control* opportunities	–	–	1.067 (6.61)***
R^2/pseudo R^2	0.184	0.183	0.177
F/Chi²	1,176.2	1,162.9	17,643.4

OLS regression analyses: unstandardized coefficients, t values in parentheses; negative binomial regression analysis: exponentiated coefficients (incidence rates ratio), z values in parentheses

*$p<0.05$; **$p<0.01$; ***$p<0.001$

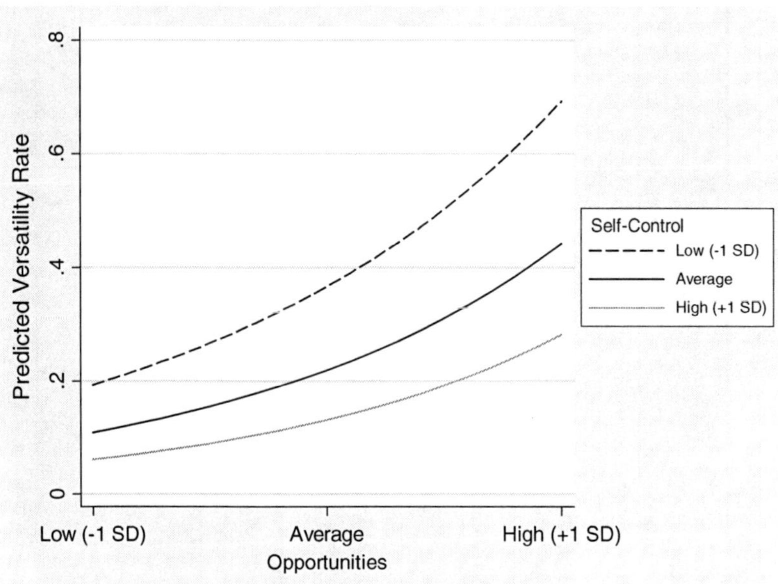

Fig. 11.4 Interaction of self-control and opportunities in predicting versatility

Also consistent with expectations, both neighborhood factors and family factors are significant predictors of versatility, holding other variables constant. The factors of parental supervision (0.784, or 1/1.276) and neighborhood disorganization (1.217) change versatility rates by more than twenty percent. These effects are independent of self-control and opportunity, as well as selected control variables. Migrant youth is also slightly more likely to have a higher versatility score than native youth (1.172, some 17%), as are those in grades 8 and 9 (compared to 7th graders). A rather counterintuitive finding is the effect of family affluence. The IRR of 1.104 suggests a weak but positive effect of family affluence on versatility. This finding may be explained by the particular way in which we have measured family affluence (see Chap. 2). This particular measure may work in less affluent countries, but in the more prosperous countries, it may measure (conspicuous) consumption behavior. Having a cell phone, for example, may be viewed as a status symbol for the lower classes.

11.4.2 Interaction of Self-Control and Opportunities

We are particularly interested in the *interaction* between self-control and opportunities. In other words, is the effect of opportunity moderated by self-control? The interaction of self-control and opportunities is displayed in Fig. 11.4, showing the buffering effect of self-control: The positive effect of opportunities on the rate of versatility decreases with increasing self-control. Whereas the difference of estimated prevalence rates predicted at high versus low values of opportunities (plus and minus one standard deviation from the average) is 0.693 – 0.193 = 0.500 if self-control is low (one standard deviation below the average), this difference is much smaller if self-control is high (one standard deviation above the average): 0.282 – 0.061 = 0.221. This finding suggests that opportunities matter much more for those with low self-control than for those with high self-control. Having said this, our data do indicate that a main independent effect of opportunities exists, even for those with high self-control.

11.4.3 Cross-national Generalizability of the Theoretical Model

The final step in our analysis is a test of the generalizability of the theoretical model. We are particularly interested to see if the effects found in the previous section differ between country clusters in interesting or important ways. The same model as above, including the control variables as well as the family and neighborhood variables, is specified for the six country clusters. Table 11.5 only shows the three (composite) variables of main interest (transformed to z-scores): Opportunity, self-control, and the interaction of opportunity and self-control. We are interested to see if the findings that applied to the total sample (see previous section) also apply similarly across country clusters, in particular we are interested in the main and interaction effects of self control and opportunity on versatility.

For comparative purposes, we want to compare the R^2, the main effects of self control and opportunity, and the interaction effect (in terms of the effect size expressed as IRR) – between the country clusters. We also want to assess how the effects in the country clusters differ from those found for the total sample.

First, for all country clusters, there remains a strong main effect of opportunity (with a factor of two and statistically significant). Second, for all country clusters, self-control has a statistically significant main effect in all country clusters, but the effect is smaller. The versatility rate is cut in about half: youths with high self-control have roughly half the variety score compared to those with low self-control. The strongest (negative) effect size (for self control) is in the Northern European cluster; the effect sizes are comparatively weaker for Latin America and the Post-Socialist countries, which, incidentally, are the two clusters with the lowest overall level of self-control. Third, and most interesting, there are significant differences between the country clusters with regard to the interaction between opportunity and self-control. In three of the country clusters: Northern Europe, Latin America, and the Post-socialist clusters, the interaction term fails to reach statistical significance. The interaction is significant in the Anglo-Saxon cluster (IRR = 1.128), the Western European countries (1.140), and the Mediterranean cluster (1.092).

Table 1[illegible].5 Effects of self-control and opportunities across country clusters

	Anglo-Saxon	Northern EU	Western EU	Mediterranean	Latin America	Post-Socialist
Self-control	0.586***	0.537***	0.570***	0.568***	0.641***	0.641***
(*z*-scores)	(−11.87)	(−15.92)	(−27.04)	(−21.25)	(−11.81)	(−20.88)
Opportunities	2.077***	1.929***	2.110***	2.024***	2.137***	1.800***
(*z*-scores)	(15.64)	(18.74)	(37.47)	(23.95)	(18.25)	(25.04)
Self-control*	1.128***	1.040	1.140***	1.092***	1.016	1.027
opportunities	(3.45)	(1.24)	(7.60)	(3.59)	(0.45)	(1.38)
Pseudo R^2	0.394***	0.322***	0.357***	0.321***	0.240***	0.273***
Chi²	1,521.5	1,949.5	5,726.7	3,197.7	1,176.7	4,335.1
N	3,545	6,610	15,887	11,107	6,209	19,165

Notes: Incidence rate ratios (exponentiated coefficients); *z* statistics in parentheses; parameters of full model (effects of control variables, family, and neighborhood not shown)
$^*p<0.05$; $^{**}p<0.01$; $^{***}p<0.001$

11.5 Concluding Observations

There is a variety of ways in which data such as ours may be used. We can simply view the more than 65,000 cases as *one huge sample*, representing most of Europe and selected other regions. This large sample, then, is used to test different propositions derived from self-control theory. The comparative features of the design are – in this approach – virtually irrelevant. On the other hand, we may take advantage of the *logic of the comparative design* of the ISRD-2 study by testing the generalizability of theoretical propositions (in the different national contexts) or by attempting to specify these theoretical propositions (i.e., in which countries or country clusters do these propositions apply, and if not, why not?). With regard to the use of the data from a comparative perspective, a common dilemma in the interpretation of the findings is whether to stress the observed *similarities* across countries (or country clusters) – and thus the generalizability of the results, or conversely to highlight the *differences* (in relative importance of variables or the strength of associations, and so on) so that we can better specify under which conditions particular propositions may hold. In most of the chapters in this book, all these strategies are employed and the current chapter is no exception.

The shorter version of the Grasmick et al. (1993) scale, when tested on the total sample, country clusters, as well as in individual countries, generally speaking performed quite well. Our analysis confirmed the existence of four distinct subscales corresponding to theoretical expectations (i.e., risk-taking, self-centeredness, impulsivity, and volatile temperament); the self-control scale was shown to be one-dimensional; the reliability (alpha) was good under all conditions; and the SC scale had a significant correlation with a behavioral measure (i.e., accident proneness). On the other hand, we also found that not all subscales performed equally well, with risk-taking appearing more robust than impulsivity. Furthermore, our comparative analysis indicated that there are some countries where the SC scale does not work as well (i.e., not according to theoretical expectations). We need to speculate about the reasons why the psychometric properties of the SC scale (and some of the subscales) appeared to vary somewhat among a handful of countries. Perhaps the translation of the questions played a role (e.g., similar problems in Surinam and the Netherlands where the same translated questionnaire was used). Or it is also possible that social desirability plays a different role in some of the countries with the more puzzling psychometric results.

The rather minor cross-national differences in the psychometric properties of the SC scale give reasons to feel quite confident about the results of our substantive analysis related to self-control theory. Our analysis shows interesting results. First, we found that there is a fairly narrow range in the mean SC values of countries: A difference of 18 points (on a 100 points scale) (a low of 53.4 and a high of 70.4), suggesting that there is a fair degree of convergence in levels of self-control among countries. On the other hand, we also found that the mean SC values differ significantly between the country clusters: the Northern European cluster (66.9) averages more ten points above the Anglo-Saxon cluster (56.5) and nine points above the

Post-socialist cluster (57.7). There was also some national variation in the mean scores of the subscales not always consistent with the larger self-control scale, in particular the volatile temperament and the self-centeredness scales. The reasons for these variations in subscales and differences in reported levels of self-control are in need of further exploration. Our analysis of the predictors of self-control (in Sect. 11.2), however, was not designed to answer that particular question. Instead, our focus was on the testing of a theoretical model (on the total sample) of the correlates of self-control (i.e., background variables, family variables, and neighborhood variables). We did find that belonging to a particular country cluster has a significant effect on self-control, controlling for a number of other factors, but we did not conduct any further analysis to determine if background variables, as well as family and neighborhood characteristics, had a comparable impact on self-control in these different country clusters. Our analysis showed that neighborhood disorganization, parental supervision and family bonding, gender, and country cluster are the five strongest predictors of self control: lowest levels of self-control are found among boys from Anglo-Saxon and Post-socialist countries, living in disorganized neighborhoods, with little parental supervision and low attachment to parents. Additional – but considerably weaker – factors are being in 8th or 9th grade (compared to 7th grade), being a second-generation immigrant, living in a one parent home, with considerable family disruption.

Self-control theory asserts that low self-control is a significant correlate of crime, regardless of culture, place, or time. Although the *levels* of self-control may vary across countries, if may very well be that the *effects* of self-control are similar across countries and country clusters. The results of our test of a theoretical model of self-control theory (including opportunities, neighborhood, and family factors) suggest several interesting conclusions. First, and consistent with our theoretical expectations, self-control has an effect on delinquency. We also found that the effects of gender and opportunities are actually stronger than the main effect of self-control. Importantly, there is a clear interaction effect of opportunities and self-control: opportunities matter more for those with low self-control than for those with high self-control. Additional significant factors having an impact of self-reported variety of delinquency are parental supervision and neighborhood disorganization, being a migrant, and being in a higher grade. Second, with regard to the cross-national generalizability of theoretical propositions, the analyses support the need for further specification of the theoretical proposed link between self-control and opportunities. When comparing country clusters, we find in all six country clusters a main effect of both self-control and opportunities (as was the case in our analysis of the combined samples), but in three of the clusters (Northern Europe, Latin America, and the Post-Socialist cluster), the interaction between opportunities and self control is no longer statistically significant. This finding demands further interpretation and exploration; it does further illustrate the power of comparative analysis as both a theory-testing and theory-development instrument.

References

Akers, R. L. and C.S. Seller. 2004. *Criminological Theories: Introduction, Evaluation, and Application*. Los Angeles: Roxbury.

Antonaccio, O. & Tittle, C.R. 2008. "Morality, Self-Control, and Crime." *Criminology* 46:479–510.

Arneklev, B.J., Grasmick, H.G., & Bursik, Jr., R.J. 1999. "Evaluating the Dimensionality and Invariance of "Low Self-Control"." *Journal of Quantitative Criminology* 15:307–331.

Arneklev, B.J., H. G. Grasmick, C. R. Title, and R.J.J. Bursik. 1993. "Low self-control and imprudent behavior." *Journal of Quantitative Criminology* 9:225–47.

Baron, S.W. 2003. "Self-Control, Social Consequences, and Criminal Behavior: Street Youth and the General Theory of Crime." *Journal of Research in Crime and Delinquency* 40:403–425.

Baron, Stephen W., David R. Forde, and Fiona M. Kay. 2007. "Self-control, risky lifestyles, and situation: the role of opportunity and context in the general theory." *Journal of Criminal Justice* 35:119–136.

Beaver, K.M., DeLisi, M., Mears, D.P. & Stewart, E. 2009. "Low Self-Control and Contact with the Criminal Justice System in a Nationally Representative Sample of Males." *Justice Quarterly* 26:695–715.

Beaver, Kevin M., John Paul Wright, and Michael O. Maume. 2008. "The effect of school classroom characteristics on low self-control: A multi-level analysis." *Journal of Criminal Justice* 36:174–181.

Bursik, R.J.J. and H. G. Grasmick. 1993. *Neighborhoods and Crime: The Dimensions of Effective Community Control*. New York: Lexington.

Burt, C. H., R. L. Simons, and L. G. Simons. 2006. A longitudinal test of the effects of parenting and the stability of self-control: negative evidence for the general theory of crime. *Criminology* 44:353–396.

Burton, Jr., V.S., Cullen, F.T., Evans, T.D., Alarid, L.F. & Dunaway, R.G. 1998. "Gender, self-control, and crime." *Journal of Research in Crime and Delinquency* 35:123–147.

Chapple, C.L. 2005. "Self-control, peer relations, and delinquency." *Justice Quarterly* 22:89–106.

Cullen, F. T., James D. Unnever, J. P. Wright, and Kevin M. Beaver. 2008. "Parenting and self-control." Pp. 61–76 in *Out of Control. Assessing the General Theory of Crime*, edited by E. Goode. Stanford, Cal.: Stanford University Press.

Delisi, M., A. Hochstetler, and D.S. Murphy. 2003. "Self-control behind bars: A validation study of the Grasmick et al. scale." *Justice Quarterly* 20:241–63.

Evans, T. David, Francis T. Cullen, Velmer S. Burton, R. Gregory Dunaway, and Michael L. Benson. 1997. "The social consequences of self-control: Testing the general theory of crime." *Criminology* 35:475-.

Feldman, S. S. and D. A. Weinberger. 1994. "Self-restraint as a mediator of family influences on boys' delinquent behavior: A longitudinal study." *Child Development* 65:195–211.

Felson, R.B., Teasdale, B. & Burchfield, K.B. 2008. "The Influence of Being under the Influence: Alcohol Effects on Adolescent Violence." *Journal of Research in Crime and Delinquency* 45:119–141.

Flora, D.B., E. J. Finkel, and V.A. Foshee. 2003. "Higher order factor structure of a self-control test: Evidence from confirmatory factor analysis with polychoric correlations." *Educational and Psychological Measurement* 63:112–27.

Forde, D.R. & Kennedy, L.W. 1997. "Risky lifestyles, routine activities, and the General Theory of Crime." *Justice Quarterly* 14:265–294.

Geis, G. 2000. "On the absence of self-control as the basis for a general theory of crime: A critique." *Theoretical Criminology* 4:35–53.

—2008. "Self-control: A hypercritical assessment." Pp. 203–216 in *Out of Control: Assessing the General Theory of Crime*, edited by E. Goode. Stanford, Cal.: Stanford University Press.

Gibbs, J.J. & Giever, D. 1995. "Self-control and its manifestations among university students: An empirical test of Gottfredson and Hirschi's general theory." *Justice Quarterly* 12:231–255.

Gibbs, J.J. Giever, D. & Martin, J.S. 1998. "Parental Management and Self-Control: An Empirical Test of Gottfredson and Hirschi's General Theory." *Journal of Research in Crime and Delinquency* 35:40–70.

Goode, Eric. 2008. "Out of Control: Assessing the General Theory of Crime." Stanford, Cal.: Stanford University Press.

—2008. "Out of control? An introduction to the general theory of crime." Pp. 3025 in *Out of Control: Assessing the General Theory of Crime*, edited by E. Goode. Stanford, Cal.: Stanford University Press.

Gottfredson, M. and T Hirschi. 2003. "Self-control and opportunity." Pp. 5–19 in *Control Theories of Crime and Delinquency*, edited by C. L. Britt and M. Gottfredson. Brunswick, N.J.: Transaction.

Gottfredson, M. R. 2005. "The empirical status of control theory in criminology." Pp. 77–100 in *Taking Stock: The Status of Criminological Theory*, edited by F. T. Cullen, J. P. Wright, and K. Blevins. Piscataway, New Jersey: Transaction.

Gottfredson, M. R. (2006). The empirical status of control theory in criminology. In F. T. Cullen, J. P. Wright, & K. Blevins (eds.), Taking Stock: The Status of Criminological Theory (pp. 77–100). New Brunswick, NJ: Transaction.

Gottfredson, M. R. and T. Hirschi. 1990. *A General Theory of Crime*. Stanford, CA: Stanford University Press.

—(1993). A control theory interpretation of psychological research on aggression. In R. B. Felson & J. T. Tedeschi (eds.), Aggression and Violence: Social Interactionist Perspectives (pp. 47–68). Washington, D.C.: American Psychological Association.

—2003. "Self-control and opportunity." in *Control Theories of Crime and Delinquency*, vol. 12, *Advances in Criminological Theory*, edited by C. L. Britt and M. R. Gottfredson. New Brunswick, N.J.: Transaction.

Gibson, C. L. (2005). A Psychometric Investigation of a Self-Control Scale: The Reliability and Validity of Grasmick et al.'s Scale for a Sample of Incarcerated Male Offenders (Doctoral Dissertation). Omhaha, NE: University of Nebraska at Omaha, School of Criminology and Criminal Justice.

Grasmick, H. G., C. R. Title, R.J.J. Bursik, and B.J. Arneklev. 1993. "Testing the core empirical implications of Gottfredson and Hirschi's General theory of Crime." *Journal of Research in Crime and Delinquenct* 30:5–29.

Greenberg, David F. 2008. "Age, sex, and racial distribution of crime." Pp. 38–48 in *Out of Control. Assessing the General Theory of Crime*, edited by E. Goode. Stanford, Cal.: Stanford University Press.

Hay, C. & Forrest, W. 2008. "Self-Control Theory and the Concept of Opportunity: The Case for a More Systematic Union." *Criminology* 46:1039–1072.

Higgins, G. E. 2004. "Gender and Self-Control Theory: Are There Differences in the Measures and the Theory's Causal Model?" *Criminal Justice Studies* 17:33–55.

Higgins, G. E and R. (2006). Sex and Self-Control Theory. Youth & Society Tewksbury, 37(4), 479. 2006. "Sex and self-control theory." *Youth & Society* 37:479.

Hirschi, T. 1969. *Causes of Delinquency*. Berkeley, Cal.: University of California Press.

—2004. Self-control and crime. In R. F. Baumeister & K. D. Vohs (Eds.), Handbook of Self-Regulation: Research, Theory, and Applications (pp. 537-552). New York: Guilford Press.

Hirschi, T and M. Gottfredson. 1983. "Age and the explanation of crime." *American Journal of Sociology* 89:552–584.

—2001. "Self-control theory." Pp. 81–96 in *Explaining Crime and Criminals*, edited by R. Paternoster and R. Bachman. Los Angeles, Cal.: Roxbury.

Hirschi, T and M. Gottfredson. 1986. "The distinction between crime and criminality." Pp. 187–201 in *The Craft of Criminology: Selected Papers. Travis Hirschi.*, edited by J. H. Laub. New Brunswick, N.J.: Transaction.

—2008. "Critiquing the critics: The authors respond." Pp. 2170232 in *Out of Control: Assessing the General Theory of Crime*, edited by E. Goode. Stanford, Cal.: Stanford University Press.

Hirschi, T. and M. R. Gottfredson. 2000. "In defense of self-control." *Theoretical Criminology* 4:55–69.
—2002/1994. "The generality of deviance." Pp. 203–219 in *The Craft of Criminology: Selected Papers. Travis Hirschi*, edited by J. H. Laub. New Brunswick, N.J.: Transaction.
Holtfreter, Kristy, Michael D. Reisig, and Travis C. Prattt. 2008. "Low self-control, routine activities, and fraud victimization." *Criminology* 46:189-.
Hope, T. L. and C. L. Chapple. 2004. "Maternal characteristics, parenting, and adolescent sexual behavior: The role of self-control." *Deviant Behavior* 26:25–45.
Hope, T. L., H. G. Grasmick, and L. J. Pointon. 2003. "The family in Gottfredson and Hirschi's general theory of crime: Structure, parenting, and self-control= La famille dans la théorie générale de Gottfredson et Hirschi: structure, filiation et contrôle de soi." *Sociological Focus* 36:291–311.
LaGrange, T. C. and R. A. Silverman. 1999. "Low self-control and opportunity: testing the general theory of crime as an explanation for gender differences in delinquency." *Criminology* 37:41–72.
Latimore, T. L, C. R Tittle, and H. G. Grasmick. 2006. "Childrearing, self-control, and crime: Additional evidence." *Sociological Inquiry* 76:343–371.
Laub, J.H. and R.J. Sampson. 2003. *Shared Beginnings, Divergent Lives: Delinquent Boys to Age 70*. Cambridge, MA: Harvard University Press.
Longshore, D. 1998. "Self-control and criminal opportunity: a prospective test of the general theory of crime." *Social Problem* 45:102–13.
Longshore, D. and S. Turner. 1998. "Self-control and criminal opportunity: Cross-sectional test of the general theory of crime." *Criminal justice and Behaviour* 25:81–98.
Longshore, D., S. Turner, and J.A. Stein. 1996. "Self-control in a criminal sample: An examination of construct validity." *Criminology* 34:209–28.
Love, Sharon. 2006. "Illicit sexual behavior: A test of self-control theory." *Deviant Behavior* 27:505–536.
MacDonald, J.M., Haviland, A. & Morral, A.R. 2009. "Assessing the Relationship between Violent and Nonviolent Criminal Activity among Serious Adolescent Offenders." *Journal of Research in Crime and Delinquency* 46:553–580.
Marcus, B. 2003. "An empirical examination of the construct validity of two alternative self-control measures." *Educational and Psychological Measurement* 63:674–706.
Mason, W. and M. Windle. 2002. "Gender, self-control, and informal social control in adolescence." *Youth & Society* 33:479.
McGloin, J.M. & Shermer, L.O. 2009. "Self-Control and Deviant Peer Network Structure." *Journal of Research in Crime and Delinquency* 46:35–72.
Meldrum, R.C., Young, J.T.N. & Weerman, F.M. 2009. "Reconsidering the Effect of Self-Control and Delinquent Peers: Implications of Measurement for Theoretical Significance." *Journal of Research in Crime and Delinquency* 46:353–376.
Moffitt, T. E. 1993. "'Life-course persistent' and 'adolescent-limited' anti-social behavior: A developmental taxonomy." *Psychological Review* 100:674–701.
Muraven, M., Pogarsky, G. & Shmueli, D. 2006. "Self-control Depletion and the General Theory of Crime." *Journal of Quantitative Criminology* 22:263–277.
Mutchnick, R., R. Martin, and W. Timothy Austin. 2009. "Travis Hirschi." Pp. 283–326 in *Criminological Thought: Pioneers Past and Present*. Upper Saddle River, N.J.: Prentice Hall.
Nagin, D. and Ray Paternoster. 2000. "Population heterogeneity and state dependence: State of the evidence and directions for future research." *Journal of Quantitative Criminology* 16:117–44.
Nakhaie, M.R., Silverman, R.A. & LaGrange, T.C. 2000. "Self-control and Resistance to School." *CRSA/ RCSA* 37:443–460.
Nofziger, S. 2008. "The "Cause" of Low Self-Control: The Influence of Maternal Self-Control." *Journal of Research in Crime and Delinquency* 45:191–224.
Oberwittler, D. and T. Naplava. 2002. "Auswirk des Erhebungsverfahrens bei Jugendbefragungen zu 'heiklen' Themen - Schulbasierte schriftliche Befragung and haushaltbasierte muendliche Befragung im Vergleichungen." *ZUMA Nachrichten* 51:49–77.

Paternoster, Ray and Ronet Bachman. 2010. "Control theories." Pp. 114–138 in *The Sage Handbook of Criminological Theory*, edited by E. McLaughlin and T. Newburn. Los Angeles: Sage.

Paternoster, Ray and R. Brame. 1998. "The structural similarity of processes generating criminal and analogous behaviors." *Criminology* 36:633–69.

Pauwels, L and R. Svensson. 2008. "How serious is the problem of item non-response in delinquency scales and eatiological variables? A cross-national inquiry into two classroom PAPA self-report studies in Antwerp and Halmstedt." *European Journal of Criminology* 5:298–308.

Pauwels, Lieven and Robert Svensson. 2009. "Adolescent lifestyle risk by gender and ethnic background: Findings from two urban samples." *European Journal of Criminology* 6:5–24.

Perrone, D., C. J. Sullivan, T. C. Pratt, and S. Margaryan. 2004. "Parental efficacy, self-control, and delinquency: A test of a general theory of crime on a nationally representative sample of youth." *International Journal of Offender Therapy and Comparative Criminology* 48:298.

Phythian, K., C. Keane, and C. Krull. 2008. "Family structure and parental behavior: Identifying the sources of adolescent self-control." *Western Criminology Review* 9:73–87.

Piquero, A.R., MacIntosh, R. & Hickman, M. 2000. "Does Self-Control Affect Survey Response? Applying Exploratory,Confirmatory, and Item Response Theory Analysis to Grasmick et al.'s Self-Control Scale." *Criminology* 38:897–930.

Piquero, A.R., MacDonald, J., Dobrin, A., Daigle, L.E. & Cullen, F.T. 2005. "Self-Control, Violent Offending, and Homicide Victimization: Assessing the General Theory of Crime." *Journal of Quantitative Criminology* 21:55–71.

Piquero, Alex R. 2008. "Measuring self-control." Pp. 26–37 in *Out of Control: Assessing the General Theory of Crime*, edited by E. Goode. Stanford, Cal.: Stanford University Press.

Piquero, A.R. & Bouffard, J.A. 2007. "Something Old, Something New: A Preliminary Investigation of Hirschi's Redefined Self-Control." *Justice Quarterly* 24:1–27.

Piquero, A. & Tibbetts, S. 1996. "Specifying the direct and indirect effects of low self-control and situational factors in offenders' decision making: Toward a more complete model of rational offending." *Justice Quarterly* 13:481–510.

Piquero, A. R., & Rosay, A. (1998). The reliability and validity of Grasmick et al.'s self-contol scale: A comment on Longshore et al. Criminology, 36, 157–173.

Polakowski, M. 1994. "Linking self-and social control with deviance: Illuminating the structure underlying a general theory of crime and its relation to deviant activity." *Journal of Quantitative Criminology* 10:41–78.

Pratt, T.C., Turner, M.G. & Piquero, A.R. 2004. "Parental Socialization and Community Context: A Longitudinal Analysis of the Structural Sources of Low Self-Control." *Journal of Research in Crime and Delinquency* 41:219–243.

Pratt, T. C. and F. T. Cullen. 2000. "The empirical status of Gottfredson and Hirschi's general theory of crime: A meta-analysis." *Criminology* 38:931–64.

Preacher, K. J. & McCallum, R. C. (2003). Repairing Tom Swift's electric factor analysis machine. Understanding Statistics, 2, 13–43.

Rebellon, Cesar J., Murray A. Strauss, and Rose Medeiros. 2008. "Self-control in global perspective: An empirical assessment of Gottfredson and Hirschi's *General Theory* within and across 32 national settings." *European Journal of Criminology* 5:331–362.

Ribeaud, Denis and Manuel Eisner. 2006. "The 'drug-crime link' from a self-control perspective: An empirical test in a Swiss youth sample." *European Journal of Criminology* 3:33–67.

Romero, E., J.A. Gomez-Fraguela, M.A. Luengo, and J. Sobral. 2003. "The self-control construct in the General theory of Crime: An investigation in terms of personality psychology." *Psychology Crime & Law* 9:61–86.

Sampson, R. J., & Laub, J. H. (1993). Crime in the Making: Pathways and Turning Points Through Life. Cambridge, MA: Harvard University Press.

Sampson, R.J. 2006. How does community context matter? Social mechanisms and the explanation of crime. In by P. O. Wikstöm and R. J. Sampson (Eds), *The Explanation of Crime: Context, Mechanisms and Development* (pp. 31–60). Cambridge: Cambridge University Press.

Savelsberg, Joachim J. "Beyond Self-Control: Analysis and Critique of Gottfredson and Hirschi's General Theory of Crime (1990). By Stefan Schulz. Berlin: Dunker & Humblot, 2006. Pp. xix-287. (book review)." *American Journal of Sociology*:1206–1208.

Schreck, C.J. 1999. "Criminal victimization and low self-control: An extension and test of a general theory of crime." *Justice Quarterly* 16:633–654.

Schreck, C.J., Stewart, E.A. & Fisher, B.S. 2006. "Self-control, Victimization, and their Influence on Risky Lifestyles: A Longitudinal Analysis Using Panel Data." *Journal of Quantitative Criminology* 22:319–340.

Schulz, S. 2004. "Problems with the Versatility Construct of Gottfredson and Hirschi's General Theory of Crime." *European Journal of Crime, Criminal Law and Criminal Justice* 12:61–82.

Simpson, Sally. S and Gilbert Geis. 2008. "The undeveloped concept of opportunity." Pp. 49–60 in *Out of Control: Assessing the General Theory of Crime*, edited by E. Goode. Stanford, Cal.: Stanford University Press.

Taylor, T.J., Peterson, D., Esbensen, F. & Freng, A. 2007. "Gang Membership as a Risk Factor for Adolescent Violent Victimization." *Journal of Research in Crime and Delinquency* 44:351–380.

Title, C. R. 1991. "Review of a General Theory of Crime." *American Journal of Sociology* 96:1609–1611.

Title, C. R., David A. Ward, and H. G. Grasmick. 2003. "Self-control and crime/deviance: Cognitive vs behavioral measures." *Journal of Quantitative Criminology* 19:333–366.

Tittle, C.R., Ward, D.A. & Grasmick, H.G. 2003. "Gender, Age, and Crime/Deviance: A Challenge to Self-Control Theory." *Journal of Research in Crime and Delinquency* 40:426–453.

—2003. "Self-control and Crime/Deviance: Cognitive vs. Behavioral Measures." *Journal of Quantitative Criminology* 19:333–365.

—2004. "Capacity for Self-Control and Individuals' Interest in Exercising Self-Control." *Journal of Quantitative Criminology* 20:143–172.

Unnever, J.D., Cullen, F.T. & Pratt, T.C. 2003. "Parental management, ADHD, and delinquent involvement: Reassessing Gottfredson and Hirschi's general theory." *Justice Quarterly* 20:471–500.

Vazsonyi, A.T., Pickering, L.E., Junger, M. & Hessing, D. 2001. "An Empirical Test of a General Theory of Crime: A Four-Nation Comparative Study of Self-Control and the Prediction of Deviance." *Journal of Research in Crime and Delinquency* 38:91–131.

Vazsonyi, A.T & Crosswhite, J.M. 2004. "A Test of Gottfredson and Hirschi'S General Theory of Crime in African American Adolescents." *Journal of Research in Crime and Delinquency* 41:407–432.

Watkins, A.M. & Melde, C. 2007. "The Effect of Self-Control on Unit and Item Nonresponse in an Adolescent Sample." *Journal of Research in Crime and Delinquency* 44:267–294.

Welch, M.R., Tittle, C.R., Yonkoski, J., Meidinger, N. & Grasmick, H.G. 2008. "Social Integration, Self-control, and Conformity." *Journal of Quantitative Criminology* 24:73–92.

Wikstöm, P.O. and Svenssson R. 2008. "Why are English youth more violent than Swedish youth? A comparative study of the role of crime propensity, lifestyles and their interaction in two cities." *European Journal of Criminology* 5:309–330.

Wikstöm, Per-Olof H. 2007. "The role of self-control in crime causation: Beyond Gottfredson and Hirschi's *General Theory of Crime*." *European Journal of Criminology* 4.

Wright, B., Caspi, A., Moffitt, T. & Silva, P. 1999. "Low Self-control, Social Bonds, and Crime: Social Causation, Social Selection, or Both?" *Criminology* 37:479–514.

Wright, J., Beaver, K., Delisi, M. & Vaughn, M. 2008. "Evidence of Negligible Parenting Influences on Self-Control, Delinquent Peers, and Delinquency in a Sample of Twins." *Justice Quarterly* 25:544–569.

Part IV
Theoretical and Policy Implications

Chapter 12
Concluding Observations: The Big Picture

Josine Junger-Tas, Dirk Enzmann, Majone Steketee, and Ineke Haen Marshall

This final chapter wants to accomplish three objectives. First, we provide an overview of the main findings of the study. Then, in order to place our findings in a wider theoretical context, we report on the results of a multilevel analysis of the data. The central question in the multilevel analysis is to determine if there are similarities or differences between the ISRD countries in terms of the influence of the variables associated with the four main theoretical perspectives utilized in this study. The third part of the chapter speculates about the implications of our study, both theoretically as well as from the perspective of policy.

12.1 Nature and Extent of Delinquency, Victimization, Substance Use, and Social Control

The highest *level of delinquency* is found in the wealthiest countries: the Anglo-Saxon, W-European, and N-European clusters, whereas the Mediterranean, Post-Socialist, and Latin-American clusters have clearly lower levels (Chap. 3). On the whole, differences in delinquency between clusters refer essentially to property offenses and much less so to violence where there is more intercountry variation. A persistent finding throughout the study is that among the three richest clusters, Northern Europe has a significantly lower delinquency level than the other two clusters, in particular, a lower violence level. The age of onset in offending is remarkably similar, with the Latin American cluster having overall a slightly higher age of onset. Shoplifting and vandalism have the lowest age of onset, whereas the age of onset of serious offenses is higher. Although in all clusters girls commit significantly fewer offenses than boys, there is a wide variation in the type of disparity. In Northern Europe, Western Europe, Mediterranean Europe, and Latin America

D. Enzmann (✉)
University of Hamburg, Hamburg, Germany
e-mail: dirk.enzmann@uni-hamburg.de

J. Junger-Tas et al., *The Many Faces of Youth Crime: Contrasting Theoretical Perspectives on Juvenile Delinquency across Countries and Cultures*,
DOI 10.1007/978-1-4419-9455-4_12, © Springer Science+Business Media, LLC 2012

the disparity between the sexes follows a parallel course with increasing age, whereas in the Anglo-Saxon and Post-Socialist clusters the disparity increases with age. These variations suggest that part of the gender differences in delinquency must be influenced by differential cultural and social–economic conditions in participating countries.

A second important aspect is *victimization* (Chap. 4). About 27% of young people have been victims of offenses, of which 20% involved theft and 7.5% involved a violent offense – robbery or assault. Moreover, 14% of the youth reported having been the victim of bullying (verbal or physical harassment or exclusion). Violent victimization rates are highest in the Post-Socialist-, Latin American-, and Anglo-Saxon cluster and lowest in Northern Europe, followed by Western Europe. This does confirm a general finding in victimology, which is that income inequality and widespread poverty are important correlates of violent crime, such as threats, assault, and robbery. As for gender, in cases of theft or bullying there is no gender difference, but boys are more often victims of violent offenses. More generally, the association between victimization and delinquency is stronger in relation to violent offenses than to property offenses. Victimization risk of juveniles aged 12–16 is only moderate at best, which may be related to a rather homogeneous lifestyle, all juveniles being still subject to compulsory education.

The third descriptive chapter (Chap. 5) refers to *substance use*, which is defined as "problem" behavior, in view of the diverging legislation on this subject in participating countries. The prevalence of alcohol use is quite high: 60% had "ever" consumed alcohol and 28% had drunk alcohol in the past month. However, in most cases alcohol use refers to beer or wine, only one-third having "ever" consumed hard liquor and 13% having drunk hard liquor in the past month. Contrary to alcohol use, which is after all a culturally accepted custom, drug use – mainly soft drugs – is reported by 10% "ever" and 4% in the past month. The rates for hard drugs are respectively 2 and 0.8%. In addition, 40% of the total sample had never used any substance. The highest alcohol consumption was found in the Post-Socialist cluster, with the exception of Bosnia, a Muslim country. In Mediterranean-Europe most alcohol is consumed during mealtimes, whereas in other countries most use takes place when young people go out at night. Indeed, the highest rates of being drunk on alcohol were found in the Post-Socialist cluster and the lowest in Mediterranean Europe. Interestingly, in all clusters there is hardly any gender difference in the use of alcohol. Where the use of hashish is concerned this is also true in the Anglo-Saxon and Northern European clusters, but in the other clusters boys consume about two times as much as do girls. Problematic drinking, in particular so-called binge-drinking (consuming five glasses or more on an evening) is frequent in Western Europe and in the Anglo-Saxon cluster (in particular in Ireland), all mainly beer-consuming countries. As for ethnicity, those who are born in a European country have a similar consumption pattern as the host country, while those who have immigrated from Asia, Africa, or Turkey have lower alcohol consumption. Drinking hard liquor and the use of hashish are highly correlated with serious delinquency.

With regard to the *social reactions to offending and victimization* (Chap. 6), 36% of all offenses were detected by parents, teachers, or the police. Parents detected twice as much as the police (21.4 vs. 11.4%). Police detection depends on the seriousness of the offense and the frequency of offending, so that those who are known to the police run a higher risk of being arrested. Other factors in this respect are having delinquent friends, substance abuse, and truancy. Parents detect more offenses in small cities than in large cities, suggesting more parental supervision and social control in small than in large cities. Moreover, parents discover their daughters' offenses considerably more often than those of their sons, indicating tighter control on girls than on boys, a finding that is confirmed in Chap. 7 on the family. Teachers want primarily an orderly and quiet class so that undisturbed teaching can go on. Therefore they tend to detect violent offenses rather than property offenses. From the perspective of the offender, the overall risk of being punished is 20%, but the risk of being punished if found out is more than twice as high (43.5%). Once detected, the highest punishment rate is for shoplifting (59.4%) and serious violent acts (48.2%). Comparing country clusters shows that there are sizable differences in punishment rates, the most punitive in this sense are the Anglo-Saxon cluster and Northern Europe, the least punitive are Mediterranean Europe and the Post-Socialist clusters. Furthermore, in all clusters punishment rates are higher for property offenses than for violent offenses, suggesting that a higher value is attached to the transgression of property than to violation of a person.

12.2 Substantive Findings About Family, School, Leisure Time, Neighborhood, and Self-control

The next part of the book examined important aspects of young peoples' life and tested different hypotheses explaining delinquent and other problem behaviour. (See Chap. 1 and Sect. 12.3 for a brief discussion of the different theoretical perspectives used.)

Family: Considering social background variables, both *family affluence* and parents' *employment* are only weakly correlated with delinquency (see Chap. 7). Family affluence as well as neighborhood cohesion are both positively related to family bonding, suggesting that material welfare has a positive influence on family life. In all clusters, single parents are considerably more likely to be unemployed, in particular in the more prosperous clusters, such as the Anglo Saxon cluster, Northern Europe, and Western Europe. Family structure differs substantially between clusters, the highest percentage of intact marriages being found in Mediterranean Europe (84%) – traditionally Catholic countries –, whereas the Latin American countries (58%) and Northern Europe (64%) have the lowest percentage of such marriages. Although Northern Europe has high divorce rates, many parents agree to share parenthood, whereas in Latin American countries there is a high number of mother only families. Family structure is related to delinquency in that being raised in a family with two biological parents is the most favorable situation, contrary to all other family arrangements.

Attachment to parents and parental control are important in successfully socializing children, but so are social support, intimate communication, and sharing activities.

Frequently spending leisure activities with parents is associated with getting along with father and mother and also with parental control. In all six clusters, family leisure has the highest correlation with parental control. Parental control has a high negative association with versatility,[1] but leisure activities moderate that impact. Our study supports social control theory, but not without qualifications. Emotional and instrumental parental support, intimate communication, and sharing activities are as important in affecting a child's behaviour as parental control.

In all ISRD countries, parents exercise more controls over their daughters than over their sons. Compared to boys, girls tend to spend also more leisure time with the family or with a small group of one to three friends. The contribution of family disruption and family *bonding* to delinquency is greater in the case of girls than in the case of boys, who are more sensitive to parental *control*. Girls score also higher than boys on self-control and lower on a positive attitude to violence.

Considering family life among immigrant groups, there is little difference in family disruption and in family *bonding* between immigrant groups and native-born youth, although living conditions of the former are worse than those of the latter in terms of employment, family affluence, and the neighborhood they live in. Immigrant youths do differ, however, in parental *supervision*, which is clearly lower than among native families. Since parental control is associated with delinquency, this goes a long way in explaining the higher delinquency rates of second-generation immigrants.

School: Repeating classes goes together with a growing lack of interest in school and is related to the absence of plans for future steps in their career (see Chap. 8). Youths who have future plans are more likely to attend well-organized schools, have a positive bond with school, and like school, whereas those who attend disorganized schools do not like school and tend to be truant more often. Although girls repeat classes and skip school as often as boys do, they have stronger bonds with school and like school better. This shows in particular in girls' plans for further education: considerably more girls than boys report that they intend to continue their education, whereas many boys want to leave school and find a job. As for ethnicity, first generation migrants repeat classes and are truant more often than natives. Second generation immigrants do better than first generation, although they tend to choose more often than natives a vocational training school instead of a higher form of education.

The strongest factor explaining serious delinquency is *truancy*, followed by attending a disorganized school, and not liking school. Those who have to repeat a class, fail to make plans for their future, which suggests an unsatisfying school career. Consequently they are more often truant, or leave school, starting to look for employment early. This is in agreement with Hirschi (1969), who stated that when youngsters are no longer attached to society – in this case a social institution such as school – they feel no longer the need to observe conventional norms and values and, since they have nothing to lose, they are free to break the law and commit offenses.

---

[1] Versatility is the sum of prevalences of 12 offenses (see Chapter 2, Sect. 2.6.1.1).

The existence of a *tracking system* is also of influence on the performance of students, in that high-ability students in a tracking system tend to perform better than comparable students in a nontracked system. On the other hand lower class kids and ethnic minorities are said to be over-represented in low tracks and they tend to fail more often, drop out of school, and misbehave more often than higher track students. All West European countries possess a tracking system, including Italy, the Czech Republic, and Hungary. Young people attending disorganized schools are three times more likely to commit serious violent offenses than youths attending well-organized schools. The existence of a tracking system, disorganized schools, and a high heterogeneity of intellectual performance are the most significant variables related to serious violent offenses. Gender, school disorganization, and attachment to school are the best predictors of property offenses. Contrary to what is generally assumed, the analysis (Chap. 8) emphasizes the importance of structural characteristics of school systems rather than individual features of students in producing problem behaviour.

Peers and lifestyle: A major determinant of young people's lifestyle and behaviour is unsupervised time spent with their friends when going out (see Chap. 9). Almost a quarter of the sample reported that they go out more often than they spend time at home and about 10% go out every evening. The likelihood of committing a serious offense among those who go out at least three times a week is six times higher than among those who do not go out as often. In Anglo-Saxon countries, young people spend more time with their peer group – and have more opportunities of offending – than in Mediterranean Europe and Latin America where they spend more time with the family. Generally, girls do not offend more often in groups than boys, except for shoplifting (girls 70% vs. boys 64%).

Asked about friends who have committed one or more of five offenses (using drugs, shoplifting, breaking and entering, threats with violence, beating someone up), about 20% declared their friends had committed one such act, 10% reported their friends had committed two- and 10% reported their friends had committed three such acts. Perhaps not surprising, the more delinquent the acts committed by friends, the more offenses the juveniles commit themselves. But they also tend to commit similar offenses as their friends: if the latter commit shoplifting, they are also more likely to shoplift themselves; this is also the case for burglary and assault. The study also tried to measure the degree of gang involvement of youth, but these questions created some confusion in European countries. A number of youths, who hardly committed any offenses, apparently defined "gang" simply as a social group to hang out with. It is probably better to define gangs as "troublesome or delinquent youth groups." Going out frequently, hanging out with friends, and a risky lifestyle are all correlated with delinquency involvement. Furthermore, those who identified themselves as gang members are more involved in delinquency and they commit also more different types of offenses.

Neighborhood: The role of the neighborhood in producing delinquency has been an important element in the analyses of the ISRD-2 material (see Chap. 10). Well-integrated neighborhoods are distinguished from disorganized ones according to answers of the respondents themselves to such statements as: "this is a close-knit neighbourhood," "people in this neighbourhood can be trusted" or "there are a lot of empty and abandoned buildings in my neighbourhood," "there is a lot of fighting; crime; drug-selling in my neighbourhood." Responses to these items were used to test aspects of social disorganization theory. High neighborhood cohesion and low neighborhood disorganization are found in Northern Europe, followed by Western-Europe, whereas most disorganized neighborhoods are found in Latin America and the Anglo-Saxon cluster. Disorganized neighborhoods are characterized by the family head's unemployment, low family affluence, single parent families, and population heterogeneity. Our analyses showed a persistent rather strong effect of neighborhood disorganization on delinquency involvement with a moderate effect of family variables, in particular parental control. This pattern is similar in all clusters.

Young people in deprived neighborhoods are also attending substandard schools, where there is much fighting, vandalizing, and stealing each other's possessions. Such students more often are truant, repeat grades, have a low degree of school bonding and are more involved in serious delinquency. Comparing the impact of family variables with that of school variables, showed that the impact of neighborhood disorganization decreased more by adding school- than family variables, whereas explained variance in the case of adding school variables is greater. These outcomes do suggest a stronger impact of the school than of the family on adolescent behavior.

Most young people – some 75–80% – whether they live in cohesive or disorganized neighborhoods spend leisure with a peer group. However, those youth living in disorganized neighborhoods have more delinquent friends than the former. Moreover the higher the degree of neighborhood disorganization, the higher the number of juveniles committing serious offenses, even among those without delinquent friends. However, we found significant interaction effects of neighborhood disorganization with deviant peer groups: the effect of delinquent friends is stronger in the more disorganized neighborhoods. Finally, in countries with high levels of delinquency, the influence of the neighborhood on serious delinquency is less important than in countries with a low level of delinquency, where the influence of a disorganized neighborhood is stronger.

Self-control: The shorter version of the Grasmick et al. (1993) scale, when tested on the total sample, country clusters, as well as in individual countries, generally speaking performed quite well (see Chap. 11). Our analysis confirmed the existence of four distinct subscales corresponding to theoretical expectations (i.e., Risk-Taking, Self-Centeredness, Impulsivity, and Volatile Temperament); when employing second-order factor analyses, the Self-Control scale was shown to be one-dimensional; the reliability (alpha) was good under all conditions; and the SC scale had a significant correlation with a behavioral measure (i.e., accident proneness). We also found that the mean SC values differ significantly between the country clusters: the Northern European cluster (66.9) averages ten points above the Anglo-Saxon cluster (56.5) and nine points above the postsocialist cluster (57.7). Neighborhood disorganization, parental supervision, and family bonding, gender, and country cluster are the five strongest predictors of self-control: The lowest levels of self-control are found among boys from Anglo-Saxon and Postsocialist countries, living in disorganized neighborhoods, with little parental supervision and low attachment to parents. Self-control has an effect on delinquency, but we also found that the effects of gender and opportunities are actually stronger than the main effect of self-control. Importantly with self-control: opportunities matter more for those with low self-control than for those with high self-control.

12.3 Testing the Cross-National Generalizability of Different Theoretical Perspectives

The ISRD-2 survey includes questions designed to test four theoretical perspectives: social bonding/social control theory, self-control theory, routine activities/opportunity theory, and social disorganization theory. The analyses presented in Chaps. 7, 8, 9, and 10 have attempted to assess different components of these perspectives, through focus on family (Chap. 7), schools (Chap. 8), lifestyle (Chap. 9), and neighborhoods (Chap. 10). Chapter 11 had an explicit theoretical focus on self-control theory. In these analyses, we made use of a large number of different variables – measuring family, school, neighborhood, lifestyle, and opportunities (see Chap. 2 for a more extensive discussion of these variables), sometimes including variables from other perspectives as well. Not surprisingly, we found that some variables and scales perform much better than others. In this section, we want to take advantage of the empirical results of the analyses reported in the preceding chapters by capitalizing on those variables that have been shown to be most important.

An important aspect of the analyses in the preceding chapters was to assess the cross-national validity of different approaches to explain delinquent behavior of juveniles. Major theoretical assumptions were confirmed by collapsing the samples of 30 countries into one big dataset. However, by collapsing the data the models thus far assumed identical effects of theoretically important variables across countries and cultures. Nevertheless, it is conceivable that there are significant national or regional variations in the associations of delinquency with theoretical variables. In order to take full advantage of the comparative nature of our study, in the following we will explicitly take into account the possible variability of delinquency and its theoretical correlates at the level of countries. Therefore, we will report on the results of multilevel models using 26 ISRD nations[2] to achieve the following objectives:

1. Determining if the associations between these predictors and delinquency are similar between countries (i.e., testing the generalizability of the findings) by investigating (a) the variability of delinquency on the country level, and (b) whether the effects of theoretically relevant predictors differ between countries.

[2] Because macro level indicators were not available for Aruba, Cyprus, the Netherlands Antilles, and Suriname, these countries will be dropped from the following analyses. One should note that 26 countries is a relatively small number of higher level units in a multilevel analysis.

2. Analyzing the effects of macro (country) level national characteristics (e.g., Human Development Index, or self-expression values based on the World Values Survey) (a) on delinquency (controlling for individual level predictors), and (b) exploring whether macro level characteristics may explain differences of the effects of individual level predictors between countries.

The variability of delinquency on the country level (1a) will be investigated by employing multilevel models with a random intercept. Selecting the most important predictors of delinquency of the four theoretical approaches, the question whether the effects differ between countries (1b) will be investigated by employing multilevel models with random slopes. Multilevel models including macro level predictors will be used to investigate whether the variability of delinquency on the country level can be explained by characteristics of the countries (2a). Allowing interactions of macro level predictors with individual level predictors (2b) will show whether differences in the effects of individual level predictors can be explained by characteristics of the countries.

To assess the effects of predictors on delinquency, we use *versatility* as the dependent variable. In our view, those kids who are involved in a relatively wide range of delinquent acts are of most theoretical and policy relevance, rather than their counterparts who only commit one or two different delinquent acts. Therefore, we defined as the delinquent group those youth who reported *three or more different delinquent acts during the last year*. Because the dependent variable is dichotomous, multilevel logistic regression models will be employed throughout this chapter.

12.3.1 Background Variables as Control Variables

The reference model (Model 0: Random intercept model) is an "empty model," that estimates the unexplained variability of delinquency (i.e., versatility) between countries. Results show that there is significant variability between countries (intercept variance $u_0=0.319$, $p<0.001$; intraclass correlation $r_{icc}=0.088$; median odds ratio = 1.715), justifying the application of multilevel modeling. The first model (Model 1) contains only background variables that will serve as controls in subsequent analyses: Grade, gender, and migrant status (Table 12.1).

All of the background variables in the first model are significant: Versatility increases significantly with grade (as a proxy for age), the odds of males to show versatile delinquent behavior are 246% higher than that of females (odds ratio = 3.46), and juveniles with migration background (first and second generation) are more likely to be delinquent (i.e., versatile) than natives (odds ratio = 1.39). The effects of Model 1 may be generalized across countries, because the effects of gender and migration status do not differ between countries, as shown by nonsignificant random slopes (RS, indicated as u_1 in the two last columns of Table 12.1).[3]

[3] Likewise, the effect of grade does not differ between countries (random effects not shown).

Table 12.1 Effects of control variables on versatility (Model 1)

	Null model	M1: Control	RS: Gender	RS: Migrant status
Grade (base: Grade 7)		$\chi^2_{(2)}=106.3$***	$\chi^2_{(2)}=106.3$***	$\chi^2_{(2)}=106.2$***
Grade 8		1.514*** (7.53)	1.515*** (7.53)	1.515*** (7.53)
Grade 9		1.721*** (10.15)	1.721*** (10.16)	1.720*** (10.14)
Gender (base: female)		3.457*** (26.32)	3.449*** (17.20)	3.459*** (26.32)
Migrant status (base: native)		1.391*** (6.87)	1.391*** (6.87)	1.360*** (4.86)
−2*LL	−10,108.9	−9,632.1	−9,632.6	−9,631.3
var(u_0)	0.319***	0.287***	0.291***	0.290***
var(u_1)			0.004	0.025

Exponentiated coefficients (odds ratios); z statistics in parentheses; cov(u_0, u_1) set to zero; significance of random effect u_1 tested via likelihood-ratio test
*$p<0.05$; **$p<0.01$; ***$p<0.001$

However, although the individual level effects of grade, gender, and migration status are significant, reducing the deviance (or log likelihood) significantly (LR $\text{Chi}^2_{(4)}=953.7$, $p<0.001$), the introduction of the control variables does not substantially change the unexplained between country variability of versatility ($u_0=0.287$).

12.3.2 Social Bonding and Social Control Theory

The basic postulate of this perspective is that strong bonds to the major social institutions will prevent delinquency. The family is viewed as the most significant institution in this view. As was shown in Chap. 7, two robust ISRD measures of family are the *family bonding* scale and *parental supervision*. Therefore, we will use these two variables in our analysis. The school is also of crucial importance in social bonding theory. Interestingly, our original measure of school bonding turned out to be less important than truancy. Skipping schools also may be viewed as an indicator of a lack of attachment to school; therefore, we use *truancy* as one of our measures of school bonding. The level of *school disorganization* – also a good predictor of delinquency – may be viewed as a measure of a (lack of perceived) social control on the youth. We decided to use this somewhat unorthodox variable as our second measure of social control related to the school.

In Model 2, we have added family bonding and parental supervision. As Table 12.2 shows, adding these variables to the model lowers the effect for all background variables with the exception of gender (male). This can be explained by the fact that in all countries there is more social control of girls than of boys (see Chap. 7), independent of the overall level of parental bonding or supervision. Family bonding and parental supervision show a strong negative effect on versatility, reducing the deviance or the log likelihood significantly (LR $\text{Chi}^2_{(2)}=1{,}727.8$, $p<0.001$), but they do not account for the differences in versatility between the countries (unexplained country level variance $u_0=0.351$ vs. 0.287). Testing random slope models

Table 12.2 Predicting versatility (0–2 vs. 3+) with family variables (Model 2)

	Null model	M1: Control		M2: Family		RS: Family bonding		RS: Parental supervision	
Grade (base: grade 7)		$\chi^2_{(2)}=106.3$***		$\chi^2_{(2)}=36.6$***		$\chi^2_{(2)}=36.5$***		$\chi^2_{(2)}=36.1$***	
Grade 8		1.514***	(7.53)	1.336***	(5.10)	1.336***	(5.10)	1.337***	(5.12)
Grade 9		1.721***	(10.15)	1.368***	(5.65)	1.367***	(5.63)	1.363***	(5.58)
Gender (base: female)		3.457***	(26.32)	3.506***	(25.59)	3.510***	(25.59)	3.511***	(25.60)
Migrant status (base: native)		1.391***	(6.87)	1.224***	(4.03)	1.224***	(4.03)	1.229***	(4.11)
Family bonding (*z*-score)				0.666***	(–21.37)	0.665***	(–18.03)	0.667***	(–21.29)
Parental supervision (*z*-score)				0.573***	(–28.66)	0.573***	(–28.61)	0.566***	(–21.62)
–2**LL*	–10,108.9	–9,632.1		–8,768.2		–8,768.1		–8,765.5	
var(u_0)	0.319***	0.287***		0.351***		0.349***		0.357***	
var(u_1)						0.003		0.006*	

Exponentiated coefficients; *z* statistics in parentheses; cov(u_0, u_1) set to zero; significance of random effect u_1 tested via likelihood-ratio test
*$p<0.05$; **$p<0.01$; ***$p<0.001$

allows to determine if the effects of these two family variables are similar for all countries. Although the effects of family bonding do not differ significantly between the countries, there are significant differences of the effects of parental supervision (LR $Chi^2_{(1)} = 5.32$, conservative $p = 0.021$).

Regarding the school variables, we know that the strongest contribution to explaining serious delinquency is provided by truancy, followed by disorganized schools. Model 3 (Table 12.3) shows that being truant increases the odds of being a versatile delinquent (three or more different offenses) by 359% (odds ratio = 4.59). As expected, school disorganization is also a significant predictor of versatility (odds ratio = 1.85). Although these factors do matter on an individual level (LR $Chi^2_{(2)} = 2{,}373.9$, $p < 0.001$), they do not explain the country differences in versatility. To the contrary, including the school factors increases the estimated variance at the country level ($u_0 = 0.398$ instead of 0.287).[4] Whereas the effects of school disorganization on versatility clearly do not differ significantly between countries, differences as to the effects of truancy are close to significance (LR $Chi^2_{(1)} = 4.71$, conservative $p = 0.030$).

In Model 4, both family variables and school variables are added into the model (Table 12.4), jointly both variables improve the model fit significantly (LR $Chi^2_{(2)} = 873.6$, $p < 0.001$). When adding these variables, the effects of the background variables grade and migrant status decrease. Truancy remains the strongest predictor of versatility (odds ratio: 3.50), but school disorganization also remains a risk factor for delinquent behavior of juveniles in this model. Compared to Model 2, the negative effects of family bonding and parental supervision are somewhat reduced; compared to school disorganization and truancy, they are smaller (supervision: 1/1.54; bonding: 1/1.35). When testing the differences of the effects of parental supervision across countries in this model, the random slope falls short of significance (LR $Chi^2_{(1)} = 2.87$, conservative $p = 0.090$); the effects of truancy, however, differ significantly by country (LR $Chi^2_{(1)} = 4.84$, conservative $p = 0.028$). In sum, with respect to the effects of family, this model is generalizable across countries and supports the basic claims of social bonding/social control theory, although the school variables show stronger effects than the family variables, and the effects of truancy differ by countries.

12.3.3 Self-control Theory

The major proposition of self-control theory claims that low self-control is a main determinant of delinquency. We found that the 12-item *Self-control Scale* (based on Grasmick et al. 1993) is a reliable and arguably valid comparative measure of self-control. The multilevel analysis includes the SC scale as the measure to test self-control theory. In Model 5 (Table 12.5), we examine the effect of self-control on versatility, including controls for background variables. Self-control has a large positive effect on last year versatility (odds ratio = 0.30 = 1/3.33). Youth with low levels of self-control are more likely to be versatile delinquents than their counterparts

[4] The increase is a methodological artifact specific to multilevel logistic regression, see Hox (2010, pp. 133–139).

Table 12.3 Predicting versatility (0–2 vs. 3+) and school variables (Model 3)

	Null model	M1: Control	M3: School	RS: School disorganization	RS: Truancy
Grade (base: grade 7)		$\chi^2_{(2)}=106.3$***	$\chi^2_{(2)}=27.0$***	$\chi^2_{(2)}=27.0$***	$\chi^2_{(2)}=27.4$***
Grade 8		1.514*** (7.53)	1.299*** (4.55)	1.300*** (4.55)	1.297*** (4.52)
Grade 9		1.721*** (10.15)	1.305*** (4.73)	1.305*** (4.73)	1.311*** (4.81)
Gender (base: female)		3.457*** (26.32)	3.308*** (24.54)	3.314*** (24.54)	3.318*** (24.56)
Migrant status (base: native)		1.391*** (6.87)	1.181** (3.27)	1.182** (3.28)	1.182*** (3.28)
School disorganization (*z*-score)			1.845*** (29.00)	1.838*** (24.22)	1.849*** (29.04)
Truancy (base: no)			4.585*** (32.87)	4.591*** (32.87)	4.709*** (23.97)
–2**LL*	–10,108.9	–9,632.1	–8,445.1	–8,445.1	–8,442.8
var(u_0)	0.319***	0.287***	0.398***	0.399***	0.399***
var(u_1)				0.003	0.040*

Exponentiated coefficients; *z* statistics in parentheses; cov(u_0, u_1) set to zero; significance of random effect u_1 tested via likelihood-ratio test
*$p<0.05$; **$p<0.01$; ***$p<0.001$

Table 12.4 Predicting versatility (0–2 vs. 3+) with family and school variables (Model 4)

	Null model	M1: Control	M4: Family + School	RS: Parental supervision	RS: Truancy
Grade (base: grade 7)		$\chi^2_{(2)} = 106.3$***	$\chi^2_{(2)} = 12.1$**	$\chi^2_{(2)} = 12.1$**	$\chi^2_{(2)} = 12.1$**
Grade 8		1.514*** (7.53)	1.221*** (3.41)	1.222*** (3.41)	1.220*** (3.38)
Grade 9		1.721*** (10.15)	1.163** (2.62)	1.160** (2.56)	1.168**
Gender (base: female)		3.457*** (26.32)	3.436*** (24.43)	3.440*** (24.43)	3.448*** (24.45)
Migrant status (base: native)		1.391*** (6.87)	1.128* (2.31)	1.129* (2.34)	1.130* (2.34)
Family bonding (*z*-score)			0.743*** (–15.00)	0.743*** (–14.96)	0.742*** (–15.00)
Parental supervision (*z*-score)			0.649*** (–21.25)	0.643*** (–16.74)	0.649*** (–21.24)
School disorganization (*z*-score)			1.712*** (24.71)	1.713*** (24.70)	1.715*** (24.76)
Truancy (base: no)			3.502*** (26.20)	3.505*** (26.19)	3.607*** (19.09)
–2**LL*	–10,108.9	–9,632.1	–8,008.3	–8,006.9	–8,005.9
var(u_0)	0.319	0.287	0.405	0.413	0.407
var(u_1)				0.005	0.044*

Exponentiated coefficients; *z* statistics in parentheses; cov(u_0, u_1) set to zero; significance of random effect u_1 tested via likelihood-ratio test
*$p < 0.05$; **$p < 0.01$; ***$p < 0.001$

Table 12.5 Predicting versatility (0–2 vs. 3+) by self-control (Model 5)

	Null model	M1: Control		M5: Self-control		RS: Self-control	
Grade		$\chi^2_{(2)}=106.3$***		$\chi^2_{(2)}=83.0$***		$\chi^2_{(2)}=82.4$***	
(base: grade 7)							
Grade 8		1.514***	(7.53)	1.423***	(6.03)	1.424***	(6.02)
Grade 9		1.721***	(10.15)	1.675***	(9.08)	1.674***	(9.04)
Gender (base: female)		3.457***	(26.32)	2.935***	(21.79)	2.948***	(21.82)
Migrant status (base: native)		1.391***	(6.87)	1.244***	(4.21)	1.245***	(4.21)
Self-control (z-score)				0.300***	(–52.03)	0.302***	(–37.75)
–2*LL	–10,108.9	–9,632.1		–8,015.4		–8,013.2	
var(u_0)	0.319	0.287		0.421		0.380	
var(u_1)						0.010*	

Exponentiated coefficients; z statistics in parentheses; cov(u_0, u_1) set to zero; significance of random effect u_1 tested via likelihood-ratio test
*$p<0.05$; **$p<0.01$; ***$p<0.001$

with higher levels of self-control. Including self-control into the model improves the model fit considerably (LR $\text{Chi}^2_{(1)}=3{,}233.3$, $p<0.001$), the effects of background variables are somewhat reduced. The random slope model shows that the effects of self-control differ between the countries (LR $\text{Chi}^2_{(2)}=4.35$, conservative $p=0.037$).

12.3.4 Routine Activities/Opportunity Theory

This perspective, broadly defined (including lifestyle theory), stresses the importance of situational factors to explain delinquency. Our analyses included a number of variables, including gang membership, types of leisure time activities, and deviant peers. We found that *lifestyle* and *deviant peers* are the most significant predictors of delinquency. In our analysis, we assess opportunity/routine activities theory by using these two variables in the multilevel analysis. Table 12.6 shows a strong relationship between having delinquent friends and versatility (odds ratio = 10.5). But the lifestyle of juveniles also has a large effect (odds ratio = 2.88). Adding lifestyle to the model improves the model fit substantially (LR $\text{Chi}^2_{(2)}=4{,}275.2$, $p<0.001$), at the same time the net effect of grade (a proxy for age) is greatly reduced. Youth having a lifestyle of spending a lot of time with a large group of friends, going out at night quite often, or spending leisure time in public places are more likely to be versatile delinquents. Model 6 further suggests that opportunities (the combination of lifestyle and delinquent friends) accounts for some of the variance in versatility between the countries, reducing the unexplained variance on the level of countries ($u_0=0.199$ vs. 0.287). A model that accounts for random effects, thus taking into account possible differences of the effects of lifestyle or delinquent friends across countries, does not fit significantly better to the data, showing that this model is generalizable across countries.

Table 12.6 Predicting versatility (0–2 vs. 3+) with opportunity variables (Model 6)

	Null model	M1: Control	M6: Opportunities	RS: Lifestyle	RS: Delinquency friends
Grade (base: grade 7)		$\chi^2_{(2)}=106.3$***	$\chi^2_{(2)}=7.5$*	$\chi^2_{(2)}=7.6$*	$\chi^2_{(2)}=7.5$*
Grade 8		1.514*** (7.53)	1.168** (2.61)	1.169** (2.62)	1.168** (2.61)
Grade 9		1.721*** (10.15)	1.137* (2.22)	1.138* (2.23)	1.137* (2.22)
Gender (base: female)		3.457*** (26.32)	3.579*** (25.67)	3.580*** (25.66)	3.581*** (25.67)
Migrant status (base: native)		1.391*** (6.87)	1.238*** (4.06)	1.238*** (4.05)	1.238*** (4.06)
Lifestyle (z-score)			2.877*** (34.60)	2.880*** (32.49)	2.877*** (34.59)
Delinquency friends (base: no)			10.46*** (35.21)	10.47*** (35.21)	10.52*** (32.38)
$-2*LL$	–10,108.9	–9,632.1	–7,494.4	–7,494.5	–7,494.4
var(u_0)	0.319	0.287	0.199	0.198	0.194
var(u_1)				0.002	0.014

Exponentiated coefficients; z statistics in parentheses; cov(u_0, u_1) set to zero; significance of random effect u_1 tested via likelihood-ratio test

*$p<0.05$; **$p<0.01$; ***$p<0.001$

Table 12.7 Predicting versatility (0–2 vs. 3+) by opportunities and self-control (Model 7)

	Null model	M1: Control		M7: Self-control + opportunities		RS: Self-control	
Grade (base: grade 7)		$\chi^2_{(2)}=106.3$***		$\chi^2_{(2)}=12.5$**		$\chi^2_{(2)}=12.5$**	
Grade 8		1.514***	(7.53)	1.169*	(2.52)	1.170*	(2.53)
Grade 9		1.721***	(10.15)	1.234***	(3.49)	1.234***	(3.49)
Gender (base: female)		3.457***	(26.32)	3.243***	(22.82)	3.259***	(22.84)
Migrant status (base: native)		1.391***	(6.87)	1.182**	(3.03)	1.184**	(3.06)
Lifestyle (*z*-score)				2.436***	(20.56)	2.454***	(20.57)
Delinquency friends (base: no)				7.639***	(29.82)	7.650***	(29.82)
Self-control (*z*-score)				0.379***	(–27.73)	0.377***	(–22.40)
Self-control* lifestyle (*z*-scores)				1.073*	(2.21)	1.079*	(2.36)
–2*LL	–10,108.9	–9,632.1		–6,797.7		–6,795.2	
var(u_0)	0.319***	0.287***		0.244***		0.231**	
var(u_1)						0.014*	

Exponentiated coefficients; *z* statistics in parentheses; cov(u_0, u_1) set to zero; significance of random effect u_1 tested via likelihood-ratio test
*$p<0.05$; **$p<0.01$; ***$p<0.001$

12.3.5 Interaction of Self-control and Opportunity

As shown in Chap. 11, there is good reason to examine the interaction between opportunities and self-control. In Chap. 11, we used a composite measure of opportunities, including *lifestyle* variables as well as *deviant peers* (delinquent friends). In the present analysis, we disentangle the opportunity effect by analyzing separately the interaction effects of deviant peers and lifestyle variables on versatility. Whereas the interaction of self-control and delinquent friends is not significant, the significant effect of the interaction of self-control and lifestyle confirms results obtained in Chap. 11 (Table 12.7). Additionally, as also found with respect to Model 5, the effects of self-control differ significantly by country (LR $\text{Chi}^2_{(1)}=5.10$, conservative $p=0.024$).

12.3.6 Social Disorganization/Collective Efficacy Theory

This perspective emphasizes the importance of a youth's immediate social environment (beyond family and school), i.e., the neighborhood. We do not have a direct measure of neighborhood disorganization; instead we use data on the youth's perception of the quality of their neighborhood. As shown in Chap. 10, two of the neighborhood-based scales proved to be useful: *neighborhood integration* and *neighborhood disorganization*. Here, we will assess the generalizability of the association of these two measures with versatility.

The results of Model 8 (Table 12.8) show that versatility tends to decrease with neighborhood integration (odds ratio = 1/1.16), whereas it clearly increases with neighborhood disorganization (odds ratio = 2.16). The inclusion of the two individual level measures of the quality of the neighborhood improves the model fit significantly (LR $Chi^2_{(2)} = 2{,}103.1$, $p < 0.001$), but at the same time increases the unexplained between country variability of versatility ($u_0 = 0.381$ vs. 0.287). The random slope models show that the effects of neighborhood integration do not differ by countries, but that the effects of neighborhood disorganization clearly differ (LR $Chi^2_{(1)} = 8.54$, conservative $p = 0.004$), thus replicating the results of Chap. 10 with respect to the nongeneralizability of the association of neighborhood disorganization and delinquency across countries.

12.3.7 Macro Level Predictors

To explore the effect of macro level predictors on delinquency, we choose three measures: (1) The Human Development Index (HDI) of 2006 (UNDP 2010), (2) a score of secular–rational values, and (3) a score of self-expression values (Inglehart and Baker 2000). The HDI was already used in Chap. 10. It is a composite measure of health (life expectancy at birth), education (mean and expected years of schooling), and standard of living (GNI per capita). Secular–rational values and self-expression values are assessed by the World Values Survey (World Values Survey Association 2009), the latter measure was used in Chap. 6, as well. The first one measures secular–rational opposed to traditional value orientations (de-emphasis of religion, family, the nation, and authority), whereas the latter measures the emphasis on self-expression values opposed to those of security; an important aspect of self-expression values are postmaterialistic value orientations. Both measures are expected to correlate positively with human development and economic security (Inglehart and Baker 2000).

Although including the HDI, secular–rational values, and self-expression values as *z*-score transformed macro level predictors simultaneously into the basic Model 1 improves the model fit not greatly (LR $Chi^2_{(2)} = 24.2$, $p < 0.001$), it reduces the unexplained country level variance of versatility considerably ($u_0 = 0.103$ vs. 0.287). Despite the fact that there are significant bivariate ecological correlations of rational secular values (weakly negative) and self-expression values (positive) with delinquency (see also Chap. 6), under controlled conditions in the multivariate analysis, only the HDI is significantly (and positively) related to the versatility of delinquent behavior: An increase of the HDI of one standard deviation corresponds to an increase of the odds of juveniles to show versatile delinquent behavior by 37%

Table 12.8 Predicting versatility (0–2 vs. 3+) by neighborhood variables (Model 8)

	Null model	M1: Control	M8: Neighborhood	RS: Neighborhood integration	RS: Neighborhood disorganization
Grade (base: grade 7)		$\chi^2_{(2)}=106.3$***	$\chi^2_{(2)}=67.6$***	$\chi^2_{(2)}=67.5$***	$\chi^2_{(2)}=68.6$***
Grade 8		1.514*** (7.53)	1.421*** (6.13)	1.421*** (6.13)	1.421*** (6.12)
Grade 9		1.721*** (10.15)	1.567*** (8.05)	1.567*** (8.05)	1.574*** (8.13)
Gender (base: female)		3.457*** (26.32)	3.143*** (23.51)	3.142*** (23.50)	3.149*** (23.49)
Migrant status (base: native)		1.391*** (6.87)	1.104 (1.92)	1.102 (1.89)	1.102 (1.89)
Neighborhood integration (z-score)			0.865*** (–6.88)	0.860*** (–5.84)	0.865*** (–6.86)
Neighborhood disorganization (z-score)			2.163*** (44.18)	2.164*** (44.13)	2.190*** (29.36)
–2*LL	–10,108.9	–9,632.1	–8,580.5	–8,578.7	–8,576.2
var(u_0)	0.319***	0.287***	0.381***	0.384***	0.382***
var(u_1)				0.003	0.008**

Exponentiated coefficients; z statistics in parentheses; cov(u_0, u_1) set to zero; significance of random effect u_1 tested via likelihood-ratio test
*$p<0.05$; **$p<0.01$; ***$p<0.001$

(odds ratio = 1.368, $p = 0.004$). Therefore, in the following we will only use this macro level predictor in a full model to explore whether it may explain differences between countries in the effects of the individual level predictors: truancy, self-control, and neighborhood disorganization.

12.3.8 Full Model

The previous tests have shown that all variables used to test social bonding/social control theory, self-control theory, routine activity/opportunity theory, and social disorganization theory are significant predictors of versatility, even when taking into account the multilevel structure of the data. Most of the effects of these predictors of versatility are similar across countries, with three exceptions: The effects of truancy, self-control, and neighborhood disorganisation differ clearly between countries, although on the average they are individual level predictors of delinquency as theoretically expected.

When combining all individual level predictors into one model (Table 12.9), there still remains substantial unexplained variability of versatility on the level of the countries ($u_0 = 0.321$). Including all the theoretically relevant variables (family, school, opportunities, self-control – plus the significant interaction of self-control and lifestyle –, and neighborhood) into the model, only the effects of self-control and neighborhood disorganization differ significantly by country, as shown by significant variances u_1 and u_2 of their slopes. The strongest effects are observed for opportunities (delinquent friends: odds ratio = 5.82; lifestyle: odds ratio = 2.13), followed by self-control (odds ratio = 1/2.07), school variables (truancy: odds ratio = 1.95; school disorganization: odds ratio = 1.16), neighborhood quality (neighborhood disorganization: odds ratio = 1.32; neighborhood integration: odds ratio = 1/1.10), and family variables (parental supervision: odds ratio = 1/1.20; family bonding: odds ratio = 1/1.17).[5] It is remarkable that the background variables grade (as a proxy for age) and migrant status are no longer significant, an exception is the strong effect of gender (odds ratio of males = 3.49).

Adding the macro level predictor HDI clearly reduces the unexplained variance of versatility on the country level by nearly a third ($u_0 = 0.221$ vs. 0.321). However, the between country variance is still significant. Cross-level interactions of HDI with self-control and neighborhood disorganization (not shown) were not significant, therefore, we must conclude that this macro level predictor cannot explain the variability of the slopes of self-control and neighborhood disorganization between countries.

[5] Strictly speaking, the size of odds ratios of dichotomous predictors and z-score transformed continuous predictors cannot be compared; however, the sequence also corresponds to the *z*-values and the outcomes of likelihood ratio tests of the Models 2–8.

Table 12.9 Full model of predicting versatility (0–2 vs. 3+) (Model 9)

	Null model	M1: Control		M9: Full model		+Macro level predictor	
Grade (base: grade7)		$\chi^2_{(2)}=106.3$***		$\chi^2_{(2)}=2.8$		$\chi^2_{(2)}=2.8$	
Grade 8		1.514***	(7.53)	1.109	(1.62)	1.109	(1.62)
Grade 9		1.721***	(10.15)	1.085	(1.29)	1.083	(1.27)
Gender (base: female)		3.457***	(26.32)	3.489***	(22.86)	3.491***	(22.88)
Migrant status (base: native)		1.391***	(6.87)	1.043	(0.73)	1.038	(0.65)
Family bonding (*z*-score)				0.852***	(–7.28)	0.853***	(–7.22)
Parental supervision (*z*-score)				0.836***	(–7.88)	0.836***	(–7.84)
School disorganization (*z*-score)				1.161***	(5.91)	1.159***	(5.88)
Truancy (base: no)				1.954***	(12.86)	1.964***	(12.96)
Lifestyle (*z*-score)				2.133***	(17.14)	2.128***	(17.11)
Delinquency friends (base: no)				5.820***	(25.19)	5.733***	(24.99)
Self-control (*z*-score)				0.483***	(–16.00)	0.482***	(–16.31)
Self-control* lifestyle (*z*-scores)				1.086*	(2.55)	1.086*	(2.53)
Neighborhood integration (*z*-score)				0.911***	(–3.96)	0.911***	(–3.96)
Neighborhood disorganization (*z*-score)				1.316***	(9.11)	1.319***	(9.30)
HDI (*z*-score)						1.353**	(3.16)
–2**LL*	–10,108.9	–9,632.1		–6,421.7		–6,417.4	
var(u_0)	0.319***	0.287***		0.321***		0.221**	
var(u_1: self-control)				0.015**		0.014**	
var(u_2:nh-disorg.)				0.009**		0.008**	

Exponentiated coefficients; *z* statistics in parentheses; covariances of random effects set to zero; significance of random effects u_1 and u_2 tested via likelihood-ratio tests
*$p<0.05$; **$p<0.01$; ***$p<0.001$

12.4 Theoretical Implications

We included four different theoretical perspectives in our study. Admittedly, our tests of these four perspectives have been rather limited because we simply lack the large amount of different indicators that would be needed in order to test the full implications of each theoretical perspective. Rather, we were able to select a small number of variables that arguably could be viewed as representing key constructs of the different perspectives, and we examined the relative importance of these theoretical variables, first alone (Models 2–8), and later (Model 9) in combination. Our findings are consistent with much existing research. All four perspectives find some support: Social bonding and social control (mostly through school-related variables followed by parental supervision), self-control (and the interaction between self-control and opportunities, respectively lifestyle), routine activities (lifestyle and delinquent friends), and social disorganization (mostly neighborhood disorganization).

Although representing different theoretical perspectives, a comparison of the respective predictors showed that all predictors are significantly related to the versatility of delinquent behavior. Most important are the opportunity factors (delinquent friends and lifestyle) and self-control, followed by truancy, neighborhood disorganization, parental supervision, and family bonding. A caveat, however, is in order: Here, we rely exclusively on cross-sectional data that cannot be used to confirm (or falsify) any causal sequence. One could argue that having delinquent friends, being truant, or living in disorganized neighborhoods (characterized by crime and incivilities) should be treated as a consequence, not a cause. The causal order assumed in the models investigated is derived from theory rather than empirically shown. In this sense, the counterargument of circularity cannot be rejected on empirical grounds.

In addition to these variables, even under controlled conditions, gender continues to be a very strong predictor of versatility. We also found that there is a need to examine interactions between different variables. This has clearly been shown for self-control and opportunities (i.e., we found that opportunities play a more important role for those youth with low self-control), but might also be true for other variables such as the effect of disorganized neighborhood and deviant peers. In short, analysis of the large combined international sample has produced findings that pretty much reproduce findings found in much existing literature on delinquency. This suggests that the key notions of these four theoretical perspectives are rather robust. Whether that suggests a need for theoretical integration or synthesis is a question that we are not prepared to address at this juncture.

The explicitly comparative nature of the ISRD study allows us to take into account the possible variability of the theoretical correlates of delinquency at the level of countries. It is the testing of the generalizability of theoretical propositions that is the most exciting and challenging part of this study. We found that countries and country clusters often differ with regard to the *levels* and nature of the main predictor variables. For example, there are significant differences in the levels of self-control between country clusters; the same is true for levels of school disorganization, parental supervision, or amount of time spent with peers, or single parent households. An important additional question is whether this also means that the *effects* of these predictor variables also differ at the country (or country cluster) level. The answer here is yes and no. For the sociodemographic variables, the effects appear similar across countries (holding other theoretical variables constant): being male, a migrant, and being in a higher grade increase the probability of versatile delinquency significantly in all 26 countries. However, this cannot be said for all theoretically derived variables: Although analysis of the total sample suggests that family (supervision), school (truancy), self-control, and neighborhood (disorganization) all have a significant effect (in the theoretically expected direction), our analysis suggests that the effects of these variables differ between countries, most certainly with respect to self-control and neighborhood disorganization. We were not able to explain between-country variation of the effects (of self-control and neighborhood disorganization) by macro level predictors such as the HDI, secular–rational, or self-expression values. This finding is most interesting, particularly in view of the fact that the HDI has been shown an important macro level predictor of versatility, underlining the importance of taking the socioeconomic situation of countries into account when studying delinquent behavior across countries.

12.5 Policy Considerations

If we consider all results of the ISRD-2 study there are a number of general outcomes, which warrant some policy recommendations.

A striking outcome is the importance of *the neighborhood* in forming a socializing environment that either promotes prosocial behavior or facilitates antisocial behavior. Whether it is the one or the other is related to the character of the particular neighborhood, in particular whether it is a well-integrated, cohesive neighborhood where neighbors know each other and are prepared to realize a shared system of values and norms by exercising social control on the youth population, or whether it is a deprived and disorganized neighborhood, where residents are unable to maintain social control on their sons (and to a lesser degree on their daughters) and youth groups show unruly, troublesome, and delinquent behavior. In that respect, it should be remembered that even in the most disorganized neighborhoods the majority of residents are law abiding and they suffer most from local criminals and youth gangs. What can authorities do to improve that situation?

- It is recommended to construct mixed neighborhoods buildings and to add higher quality houses to existent social housing in order to attract a more prosperous middle class population. This helps to improve the neighborhood's economic and social situation and to create a climate where there will be more consensus among residents about prevailing norms and values and more efforts to try to realize these in their own environment.
- It is also important that in these neighborhoods social services, health care, high-quality schools, and recreation possibilities, comparable to those found in most middle class neighborhoods, are established. The families in deprived neighborhoods are very vulnerable, because of unemployment, physical illness, psychosocial problems, debts, or alcohol problems, and they are often unable to keep their children in line, to transfer prevailing norms and values, and to support their children in their school career. One reason for higher serious delinquency rates among some groups of migrants than among natives is the fact that their parents exercise less control over their offspring than native parents and are unable to support them when having problems. Social services offer assistance and support

to residents who need help in the form of budget management, parent training, and child care services, allowing single mothers to look for a job.

- The presence of small businesses and shops may be useful too, in order to create more prosperity as well as job possibilities for young people. Promising experiences have been conducted by vocational schools. These schools provide work practice and employment for their students by establishing good relationships and regular contacts with small enterprises and shopkeepers in their environment.
- Adding more "blue on the streets" – although definitely an appealing solution in the eyes of many – may turn out to be counterproductive, unless it is done with utmost caution and respect for maintaining neighborhood integrity. Heightened police presence and surveillance all too easily results in the stigmatization of certain neighborhoods and ethnic groups. That is not to imply that the police has no role to play in the prevention of juvenile crime. In a number of countries, community policing, i.e., using neighborhood officers with intimate knowledge of the specific problems of residents, has proved to be fairly successful. However, community policing should explicitly try to activate and strengthen the responsibilities of community members. Indeed, our findings suggest that promoting social integration and improvement of networks including resources of the inhabitants is by far to be preferred over the simple expansion of police presence in the more problematic neighborhoods.

The *school* – the bond with school and school achievement – has a crucial effect on young people's behavior. Unfortunately, adolescents living in deprived neighborhoods – natives and migrants alike – rather often attend disorganized schools and this is strongly related to truancy and offending. Even those who live in well-integrated, cohesive neighborhoods but attend disorganized schools are more likely to be truant and to commit offenses than those attending well-organized schools. If one wishes to prevent delinquency, investing in education should be placed high on the agenda. Education is the highway to better jobs, higher income, more welfare, better health, and less crime. Four different measures are relevant in this respect.

- First, early education (age 3–5), in particular for lower working class and ethnic minority children, has proved to be very effective in promoting a positive school career, allowing young people later to find a good job (Schweinhart et al. 1993). Moreover, following these children into adulthood showed that their involvement with the law was considerably lower than that of a control group.
- Second, local authorities in Norway, Sweden, the UK, and the Netherlands developed so-called "Large schools" in deprived neighborhoods. The school's functions are enlarged by introducing social work services within the school, lengthening the school day with recreational activities, and including parent-training programs and social competence programs for pupils. Most of such primary schools include at the same location crèches, kindergarten, a special education school, and after school programs, whereas social welfare services, health services, child care organizations, and the local police are all present under the same roof or in the direct environment.
- A third measure refers to the quality of the schools. It is a sad fact that children in deprived neighborhoods, who should attend the best schools with high-quality

teachers, get instead low-quality education, preparing them inadequately for useful participation in society. Primary schools, and even more so secondary schools in difficult neighborhoods, should be run by highly qualified teachers. Some countries pay a bonus to teachers willing to work in these neighborhoods, rewarding the teachers for working with difficult, hard to discipline children instead of quiet, orderly, middle class children.

- The fourth measure is based on our finding of the effects of a school tracking system on violent offending, multilevel analysis showing more violence in countries with a tracking system than in countries without such a system. One option in this case, apart from changing the entire education system, is to introduce more flexibility, allowing students to continue their education by attending schools of gradually higher levels. In this way, after having achieved successfully a lower track school students can attend a higher track school, eventually continuing in this way up to university. Experiences with "stacking" different school levels have been very successful in the Netherlands, in particular for young migrants.

Most young people have a *group of friends* they like to spend time – and to hang out with, without this leading necessarily to troublesome or delinquent behavior. For example, in countries with a warmer climate – such as in Southern Europe – leisure time with peers is usually spent outside without this being related to delinquency. However, two study outcomes warrant special attention. The first outcome is that in a number of western and postsocialist countries so-called *binge drinking* on weekend nights leads to outbursts of vandalism and violence and other forms of troublesome behavior, whereas drinking heavily endangers seriously young people's health and their future. The second outcome is that, related to the degree of neighborhood disorganization, both the respondent and his peer group tend to commit increasingly serious offenses.

- To combat excessive use of alcohol by young people several measures are in order, some of which have already been taken in some countries. Most of these are addressed to the young people themselves, such as increasing by law the age of buying and drinking alcohol up to age 18 or 21; reducing the availability of alcohol to some specialized shops, as has been done in Scandinavian countries; increasing the price of alcohol, a quite effective measure as shown in evaluation studies. One might also think of taking measures against the owners of bars, cafés, and clubhouses, since they usually just go on serving alcohol, independent of the clients' state of drunkenness. Adequate measures would be to require strict age control, not serving drinks anymore to young people under the influence of alcohol, all this under the control of local authorities and the threat of withdrawing the authorization to conduct their business.
- The second problem requires different measures. Because of their cramped housing arrangements, these young people are forced to spend most leisure time on the streets. This makes it important to create special recreation possibilities, such as high-quality youth services, modern facilities, and active sports organizations. For example, some ethnic groups who want to preserve their culture and group cohesion organize local festivities, sports events, and family outings, the result of which

is more social control on young people, less delinquency, and less involvement with the juvenile justice system. Providing attractive recreation options to adolescents goes a long way to avoid hanging out with peers on the streets and developing troublesome behavior out of boredom, which may deteriorate into delinquency.

- However, a more serious problem is presented by the young people living in highly deprived neighborhoods, who commit serious offenses or participate in gangs, running the risk of developing a delinquent career. In many such cases, prevention is no longer an option and intervention by the juvenile justice system is unavoidable. Considering their young age, placing them in an institution would be counter effective, research showing high recidivism rates after leaving institutional placement. A much better option is intense supervision of the youth and his family while administering one of the well-structured and effective ambulatory programs that are available. One example is Multisystemic therapy that has been tested in the United States, Norway, Canada, Switzerland, and the Netherlands, demonstrating its effectiveness. Its objectives are to improve parental discipline, to reduce involvement with deviant, violent peers, to improve school/ work achievement, and to improve problem-solving skills of the family. There are other programs, the most effective of which include leading the juvenile back to school while helping him to succeed, or/and leading him to employment. In all cases, however, being successful and effective requires intense supervision and control on young people, their family, and their friends.

Not all policy recommendations are cross-nationally transferrable, of course. Our study has shown that youth problems exist – in greater or lesser degree – in all ISRD countries, and that – to a large degree – similar factors appear to play a role in these problems. However, we also have shown that there are important differences between countries and country clusters with regard to the dimensions and correlates of these problems. Therefore, policies need to be adapted to local cultures and contexts.

References

Grasmick, H. G., Title, C. R., & Arneklev, B. J. (1993). Testing the core empirical implications of Gottfredson and Hirschi's general theory of crime. *Journal of Research in Crime and Delinquency, 30*, 5-29.

Hirschi, T. (1969). *Causes of Delinquency*. Berkeley, CA: University of California Press.

Hox, J. J. (2010). *Multilevel Analysis: Techniques and Applications*. New York (2nd ed.): Routledge.

Inglehart, R. & Baker, W. E. (2000). Modernization, cultural change, and the persistence of traditional values. *American Sociological Review, 65*, 19-51.

Schweinhart, L. J., Barnes, H. V. & Weikart, D. P. (1993). *Significant Benefits: The High/Scope Perry Preschool Study through Age 27* (Monographs of the High/Scope Educational Research Foundation, 10). Ypsilanti, MI: High/Scope Press.

UNDP (2010). *United Nations Development Programme: International Human Development Indicators*. [http://hdrstats.undp.org/en/tables/default.html]

World Values Survey Association (2009). *Word Values Survey 2005 Official Data File v. 20090901*. World Values Survey Association. [http://www.worldvaluessurvey.org]

Index

A

Absenteeism, 41, 267
Abstinence, 120, 121, 123, 132, 133. *See also* Alcohol use; Drug use; Substance use
Accidents
  and delinquency/offending, 134, 187, 258, 285
  and self-control, 285, 297
Administrator's form/questionnaire, 58–59
Affluence, 52, 172, 173, 176, 187–189, 192, 193, 201, 203–205, 261, 264, 280, 306,–309, 314–316, 331, 332, 334. *See also* Social class
Age. *See also* Grade
  and alcohol use, 51, 139
  cohort, 33
  and delinquency/offending, 77, 81–84, 286
  and deviant peers, 238
  distribution, 33, 34, 82, 83, 116
  and drug use, 51
  and gang membership, 239
  and grade, 45, 171, 180, 278
  and life-style, 100, 180
  of migration, 33, 166, 290, 336
  of onset, 4, 14, 17, 21, 82, 83, 91, 119, 126, 127, 329
  and risk behavior, 51
  of sample, 276, 282
  and victimization, 157, 329
Alcohol policy, 121
Alcohol use. *See also* Substance use
  beer, 119, 330
  binge drinking, 128, 137
  and delinquency/offending, 119
  and drug use, 44
  drunk, 119, 128
  hard liquor, 330 (*see also* Spirits)
  incidence, 35, 74–75, 119 (*see also* Frequency)
  prevalence, 119
  and risk behavior, 51–52
  and victimization, 44
  wine, 119, 330
Alpha coefficient, 295. *See also* Reliability; Scales
Analysis. *See also* Correlation; Design
  bi-variate, 115
  comparative, 21, 25, 87, 113, 293, 297, 319, 320
  and country clusters, 125, 296, 309, 314
  descriptive, 16, 32
  explanatory, 102
  factor analysis, 293, 295–297
  multi-level, 25–26, 206, 212, 228, 271, 277–280, 282, 329, 335, 339, 342, 352
  multivariate, 34, 84, 345
  psychometric, 47, 61, 293, 298
  and theory-testing, 320
Anglo-Saxon cluster. *See also* Canada; Ireland; United States
  and alcohol use, 127
  and delinquency/offending, 69, 76, 79, 84
  and drug use, 125, 137
  and risk behavior, 156, 249
  and victimization, 99, 156
Armenia, 5, 16, 39, 41, 52, 97–99, 120–122, 125, 139, 145, 148, 150–153, 156, 162, 177, 179, 221, 223, 240, 247, 293, 295, 299. *See also* Post-socialist cluster
Aruba, 5, 16, 26, 31, 32, 37, 74, 97, 120, 139, 145, 159, 161, 162, 300, 335. *See also* Latin America

J. Junger-Tas et al., *The Many Faces of Youth Crime: Contrasting Theoretical Perspectives on Juvenile Delinquency across Countries and Cultures*, DOI 10.1007/978-1-4419-9455-4, © Springer Science+Business Media, LLC 2012

Assault. *See* Offenses
Attachment. *See also* Bonding
  family, 10, 53–54, 309
  neighborhood, 55–56, 108
  parents, 10, 54, 102, 105, 107, 185, 192–194, 206, 302, 331, 335
  school, 10, 55, 223, 226, 228, 230, 232, 234, 266, 333, 337
Attitudes. *See also* Scales
  towards neighborhood, 251
  towards parents, 130, 195, 211
  towards school, 251
  towards violence, pro-violent, 57, 102, 136, 195, 200
Austria, 5, 16, 41, 97, 99, 102, 125, 145, 148, 260, 300. *See also* Western-European cluster

B

Background factors. *See also* Affluence; Age; City size; Gender; Immigrants
  and alcohol use, 51
  and country clusters, 14–16
  and delinquency/offending, 17
  demographic, 131–134, 309
  and drug use, 51
  and risk behavior, 51–52
  socio-economic, 52–53
  and victimization, 52
Behavior, delinquent, 171, 178, 310. *See also* Delinquency; Offending
Belgium, 5, 16, 26, 44, 86, 101, 122, 148, 162, 247, 300. *See also* Western-European cluster
Bicycle theft. *See* Offenses
Binomial regression. *See* Regression
Bonding. *See also* Attachment
  family/parents, 115, 136, 186, 188–189, 192–194, 197, 198, 200, 201, 203, 205, 206, 248, 251, 253, 263, 264, 275, 276, 304, 312, 320, 331, 332, 337, 339, 347
  neighborhood, 55, 259, 260, 263, 279, 281, 305, 309
  peers, 10
  school, 55, 212–217, 267, 270, 334, 337
  social bonding theory, 9–10, 54, 285, 304, 310, 335, 337–339, 347, 349 (*see also* Social control, theory)
Bosnia-Herzegovina, 31, 148, 162, 221, 223, 247. *See also* Post-socialist cluster
Boys, 57, 80, 82–84, 89, 91, 99, 100, 111, 113, 115, 118, 124, 131, 132, 135, 139, 187, 195–198, 200, 201, 214, 218, 230, 240, 241, 243, 246, 247, 249, 251, 254, 264, 278, 305, 320, 329–333, 335, 337. *See also* Males
Bullying, 4, 23, 52, 95–97, 100–102, 105, 113, 116, 145, 151, 232, 330. *See also* Victimization
Burglary. *See* Offenses

C

Canada, 4, 15, 26, 27, 32, 35, 40, 42–44, 47, 353. *See also* Anglo-Saxon cluster
Car break, theft from car. *See* Offenses
Carrying a weapon. *See* Offenses
Car theft(s). *See* Offenses
Central and Eastern Europe. *See* Post-socialist; Post-socialist cluster
Citizenship, 211. *See also* Ethnic minority groups; Migrants; Nationality; Native
City size
  and alcohol use, 133
  and delinquency/offending, 79
  and drug use, 133
  large, 153, 155, 157
  medium, 28, 133, 153, 155
  and reporting to police, 156, 180
  and risk behavior, 180
  and sampling, 156, 163
  small, 79
  and victimization, 157, 158
Cluster, 14, 23, 69, 97, 117, 145, 188, 214, 239, 259, 290, 329 . *See also* Anglo-Saxon; Country cluster; Latin America; Mediterranean country cluster; Northern-European cluster; Post-Socialist; Western-European cluster
  analysis, 125, 296 (*see also* Sample)
  differences, 16, 27, 83, 113, 188, 189
Cohesion, 202, 352. *See also* Integration; Social disorganization theory
  and neighborhoods, 56, 186, 189, 206, 259, 263, 267, 331, 334
Collective efficacy, 9, 12, 17, 186, 188, 194, 259, 270, 304, 344–345. *See also* Social disorganization theory
Comparative design, 5–8, 21, 23, 25, 61, 319. *See also* Cross-national design; Design; Standardization
Computer hacking, 48. *See also* Hacking; Offenses
Computerized survey (administration), 47, 59

Consent. *See also* Response rate
active, 42
informed, 42
parental, 36–38, 42–44
passive, 42, 43
procedure, 36, 42
schools, 36, 41
student/pupil, 41, 42
teachers, 43
Co-offending, 21, 237. *See also* Delinquent groups; Gangs; Group offending
Cooperation. *See* Consent; Response rate
multi-collinearity,
Country cluster. *See also* Anglo-Saxon; Latin America; Mediterranean country cluster; Northern-European cluster; Post-Socialist; Southern European cluster; Western-European cluster
and alcohol use, 117, 125, 128, 131, 264
and delinquency/offending, 16, 25
and drug use, 85, 117, 125, 130
and risk behavior, 52
Saint-Arnaud and Bernard, 23–25
and victimization, 25
Country-level indicators, 25, 219, 223, 227
Crime. *See* Delinquency; Offending
Crime rates, statistics, official, 144, 148, 150, 167, 180
Criminological theory, 6, 22, 27. *See also* Hypothesis; Theory
Cross-national design, 4. *See also* Comparative design
Cyprus, 5, 16, 25, 28, 38, 39, 69–72, 74, 97–99, 103, 105, 121–125, 145, 146, 149, 160, 161, 220, 221, 293, 299, 335. *See also* Mediterranean country cluster
Czech Republic, 5, 16, 27, 28, 31, 36, 37, 41, 42, 44, 70, 97–99, 101, 105, 121–125, 147, 148, 162, 220, 221, 240, 333. *See also* Post-Socialist cluster

D

Data coding, 6, 7
Data collection. *See also* Consent; Design; Response rate; Sample
administrator's form/administrator's questionnaire, 58–60
instructions, 52
research protocol, 7
structural indicators collection form, 30
student questionnaire, 46–47
survey manager, 8
teacher questionnaire, 46
Data entry, 5–9
Data, missing, 8, 30, 222, 225
Data weighting, 32–33
De-commodification, 23. *See also* Country cluster; Esping-Andersen; Saint-Arnaud and Bernard
Delinquency. *See also* Offending
and age, 4, 14, 17, 81–83, 153, 157, 162, 166, 167, 178, 180, 239, 285,–287, 329
and city size, 28–32, 39, 60, 79, 157, 180, 306
and country clusters, 14–16, 23–25, 32, 43, 44, 69, 84, 90, 117, 188, 193, 198, 200, 214, 245, 253, 290, 293, 298, 300, 301, 306, 310, 314, 320, 331, 334, 349, 353
and family, 160, 171–173, 197, 242, 251, 331, 333
frequency, 13, 14, 16, 50, 56, 78, 119, 171, 180, 188, 194, 198, 218, 239, 276, 281, 290 (*see also* Incidence)
and gender, 80, 81, 83, 153, 156, 165, 166, 171, 180
and grade, 81, 148, 153–157, 165–167, 171–180
incidence, 4, 12, 21, 32, 35, 41, 44, 49, 50, 69, 144, 158, 314 (*see also* Frequency)
and lifestyles, 116, 136, 237–254, 271, 311, 312
measure of, 24, 30, 49–51, 186, 194, 251, 291, 303, 310, 312, 337, 339, 344, 345 (*see also* Operationalization; Scales)
and migrant, 86–91, 135, 171, 198, 202, 223, 229, 251, 252, 258, 278, 320, 336, 339, 342–344, 347, 349 (*see also* Ethnic minority groups; Native)
and neighborhood, 55–56, 103, 180, 290, 298, 304–306, 310–314, 320, 331–335, 344, 345, 347–352
non-serious, 74–78, 82, 192, 196, 197, 282 (*see also* Minor)
and opportunities, 11, 71, 217, 233, 280, 288, 305, 310–318, 320, 333, 335, 342–344, 347, 349
and peers/friends, 10, 11, 14, 154–157, 159, 171, 198, 218, 219, 227, 237–254, 271, 282, 285, 310–312, 333, 342, 347, 349, 352, 353
prevalence, 27, 30, 32, 40, 44, 69–74, 79–81 (*see also* Last year; Life-time; Recent)
property, 80
rates, 13, 69, 78–80, 82, 84, 91, 233, 258, 332, 350

Delinquency. *See also* Offending (*cont.*)
and school, 81, 85, 165–168
and self-control, 178, 181
serious, 50, 79, 188, 191, 197, 206, 267, 273, 278–282, 330, 332, 334, 339, 350 (*see also* Rare)
and social disorganization, 9, 12, 17, 102, 119, 135, 204, 206, 258, 259, 266, 281, 282, 334, 335, 345, 347 (*see also* Neighborhood)
versatility (diversity variety, variability), 4, 21, 188, 212, 252, 263, 270, 336, 345
violent, 238
Delinquent behavior, 27, 164, 165, 167, 171, 173, 178, 179, 181, 310, 335, 336, 339, 345, 349, 350, 352
Delinquent groups, 197, 238, 239, 246, 251, 254, 336
Denmark, 5, 13, 16, 28, 37, 70–72, 74, 98, 99, 101, 103, 105, 120–122, 124, 125, 145, 146, 148, 157–161, 177, 178, 220, 221, 299. *See also* Northern-European cluster
Design. *See also* Comparative design; Cross-national design; Standardization
cross-sectional, 4
self-report survey, 4
victimization survey, 3
Design effect, 45. *See also* Sample
Detection, 14, 17, 79, 143, 144, 158–174, 177, 179, 180, 330. *See also* Punishment; Social control; Social response
Deviant/delinquent friends, 10, 56, 102–104, 108, 110–115, 143, 154, 156, 172, 173, 185, 186, 228, 232, 237–239, 243–254, 272, 281, 286, 289, 303, 313, 331, 334, 342, 344, 347, 349, 353. *See also* Peer groups
Deviant peers, 328, 342, 344, 349
Disorganization. *See also* Neighborhood
and country clusters, 17, 188, 193, 198, 200, 206, 214, 223, 264, 275, 309, 314, 320, 334, 349
and delinquency/offending, 9, 12, 102, 111, 113, 273, 337
delinquent subcultures, 57
(Social) disorganization theory, 204, 206, 258, 259, 266, 281, 334, 335, 347 (*see also* Collective efficacy)
Diversity. *See* Versatility
Drug dealing. *See* Offenses
Drug use
hard drugs, 108, 117, 119–122, 126, 132, 134, 171, 244, 330
hashish (*see* marijuana)
incidence, frequency, 13, 35, 44, 50, 74–75, 119, 172, 239, 330
last month, 51, 119, 120, 131–133, 135, 171 (*see also* Recent)
life time, 121, 122, 132, 171, 172 (*see also* Ever)
LSD, heroin, cocaine, speed, 51, 119, 122, 133
marijuana, 51, 52, 118–120, 126, 131, 132, 135, 244 (*see also* soft drugs)
prevalence, 43, 44, 117, 120, 122–124
soft drugs, 85, 92, 118–122, 132, 135, 330
XTC, 51, 108
Dutch Antilles, 16, 70. *See also* Latin America; Netherlands Antilles

E

Education, 7, 8, 15–17, 24, 35, 36, 40, 41, 52, 55, 60, 81, 85, 87, 166, 187, 205, 211, 214, 218, 225, 233, 266, 279, 280, 304, 330, 332, 345, 351, 352. *See also* Grade; School
Epidata. *See* Data entry
Equivalence of measures, 22, 47. *See also* Comparative design; Questionnaire
Esping-Andersen, 14–16, 23, 69. *See also* Country cluster; De-commodification
Estonia, 4, 5, 16, 27, 28, 31, 37, 41, 70–72, 74, 97, 98, 101, 104, 105, 120–124, 128, 133, 147, 149, 160–162, 177, 220, 221, 240, 299, 300. *See also* Post-socialist cluster
Ethnicity/Ethnic minority group. *See also* Immigrants
and alcohol use, 133, 330
country of origin, 53, 86, 87, 89
and delinquency/offending, 17, 214, 218, 253, 270, 330, 333
and drug use, 53, 267
host country, 34, 81, 86, 90, 92, 191, 202, 330
language, 8, 43, 53, 58, 81
and risk behavior, 48, 51–55, 172, 173, 310
and victimization, 17, 330
European School Survey Project on Alcohol and Other Drugs (ESPAD), 4, 61, 118, 122–125, 139
Ever. See Life time
Extortion, 48–50, 52, 57, 75, 78, 85, 106, 109, 159, 163, 219, 243–245, 277, 313. *See also* Robbery

F

Family. *See also* Parents; Social bonding; Social control
affluence, 52, 172, 173, 187–188, 192, 193, 201, 203–205, 261, 264, 306, 307, 309, 314–316, 331, 332, 334
and alcohol use, 51, 136, 330
bonds, 9, 10, 185, 232, 270, 285, 287, 332, 337 (*see also* Attachment; Scales)
composition/family structure, 17, 54, 107, 187, 189–193, 202, 262, 331
control, 180, 200, 205, 290
and country clusters, 14, 17, 23–25, 84, 188, 189, 193, 198, 200, 206, 239–240, 253, 264, 275, 298, 306, 307, 309, 310, 314, 317, 331, 334, 349, 353
and delinquency/offending, 10, 14, 17
disruption, 54, 57, 186, 190, 194, 198–202, 204, 263–266, 275–277, 281, 304, 308, 320, 332
and drug use, 52, 108
and ethnic minorities/migrant, 14, 33, 86, 202, 282
and etiology/genesis of criminal behavior, 174, 286, 289
and gender, 17, 102, 195–201, 334
and leisure time, 10, 53, 101, 194, 195, 200, 206, 233, 237, 239, 241, 242, 252, 263, 313, 331, 332, 352
lone or single parent family, 166, 168, 169
parental management, 185, 186, 303, 304, 309, 310
parental supervision, 54, 102, 107, 111, 163, 166, 167, 172, 173, 193, 206, 234, 270, 304, 306, 308–310, 312, 314–316, 320, 331, 332, 334, 337–339, 341, 347–349
and risk behavior, 17, 172
and victimization, 17, 102, 111, 113
Females, 33, 91, 156, 157, 166, 167, 171–174, 196–198, 200, 211, 214, 305, 309, 310, 336. *See also* Gender; Girls
Finland, 4, 5, 13, 16, 28, 31, 37, 39, 70–72, 74, 97, 98, 103, 105, 121, 122, 124, 128, 146, 148–150, 157, 159–162, 220, 221, 299. *See also* Northern-European cluster
France, 5, 16, 27, 28, 31, 38, 40, 43, 56, 70–72, 74, 86, 88, 97, 98, 103, 105, 118, 120–125, 146, 149, 156, 160, 161, 220, 221, 247, 299, 300. *See also* Western-European cluster
Frequency. *See also* Incidence; Rates
alcohol use, 51, 119, 330
delinquency/offending, 14, 16, 50, 51, 56, 77, 78, 119, 171, 172, 180, 194, 198, 218, 239, 276, 281, 290, 312
drug use, 51, 119, 171, 239, 330
reporting, 17, 50, 144, 153, 154, 156, 157, 180
risk behavior, 51, 172
victimization, 14, 16, 33, 50, 52, 111, 144, 145, 153, 154, 156, 157, 180, 330
Friends, 9, 10, 53, 56, 57, 102, 108–115, 129, 136, 139, 154, 156, 172, 173, 185, 186, 194, 200, 211, 217, 237–242, 244–246, 248–254, 261, 271–273, 276, 277, 281, 311, 313, 331–334, 342–344, 347–349, 353. *See also* Gangs; Peer groups

G

Gangs. *See also* Friends; Leisure; Peer groups; Troublesome groups; Youth
and alcohol use, 253, 350
and country cluster, 253, 353
definition, 247
and delinquency/offending, 237, 253, 273, 333
and drug use, 253
Eurogang, 237
and gender, 247, 248, 333
measurement, 253, 333
membership, 247, 273, 276
and neighborhood, 273, 333–334, 350, 353
and risk behavior, 350, 353
and victimization, 237
Gender. *See also* Boys; Females; Girls; Males
and age of onset, 17, 81, 83, 330
and alcohol use, 131, 135, 330
and delinquency/offending, 16, 17, 33, 82–84, 106, 153, 154, 156, 165, 171, 180, 194, 197, 218, 249–252, 330
distribution, 33, 34, 82–84, 111, 290
and drug use, 131, 132, 135, 153, 171, 267, 330
and family, 17, 102, 107, 111, 113, 166, 171, 195–201, 203, 204, 240, 251, 252, 254, 263–267, 276, 290, 304–307, 310, 314, 315, 320, 332, 334, 335
gender gap, discrepancies, 80, 171, 196, 201
and life-styles, leisure, 101, 102, 195, 205, 249–252, 254, 263, 334, 342
and peers, 101, 156, 198, 218, 223, 227, 240, 247–252, 254, 310, 333, 342, 344, 349
and risk behavior, 310
and socialization, 84, 197, 198, 267, 305
and victimization, 17, 99–103, 106, 109, 111, 180, 289, 330

Gender differences, 80, 82, 131, 132, 135, 197–200, 240, 247, 249–252, 305, 330
Generalizability, 32, 285–320, 334–349. *See also* Comparative design; Theory, testing
General theory of crime, 10, 11, 57, 186, 197, 285–289, 291, 304, 306. *See also* Self-control, theory
Germany, 4, 5, 13, 16, 27, 28, 38, 41, 70–72, 74, 86, 97, 98, 101, 103, 105, 121, 122, 124, 145, 146, 148, 159, 161, 162, 220, 221, 233, 260, 299, 300. *See also* Western-European cluster
Girls, 80, 82–84, 91, 99, 100, 110–114, 118, 131, 132, 135, 139, 187, 195–198, 200, 201, 214, 229–232, 240, 241, 243, 246–249, 251, 254, 264, 278, 305, 329–333, 337. *See also* Females; Gender
Gottfredson and Hirschi theory, 10, 11, 57, 117, 119, 134, 186, 187, 193, 195, 197, 205, 206, 211, 219, 234, 267, 285–291, 297, 303–306, 309–311. *See also* General theory of crime; Self-control, theory
Grade. *See also* Education; School
  eight, 101, 108
  ninth, 7, 13, 31, 34, 36, 40, 45, 124, 133, 148, 278
  seventh, 7, 13, 31, 36, 40, 148, 278
Grasmick, H.G., 11, 12, 57, 61, 186, 195, 197, 257, 258, 267, 288, 290–292, 294, 297, 304, 319, 334, 339. *See also* Scales; Self-Control
Group fight, 48–50, 78, 106, 155, 163, 168, 174–176, 243. *See also* Offenses
Group offending. *See* Co-offending; Deviant/delinquent friends; Gangs

H

Hacking, 48, 49, 243
Hard liquor, 132, 330
Herzegovina, 27, 31, 37, 41, 97–99, 101, 105, 120–123, 147, 148, 161, 220, 221, 223, 247. *See also* Post-socialist cluster
Home country. *See* Immigrants
Host country. *See* Immigrants
Hungary, 5, 16, 24, 27, 28, 31, 37, 70–72, 74, 97–99, 104, 105, 120–124, 128, 145, 147–149, 160–162, 177, 178, 220, 221, 247, 299, 300, 333. *See also* Post-socialist cluster
Hypothesis, 23, 27, 30, 44, 171–173, 226, 227, 289, 306. *See also* Theory
Hypothesis-testing, 44

I

Iceland, 5, 16, 24, 28, 30–32, 34, 70–72, 74, 97, 98, 101, 103, 105, 120–124, 133, 145, 146, 148–150, 160–162, 220, 221, 223, 247, 299, 300. *See also* Northern-European cluster
Immigrants. *See also* Ethnic minority groups
  and alcohol use, 133
  and delinquency/offending, 14, 81, 86, 88, 202, 216, 279
  and drug use, 86, 133, 202, 206
  first generation, 14, 87, 133, 203, 205, 214, 262, 306, 332
  natives, 202, 203, 214, 332
  and reporting to police, 14
  and risk behavior, 52
  second generation, 14, 53, 133, 203, 205, 262, 306, 309, 320, 332
  and victimization, 14
Incidence, 13, 14, 21, 32, 35, 41, 44, 49, 50, 69, 74–75, 119, 129, 144, 145, 151, 152, 157, 158, 179, 200, 314. *See also* Frequency
Indicators, structural. *See* Structural indicators
Integration, neighborhood, 56, 108, 110, 112, 114, 188, 206, 252, 258–260, 268, 269, 277–279, 305, 308, 309, 312, 345–348
Interaction
  neighbourhood and deviant peers, 238, 344, 349
  opportunity and self-control, 9, 10, 313, 314, 316–317, 344
  testing for, 32, 320, 349
International Crime Victimization Survey (ICVS), 3, 14, 60, 61, 79, 95, 97, 144, 158
International Self-Report Delinquency Study (ISRD)
  International Self-Report Delinquency Study–1 (ISRD1), 5–7, 9, 13, 16, 48, 52, 53, 122, 123, 162, 163, 233, 239, 249
  International Self-Report Delinquency Study–2 (ISRD2), 6–9, 22, 48, 291, 294, 297, 298, 304, 306
Interviewer's form. *See* Administrator's form/questionnaire
Ireland, 5, 16, 28, 38, 70–72, 74, 77, 78, 98, 103, 104, 120, 121, 123, 124, 128, 146, 148, 149, 160–162, 220, 221, 247, 253, 280, 299, 300. *See also* Anglo-Saxon cluster
Italy, 5, 16, 28, 29, 31, 32, 38, 41, 70–72, 74, 86, 87, 97–99, 101, 103, 105, 118, 121–123, 125, 145, 146, 149, 160–162, 220, 221, 293, 295, 299, 300, 333. *See also* Mediterranean country cluster

L

Last month. *See* Frequency; Incidence; Prevalence; Versatility
Last year. *See* Frequency; Incidence; Prevalence; Versatility
Latin America. *See also* Country cluster
  and alcohol use, 125, 128, 264
  and delinquency/offending, 32, 79, 80, 84, 86, 87, 90, 92, 189, 191, 192, 200, 205, 216, 320, 333, 334
  and drug use, 264
  and risk behavior, 310
  and victimization, 32, 97, 329
Leisure. *See also* Lifestyle
  activities, 9–11, 56, 232, 240, 342
  and alcohol use, 56, 70, 352
  and delinquency/offending, 9, 10, 14, 56, 195, 233, 239, 242, 249, 253, 263, 331–335, 342, 352
  and drug use, 57, 239, 333
  with family, 53, 109, 185, 194, 195, 200, 205, 206, 231–235, 241, 252, 263, 313, 352
  with large group, 56, 200, 241–243, 252, 254, 313, 342
  at night, 56, 194, 239, 242, 313, 342, 352
  and peer group, 10, 11, 14, 101, 195, 200, 237, 239–242, 249, 252, 274, 334, 342, 352 (*see also* Friends)
  at public places, 56, 238–242, 249, 252, 254, 281, 313, 342
  and risk behavior, 10, 99, 185, 244, 249, 252
  and victimization, 11, 14, 101, 102, 109
Life events
  family disruption, 54, 57, 186
  scale, 54, 57
  serious, traumatic, 57, 107, 111
Lifestyle
  and alcohol use, 70, 119, 135, 136, 238, 239, 244, 245, 312
  delinquency/offending, 14, 56, 102, 108, 115, 237–239, 245, 249, 251–254, 258, 271, 333, 334, 344, 349
  drug use, 57, 108, 119, 135, 136, 238, 239, 243–245, 252, 253
  life style scale, 56, 242, 312
  life style theory, 342 (*see also* Opportunity; Routine activity)
  and risk behavior, 102, 113, 119, 135, 239, 244, 249, 251
  and victimization, 14, 17, 95, 100–102, 106, 108, 110, 111, 113–116, 180, 330
Life-time, 13, 49, 50, 69–71, 76, 91, 118–121, 124, 125, 128, 131–133. *See also* Frequency; Incidence; Prevalence; Versatility
Lithuania, 4, 5, 16, 28, 37, 70, 98, 104, 120–123, 133, 147, 161, 177, 220, 221, 293, 295, 300
Logistic regression. *See* Regression

M

Macro-level indicators, 14, 25, 27, 59, 60, 233, 336, 345–348, 350
Males, 33, 80, 84, 91, 99, 106, 131, 132, 136, 155–157, 166, 167, 171–174, 195–201, 214, 247, 248, 251, 252, 278, 305, 307, 309, 310, 314, 315, 336, 337, 347, 349. *See also* Boys; Gender differences
Mediterranean country cluster. *See also* Cyprus; Italy; Portugal; Southern European cluster; Spain
  and alcohol use, 118, 120, 125, 127, 129, 130, 132, 137, 330
  and delinquency/offending, 25, 32, 33, 71, 73, 79, 84, 118, 137, 150, 152, 156, 179, 180, 223, 224, 249, 250, 301, 329–331
  and drug use, 118, 120, 125, 130, 132, 264, 330, 333
  and risk behavior, 310
  and victimization, 25, 97, 98, 150, 179, 329–331
Methodology, 4–9, 12–16, 21–62, 77, 219–227. *See also* Comparative design; Data collection; Questionnaire; Reliability; Sample; Self-report survey; Standardization; Validity
Migrants, 33, 34, 86–90, 92, 107, 113, 115, 133, 135, 153, 156, 166, 168, 173, 202, 203, 248, 332, 350–352. *See also* Ethnic minority groups; Immigrants
Minor, 14, 50, 53, 73, 137, 159, 165, 175, 188, 201–204, 251
Multi-level analysis, 206, 212, 228, 271, 277–280, 282, 328, 339, 342, 352. *See also* Structural indicators

N

Nationality, 87. *See also* Ethnicity; Immigrants
Native, 34, 88, 153, 155, 172, 202–204, 309

Neighbo(u)rhood. *See also* Social disorganization theory
  and alcohol use, 119, 136, 171, 264
  attachment, bonding, 55, 108, 110, 112, 114, 259, 260, 266, 279, 281
  collective efficacy, 11, 17, 186, 188, 194, 259, 270, 304, 344, 345
  and country clusters, 188, 193, 198, 200, 206, 253, 264, 275, 290, 298, 306, 310, 314, 317, 334
  and delinquency/offending, 85, 172, 173, 251–253, 266, 279–281, 351
  disorganization, 102, 108, 110–114, 136, 188, 189, 192, 193, 198–200, 203–205, 248, 252, 259–262, 264–279, 281, 282
  and drug use, 119, 136, 171, 172, 267
  and informal social control, 12, 258, 260
  integration, cohesion, 108, 110, 112, 114, 188, 189, 206, 252, 259–260, 263, 267–269, 277, 279
  and the peer group, 85, 200, 259, 271–277, 281, 352 (*see also* Delinquency; Gangs)
  and risk behavior, 172
  and victimization, 102–104, 108, 110–114, 180, 331–335
Netherlands Antilles, 26, 37, 74, 97, 98, 105, 220. *See also* Latin America
Netherlands, The, 5, 16, 44, 99, 121, 123, 148, 161, 162, 177, 293, 295, 296, 300, 352, 353. *See also* Western-European cluster
Northern-European cluster, 24, 25, 32, 34, 42, 98, 101, 125, 157, 176, 179, 189, 300, 301, 310, 317, 319, 320, 329, 330, 334

O

Offending. *See also* Delinquency; Delinquent behavior
  and age, 4, 14, 17, 81–83, 153, 157, 162, 166, 167, 178, 180, 239, 285–287, 329
  and city size, 79, 153, 155, 157, 163, 164, 180
  and country clusters, 32, 71, 83, 90, 145, 150–153, 156, 160, 161, 174–177, 179, 223, 331
  and family, 160, 171–173, 197, 242, 251, 331, 333
  and gender, 80, 81, 83, 153, 156, 165, 166, 171, 180
  and grade, 81, 148, 153–157, 165–167, 171, 180
  as group behavior, 173 (*see also* Co-offending)
  and lifestyles, 237, 239, 241–248
  and neighborhood, 85, 172, 173, 251–253, 266, 279–281, 351
  and opportunities, 79, 233, 241, 280
  and peers/friends, 85, 154–156, 159, 172, 237, 239–, 241–243, 249–253
  and school, 81, 85, 165–168
  and self-control, 178, 181
Offenses
  assault, 49, 74, 78, 109, 153–156
  bicycle/motorbike theft, 49, 175, 219
  burglary, 49, 281, 333
  car break (*see* theft from car)
  carrying weapon, 49, 109, 159, 168, 176, 180
  car theft, 49, 82, 106, 159, 175, 219
  computer hacking, 48
  downloading, 48
  drug dealing, 49, 82, 86, 176
  extortion, 49, 83, 109, 159, 219 (*see also* Robbery)
  group fight, 49, 78, 109, 155, 168, 174, 175
  purse/bag snatching, 85, 86, 91
  robbery, 49, 82, 85, 92, 109, 143, 145, 153, 156, 281, 330 (*see also* Extortion)
  shoplifting, 49, 50, 74, 76, 80, 85, 92, 109, 159, 164, 166–168, 170, 174, 219, 281, 329, 331, 333
  theft, 49, 82, 85, 88, 106, 109, 143, 159, 175, 219
  theft from car, 49, 82, 106, 159, 175, 219
  vandalism, 49, 74, 76, 82, 85, 92, 109, 164, 166–168, 170, 174, 176, 281
Offenses, grouped
  non-serious, minor, frequent, 49, 71, 74–76, 78, 79, 81, 88, 109, 144, 159, 165, 195, 196, 217, 223, 228, 272
  property, 49, 70–73, 75, 80, 81, 89, 90, 106, 116, 135, 137, 139, 153–157, 159, 164–170, 174–177, 179, 180, 196, 202, 203, 280, 281
  serious, rare, 49, 71–74, 76, 78, 79, 82, 88, 90–92, 109, 134, 136, 139, 195, 223, 227, 240, 272, 273, 276–279, 281, 333, 352, 353
  violent, 49, 71, 72, 89–91, 96, 106, 109, 111, 113, 115, 116, 136, 159, 163, 164, 166–168, 170, 174–177, 180, 196, 200, 202, 203, 213, 219, 222, 223, 227–230, 232, 233, 237, 251, 253, 280, 330, 331, 333
Operationalization, 312, 313
Opportunity. *See also* Life style; Routine activity
  and alcohol use, 35, 56, 238

and delinquency/offending, 11, 71, 217, 233, 280, 288, 305, 310–318, 320, 333, 335, 342–344, 347, 349
and drug use, 23, 35
measurement of, 56
and risk behavior, 310
and self-control, 9, 197, 253, 286, 290, 310–317
theory, 9, 11–12, 17, 280, 335, 342–344, 347
and victimization, 11, 17, 35

P

Parental consent. *See* Consent
Parental supervision, 54, 102–104, 107, 111, 163, 167, 172, 173, 193, 234, 270, 304, 306, 308–312, 314–316, 320, 331, 332, 334, 335, 337–339, 341, 347–349
Parents, 8–11, 14, 36–39, 41, 42, 51, 52, 58, 102–105, 107, 110–115, 129, 130, 133, 143, 159–173, 178–180, 185–195, 197, 198, 200, 202, 205, 206, 211, 234, 238, 240, 253, 254, 259, 263, 264, 267, 271, 276, 280, 303–305, 311, 320, 330–332, 335, 350. *See also* Family
Participation rate, 37–40. *See also* Prevalence
Peer groups. *See also* Deviant peers; Friends; Gangs
and alcohol use, 352
delinquency/offending, 10, 11, 14, 85, 154–157, 159, 171, 172, 198, 218, 219, 227, 237–254, 271, 282, 285, 310–312, 333, 342, 347, 349, 352, 353
delinquent, 154–157, 172, 271–276, 281, 282, 334
and drug use, 85, 92, 333
and leisure time, 10, 11, 14, 101, 195, 200, 237, 239–242, 249, 252, 274, 334, 342, 352
and lifestyle, 249–252, 271, 333
and opportunity, 11, 197, 198, 238, 244, 253, 310–312, 342, 344
and risk behavior, 310
selection of, 218, 271
victimization, 11, 17, 35
Peterborough study, 77, 78
Pilot study, 6, 60
PISA, 4, 219, 221–226, 228, 230, 233
Poland, 4, 5, 13, 16, 28, 34, 37, 41, 42, 44, 70, 97–99, 101, 104, 118, 121, 122, 147, 148, 150, 158, 161, 162, 220, 221
Police
Policy
alcohol, 35, 119
crime, 50, 60, 163, 167
drug, 35, 121, 123, 126
penal, 167
welfare, 24
youth, 6
Portugal, 5, 16, 24, 27, 28, 31, 38, 41, 69–72, 74, 97–100, 103, 105, 120, 121, 123, 124, 145, 146, 149, 150, 161, 162, 178, 220, 293, 299, 300. *See also* Mediterranean country cluster
Post-socialist cluster. *See also* Armenia; Bosnia-Herzegovina; Czech Republic; Estonia; Hungary; Lithuania; Poland; Russia; Slovenia
and alcohol use, 330
and delinquency/offending, 71, 73, 79, 80, 84, 179, 192, 320, 330
and drug use, 330
and risk behavior, 301
and victimization, 179, 330
Prevalence
alcohol use, 43, 44, 51, 117–120, 125
delinquency/offending, 4, 5, 13, 16, 27, 30, 32, 41, 44, 49, 50, 69, 71, 77, 79, 80, 88, 144, 152, 154, 171, 191, 233, 242, 279
drug use, 44, 117–119, 125, 171, 330
reporting, 153
risk behavior, 50, 51, 144, 153–156, 158
victimization, 27, 32, 44, 117, 144, 153, 154, 156, 330
Property offenses. *See* Offenses
Punishment, 17, 130, 143, 173–181, 331

Q

Questionnaire. *See also* Data collection; Validity
format, 53
items, 8, 47, 48, 56–58, 107, 144, 244
length, 9, 292
translation, 8, 58, 319

R

Rare, 4, 49, 74, 77, 223, 241, 248, 282
Recent, 12, 22, 77, 81, 120, 123, 177, 193, 285, 291, 296, 303, 305, 311, 313. *See also* Frequency; Incidence; Last month; Last year; Prevalence; Versatility
Reliability, 4, 5, 22, 47, 57, 61, 290, 291, 293–298, 301, 319, 334. *See also* Scales
Reporting, 3, 17, 39, 50, 52, 143–146, 148–158, 163, 165, 179, 180, 273
Representativeness, 13, 27, 30, 35, 39, 43. *See also* Sample

Research protocol, 7. *See also* Design; Questionnaire; Sample
Response rate, 39, 42, 44, 46, 78. *See also* Consent
Risk behavior(u)r
  and alcohol use, 51
  and delinquency/offending, 48–51
  and drug use, 51
  friends, 53
  truancy, 51, 52, 55, 172
  and victimization, 52
Robbery, 48–50, 52, 75, 78, 82, 85, 92, 95–99, 101–103, 106, 109, 111–113, 115, 137, 143–146, 148, 150–154, 156, 158, 175, 179, 243, 280, 281, 313, 330. *See also* Extortion
Routine activity, 115, 232, 238, 313, 347
Russia, 13, 16, 24, 28, 30, 37, 40, 41, 70, 72, 74, 97, 98, 101, 104, 105, 120–122, 124, 125, 133, 139, 147–150, 157, 160, 161, 177, 178, 220, 221, 240, 260, 293, 295, 296, 299, 300. *See also* Post-socialist cluster

S
Saint-Arnaud and Bernard, 24
Sample. *See also* Design; Methodology
  city-based, 7, 13, 27–32, 153
  classroom-based, school-based, 7, 17, 35–36, 38, 40, 43–46, 58, 291
  multi-stage, 36
  national random, 13, 27
  non-response, 36, 40, 41, 44
  participation rate, 37–40, 43
  population, 35
  protocol, guidelines, 28, 35
  random sample, 8, 13, 35, 78, 297
  refusal to participate, 41
  response rate, 39
  sample bias, 35
  sampling error, 30, 37, 44
  sampling frame, 26, 36, 39, 40
  sampling unit, 45
  size, 31, 32, 45, 111, 145, 154, 212, 300, 309, 310
  stratification variables, 45
  weighting, 32–33
Scales. *See also* Reliability; Validity
  attachment, 54, 55, 104, 105, 107, 108, 110–115, 185, 187, 192, 194, 206, 223, 310, 331, 333, 337
  attitudes toward violence, 57
  family, 53–54, 186–189, 195, 197, 212
  life style, 56
  neighborhood, 55–56
  opportunity, 56
  school, 55
  self-control, 57–58
School. *See also* Teachers; Tracking; Truancy
  achievement, 46, 266, 267, 351
  and alcohol use, 51
  aspiration, 55
  attachment, 55 (*see also* bonds)
  bonds, bonding, 54–56
  cooperation, 44
  and delinquency/offending, 48–52
  disorganization, 55, 56
  and drug use, 51
  level, 55
  and risk behavior, 51–52
  truancy, 55
  and victimization, 52
School type
  level, 13
  type, 36, 38
Self-control. *See also* General theory of crime; Self-control scale
  and alcohol use, 51, 70, 117, 119–121, 124–129, 131, 133, 135–137, 139, 330
  and country clusters, 14–16, 23–25, 43, 44, 69, 71, 75, 83, 84, 90, 91, 117, 125, 127, 128, 130–134, 145, 150–153, 156, 160, 162, 174–177, 179, 189, 193, 198, 200, 206, 214, 223, 239–242, 246, 294, 296, 298–302
  and delinquency/offending, 57, 69–92, 193–195, 211–234, 310–318, 339–342
  and drug use, 51, 57, 61, 108, 117–123, 131, 132, 135, 136, 171, 212, 225, 238, 239, 243, 245, 267, 330
  and the family, 54, 185–205
  impulsivity, 186, 287, 301–303
  and opportunity, 11–12, 288, 316–317, 344
  and parental supervision, 54, 206, 309
  and peers, 14, 237–254, 285, 310
  and risk-behavior, 51, 172, 173, 310
  risk-taking, 57, 58, 301–303
  self-centeredness, 57, 58, 186, 301–303
  temperament, volatile, 57, 58, 301, 302
  theory, 10–11, 186, 195, 204–206, 285–320, 339–342, 347
  and victimization, 52, 95–116, 144–158, 163, 329–331

Self-control scale. *See also* Scales; Self-control
and country clusters, 14–16, 23, 125, 298–302, 334
dimensionality, 290, 291, 293–294
psychometric properties, 58, 61, 291, 293, 319
reliability, alpha, 57–58, 61, 62, 290, 291, 293–294, 297
validity, 290, 297
Self-report method/self-report survey, 4–6, 29, 40, 47, 77–79
Slovenia, 16, 24, 28, 37, 39, 42, 70–72, 74, 97, 98, 105, 121, 122, 124, 125, 147–150, 160, 161, 178, 220, 221, 299. *See also* Post-socialist cluster
Social bonding. *See also* Social control
and alcohol use, 51, 337–338
and delinquency/offending, 9–10, 56, 285, 337, 339, 347, 349
and drug use, 330, 337–339
and risk behavior, 51–52, 310
and substance abuse, 331
theory, 9, 10, 54, 285, 337
and victimization, 329–331
Social class, 12, 186, 187, 189
Social control. *See also* Family; Neighborhood; School; Social bonding
and country clusters, 11, 17, 71, 75, 162, 174–177, 179, 214, 223, 239, 264, 290, 331, 334, 349, 353
and family, 10, 14, 84, 109, 166, 171–173, 185–206, 218, 234, 261, 270, 281, 285, 331, 332, 334, 335, 337–339, 341, 345, 347, 349, 350, 352, 353
and gender, 17, 30, 33, 171, 337
informal, 12, 40, 71, 143, 153, 159, 163, 165, 246, 258, 260, 263, 285, 312
and school, 9, 55, 102, 211–234, 337
and social background, 187–189, 192, 193, 200, 204, 205, 264, 331
social capital, 285
surveillance, 72, 154, 167, 196, 351
theory, 9–10, 17, 185–187, 203, 212, 216, 232, 282, 332, 335, 337–339, 347
Social disorganization theory, 9, 12, 102, 119, 135, 204, 206, 258–260, 266, 281, 282, 334, 335, 344–345, 347, 349
Social response, 14, 16, 17, 143–181
Southern European cluster, 5, 53, 86, 87, 97, 99, 189, 191, 215, 239, 249, 352. *See also* Mediterranean country cluster
Spain, 5, 16, 24, 26, 28, 38, 42, 70, 72, 74, 88, 97, 98, 103, 105, 120–123, 146, 149, 150, 160, 161, 178, 220, 221, 299, 300. *See also* Mediterranean country cluster
Spirits, 51, 109, 120, 125–127, 130–134, 172. *See also* Hard liquor
Standardization/standardized, 4–8, 21, 30, 36, 41, 46, 50, 52, 58, 61, 78, 143, 308, 315. *See also* Data collection; Data entry; Questionnaire; Sample
Structural indicators, 7, 14, 30, 46, 59, 60, 279. *See also* Country-level indicators; Data Collection; Macro-level indicators; Multi-level analysis
Substance use, 16, 17, 57, 117–139, 218, 239, 244, 245, 252, 253, 329, 330. *See also* Alcohol use; Drug use
Surinam, 16, 24, 26–28, 39, 40, 52, 58, 70, 72, 74, 86, 97, 98, 101, 103, 105, 120–122, 145, 147–153, 156, 160, 161, 179, 216, 220, 293, 295, 296, 299, 300, 319. *See also* Latin America
Survey. *See* Self-report survey
Sweden, 16, 24, 28, 31, 37, 39, 70–72, 74, 97, 98, 100, 103, 105, 118, 121, 122, 127, 146, 148–150, 160, 161, 177–179, 220, 221, 247, 299, 351. *See also* Northern-European cluster
Switzerland, 5, 7, 16, 24, 25, 27, 28, 31, 38, 58, 59, 70–72, 74, 86, 97–99, 101, 103, 105, 120–124, 128, 145, 146, 148–150, 160, 161, 178, 220, 221, 233, 247, 299, 300, 353. *See also* Western-European cluster

T

Teachers, 10, 38, 39, 51, 55, 108, 143, 159, 164, 165, 180, 211–212, 218, 225, 232, 238, 267, 270, 330, 331, 352. *See also* Education; School
Theft. *See* Offenses
Theory
general theory, 10, 11, 57, 186, 197, 253, 285–291, 304–306 (*see also* Self-control, theory)
integration, 25, 56, 108, 110, 112, 114, 188, 206, 221, 225, 231, 251, 252, 258–260, 268, 269, 277–279, 305, 308–309, 312, 345–349
macro-level, 14, 25, 27, 59, 60
opportunity, 9, 11–12, 17, 280, 335, 342–344, 347
routine activity, 115, 232, 238, 313, 347
self-control, 9–12, 17, 186, 195, 204–206, 285–320, 335, 339–342, 347

Theory (*cont.*)
- social control, 9–10, 17, 185–187, 203, 212, 216, 232, 282, 332, 335, 337–339, 347 (*see also* Social bonding)
- social disorganization, collective efficacy, 9, 12, 102, 119, 135, 204, 206, 258–260, 266, 281, 282, 334, 335, 344–345, 347, 349
- social learning, 310
- testing, 17, 32, 320

Tracking, 212, 217–220, 225, 226, 333, 352
Troublesome groups, 273
Truancy, 51, 52, 55, 102, 109, 111, 113, 172, 212–216, 224, 226, 248, 253, 256, 266–270, 275–277, 282, 331, 337, 339–341, 347–351. *See also* Risk behavior; School

U

Unemployment, 15, 16, 23, 30, 187–190, 192, 202, 203, 205, 206, 222, 226, 229, 230, 233, 263, 281, 282, 334, 350. *See also* Social class
United States, 16, 24, 28, 70, 74, 77, 78, 86, 120, 121, 123, 150, 203, 220, 221, 247, 253, 273, 353. *See also* Anglo-Saxon cluster

V

Validity, 4, 5, 17, 22, 40, 47, 61, 188, 203, 216, 290, 293, 297, 298, 335. *See also* Data; Questionnaire; Scales
Variety. *See* Versatility
Venezuela, 16, 24, 26–28, 37, 41, 44, 52, 69–72, 74, 97, 98, 103, 105, 120–122, 139, 147, 149–150, 160–162, 178, 216, 220, 299. *See also* Latin America
Versatility (diversity, variety)
- and country cluster, 77, 131, 132, 134
- and family, 200
- and frequency, 50, 76, 78, 111
- and gender, 80, 91, 132, 201, 215, 216, 264–266, 268, 269, 277, 337–338, 340–344, 346, 348
- and grade, 14, 55, 77, 81, 134, 138, 188, 197, 198, 213, 214, 243, 264–266, 268, 269, 277, 307, 309, 310, 315, 320, 337–344, 346, 348, 349
- last month, 51, 134–138, 172, 245
- last year, 76, 135, 138, 191, 242, 250, 252, 274, 339
- and leisure, 14, 56, 101, 188, 194, 200, 205, 206, 233, 242, 249, 252, 263, 270, 274, 281, 313, 332, 342
- life time, ever, 76, 91, 118, 131, 132
- and migrants, 14, 90, 92, 136, 203, 205, 214, 263, 306, 332, 350
- and neighborhood, 55–56, 103, 104, 274, 312, 313, 315–317, 332, 344–353
- and opportunity, 7, 17, 22, 56, 217, 281, 312–314, 316, 317, 342–344
- and (deviant) peers, 14, 237–254, 312
- and school, 4, 14, 17, 77, 96, 135, 212–216, 251, 252, 267–271, 275–277, 281, 312, 337, 340, 341, 344–353
- and self-control, 14, 16, 17, 134–136, 193–195, 200, 201, 203, 204, 206, 251, 252, 254, 275–277, 285–320, 332, 339, 340, 342, 344, 347–350
- and seriousness, 14, 50, 76

Victimization
- and alcohol use, 44, 51, 71, 117, 119–121, 124–129, 131, 133, 135–137, 139, 330
- assault, 52, 96, 98–99, 101–103, 106, 113–115, 148, 151, 330
- bullying, 23, 52, 95–98, 100–102, 105, 113, 145, 151, 232, 330
- and city size, 153, 155, 156, 163
- and country clusters, 14–16, 25, 31, 117, 144–146, 151–153, 155–157, 179, 290, 331
- and delinquency/offending, 32, 180, 329, 330
- and drug use, 51
- and ethnicity, immigrant, 14, 16, 17, 25, 32, 44, 117, 145, 150, 151, 153, 156, 179, 330
- frequency, incidence, 153–157, 162
- and lifestyles, 100, 101, 116, 136, 237–254, 271, 311, 312
- prevalence, 153–155, 330
- property, 153–157, 159, 330
- and reporting to police, 50
- and risk behavior, 48, 51, 52, 172, 173, 310
- robbery, 111–113, 146
- and school grade, 100, 101, 108, 268
- theft, 109, 110, 113, 115
- violent, 95, 97–99, 101, 102, 106, 330

Violence
  attitude towards, 107, 113, 186, 195, 200, 205, 248, 251–254, 276
  violence scale, 4, 12, 57, 72, 73, 80, 81, 89, 90, 107, 114, 137, 165, 175, 198–201, 204, 213, 228, 248, 252, 272, 275, 277, 329, 332, 352

W

Western-European cluster, 25, 134, 162, 179, 180, 300, 310

Y

Youth
  culture, 217
  gangs, 350

CPSIA information can be obtained at www.ICGtesting.com
Printed in the USA
LVOW082121141211

259489LV00007B/26/P

9 781441 994547

0 1341 1381878 2